Mosaic Art Today

Jeffrey B. Snyder, Editor

Schiffer Publishing Ltd

4880 Lower Valley Road • Atglen, PA 19310

Other Schiffer Books by the Editor:
Art Glass Today. ISBN: 9780764334641. $50.00
Art Jewelry Today 3. ISBN: 9780764338830. $50.00
Art Jewelry Today 2. ISBN: 9780764330650. $50.00
Ceramics Today. ISBN: 9780764334658. $50.00
Ironwork Today 3: Inside and Out. ISBN: 9780764338762. $50.00
Ironwork Today 2. ISBN: 9780764330643. $50.00
Printmakers Today. ISBN: 9780764334627. $50.00
Wood Art Today 2. ISBN: 9780764334634. $50.00

Other Schiffer Books on Related Subjects:
A Beginner's Guide to Mosaics: Four Decorative Projects. Alexandra Carron. ISBN: 9780764340963. $19.99
Fused Glass Mosaics: Master Class Techniques with Martin Cheek. Martin Cheek. ISBN: 9780764339332. $34.99
The Mosaics of Louis Comfort Tiffany. Edith Crouch. ISBN: 9780764331411. $99.99

Library of Congress Control Number: 2012935731

Designed by Bruce Waters
Type set in DeVinne BT/News Gothic BT

ISBN: 978-0-7643-4001-7
Printed in Hong Kong

Schiffer Books are available at special discounts for bulk purchases for sales promotions or premiums. Special editions, including personalized covers, corporate imprints, and excerpts can be created in large quantities for special needs. For more information contact the publisher:

Published by Schiffer Publishing Ltd.
4880 Lower Valley Road
Atglen, PA 19310
Phone: (610) 593-1777; Fax: (610) 593-2002
E-mail: Info@schifferbooks.com

For the largest selection of fine reference books on this and related subjects, please visit our website at **www.schifferbooks.com**
We are always looking for people to write books on new and related subjects. If you have an idea for a book, please contact us at
proposals@schifferbooks.com

This book may be purchased from the publisher.
Please try your bookstore first.
You may write for a free catalog.

In Europe, Schiffer books are distributed by
Bushwood Books
6 Marksbury Ave.
Kew Gardens
Surrey TW9 4JF England
Phone: 44 (0) 20 8392 8585; Fax: 44 (0) 20 8392 9876
E-mail: info@bushwoodbooks.co.uk
Website: www.bushwoodbooks.co.uk

Acknowledgments

I thank the artists and galleries who assisted in this project. Without their efforts, this book would not have been possible.

I wish to acknowledge The Society of American Mosaic Artists (SAMA) and the British Association for Modern Mosaic (BAMM) for all they do to encourage and promote mosaic artists and their work.

Finally, I thank my publisher, coworkers, church, friends, and family, who keep my spirits high and the books coming.

Contents

Introduction

Mosaic art is created by setting small colored pieces of glass, marble, china, ceramics, pebbles, shells, and mirror set in adhesive, plaster, or cement to create beautiful, unified pictures and patterns. As a decorative art form, mosaic art has a long and distinguished history. Archaeologists have recovered well designed, advanced mosaics from among the early civilizations of Mesopotamia and Sumeria, mosaics roughly five thousand years old. In the fifth or sixth centuries BC, the Greeks preferred black and white pebbles when creating artfully decorated mosaic floors. Both Greeks and Romans began their mosaic art development on floors and later moved to walls. I have seen some impressive Roman floors in Italy in Rome's Palatine Hill excavations of high society homes of the ancient empire.

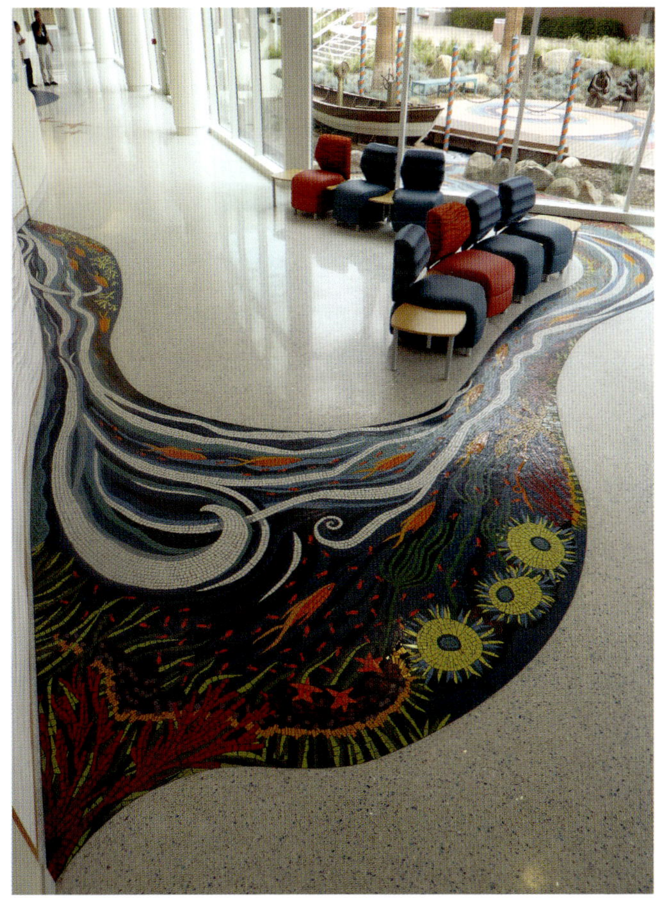

Kim Emerson. *River of Life.* Main lobby floor and garden mosaic. 2009-2010. Ceramic tile. Hand-cut tesserae/tape technique/direct method. 500 square feet. Rady Children's Hospital, Acute Care Pavilion, Carley's Magical Gardens, San Diego, California. *Photo by the artist*

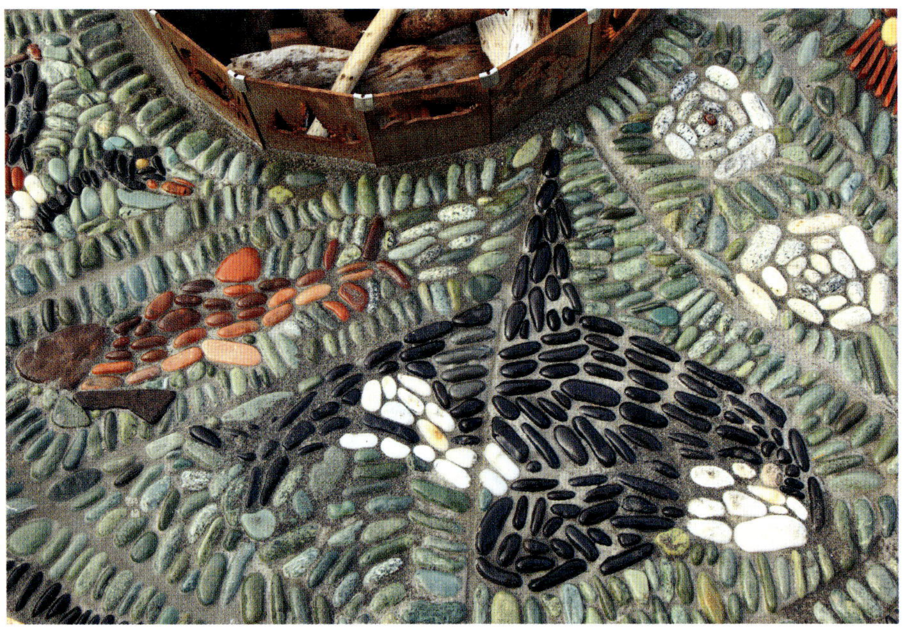

Richard S. Davis. Private Commission: Beach Suite. 2010. Sea life pebble mosaic. Pebbles, tumbled glass, reinforced cement, cementitious non-shrink grout. 7' in diameter. *Photo by Michael Stadler*

Today's mosaic artists may receive training from some of the best art schools in the United States and Europe. They are supported in their endeavors by professional organizations, including The Society of American Mosaic Artists (SAMA) and the British Association for Modern Mosaic (BAMM). These twenty-first century artists build upon the vibrant works of their predecessors, innovating with this ancient medium to create new and startling works of art that push the envelope of what may be accomplished and provide relevant messages to today's viewers. The works of art presented here include an astonishing array of forms, from the classic floors and wall art to a wide range of sculptural forms, some of which are intended for hands-on interaction.

Terminology

There are a few common terms used regularly by the artists throughout this book that are worth defining. There are many other terms involved with mosaic art, including Andimenti, which describes the movement and flow of small pieces of materials (tesserae) used to make mosaics, but the focus here will be on the terms the artists themselves employ that may be unfamiliar to newcomers to this art medium.

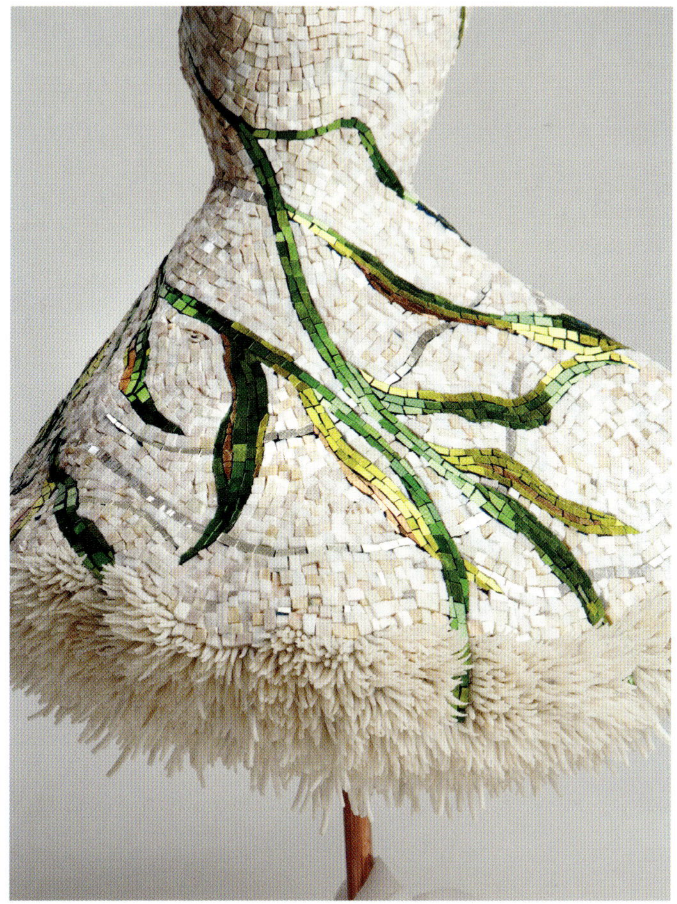

Julie Richey Mosaics, LLC. *La Corrente (The Current).* 2010. Marble, Italian, and Mexican smalti, 24k gold leaf smalti, chalcedony, and seashells on mixed media base. 29" x 22" x 22". *Photo by Stacy Bratton, www. stacybrattonphotography.com*

Materials and Patterns

Tesserae: Small, thin pieces of material used to create mosaic art. As stated previously, the range of materials can be quite broad, including glass, china, ceramic, pebble, shell, marble, and mirror.

Smalti (or smalto singular): Colored or colorless fused glass produced in an array of thousands of vibrant colors. It is durable, stable, and easily cut glass.

Vitreous tile: Square tiles of glass formed in molds from glass past. These tiles usually measure 3/4" x 3/4" and feature smooth tops and ridged bottoms that adhere well when placed.

Pique assiette or picassiette: Creating mosaic art from fragments of broken pottery.

Opus: Various ways the pieces are cut and placed. There are many opus forms, including:

Opus Palladianum: Irregularly fitting forms referred to as "crazy paving."

Opus Tessellatum: Regular, straight lines of tesserae.

Opus Regulatum: Grids of horizontal and vertical lines.

Opus Romano: Patterns made with molds.

Opus Vermiculatum: Flowing tesserae lines.

Placement

There are also two techniques for placement worth exploring, the direct and indirect techniques. The direct technique involves placing each piece directly into the setting bed of adhesive at the location where the mosaic artwork will reside. The most common uses of the direct method today are in the creation of mosaic panels intended to hang on the wall and for wall mosaics. This method affords the artist with a great deal of control over the placement of the individual tiles, allowing the pieces to be set specifically for feel and texture while manipulating pieces to adjust for the on site lighting. Indirect techniques are used when it is impractical to work directly on site. These techniques require the mosaic to be supported in transit by paper or panels. Using paper, the mosaic is glued to the paper for transit with the backing exposed. When placed, the paper is removed. This works with large projects. Also used for large art projects, mosaics may be created in panels off site, brought to the site, and placed together on site to create the entire work.

Organization of the Book

All of the artwork presented here is organized by artist. The artists are arranged alphabetically and all of their works are shown together to give the reader a sense of each artist's range. The artist's statements and explanations of their works are provided for those who wish to know more about the artist's motivation and intent. The range of artwork presented here is vast and inspiring. It is also a snapshot of what is happening in mosaic art today.

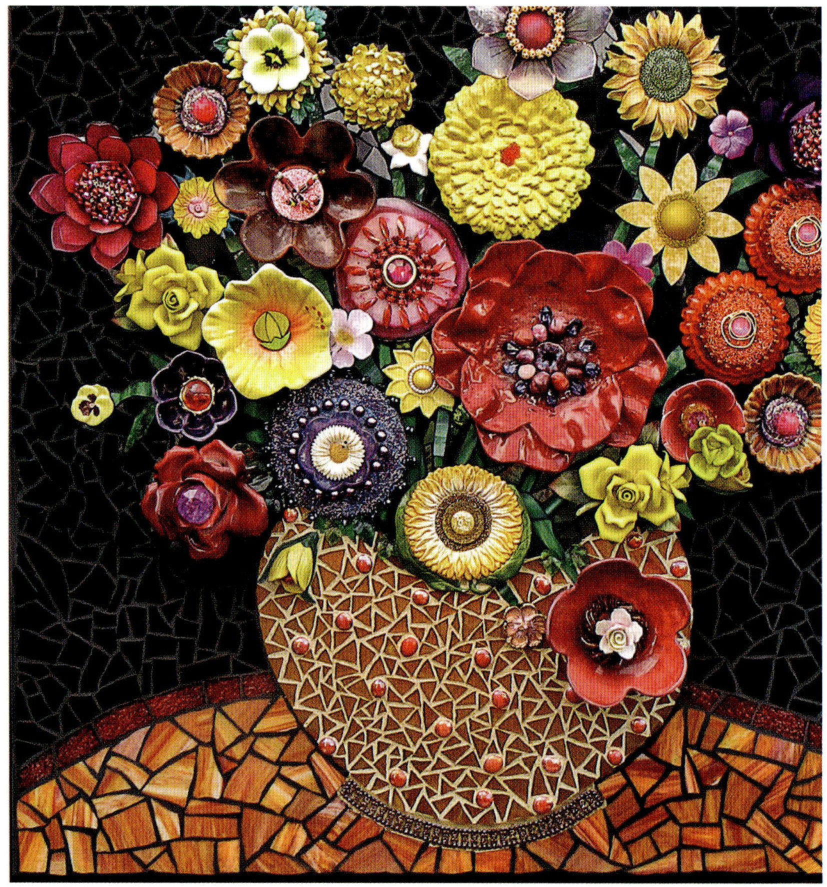

Suzan Germond. *Big Bouquet.* 2008. Mixed media mosaic with glass, beads, jewelry, and found objects. 36' x 36" x 4'. *Photo by artist*

The Artists and Their Works

Doreen Adams

Malibu, California, Doreen@creativeartmosaics.com

One tesserae at a time, painstaking, laborious, such is the truth of mosaic art. *Opus veritas*.

—Massimiliano Salviati

Artist's Statement

Born in 1948 and growing up in the Scottish countryside I was very lucky to experience and connect with nature. "Today's kids are increasingly disconnected from the natural world," says child advocacy expert Richard Louv and author of *Last Child in the Woods*. Through my art I want to reacquaint our children and ourselves with nature and the power of imagination. Adding imagination to our lives liberates us from many of our limitations.

In 2004 I was introduced to the art of mosaics. After extensive research of techniques and materials I gravitated to a Venetian glass called "smalti." Drawn to its luminosity and vivid colors, I began using the technique of cutting and laying the tesserae to make an image known in mosaicing circles as "painting with glass." Combining my nostalgia for the past, my sense of wonder about everything in nature, my painstaking and instinctual attention to detail, and the challenge of making each piece work towards the complete work, I ignited a new found passion and experienced instant success.

"The work of art must seize upon you, wrap you up in itself and carry you away. It is the means by which the artist conveys his passion. It is the current which he puts forth, which sweeps you along in his passion."

—Pierre August Renoir

About the Artwork

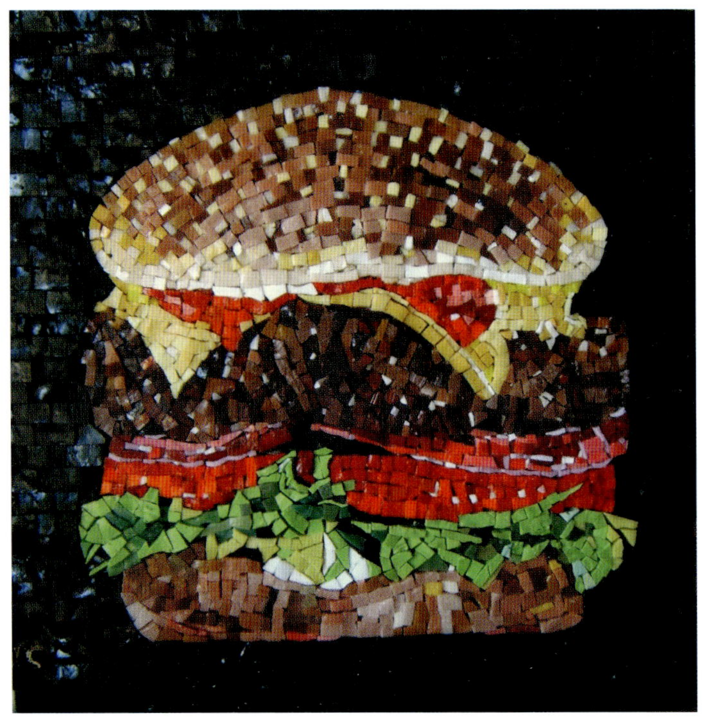

(Detail opposite page.)

Cheeseburger: The cheeseburger was invented in 1928 in Los Angeles County, California, USA, although some controversy still exists regarding this burger with a slice of cheese on top. I think I may be the first artist to render a cheeseburger in smalti. When I decided to mosaic the cheeseburger it was mainly because I wanted to do a small piece that wouldn't take months to complete. My vision was to render this 2D cheeseburger as realistically as possible in the hopes of making the viewers' mouths water or at least crack a smile. I apologize to the vegetarians; perhaps I will break out the smalti and mosaic some broccoli or cauliflower next.

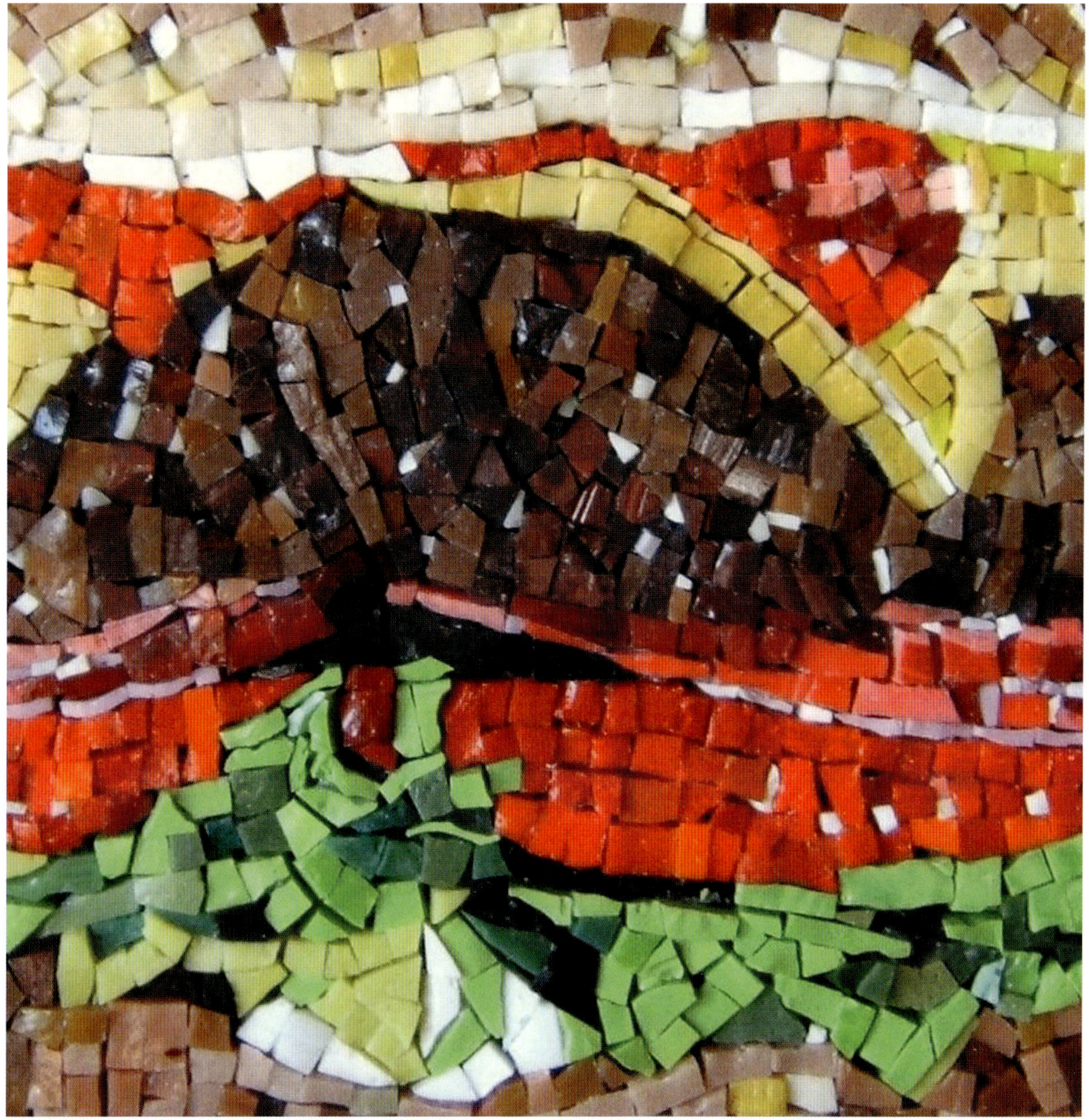

Doreen Adams. *Cheeseburger.* 2008. Venetian & Mexican smalti. Direct method, 2D. 12" x 12" x 1".
Art & Photography by Doreen Adams

White Rabbit: "Oh Dear! Oh Dear! I shall be late!"— The White Rabbit: This is one of a series of mosaics I have made investigating the themes of Lewis Carroll's *Alice's Adventures in Wonderland*. I chose to render The White Rabbit larger than life to accentuate his urgency as he rushed through the scene checking his watch. Depicting the lushness and tranquility of an English meadow in the corresponding close detail, however, required the kind of commitment that makes a mosaic a labor of love. Every piece of glass was thoughtfully and carefully chosen to infuse as much movement, emotion, realism, and humor into the scene as possible.

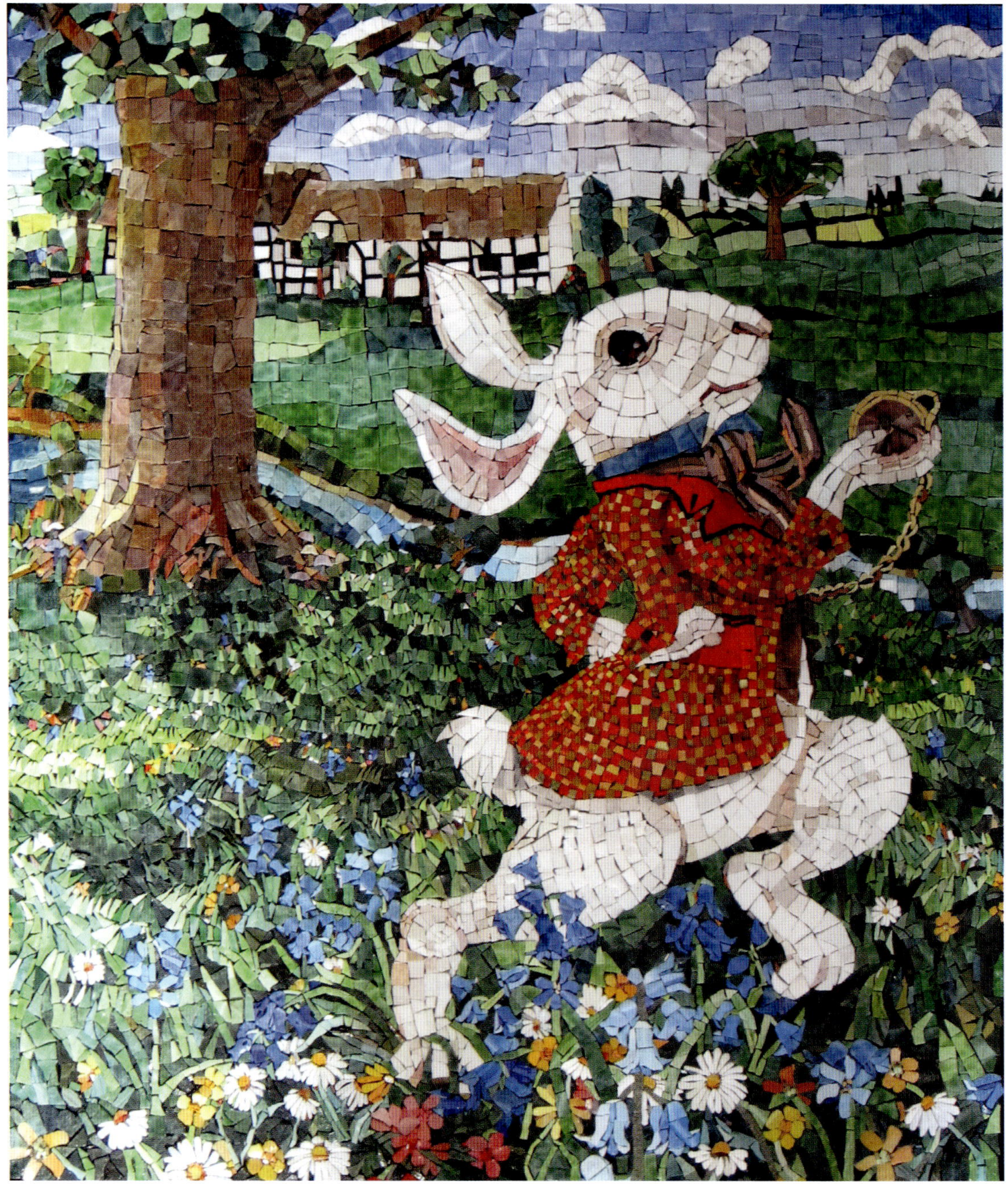

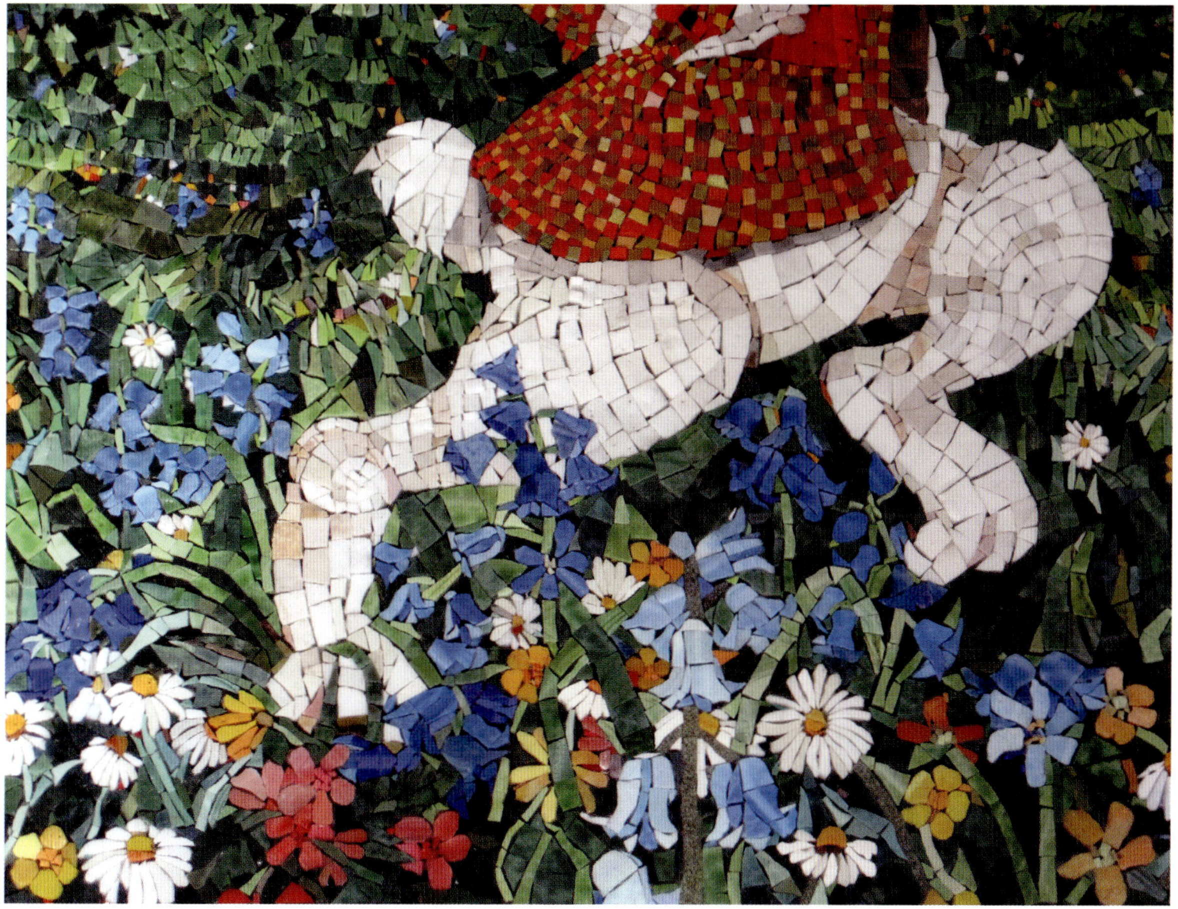

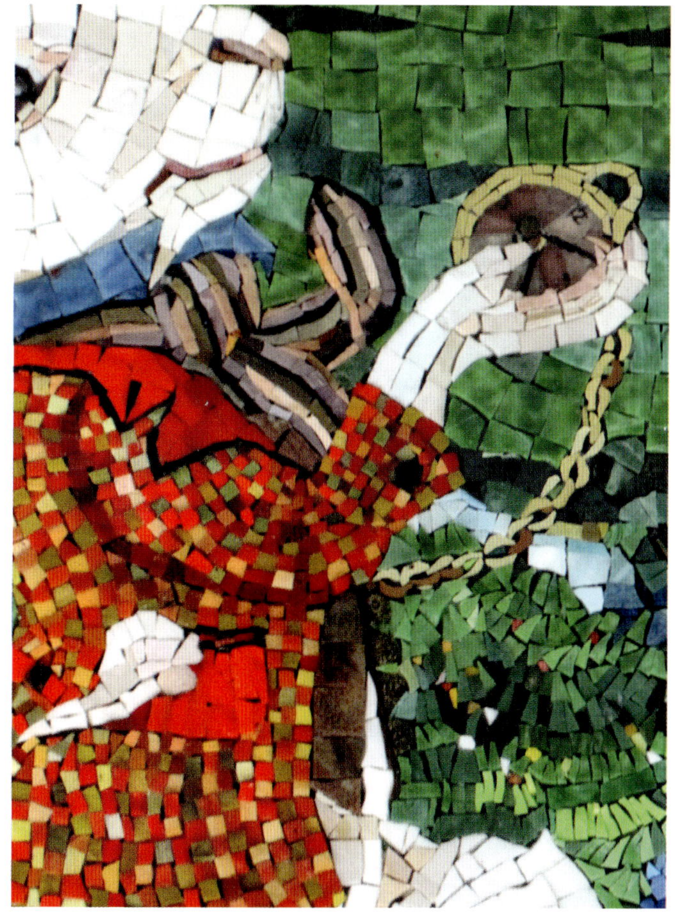

Doreen Adams. *White Rabbit: "Oh Dear! Oh Dear! I shall be late!" —The White Rabbit.* 2008. Venetian & Mexican smalti, millefiori. Direct method, 2D. 30" x 26" x 1". *Art & Photography by Doreen Adams*

Cheshire Cat: Cheshire Cat with his famous grin is the fourth mosaic in my series. His teeth, although correct in quantity, I rendered more human-like to avoid a fierce or foreboding appearance. My intent was to give this mighty oak tree a strong, textured appearance without taking the focus away from Alice or the cat. To capture the wonder on her face as she timidly approached this grinning cat. She asked him. "Would you tell me please, which way I ought to go from here?"

"That depends a good deal on where you want to get to," said the cat.

I know which way I am going. My success with *White Rabbit* and *"Who Are You?" said the Caterpillar* has given me the incentive and commitment to complete the series by 2015 and present my body of work on the 150th anniversary of one of the most influential books of all time.

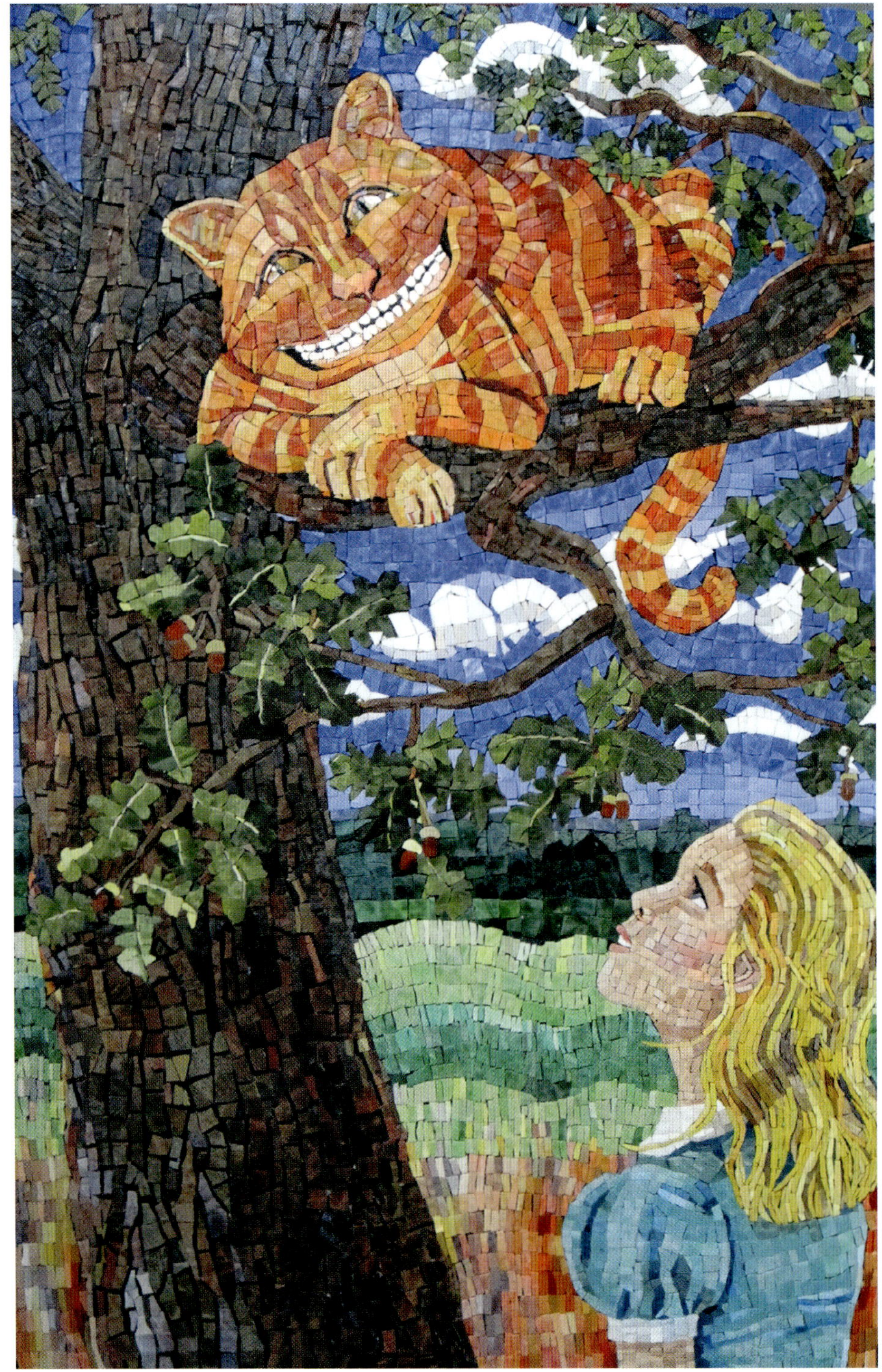

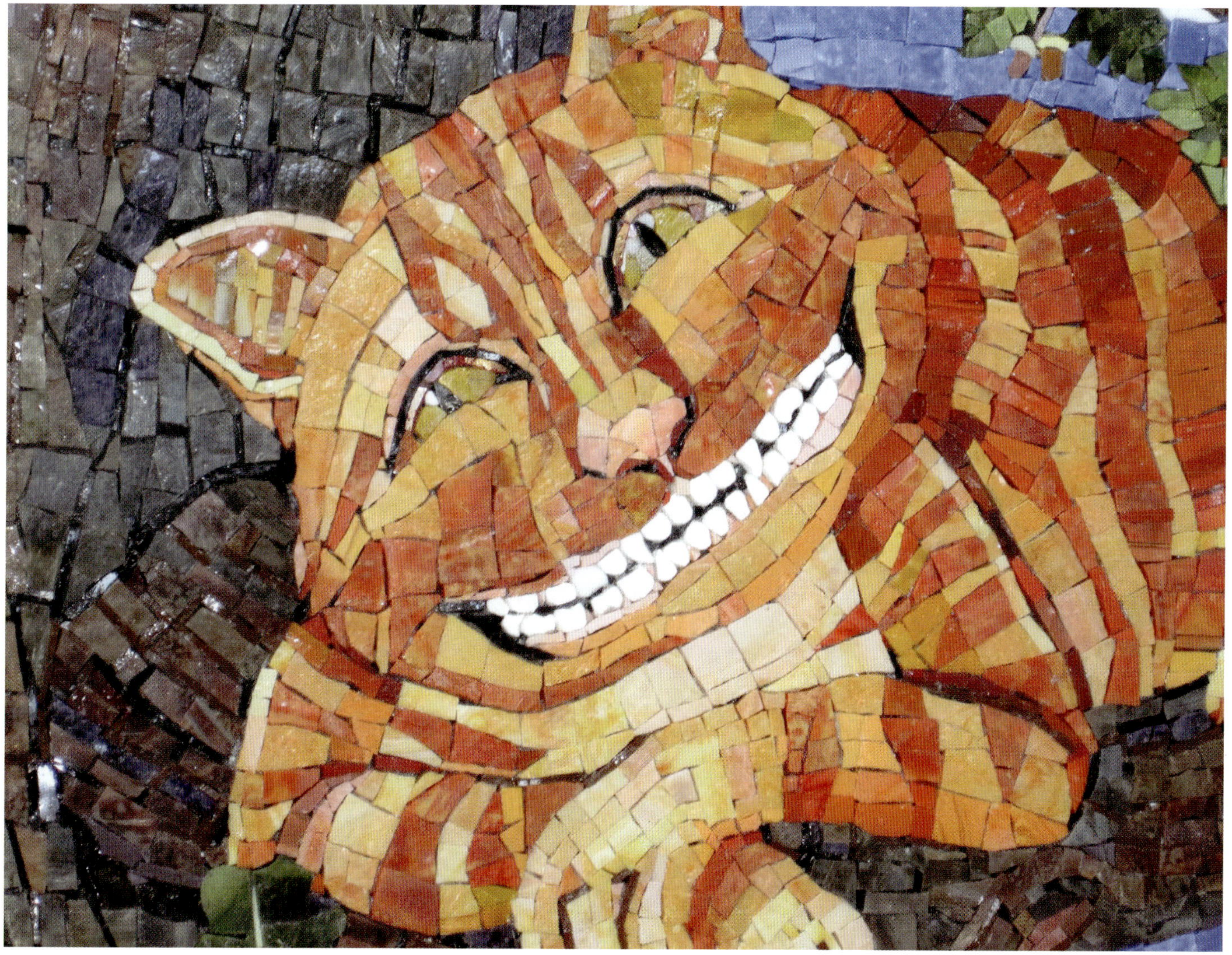

Doreen Adams. *Cheshire Cat*. 2009. Venetian & Mexican smalti, iridized smalti, contorno. Direct method, 2D. 36" x 24" x 1". *Art & Photography by Doreen Adams*

"Who Are You?" said the Caterpillar: This is the fifth and most recent mosaic investigating the themes of Lewis Carroll's *Alice's Adventures in Wonderland*, one of the most influential books of all time and one of my personal favorites. My vision and style coupled with my passion for telling a story using this medium becomes stronger with each mosaic. The clusters of wild woodland strawberries, the swirls of smoke, the beams of light, and hint of blue sky spontaneously provided the atmosphere I envisioned. The mushroom, caterpillar, and hookah I kept true to my original sketch. I achieved my goal to give this quirky blue caterpillar a sleepy yet inquisitive expression. My art restores my sense of wonder and helps me reconnect one-on-one with nature, as I did when I was a child growing up in Scotland.

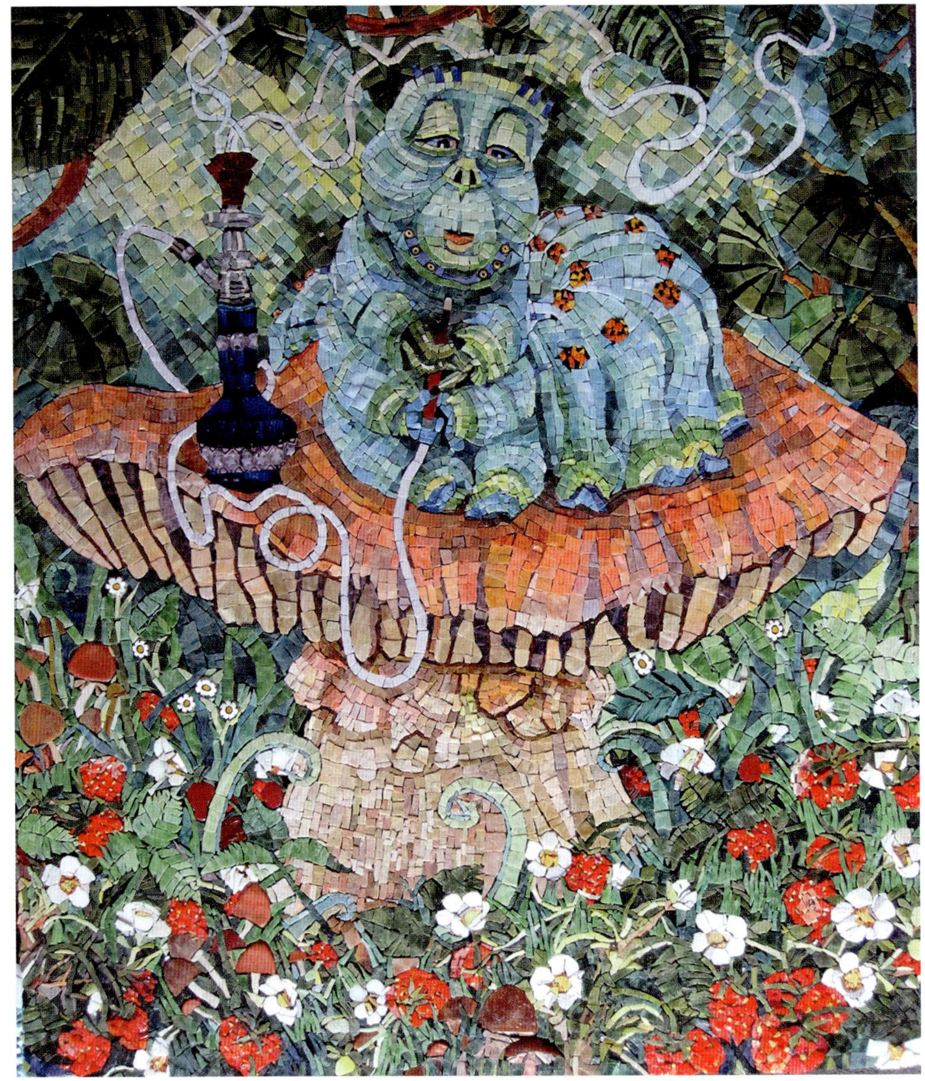

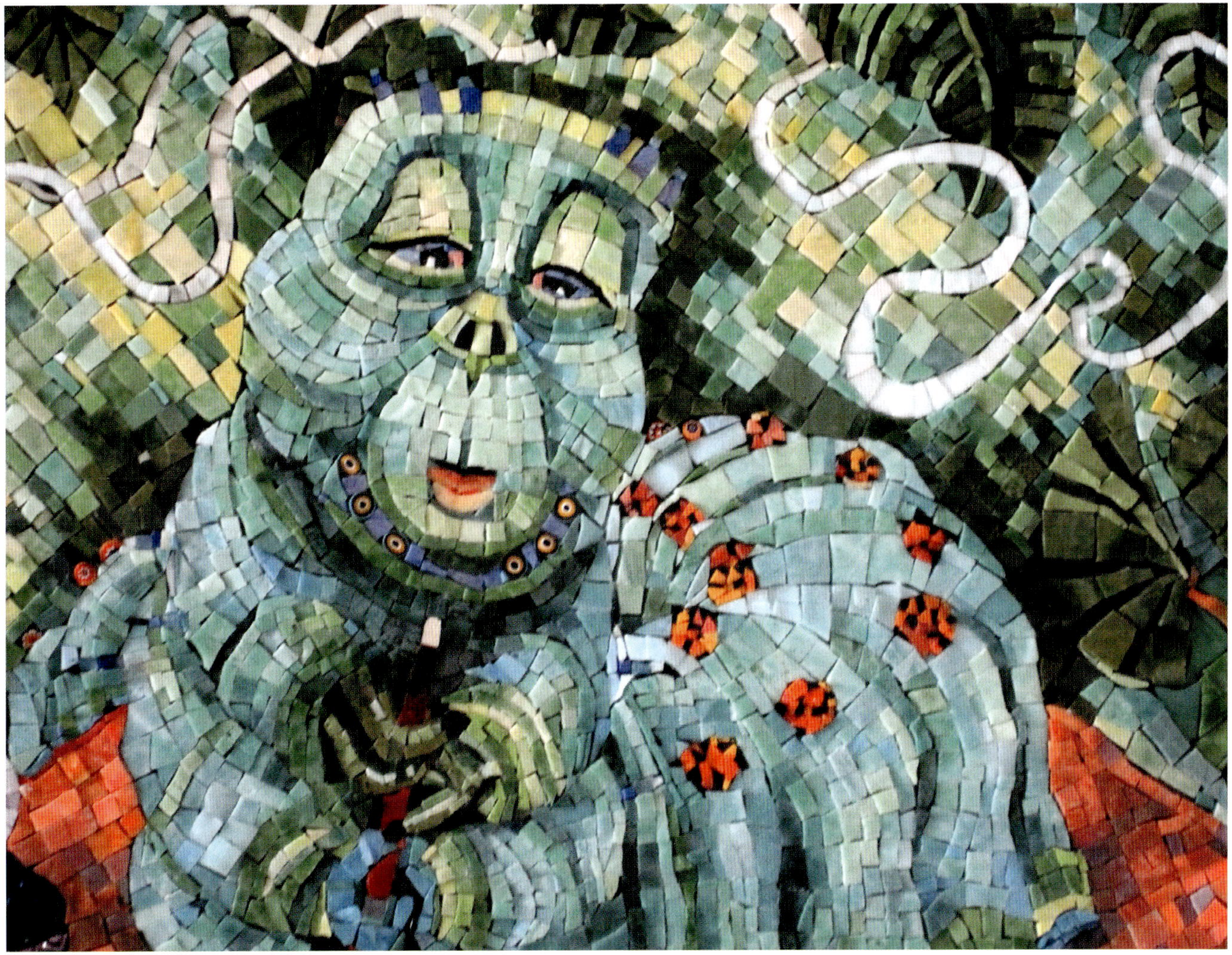

Doreen Adams. *"Who Are You?" said the Caterpillar.* 2010. Venetian & Mexican smalti, Transparent smalti, contorno, studio piastrini, millefiori, glass pebbles. Direct method, 2D. 30" x 26" x 1". *Art & Photography by Doreen Adams*

Linda Billet

Hummelstown, Pennsylvania, contactme@lindabillet.com

Artist's Statement

I absolutely LOVE working with glass. I feel it gives me an unfair advantage because it is just so beautiful before I even touch it. I fuse glass and I mosaic it, but then a lot of really magical things happen when I combine those two crafts. I try whenever possible to incorporate depth and dimension in my work. Glass is the best way I know to do that. Combining different thicknesses of my fused glass and regular stained glass creates texture on the surface, or if the thicker glass is set in, the visual texture will be the result of mixing opaque material with transparent material. Unless commissioned, most of the ideas for my work come from things in my life that make me happy. The rest of my ideas just start with a unique piece of glass that sets the direction of the rest of the piece. There are not too many things that make me happier than being in my studio working with my dogs.

About the Artwork

DiAngelo Backsplash: This client loves hiking. The request was for a forest feel. All tesserae is 1/8" stained glass, some of which is glass that I fused.

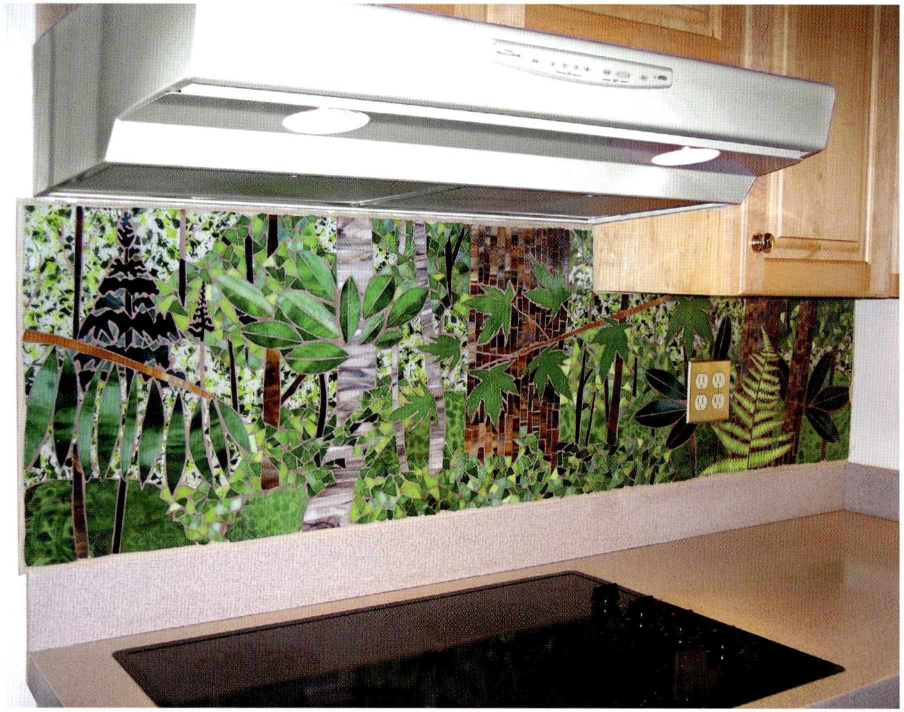

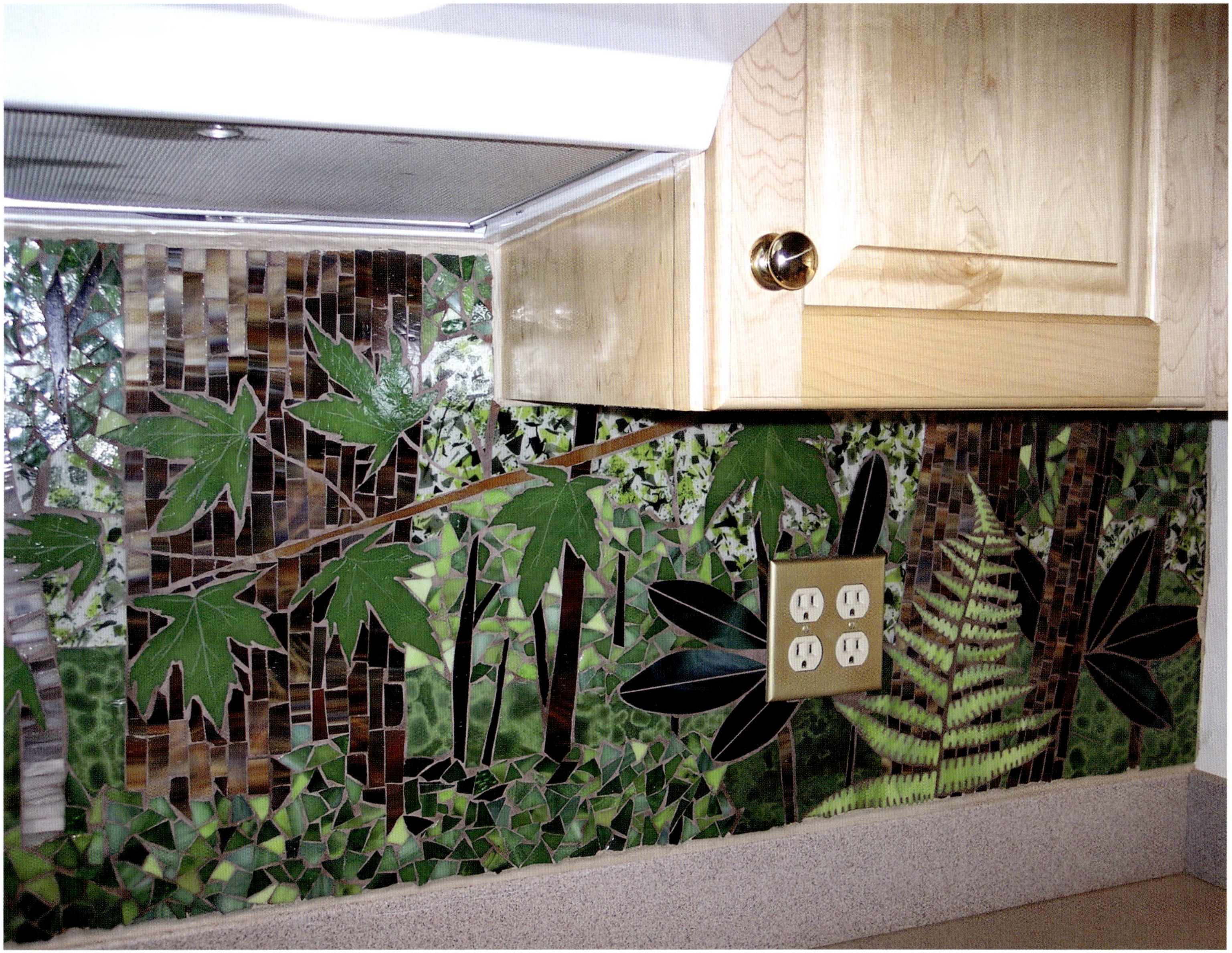

Linda Billet. Backsplash. 2007. Stained glass and fused glass, weldbond on cement board with grout. 3' x 6'.
Photography by Linda Billet

Pink Lady: The key to this piece is the striation in the pink glass, which made the feathers a fun feature. The eye is fused 1/8" glass with regular 1/8" glass.

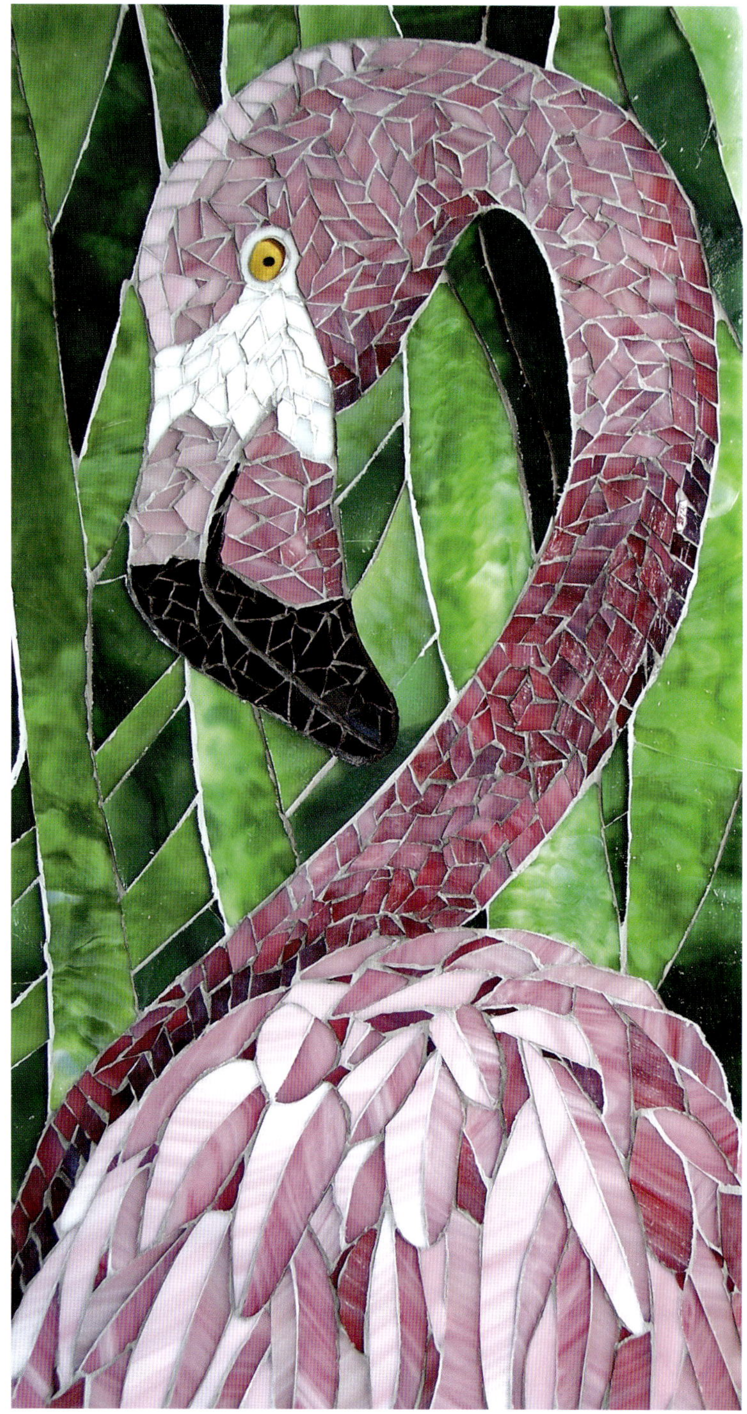

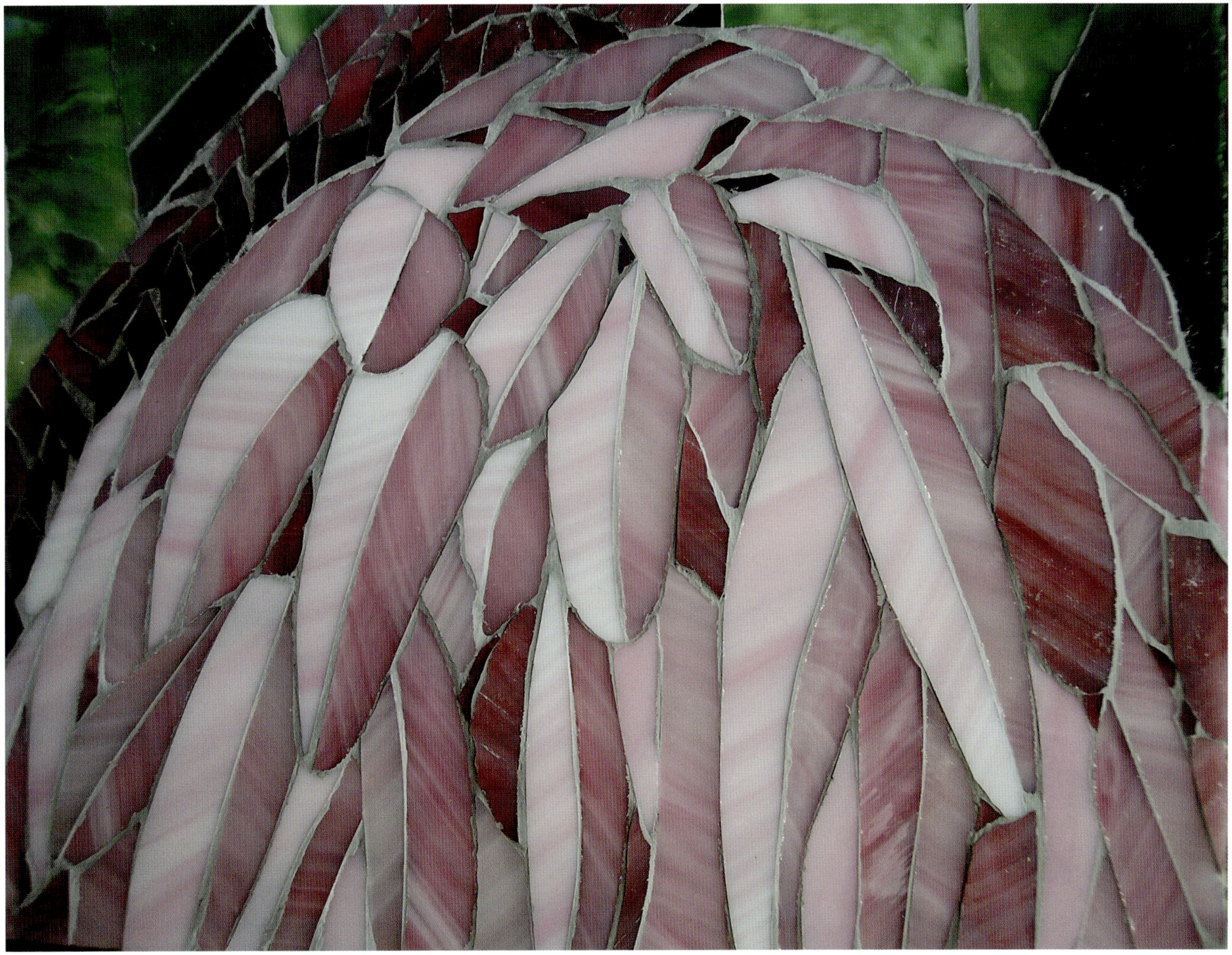

Linda Billet. *Pink Lady*. 2008. Stained glass, weldbond on cement board with grout. Approximately 24" x 12".
Photography by Linda Billet

Tink: This was a gift for a friend. Her dog, Tinkerbell, looks up at you with eyes that you can't say no to. All tesserae are regular stained glass.

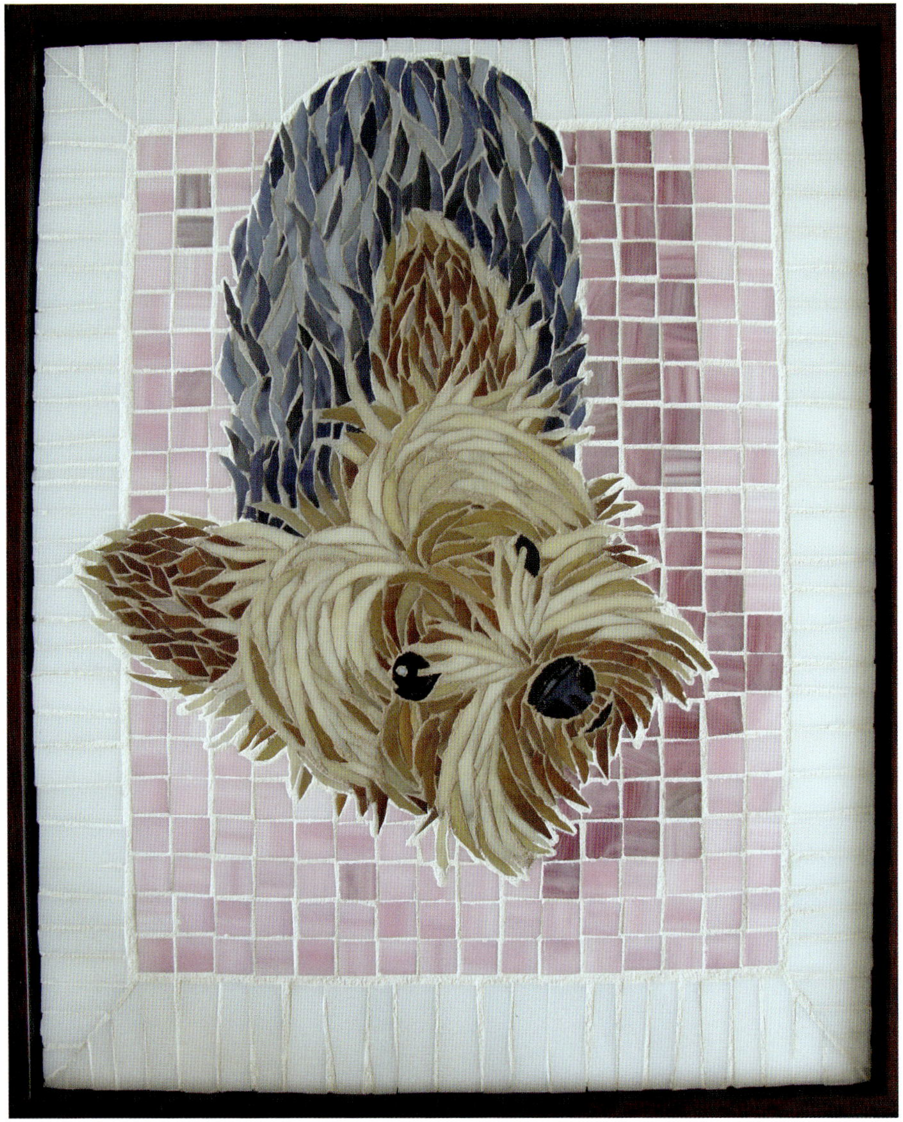

Linda Billet. *Tink*. 2009. Stained glass, weldbond on cement board with grout. 14" x 11". *Photography by Linda Billet*

Twinkle: The substrate of this mosaic is mirror where the iris is. The iris is made of some transparent glass so that with the mirror behind it you can look into the eye as you would a real eye. All tesserae are regular stained glass.

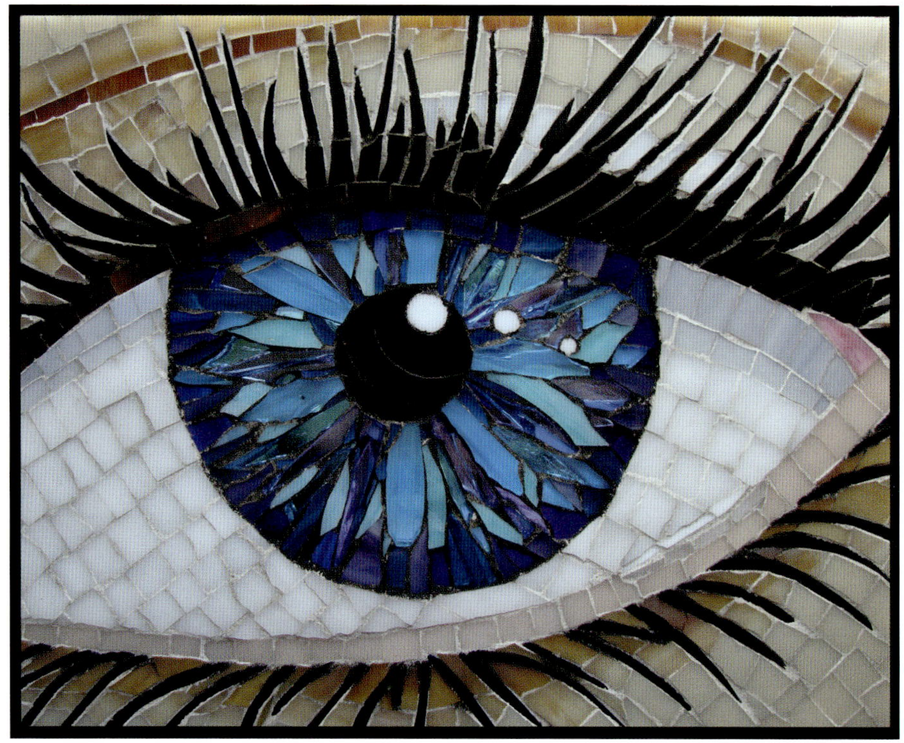

Linda Billet. *Twinkle*. 2009. Stained glass, weldbond on foam board and mirror with grout. 8" x 10". *Photography by Linda Billet*

Follow Your Bliss is actually a self-portrait. I love looking up at the sun while underwater and this mosaic is basically my life's philosophy. The mosaic is regular 1/8" stained glass with 1/4" fused glass set in so the surface is level.

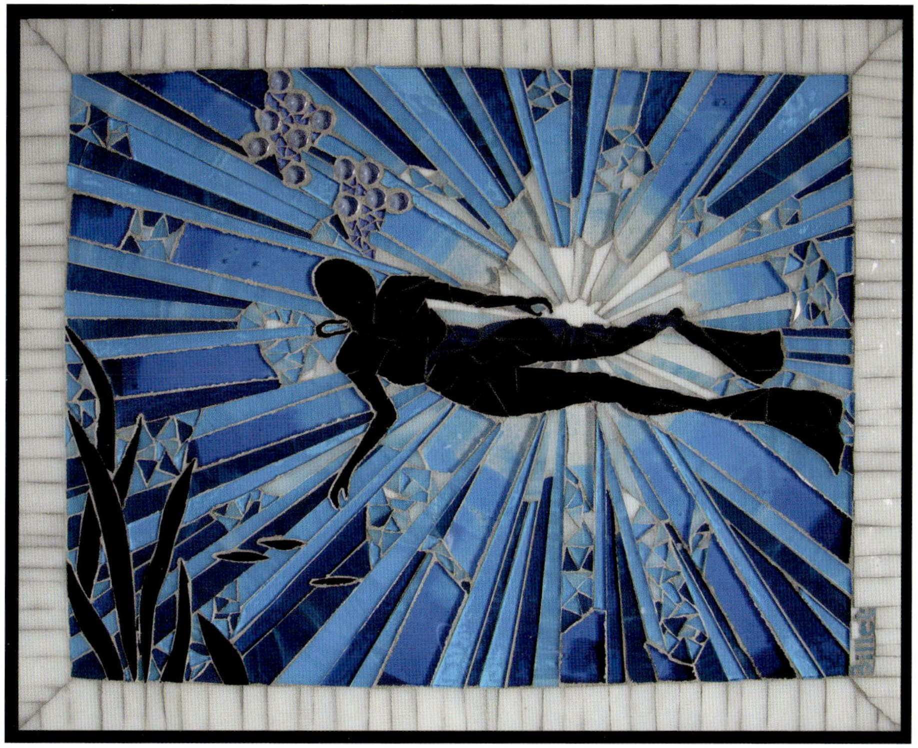

Linda Billet. *Follow Your Bliss*. 2010. Stained glass, fused glass, weldbond on foam board and mirror with grout. 16" x 20". *Photography by Linda Billet*

End of the Route: This work was a donation that permanently hangs in the Hummelstown Library in Pennsylvania. The mosaic is of the National Hotel, from a photo given to me by the library. Before the hotel burnt down, it stood on the property where the new library has been built. In researching information about the appearance of the hotel, I found out that it had been on the mail route of a friend and former co-worker. Because of that, I parked a mail jeep alongside the curb in the mosaic. It is the same kind of jeep that I drove when I was a postal employee. I also made a stop motion video of the mosaic's construction.

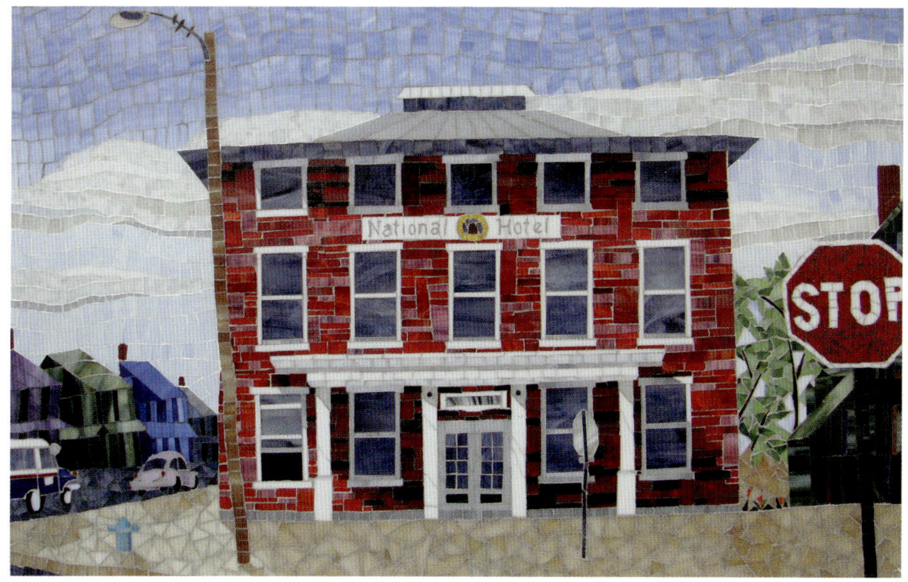

Linda Billet. *End of the Route*. 2010. Stained glass, weldbond on cement board with grout. 3' x 4'. *Photography by Linda Billet*

Fultz Fireplace: This was a commission for a client that loves floral motifs. She had wanted red and green with a bit of blue and then black involved.

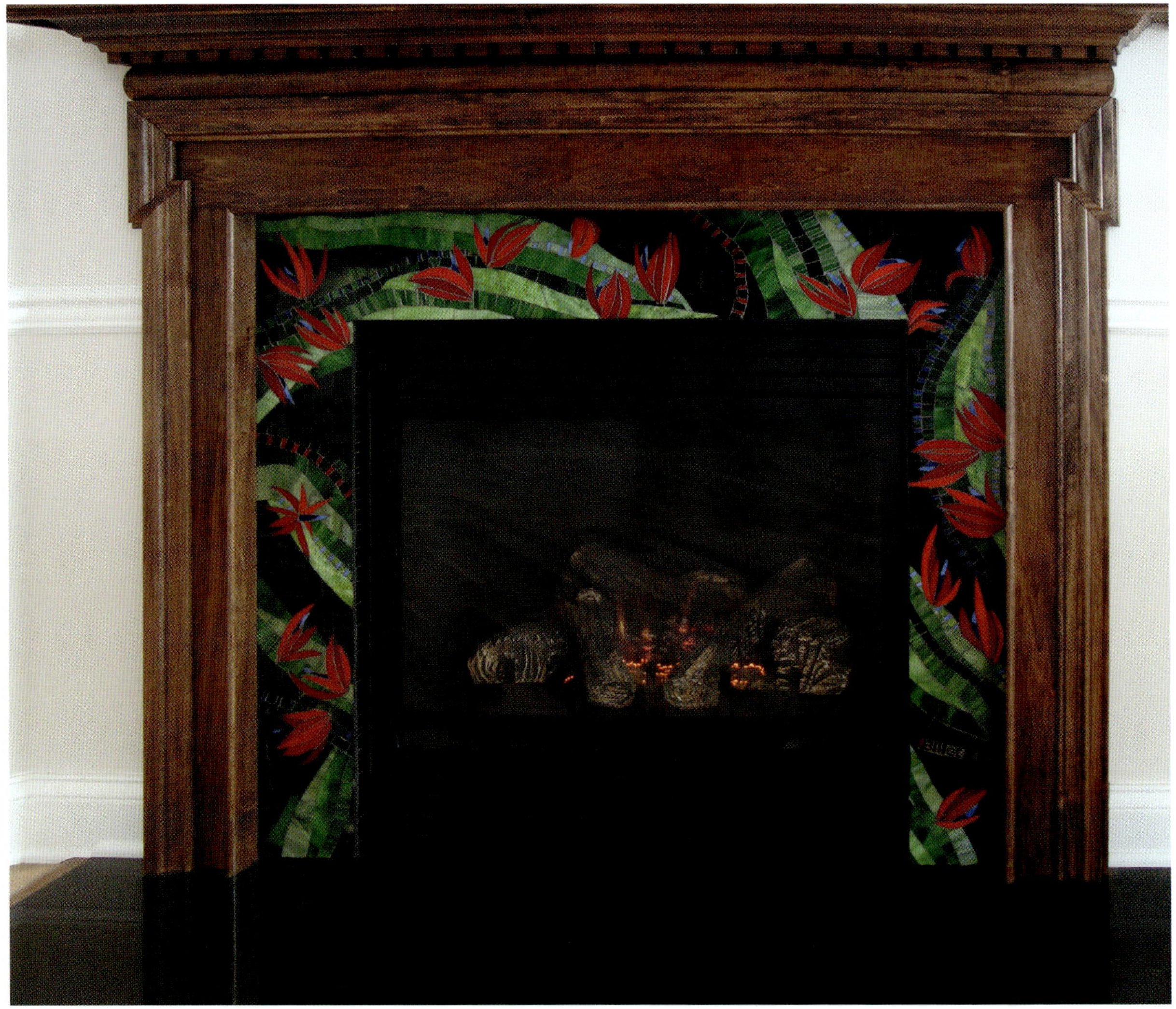

Linda Billet. Fireplace. 2010. Stained glass, thinset on cement board with grout. Approximately 4' x 5'. *Photography by Linda Billet*

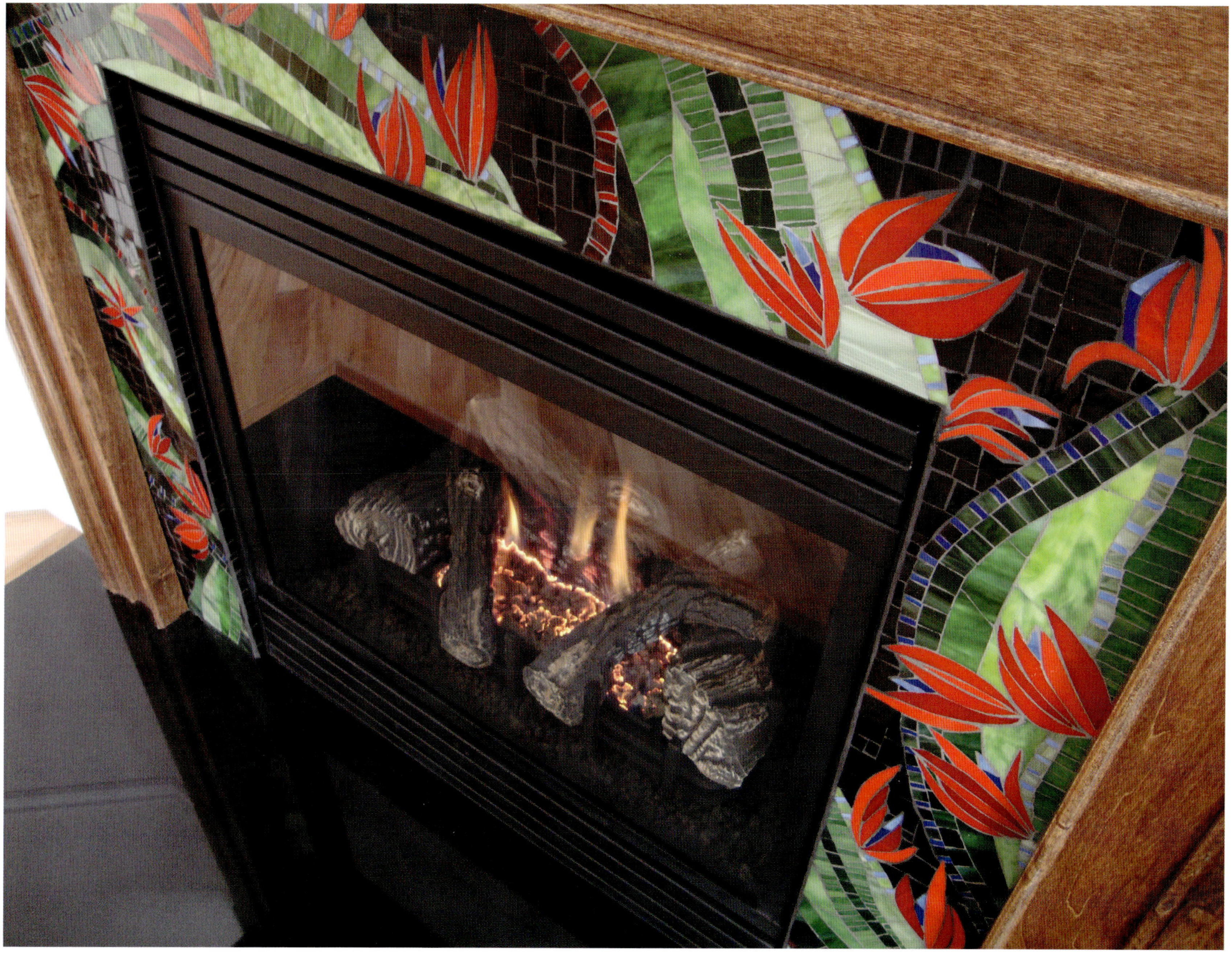

True: When I called my brother and was telling him about this chocolate mosaic, he asked if I included a half eaten chocolate that was discarded because it was a weird flavor. I had indeed thought about that and it is part of the frame. The chocolates in *True* are all fused glass (about 1/4" thick) and the rest of the glass is regular 1/8" stained glass.

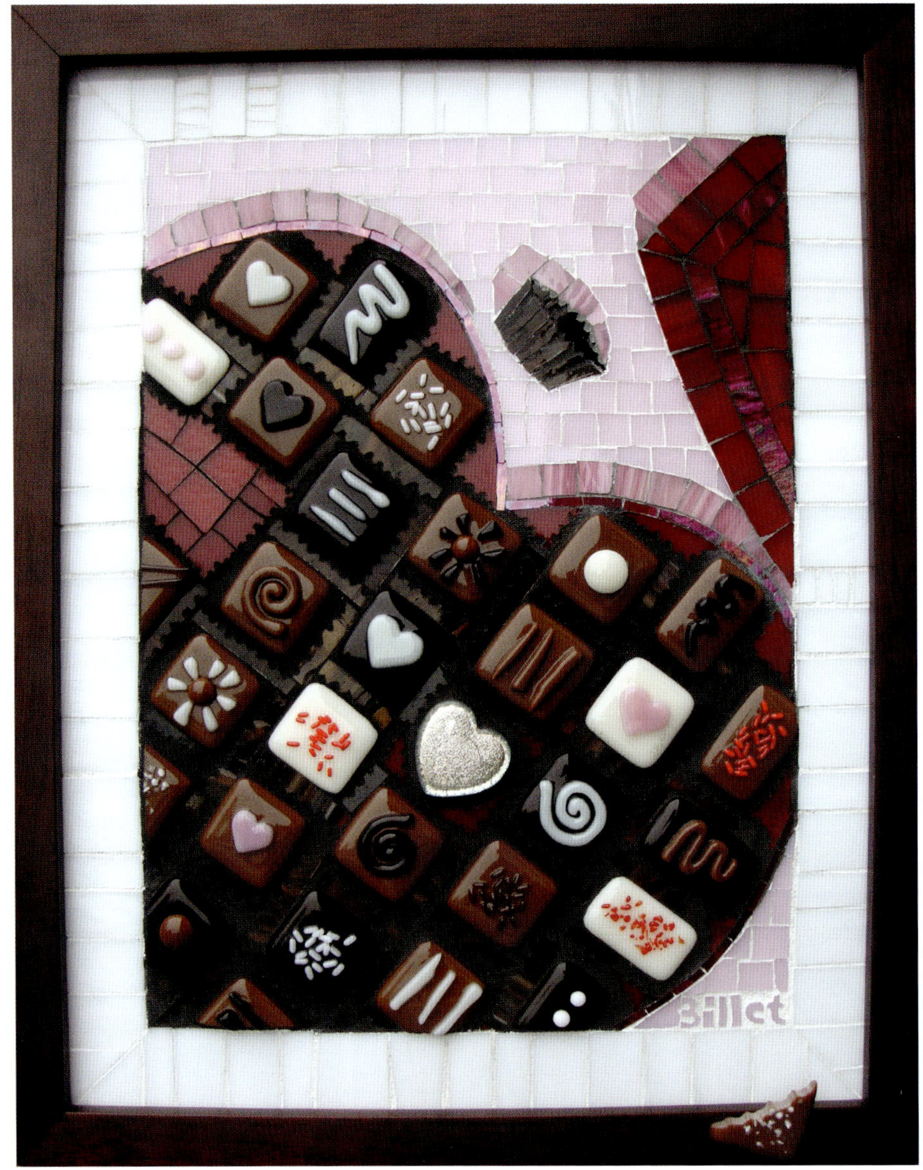

Linda Billet. *True.* 2011. Stained glass, fused glass, weldbond on cement board with grout. 11" x 14". *Photo: Linda Billet*

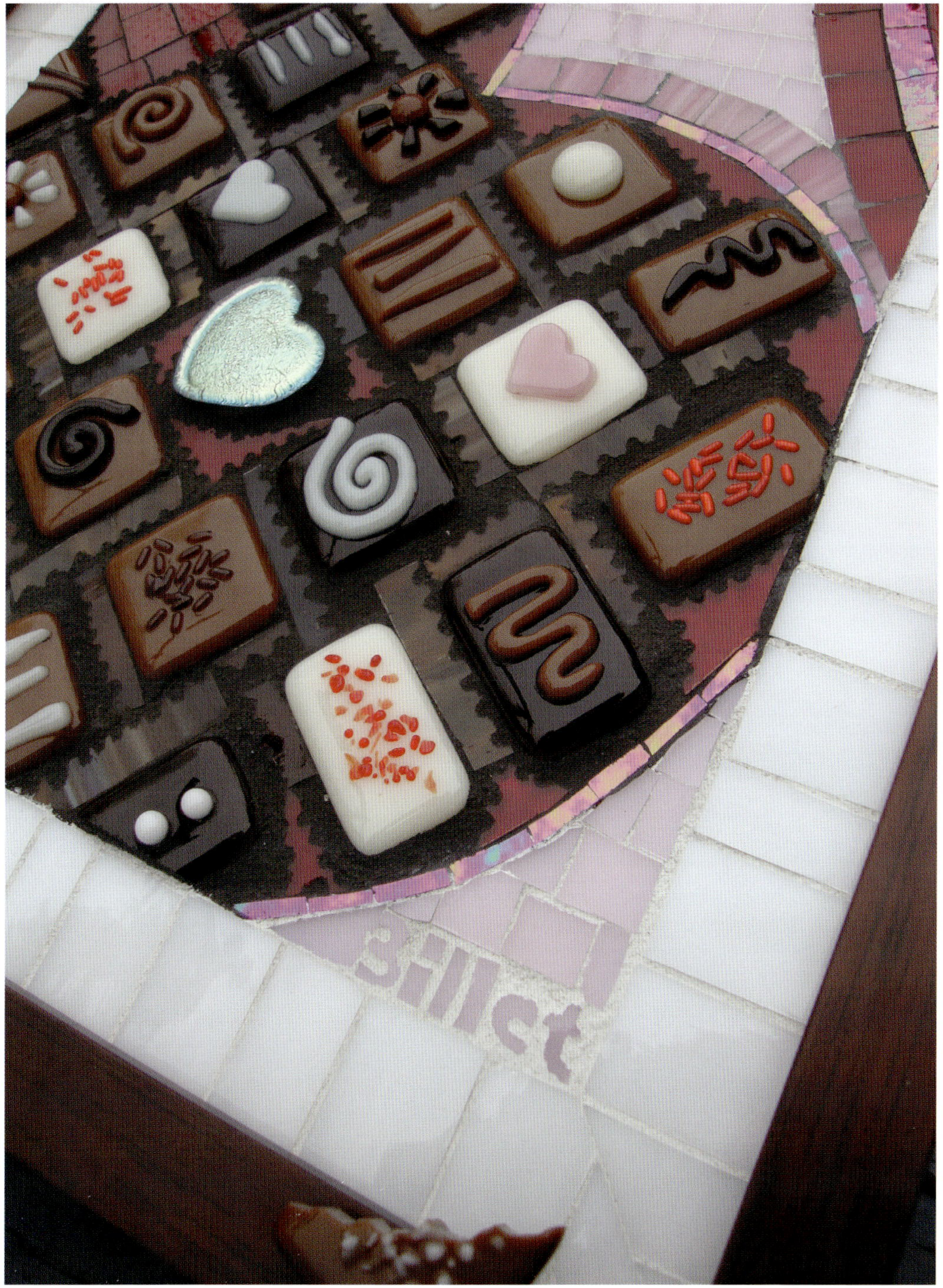
Billet

Carrie Bonnet

San Francisco, California, Carriebonnet@yahoo.com

Artist's Statement

When I paint, I paint what I want to see. When I mosaic, I enter into a mental zone and just go. This is a place where lack of control somehow becomes control and by the end of the piece, after it's grouted, I am always surprised but what reveals itself. When Lisa Bookstein (Mosaic Artist and Teacher and HR manager at Heath Ceramics) introduced me to the mosaic art form in one of her mosaic classes in 2009, I became addicted to the medium and the challenge of understanding how to manipulate it. When I paint, I love to make figures and faces. With mosaic, I try to make the tile look like paint, to make it blend, to show light and shading. I am intrigued by all the choices, both known and unknown, that the mosaic technique involves: substrate, theme, type of material, cut of the tile or the glass or any medium, grout lines, color of grout, use of grout, multi-grouts? My figure drawing teacher, Michael Markowitz, once said, "First master the medium and then let it go." As an artist, it is my goal to master the mosaic technique and then let it all go and allow my art to lead the way.

The Artwork

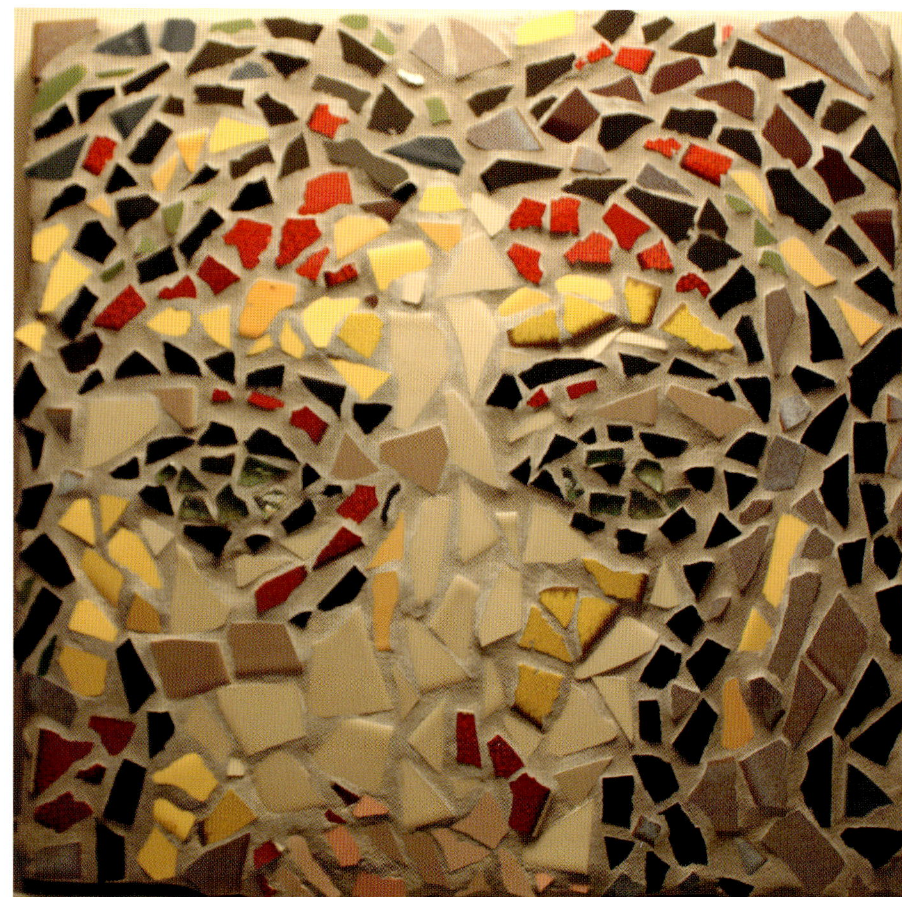

Carrie Bonnet. *First Face –Attempt.* 2009. Ceramic tile, glass, grout, thin set cement, hardibacker. First attempt at the medium. 10" x 11".

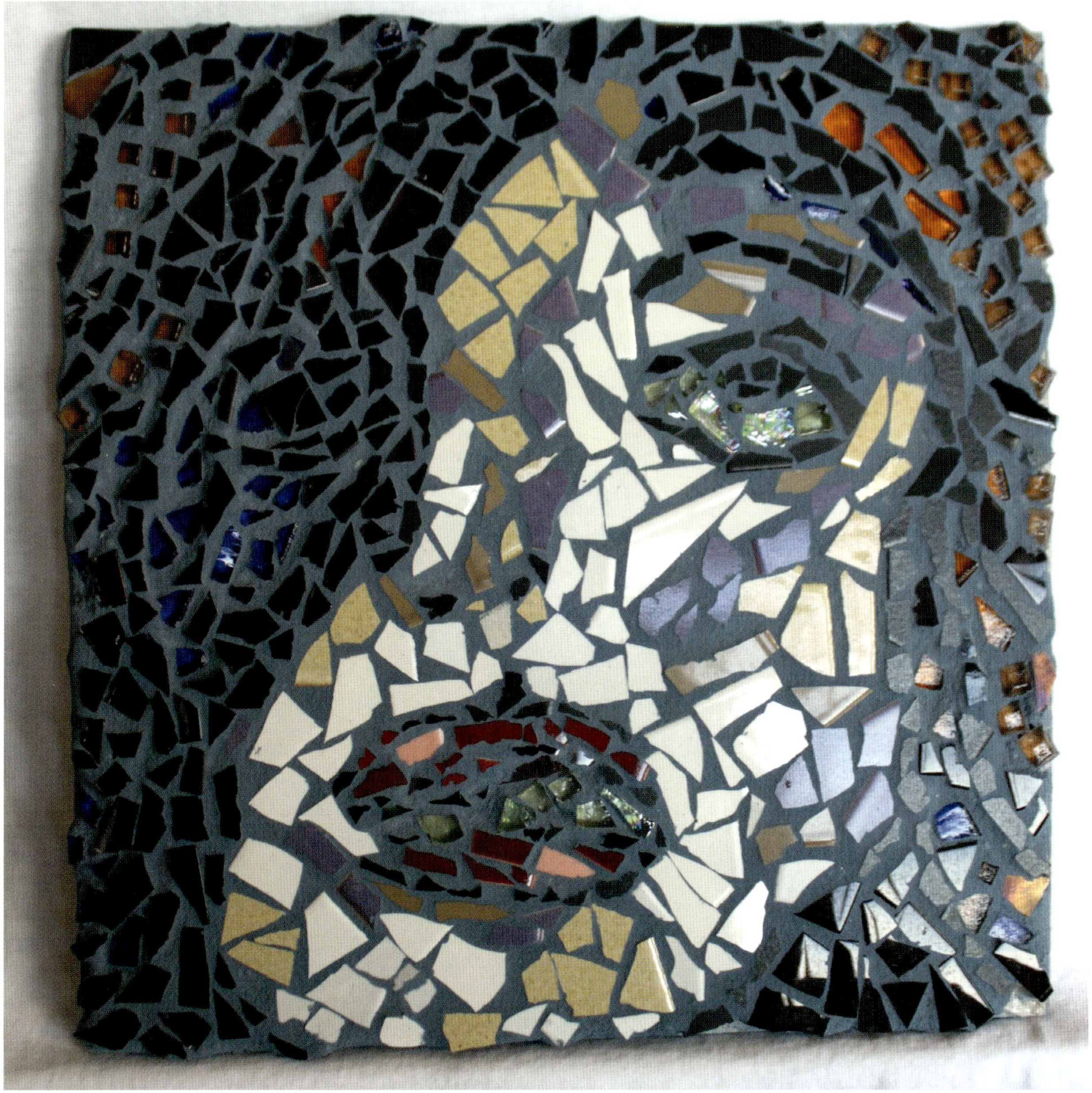

Carrie Bonnet. *Second Face–Letting Go.* 2010. Glass, ceramic tile, grout, glue, hardibacker. Learning grout lines. 11" x 11".

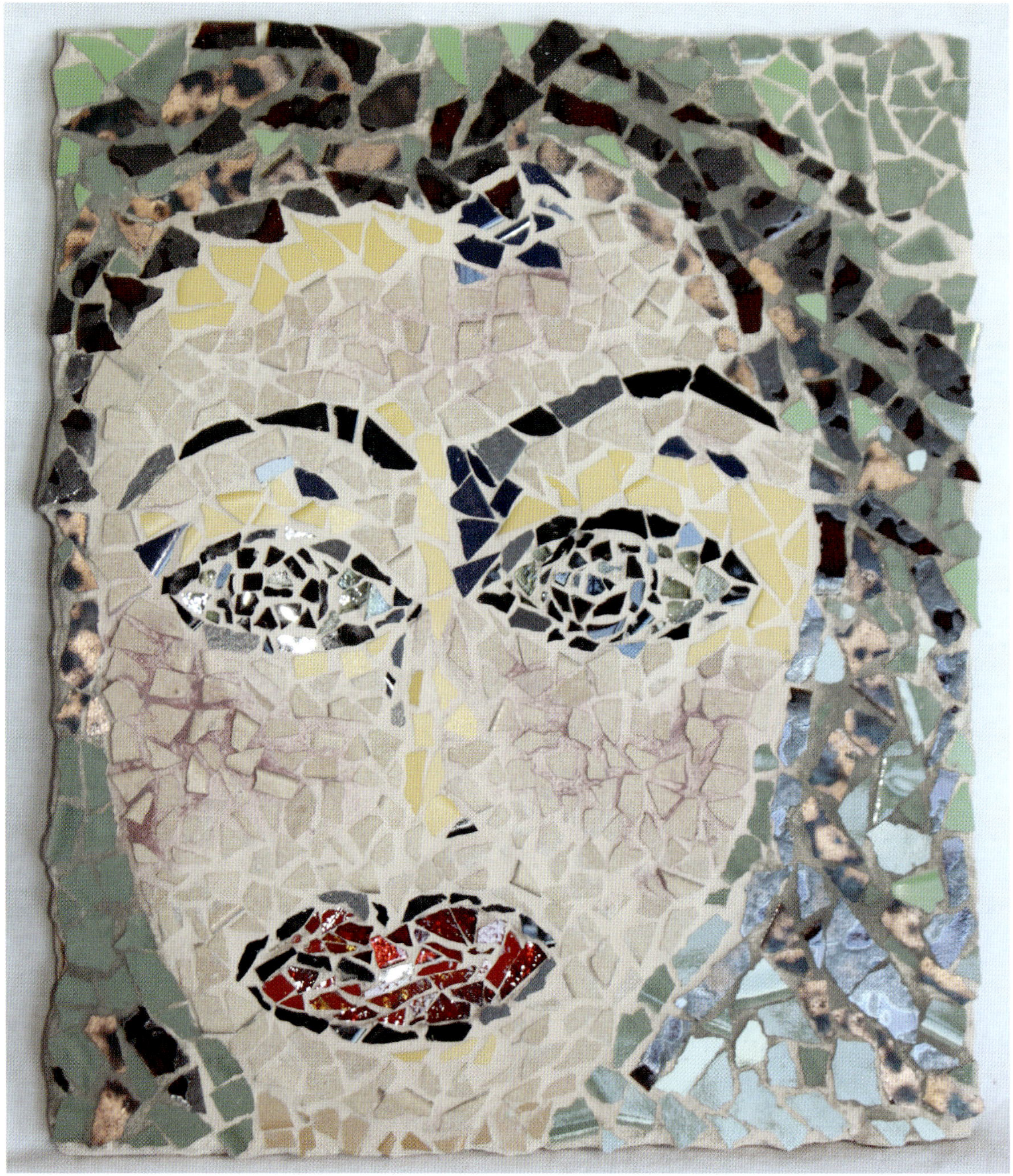

Carrie Bonnet. *Third Face–Control*. 2010. Ceramic tile, glass, grout, glue, hardibacker. Learning using multiple grouts as paint. 9" x 11".

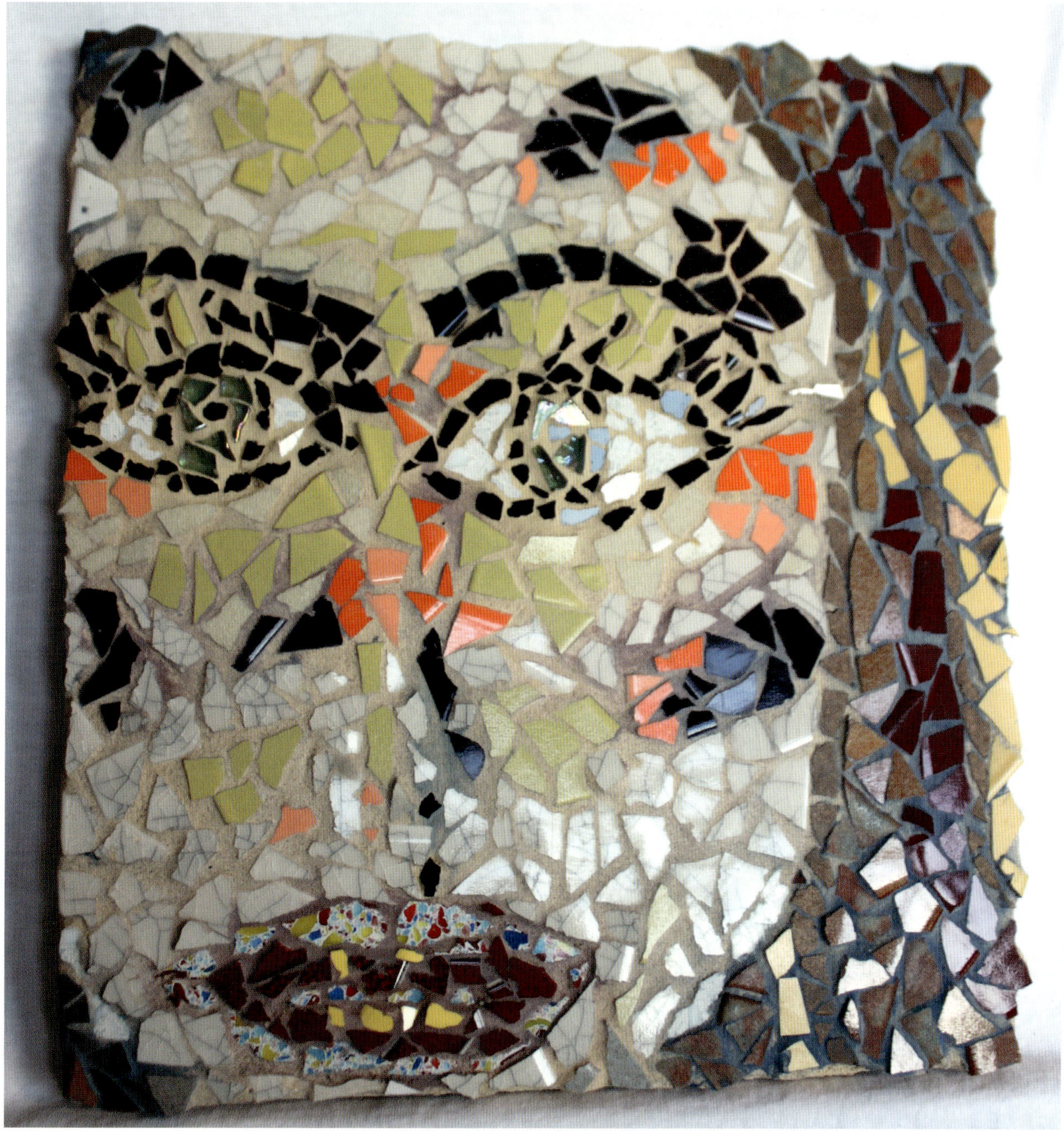

Carrie Bonnet. *Fourth Face–Achieving*. 2010. Ceramic tile, glass, grout, glue, hardibacker. Almost like paint. 9" x 11".

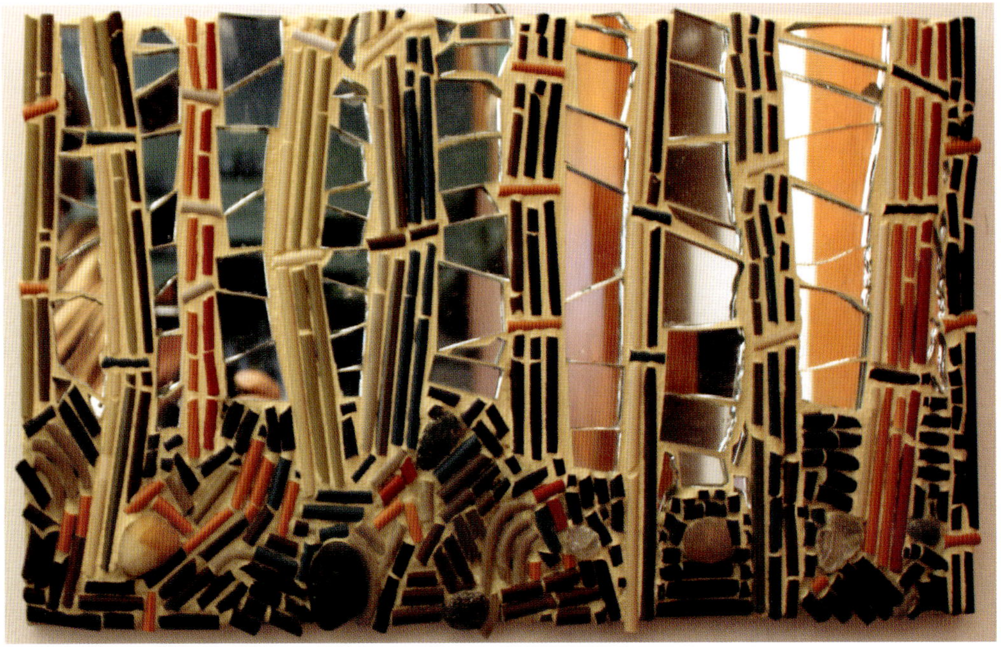

Carrie Bonnet. *Bamboo.* 2010. Heath Ceramic paint/ceramic tester logs, mirror, rocks, grout, glue, hardibacker. Testing multiple grouts and Dana's wedding present. 9.5" x 18".

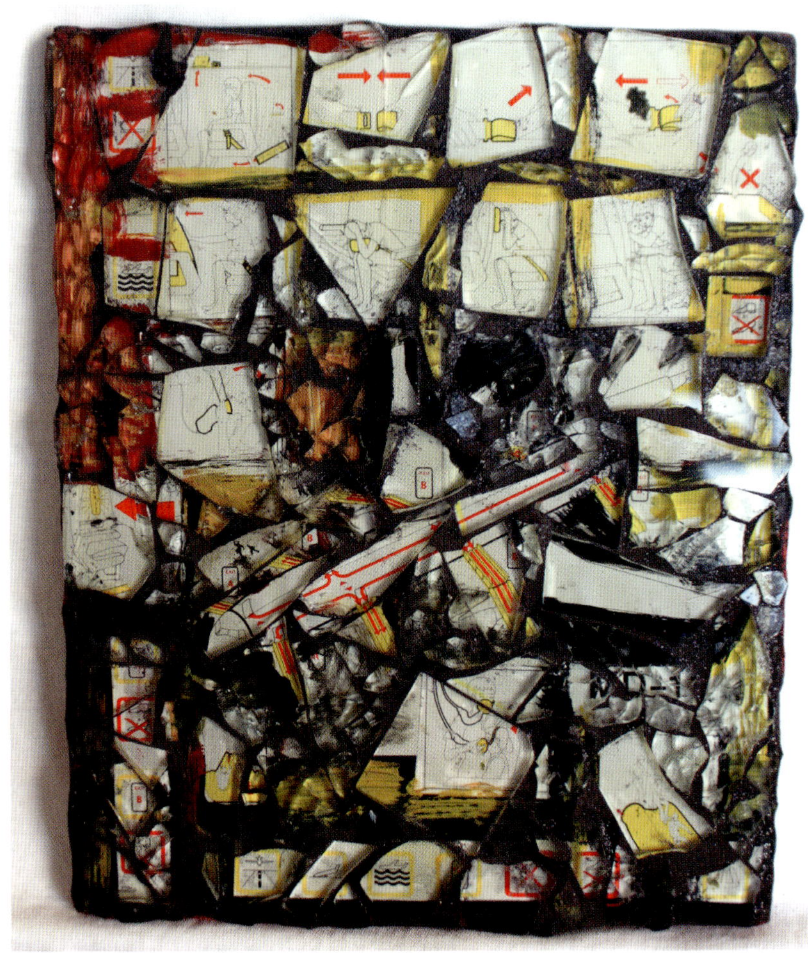

Carrie Bonnet. *Airplane Manual*. 2010. Airplane manual, paint, tempered glass, grout, tint, sealant, glitter, epoxy, hardibacker. Ellen Blakely inspired. 8" x 9".

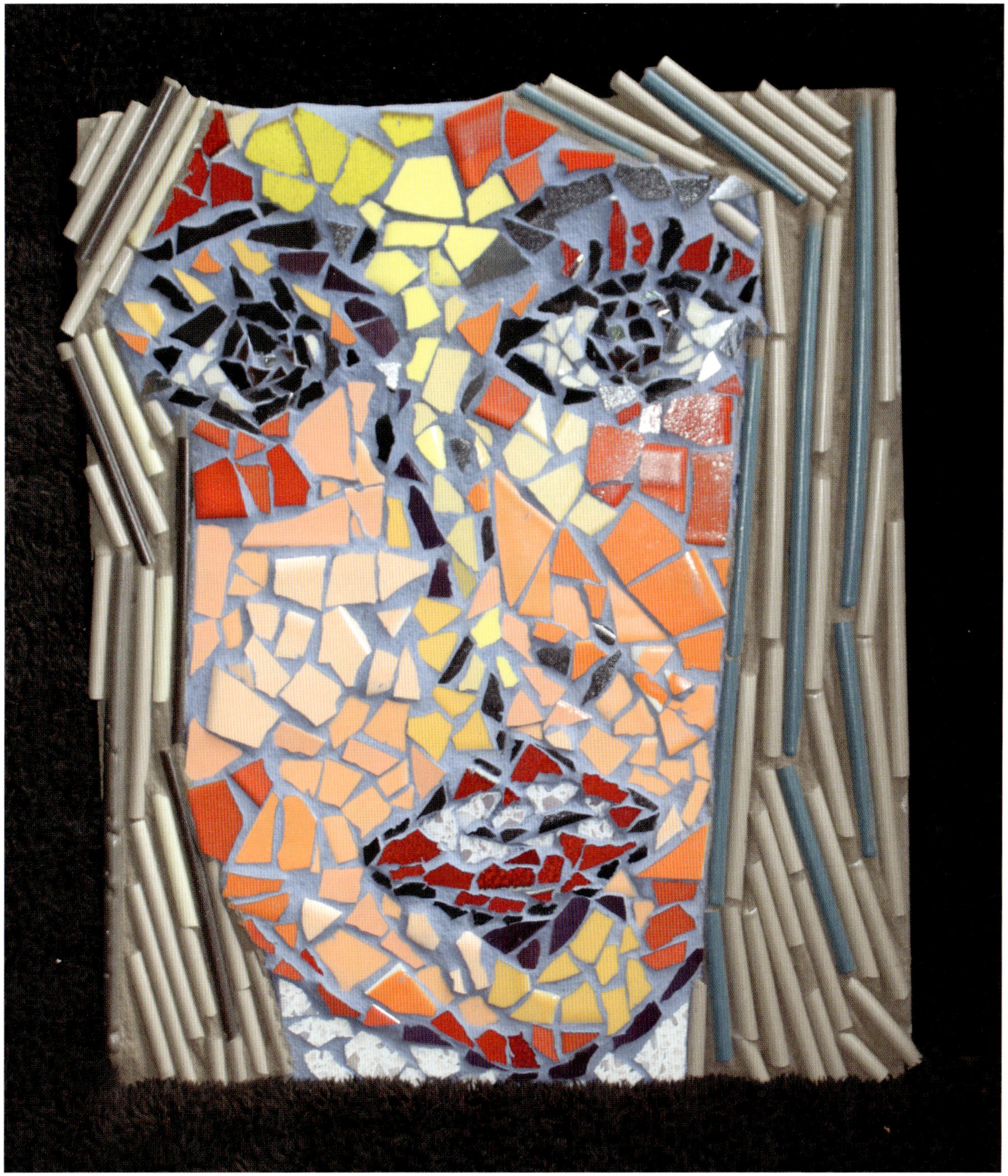

Carrie Bonnet. *Fifth Face.* 2011. Ceramic tile, glass, grout, glue, hardibacker. Mixing tile like paint.

Valerie Bretl

Cedar Key, Florida & Bristol, Rhode Island, vbretl@msn.com

Artist's Statement

As a child in kindergarten, I enjoyed cut-and-paste rather than clay or paint. Later, I became good at drawing but still preferred gluing things together into images. Like many mosaic artists, I began working with broken plates, then ceramic tiles, and most recently with cracked stone.

For me, working with cracked stone is like a lost soul finding home. The timeless quality of stone resonates with my designs as if nature had placed the pieces. My stone mosaics have no inclusions of other material to compromise the beauty of the natural rocks. Alternately, I use one of a kind stoneware tiles made at a local pottery and ceramic tile imported from Portugal.

I live in Florida during the winter where brilliant sunlight plays on my subjects of birds, trees, and people amidst nature. I find motivation there and my representational style comes as second nature. During the summer, I exhibit the mosaics at my Rhode Island gallery, Mosaic Arts.

My designs are created before I choose between ceramic or stone materials. Rather than make designs to fit the materials, I select materials that best suit the design. There are so many materials available to a mosaic artist that I am inspired by the possibilities ahead.

About the Artwork

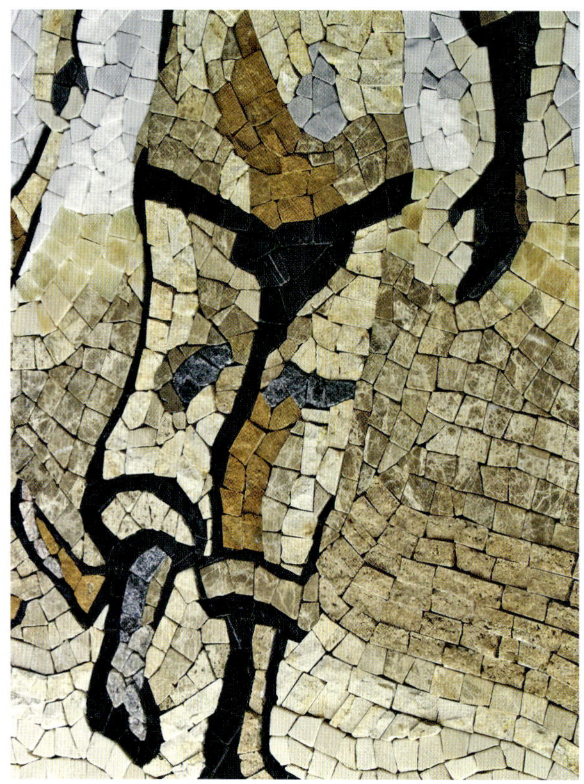

Beach Day: My intent for this mosaic was to have a family meld into their beach experience. After creating the family, I made the surround, not noticing that the family actually was disappearing into the background. This disaster just needed replacements of darker stones.

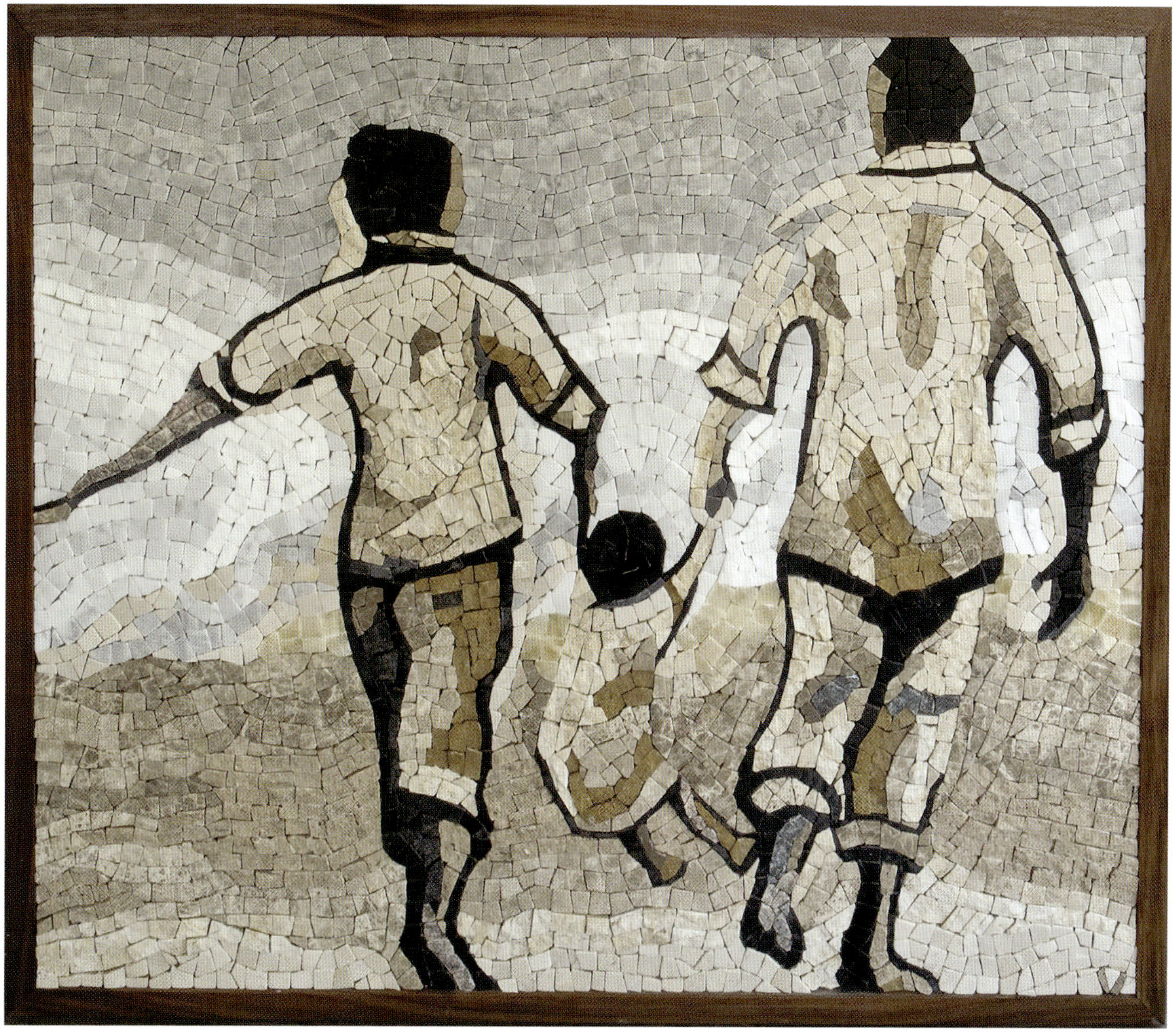

Valerie Bretl. *Beach Day*. 30" x 25.5". *Photographs by Bill Kilborn* (Detail opposite page.)

Beaks: I ordered stones from Holland to complete this mosaic for an upcoming exhibit. The stone arrived about two months later, having been sent by boat and held in customs where officials could not believe it was rocks.

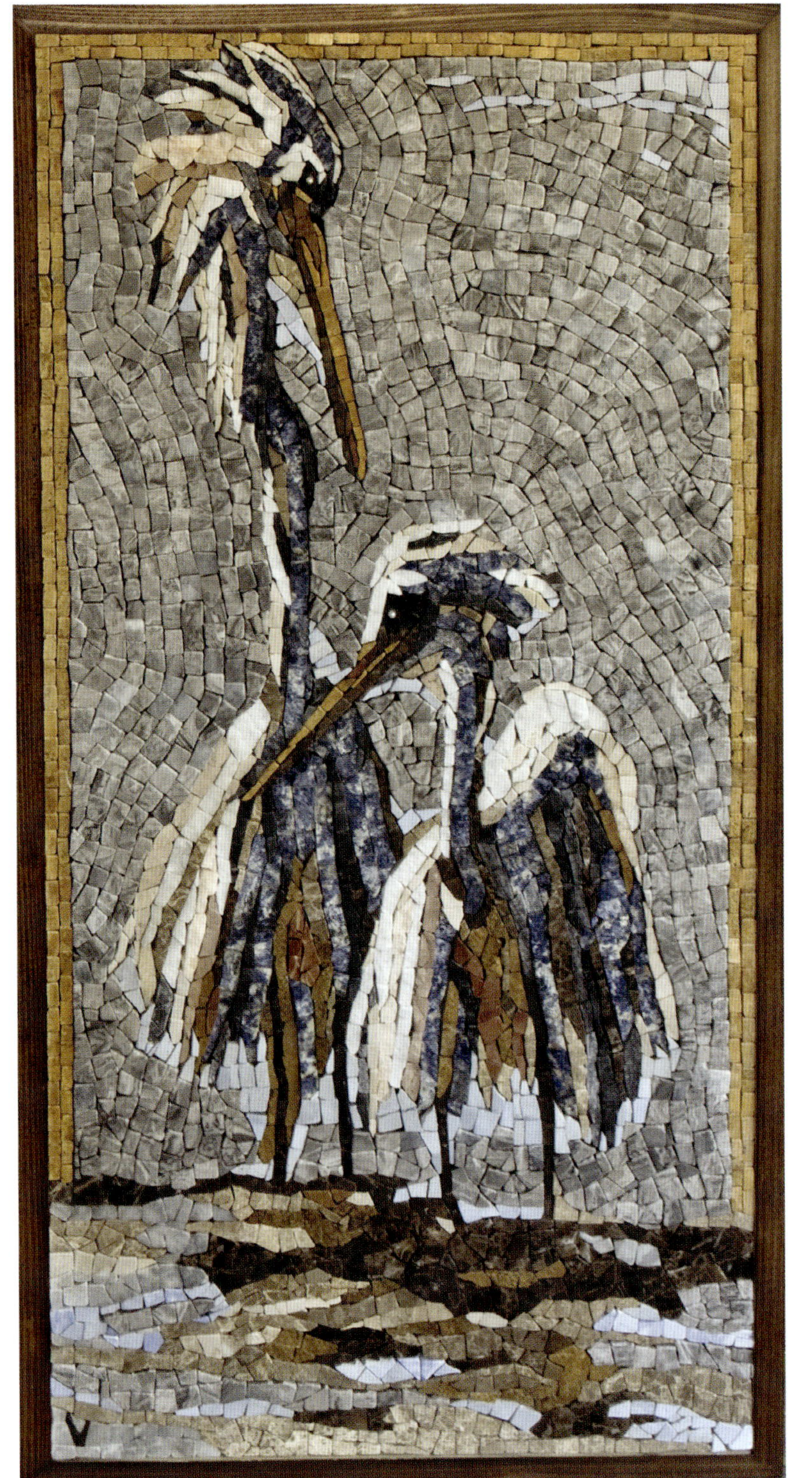

Valerie Bretl. *Beaks*. 18" x 34". *Photographs by Bill Kilborn*

Becoming the Garden: I was daunted by the hundreds of small pieces needed to make this delicate mosaic. Anxious for completion, I made rushed color choices that needed changing and learned the lesson of patience.

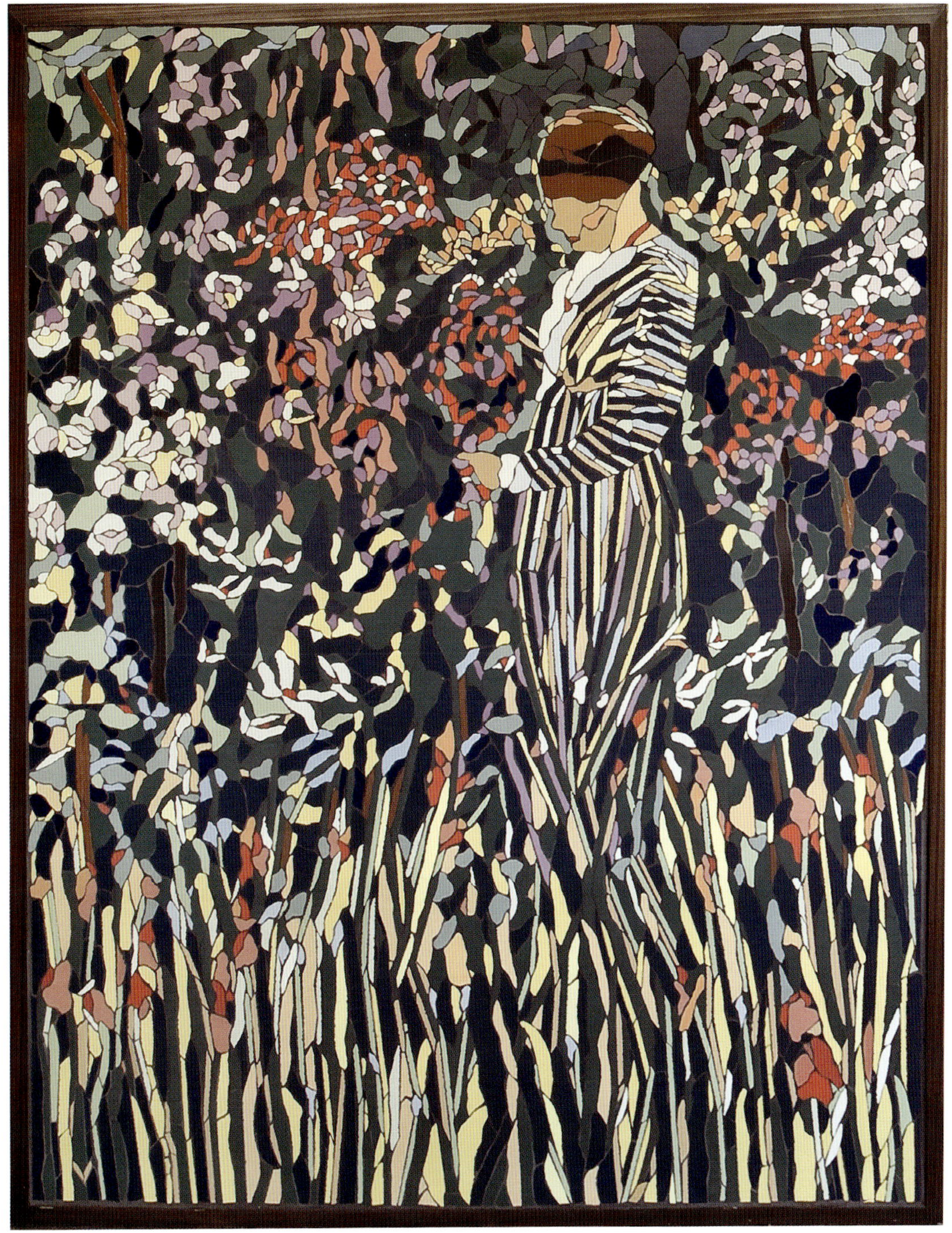

Valerie Bretl. *Becoming the Garden.* 33.5" x 42". *Photographs by Bill Kilborn*

Dove: After creating the headscarf and skirt design from stoneware tile, I was impressed with my technique. Perhaps a thousand years from now a person will find this mosaic and see that some of us loved peace.

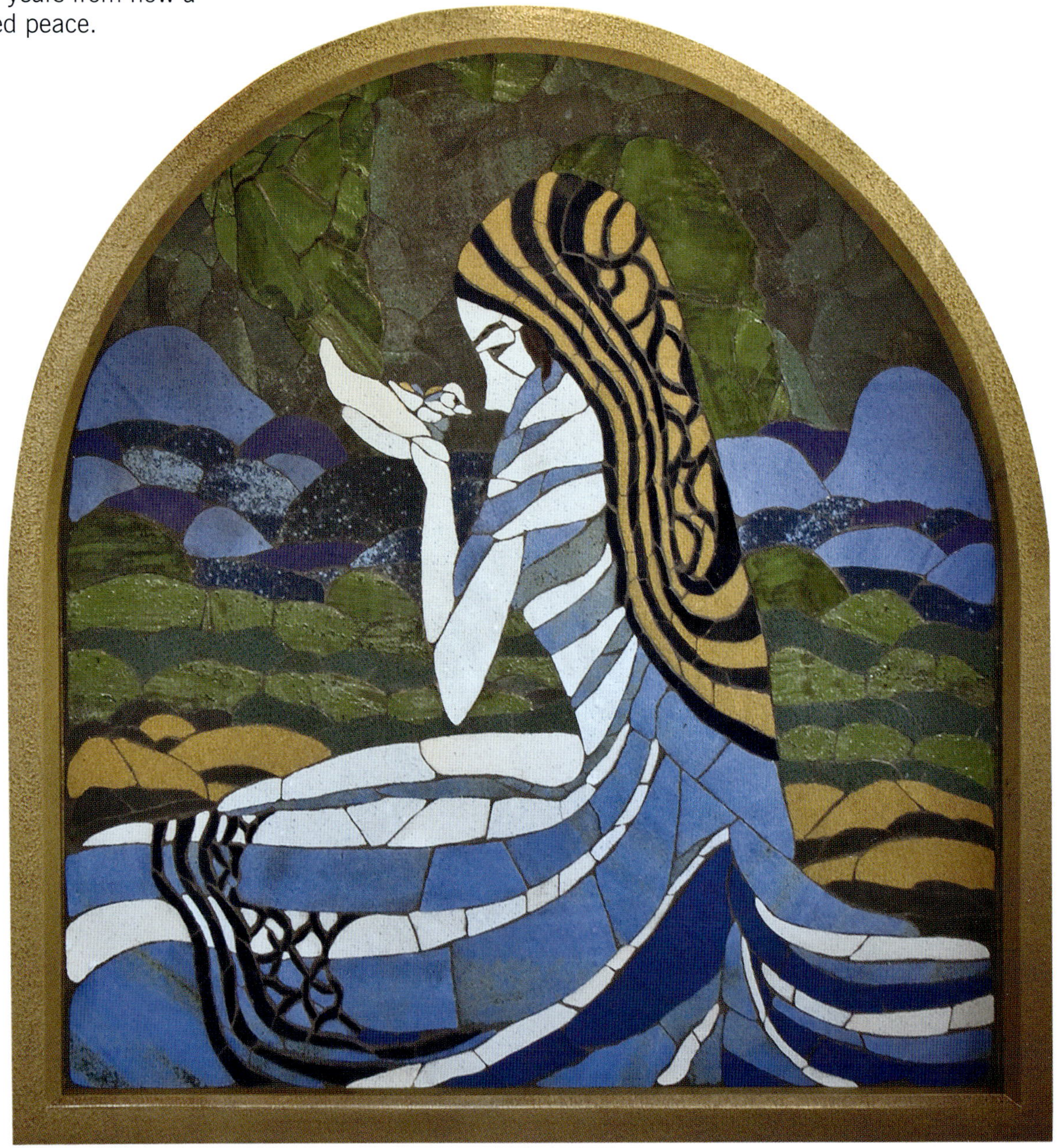

Valerie Bretl. *Dove.* 30" x 31" *Photographs by Bill Kilborn*

Last Dance: This mosaic marks the end of my time using repurposed dishes as materials. After creating thirty mosaics, I sadly had my "last dance" with broken plates.

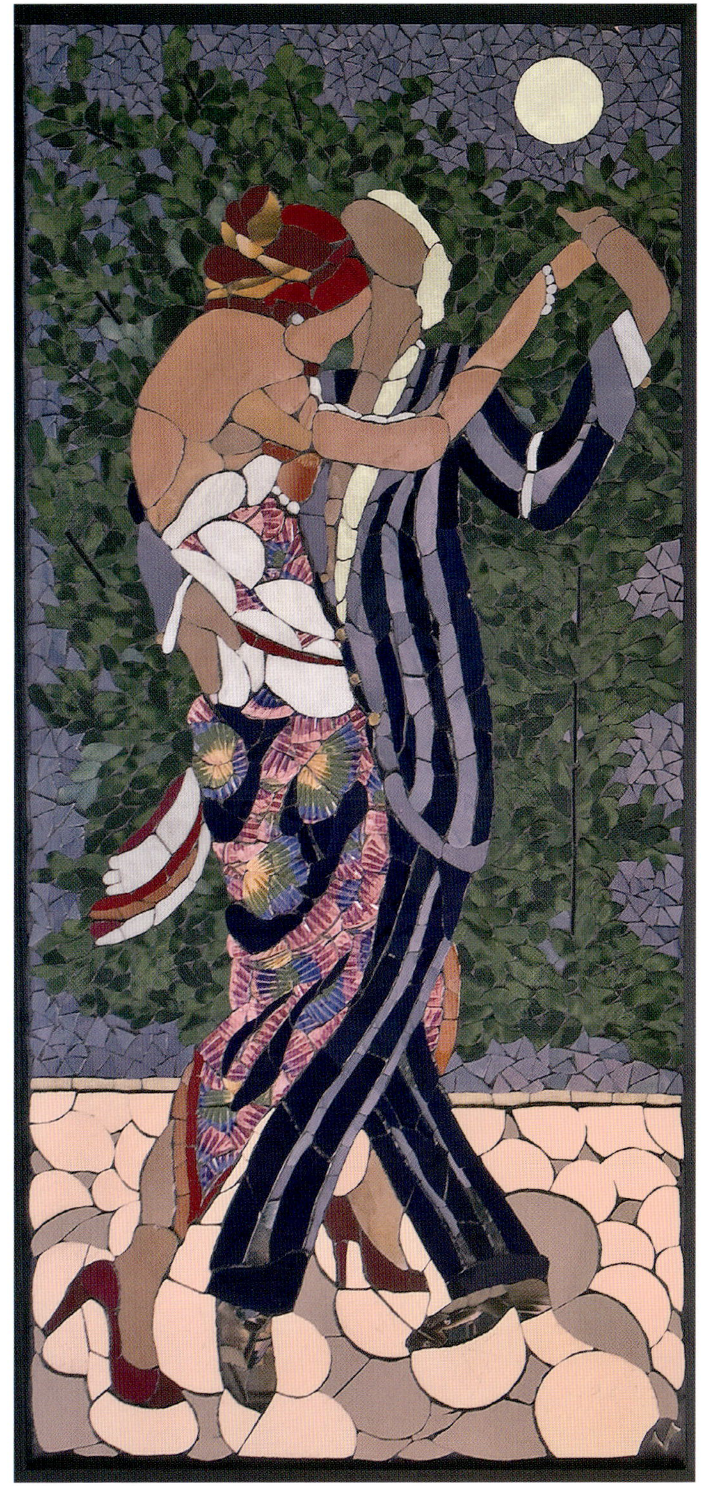

Valerie Bretl. *Last Dance.* 18" x 37". *Photographs by Bill Kilborn*

Misty: This mosaic was designed to be a mystic Sufi dancer, then he seemed to become a pine tree and finished as a dress in the twilight. Stones can play tricks on the eyes.

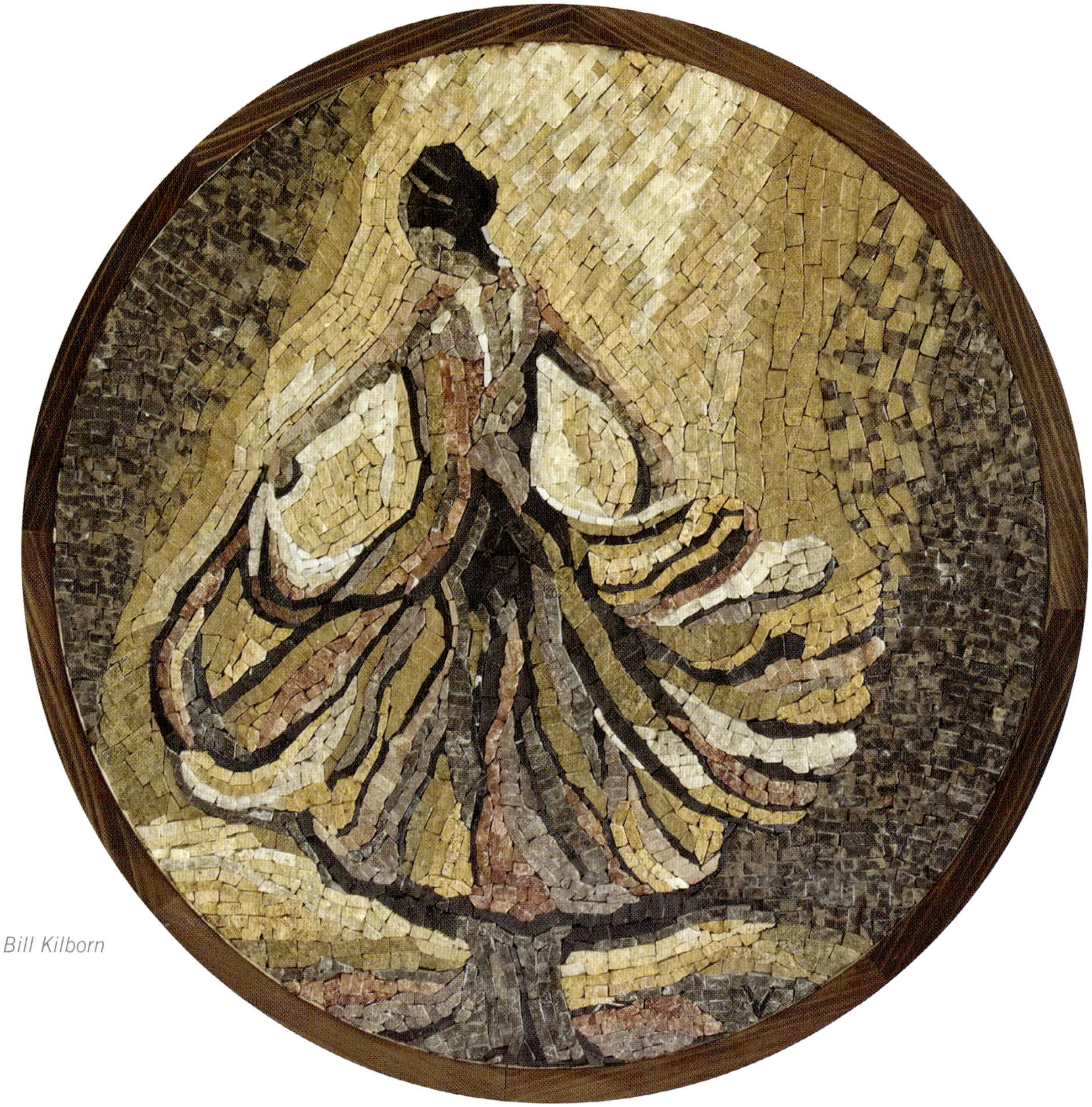

Valerie Bretl. *Misty.* 25.5" round. *Photographs by Bill Kilborn*
(Detail opposite page.)

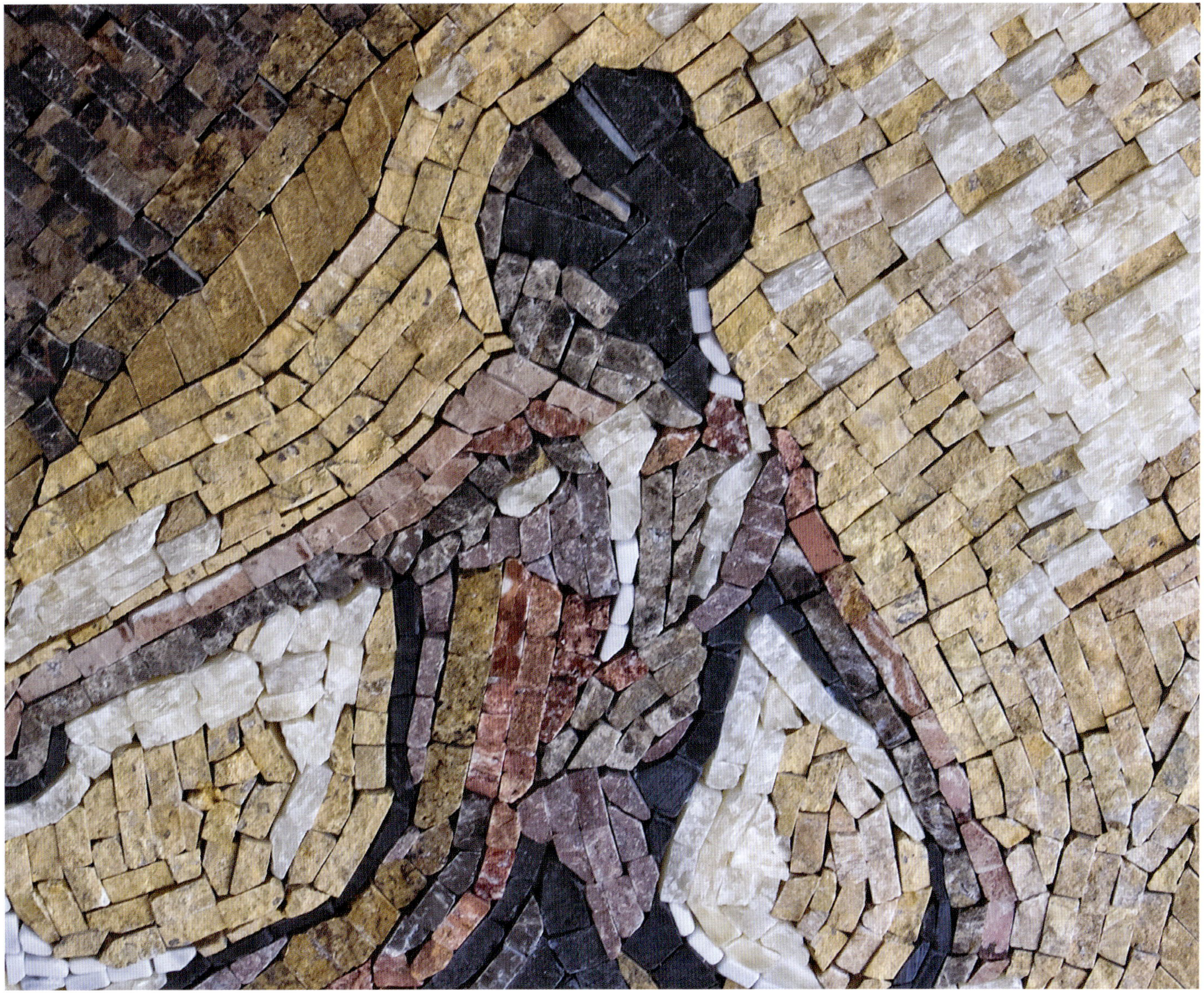

Sun Hat: Tiles for this work came from a local pottery where glazes vary due to weather conditions, and uncertainty is balanced by beautiful surprises. Large stoneware pieces convey boldness in this mosaic of a cancer survivor.

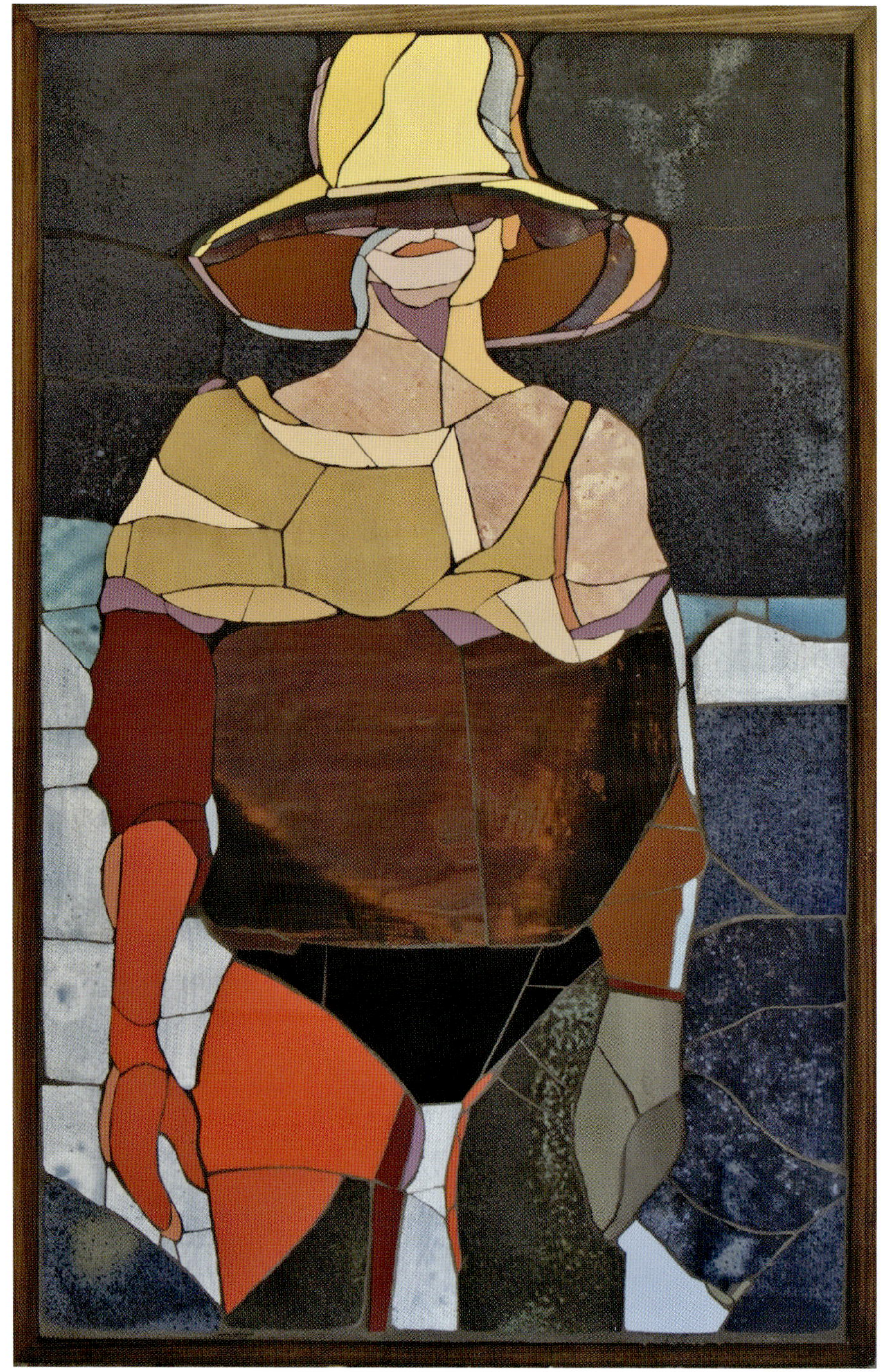

Valerie Bretl. *Sun Hat.* 22.5" x 34.5".
Photographs by Bill Kilborn

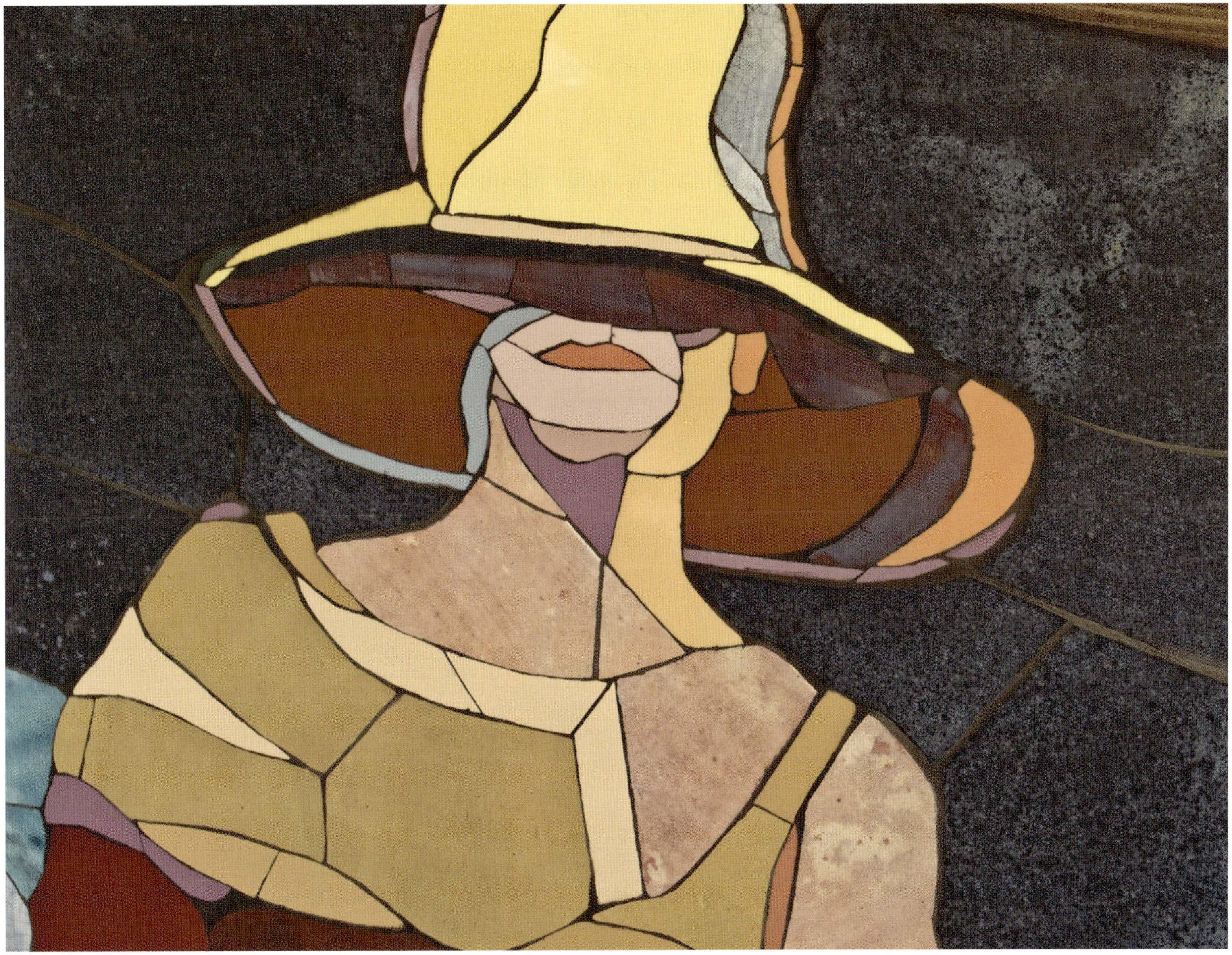

Sisters: There was a boundless feeling working with this readily available imported tile. I freely experimented with curved shapes and color tones for this mosaic depicting a downhill walk.

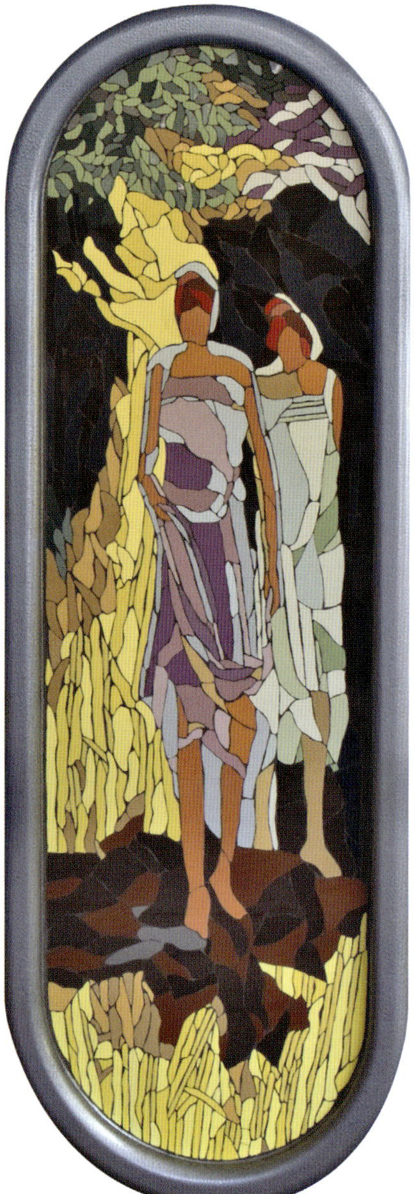

Valerie Bretl. *Sisters.* 15" x 44".
Photographs by Bill Kilborn
(Detail opposite page.)

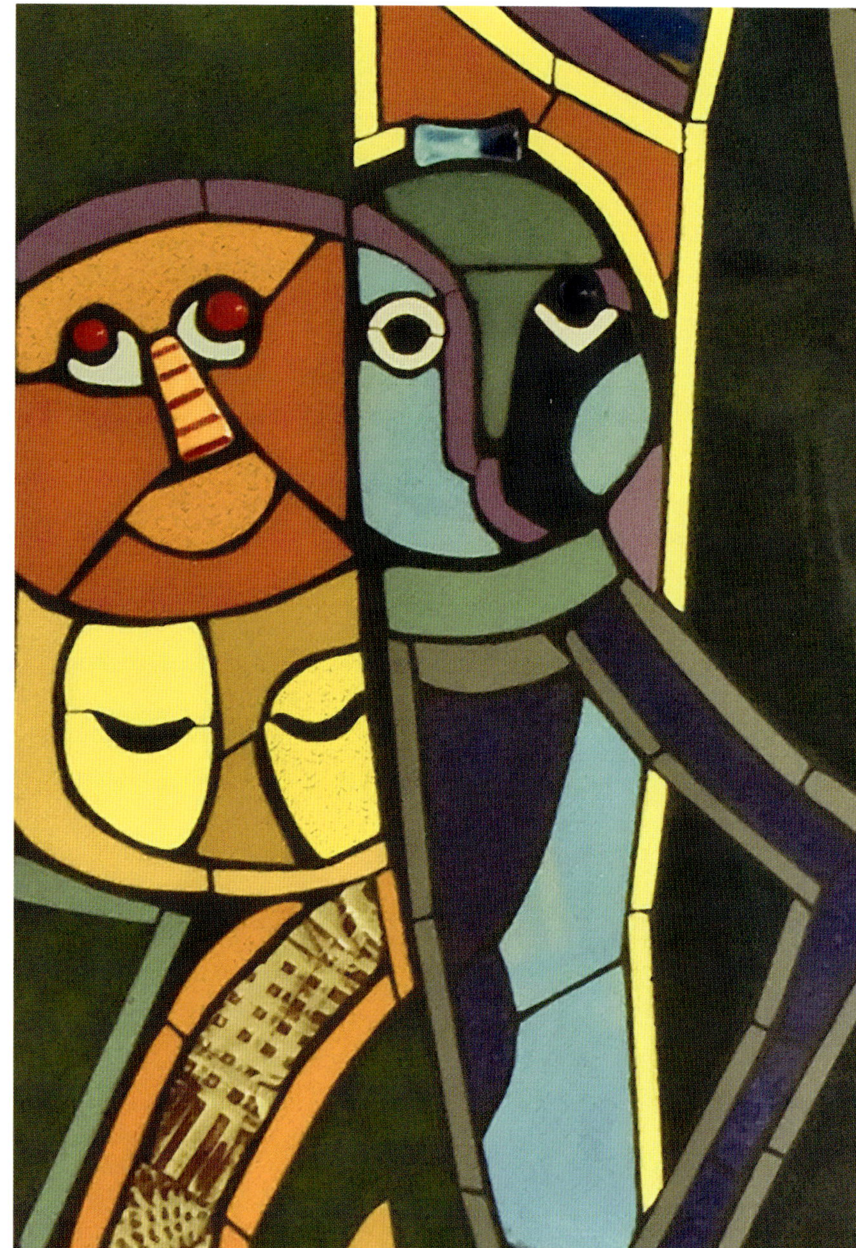

Tree Party: This triptych, located at the Island Hotel in Cedar Key, Florida, was my first mosaic following an illness spent watching trees. Perhaps the trees and I gave new life to each other.

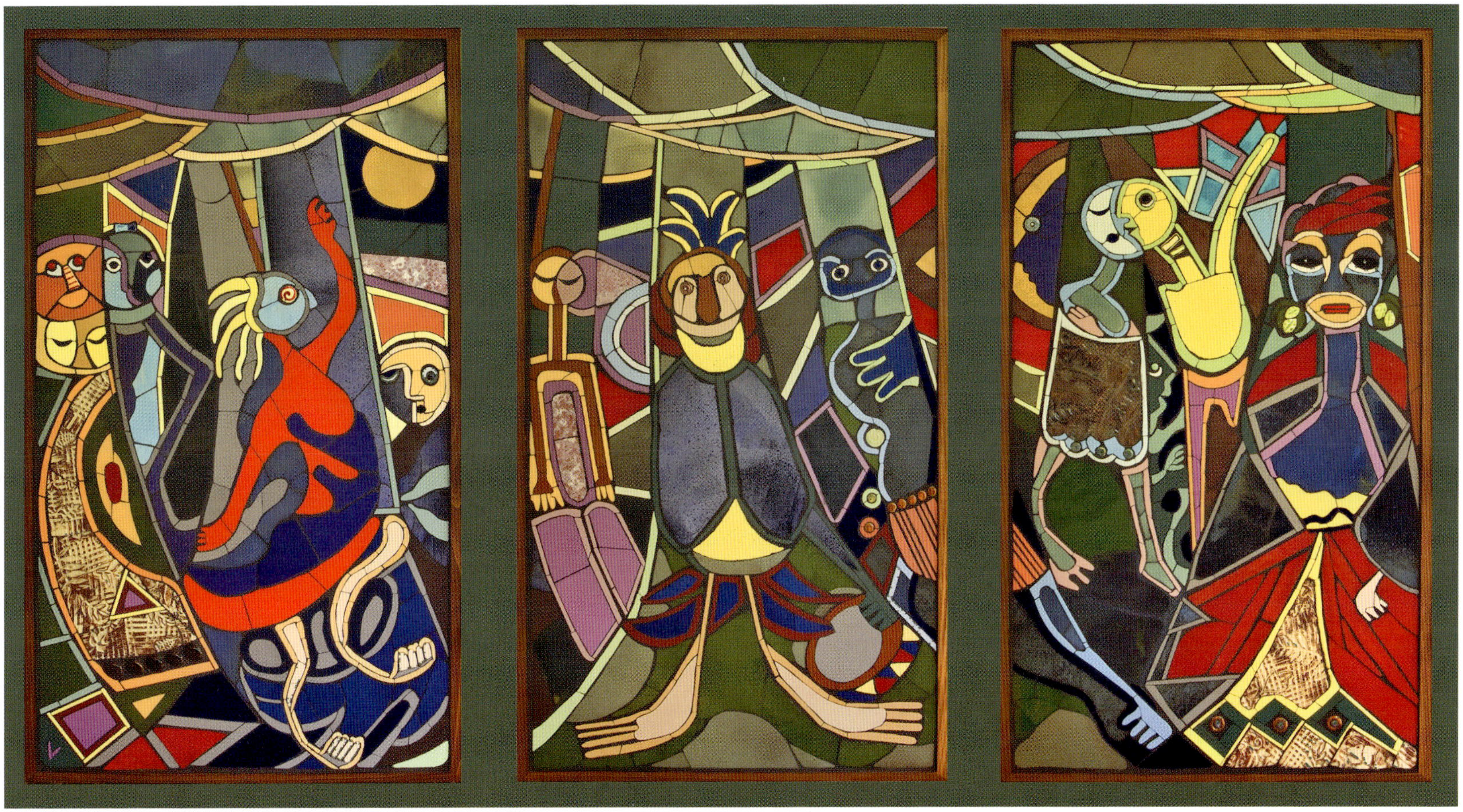

Valerie Bretl. *Tree Party*. 26" x 44" x 3". *Photographs by Bill Kilborn* (Detail opposite page.)

Jeannette M. Brossart

Durham, North Carolina, info@mothernaturemosaics.com

Artist's Statement

Art allows us to experience the spirit of our human senses, and individualize our conception of the world around us. My science background has emphasized that living things are made from tiny building blocks, and it is their precise arrangement that allows for a variety of species. I feel that the ancient art of mosaic is the perfect representation and translation of these two disciplines.

My mosaic designs revolve around nature themes, and often human or animal subjects, where energy abounds. I have discovered that the physicality of hand cutting the tesserae, laying them in a specific arrangement, taking into consideration size, shape, color, texture, direction, flow, as well as the interstices between the pieces, enables me to feel as if I am creating life within the realm of artistic expression. One individual piece of a mosaic may blend into the background, or stand apart and draw attention. It is challenging and exhilarating to transform a 3/4" square of glass into a bird feather, human pupil, or leaf blowing in the wind.

I am experimenting with creating sculptural forms with custom cement mixes, fiberglass mesh, and other repurposed and found materials for mosaic application. I am aware of my personal challenge to reuse materials, as well as the global benefits to taking advantage of these items, and showcasing their viability and beauty in a unique way.

I bring a fresh appreciation for the art medium of mosaic, as well as the amazing detail of our living world. I use glass tesserae most often since the reflective quality and brilliance of color give beauty and energy to my work. I sometimes juxtapose glass with slate, ceramic, mirror, or pebbles for texture and homage to earthy materials. My work considers the versatility and permanence of the medium, since it can be suitable for indoor or outdoor applications, wet or dry conditions, and a wide range of temperatures. In this way, my art has practical considerations and may be used beyond the confines of a gallery wall to enhance the aesthetics of our manufactured world, and bring to those spaces a celebration of the animation and vigor of life.

About the Artwork

Effervescence (6th St. Walls): Mural is on three sides of a LEED silver certified parking/retail structure in Charlotte, North Carolina. Simple bursting design gives the illusion of the artwork filling up the available space, while staying in the budget of the client. The circular details are enhanced by the use of color and pattern; none of the almost 300 circles are the same. Glow-in-the-dark tile is used between the touching circles to create an effervescent glow, as well as simple patterning in the floating circles.

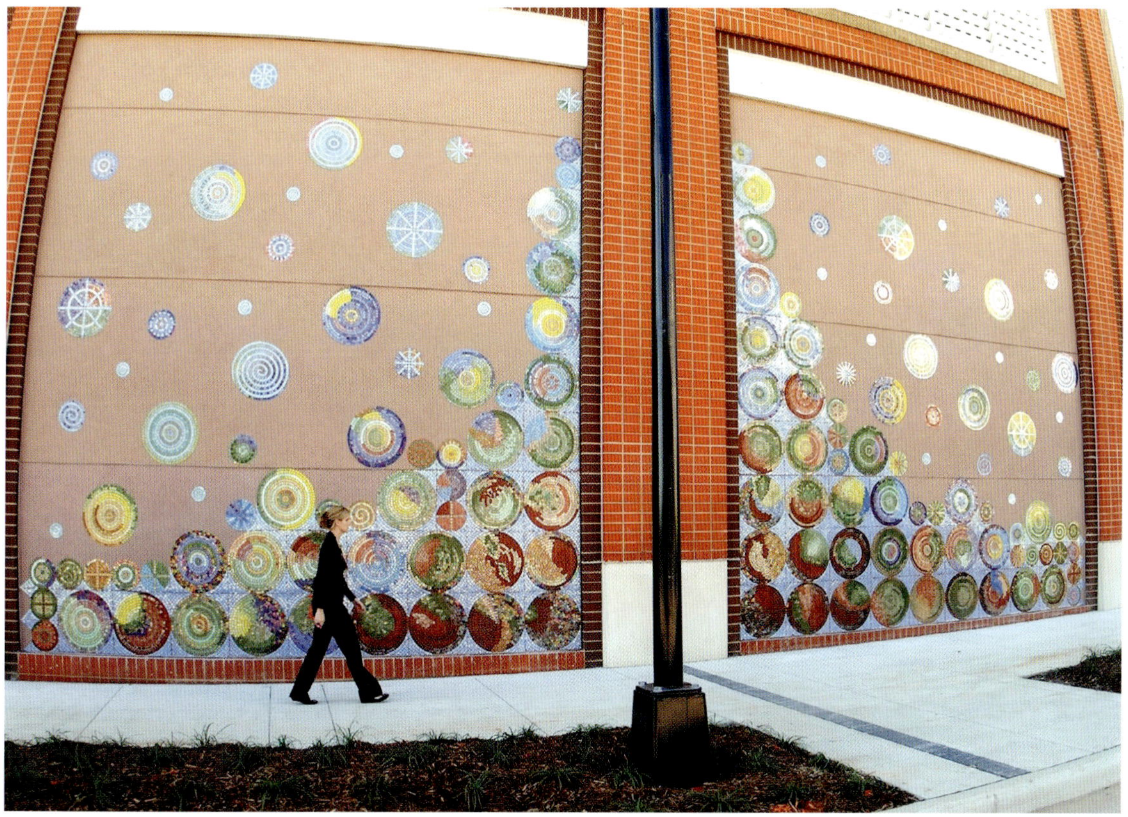

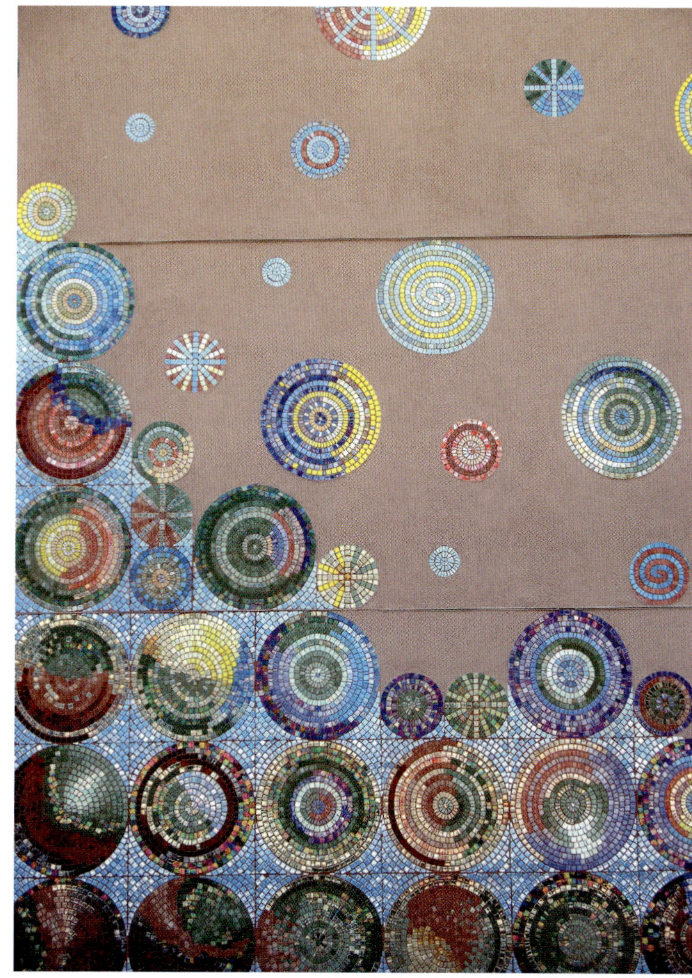

Jeannette M. Brossart. *Effervescence (6th St. Walls)*. 2009. Recycled glass tile. Artist designed and fabricated alone, with help for installation. Mosaic, installed over approximately 2000 sq. ft. of exterior wall and column space. These focal walls are 21' x 19' each; approximately 575 sq. ft. of recycled glass tile. *Photo by Mark Fortenberry, Charlotte, North Carolina*

We Are The Problem, We Are The Solution: This piece was created for a juried show featuring 90% repurposed, scrap, discard, and recycled materials. It has too many features to list, including moving light switch, horseshoe, brass finials, silverware, porcelain figurines, watch faces, hinges, glass, ceramic, shell, metal. Almost, but not literally, the kitchen sink. It has been shown at several sculpture shows, and is a fanciful reminder of the problems of human consumption.

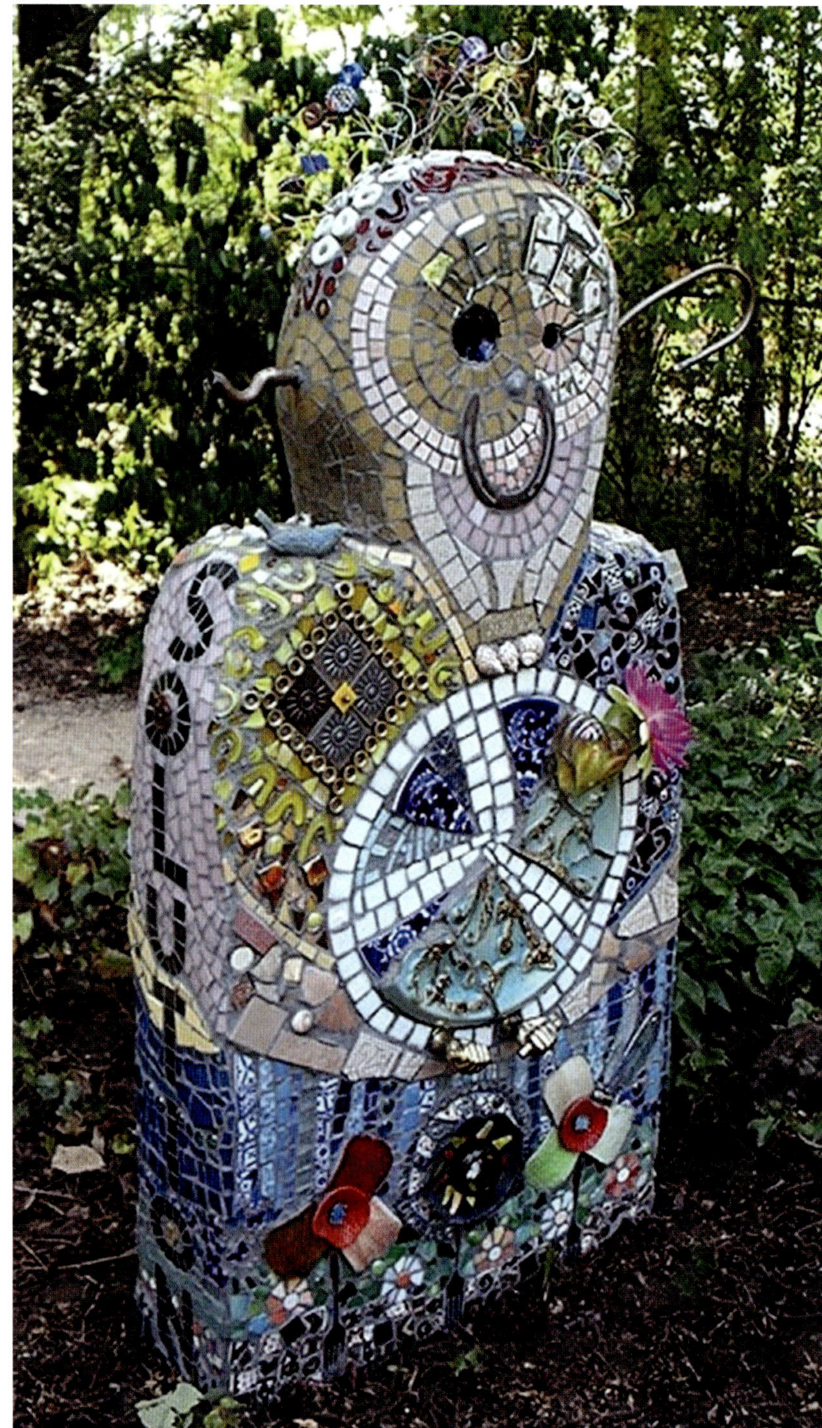

Jeannette M. Brossart. *We Are The Problem, We Are The Solution.* 2009. Carved and fused polystyrene, fiberglass, cement, applied mixed mosaic. 4' 8" x 2' x 1'.

Moon Birds: This piece was part of a private commission to create nature scenes to be inset in a pool deck. Each inset had its own shape and required some creative strategies for subject matter as well as installation. The moon is created with glow-in-the-dark recycled glass tile, and shines at night for extra illumination in the exterior pool area.

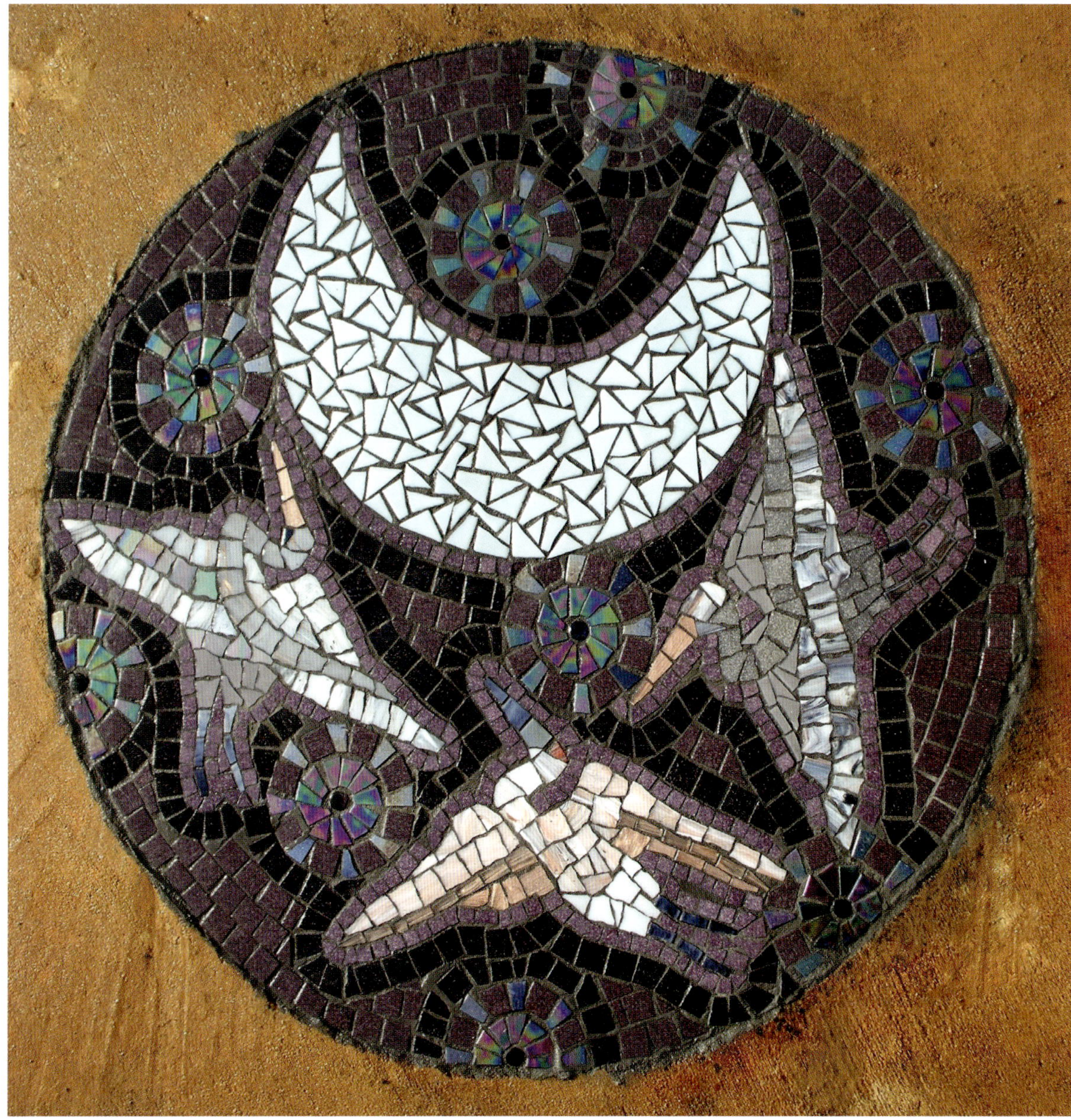

Jeannette M. Brossart. *Moon Birds*. 2009. Glass tile mosaic. 27" diameter pavement inset.

Currently Nesting: This work was created for an annual juried show featuring work created with 95% repurposed, scrap, discard, or recycled materials. An old tobacco cart is the base of the nest, with a variety of electrical, plumbing, and construction discards. A friend was showing me some welding and encouraged me to give it a try. So, of course, I had to dream up a piece that incorporated mosaic. *Currently Nesting* is a reference to the recent need for people to feel "wired in" and connected at all times, juxtaposed with the classic, natural iconic beauty of a bird's nest. Reiterating the question of how much is really enough in today's electronic world.

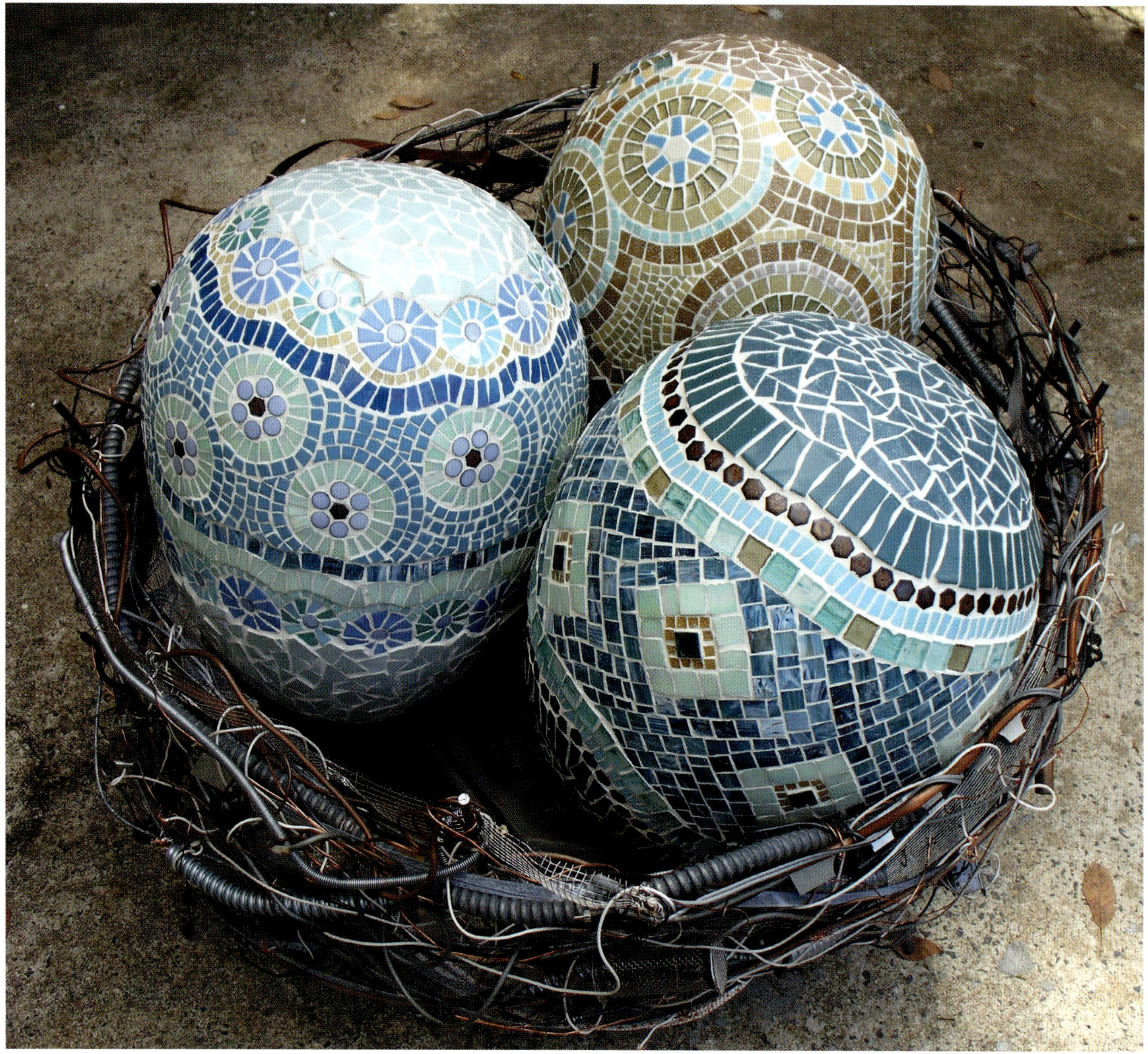

Jeannette M. Brossart. *Currently Nesting*. 2010. Welded and woven scrap metal nest, polystyrene, fiberglass, cement with applied glass and porcelain mosaic. 3' x 4' x 4'. Eggs: each 2' long.

First Bud: This work was a personal challenge of size and logistics of creating a sculptural piece larger than my workspace and with suitable engineering to be transported and moved with man (woman) power. The form was simply taken from the budding branches of trees in spring, with the promise of green to come.

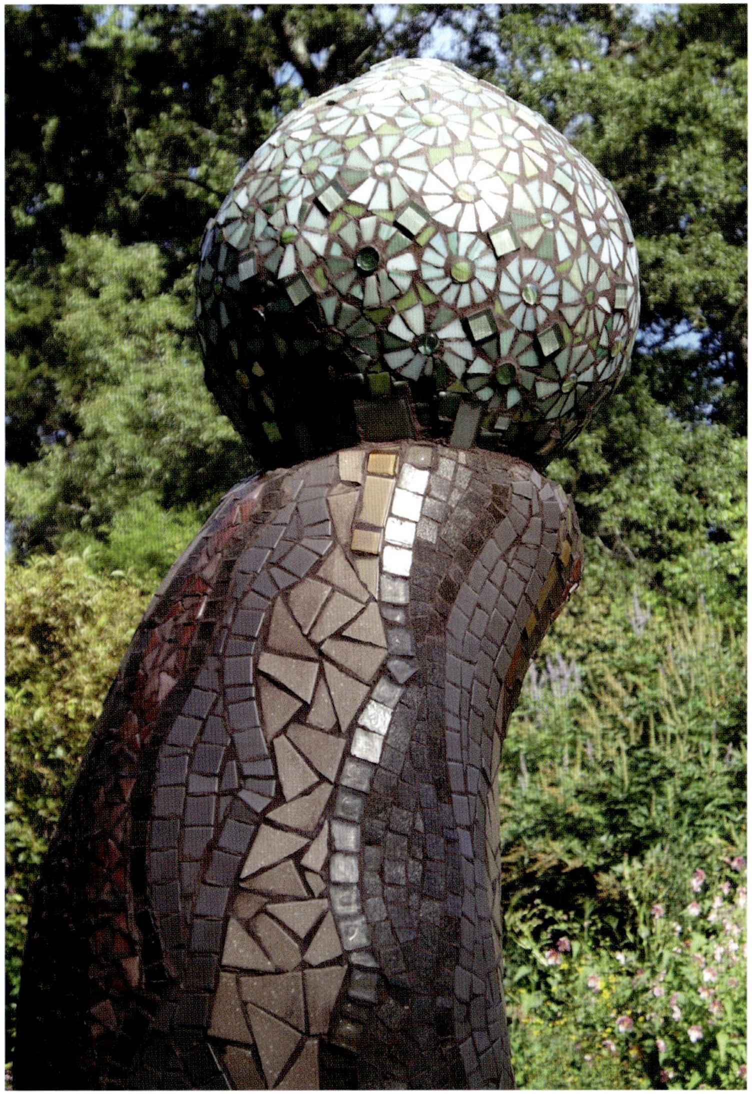

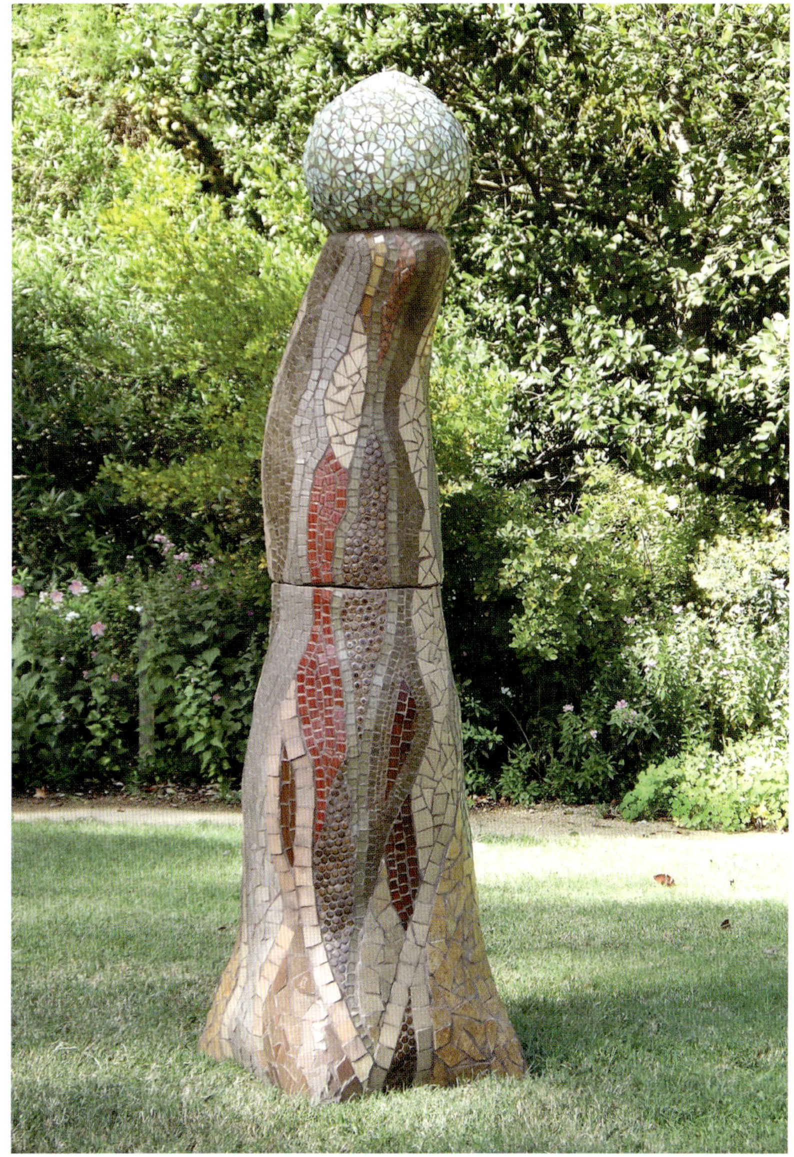

Jeannette M. Brossart. *First Bud*. 2010. Carved polystyrene, fiberglass, and cement base, with applied glass and porcelain mosaic. 8' x 2' x 2'.

Ilona Brustad

Ann Arbor, Michigan, imbrustad@aol.com

Artist's Statement

When I took my first mosaic workshop, my response was immediate and intense. I needed to make mosaics. As a painter for twenty years, I had always been charmed by the intense colors of Rouault and the primitive painters of Haiti. Consequently, I found the shift to the color and texture possibilities of mosaics natural and intriguing. Since that first mosaic class, I have experimented with a variety of materials, including glass, porcelain, stones, beads, found objects, and handmade tiles, to create unique, innovative work.

About the Artwork

Light Show: *Light Show* is unusual in being both a painting and a mosaic. I was trying to create a visual and physical sense of space by using pieces of glass for the water and small rock formations and painting the sky and water as it receded. (opposite page)

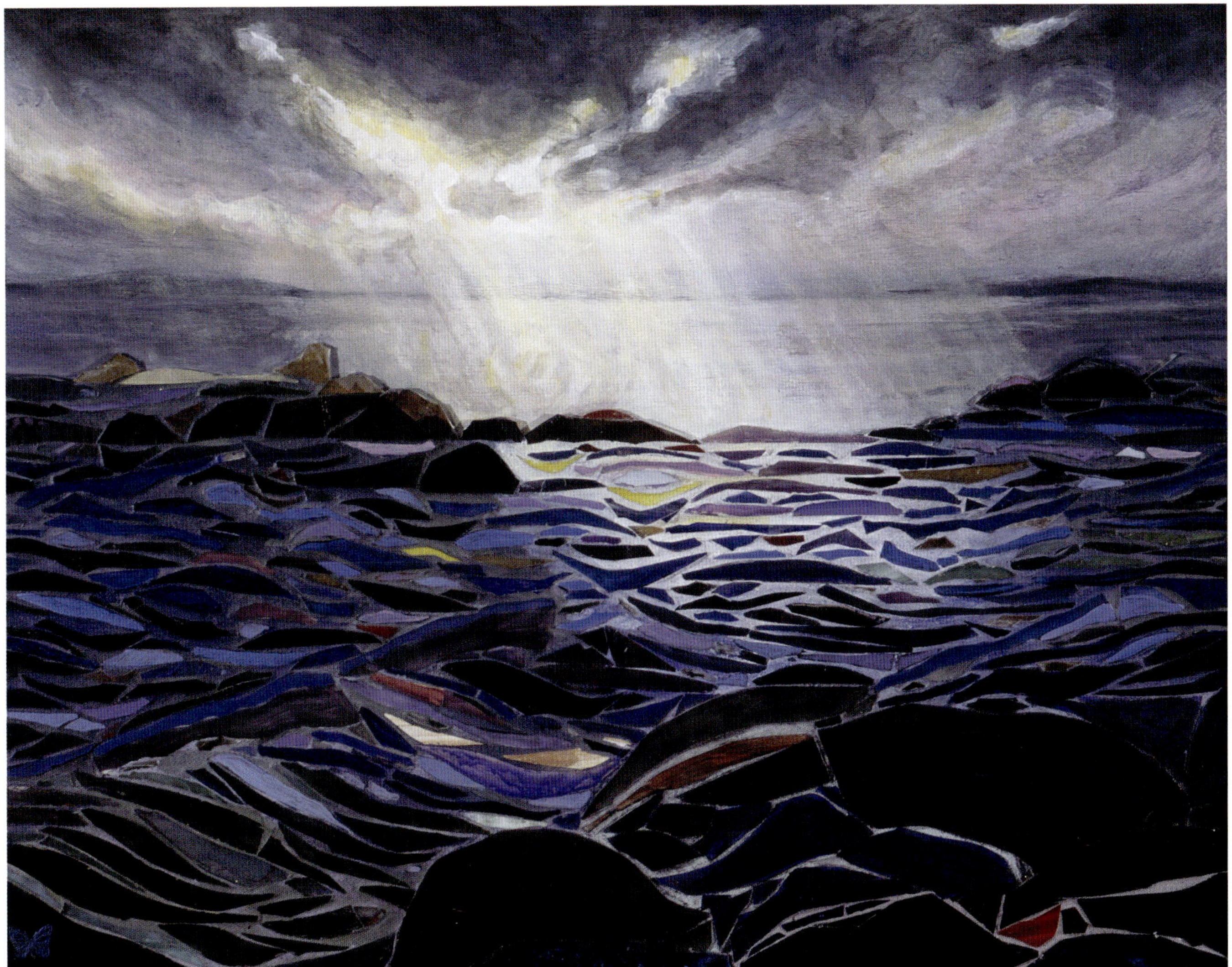

Ilona Brustad. *Light Show*. 2007. Glass and acrylic paint. 24" x 32". *Patrick Young, photographer*

Yearning to Fly: *Yearning to Fly* is an autobiographical work referring to a time in my youth when I felt alienated and alone. I wanted to be like everyone else and to "fly with the flock" instead of being left behind.

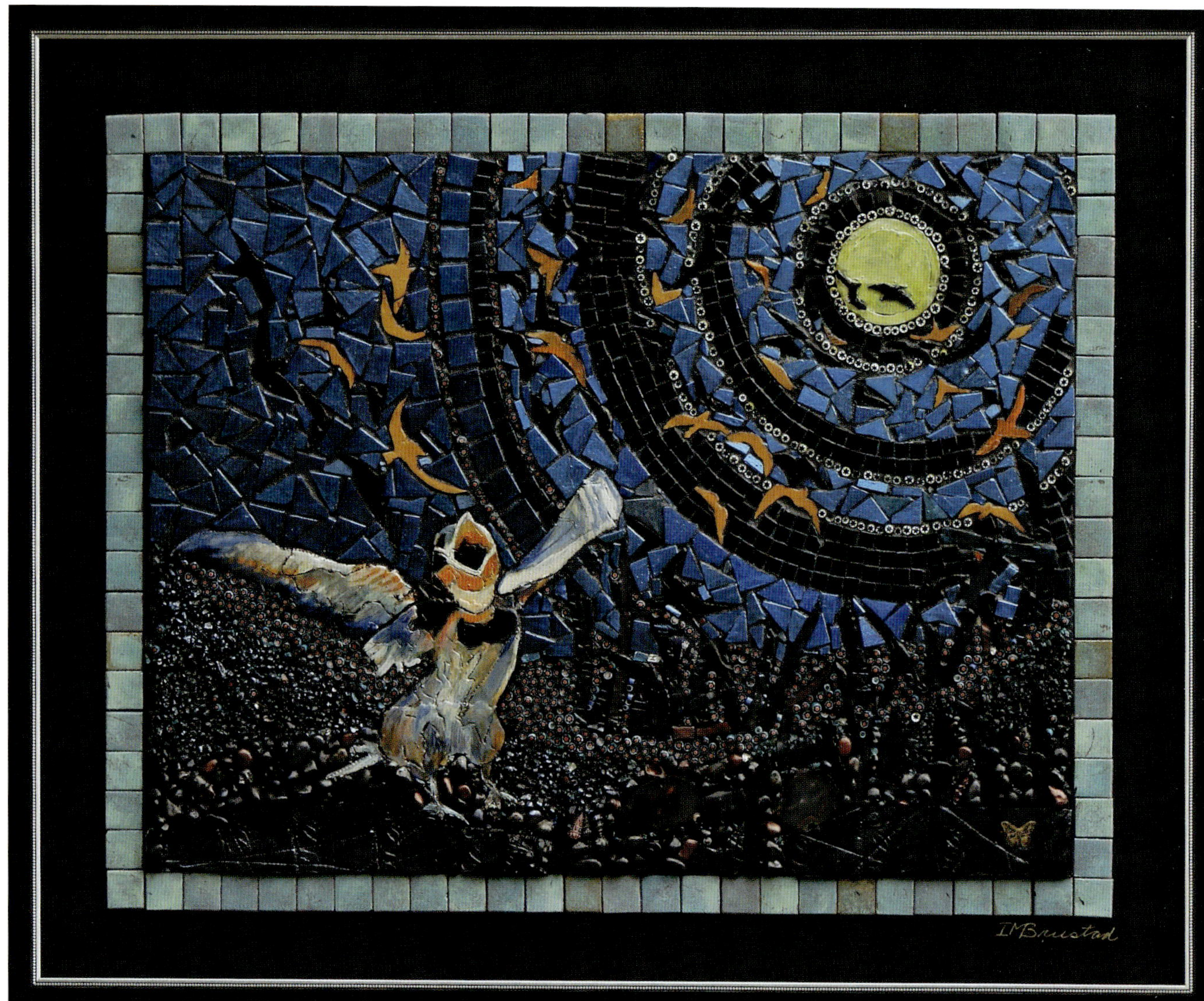

Ilona Brustad. *Yearning to Fly*. 2009. Stained glass, polymer tiles, millefiori, pebbles, acrylic paint. 25" x 31".

Nautilus: I made the mosaic *Nautilus* especially for a performance of Saint Saens' symphony *Carnival of the Animals*. A local orchestra performed this symphony using artists' interpretations of the various movements. I chose the movement *Fossils*. During the performance the artwork was projected on the screen behind the orchestra. It was very dramatic and pleasing to see my work projected on a large screen.

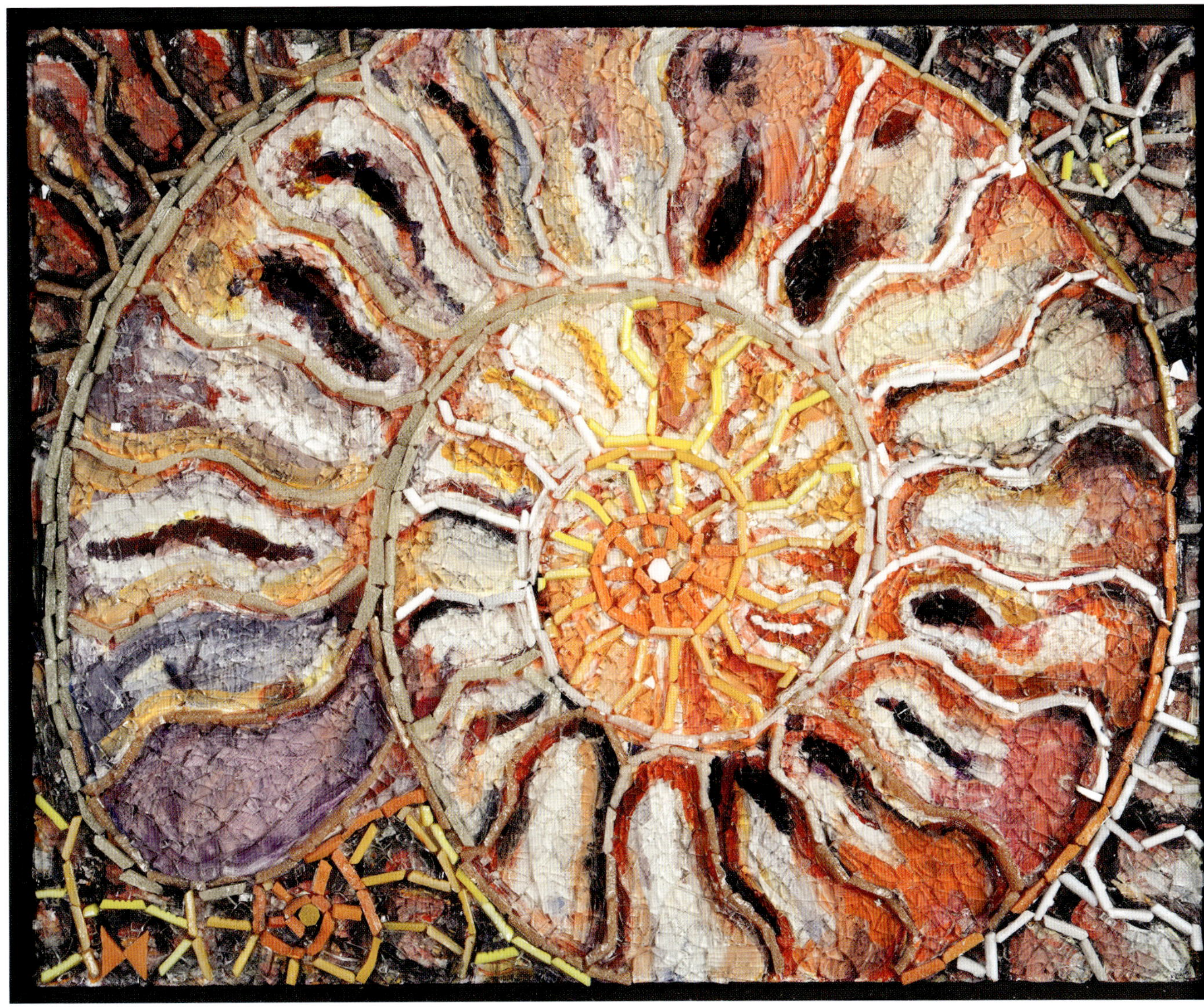

Ilona Brustad. *Nautilus*. 2010. Tempered glass, vitreous glass, acrylic paint. 16" x 20". *Patrick Young, photographer*

Susan Burton—Art Explorations

Marseilles, Illinois, www.artexplosions.com

Artist's Statement

My original and innovative work ranges from anything made in glass ... small gifts to large focal pieces and outdoor sculptures, which can be used for both commercial and residential applications. I enjoy experimenting and continue to work from traditional perspective as well as limit testing medium contradictions. Attention to detail as well as structural execution and use of the rainbow colors have come together from years of experience creating the unusual and unique. Welcome to my passion.

My journey has been a creative and spiritual process inspired by testing limits of mediums and myself. The power of symbols, light, and discovering my innate skills influence my work on a cellular level.

About the Artwork

Catharsis Two: "Catharsis Birth:" Self-portrait of the artist. She took a look within and was created. Catharsis is the powerful emotional, psychological, and physical process that consists of bringing to the surface, intensifying, and purging the emotions. The goal of this self-portrait was to take tears, neuro-nets, energy spirals, third eye, love, and healing powers in a process of cleansing and releasing of emotions. Something beautiful has come from the depths of sadness. This is a powerful experience for any artist. (opposite Page)

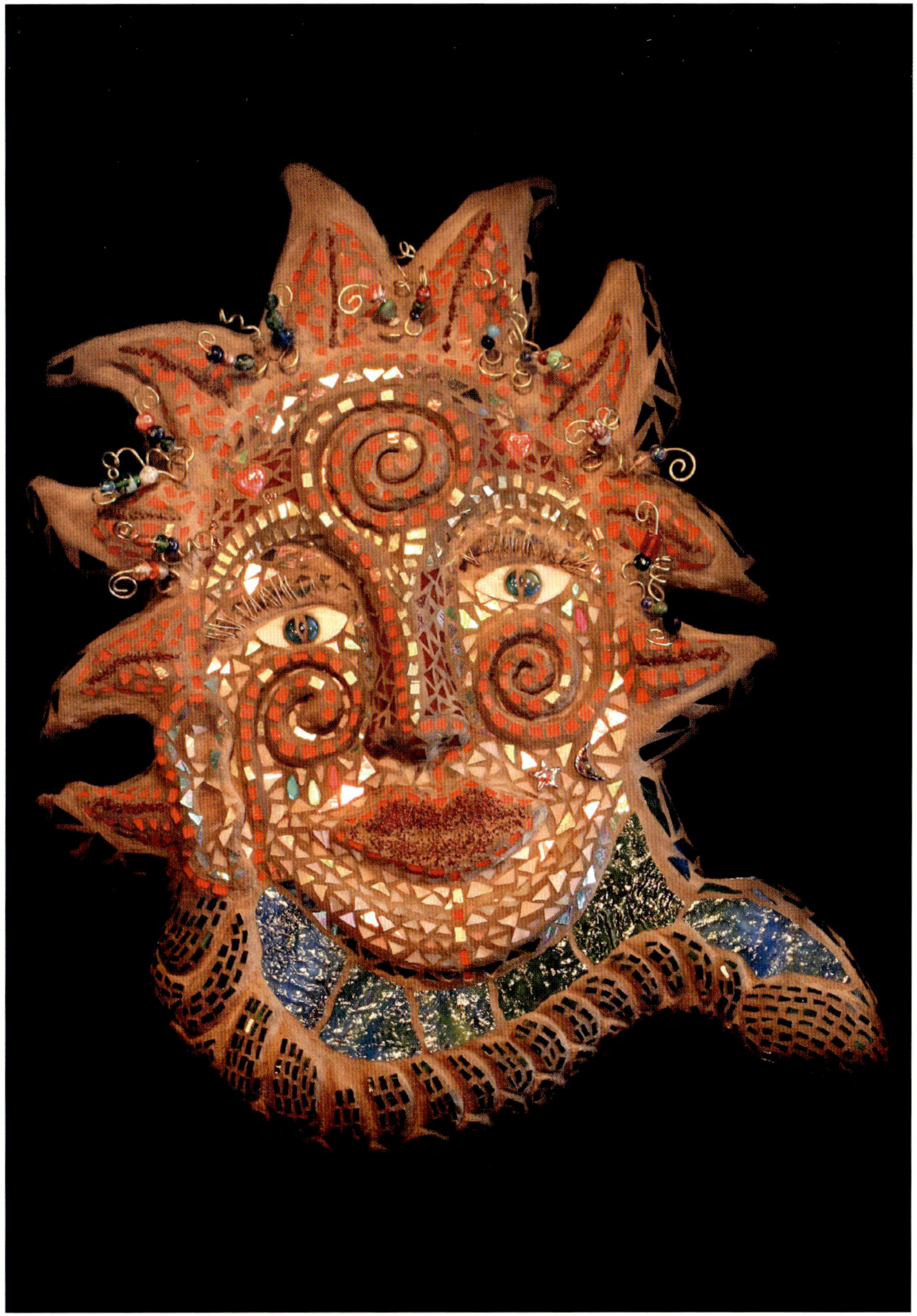

Susan Burton—Art Explorations. *Catharsis Two: "Catharsis Birth."*
Mosaic, two dimensional. Sculpted foam. 30" x 23".

Combination: Creation of a beautiful symbol of beliefs combines them all into one. The movement of andamento and color create for me the beginning and blending of all belief systems flowing together into one beautiful motion. This symbol is a reminder to explore myself without the influence of others.

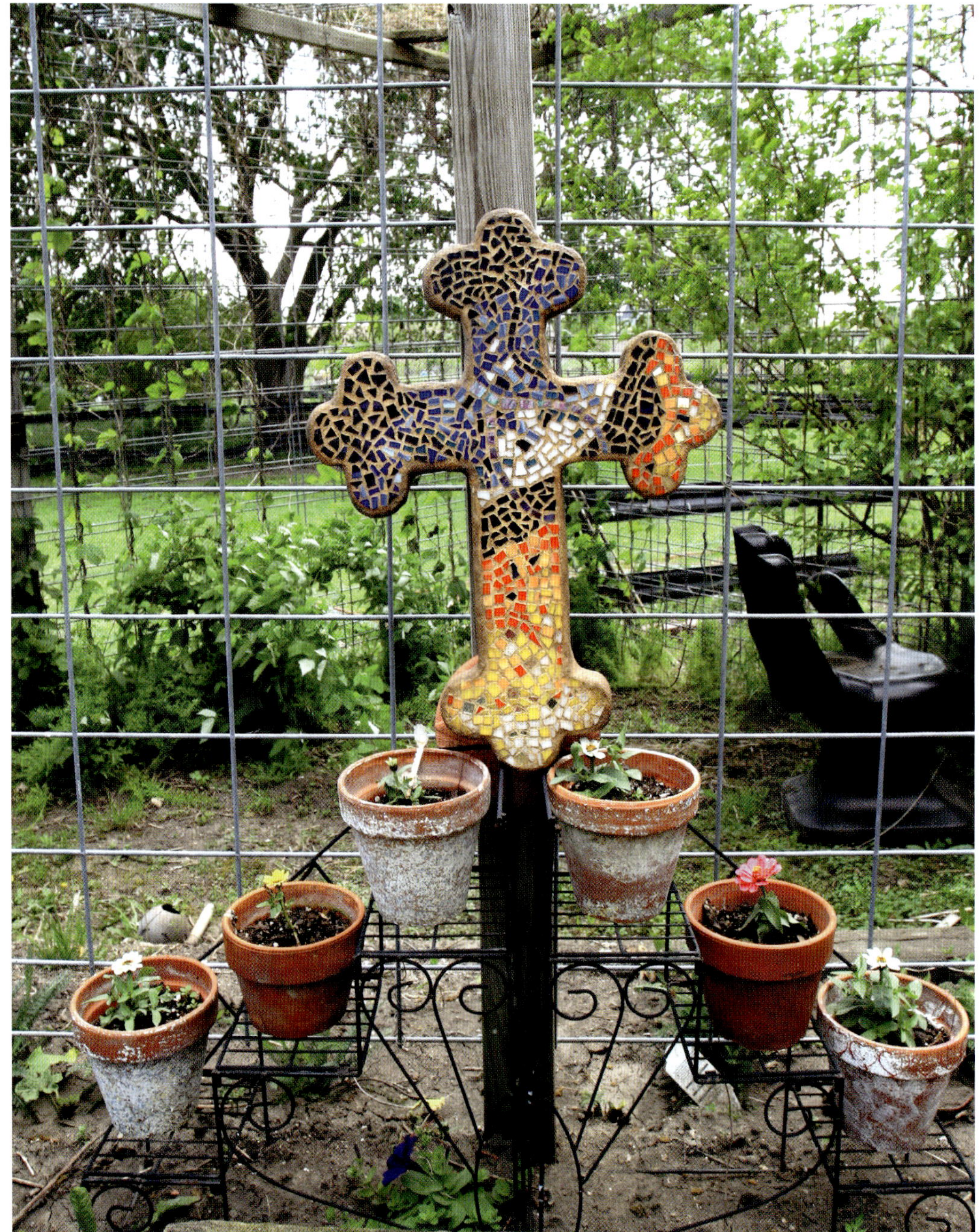

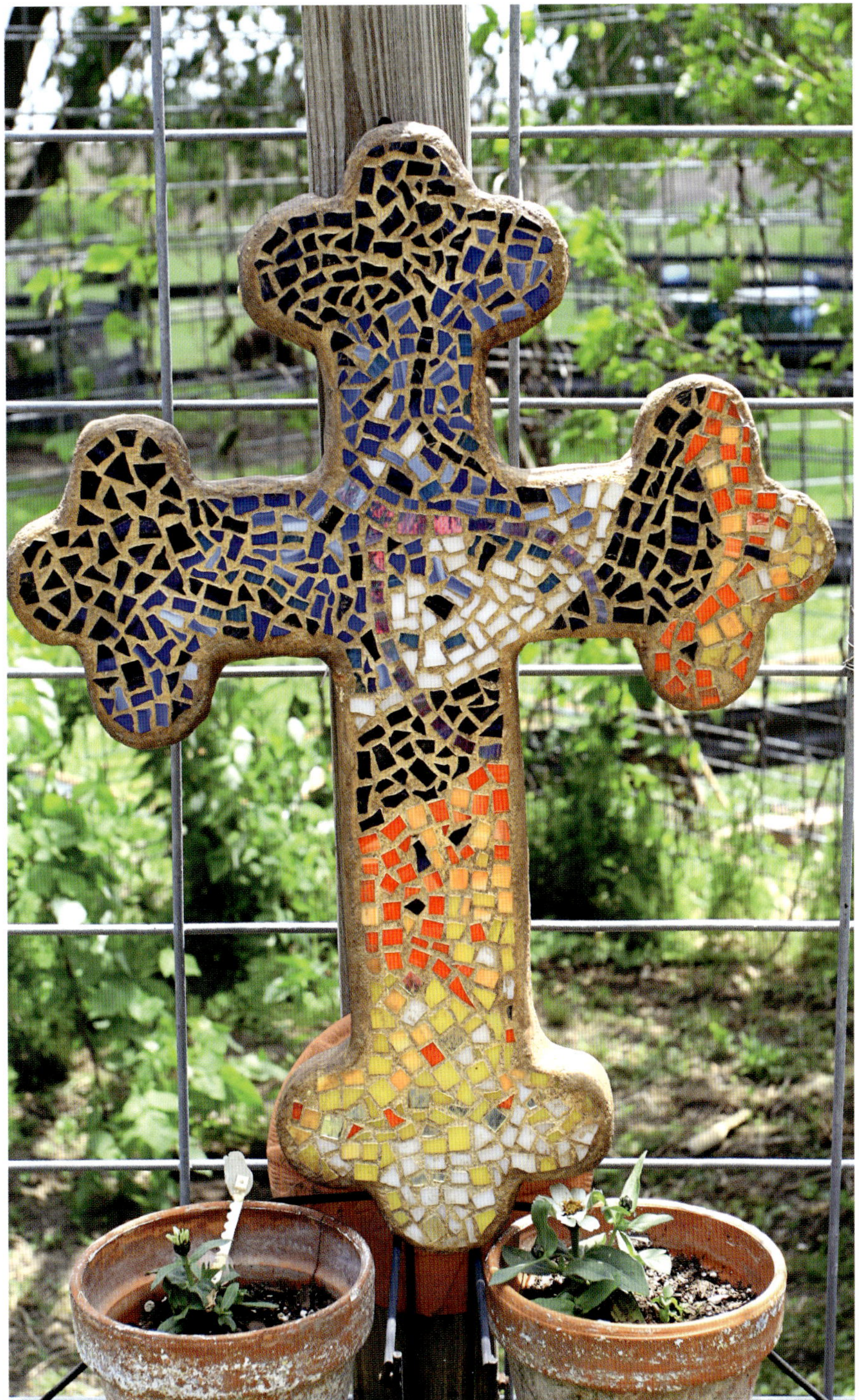

Susan Burton—Art Explorations.
Combination. Mosaic, two dimensional.
Sculpted foam. 24" x 18".

Listen to Your Heart One: "Meditation Spiral:" An intense study of the heart, this is meant to be a reminder to myself and others to "listen" to that intuitive self. It helps us remember what we have forgotten, keeping our eyes open and shut at the same time. Once again, I was transformed by this intense study. The spiral is present to once again invite a visual meditation. White light energy streaks all around, bathing the heart in its purity. This heart serves as a reminder that we all know collectively everything it is that we need to know. We just need to "Listen to Our Hearts." (Detail opposite page.)

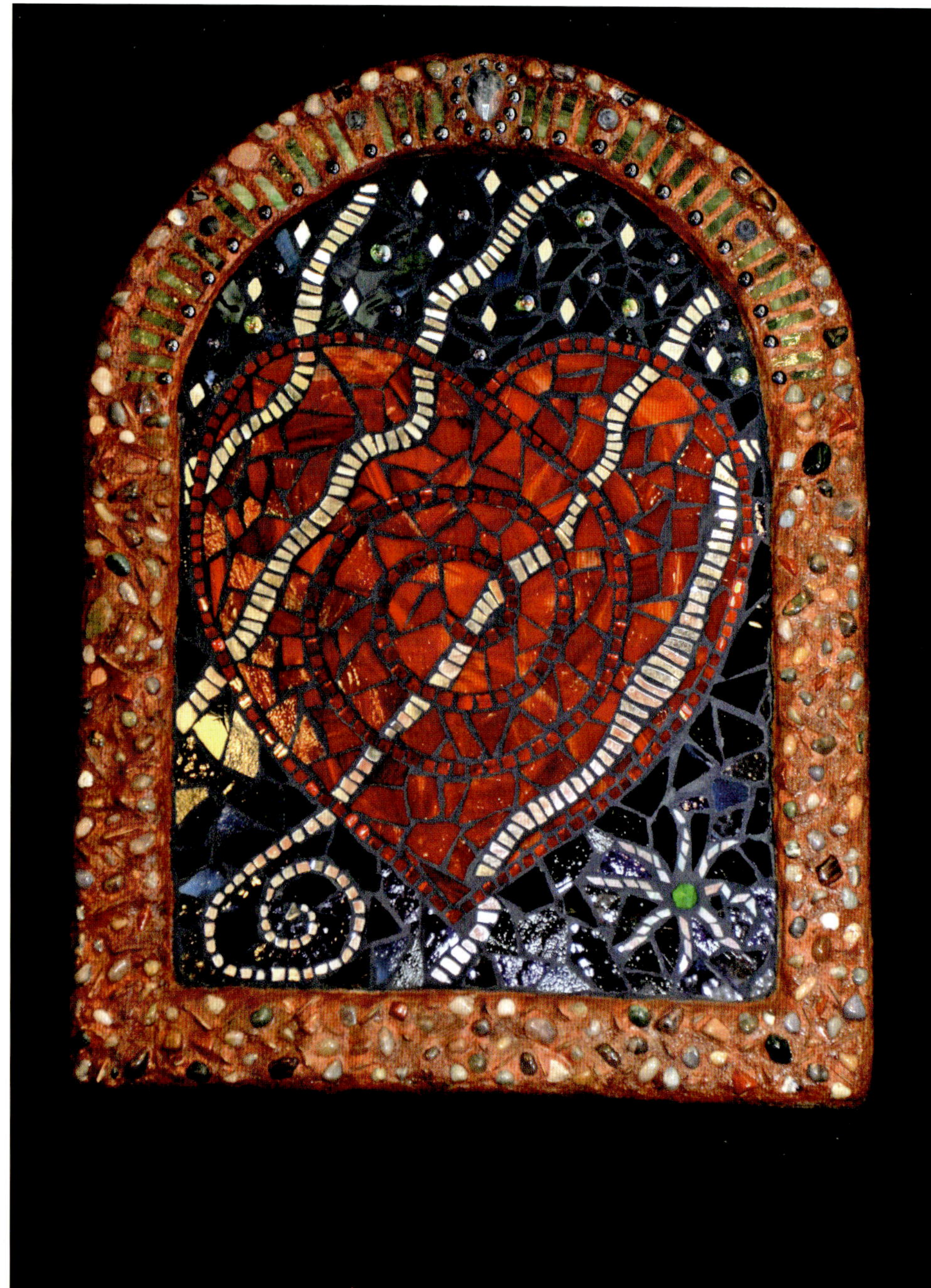

Susan Burton—Art Explorations. *Listen to Your Heart One: "Meditation Spiral."* Mosaic, two dimensional. Sculpted foam. 32" x 25". (Detail opposite page.)

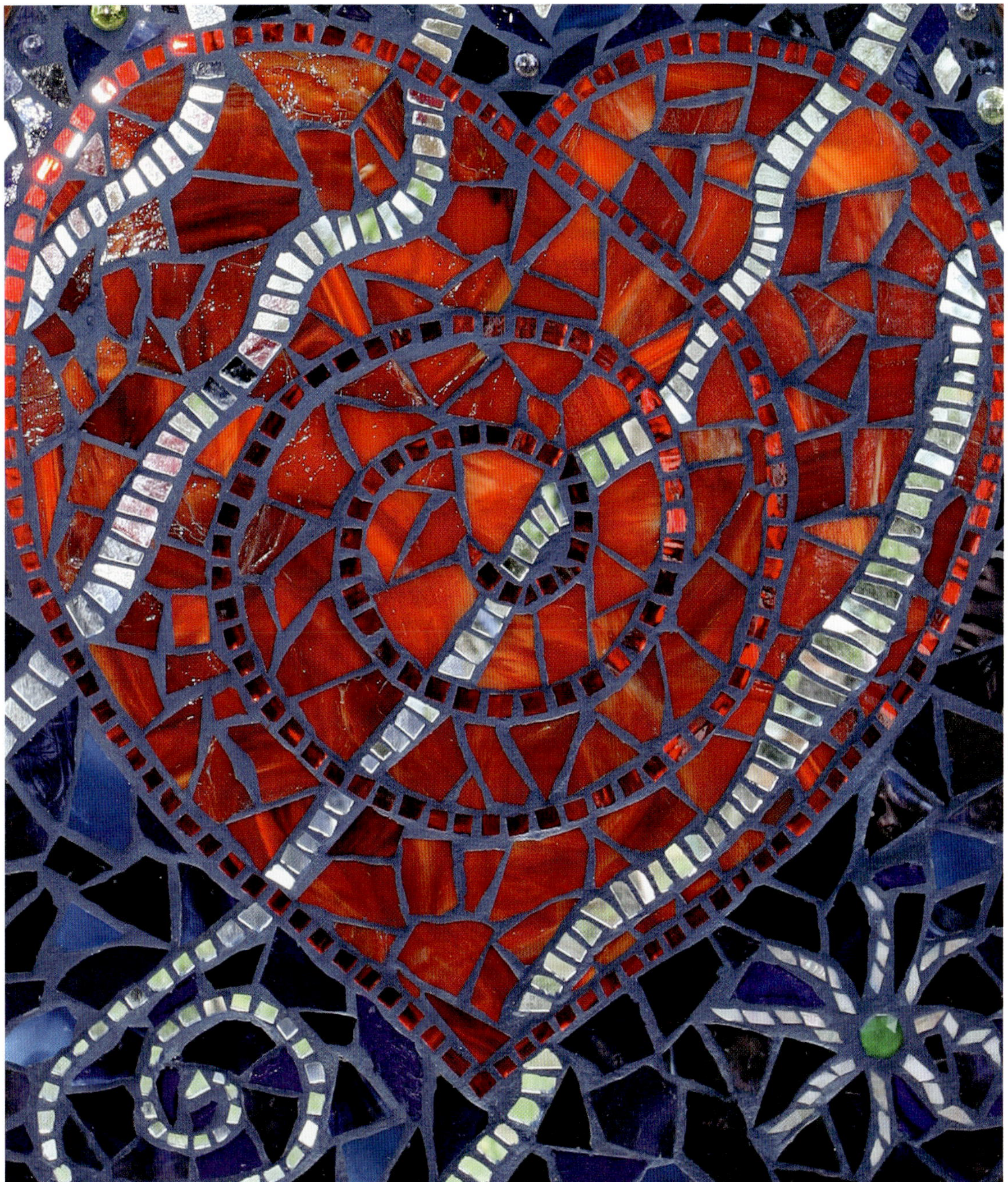

Transformation Eight: "Rays of Touch:" One day last fall I came home, began working, and had no idea what I was creating. It seems I stepped into a way of spiritual creation. This art came to me in a vision from beyond my normal knowing.

It is called *Transformation* because it opens my eyes to letting a special process happen. Keeping the eyes open while shut at the same time, finding a deep intuitive creative potential! I used Styrofoam, carved, painted, brushed, and glued for hours. Next came buckets of scrap glass followed by hours of gluing. Then cementing, cementing, and more cementing. After exactly 128 hours of hard work, a 38" diameter and 34 pound baby was born. This incredible symbol of *Transformation* was in existence.

I, as an artist, would never be the same. The piece represents a shift in consciousness, an opening up of who I really am. It represents the elements of fire, water, air, and earth. You can trace the spiral using a finger or your mind in an amazing meditation. As you pass by each chakra color, the spiral draws you into the center for a powerful grounding. This piece literally draws you into a profound place within for each person who sees it.

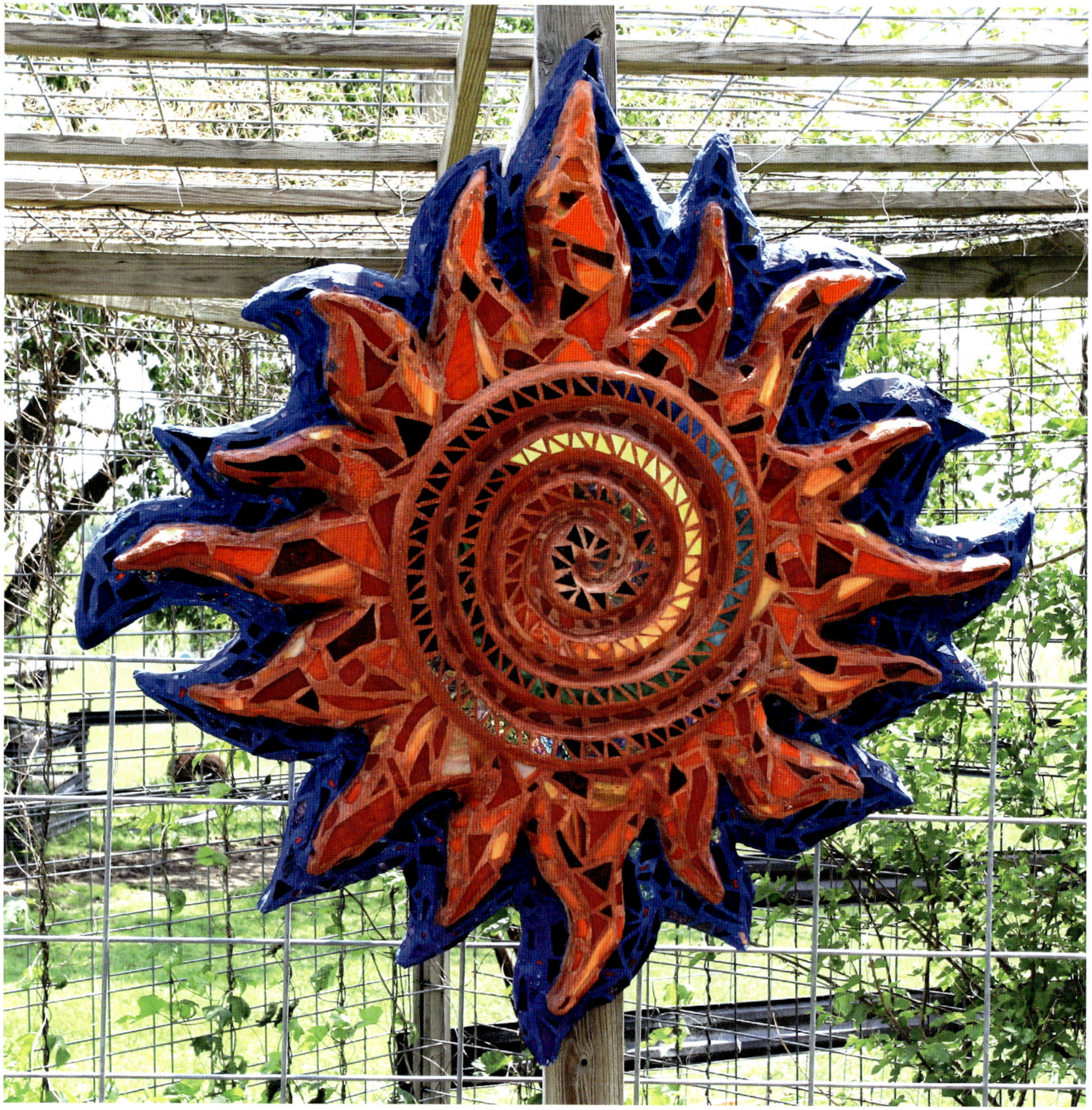

Susan Burton—Art Explorations. *Transformation Eight: "Rays of Touch."* Mosaic, two dimensional. Sculpted foam. 38" diameter, 34 pounds.

Martin Cheek

Kent, United Kingdom, martin@martincheekmosaics.com

Artist's Statement

I have become increasingly interested in the applied arts, particularly mosaic, which is becoming more and more popular both as an art form and as a decorative medium. I regard my mosaic work as logical progression from my career in animation, both of which involve building a coherent whole, displaying character and movement, from thousands of tiny elements. I am particularly inspired by the natural world and take the challenge of capturing its organic grace in such a seemingly uncompromising medium.

About the Artwork

Purple Peacock: Birds are a favorite subject of mine as one sees from the sheer number of mosaics that I make of them! So much so in fact that I have separated the peacocks and given them their own gallery.

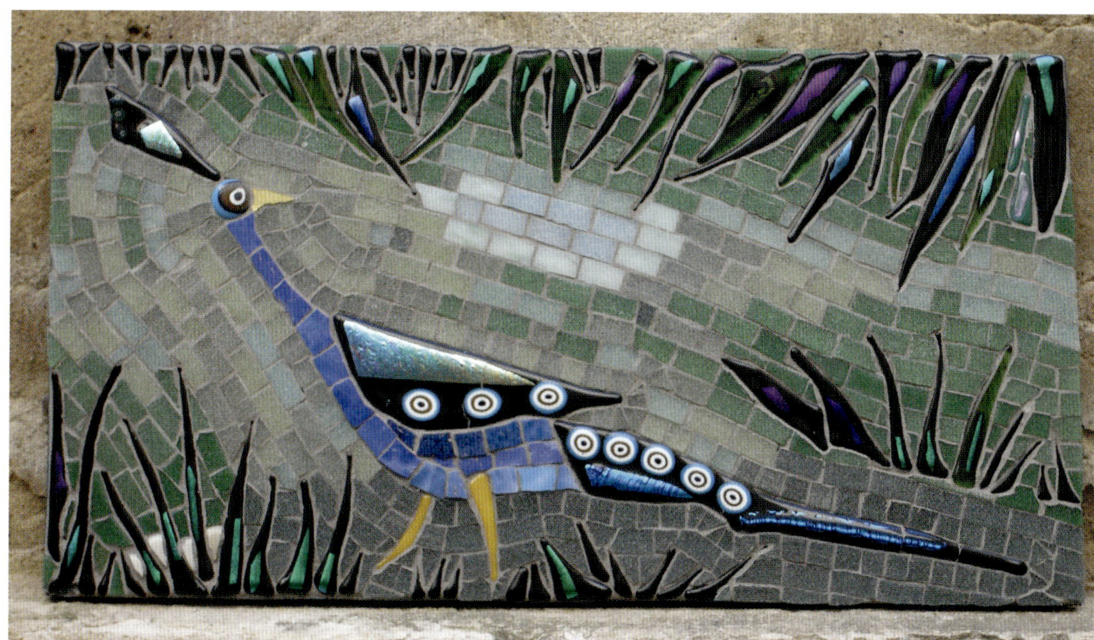

Martin Cheek. *Purple Peacock*. Glass fusions and vitreous glass. 19" x 11" (48cm x 28cm).

Barbados Floor: My brief was to design a mosaic floor that would capture life on a Caribbean island. I was given a list of all things Bajan, which include dominoes, cocktails, and breadfruit trees.

The actual mosaic was made in Mexico. I spent six weeks in the mosaic factory, overseeing the work. This is the first time that I have not made everything by myself in England, but the sheer size of the floor meant that it was simply not possible for me to work fast enough to finish it on time.

The mosaic was made in many small parts—like pieces of a huge jigsaw puzzle. The design is firstly drawn onto strong brown craft paper and then cut up into the "jigsaw" not in even squares but in haphazard zigzags so that the joins don't show so obviously on the finished floor. Each piece of mosaic was then boxed up and shipped to Barbados to be laid down in situ. The mosaic is made "indirect," in other words it is upside down and back to front, the paper side being the final surface. Thus the finished mosaic is perfectly flat.

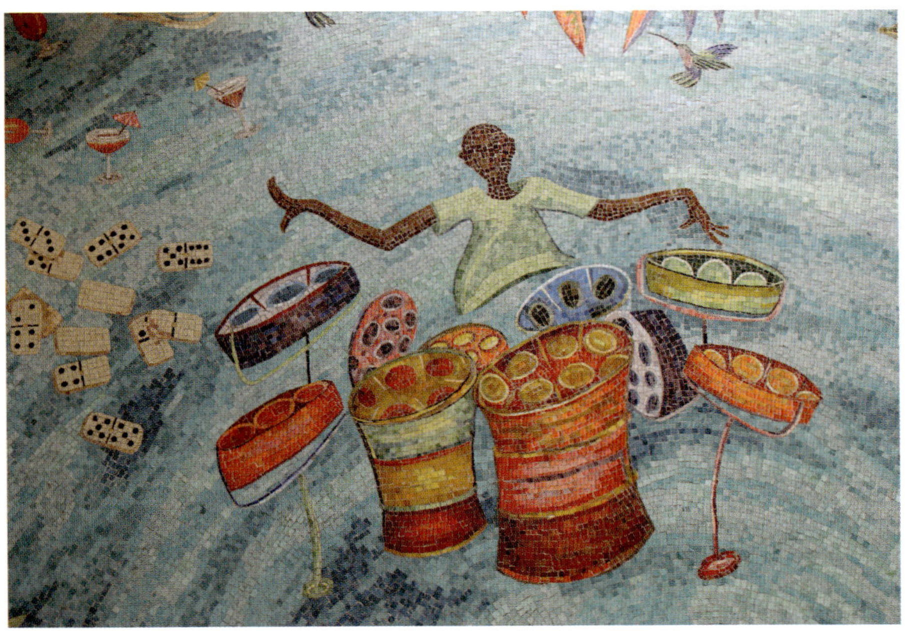

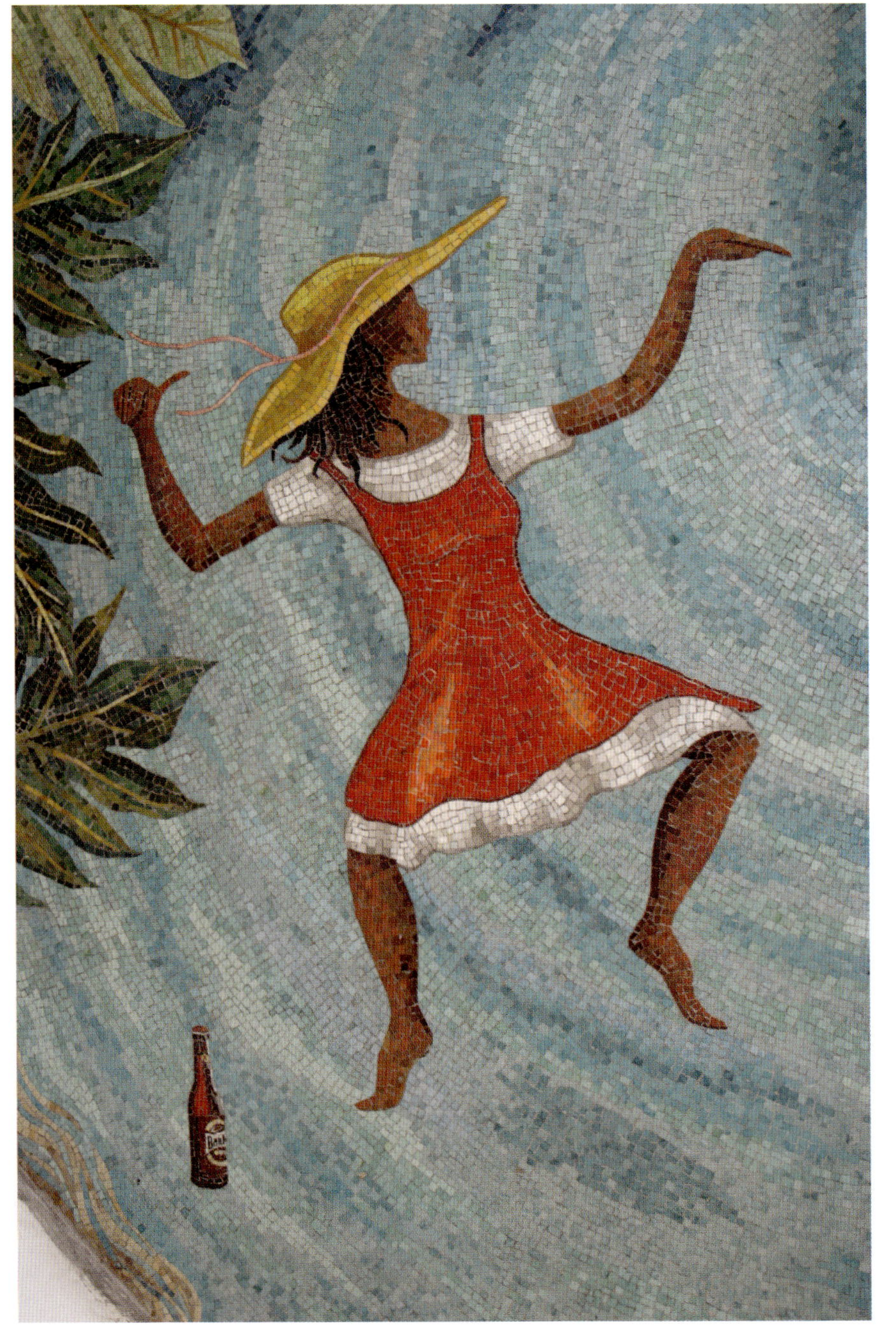

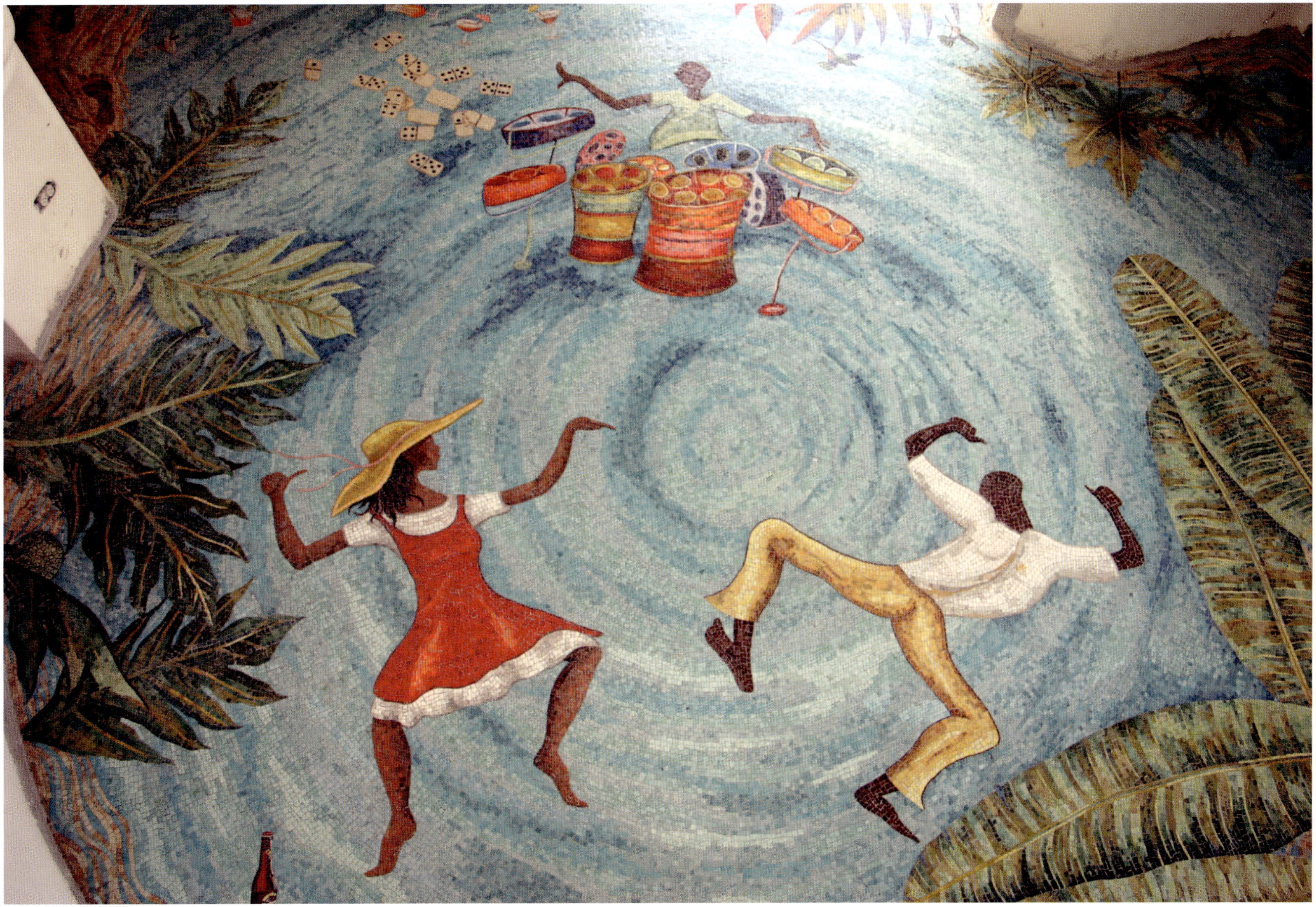

Martin Cheek. *Barbados Floor*. Mexican smalti. 49' x 66' (15m x 20m). (Details opposite page.)

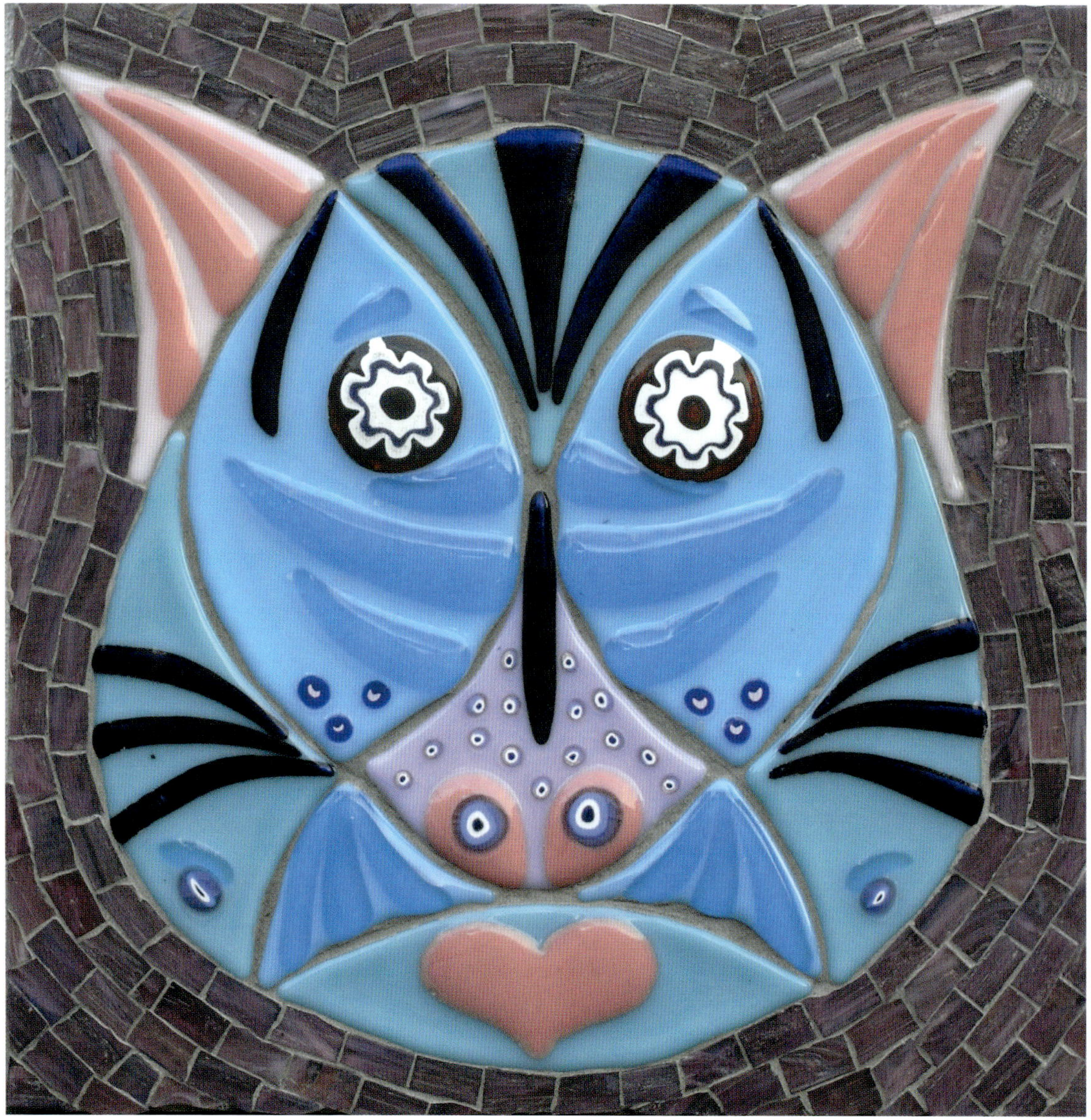

Martin Cheek. *Fishface*. Glass fusions, Mexican smalti, brass wire, and vitreous glass. 12" x 12" (30cm x 30cm).

Sara's Butterfly Dance is a memorial mosaic to Sara—the daughter of Alison, a friend of mine. Sara was a gifted ballet dancer. So the mosaic is supposed to represent—though hopefully in a subtle way—Sara in paradise. As Sara dances, she conjures up butterflies—who swoop and fly around her.

It is meant to be funny and uplifting—but when you know the story behind it—it's poignant and a bit sad. This mosaic hangs in the reception to the LITU (Liver Improvement Treatment Unit) at King's Hospital in London.

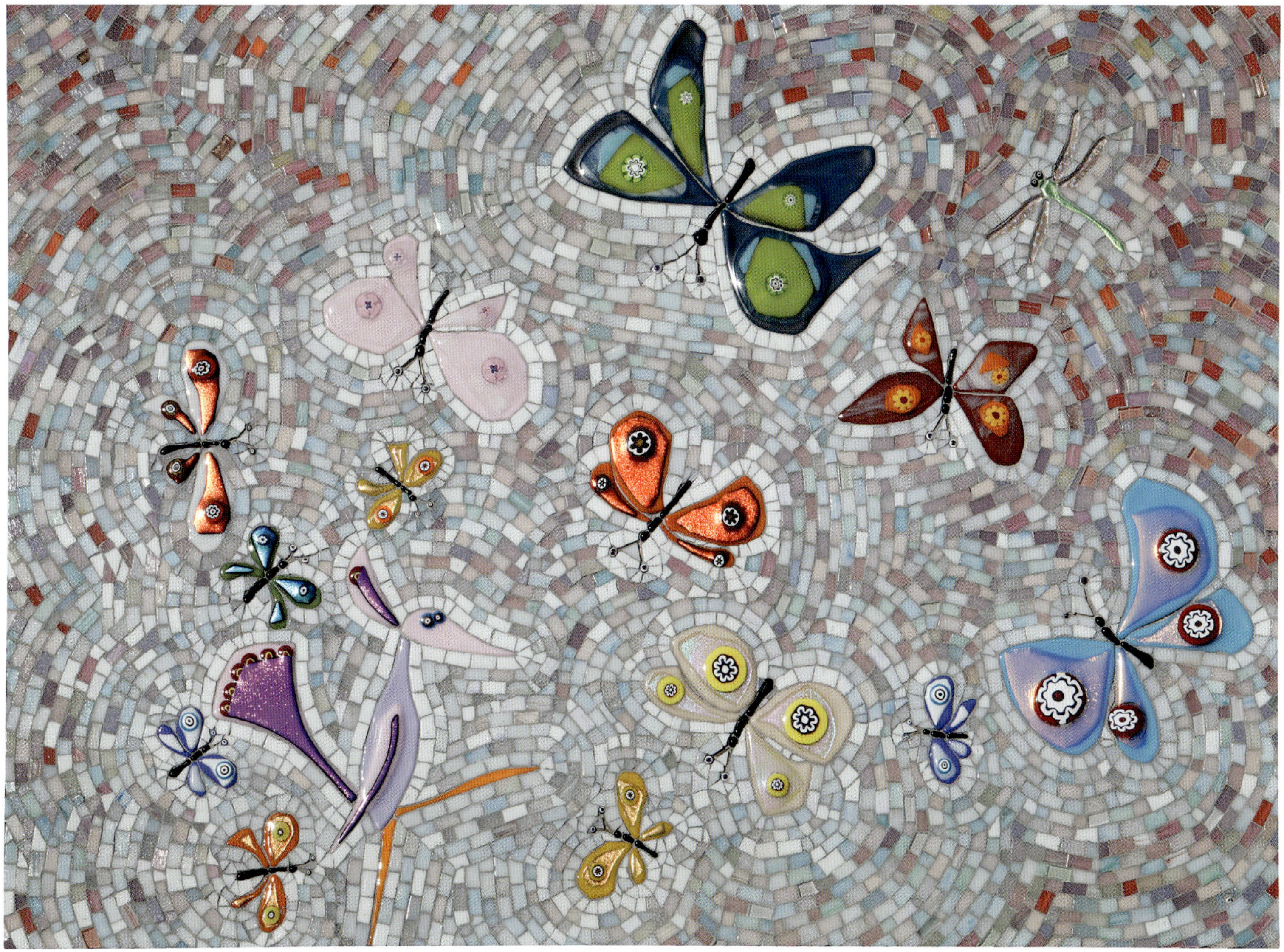

Martin Cheek. *Sara's Butterfly Dance*. Glass fusions and vitreous glass. 39" x 28" (100cm x 72cm).

Lynne Chinn

Plano, Texas, info@lcmosaics.com

Artist's Statement

For me, being an artist is not something I chose—it is who and what I am and always was. My ideas are constant and internally driven and they come from my everyday life experiences. The things I see or do, the people I know, and the places I travel to. Lately, I have been fascinated with the idea of making glass and stone mosaics that appear light and airy as though they are lightly draped fabric softly billowing in the wind. It is my intent to make them appear to be minimal and subtle, to impart for the viewer a seemingly effortlessness in their creation, which in turn creates a feeling of calmness and serenity.

To this end, I work within a mostly monochromatic color scheme and am very deliberate about the harmonization of the hues, shades, and tints. In shaping the tesserae I can manipulate their texture and appearance, and then I work diligently with the fit and ease of the pieces as they touch and transition from one to the other to create movement and flow.

In my 2- and 3-dimensional mosaic art works, I use the tesserae and its andamento as my textural brush strokes. Generating my own processes for the artwork I create is as important to me as the finished pieces I construct. Mosaic is mesmerizing and it is like life; choice, judgment, magic, frustration, coordination, shaping, fitting, adhering, beauty, joy, quality, and effort.

About the Artwork

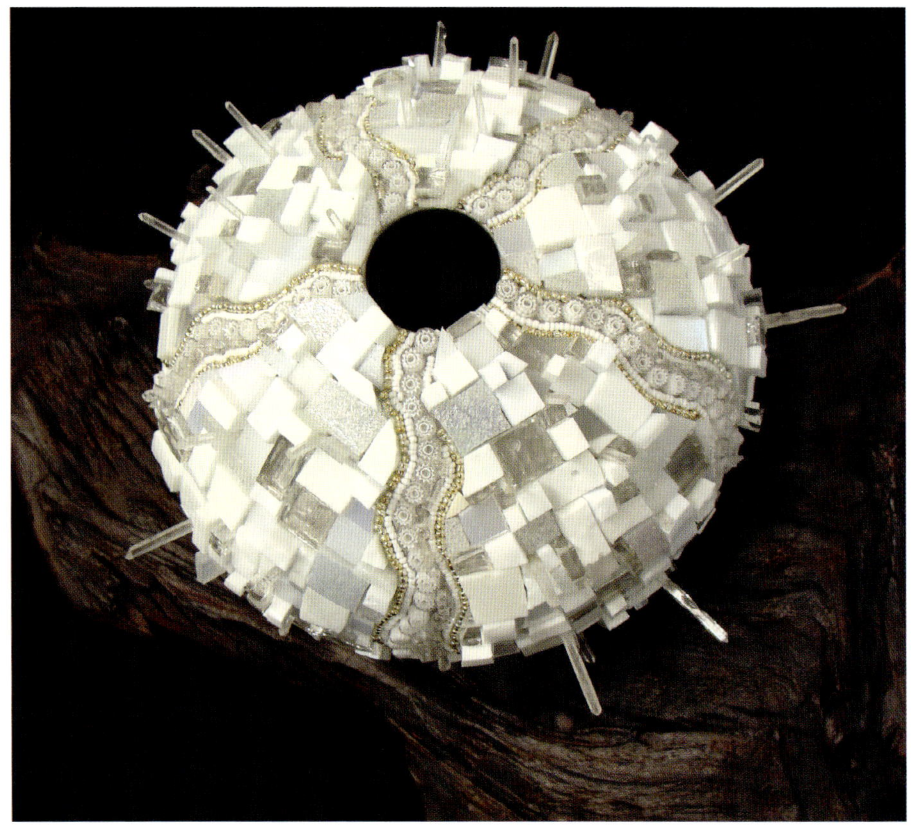

Lynne Chin. *Sputnik.* 2007. Smalti, 24k gold smalti, millefiori, quartz crystals, vitreous glass, and glass beads. Direct method. 5" x 8" x 8". *Photo by the artist*

Winged Geode is a metaphor for Americans and what our "politically correct" society has forced us to become. On the outside, for fear of reprisal, we show the world our bland smiles, polite customs, and soft attitudes, not daring to say what we really feel about the current political situation.

In fact, if we could show our true interior natures and speak our true feelings, they may be brassy, sharp, and rough, but infinitely more straightforward and far more interesting. With this in mind, the idea for the exterior was to produce something visually soft, pretty, and light weight. By using a limited color palette and creating a variety of textures, shapes, and cuts of tesserae placed in specific patterns, I made the enveloping wings, feathers, and down. The interior is intended to appear as a hard, jagged, colorful, sparkly core of a Geode.

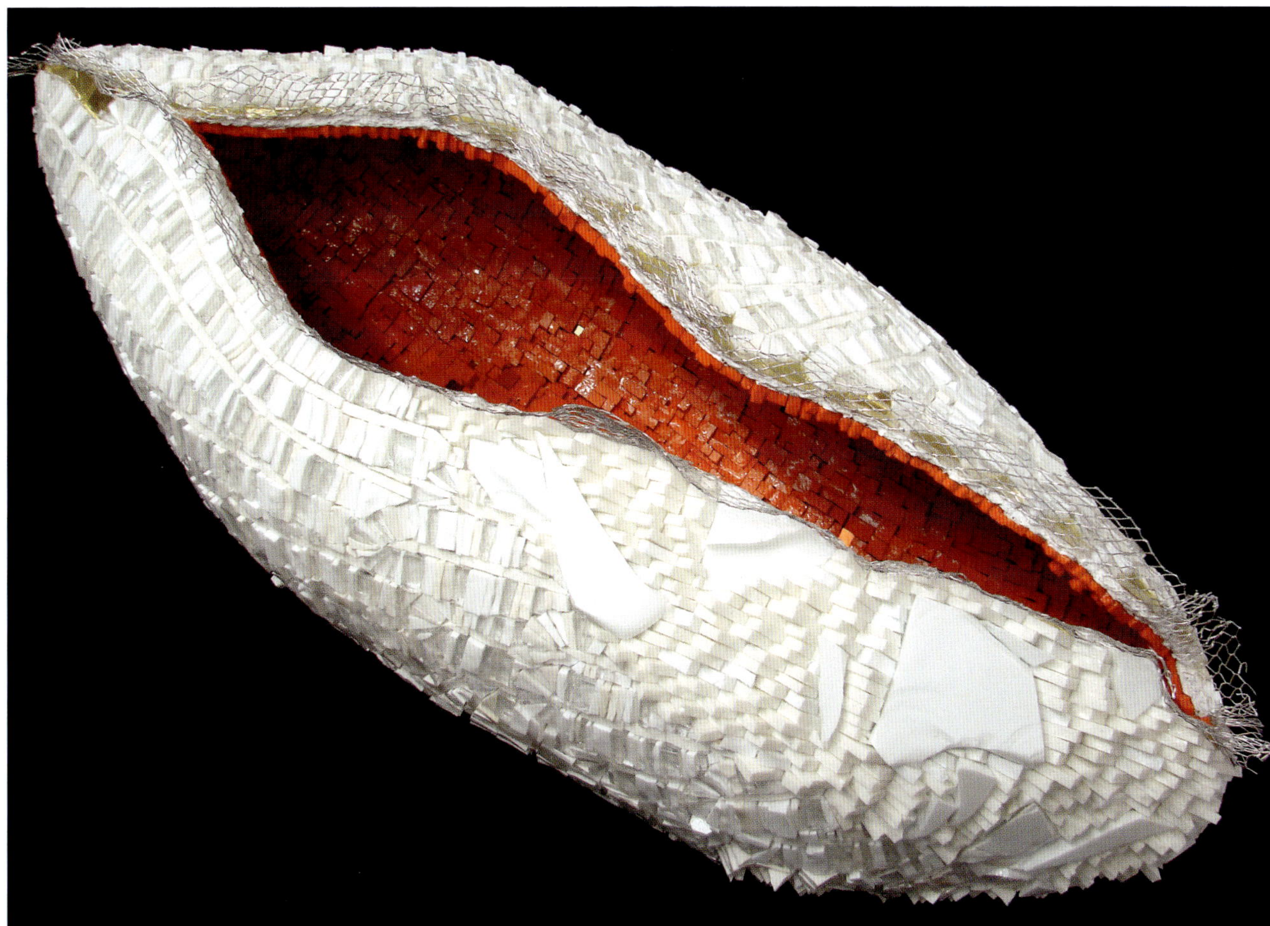

Lynne Chinn. *Winged Geode*. 2007. Smalti, transparenti, 24k gold smalti, and colored gold. Direct method. 9" x 29 1/2" x 13". *Photo by the artist*

Geode: The idea behind the sculptural form of *Geode* was simply an experiment I devised for applying glass mosaic tiles to difficult sculptural forms. In creating my underlayments, I worked to create shapes that could be awkward to mosaic, with hard to reach interior places as well as covered and hidden folds. Each switchback and every convex and concave shape of the substrates in this exploding seed-pod shape gibes a new and interesting view of the cut glass, imparting the maximum amount of shimmer and excitement.

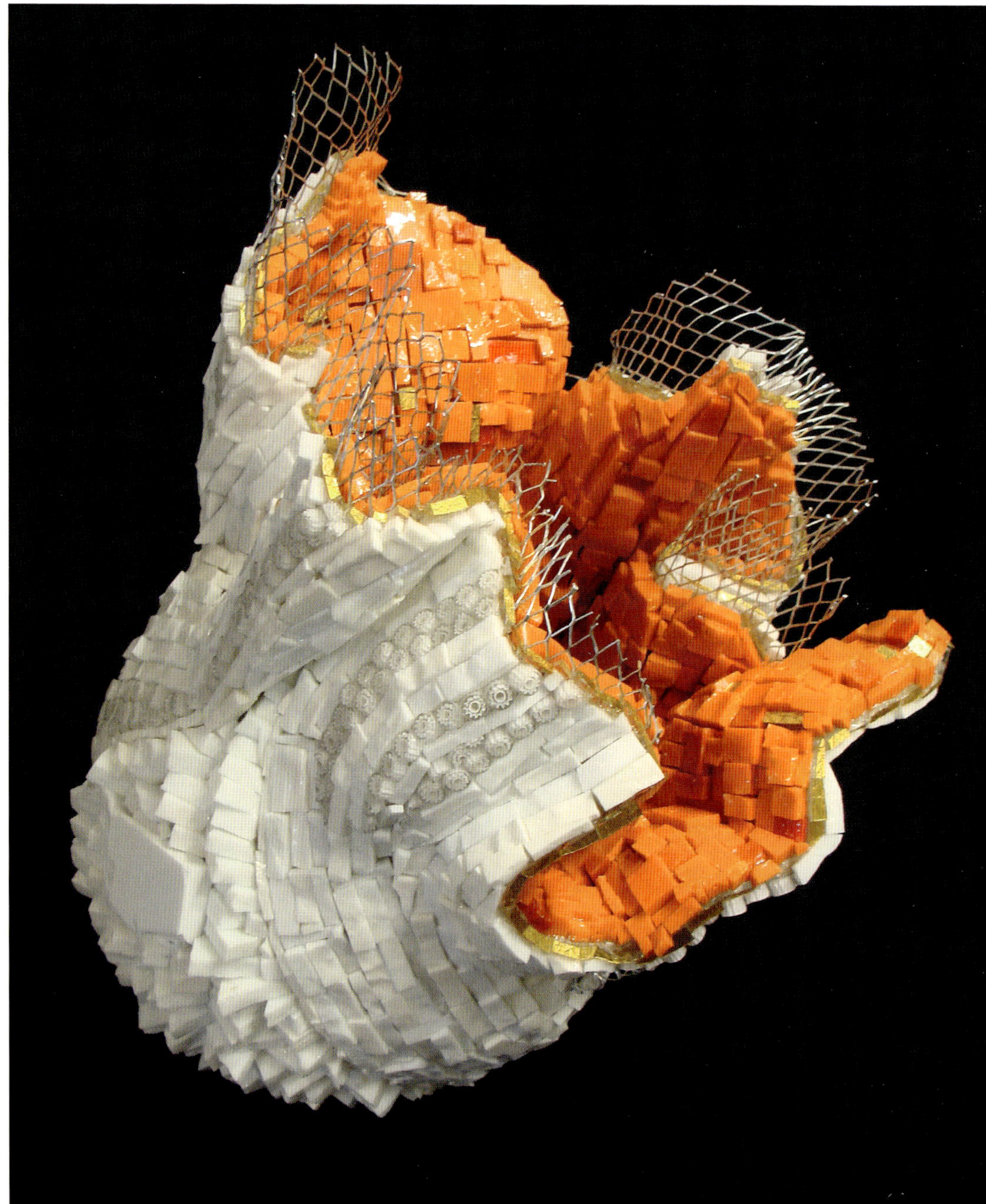

Lynne Chin. *Geode*. 2008. Smalti, 24k gold smalti, and millefiori. Direct method. 10 1/2" x 9 1/2" x 8". *Photo by the artist*

Undulate: Lately I have been fascinated with the idea of making large-scale glass and stone mosaics that appear light and airy. To that end, I conceived of the idea to depict rough-hewn handmade cloth lightly draped over a piece of tightly woven brocade material. With a mostly monochromatic color scheme, I worked to create a visually pleasing and exciting andamento, keeping motion and texture in mind. As the hard-edged, unforgiving tesserae undulate over the soft folds of fabric, they sparkle and dance, creating gentle highlights and shadows.

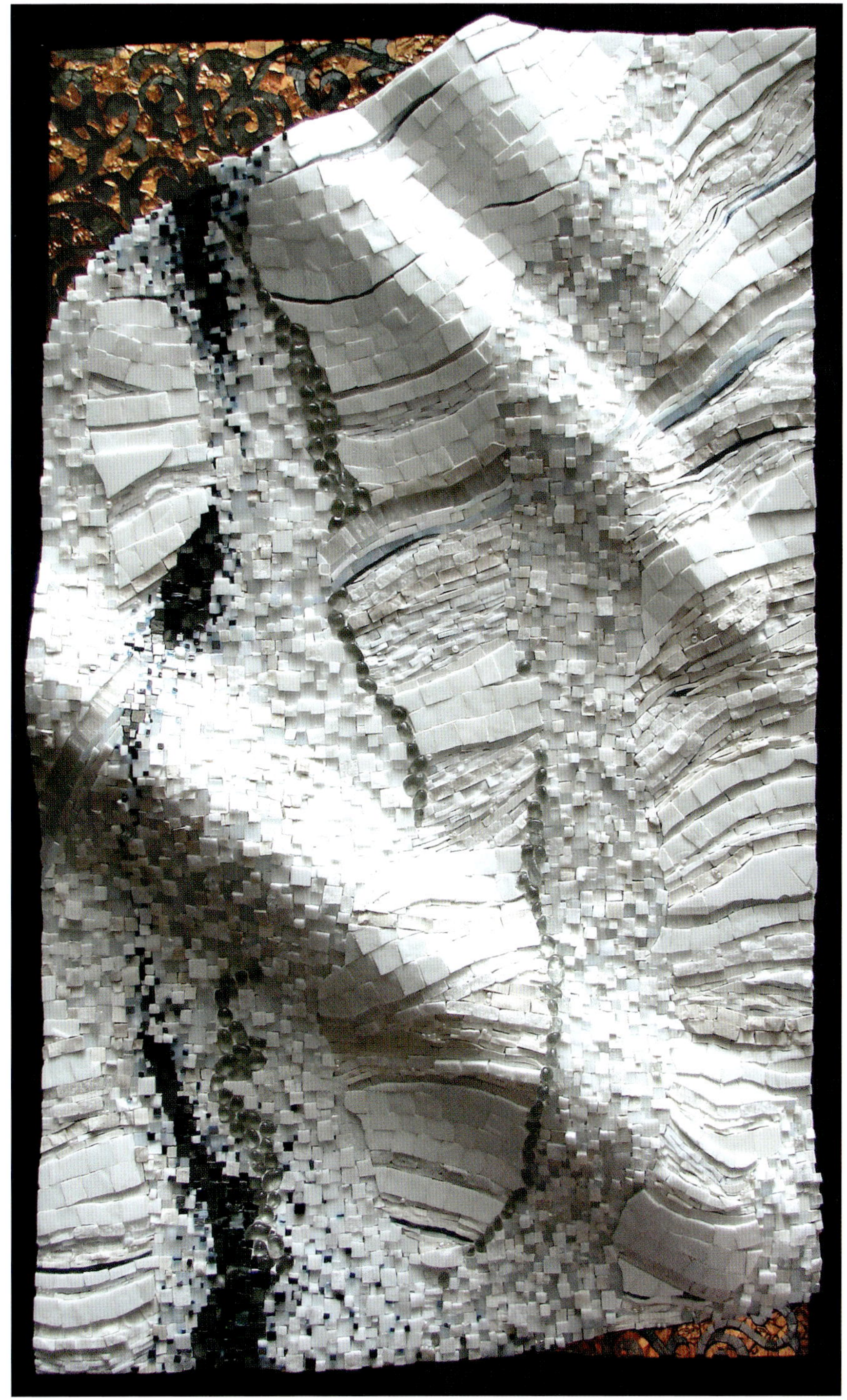

Lynne Chin. *Undulate.* 2008. Smalti, 24k colored gold smalti, copper smalti, marble, vitreous glass, stained glass, porcelain, polymer clay, pearls, and selenite. Direct method. 30 1/4" x 18" x 2 1/4". *Photo by the artist*

Urchin: Gaia: My inspiration for *Urchin: Gaia* was an imaginary sea creature in the shape of a giant sea urchin, which celebrates air and water, two elemental forces of the earth's biosphere. The fluidly swirling pattern of alternating blue, green, and white tesserae are meant to evoke images of the earth's sparkling and self-renewing oceans and the geometrically set textural white areas, her puffy cloud cover as seen from space. The aluminum sculptural wire is shaped to elicit ideas of the creature's flowing and ethereal underwater life.

The specially cut, shaped, and placed glass, gold, and marble pieces encircle the spherical shape symbolizing the ancient and universal symbols of unity, wholeness, and infinity, the goddess, and female power.

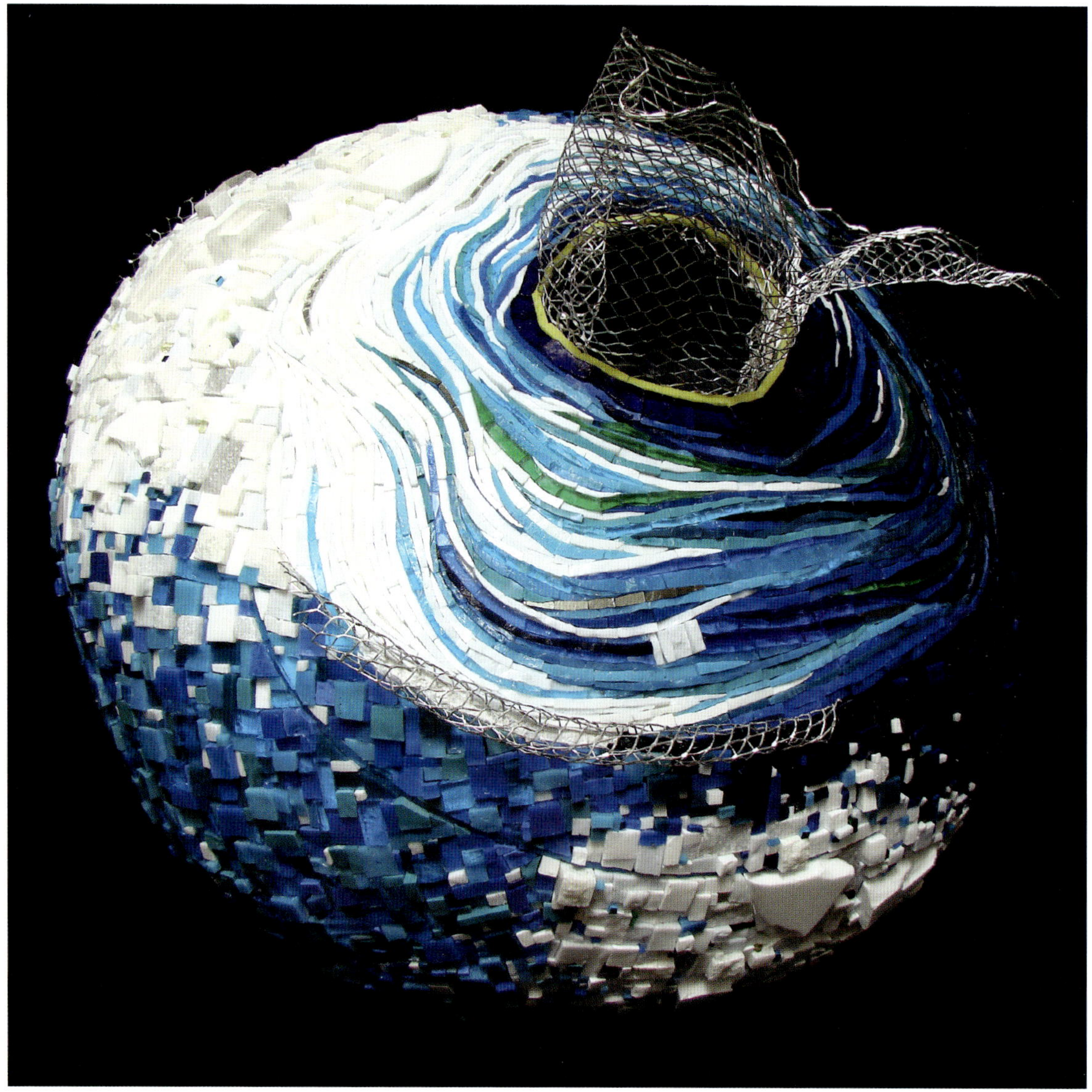

Lynne Chin. *Urchin: Gaia*. 2009. Smalti, transparenti, 24k white gold smalti, and colored gold, marble, selenite, quartz, calcite, and vitreous glass. Direct method. 13 1/2" x 17" x 16". *Photo by the artist*

Astral: My inspiration for *Astral* was the imagery that is now available to us from the Hubble Space Telescope. Celestial bodies, stars, planets, and a field of space debris from a supernova explosion are the elements I chose for the design. I incorporated natural stones and minerals to further enhance the idea of a primordial night sky. The swirling and flowing movement of the tesserae are meant to evoke the idea of endless space. The geometrically set stones in which the tesserae are set at various depths to enhance the texture, depict the swath of space debris.

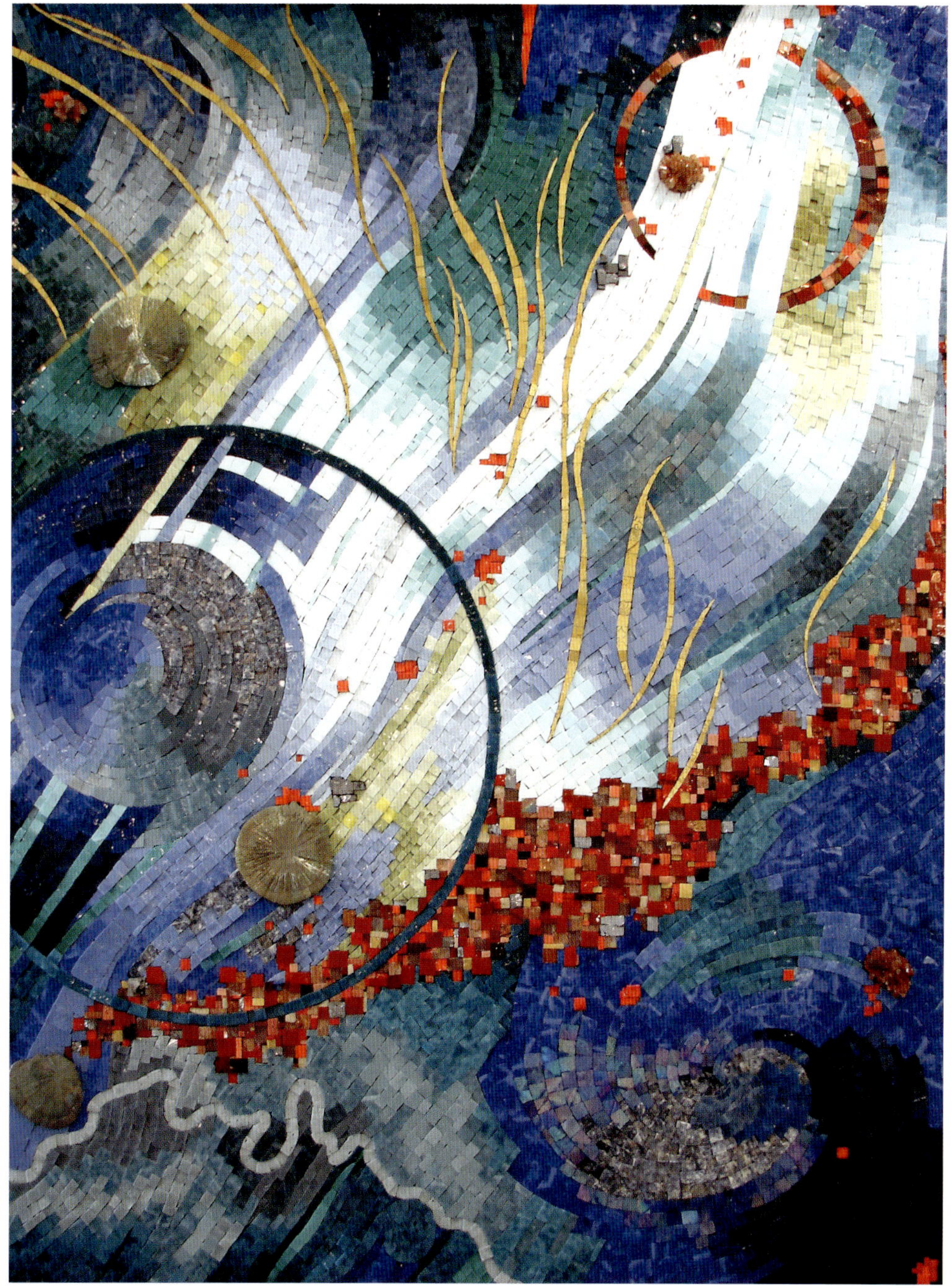

Lynne Chin. *Astral.* 2010. Smalti, iridized smalti, 24k gold, copper, and titanium smalti, vitreous glass, pyrite suns, pyrite clusters, aragonite clusters, imperial sodalite. Direct method. 44" x 33 1/2". *Photo by the artist*

Ammette Cossentine—Alla Bizantina

Charlotte, North Carolina, www.bizantinamosaics.com

Artist's Statement

Creating a mosaic brings me joy, peace, and engages my mind as nothing else could. The design, the tesserae, and the colors all challenge me, yet provide me with a tranquil release of my inner self.

About the Artwork

BreakThrough: This piece represents a time in my mosaic career when I made the decision to break free of doing more "commercial" mosaics and becoming freer with my interpretation of design and color. Why not pink hair? The gold wall on the right represents barriers we all face in life. They could be professional, personal, health … etc. This woman has a determined look on her face and is moving forward in her life, through her barrier.

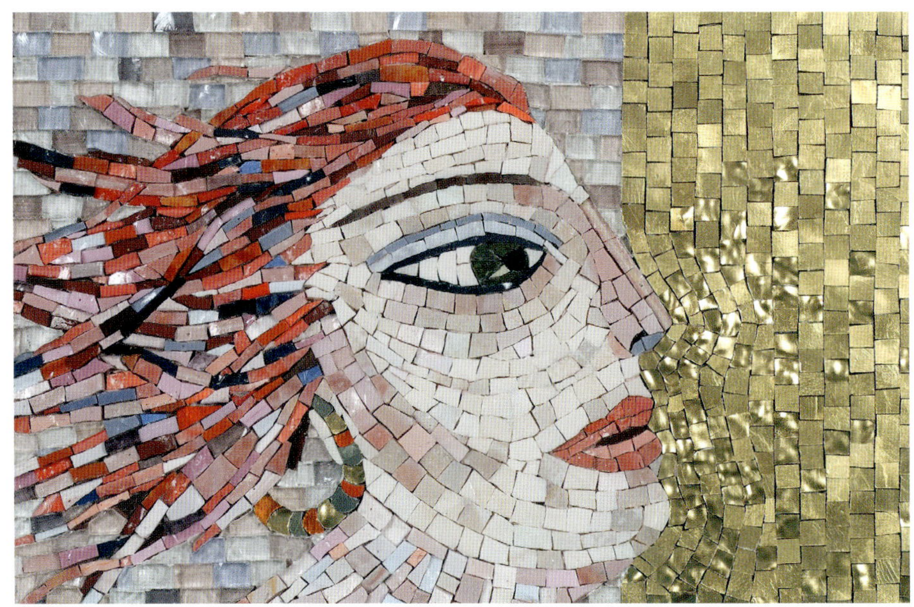

Ammette Cossentine—Alla Bizantina. *BreakThrough.* 2008. Smalti, transparent smalti, metallic smalti. 12" x 15".

A Journey Begun: Given as a wedding gift, this mosaic depicts the happy couple as they begin their journey together as husband and wife. I wish them nothing but fields of flowers and happiness. The clouds have silver linings and the sun's rays, shining upward, mean hope and all things good.

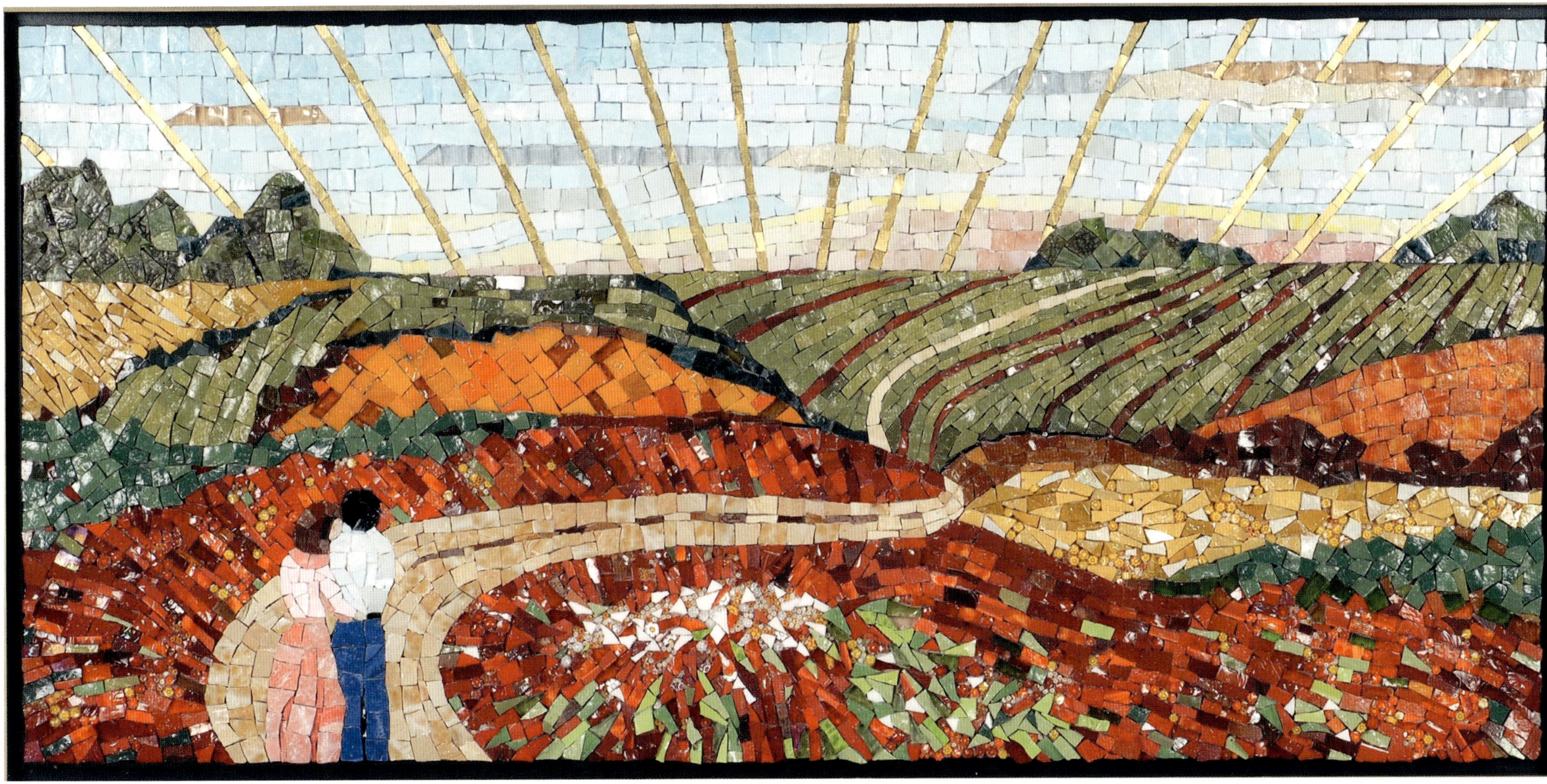

Ammette Cossentine—Alla Bizantina. *A Journey Begun.* 2009. Smalti, millefiori. 15" x 31".

Moving On: Sometimes we all feel like we just have to get out of certain situations. Why can't this bird do the same? She's packed up her brood and is moving on!

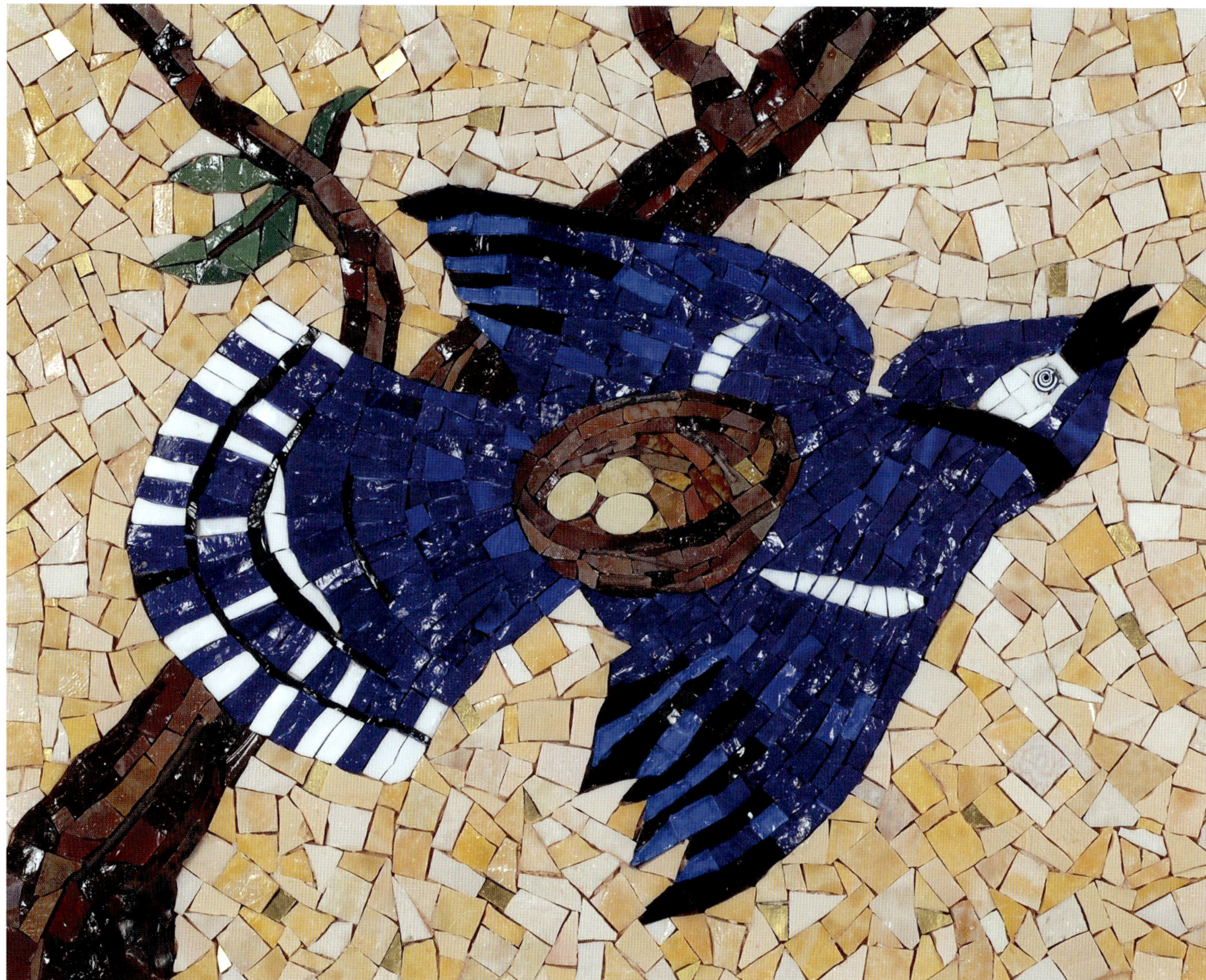

Ammette Cossentine—Alla Bizantina. *Moving On.* 2010. Smalti, obsidian points, branches. 11" x 14".

Repast: The chair is pulled out, asking the viewer to join this family at their table. Will you join? Mom is busy serving, Dad is ready to dig in, and junior is looking at you, asking for your company. Even mama bird is flying to feed her young.

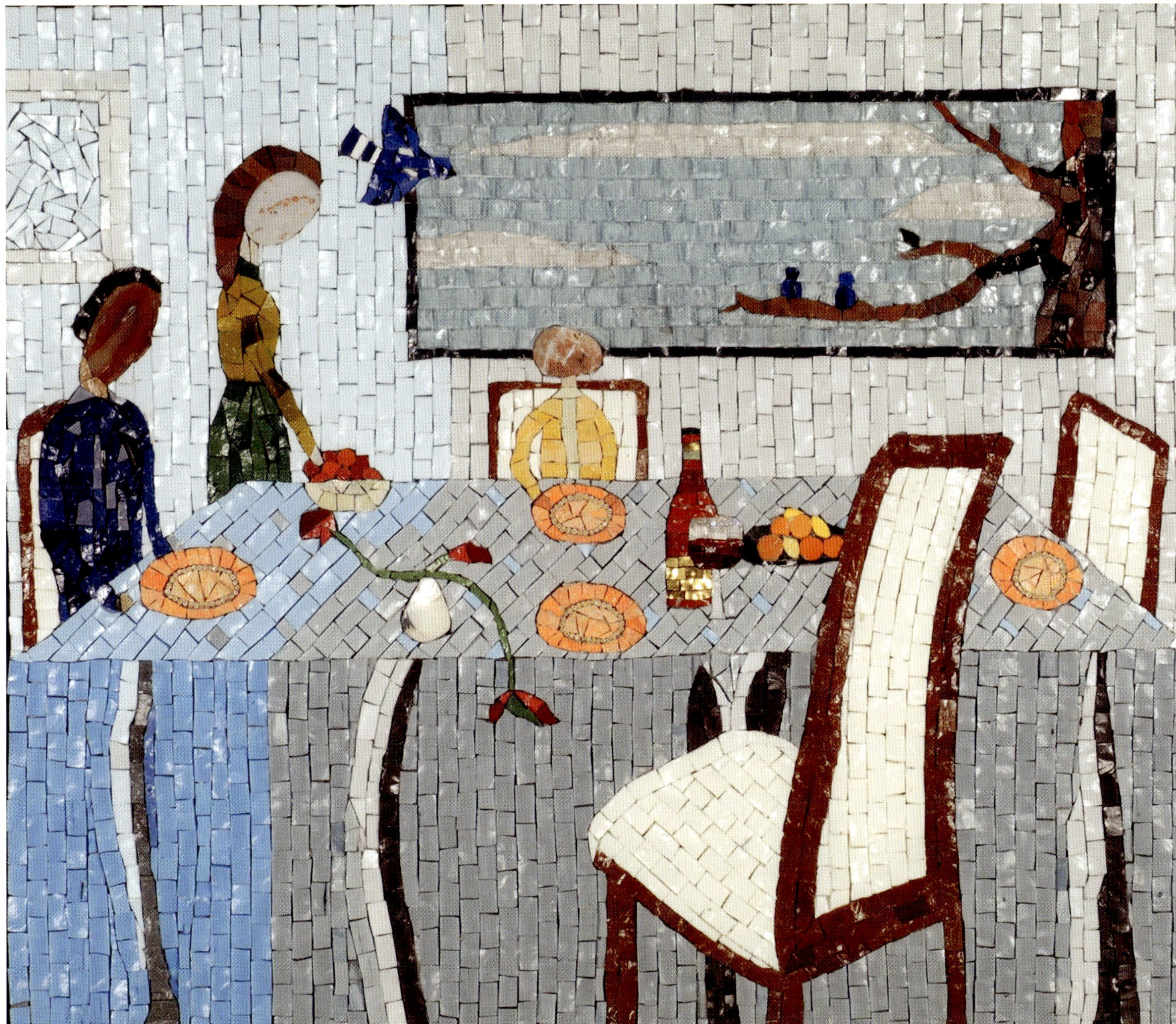

Ammette Cossentine—Alla Bizantina. *Repast.* 2010. Smalti, agate slices, oyster shell. 20" x 24".

Richard S. Davis

Clinton, Washington, rshevlin@whidbey.net

Artist's Statement

In my first decade of making mosaics, my technique has been heavily influenced by the materials I've collected from frequent trips to salvage yards and garage sales. This was partially the result of learning to make mosaics in New Zealand, where mosaic materials were in short supply in 1999, and I was taught to make the best of the situation. Having moved to Whidbey Island in 2007, there are fewer opportunities to collect recycled materials. However, living very near Puget Sound beaches provides almost unlimited Styrofoam chunks and pebbles that can influence the direction of future artwork. I continue to add to my inventory "stash" of found materials whenever I can.

In the past few years my wife and I have travelled to Uzbekistan, Krygyzstan, Tunisia, Egypt, Morocco, India, and throughout Europe. Traveling provides endless inspiration and imagery for future projects.

About the Artwork

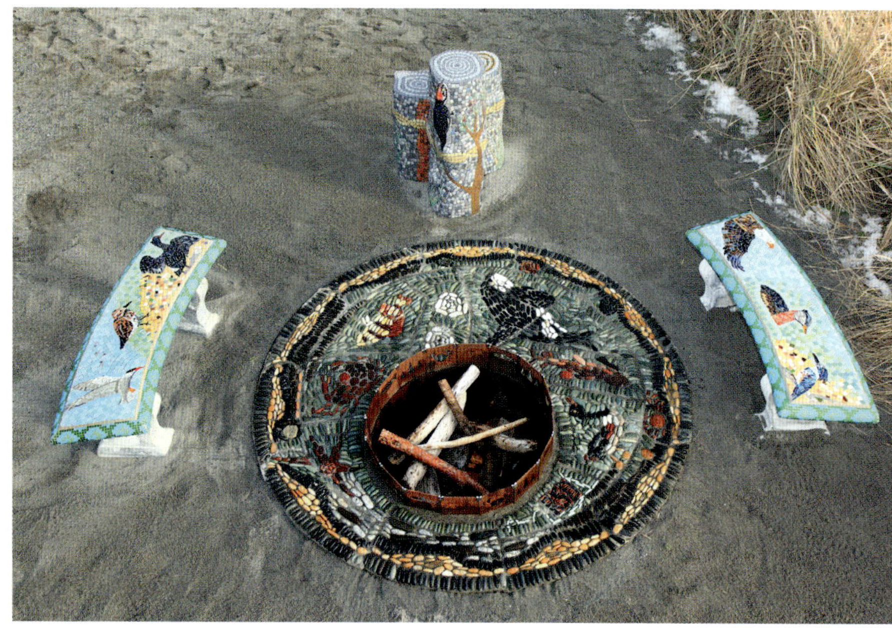

Richard S. Davis. Private Commission: Beach Suite. 2010. Beach Suite overview. 14' across x 12' across. *Photo by Michael Stadler*

Private Commission, Beach Suite, 2010 Pebble Mosaic

I received this commission through a local nursery that has been carrying some of my smaller artworks. The client had already purchased new metal cutout surrounds for their fire pit when I was put in contact with them. They told me they wanted to improve the appearance of the surrounding area with a pebble mosaic. I explained that not only would this be my first pebble mosaic, but that I rarely worked with realistic imagery. Despite these caveats they hired me.

My first surprise was the cost of appropriately shaped and colored pebbles. I immediately changed tack by deciding to collect pebbles on our local beaches instead. I even got the client to join in the collecting with me for a short period. We agreed to add their beach glass collection to the mosaic's materials where possible.

Whidbey Island's diverse animal and plant sea life was selected as the theme. Because of the scale of the project and the fact that I would be building the mosaics across the island at my home studio I needed to build the pebble mosaic in components that could be managed by one person and later combined into an overall visual scheme. To make the seams between the pebble mosaic components less visible I constructed twenty-two different forms from wood and syntactic polyurethane molding. Using the reverse method, I filled each form with pebbles, cementitious non-shrink grout, and, finally, reinforced concrete to hold everything in position. The final pebble mosaic puzzle pieces were de-molded and transported to the client's beachfront home where the pieces were reassembled and mortared together around the fire pit. The Orca whale's eye is a pebble I picked up on a beach in Sicily.

Richard S. Davis. Private Commission: Beach Suite. 2010. Sea life pebble mosaic. Pebbles, tumbled glass, reinforced cement, cementitious non-shrink grout. 7' in diameter. *Photo by Michael Stadler*

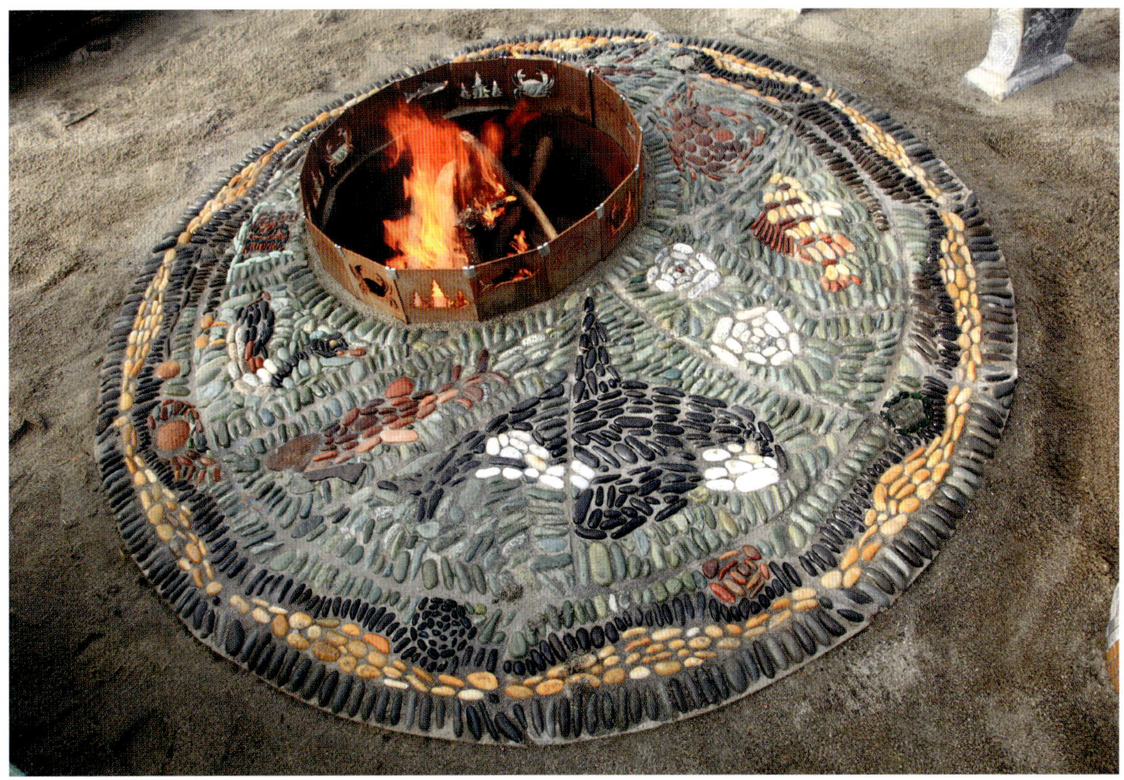

Benches

The client provided two cement benches to be covered in mosaic, and we choose native shore bird life as the subject. A bald eagle, tern, cormorant, kingfisher, sandpiper, and a harlequin duck adorn the benches. The mosaic was made by the paper-faced reverse technique in the studio and then applied to the benches on site. The bench borders were made using an indented plastic tray to create a uniform repetitive strip. I used mostly salvaged 3/8" tile removed from sections of an old wallpaper motif originally created by Bisazza tile.

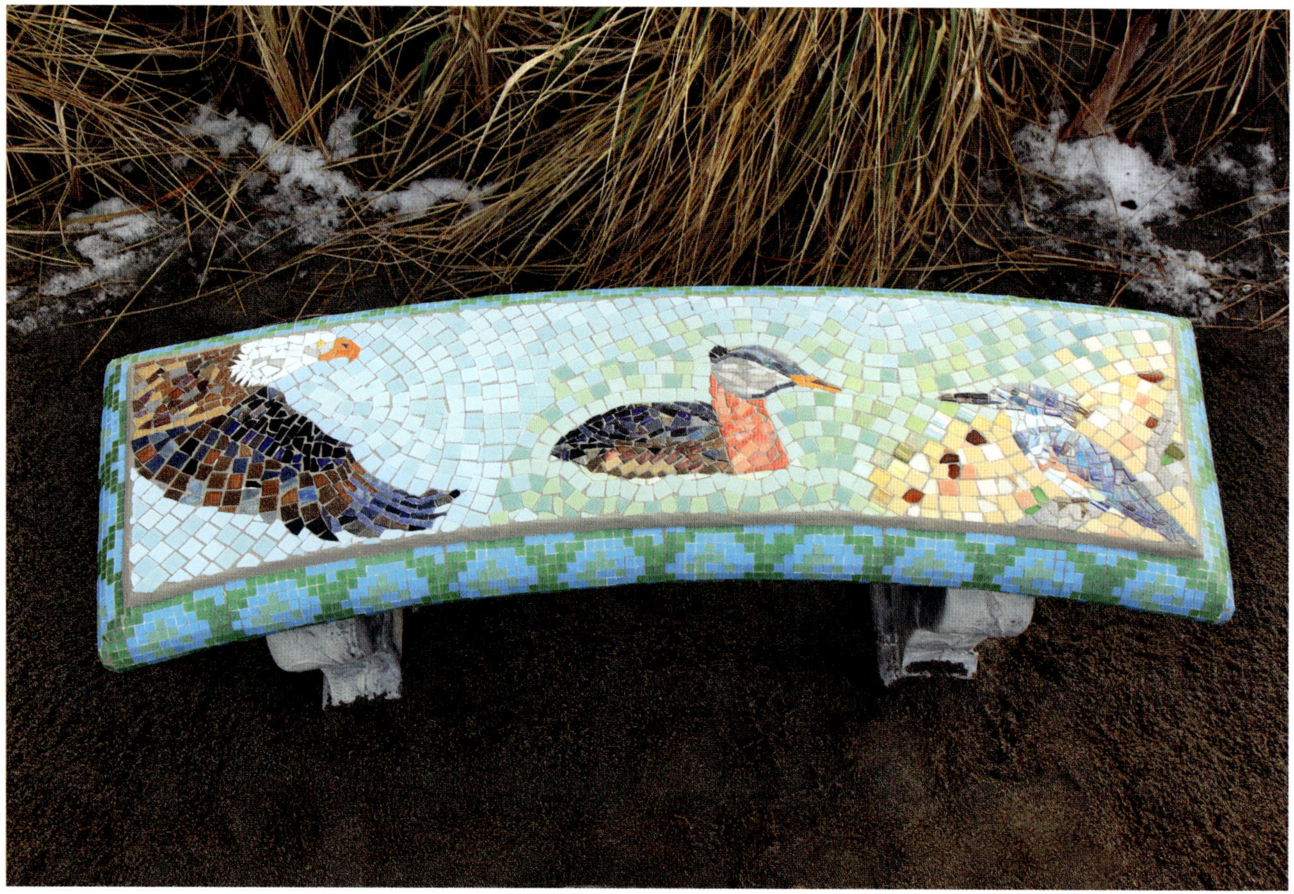

Richard S. Davis. Private Commission: Beach Suite. 2010. Bird Bench Vitreous glass, beach glass, thin set mortar and epoxy grout. 18" x 4'. *Photo by Michael Stadler*

Bollard Table

I suggested to the client that the table be unusual since it was not to be used for dining but for cocktails and casual BBQ cooking. As part of our sea life shore theme, I suggested the table imitate the driftwood bollards that are found all over Whidbey Island in driveways and gardens. This approach would result in a three level table. We agreed the bollard table would be covered in beach grasses, flowers, a few birds and small animals, and that a rope chain would appear to hold the three driftwood logs together.

I used large pieces of Styrofoam that had washed up on the beach as the base form. These were carved and glued together until they resembled driftwood log sections. The log sections were then covered in fiberglass mesh and cement. Vitreous glass mosaics were applied using both the direct method and the paper-faced reverse method due to the uneven and round character of the logs. It was very satisfying to know that beach glass and Styrofoam garbage washed up on the beach is now returned to the beach as art!

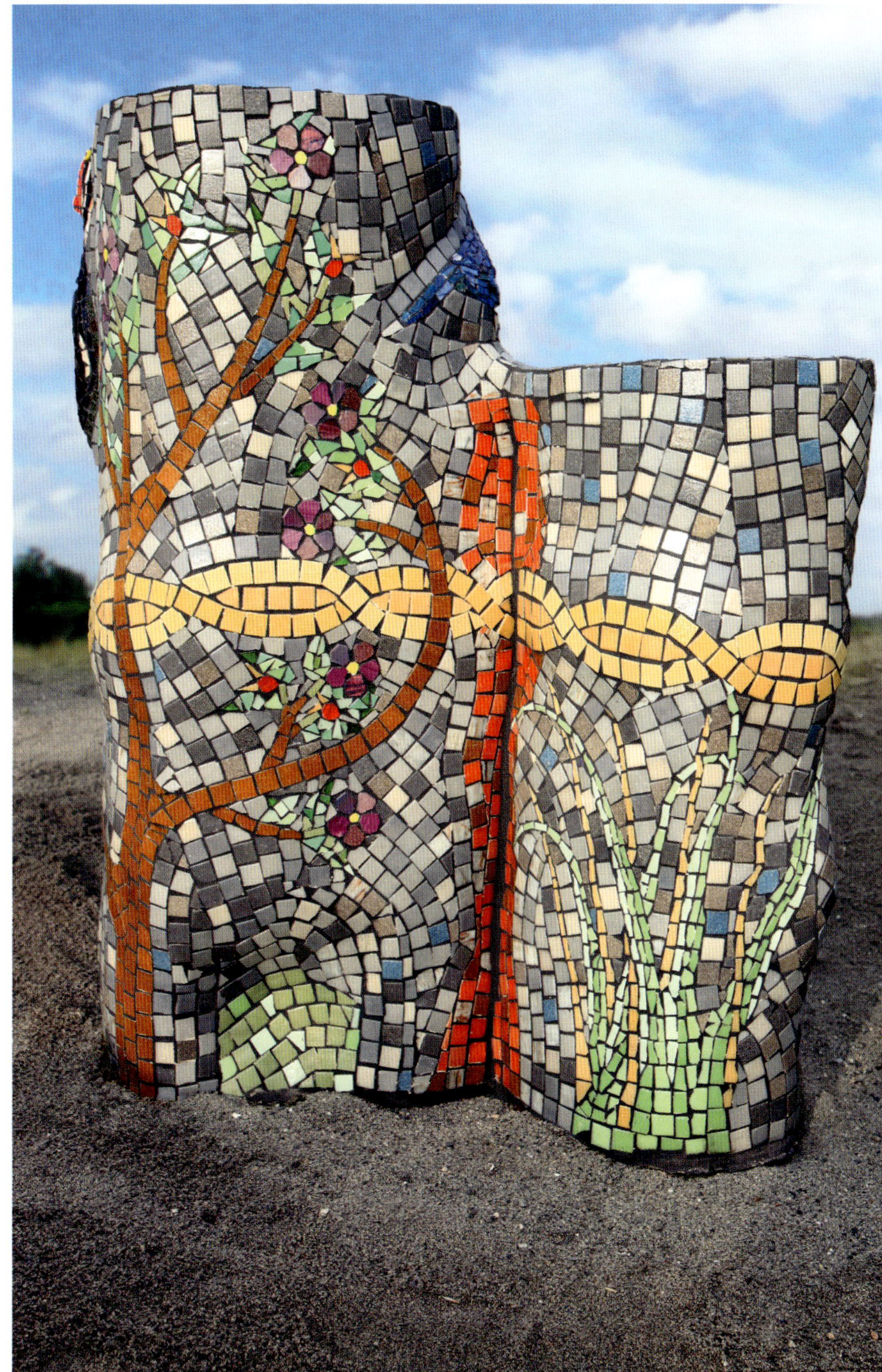

Richard S. Davis. Bollard Table. Private Commission: Beach Suite. 2010. Styrofoam, fiberglass mesh, concrete, vitreous glass, beach glass, thin set mortar, and epoxy grout. 36" x 3' in diameter. *Photo by Michael Stadler*

Art-Isle Home Master Bath, 2011

The original theme of my new master bath was to be "sunrise," but the theme changed with the discovery of 110 hand-painted Portuguese floral tiles from the 1960s at a salvage business. The decision to use the Portuguese tiles around the toilet stall converted the already loose sunrise theme into an autumn one. I chose autumn because I'd already laboriously collected many ceramic and glass tiles in shades of yellow, red, and orange over a three-year period and I was determined these not be wasted!

The master bath project was part of a new home construction and took more than two years from beginning to end, with different sections being finished along the way. The shower mosaic was made in the paper-faced reverse technique as it allows a relatively easy and inexpensive method for lying out and rearranging tile patterns. Tiles were cut with a wet saw where necessary. Some oddly shaped ceramic tiles made perfect tree silhouettes, and stained glass sections were sometimes added "as found." Overall, the mosaic's materials in the shower were manufactured by at least twenty-five different companies. An additional fifteen manufacturers made the materials for the remainder of the bathroom. The plethora of types of materials is both a blessing and a bane in that the artist has to marry and reconcile the varying thicknesses and textures of the assorted materials to create the continuous smooth surface required by a floor or shower wall.

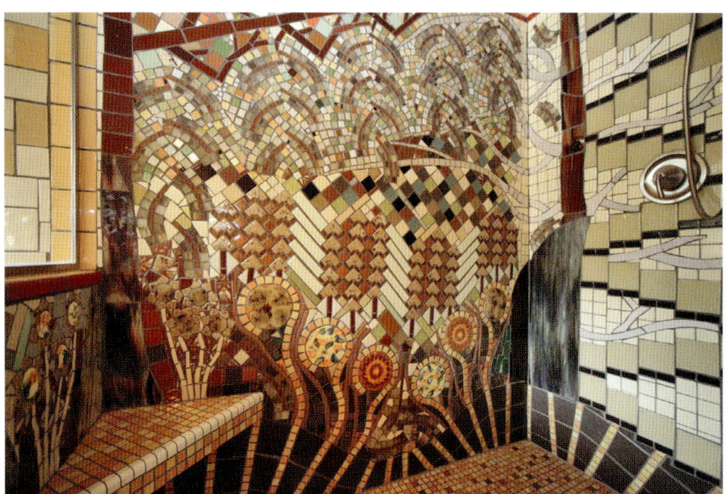

Richard S. Davis. Art-Isle Home Master Bath. 2008-2011. Six different types of glass tiles, glazed and unglazed ceramic tiles, marble "gems," stained glass, thin set mortar and grout. Autumn bench. 69" x 38" x 82". *Photo by Michael Stadler*

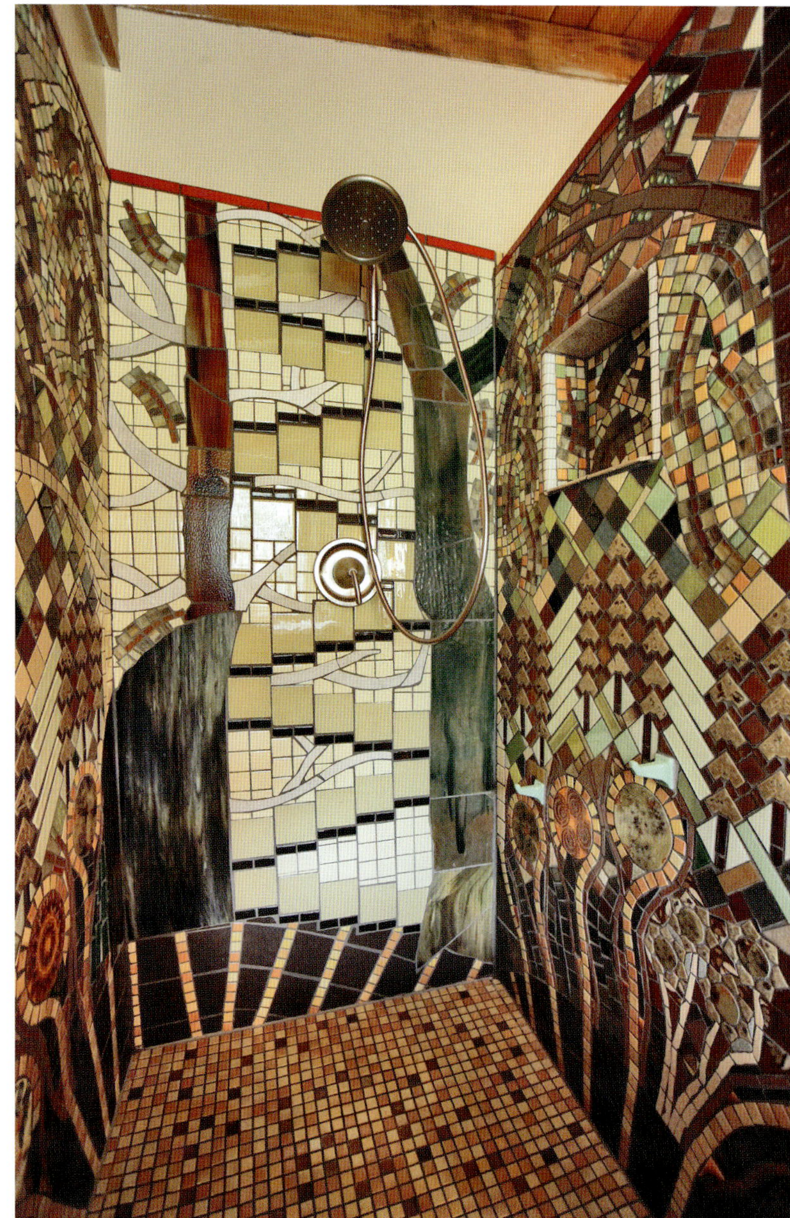

Richard S. Davis. Art-Isle Home Master Bath. 2008-2011. Six different types of glass tiles, glazed and unglazed ceramic tiles, marble "gems," stained glass, thin set mortar and grout. Autumn shower faucet, back wall. 38" x 82". *Photo by Michael Stadler*

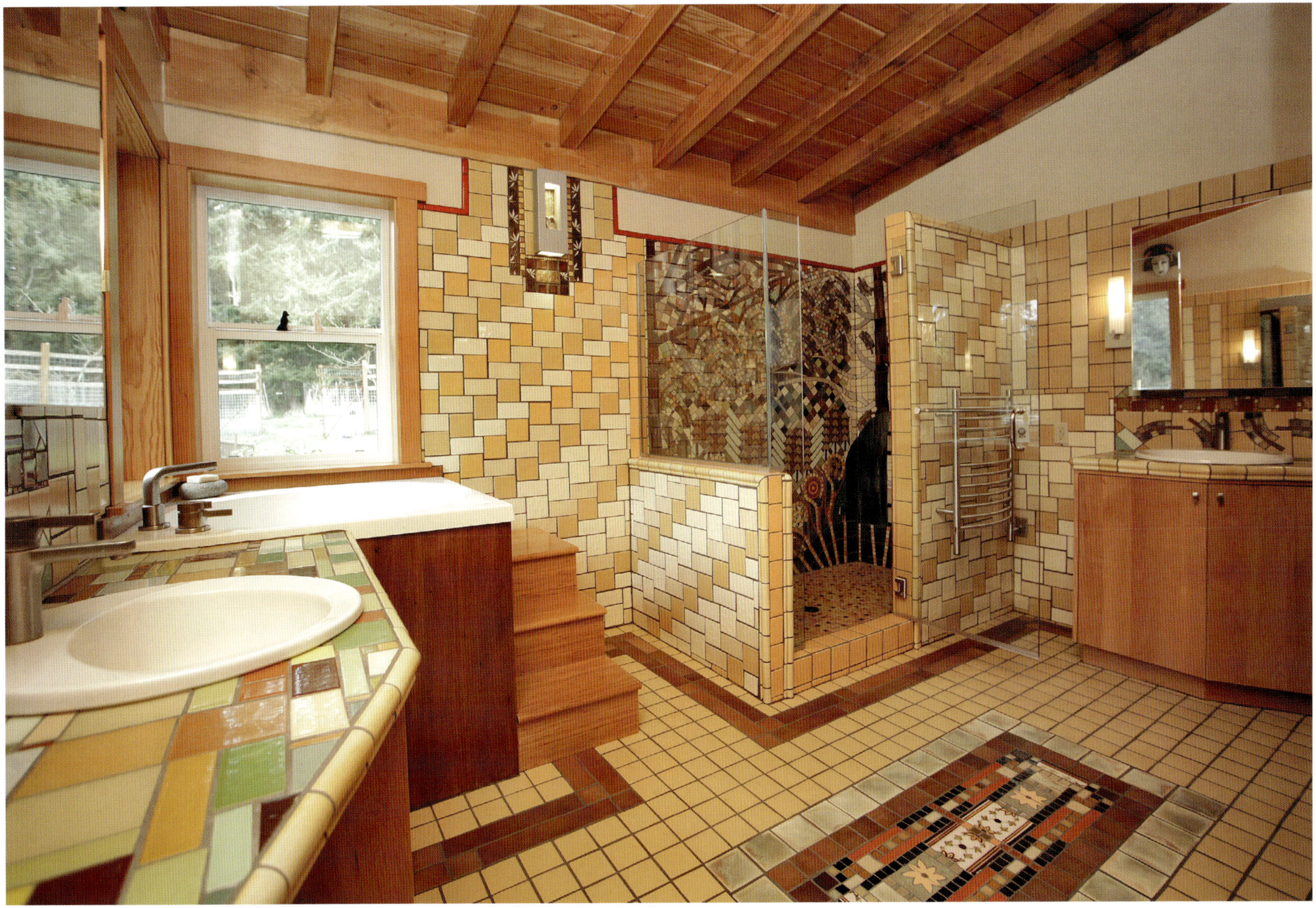

Richard S. Davis. Art-Isle Home Master Bath. 2008-2011. Six different types of glass tiles, glazed and unglazed ceramic tiles, marble "gems," stained glass, thin set mortar and grout. Bathroom overview: 12' x 12'. *Photo by Michael Stadler*

Gary Drostle

London, United Kingdom, gary@drostle.com

Artist's Statement

A simple ancient hand print can be seen as lying at the core of my artistic vision, it's origin is perhaps human kind's most ancient creative expression and can be seen in cave paintings over 50,000 years old, the signature of the first mural artists. Of course it's not a print, rather the impression left after the hand has been removed and as such symbolizes the marks left on the environment by people now departed. It is this profoundly democratic view of art for all, on the street, enhancing and changing our environment, interacting with people, landscape, and architecture, reflecting a sense of place through the expression of our history and humanity that inspires me.

The Artwork

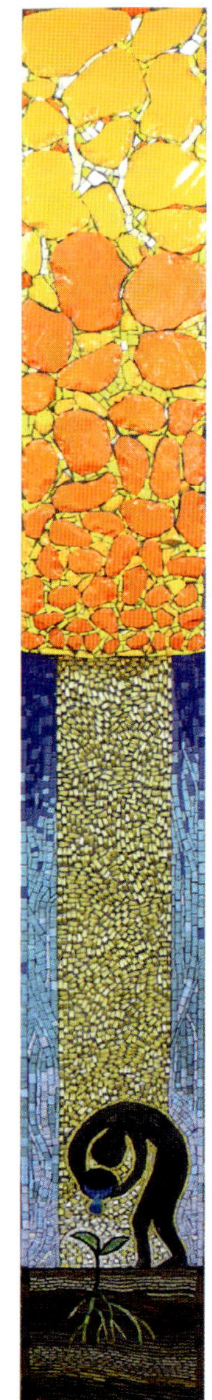

Gary Drostle. West Green Children's Mural. Exterior Wall. 1987. Emulsion on flush rendered brick. Design & fabrication. Mural with children from West Green School. 8' x 36'.

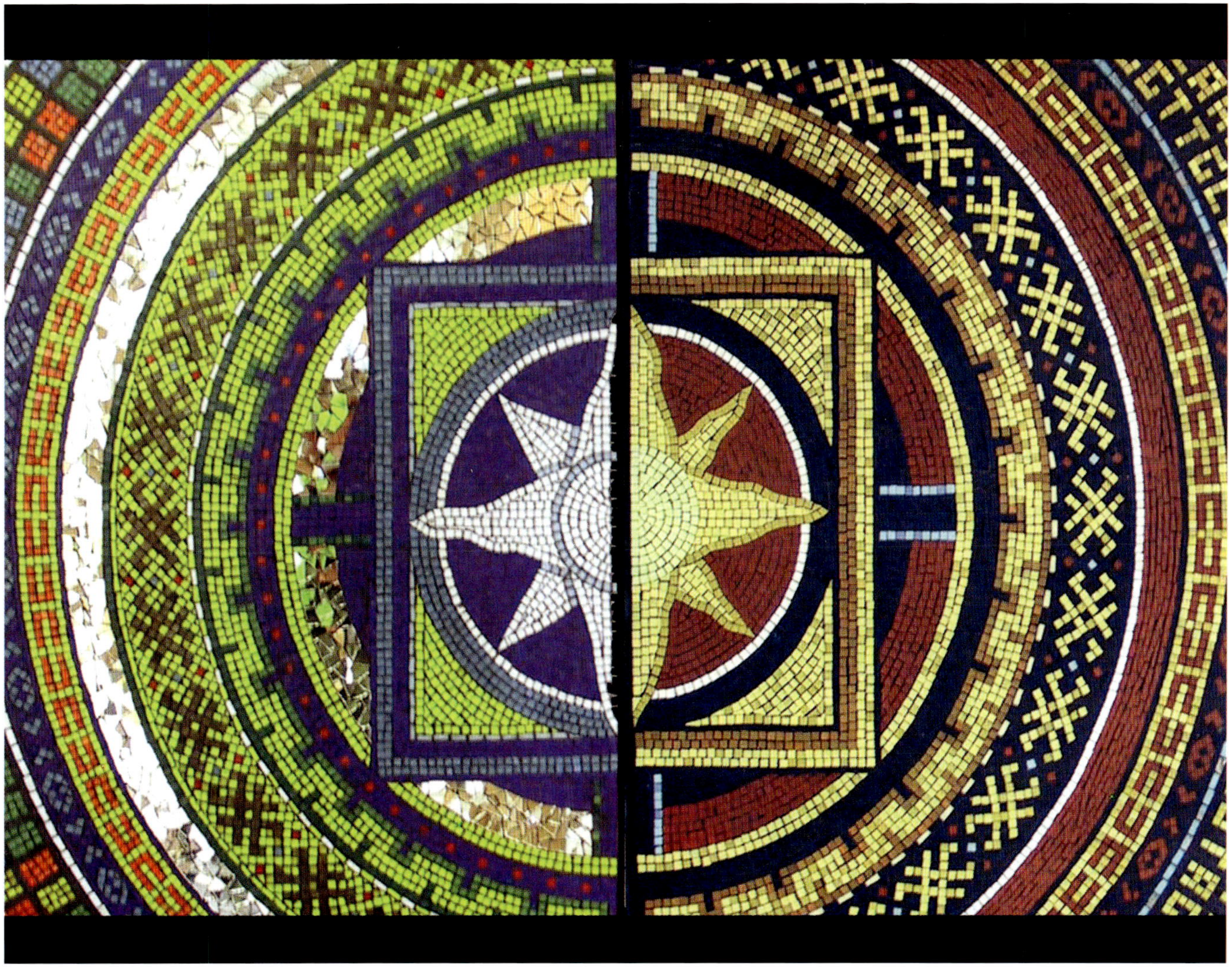

Gary Drostle. *Body & Spirit Mosaic*. Wall mosaic. Interior wall. 2005. Glass & ceramic mosaic. 6 1/2' (2m) diameter.

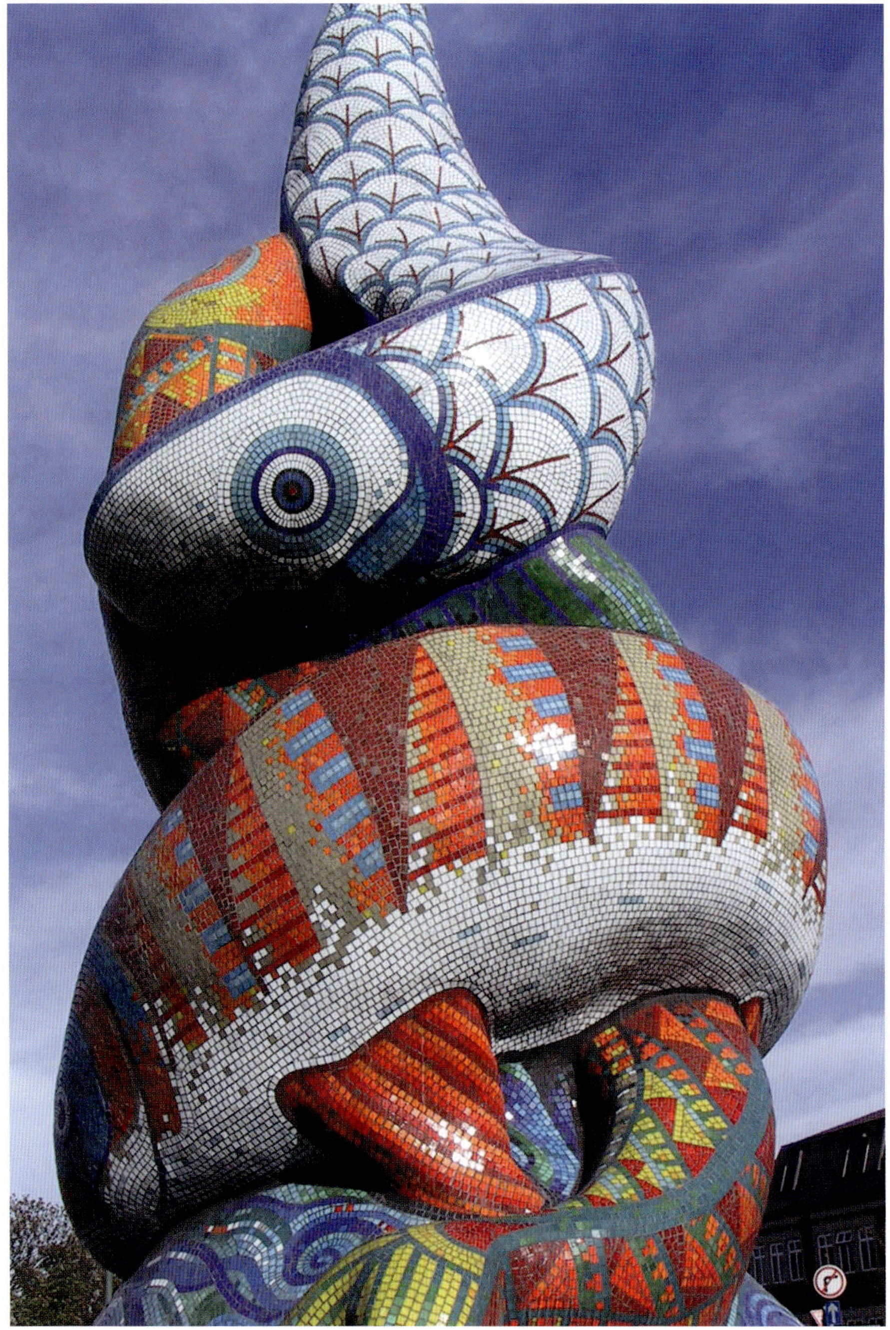

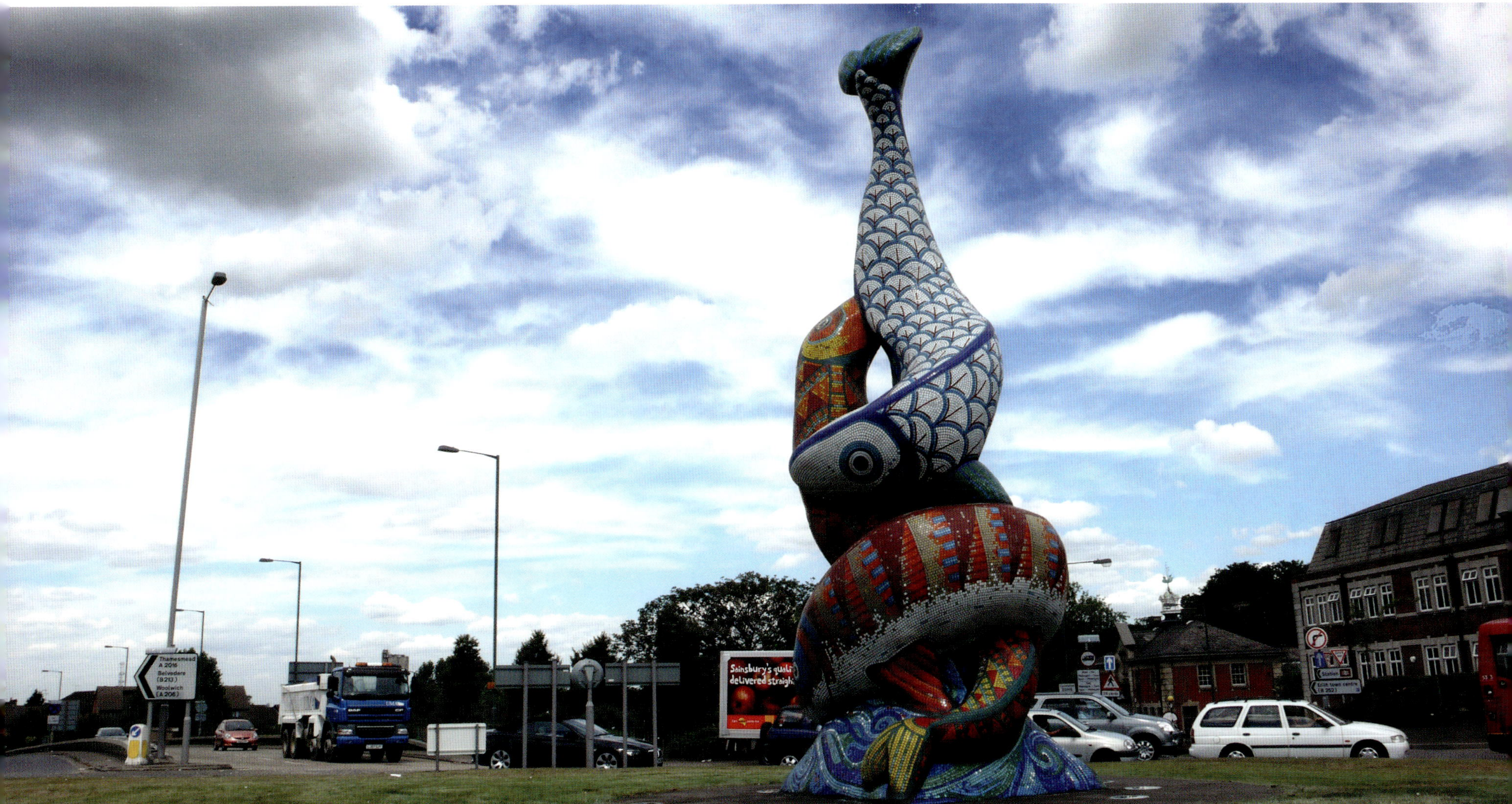

Gary Drostle. *Erith Fish*. Roundabout mosaic sculpture. 2006. Glass mosaic on concrete form. 24 1/2' (7.5m) high. (Detail opposite page.)

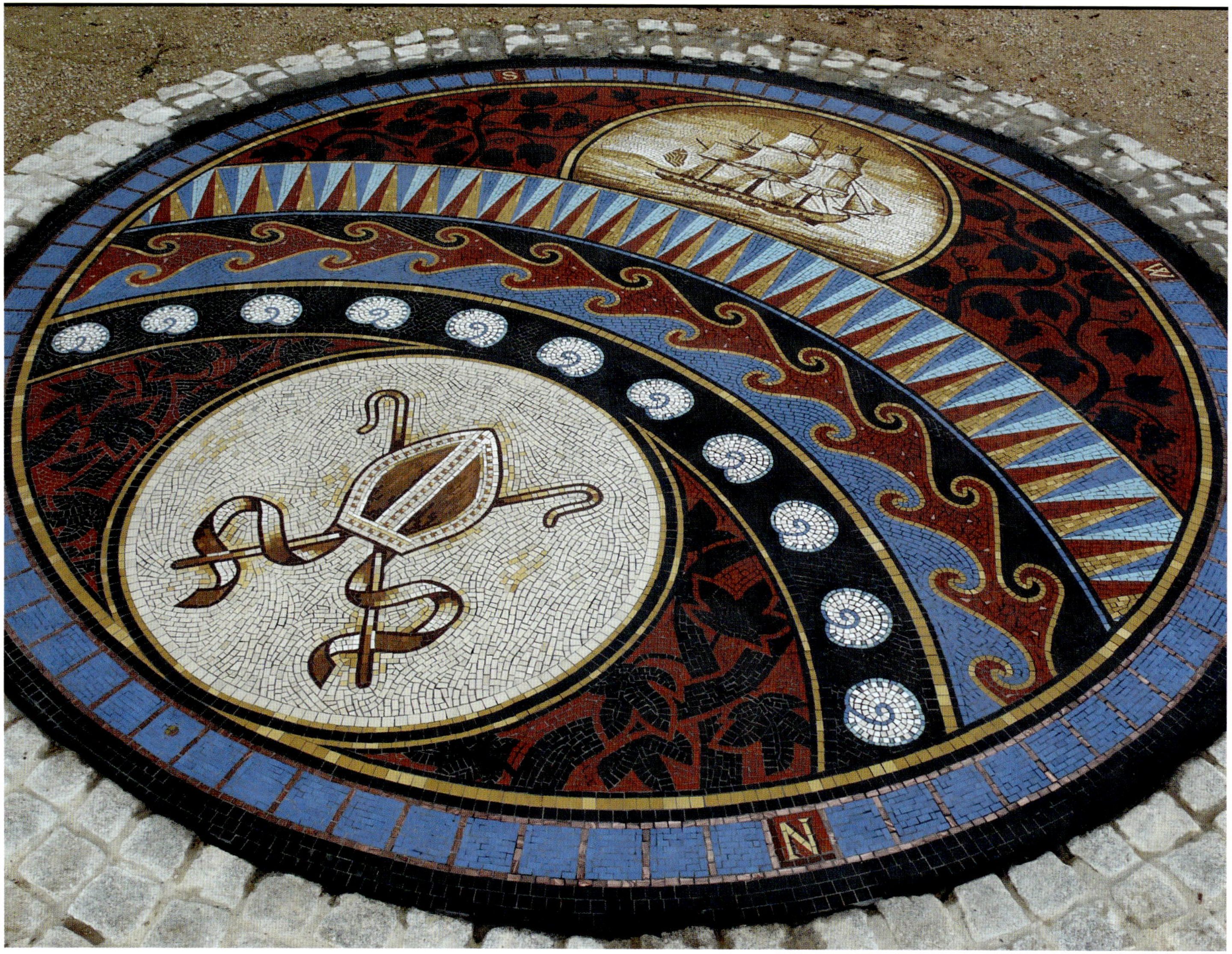

Gary Drostle. *Bishop's Walk Mosaic*. Mosaic pavement. 2008. Unglazed ceramic and glass. 10' (3m) diameter. (Detail opposite page.)

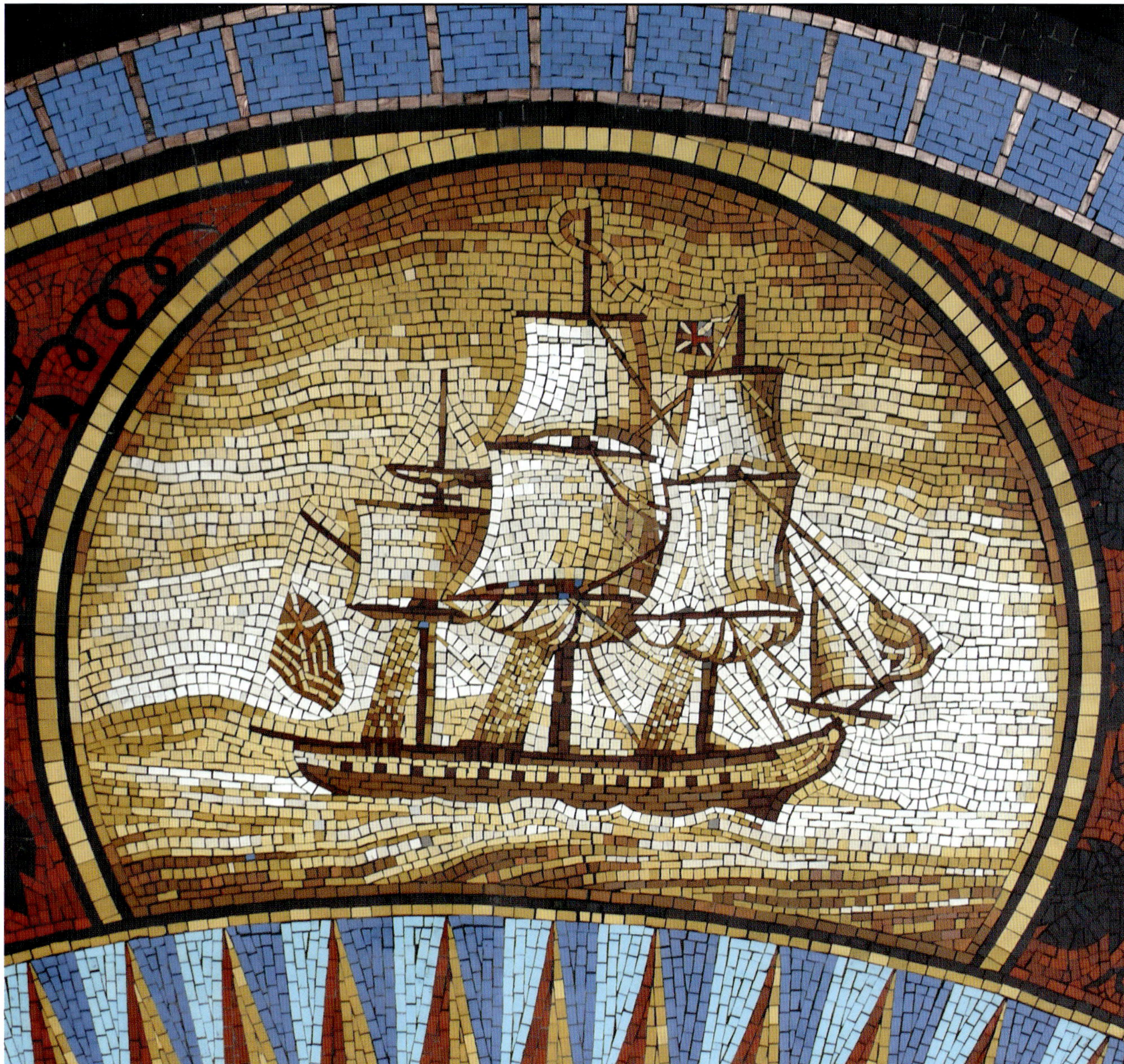

Wade Eldean

Macatawa, Michigan, wadeeldean@hotmail.com

Artist's Statement

My artwork contains representations and celebrations of the irresistible qualities, such as innovation, naiveté, love, instinct, and play that children appear to innately possess. My work, at its nexus, celebrates and reminds the viewer of the important role and relationship we have in society with our children.

A mosaic, when creating a portrait, is a rather crude and painstaking medium. There are no layers, colors are limited, forming shapes is restrictive, and soft edges and blending of colors is virtually non-existent. However, when viewing the mosaic after it is completed, the mosaic takes on many of these subtle characteristics that it resisted during creation. Mosaics are a challenging, fun, and rewarding medium with amazing visual results!

The Artwork

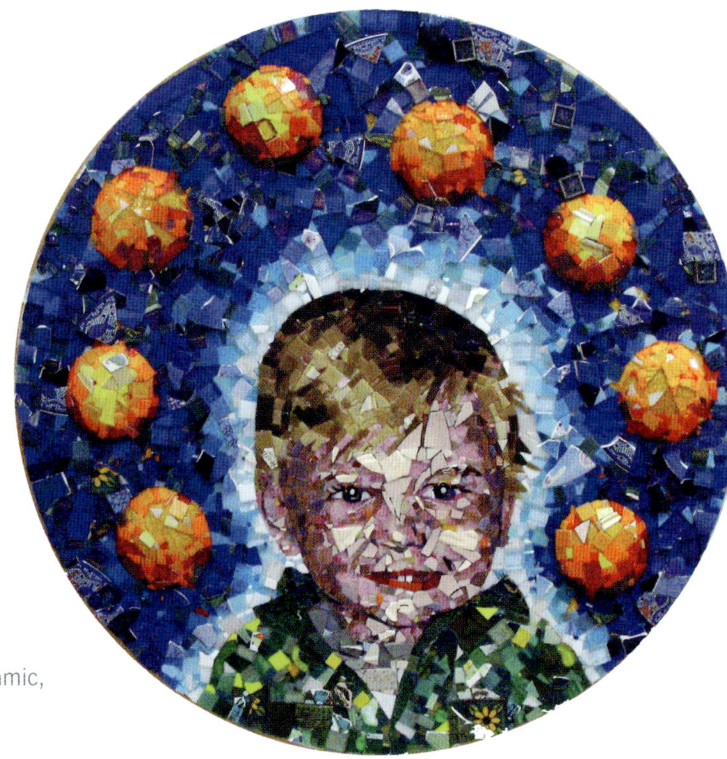

Wade Eldean. *Grandson Alexander*. 2009. Mosaic with glass, tile, ceramic, and plastic on board. 36" round x 2" deep. *Photo by Wade Eldean*

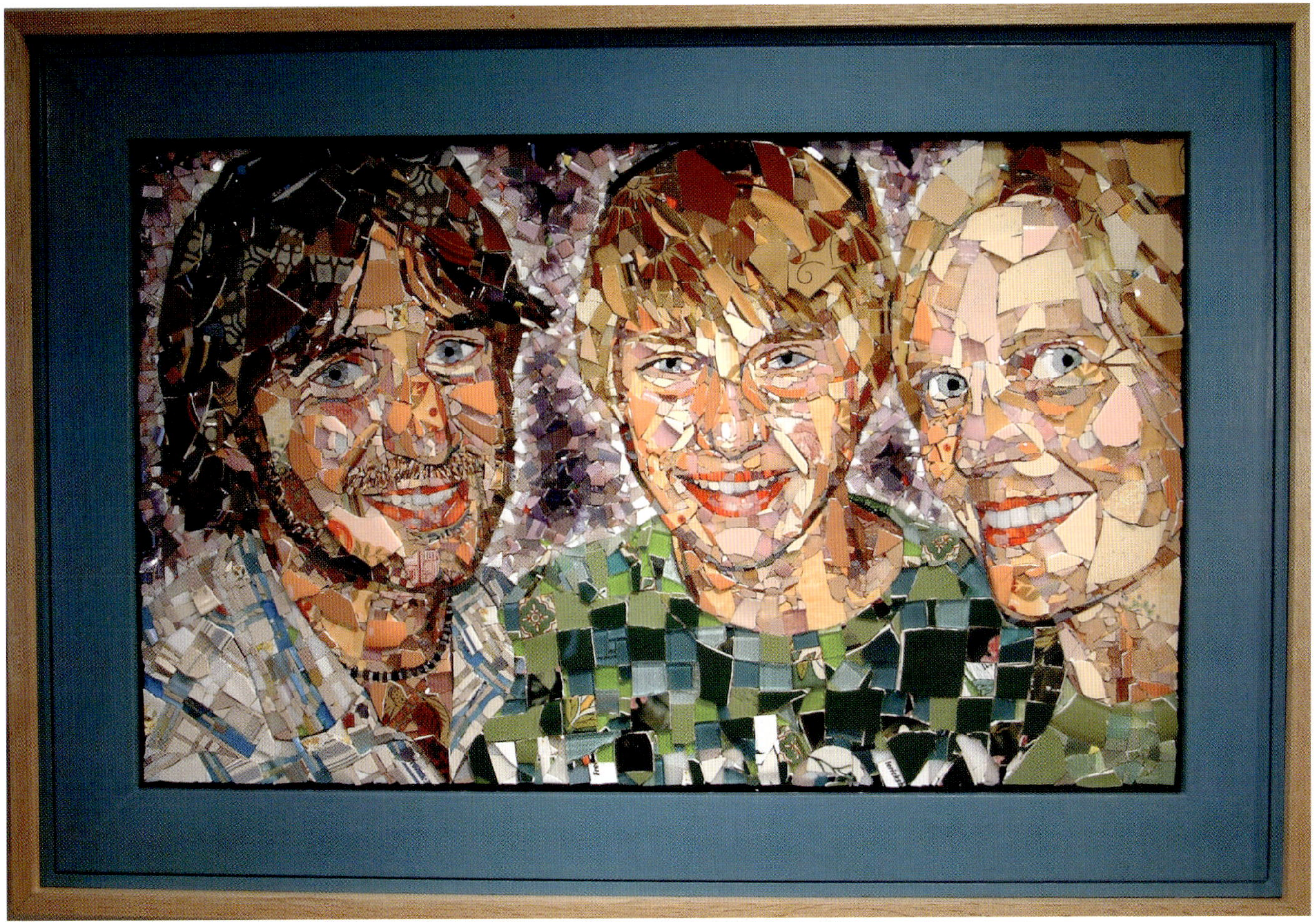

Wade Eldean. *Wade, Ryan, & Kris –A Family (Self) Portrait*. 2010. Mosaic with glass, tile, ceramic, and plastic on board. 30" x 44" framed. *Photo by Wade Eldean*

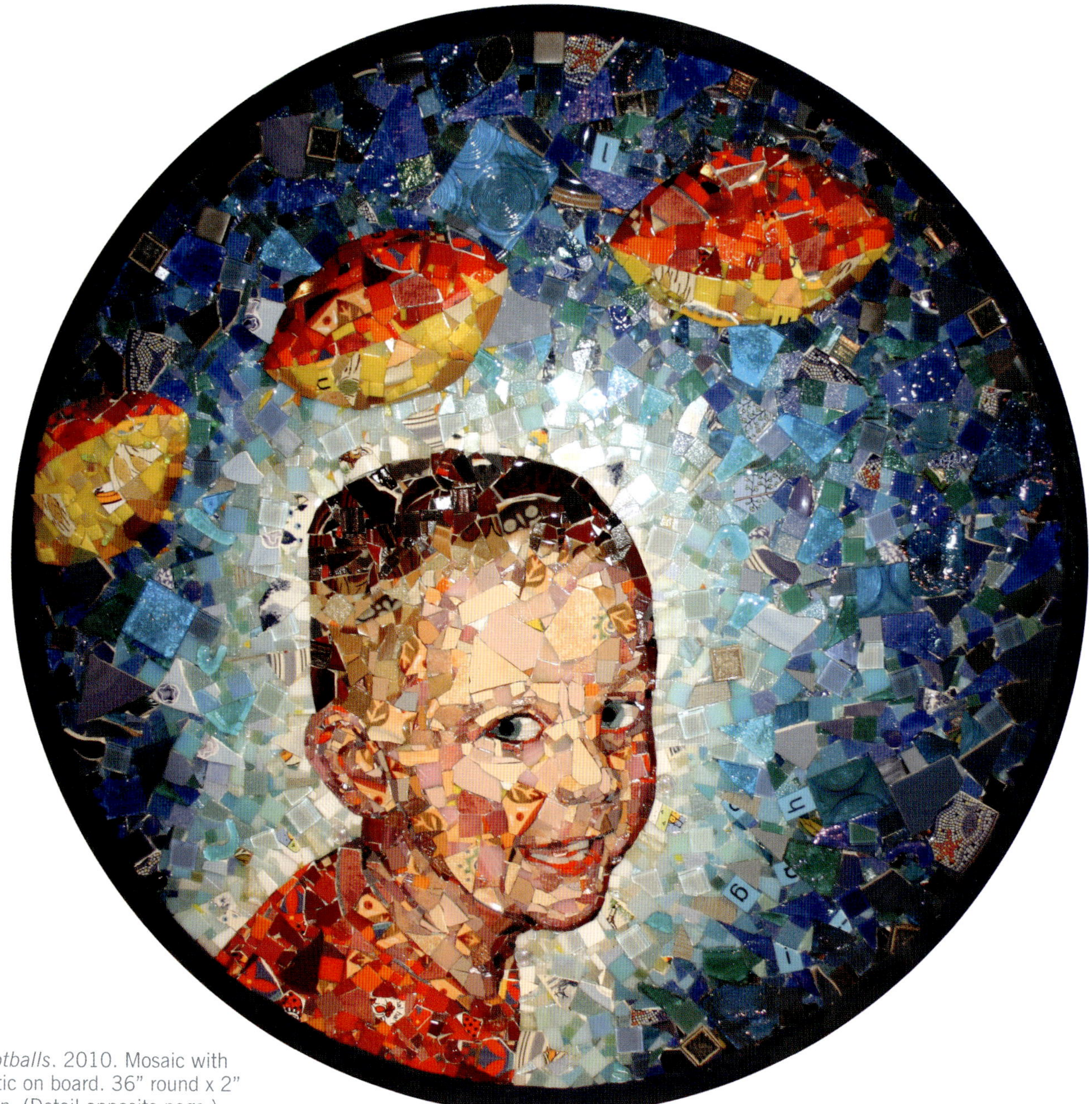

Wade Eldean. *Gavin with Footballs*. 2010. Mosaic with glass, tile, ceramic, and plastic on board. 36" round x 2" deep. *Photos by Wade Eldean* (Detail opposite page.)

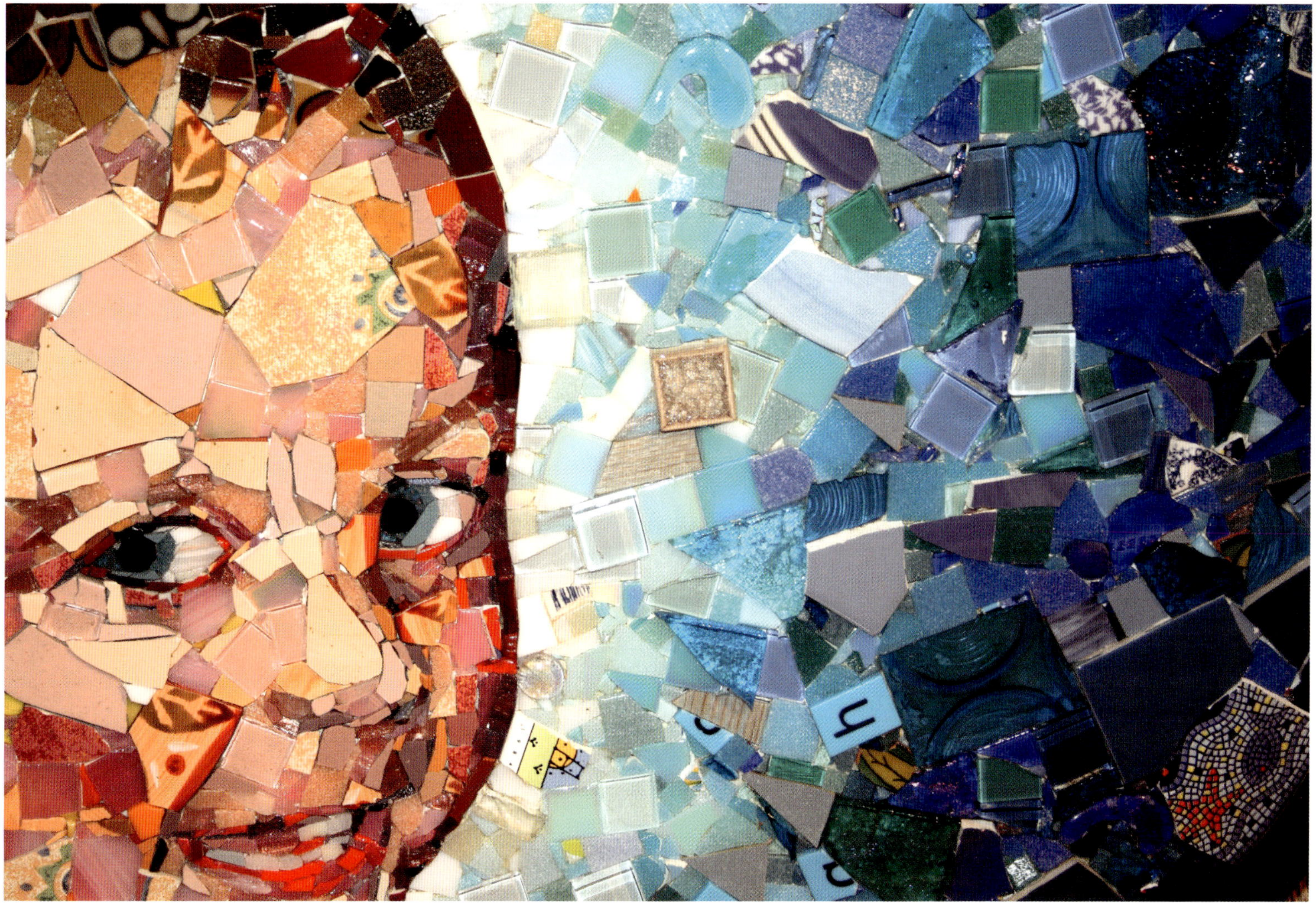

Olena A. Ellis

Wasilla, Alaska

Artist's Statement

Mosaics are like life to me. We have these different pieces which seem disjointed, but when put together they create an image, which is the landscape of our lives. Every piece I make is a journey and each piece takes on a life of its own.

I am a self-taught mosaic artist. I am an intuitive artist; if I like how it looks that is what I will go with. Each art piece is its own story. I only create pieces I would be willing to hang in my own home. I begin with an idea of something "I want" and do not know what the finished product will look like. Mosaic is a form of meditation or silent prayer in that I get lost in my work. I focus on one piece at a time. If I find myself struggling with a section, I have learned to move to another section or step away. When I return to that section with fresh eyes, it usually just falls into place. I call this my getting out of my own way process. Art is definitely a spiritual process for me and I hope my art touches or opens people when they see it.

About the Artwork

Kokopelli and Kokopelli Mama Spiral Dance: This is an up-cycled table that I made into a new table with a mosaic design. Kokopelli is my love, however Kokopelli Mama just does not get the air time of her counterpart. My original thought was for the table to be a yin-yang with Kokopelli and Kokopelli-Mama. As you can see, they came to life and are not in petroglyph form or a formal yin-yang design. Their flute playing is creating energy together, bringing light into their relationship, which radiates out from them. I used various glass tiles for this piece and wood edged the sides.

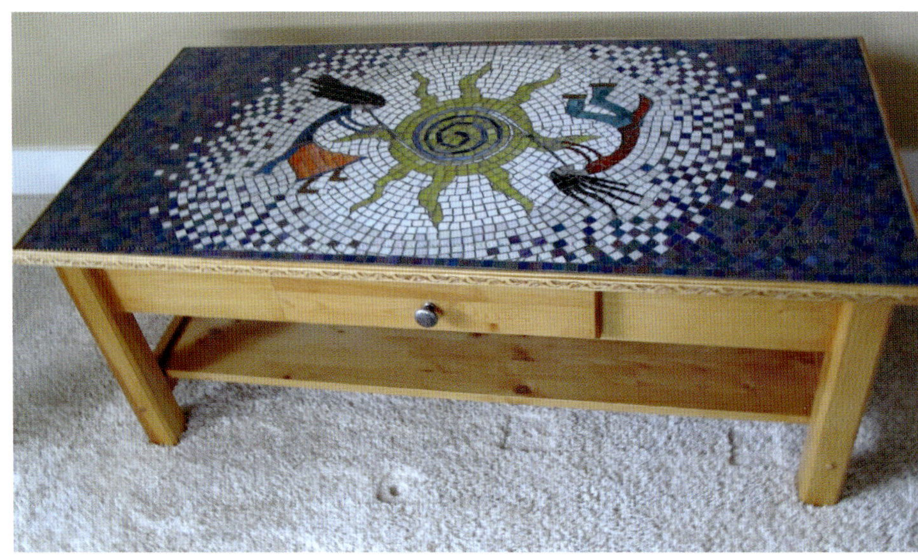

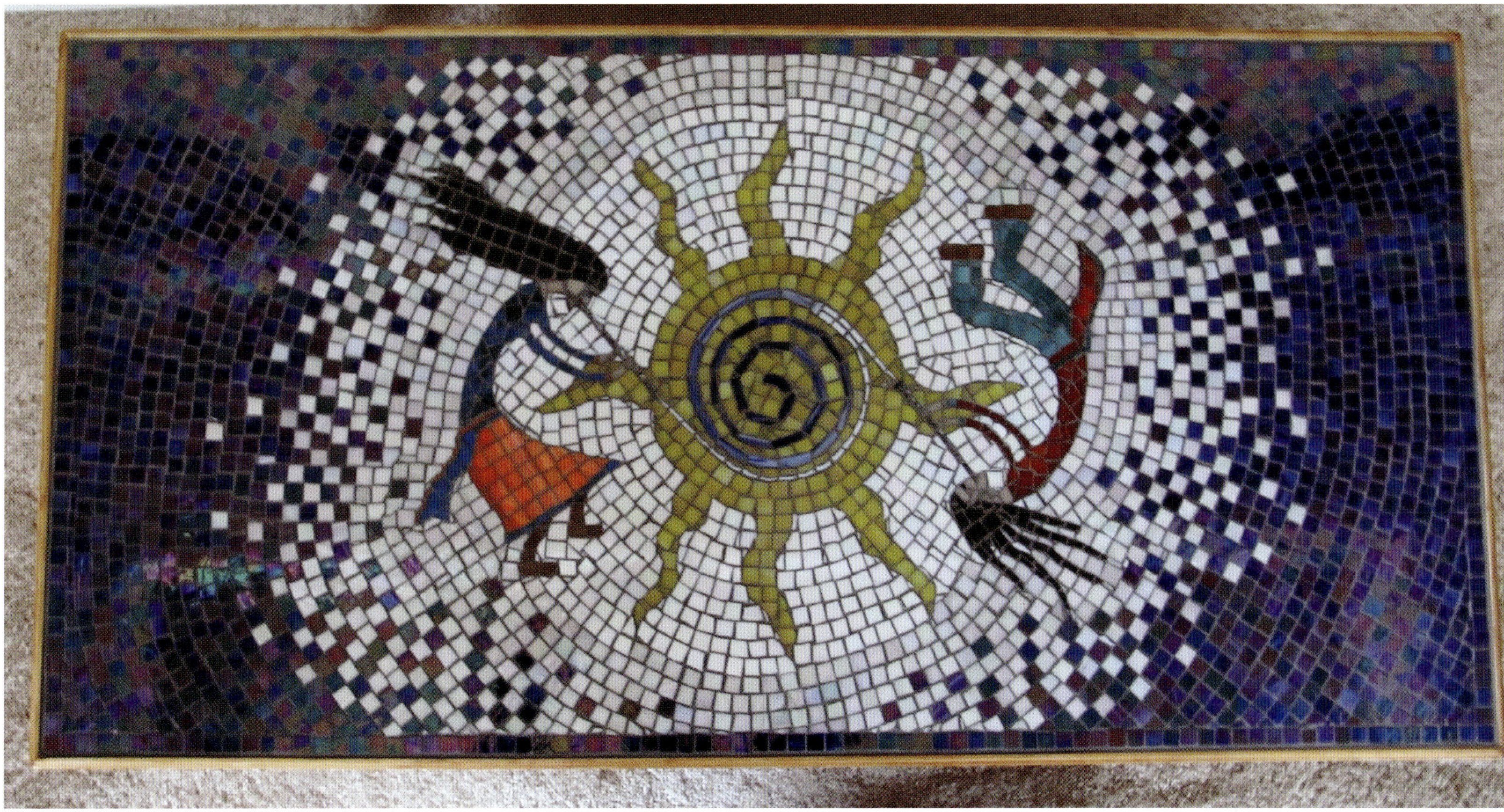

Olena A. Ellis. *Kokopelli and Kokopelli Mama Spiral Dance*. 2009. The table measures 18" tall, 23 3/4" x 47 3/4".

Mosaic Interpretation of Gustav Klimt's "The Kiss!:" My interpretation is slightly different, as she is not kneeling, feeling that relationships need two people standing and supporting one another. There are glass tiles, (glitter, mirror, stained, fused, etc.), and "baubles/trinkets/embellishments" used in this piece. Some items are attached directly onto the tiles, after grouting. This piece is wood edged.

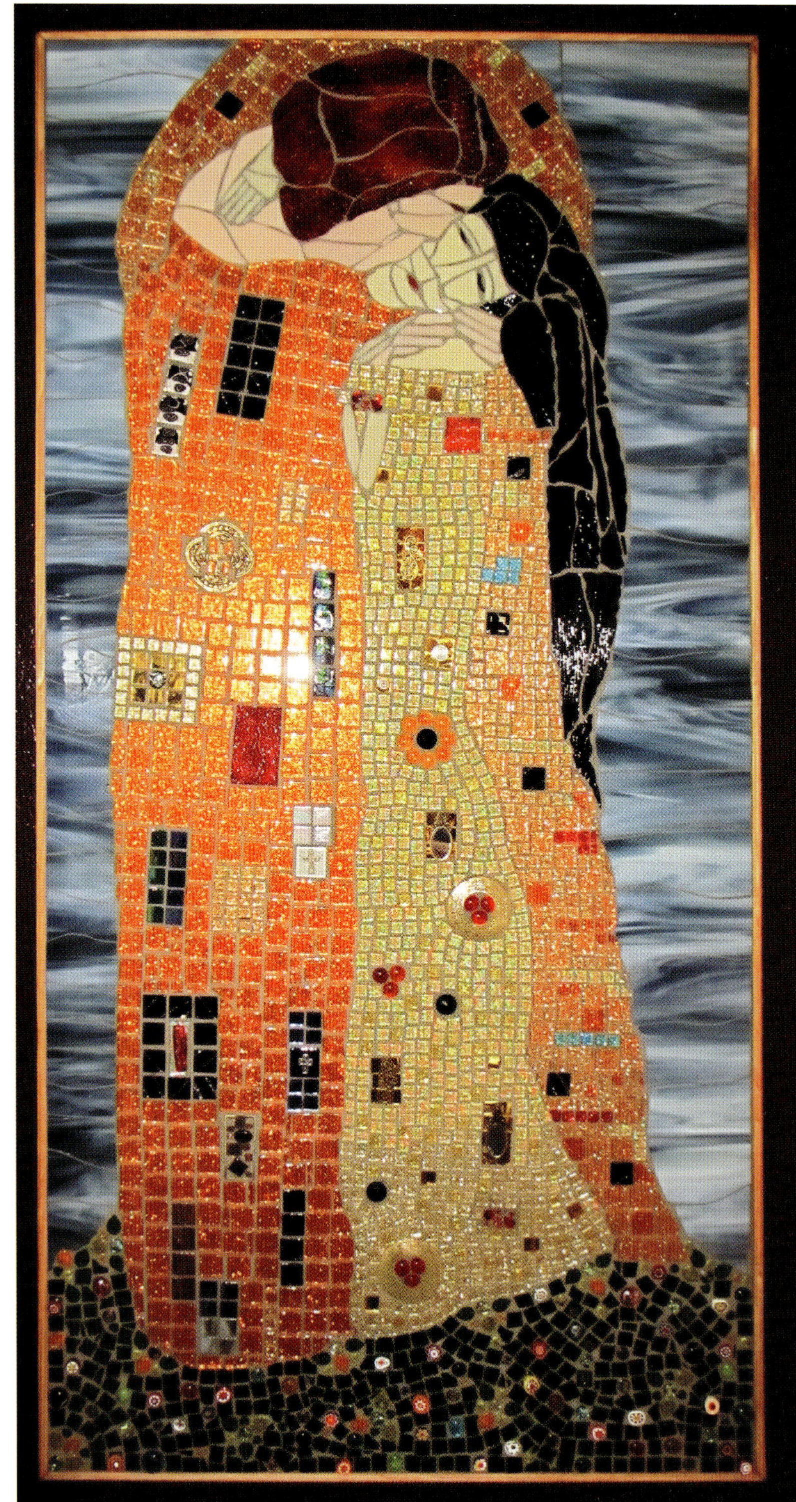

Olena A. Ellis. *Mosaic Interpretation of Gustav Klimt's "The Kiss."* 2010. 24 3/4" x 49 3/4".

Prayer Abundance Bowl: We are surrounded by abundance all the time. We can get caught up in day to day living and may forget that we are part of the bigger picture. These bowls are a reminder to empty ourselves and remain open to abundance coming into our lives. To take moments to be grateful and welcoming to the abundance that surrounds us. I began with an empty wood Asian bowl and added tiles or "shinnies'" to each bowl. In addition, each *Abundance Bowl* has therapeutic "Abundance" oil added to the grout and wood to support the intentions you place in your bowl.

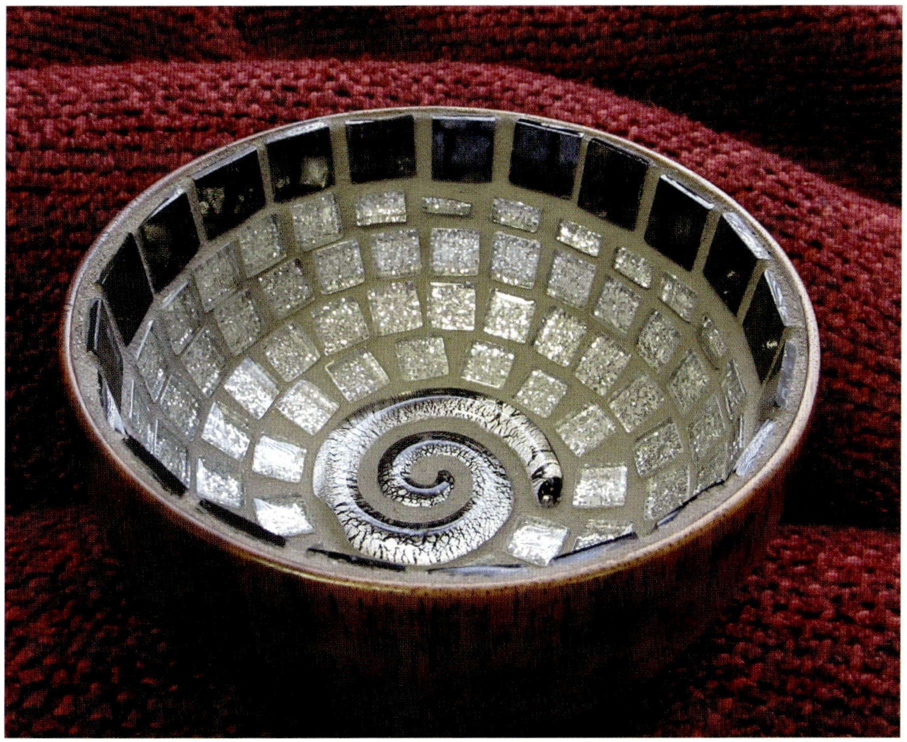

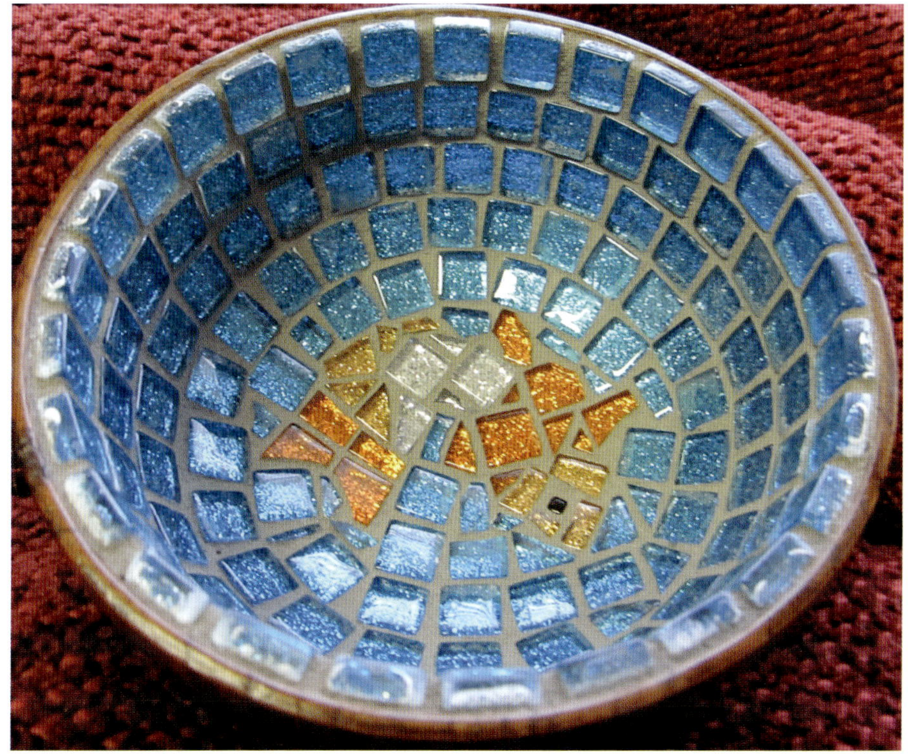

Olena A. Ellis. *Prayer Abundance Bowls*. Bowl. 2011. 2 3/4" x 4 1/2".

Koi Pond: There is a feeling of peace and tranquility one gets when looking into a koi pond.

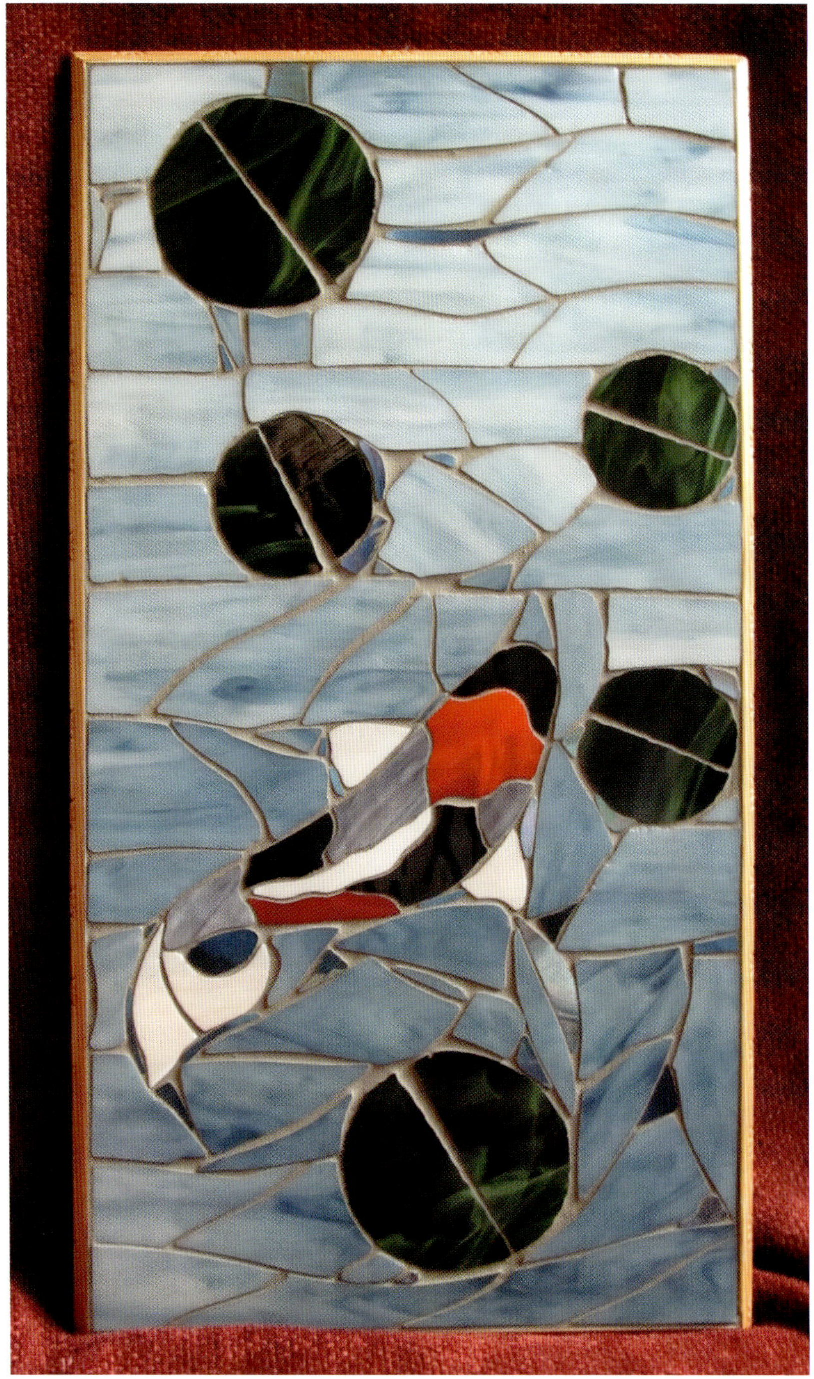

Olena A. Ellis. *Koi Pond.* 2011. 24 1/2" x 12 1/2".

Northwest Raven: The Raven is my teacher and I love the simplicity of the Northwest Art, so I created this piece. The Raven is called upon in Native ceremony for healing purposes and is thought to provide long-distance healing. The variegated stained glass in the background is a spiritual representation.

Olena A. Ellis. *Northwest Raven*. 2011. 24 1/2" x 12 1/2".

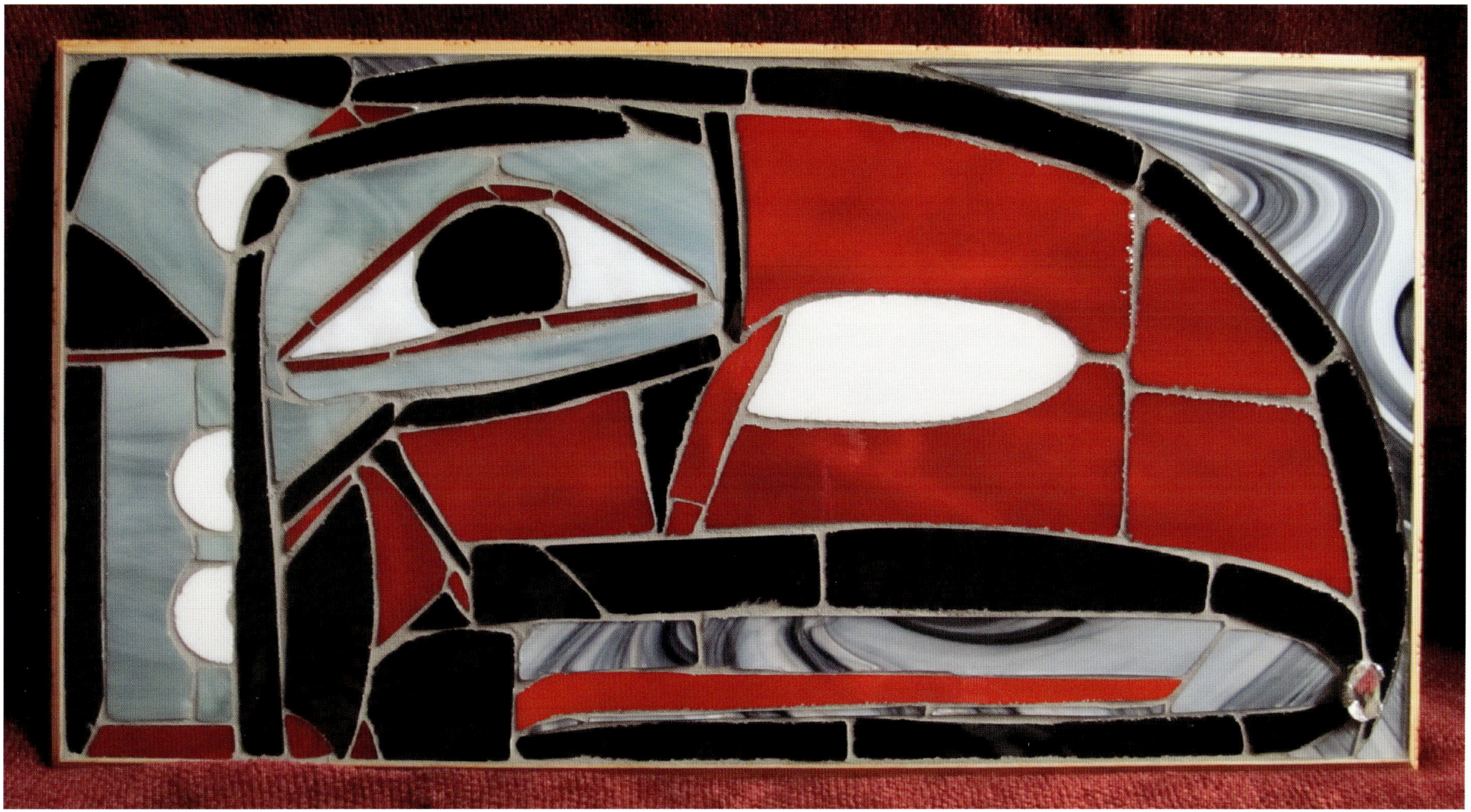

Kim Emerson

San Diego, California, kim@kimemersonmosaics.com

Artist's Statement

Expression as an artist for me comes through the medium of mosaics in the form of murals and three-dimensional sculpture. I carefully cut geometric pieces of glass, ceramic tile, and/or found objects and "puzzle" them together to create something representational or abstract. Mosaics are like permanent textured paintings that reflect light and shadows. Most of my work is designed to be site specific. The challenge for me is to design in harmony with the natural landscape or existing architectural design, thus reflecting environment and culture.

I have always been fascinated by the historic and pre-historic context of humanity in its relationship with nature and how our world is constantly changing. Motifs from nature and our ancient predecessors guide me in my work. The word "mosaic" of late has become a metaphor to describe the diversity in which we live. For me, the world is a mosaic made up of various cultures, conditionings, environment, time, and space, each having its unique circumstance and yet bonded by the cement of life itself.

About the Artwork

Water Henge: H2o = Life: This public art project tells the story of the history of water in the Los Angeles basin. The sculptures are arranged in a circular configuration that invites visitors to gather, explore, and learn. The orange ceramic tiles have engraved written facts about the various epochs of time going back 40 million years. The largest sculpture stands 13' high and represents a time when the entire area was covered by ocean. Images of ancient underwater fish and scenery are found in the details. The second largest sculpture represents a time when dinosaurs or pre-historic animals roamed the marshlands. Imagery of dinosaur bones and skeletons make up the mosaic design. The third smallest sculpture represents animal life with mosaic images of paw prints. The fourth smallest sculpture, also a bench to sit upon, represents the plant life of the area. The sculptures are placed around the circle in a fashion that expresses that the water over time receded to what it is today as they appear smaller, more rounded, and eroded. The tallest sculpture features a powder coated plate steel "sun" cut-out that casts a shadow onto the smallest centrally located sculpture on the fall and spring equinoxes.

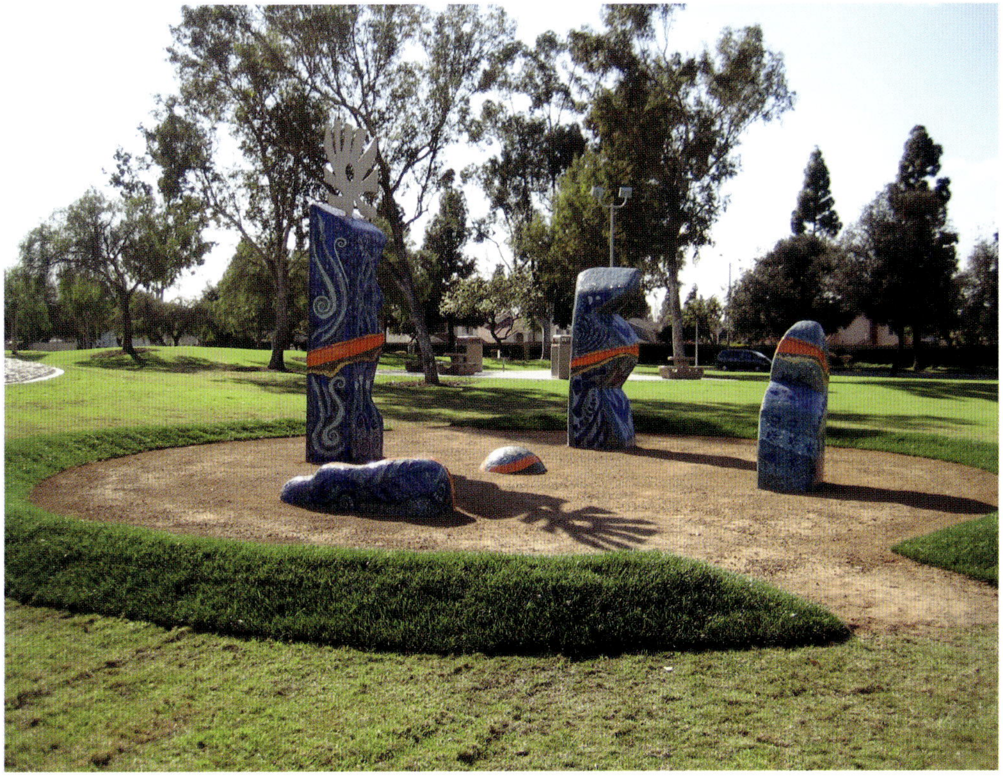

Kim Emerson. *Water Henge: H2o = Life.* Five freestanding mosaic sculptures surrounded by a circular grass mound or "henge." 2009. Sculpted expanded polystyrene (EPS), rebar, cement, cut/painted plate steel and ceramic tile. Hand-cut tesserae/tape technique/direct method. 13' high (tallest sculpture) x 20' in diameter (henge). Cerritos Regional Community Park, City of Cerritos, California. *Photo by the artist*

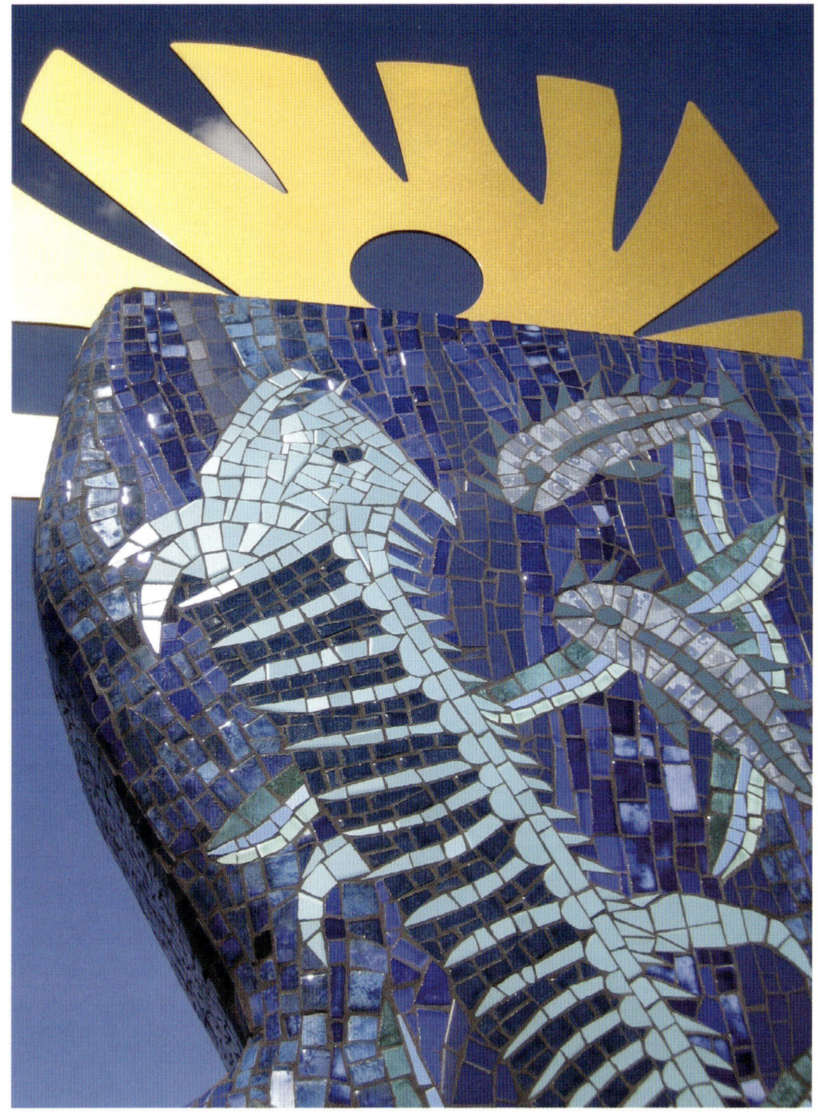

***Marisa, Marisa the Magical Bird. She'll grant all your wishes,** just leave the words* is what is written upon a small secret bronze door where children can leave their own written wishes inside a special moveable locket. This large mosaic and bronze children's play sculpture bird at Carley's Magical Gardens was designed especially for hematology/oncology patients. This very special sculpture is a magical and powerful example of how art can promote healing in the health care environment. *Marisa the Magical Bird* was a collaboration with mosaic artist Kim Emerson and bronze sculptors T.J. Dixon and James Nelson. The bird's moveable head is cast bronze, the sturdy affixed wings and tail were carved by the artist out of expanded polystyrene (EPS), and then coated with cement. These three-dimensional cement surfaces are covered with hand-cut mosaic tesserae that were applied piece-by-piece using the direct method. Marisa's ten-foot long tail of feathers functions as a slide which children enjoy and play. She is gracefully perched on top a mound of soft green turf at the center of the garden where she is cherished by all.

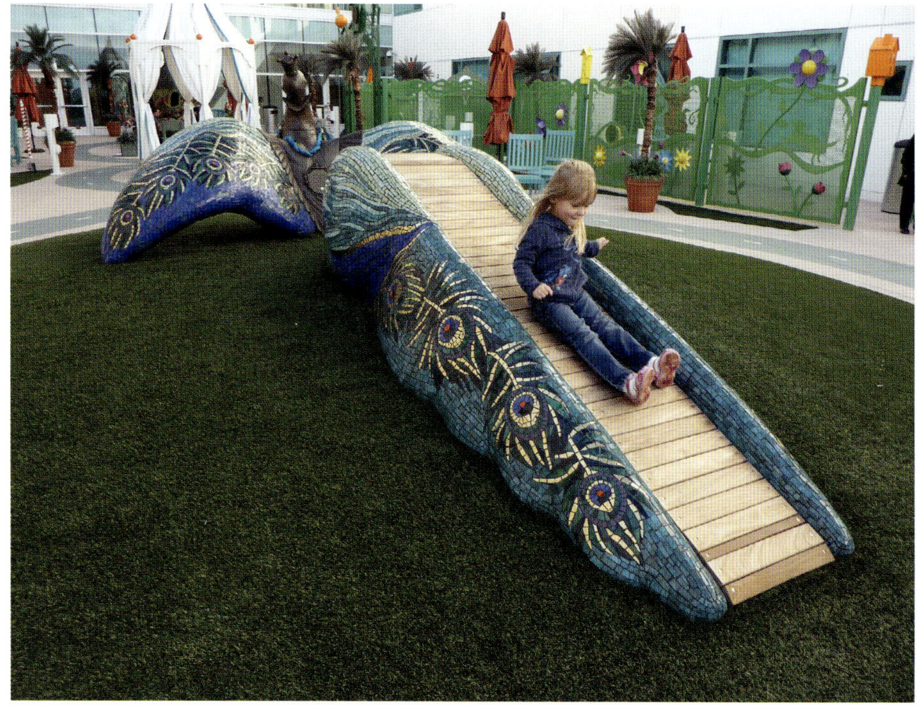

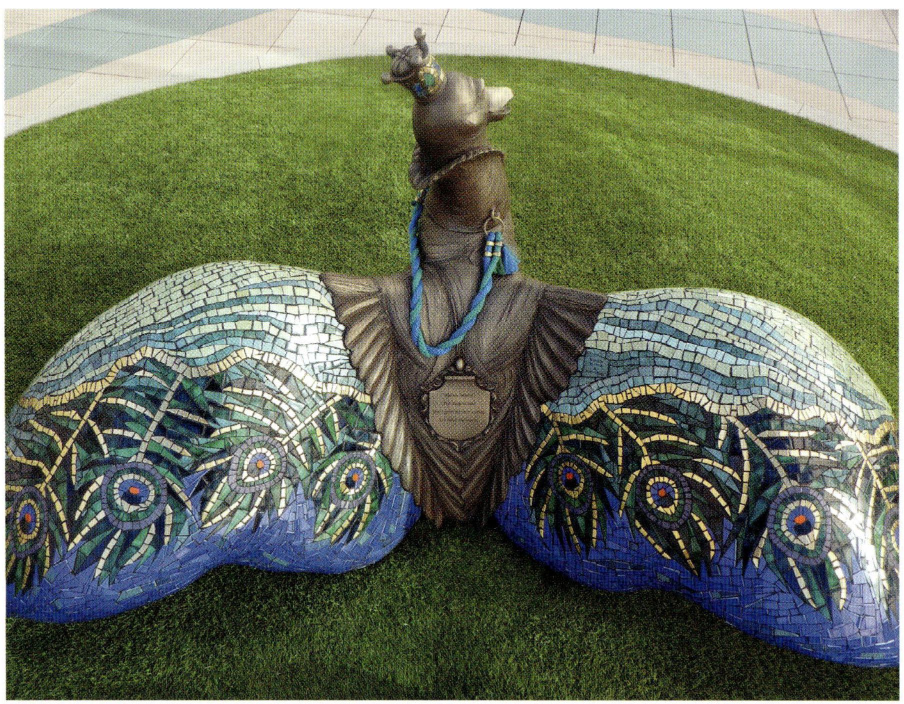

Kim Emerson. *Marisa the Magical Bird.* Children's play sculpture. 2009-2010. Sculpted expanded polystyrene (EPS), rebar, cement, cast bronze, and ceramic tile. Hand-cut tesserae/direct method. 12' x 3' x 20'. Rady Children's Hospital, Acute Care Pavilion, Carley's Magical Gardens, San Diego, California. Design collaboration & cast bronze head by sculptors T.J. Dixon and James Nelson. *Photos by the artist*

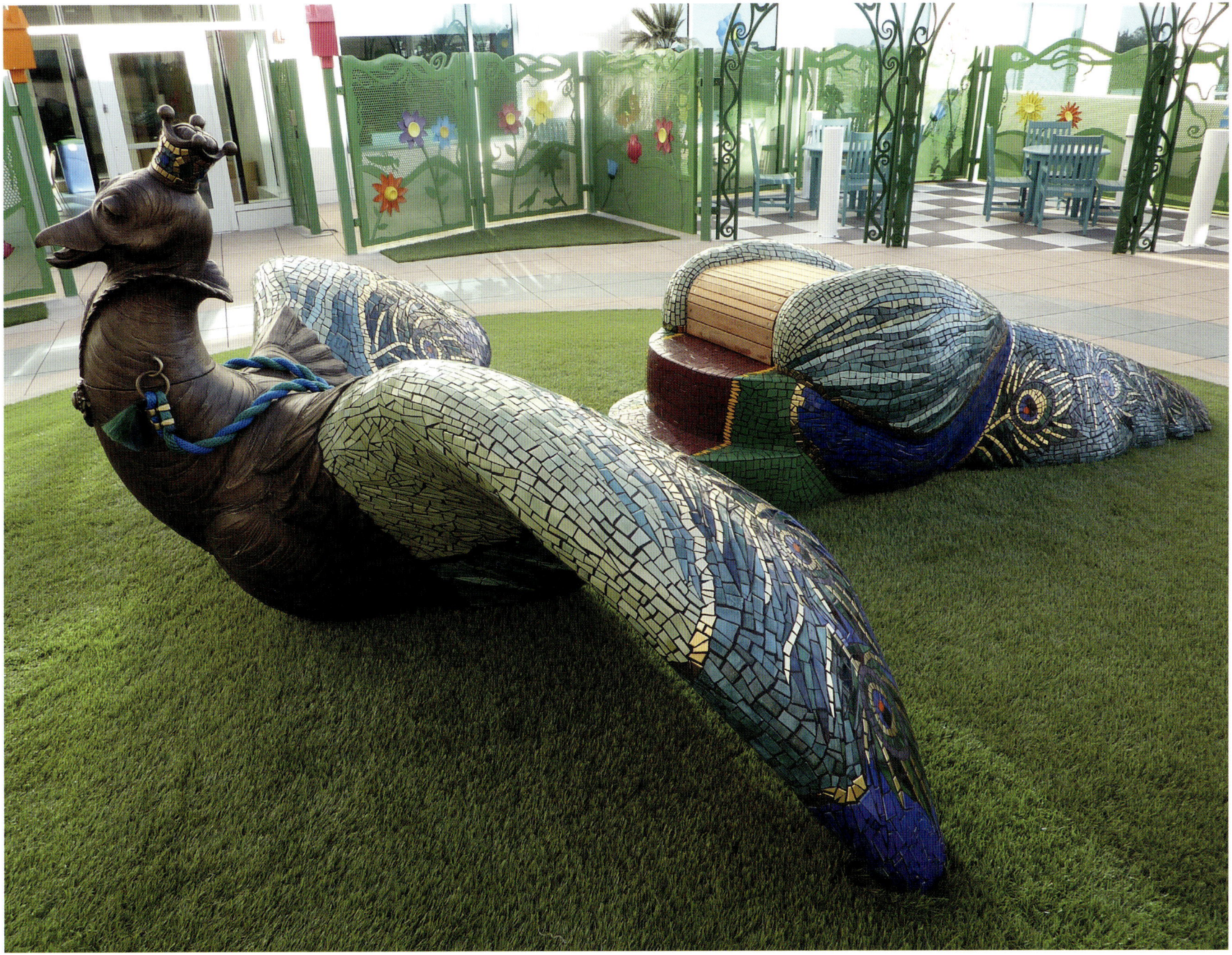

The ***River of Life*** main lobby floor mosaic was planned early in the design process of the newly constructed Acute Care Pavilion at Rady Children's Hospital in San Diego, California. The success of public art and design often depends on how early the artist's craft and vision can be applied to the architect's conceptual design. This is one such exemplary project. Throughout the entire health facility the theme of ocean is visible in many other decorative elements on all four floors. The *River of Life*, lush in design with fish, waves, and underwater scenery, begins inside the main lobby at the ripple textured plaster wall. The mosaic is recessed into a white with blue glass chip terrazzo floor surrounding it on all sides. The mosaic twists and turns across the main lobby area making its way to the window where it appears to flow under and through to the outside of the building. Visible through the window from the inside, from above levels, and accessible from the outside, the *River of Life* floor mosaic continues to flow. The edges of the mosaic outside in the garden area are enclosed with large natural granite boulders. As the mosaic gradually slopes downward it appears as if it flows under a wooden bridge next to a real teak wooden boat. It appears again in a large spiral design recessed in warm colored concrete.

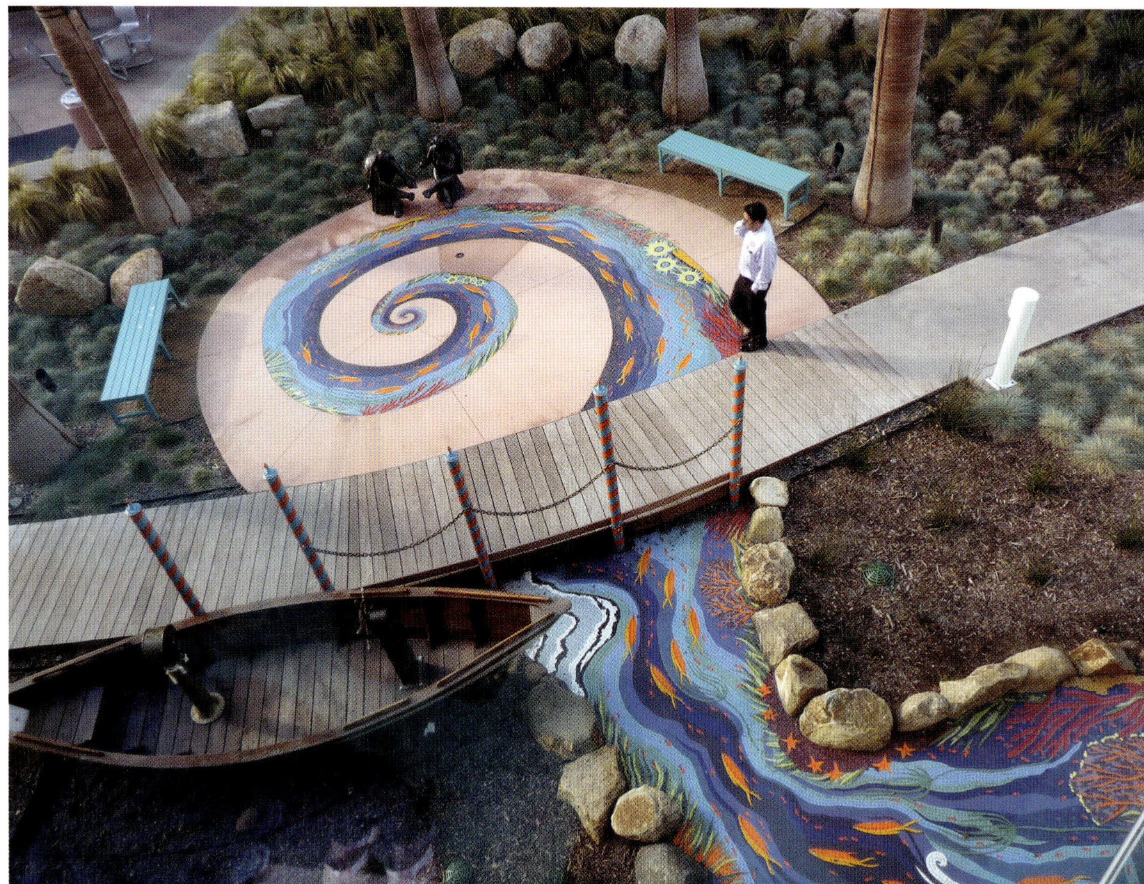

Kim Emerson. *River of Life.* Main lobby floor and garden mosaic. 2009-2010. Ceramic tile. Hand-cut tesserae/tape technique/direct method. 500 square feet. Rady Children's Hospital, Acute Care Pavilion, Carley's Magical Gardens, San Diego, California. *Photo by the artist*

Wild Flowers of the Sonoran Desert: This project is a wonderful example of how mosaic art can be utilized in a traditional form of fund raising for a deserving non-profit organization. Presentation Design Group (PDG) designed the walls that prominently display written sponsor names, the history of the ABHOW (American Baptist Homes of the West) Foundation, and photographic images of the surrounding area. The two large 6' by 6' panels were designed for the mosaics that celebrate and feature specific flowers of the Arizona desert. The mosaics are made up of a combination of hand-cut ceramic tile and various textured elements of glass baubles and natural stone. The centers of some flowers are filled with Mexican smalti, a Byzantine style of glass. Before the project was installed, the corner where it is located was lifeless, anonymous, and bland. Now this area of the retirement community has become a special gathering place for social activity and appreciation of the foundation donors. Another result of the success of the project, the flower designs in mosaic have since been reproduced on many printed publications and promotional materials. These mosaics have become a trademark image or marketing tool that helps promote the ABHOW Foundation.

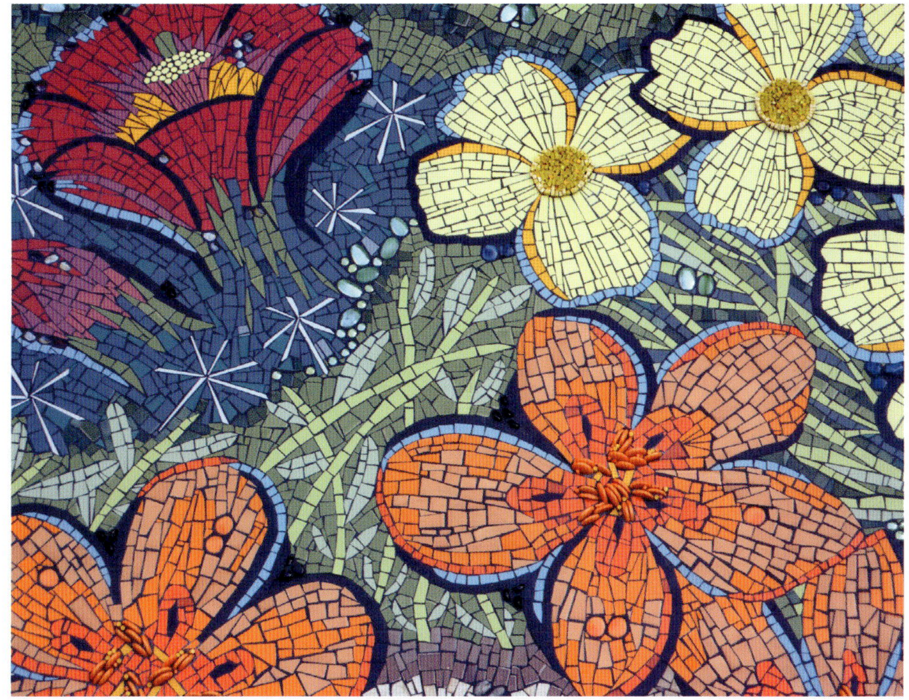

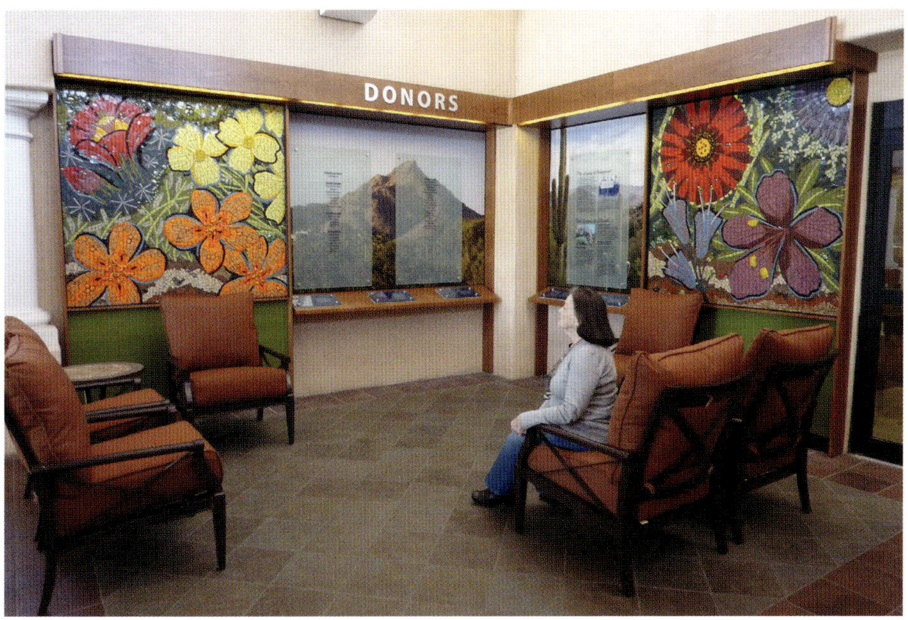

Kim Emerson. *Wild Flowers of the Sonoran Desert.* Two donor wall mosaic murals. 2009-2010. Ceramic tile, glass tile, Mexican smalti, glass baubles, and natural pebbles. Hand-cut tesserae/tape technique/direct method. 6' x 6' (each panel). The Terraces of Phoenix, A Retirement Community, ABHOW Foundation, Phoenix, Arizona. Design collaboration with Presentation Design Group. *Photo by the artist*

Faducci LLC

North San Juan, California, www.faducci.com

Artist's Statement

It is my strong belief that the best civic artwork forges connections between people and their physical environment, celebrates the unique qualities of a place, and communicates our ideas, dreams, and goals for our communities to each other. Unified by an aesthetic of care, public art becomes a physical manifestation of the values we hold in common. We are committed to the creation of art which is beautiful and meant to be shared.

About the Artwork

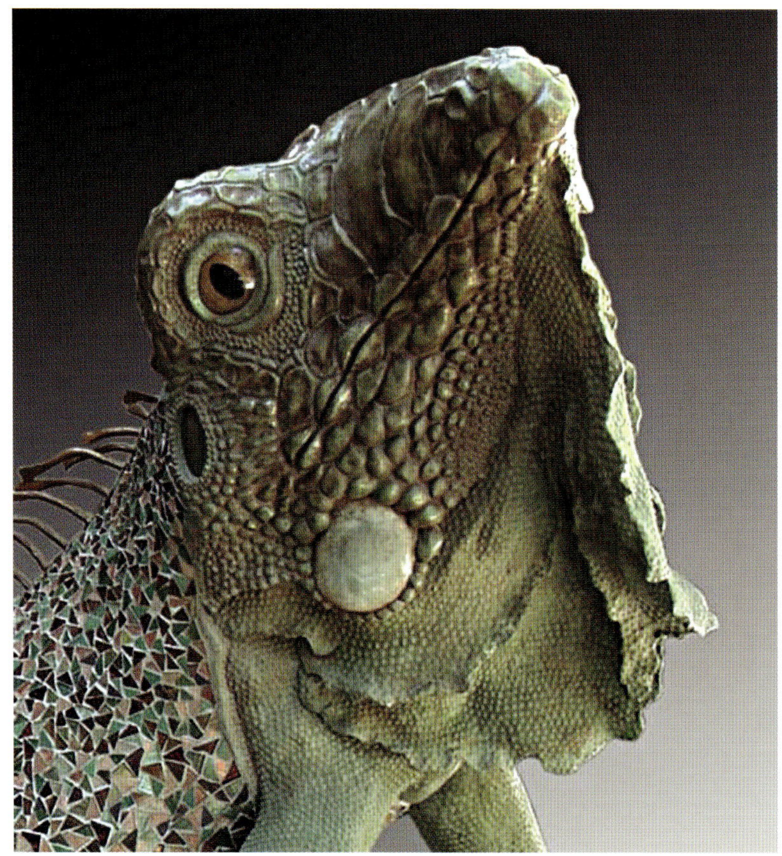

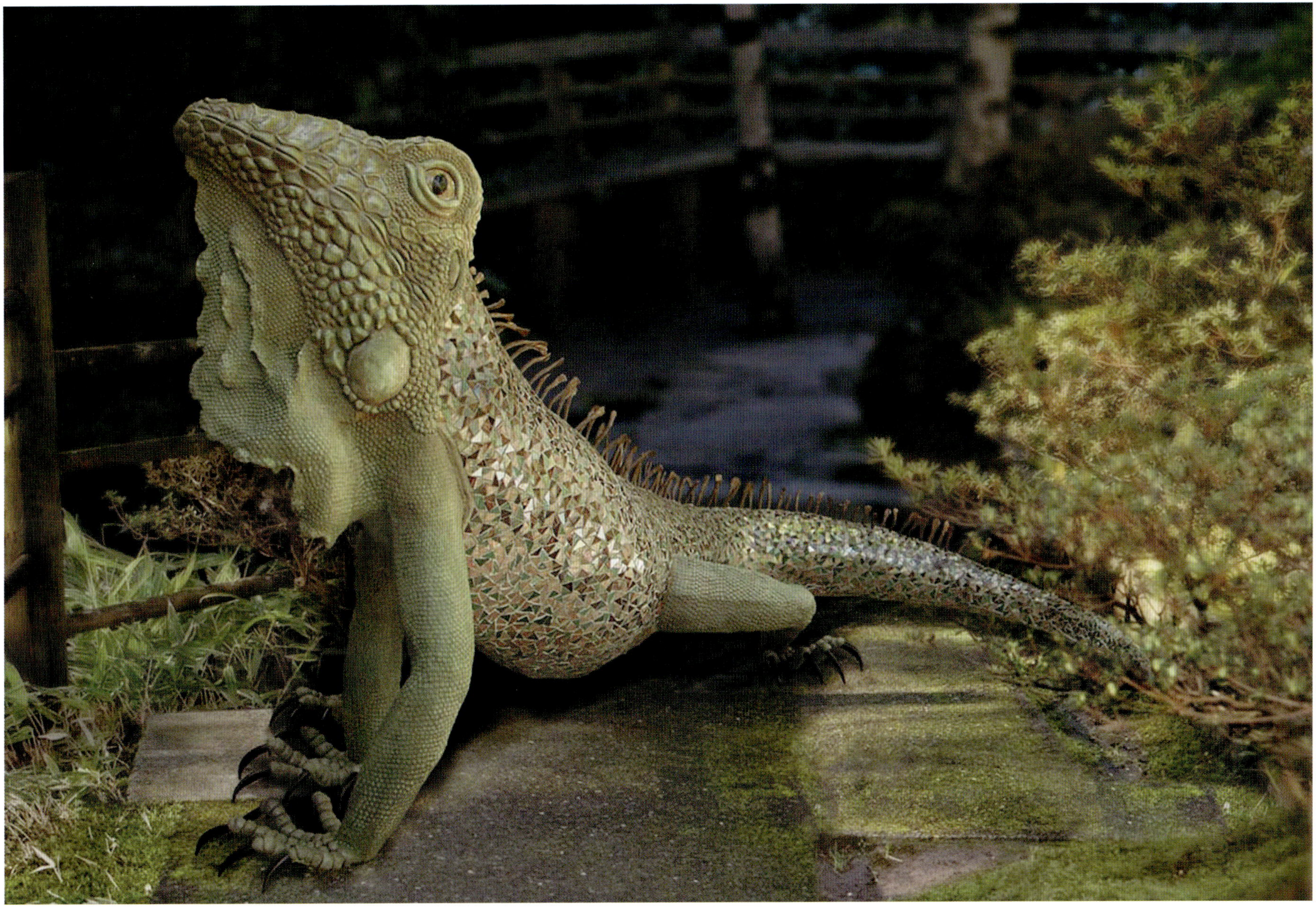

Faducci LLC. *Galapagos Sea Iguana*. 2007. Cement, steel, glass. 145" x 37". *Private Collection* (Detail opposite page.)

3 Dogs: Local artist Solomon Bassoff of Faducci recently completed three lifelike dog sculptures for a private collector. All three dogs were favorite pets that had passed on. The trio was presented as a surprise holiday gift for the collector's husband. The sculptures will be placed near the home entryways as a year round greeting for visitors.

All sculptures are created of hand sculpted cement. Two are accented in reflective Italian glass mosaic. The third sculpture, a border collie, has an applied black granite mosaic body. Each dog was created life-sized and as realistically as possible.

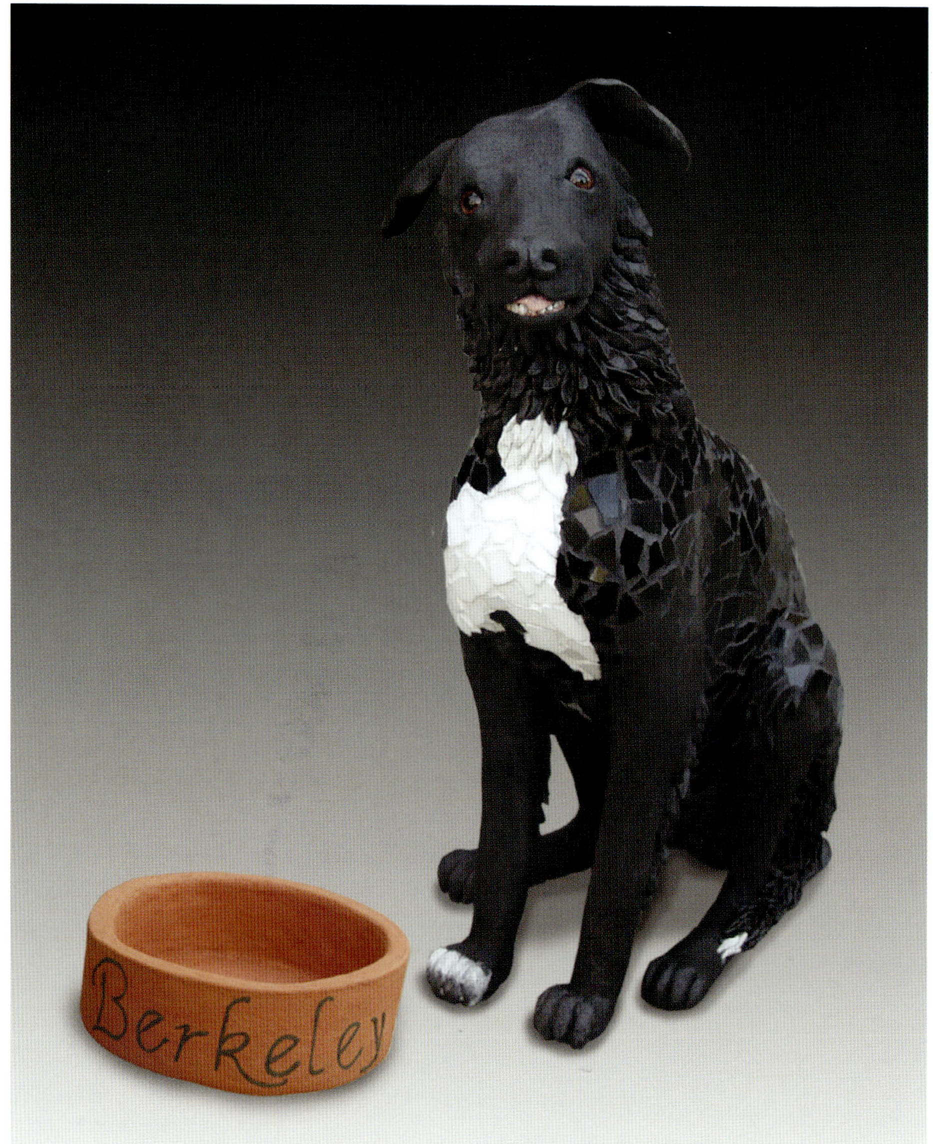

Faducci LLC. *3 Dogs*. 2008. Cement, steel, glass, granite, and marble. 38" x 26", 18" x 23", 32" x 18". *Private Collection* (above and opposite page)

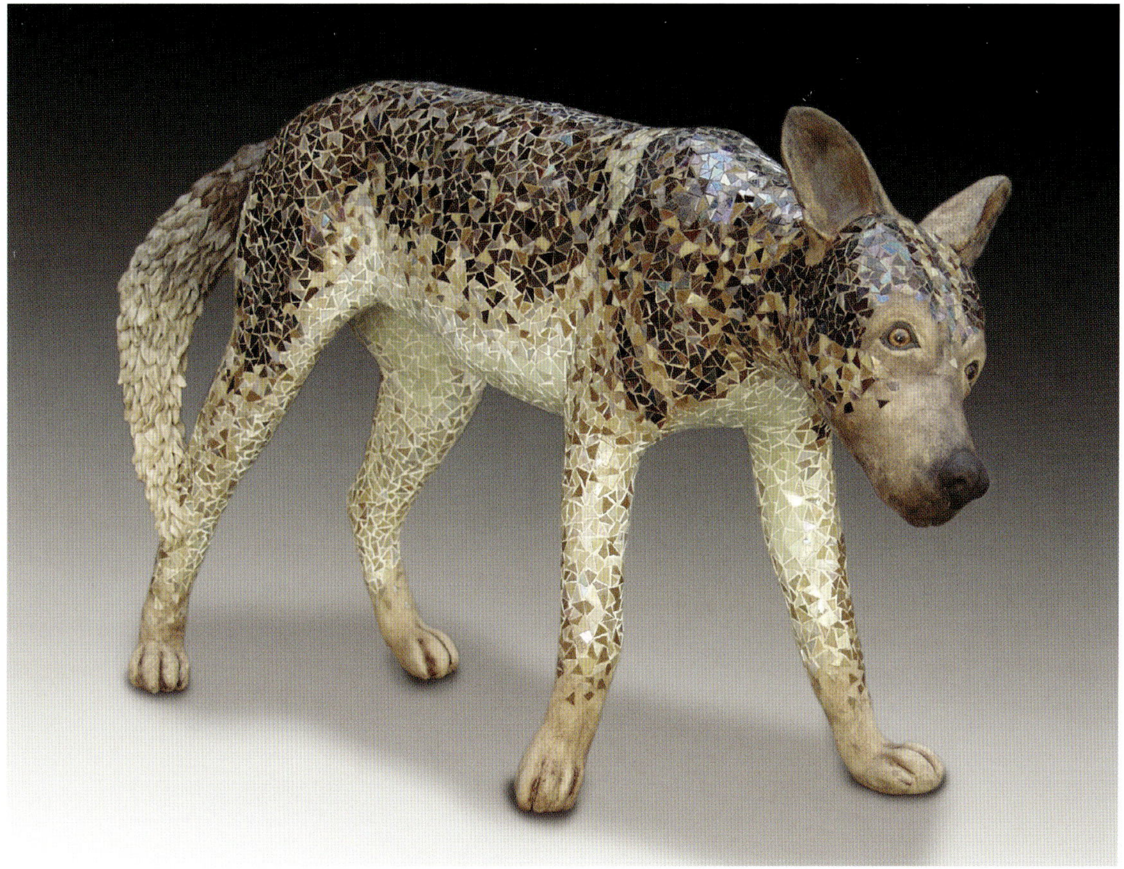

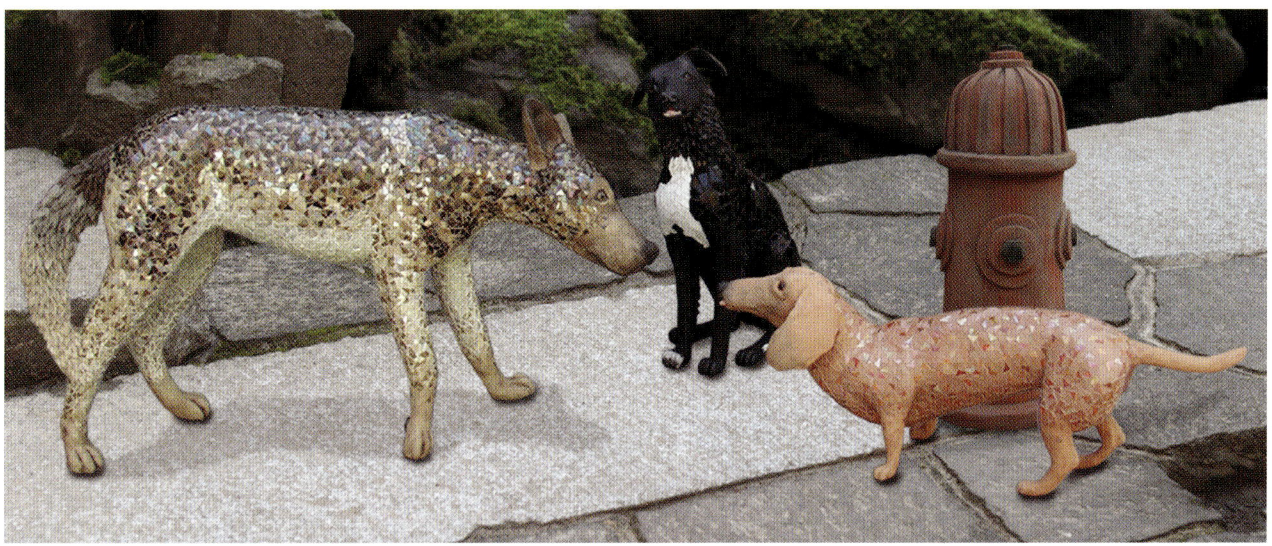

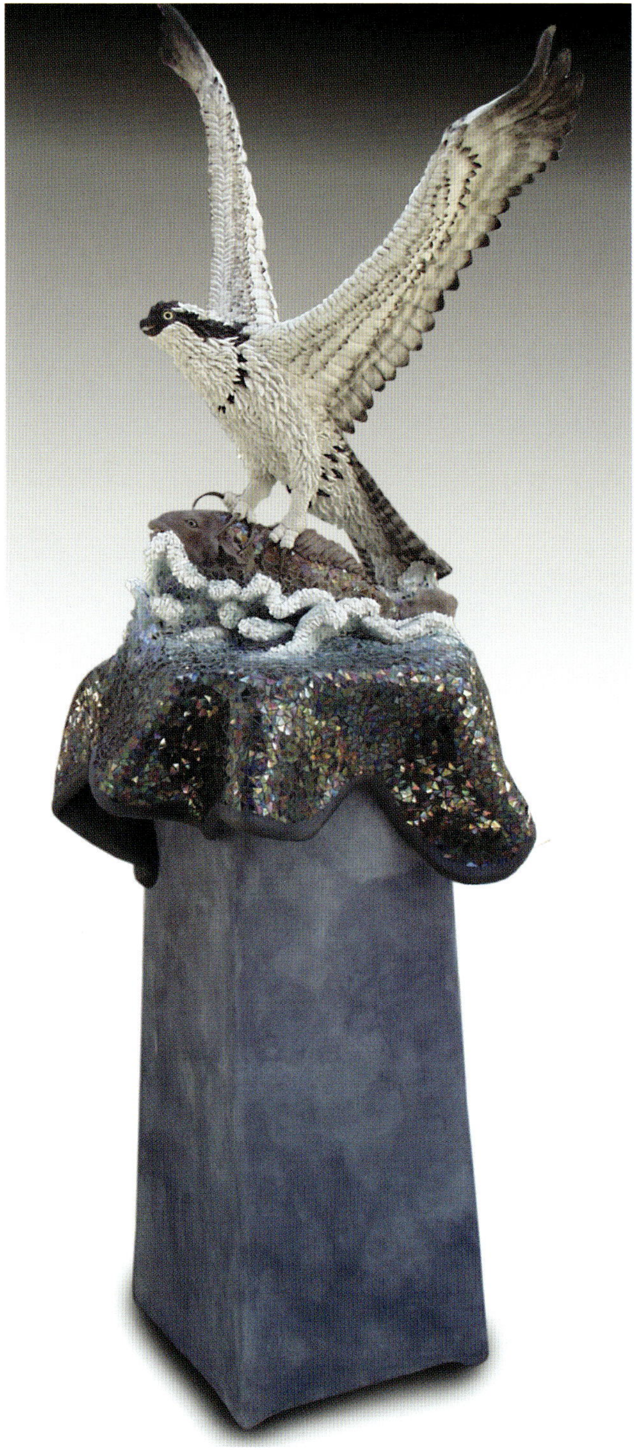

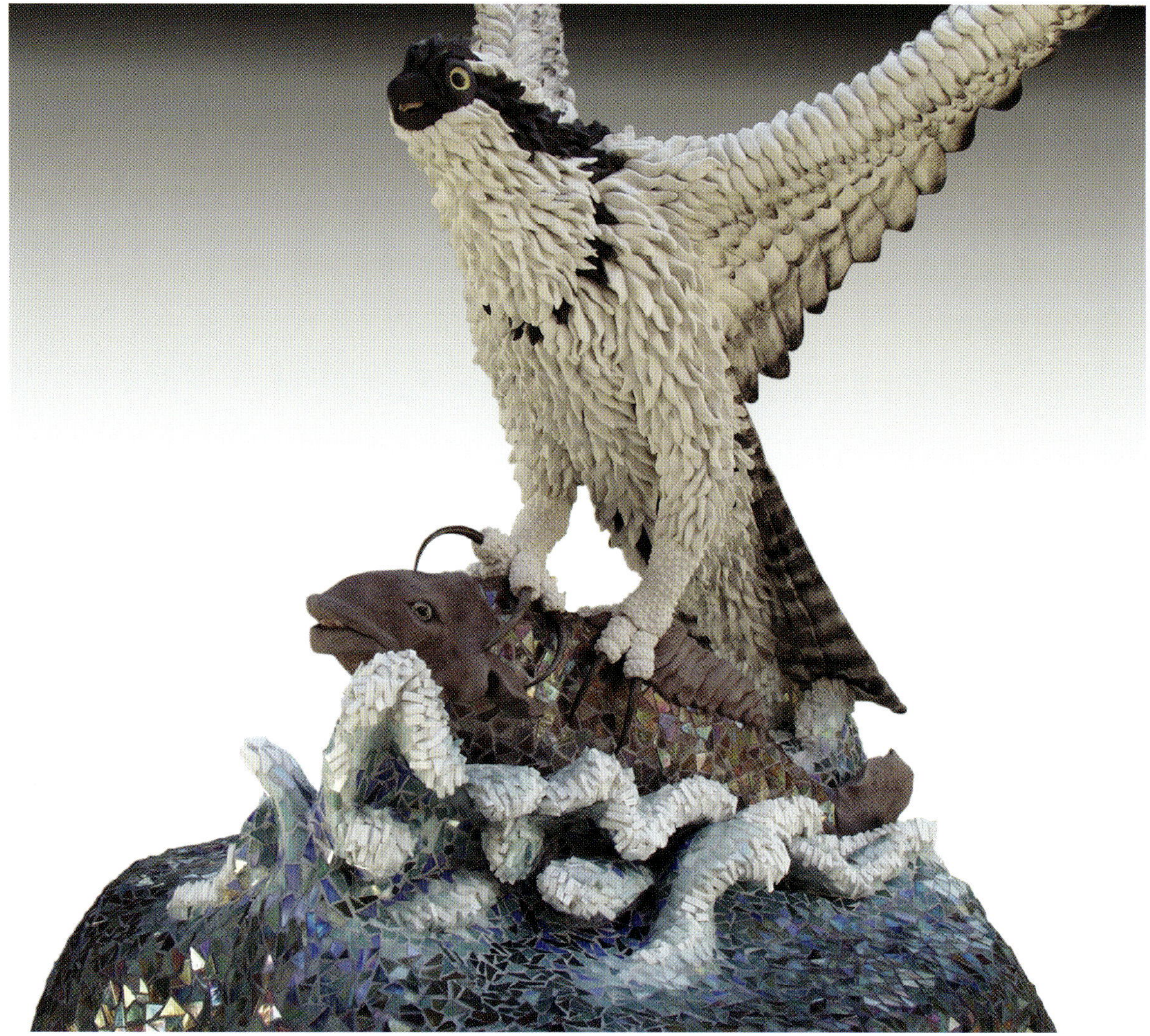

Faducci LLC. *Osprey Catching Fish.* 2009. Cement, steel, glass.
23" x 84". *Private Collection*

Caterpillar with 7 Pairs of Shoes: The whimsical piece, an 8' long cement whimsical rendition of a Monarch caterpillar, includes a different shoe and sock on each of the caterpillar's many feet. The artists consider their work unique for "its infusion of bright color and lifelike textures into hand-sculpted, cement forms." Bassoff and Mottarella create their works by forming cement around a steel and wire armature. They permanently color the cement with natural mineral pigments, adding other materials that enhance the cement's strength and frost resistance. Many of their pieces include glass mosaic.

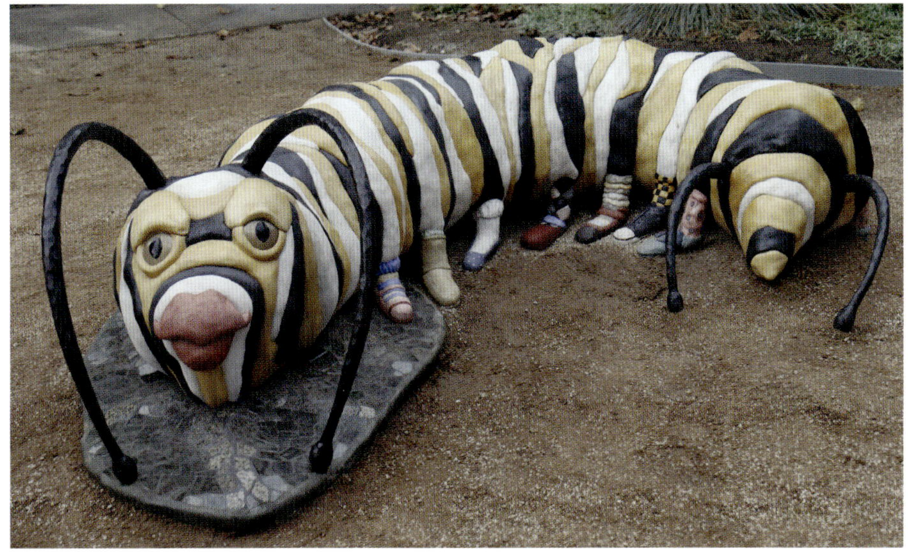

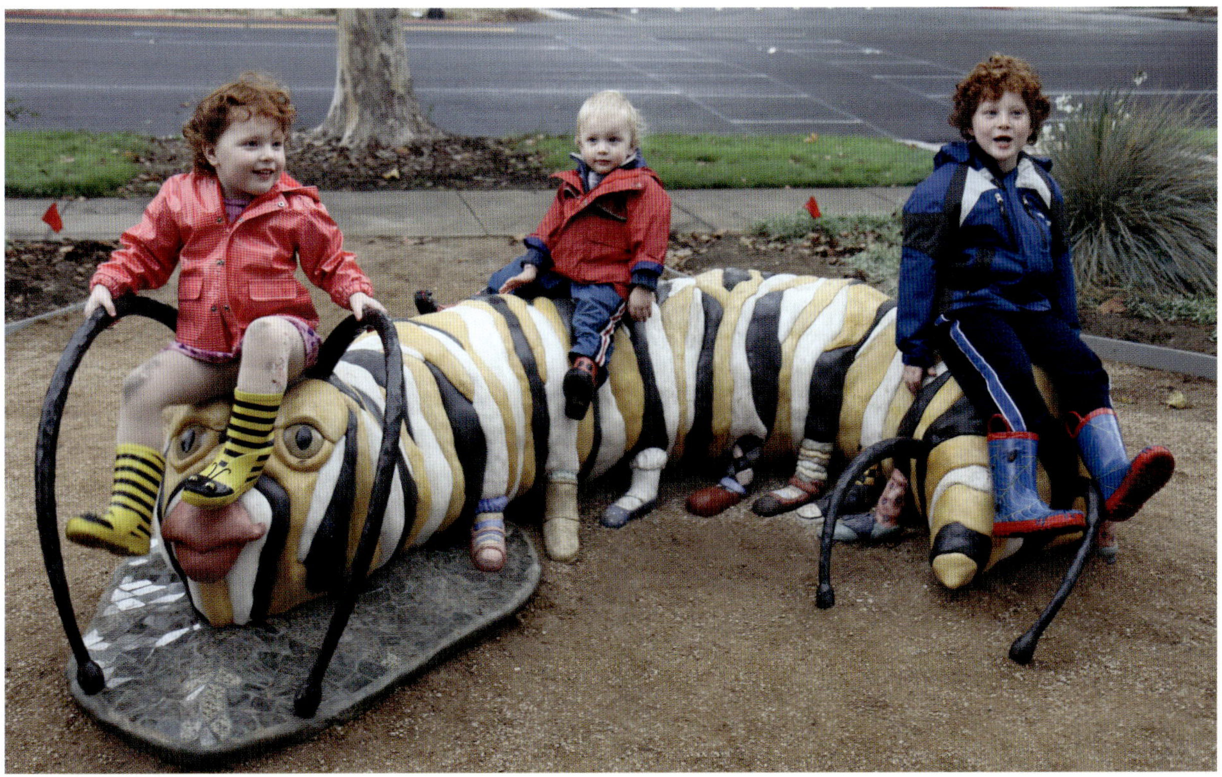

Faducci LLC. *Caterpillar with Shoes*. 2010. Cement, steel, granite. 96" x 64" x 29". *Commissioned by City of Davis, California*

Cynthia Fisher

Charlemont, Massachusetts, cindy@bigbangmosaics.com

Artist's Statement

The process of creating an abstract mosaic begins weeks or even months in advance of actually laying tesserae. First I identify a concept to explore; concepts often arise from observations. I process how to depict my ideas with choice of materials, andamento (or how the tesserae will be laid), and explore new ways to achieve desired visual effects. I love the planning process when I can mull over the various possibilities and directions to go. Now I am ready to begin, and I start with a simple line drawing. When finally laying tesserae, I find many of the ideas I have cogitated fall by the wayside and I respond to the materials and allow the process itself to determine how the mosaic comes together. When stuck, I refer back to my idea list, and what I was trying to achieve. My favorite part of all is when the left brain gets out of the way and I am working intuitively, viscerally responding to the materials and process. Each mosaic is an experiment, thus some are more successful than others.

My work is steadily evolving since I began creating mosaics in 2000. Originally my style was graphic and subject oriented, influenced by my prior career as a children's book illustrator; over time my oeuvre has become increasingly more painterly, with a livelier *andamento* and more sophisticated use of color. A wider array of materials is an exciting fresh direction adding new elements to work out: size, from larger stained glass pieces; pattern, incorporating broken pottery; and texture from smalti, rock, and marble. I will continue exploring these materials abstractly, and remain passionately committed to challenging myself in this art form.

About the Artwork

Spawning Salmon: *Spawning Salmon* is a favorite mosaic of mine, predominantly assembled with vitreous glass and unglazed porcelain, materials often overlooked by mosaic artists today. When used thoughtfully I believe one can achieve striking results with these more "plebian" materials. The idea for this piece started with a photograph. I then researched Sockeye Salmon life cycles, habitat characteristics, migration routes, and spawning facts and included some of these elements in the mosaic. This mosaic is fairly representational, though I particularly like when the fish break up and appear more fractured and abstract.

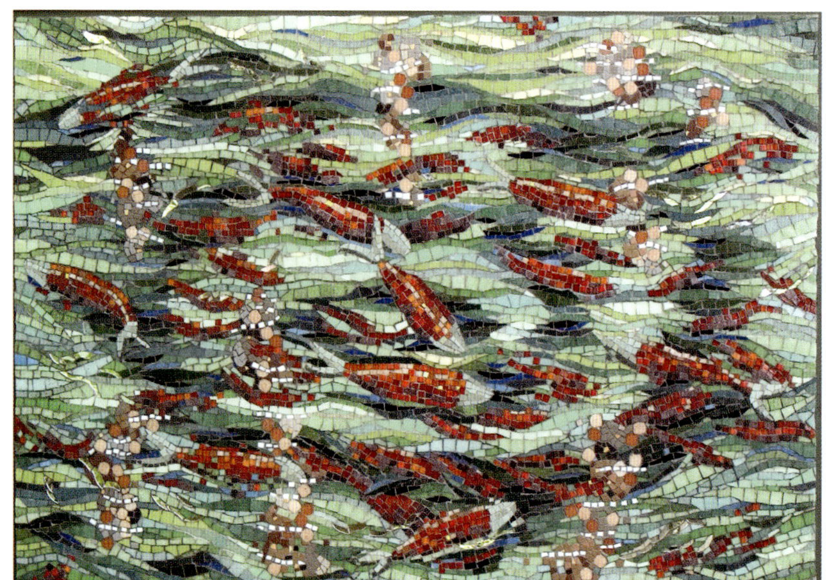

Cynthia Fisher. *Spawning Salmon*. 2-D wall art. 2006. Vitreous glass, unglazed porcelain, mirror, gold smalti. 54" x 40". *Photograph by artist*

Chesapeake Bay Wetland: The Chesapeake Bay mosaic is a floor medallion of a wetland scene depicting a Great Blue Heron, Blue Crab and a species of turtle found in the area. It was a challenge to get an accurate view of how this all might look from above. I particularly enjoyed working on the reflections and getting a feeling of flowing water. This mosaic was sent to the homeowner in two halves with a center strip to bridge the space where the panels come together. My regret was the tile installer did not use my suggested dark grout, so for me this piece is a bit too fractured looking.

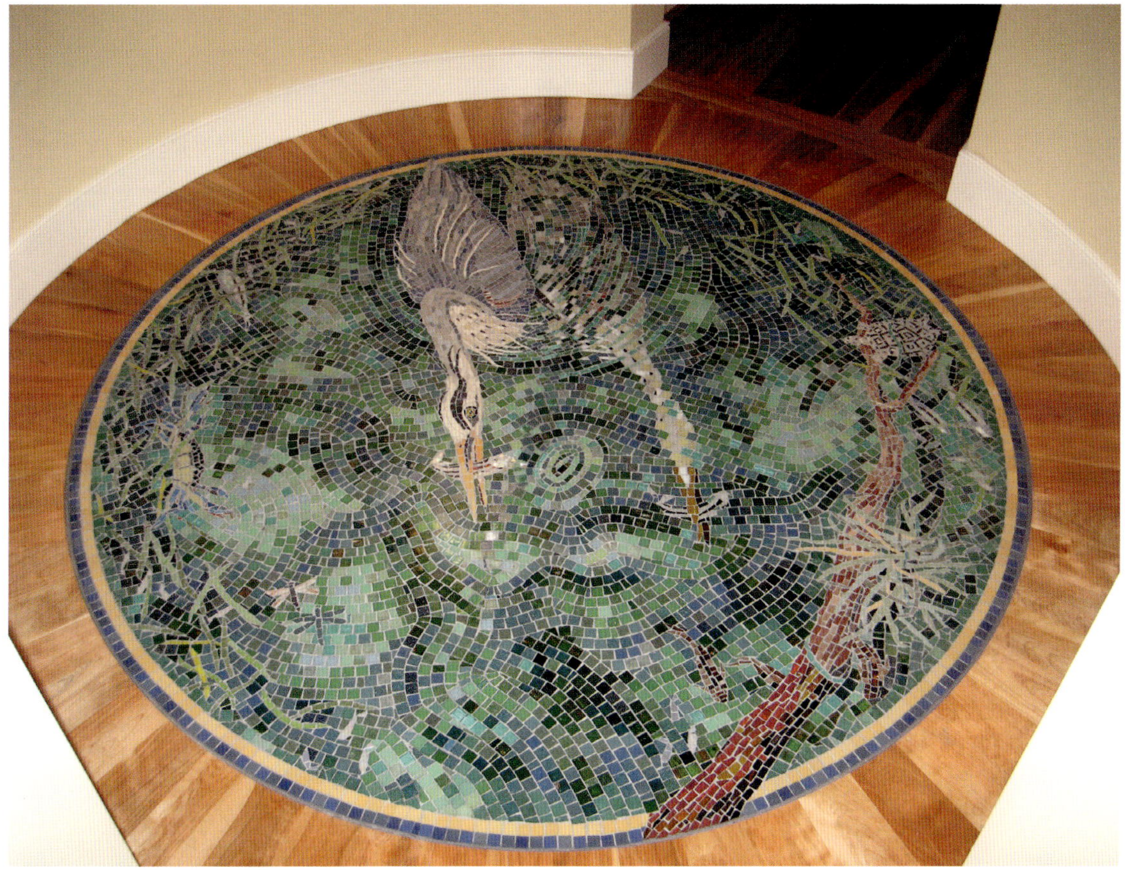

Cynthia Fisher. *Chesapeake Bay Wetland*. Floor medallion. 2007. Vitreous glass, unglazed porcelain, mirror. 72". *Photograph by David Lavine*

Pavement Fractals: As an avid road cyclist, I am looking down at the road a lot. I noticed that when pavement starts to break up it does so in the same manner, technically called a repeating fractal. Shapes are to a certain extent random, but display "self-similarity," the primary characteristic of a repeating fractal. In this case the fractal is geometric and so mosaics were a perfect medium to depict this process. I began with several vertical and horizontal lines and assembled the piece, always keeping in mind the rules of fractal formation. My first truly abstract piece, I loved the process of not knowing exactly where I was going while working on it. This piece was my mosaic epiphany, by choice of materials, subject, limited palette, and approach. In all my mosaics, my goal is to keep the viewer's eye attentively roaming.

Cynthia Fisher. *Pavement Fractals.* 2-D wall art. 2009. Vitreous glass, unglazed porcelain, smalti, grout, rocks, broken pottery, beads, stained glass, glass rods. 32" x 18". *Photograph by artist*

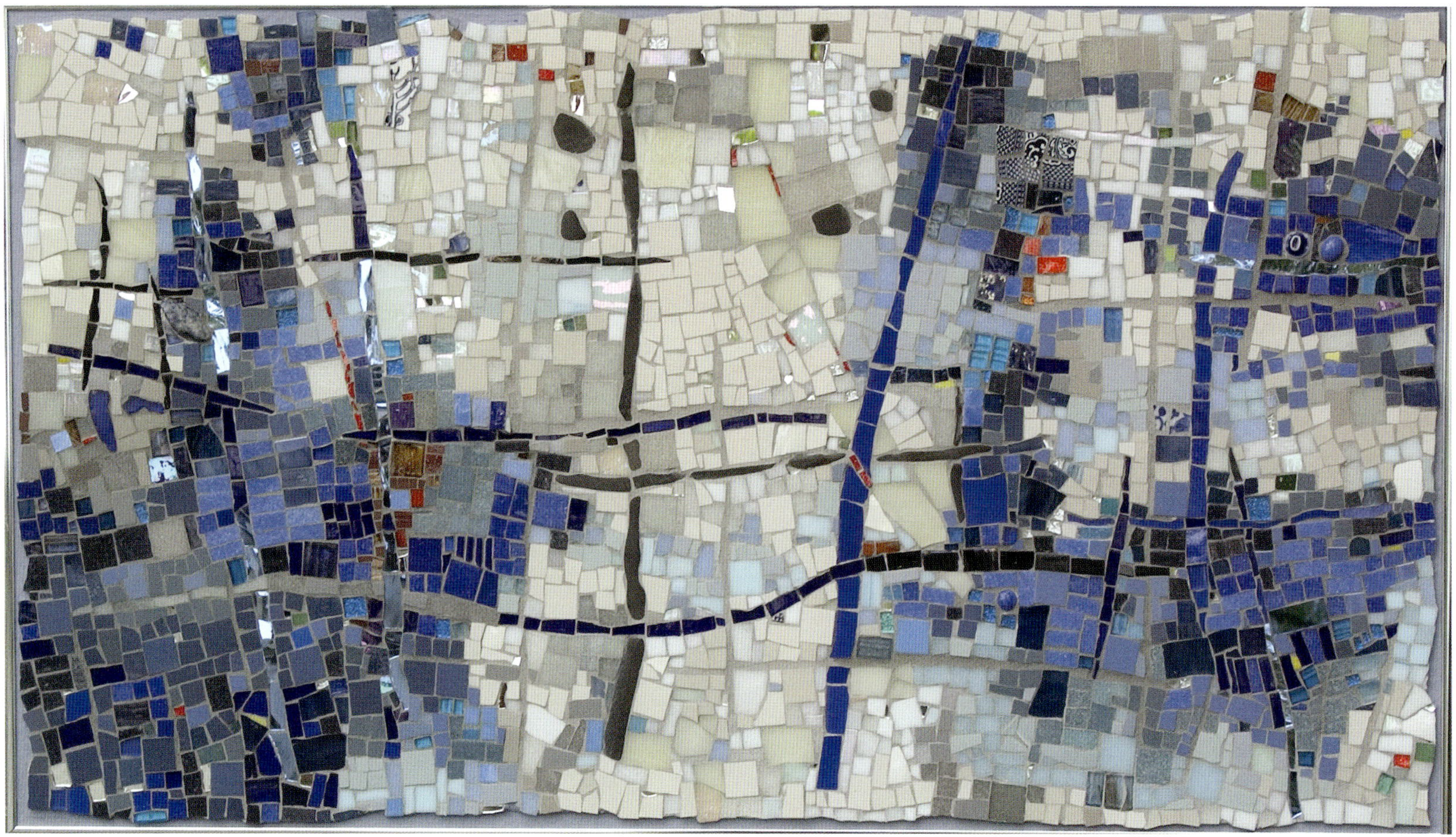

To Everything There Is a Season: I try new things with each mosaic I create, and always have several specific goals. For this mosaic my intent was to lay the tile more horizontally but try to direct the eye vertically by color and value choices; to depict the chaotic color of the fall season without any realistic elements; to use larger stained glass shapes that integrate seamlessly with the smaller bits. This is my second fully abstract mosaic. I particularly enjoyed laying out the color and value passages. Sometimes I introduced shifts gradually with more subtlety; at other times I wanted a bolder sequence. Successful elements include the use of pottery shards for added visual interest, the contrast of shiny versus flat with the glass and unglazed porcelain, and the texture of grout and its choice instead of tesserae in the areas adjacent to the mirror pieces.

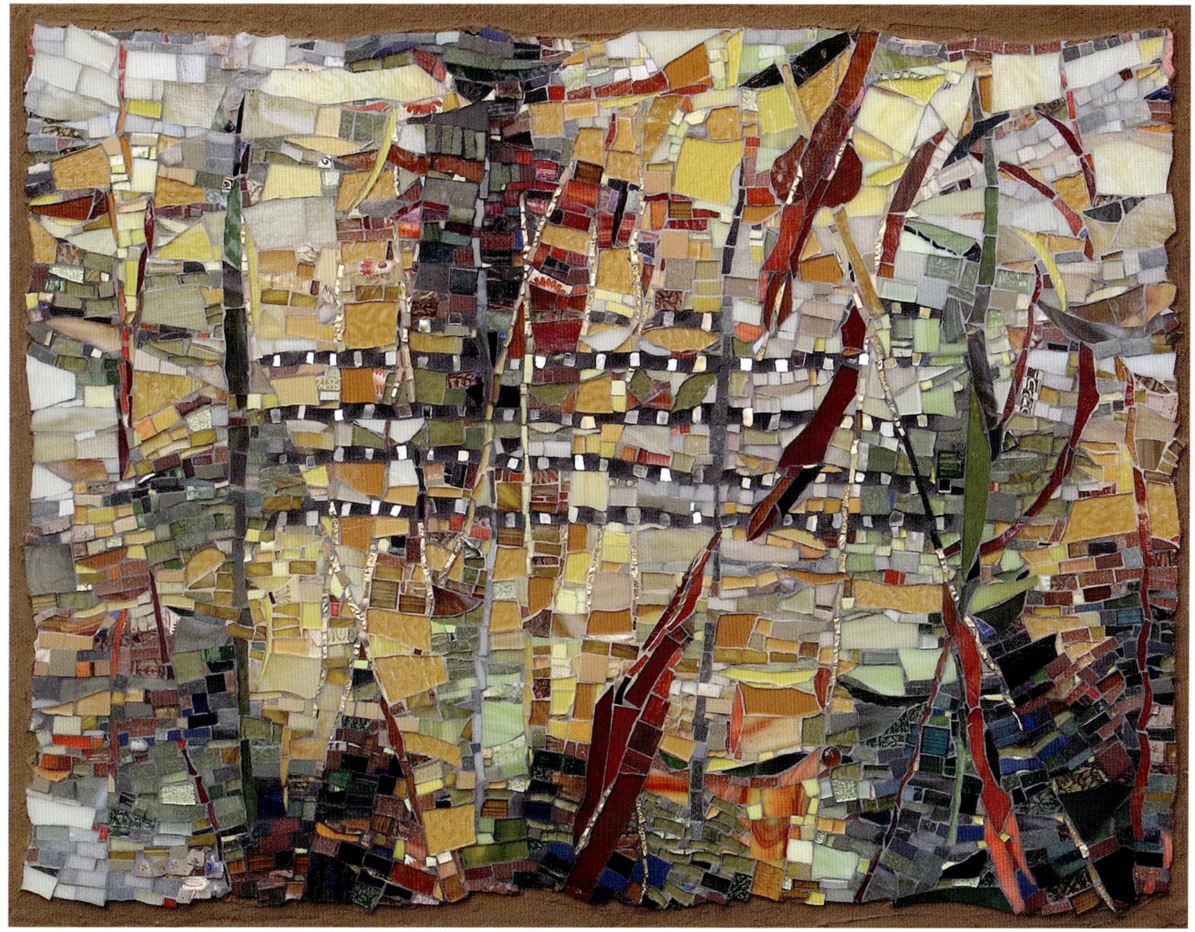

Cynthia Fisher. *To Everything There Is a Season*. 2-D wall art. 2009. Vitreous glass, unglazed porcelain, smalti, grout, rocks, broken pottery, beads, stained glass, mirror. 33" x 25". *Photograph by artist*

Stochastic Properties: In this mosaic, my starting point was a line drawing of *stochastic mixing layers. "A stochastic process is one whose behavior is non-deterministic, in that a system's subsequent state is determined both by the process's predictable actions and by a random element."* Wikipedia. The "predictable actions" are the layers which start out as vertical mosaic columns on top and bottom. The silver and green mirror bits are introduces as the random elements. How they interact and are thrown about when they meet evolved with the laying of the mosaic. As with my other abstract work, I am trying several different things at a time; in this case I was also working the composition in a series of 1 1/2" horizontal rows, wherein the expanded grout line becomes an important visual element.

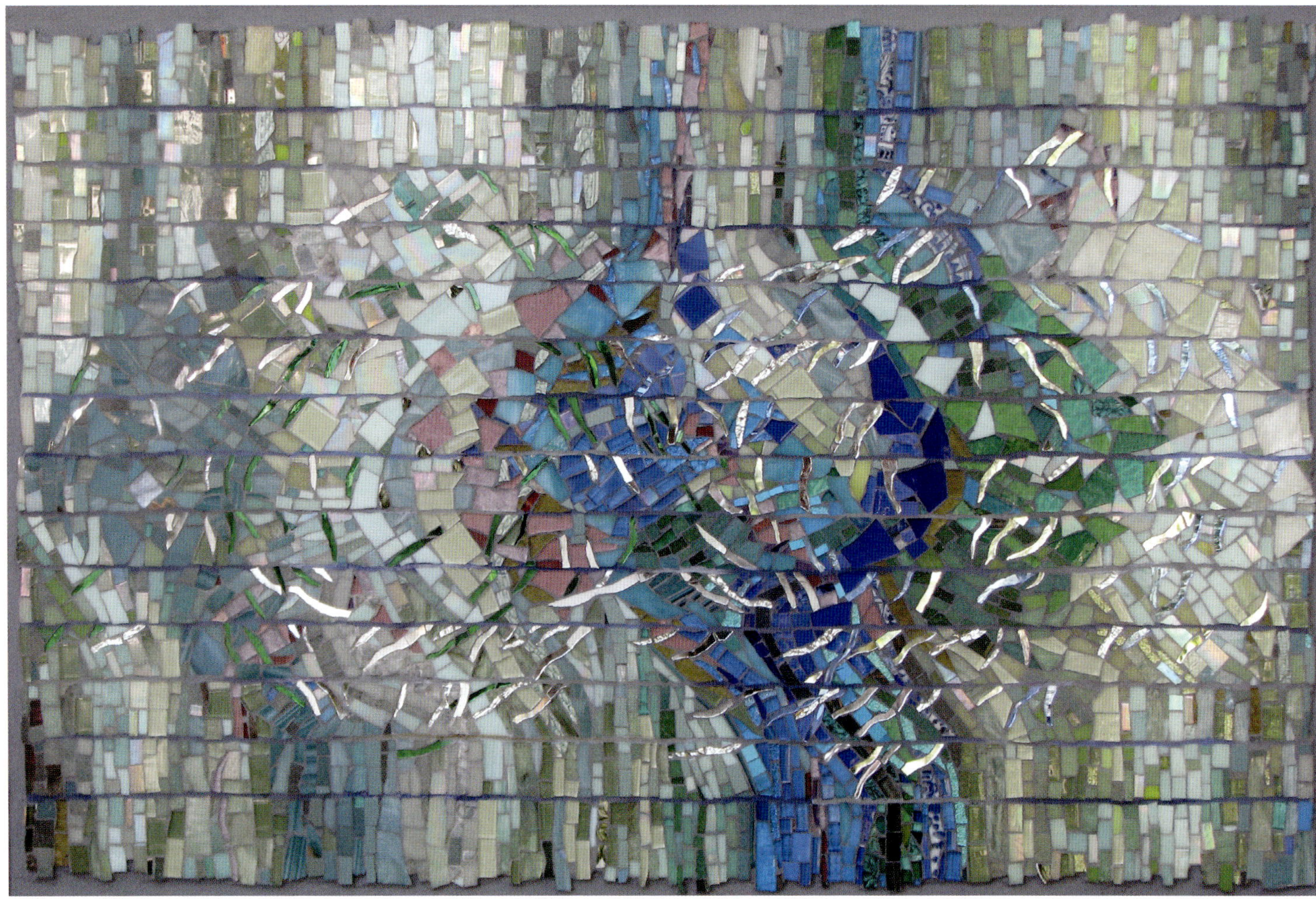

Cynthia Fisher. *Stochastic Properties*. 2-D wall art. 2009. Vitreous glass, unglazed porcelain, smalti, grout, rocks, broken pottery, stained glass, mirror. 36" x 24". *Photograph by artist*

Naples Pediatric Dental Clinic: Public art is a difficult field to break into, especially if one lives in a state that does not have a "percent for art" program. Florida, however, is such a state, and one in which the importance of public art in a community is recognized and valued. Called "Art in State Buildings," Florida's program is one that other states should model! This mosaic of three young kids on the back of an alligator is located at a University of Florida children's dental clinic in Naples. My original proposal was for kids on a toothy T-Rex as appropriate for a dental clinic; this was changed to the UF mascot, an alligator. It really looks great with the other art in the building, colorful suspended sea creatures.

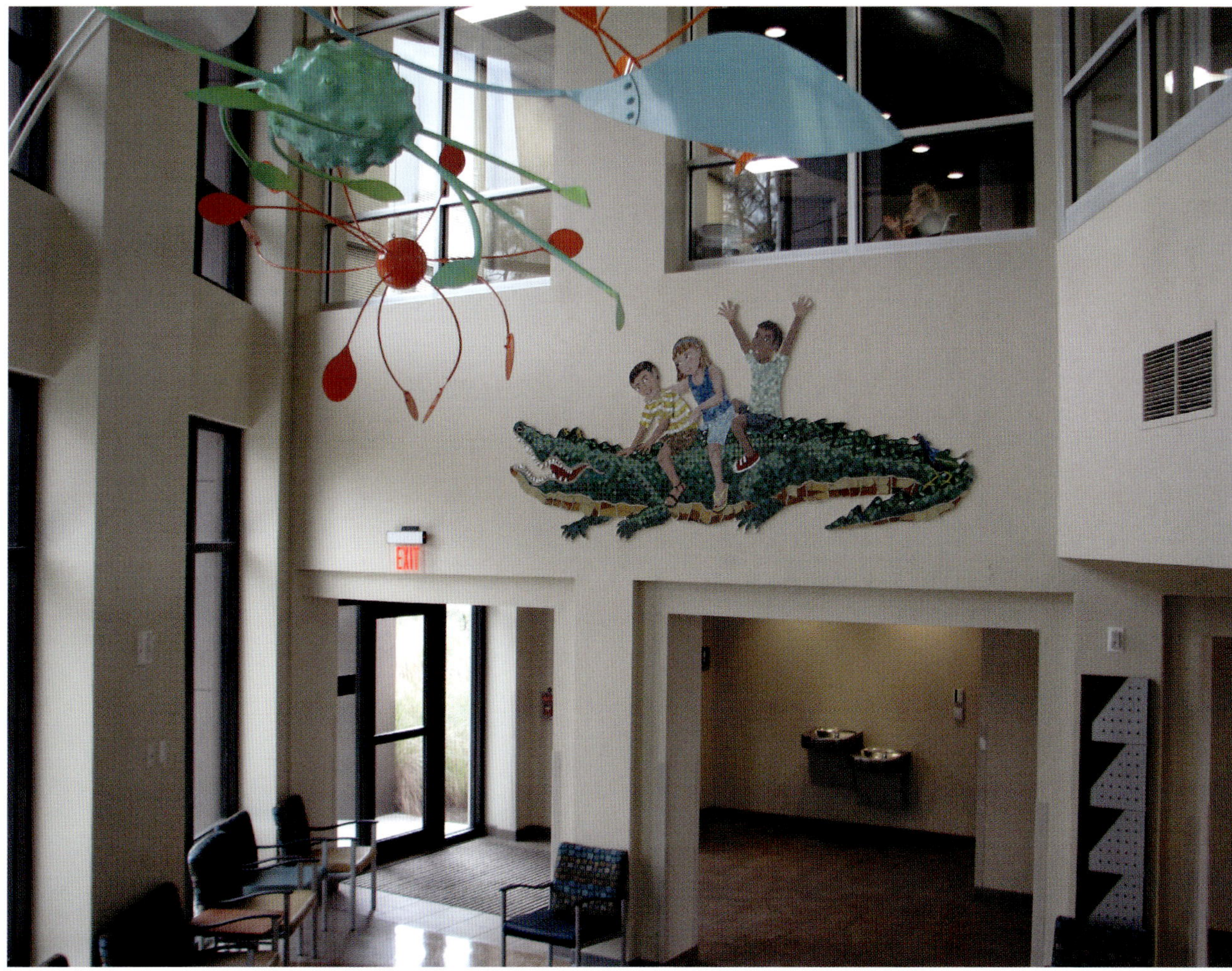

Cynthia Fisher. Naples Dental Clinic. 2-D wall art. 2010. Vitreous glass, unglazed porcelain. 132" x 48". *Photograph by artist*

Ilona Landau Fried

Denver, Colorado, ilona@mixedmediamosaics.com

Artist's Statement

The tactile quality and the permanence of mosaics are what drew me to this ancient medium after years of auditioning other art forms. Discovering, touching, and arranging diverse materials intrigues me and the process of creating mosaics challenges me mentally and spiritually. Although I have traveled to dozens of countries and enjoy mountain adventures almost every week, art making is a journey unlike any other.

I've created mosaics of sushi, cityscapes, landscapes, and characters from my imagination. Currently, my work focuses on using shapes and saturated colors to translate the world and my interior experience into mosaic. Lately I have been experimenting with non-parallel intersecting lines and the "skewed" grid that they form; I enjoy the challenge of creating visual distinctiveness within each segment while trying to make sure that each relates to its neighbors and to the mosaic as a whole. This method allows me to incorporate a wide range of materials—many types of glass, semiprecious stones, ceramic, shell beads, found objects—into my art while still maintaining a focus and theme.

The Artwork

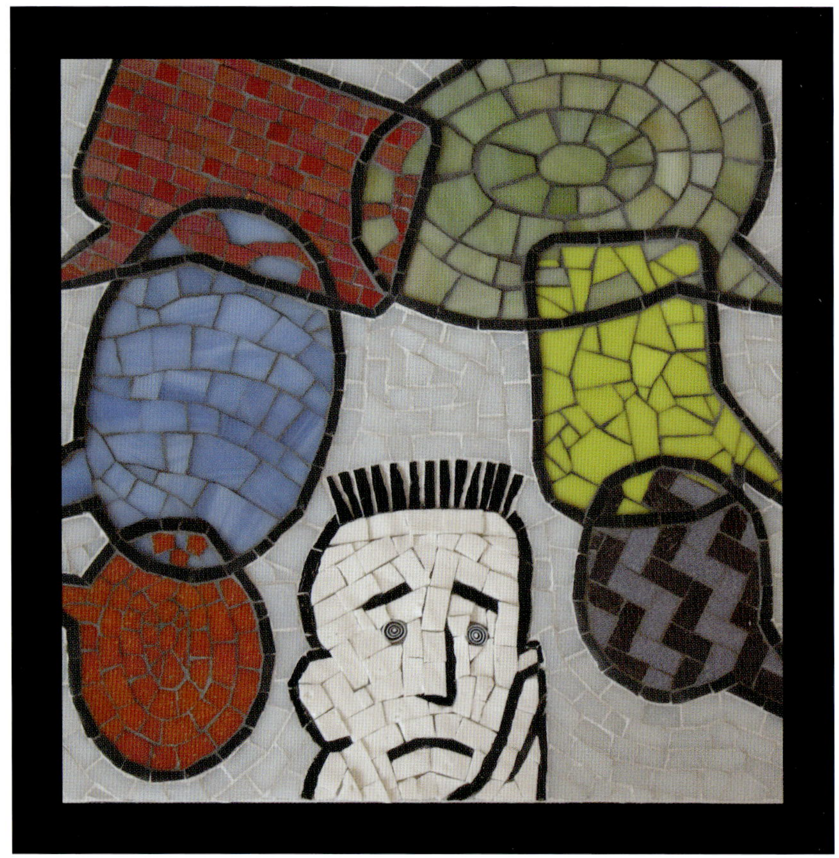

Ilona Landau Fried. *Mixed Messages.* 2-D wall panel. 2009. Stained glass, smalti, unglazed ceramic, vitreous tile. Mosaic. 12" x 12". *Photo by Ilona Landau Fried*

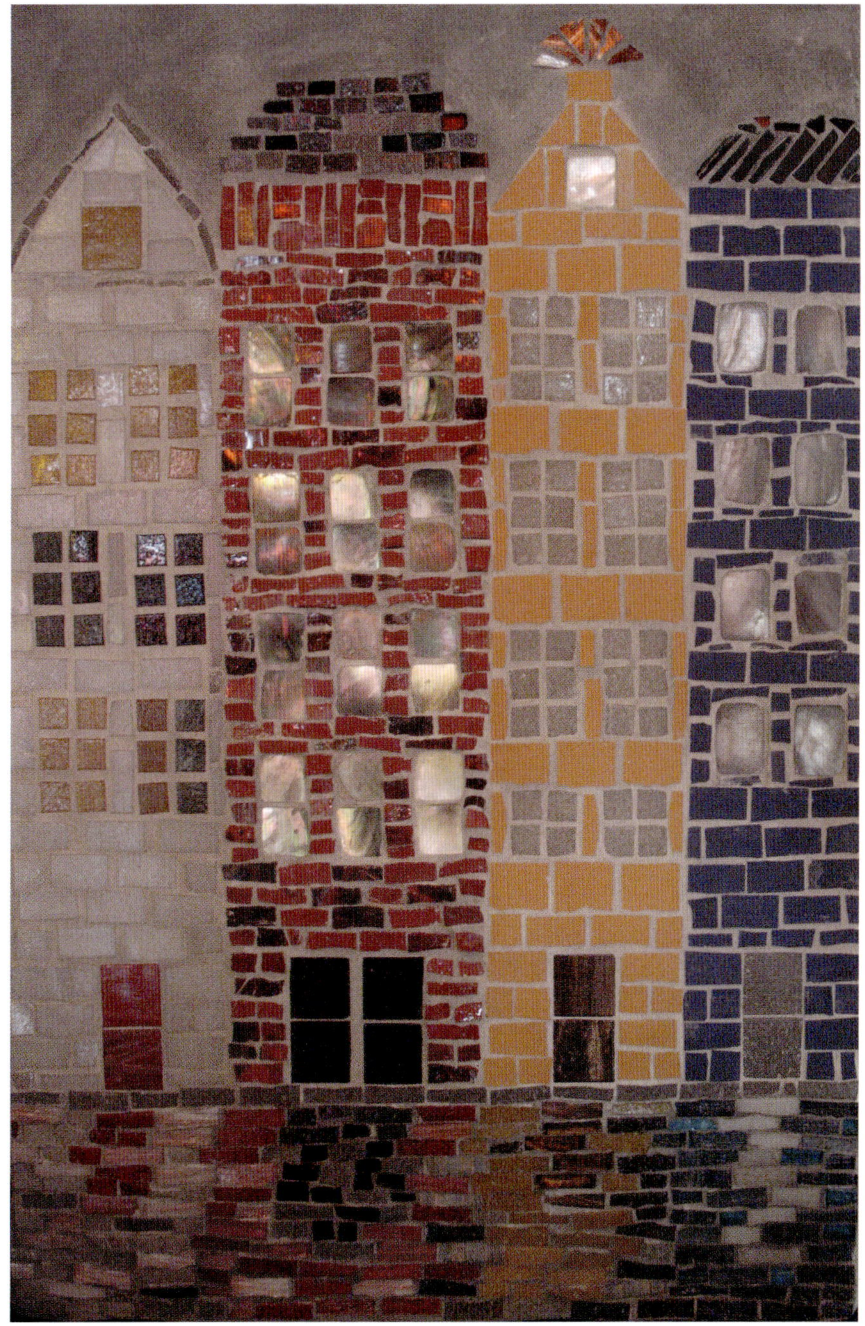

Ilona Landau Fried. *Amsterdam Canal.* 2-D wall panel. 2007. Unglazed ceramic tile, shell beads, vitreous tile. Mosaic. 11" x 16". *Photos by Ilona Landau Fried*

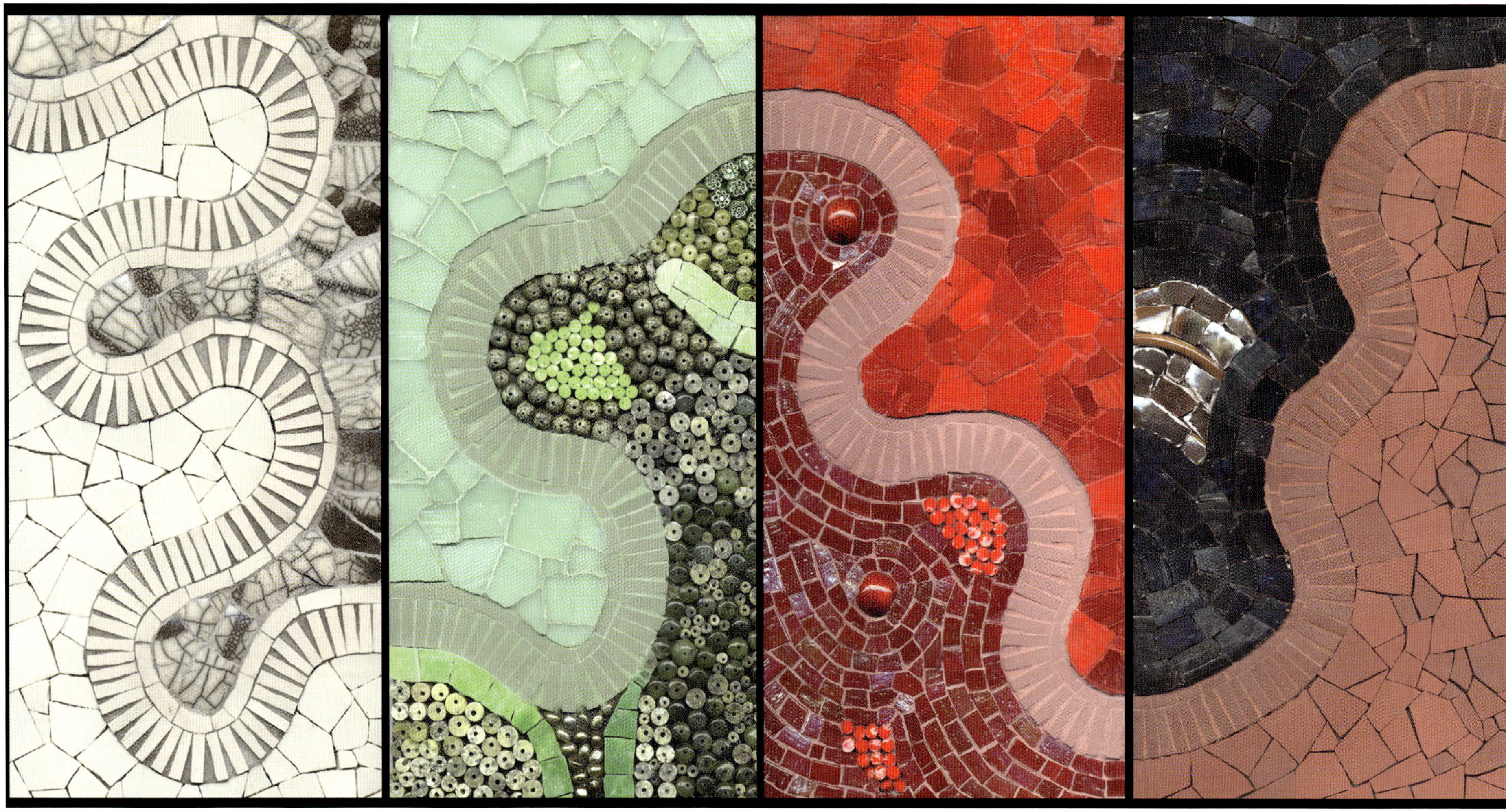

Ilona Landau Fried. *Journey*. 2-D wall panels. 2009. Recycled glass tile, unglazed ceramic tile, raku shards, ceramic and stone beads, moretti glass rods, smalti. Mosaic. Four panels, each 6" x 12". *Photo by Ilona Landau Fried*

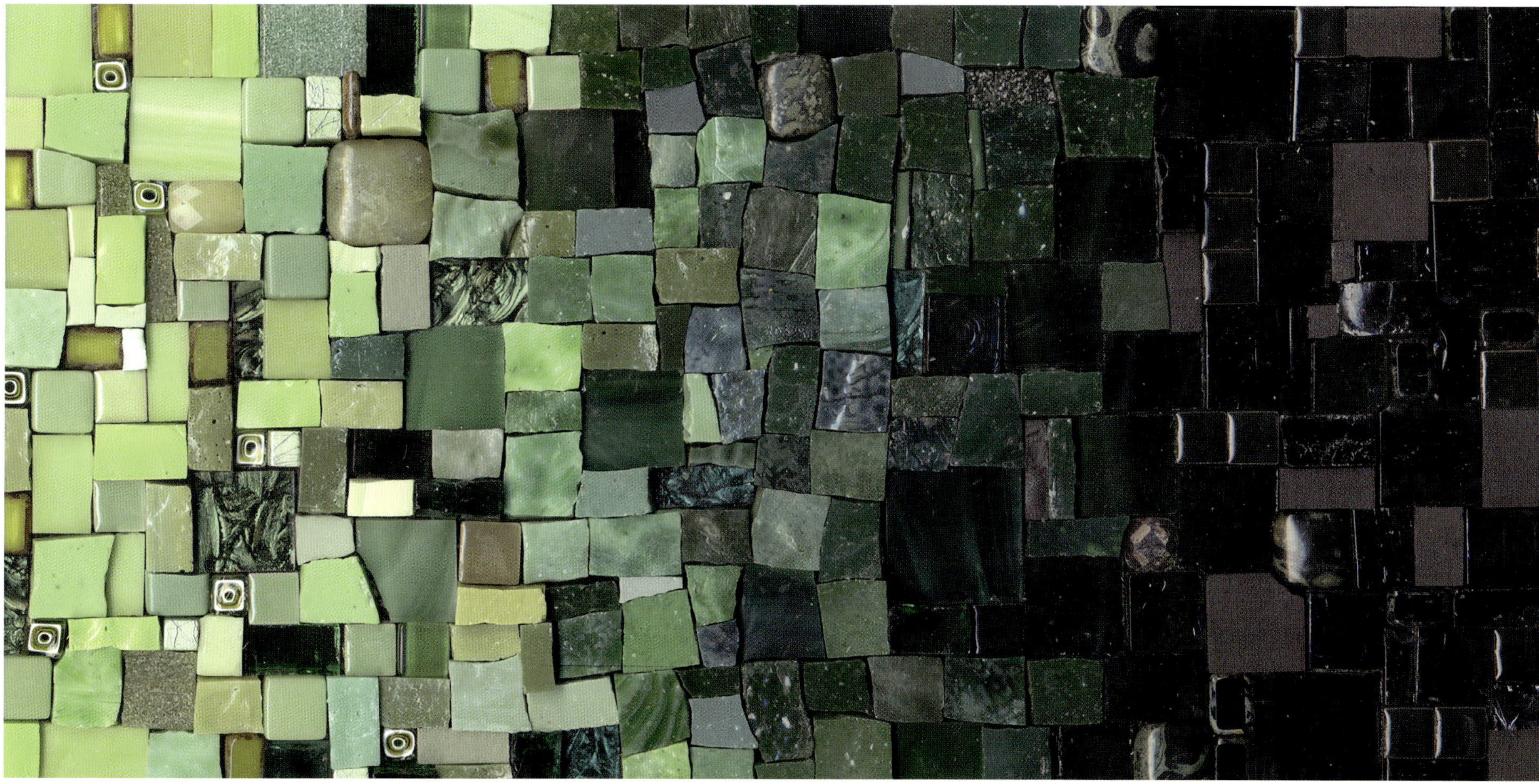

Ilona Landau Fried. *Disappearance.* 2-D wall panel. 2009. Stained glass, vitreous tile, smalti, millefiori, beads of stone, glass and metal, Van Gogh glass. Mosaic. 12" x 6". *Photo by Ilona Landau Fried*

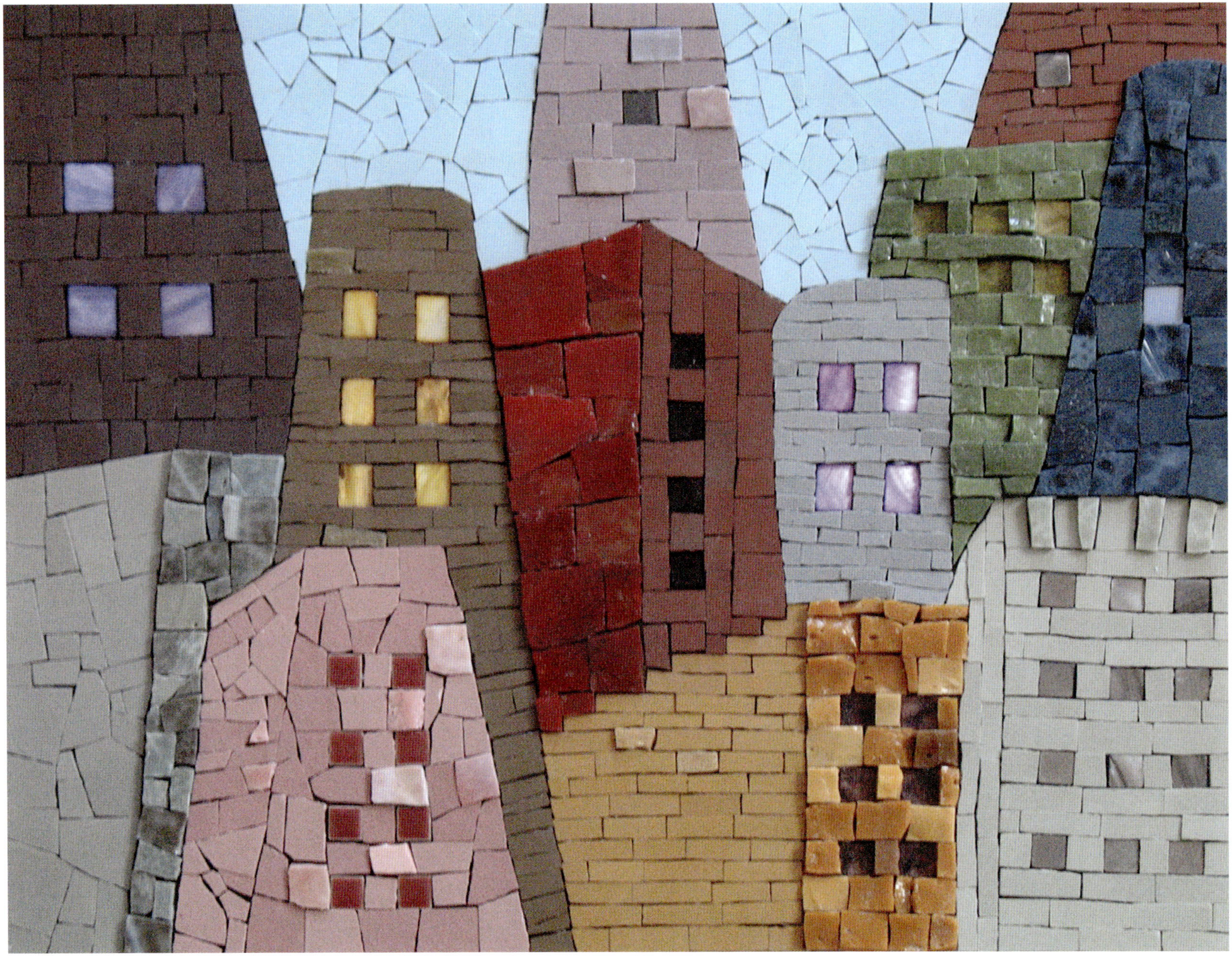

Ilona Landau Fried. *City of Then and Now.* 2-D wall panel. 2010. Smalti, unglazed ceramic tile, shell beads, glazed ceramic. Mosaic. 14" x 11". *Photo by Ilona Landau Fried*

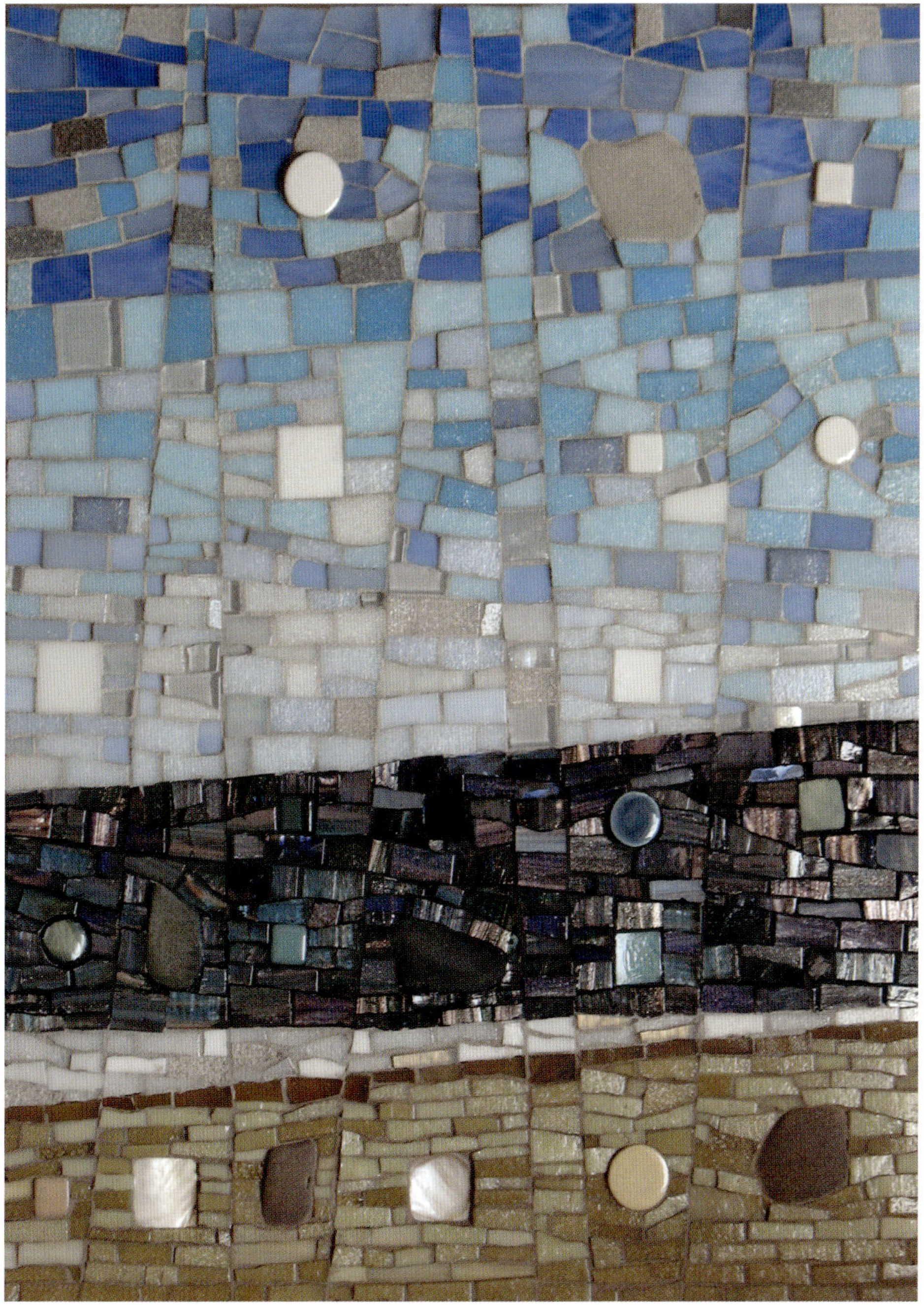

Ilona Landau Fried. *Walk on the Beach*. 2-D wall panel. 2011. Glazed ceramic, shell beads, stained glass, beach glass, vitreous tile. Mosaic. 11" x 14". *Photo by Ilona Landau Fried*

Suzan Germond

Austin, Texas, majormosaics@sbcglobal.net

Artist's Statement

I am passionate about this art form because it can be used in so many compelling ways. I can make mosaics that are decorative, functional, architectural or purely fine art. No defined limits give me a creative freedom and spontaneity of choice when I go to my studio each day. It is important to continue to refine my techniques so that no matter what type of mosaic I make it is of excellent quality and refined workmanship. I believe studying with world masters has elevated my own vision and skills over the twelve years of dedication to this art form.

My work is colorful, whimsical, and highly detailed. Creating texture and pattern with a variety of materials such as glass, tile, beads, jewels, and found objects inspires me. When possible I layer these materials so that the viewer is compelled to look at the art piece repeatedly to see all the various components. I often use unexpected found objects to translate something old or discarded into a part of an art piece. This re-contexting adds another dimension to my work, which gives me, and I hope, the viewer added pleasure to see objects imaginatively transformed.

About the Artwork

Big Bouquet: This large still life has a dimensional bouquet made of a variety of materials, including plates, bowls, ceramics, beads, and jewelry. The background is made of hand cut glass.

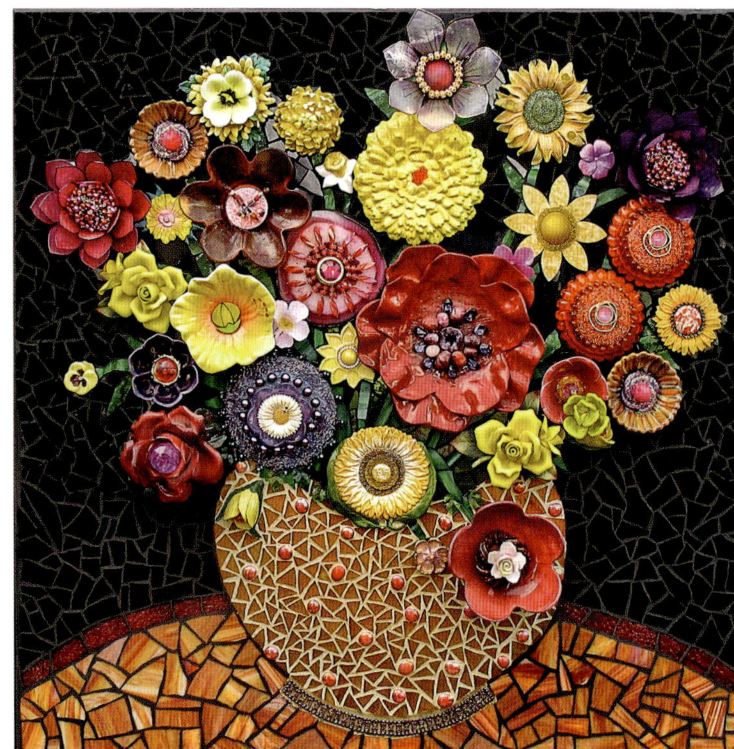

Suzan Germond. *Big Bouquet.* 2008. Mixed media mosaic with glass, beads, jewelry, and found objects. 36' x 36" x 4'. *Photo by artist*

Mustang: This large glass mosaic was created for an elementary school whose mascot was the mustang. I tried to represent a stylized horse in motion moving forward encouraging the students to also charge forward. The 4th grade art class participated in gluing on the flat back green marble border.

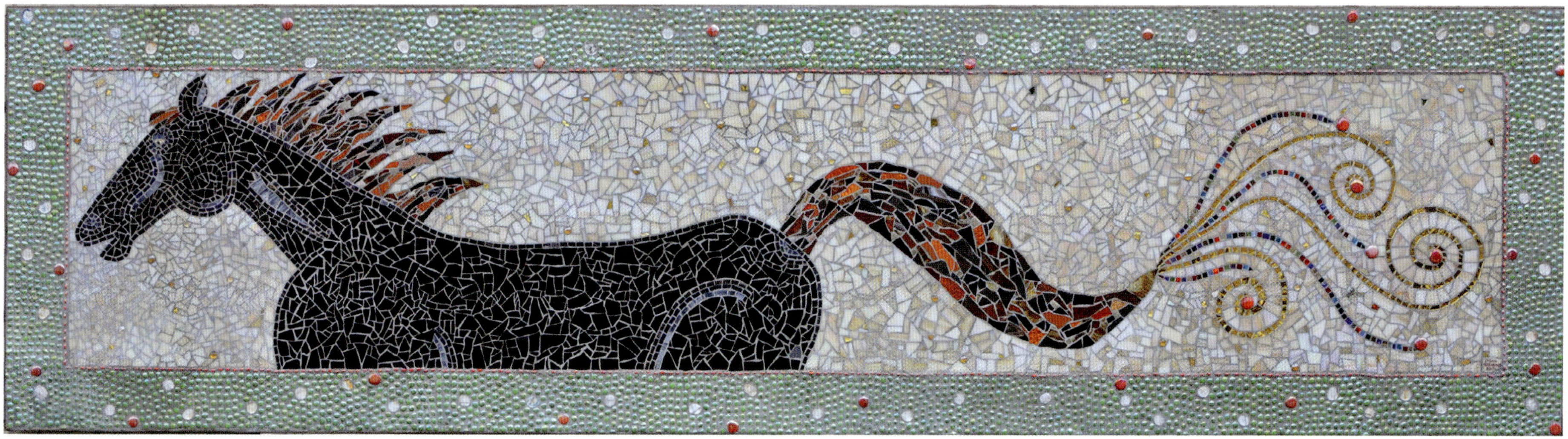

Suzan Germond. *Mustang.* Exterior glass mosaic. 2005. Glass, colored mirror, flat back marbles. 14' x 4'. *Photo by artist*

Lost: This abstract mosaic has a richly textured field of red in a variety of hues. It is intersected by a white and ivory band that contains one small red ball which seems out of its natural place, hence the title *Lost*. The density and texture of different materials create a rich visual field.

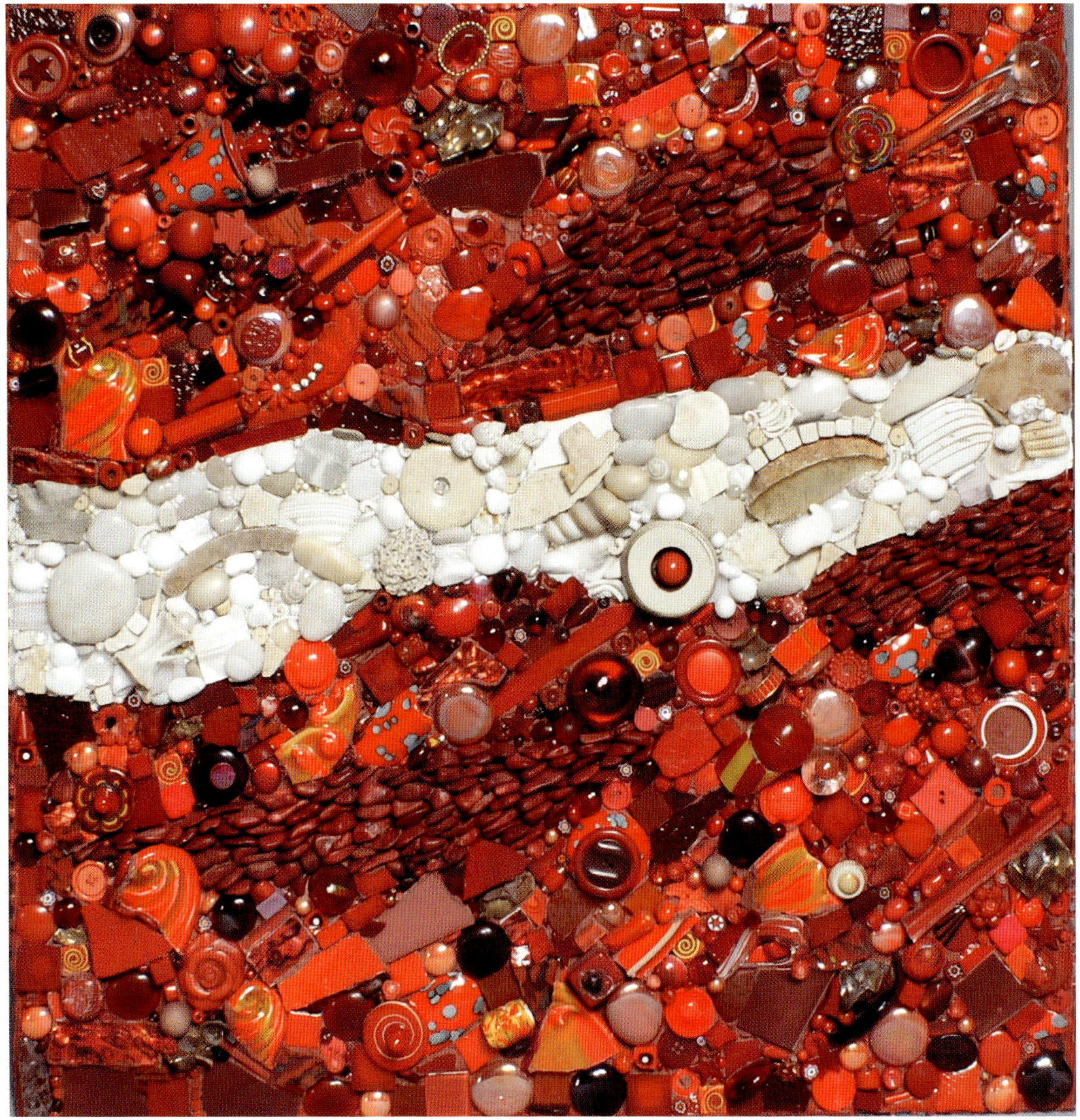

Suzan Germond. *Lost.* 2010. Mixed media mosaic with natural material such as stone, pebbles, shells and buttons, beads, glass shards, toy pieces, jewelry, tile, and ceramics. 36" x 36". *Photo by Leroy Lawson*

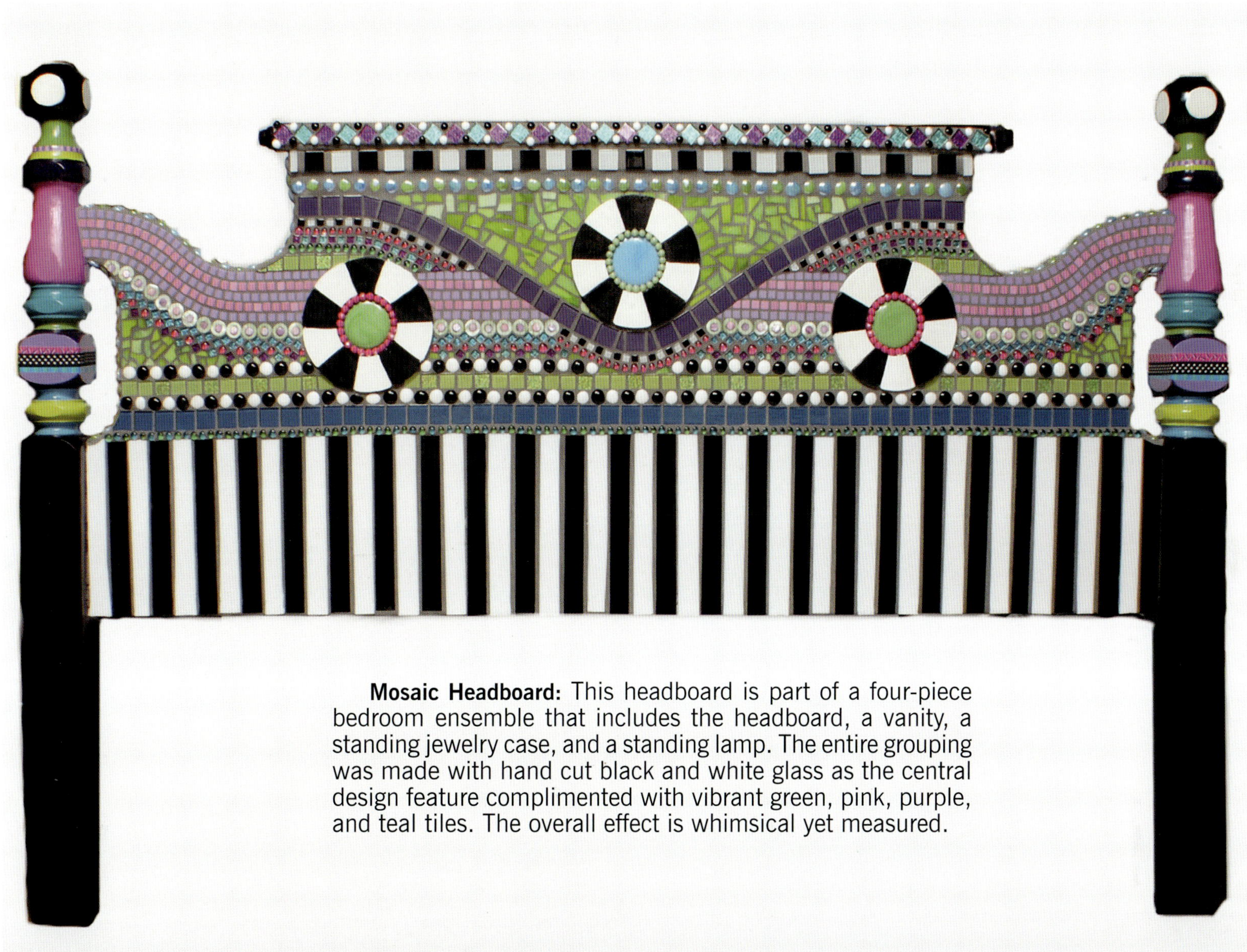

Mosaic Headboard: This headboard is part of a four-piece bedroom ensemble that includes the headboard, a vanity, a standing jewelry case, and a standing lamp. The entire grouping was made with hand cut black and white glass as the central design feature complimented with vibrant green, pink, purple, and teal tiles. The overall effect is whimsical yet measured.

Suzan Germond. Mosaic Headboard. 2010. Mixed media mosaic. 5' x 3' x 6". *Photo by Leroy Lawson*

Watch Dog: This is a life size dog made from metal and concrete that is covered in hand cut black glass. The flowers have petals cut from china and the centerpiece of each flower is a watch face. I wanted to make the title a literal part of the piece.

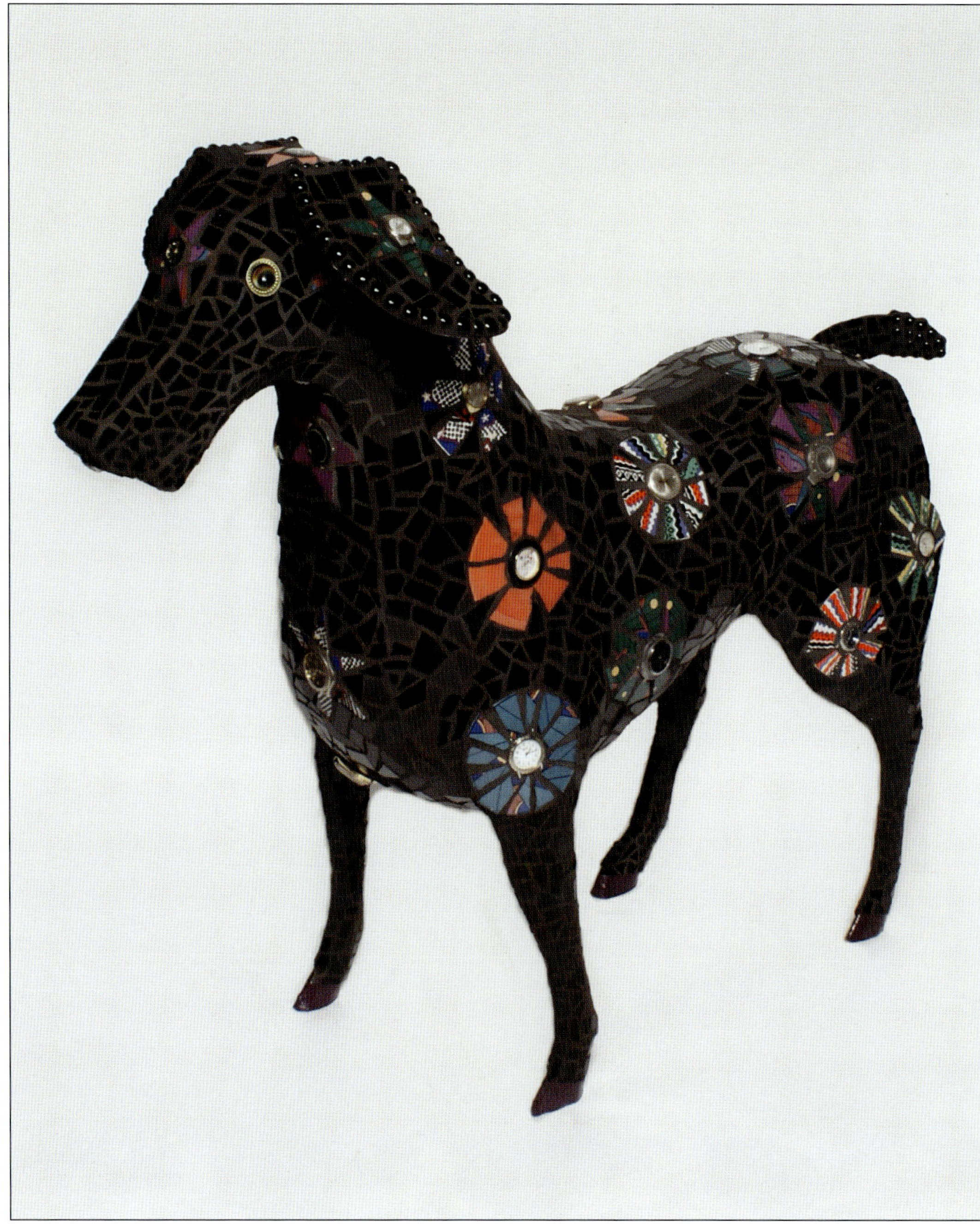

Suzan Germond. *Watch Dog*. 2010. Mixed media mosaic using black glass, china, and watch faces. 36" x 24" x 12". *Photo by Leroy Lawson*

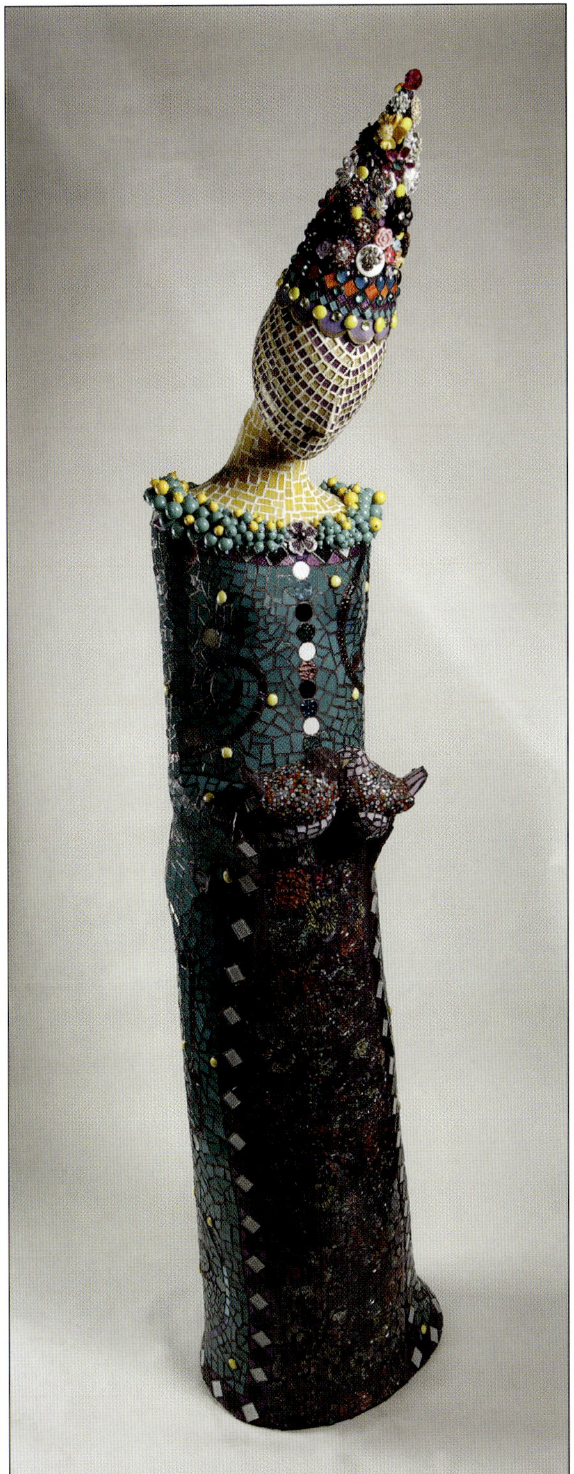

Lady-in-waiting in the Garden: This life size sculpture was hand built with clay barrels and covered with hand cut teal glass, diachroic glass, tempered glass, black and white crystal tiles, mirror, and jewelry. The cone hat was covered with vintage jewelry and handmade jewelry. The lady is in a contemplative pose holding two birds in her hands. I wanted her to have a solemn quality combined with the vibrant materials.

Suzan Germond. *Lady-in-waiting in the Garden.* 2011. Mixed media mosaic. 70" x 34". *Photo by Leroy Lawson*

Kim Grant

Spence, Australia, kim@kimgrantmosaics.com

Artist's Statement

I find myself drawn to a couple things simultaneously: order and chaos. With numbers, the mathematics that is around us every day, I find order, in nature, in the doodle I unconsciously draw, in outer space ... Numbers are all around us and there are no coincidences with numbers, at least that is what I have found to be true. With the unknown I find I can revel in chaos. Fearless non-planning and spontaneity which manifests as "working organically," allowing myself to breathe unconsciously and trust in the process.

About the Artwork

Celestial Horizon: This installation resides just outside Melbourne, Australia, up high in the lovely mountains of the Dandenong Ranges. I created this installation in about five days.

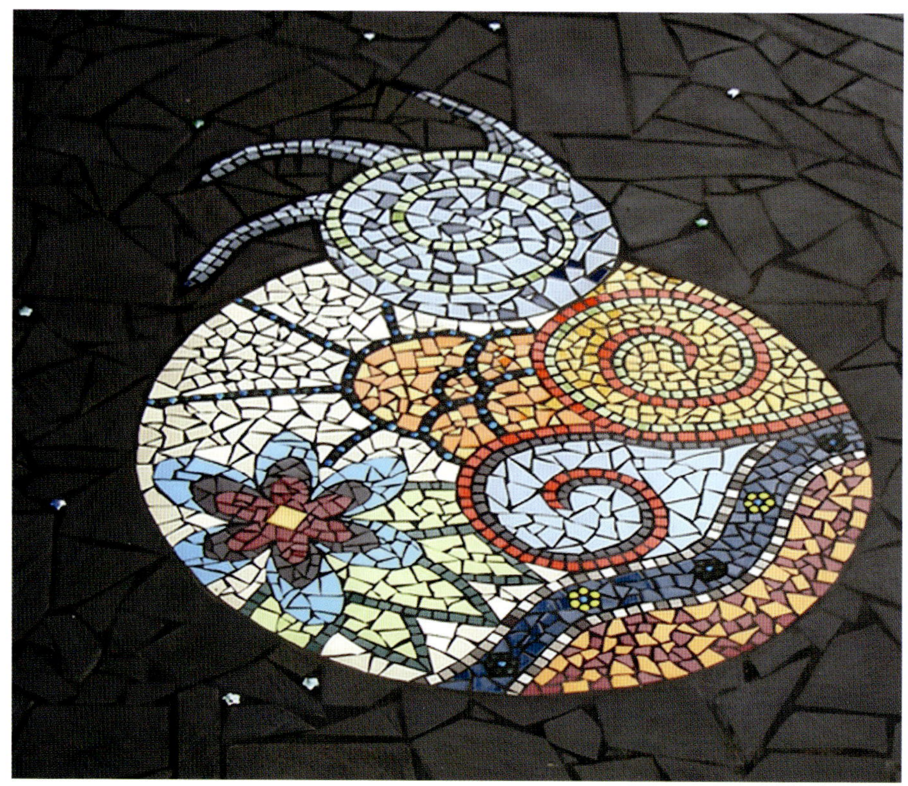

Kim Grant. *Celestial Horizon*. Mosaic floor installation. 2008. Ceramic, glass gems. 13' x 5' (3.85m x 1.65m). *Photo by Kim Grant*

Discovery Garden: This installation was my first community project involving a preschool. It is a culmination of a few designs created by some of the children aged four years old. I created much of the work on mesh in my studio and then taught interested families of the school how to set tile direct to the wall over a number of weekends. It allowed for some wonderful spontaneity from children as young as two (some glass gem fireflies and flowers, if you look carefully) and helped to boost a wonderful community spirit.

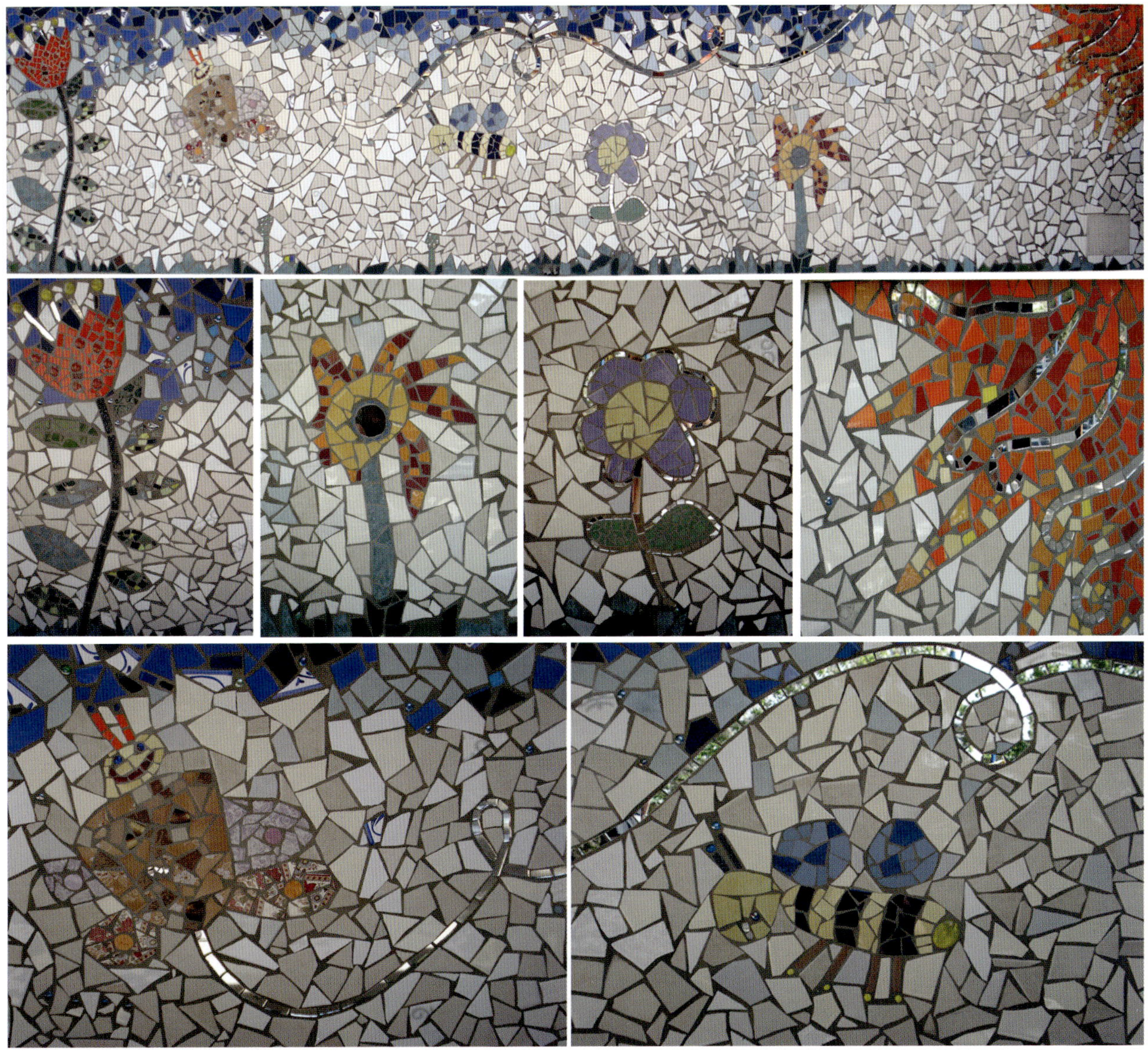

Kim Grant. *Discovery Garden*. A Community Project. 2008. Ceramic, glass gems, mirror. 17' x 3' (5.25m x 1m). *Photo by Kim Grant*

Sir Elton: The clients who commissioned me to do this piece had seen my first chicken titled *Liberace*. They wanted something similarly whimsical, outrageous, and fun.

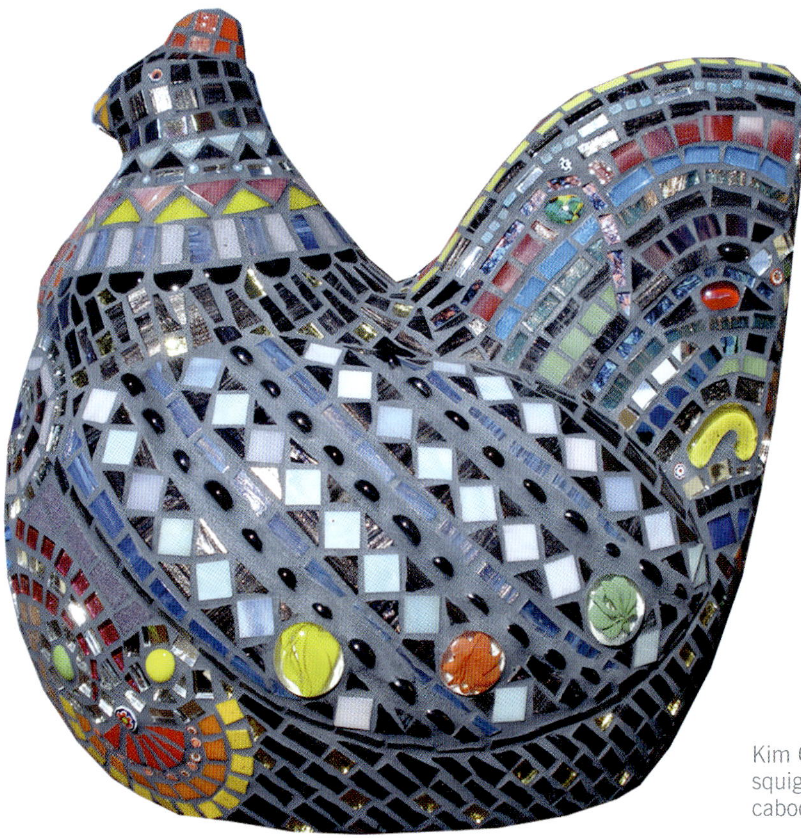

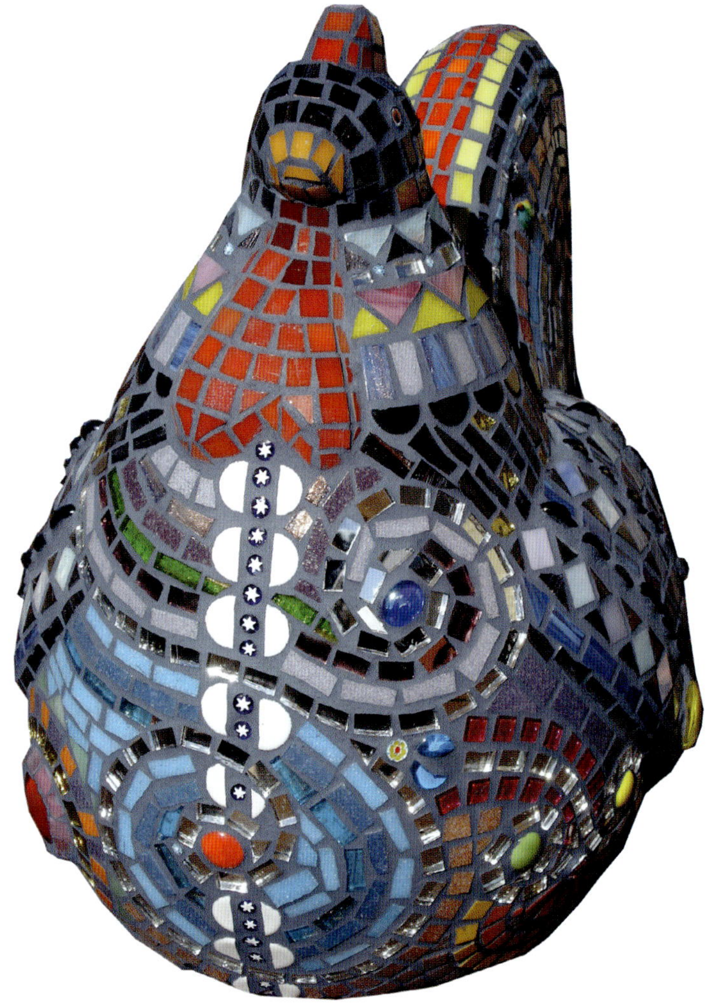

Kim Grant. *Sir Elton.* 2008. Vitreous glass, Van Gogh glass, glass gems, glass squiggles, millefiori, ceramic, mirror, gold, iridized glass, glitter tile, fused glass cabochons. 16" x 10" x 15" (40cm x 26cm x 38cm). *Photo by Kim Grant*

Mermaid Dreaming: This installation now resides in a private residence in Canberra, Australia. It was a collaboration with my sister, Natalie Grant, who sketched out the entire thing one afternoon on the wall.

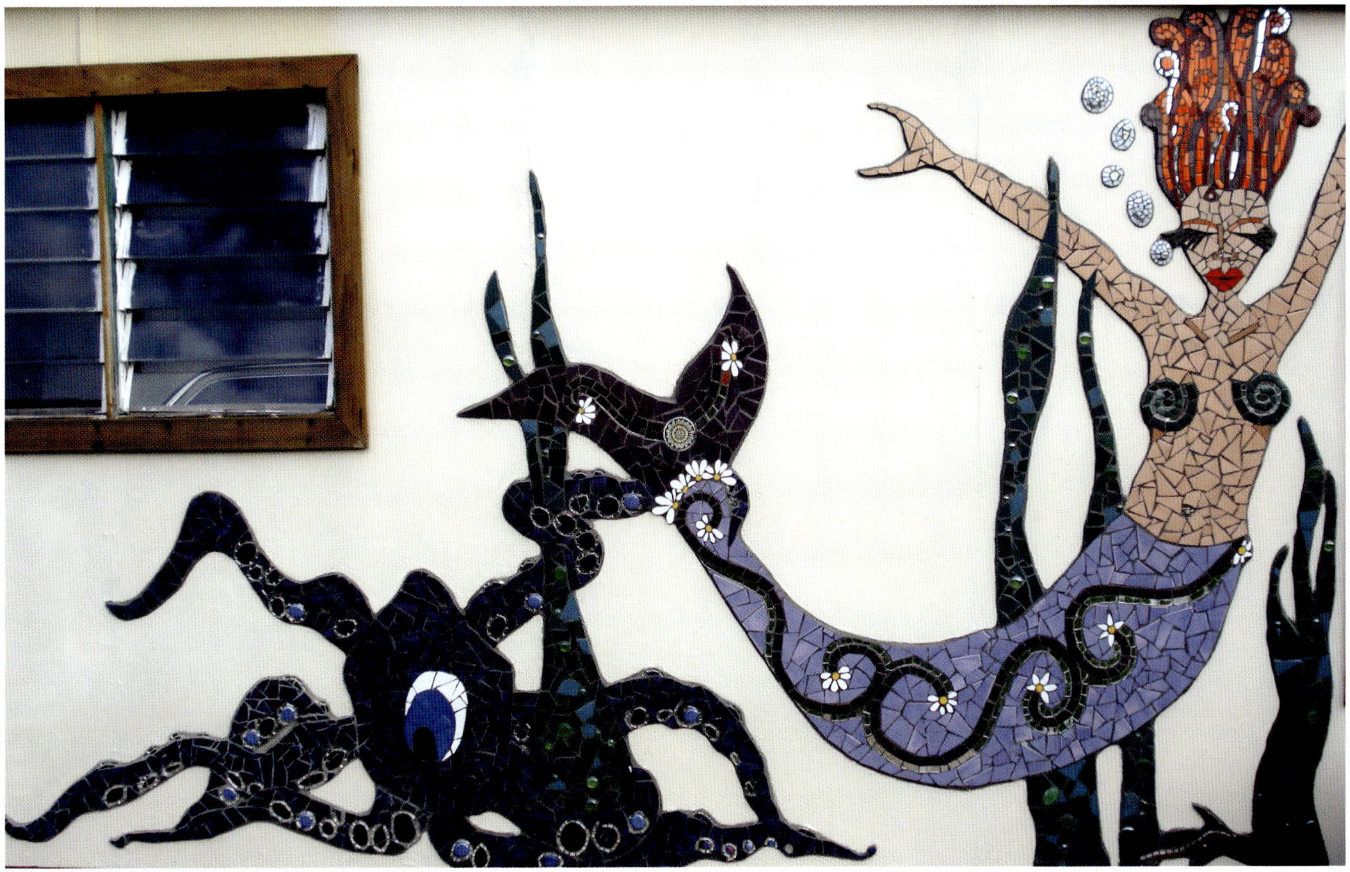

Kim Grant. *Mermaid Dreaming.* 2009. Ceramic, glass gems, mirror, iridized glass, opalescent vitreous tile. 16' x 9' (5m x 2.7m). *Photo by Kim Grant*

Priscilla — Queen of the Pond: This was a commission for a couple in Paris, France, who had seen *Sir Elton*, another commission of a chicken that now lives in Seoul, Korea. They fancied a chicken at first until settling on this fish. With my 3D pieces, I simply breathe life into what would otherwise be an inanimate object.

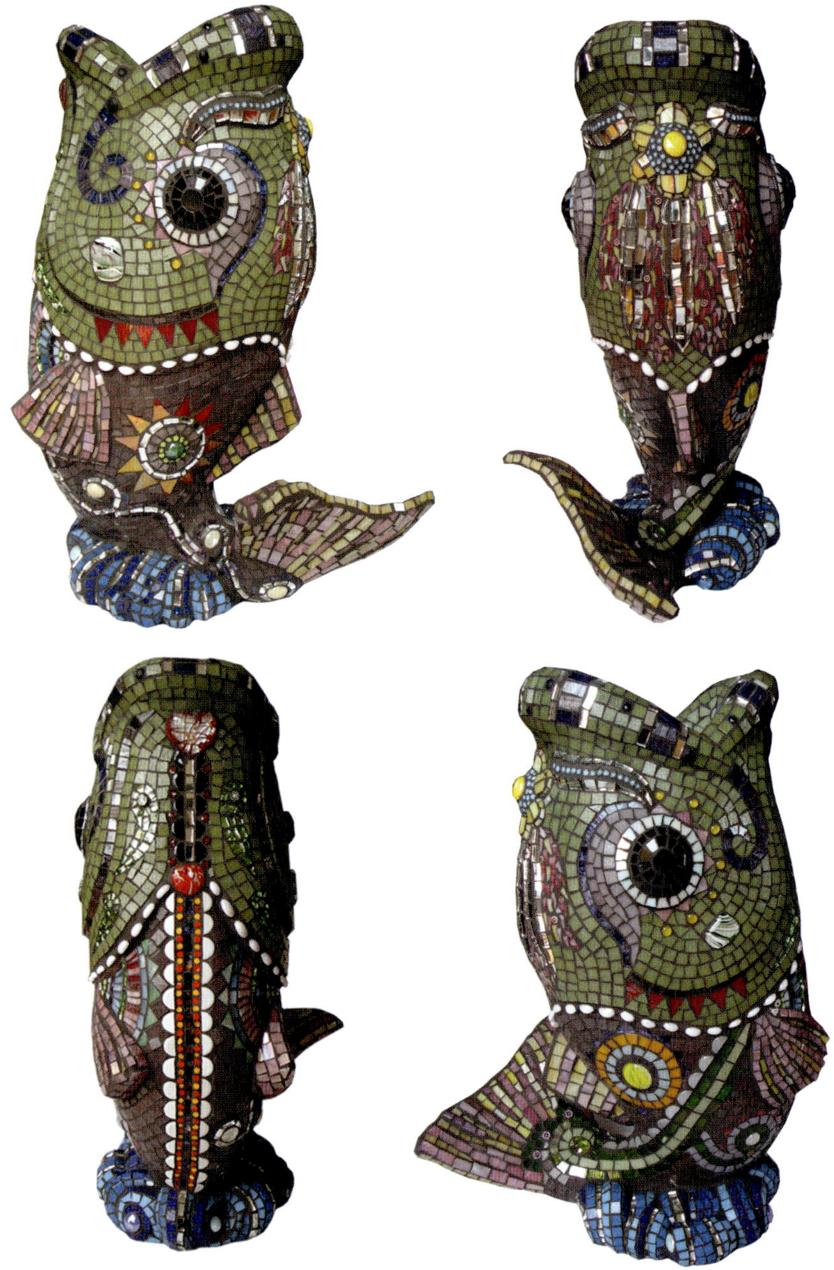

Kim Grant. *Priscilla — Queen of the Pond.* 2010. Stained glass, vitreous glass, fused glass, glass gems, millefiori, mirror, ceramic on pre formed substrate. 20" x 12" x 13" (50cm x 30cm x 33cm).

Shroom: With my 3D pieces, I simply breathe life into what would otherwise be an inanimate object. When I saw the mushroom in its former life, it beckoned for that breath.

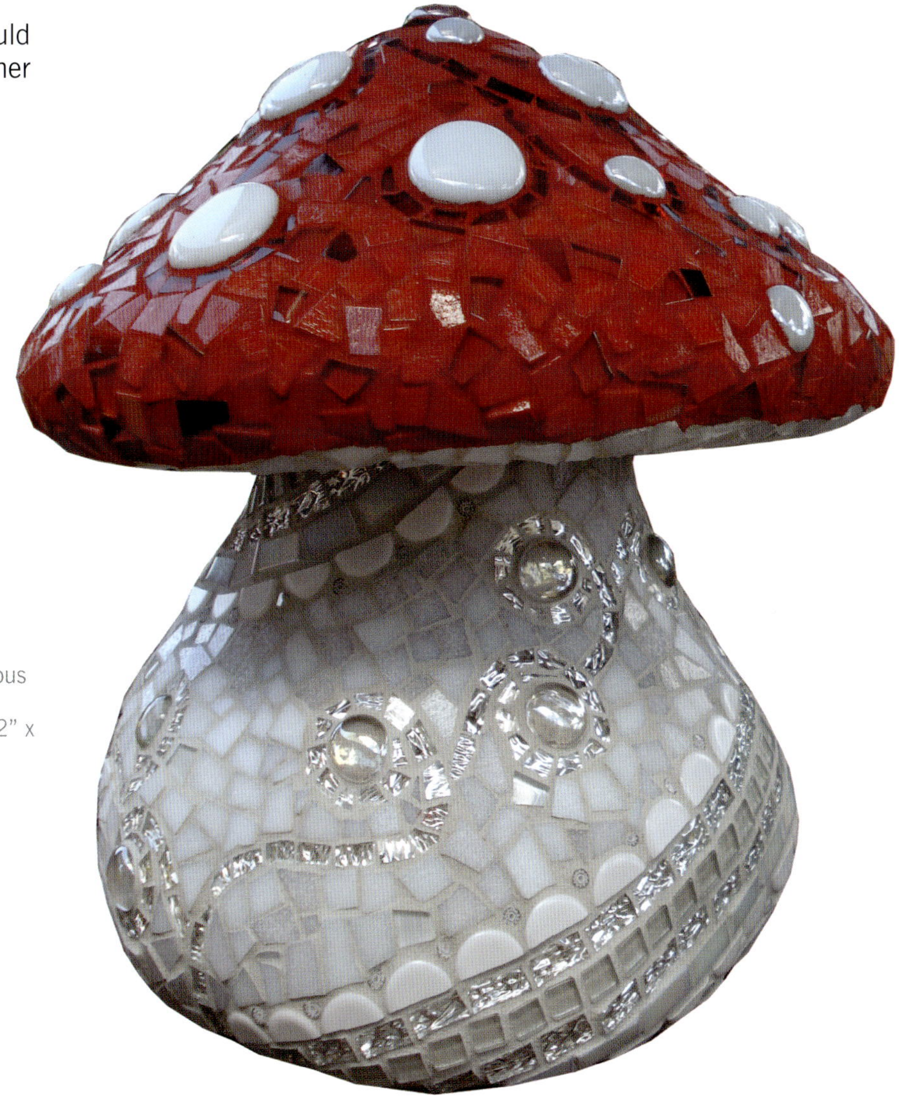

Kim Grant. *Shroom*. 2011. Vitreous glass, opalescent vitreous glass, glass gems, millefiori, textured mirror, colored mirror, ceramic, crystal glass tile on pre-formed substrate. 12" x 12" x 12" (30cm x 30cm x 30cm). *Photo by Kim Grant*

Chris Heisinger

Evanston, Illinois, Chrisheisinger@hotmail.com

Artist's Statement

I have traveled to various wild forests and woods and am amazed by the beauty and high energy of all of those magnificent places. These are the places I stop and become one with the environment. The colors, sounds, and smells are intense and profound. It is these experiences that I try to capture in time within my art.

By being aware of the fragility of nature and our ecosystem, I try to use as much recycled materials as possible with all my artwork. Most of my window pieces are actually old recycled window frames and a significant amount of the stained glass used in the pieces are either scraps from other projects or glass that would have otherwise been thrown out.

The Artwork

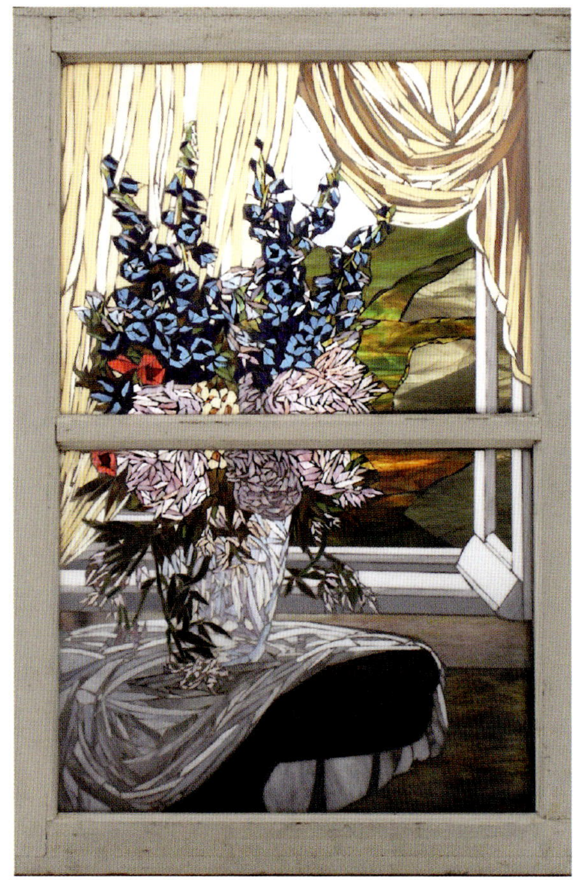

Chris Heisinger. *Peonies in the Sun*. Window. 2008. Stained glass. 36" x 24".

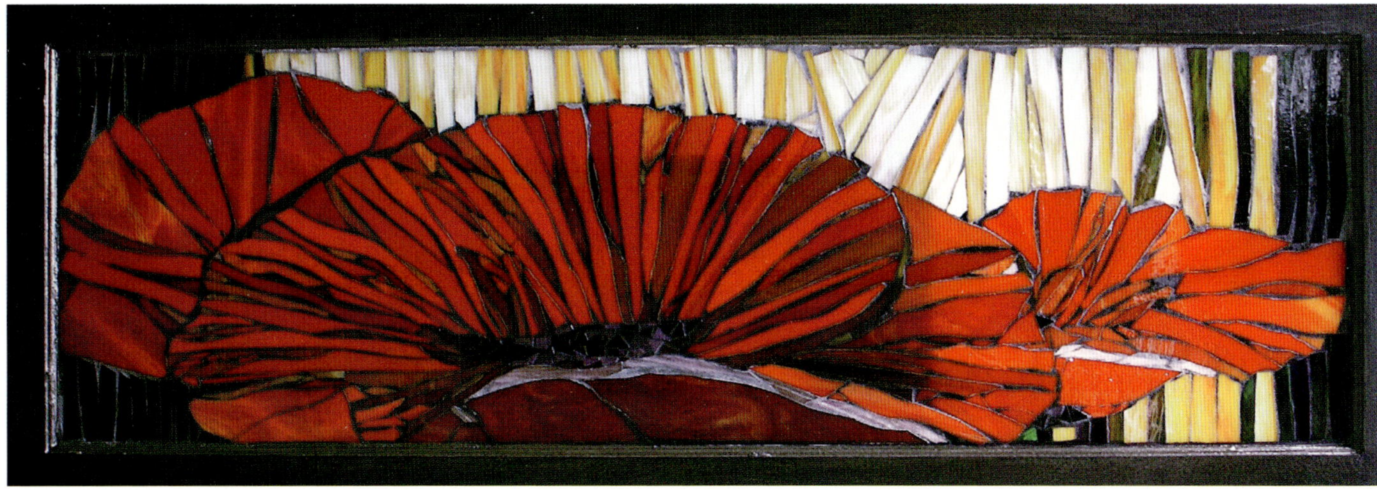

Chris Heisinger. *Splendid Poppies.* Window. 2009. Stained glass. 18" x 50".

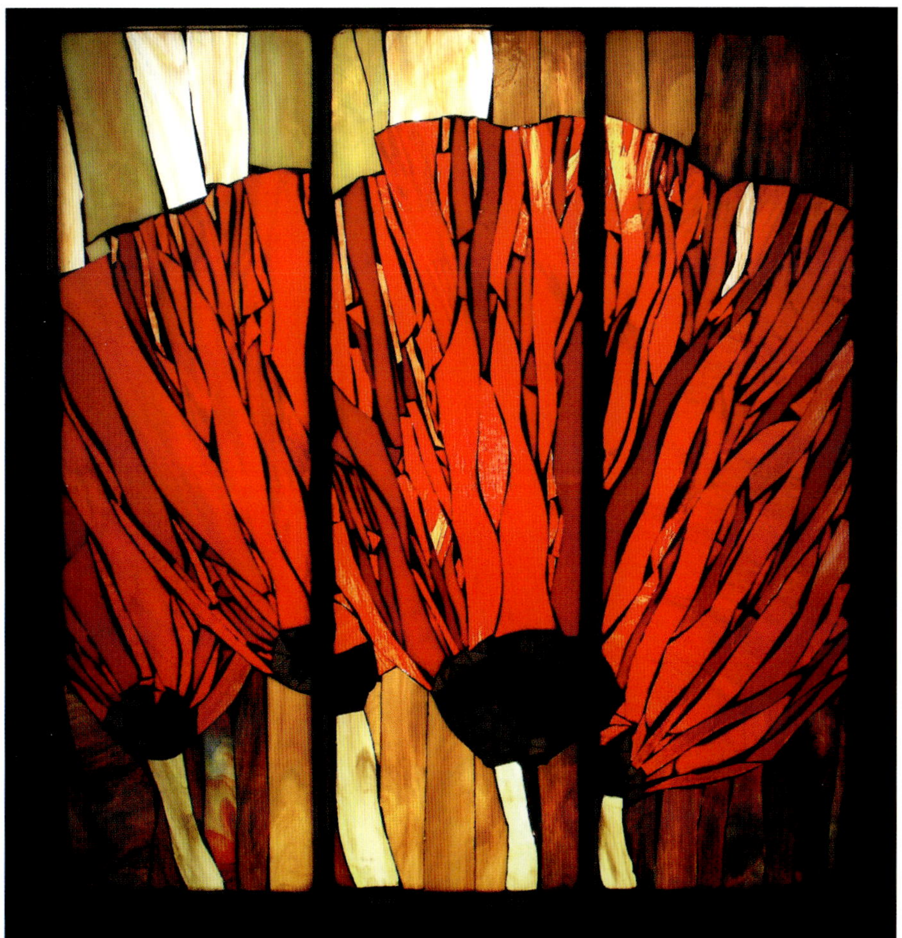

Chris Heisinger. *Poppies / Poppies*. Window. 2009. Stained glass mosaic with tiles. 33" x 32".

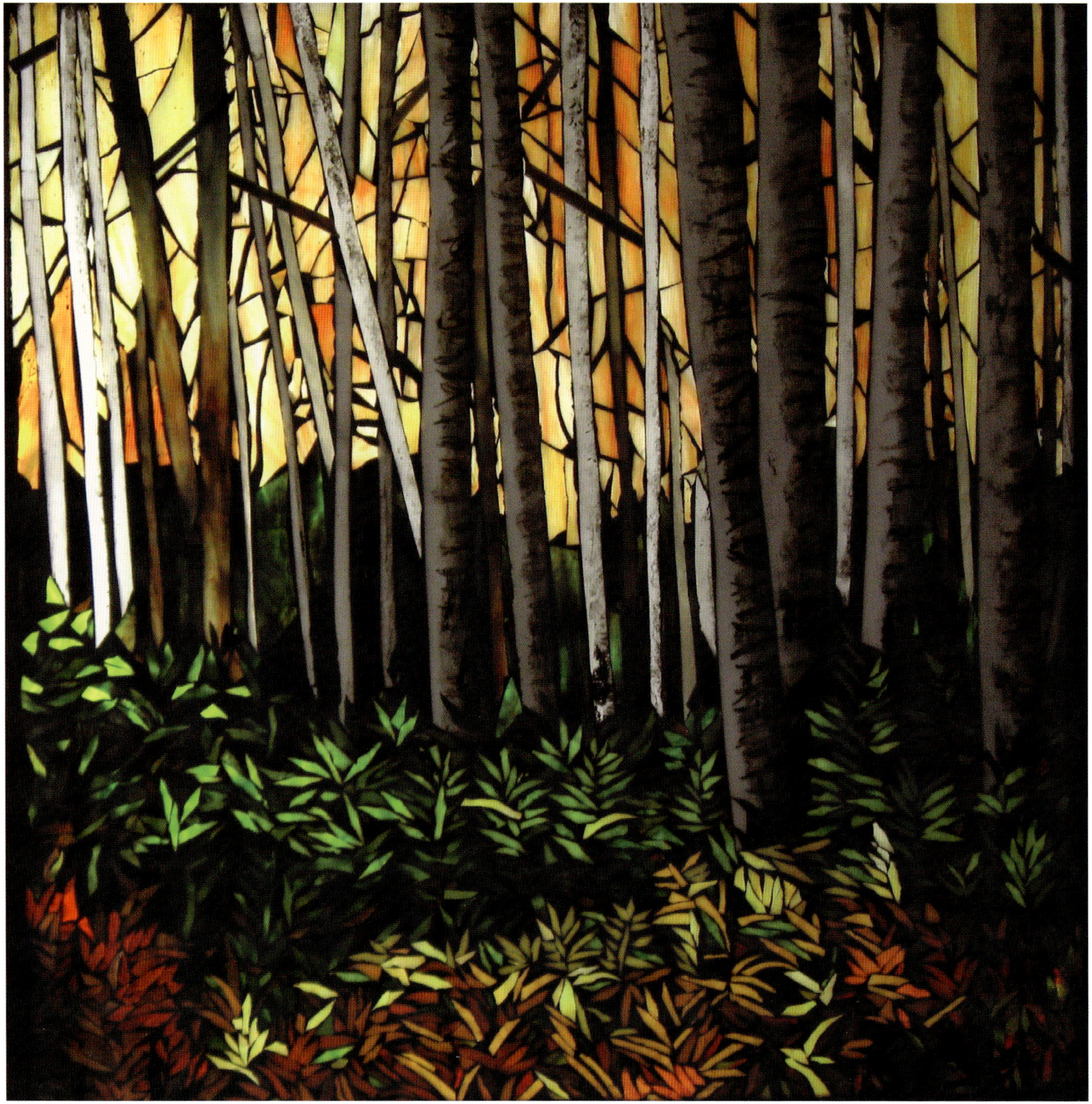

Chris Heisinger. *Evening Forest.* Window. 2009. Stained glass. 28" x 29".

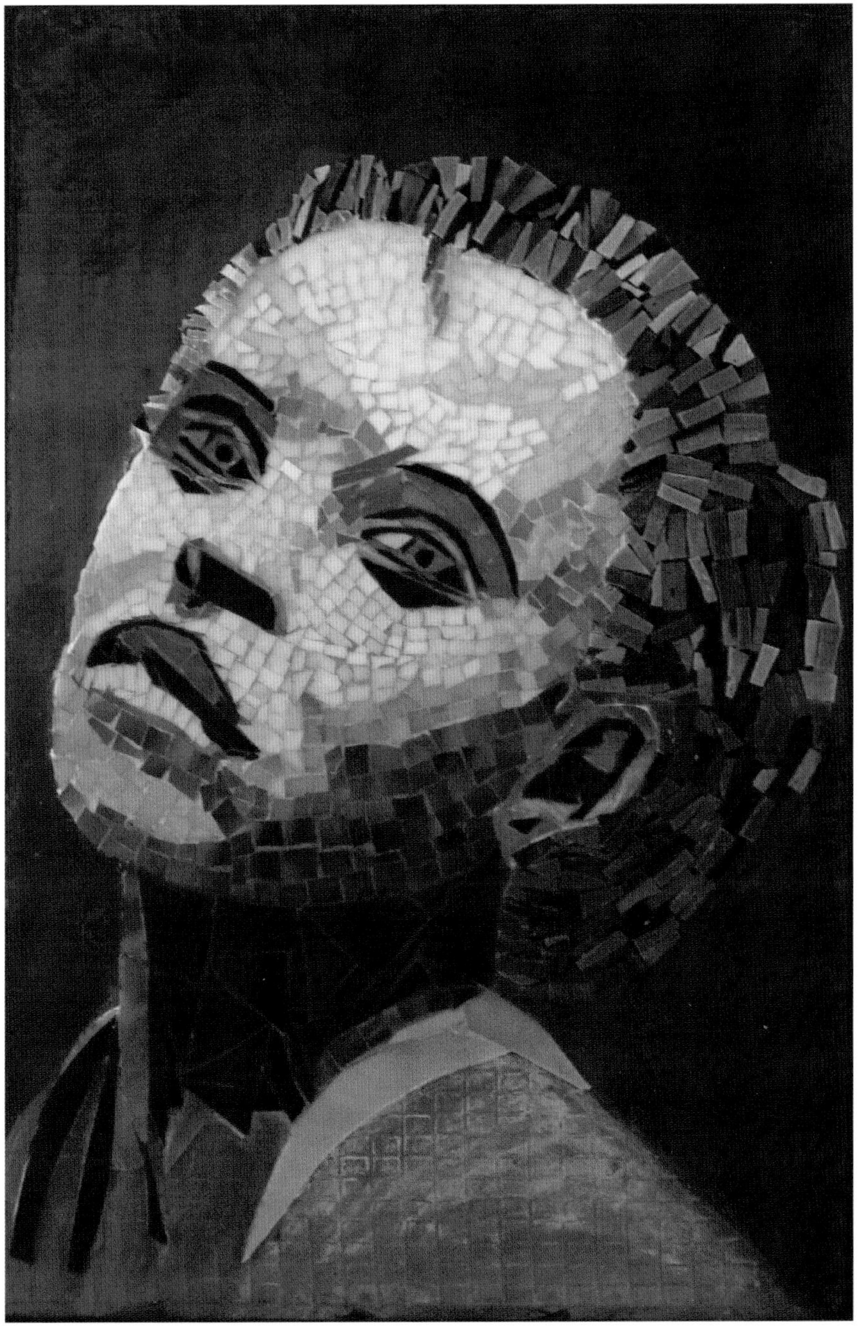

Chris Heisinger. *Beauty in Black and White*. Wall art. 2010. Stained glass, smalti on Wedi Board. 14" x 18".

Rhoda Heisler

Skillman, New Jersey, rhondaheisler@gmail.com

Artist's Statement

As a former painter, now full-time mosaicist, I consider myself primarily a colorist and draw inspiration from my chosen material: the rich, one-of-a-kind color and pattern variations in the stained glass sheets that I personally select at the distributor's showroom. (I never use pre-molded tile in standard squares.) I am particularly drawn to glass that has a richly patterned underside or unusual texture or surface contours, the better to reflect light.

Back at the studio, I settle on a color palette, arrange my materials (sometimes including rock, slate, minerals, shells, and ceramic) around me, and begin to sketch abstract designs on paper in colored pencil. Once I have a basic design and color distribution that pleases me, I determine the size of the panel(s) and transfer the elements of the sketch in a very loose way to the substrate, knowing that the design will evolve and grow more complex as the mosaic is created.

I begin the mosaic by cutting into the glass with traditional glass-cutting tools to create the principal design motifs in the composition. In my abstract compositions, many of these motifs take form as free, gestural strokes, similar to the way I would wield a paintbrush. As I cut my tesserae out of the sheet, I act as an editor, choosing the best areas of pattern and texture, and then the choicest bits of color that I can further trim to fit the design. In creating the mosaic, I often cut larger pieces of hand cut glass or tile into smaller tesserae, then glue these tesserae directly to the substrate. I try to work spontaneously and expressively, and in creating the mosaic surface I pay close attention to the same formal elements that challenged me as a painter: color, line, shape, scale, pattern, texture, and the reflective properties of light. Metallic elements add richness and flash. I generally grout in several colors, to enhance the painterly effect. Usually, the title of the piece comes to me somewhere in the process of creating the mosaic.

About the Artwork

Breakaway (2006) was the first abstract in which I used the rose/purple/persimmon/mustard/brown/bruise color palette, with black/ivory/metallic accents.

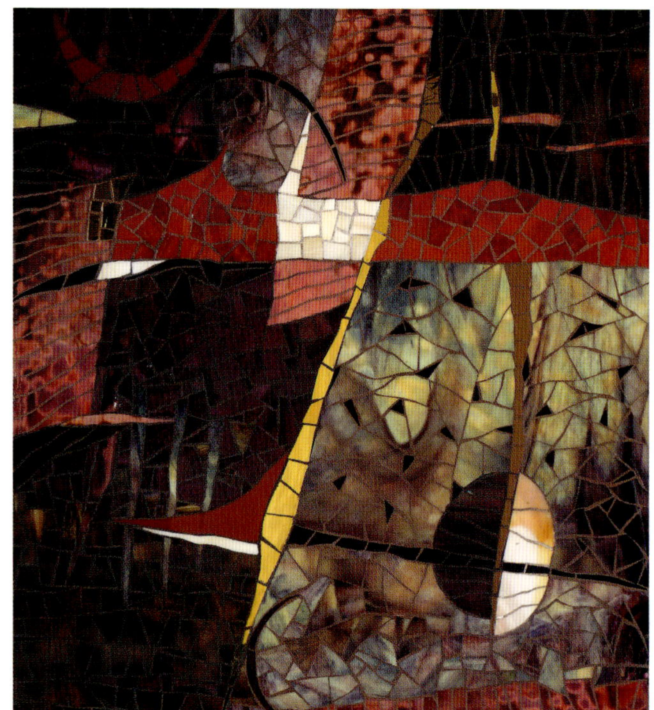

Rhonda Heisler. *Breakaway.* One-of-a-kind single panel mosaic abstract. 2006. Hand cut opaque and metallic stained glass. 25" x 23". *Photo by Ross Stout*

Breakaway II (2006) was commissioned for the lobby of Integrated Health Center, a medical building in Allentown, Pennsylvania. The builder and design supervisor had been very taken with the original Breakaway mosaic and wanted something with the same abstract elements and in the same color palette, but in a two-panel composition to hang opposite the main elevator doors. So I created what I like to think of as a jazz riff off the original design, with some new motifs added.

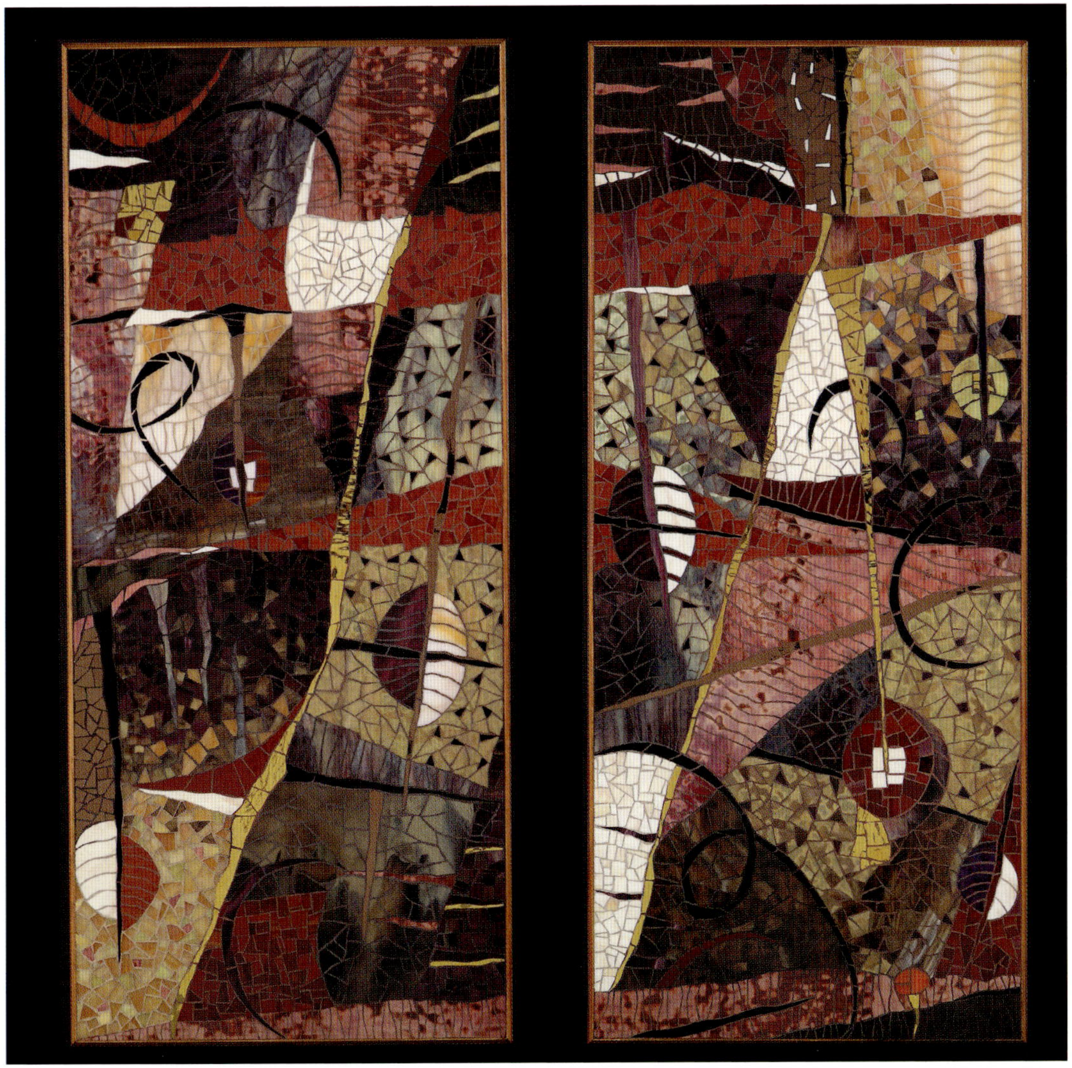

Rhonda Heisler. *Breakaway II.* One-of-a-kind two-panel mosaic abstract. 2006. Hand cut opaque and metallic stained glass. 54" x 24" each panel. *Photo by Ross Stout*

From This All Flows (2006) represents the first time I incorporated colored agates into a mosaic. The swirling patterns in the polished slices of stone suggested something elemental to me, and so this became my principal motif. I used a wet saw to cut more spirals and arcs of out the glass.

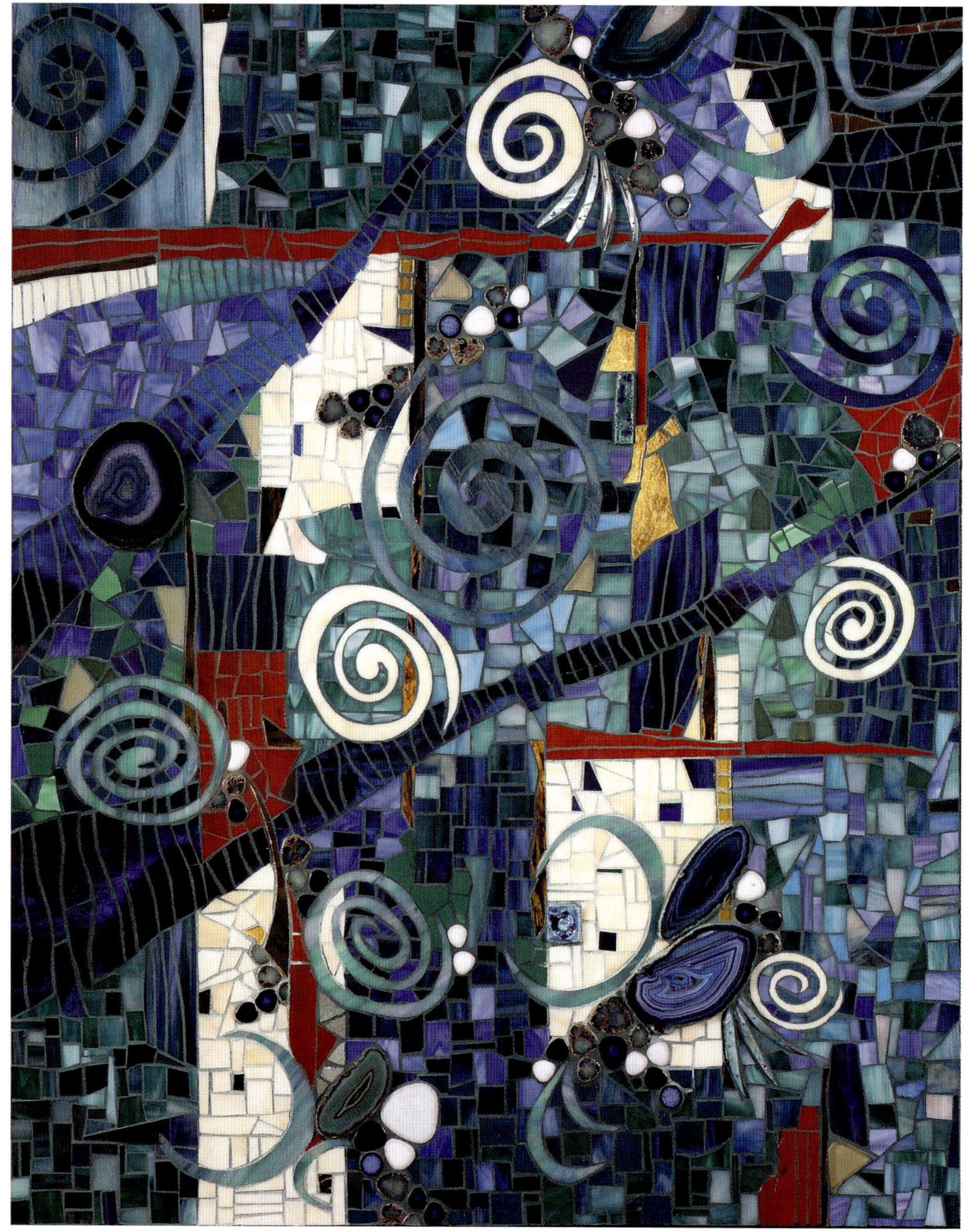

Rhonda Heisler. *From This All Flows.* One-of-a-kind 2-D mosaic abstract. 2006. Opaque and metallic stained glass, agates, shells, glazed and unglazed ceramic, smalti. 35" x 29". *Photo by Ross Stout*

In ***Progression II*** (2006) and ***Progression III*** (2007), I am still working with some of the same design elements I came up with for the *Breakaway* series, though in new color palettes and in horizontal formats.

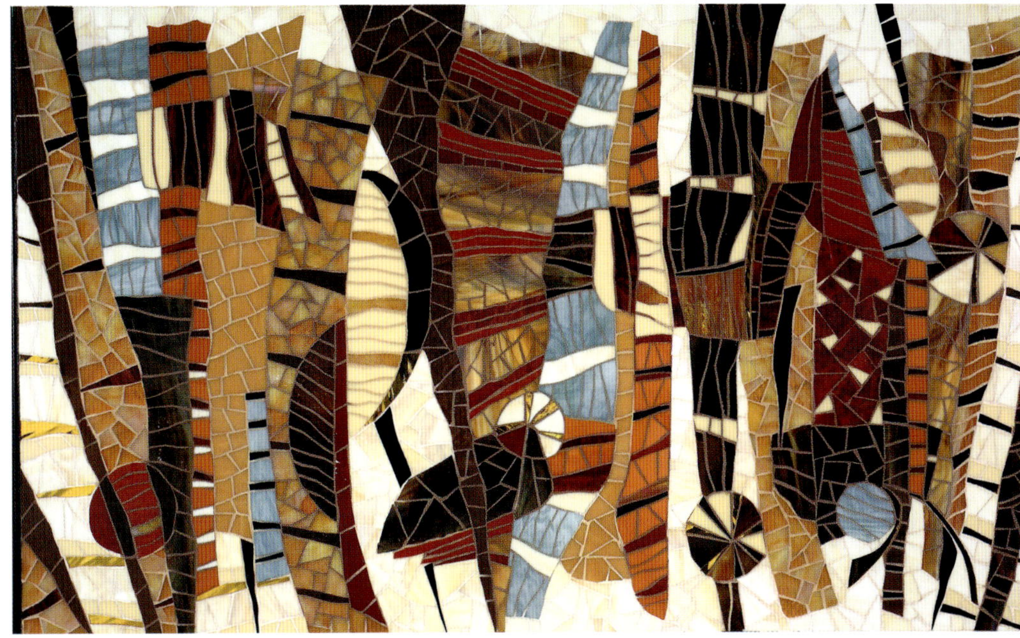

Rhonda Heisler. *Progression II.* One-of-a-kind single-panel mosaic abstract. 2006. Hand cut opaque and metallic stained glass. 24" x 40". *Photo by Ross Stout*

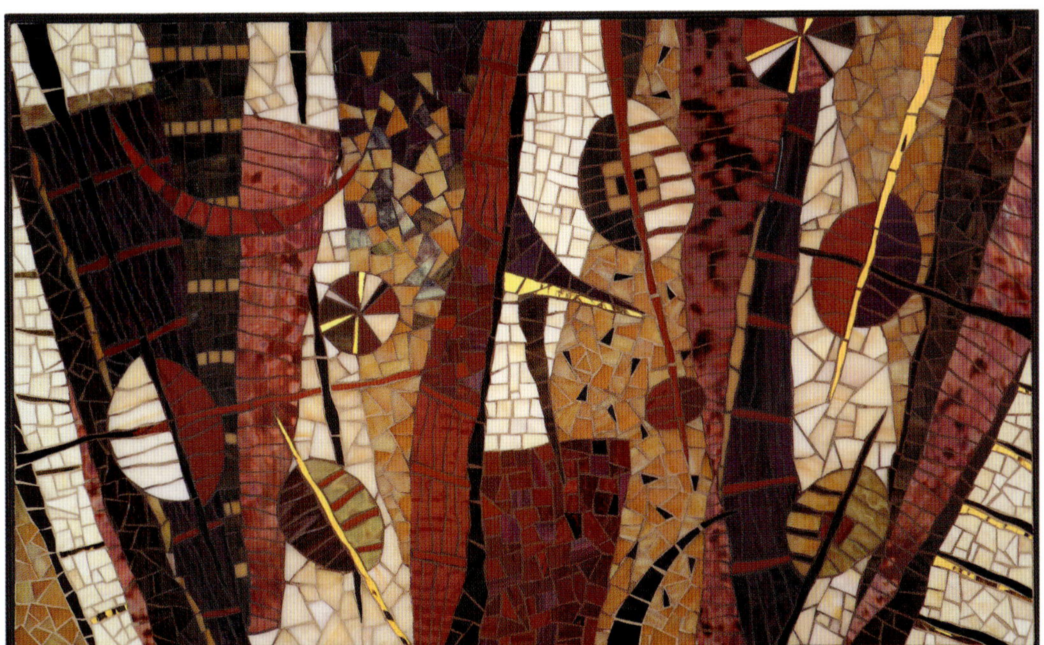

Rhonda Heisler. *Progression III.* One-of-a-kind single-panel mosaic abstract. 2007. Hand cut opaque and metallic stained glass. 24" x 40". *Photo by Ross Stout*

The ***Encoded*** mosaics were inspired by a series of close-up photos of autumn leaves I shot while walking along the Appalachian Trail in the Blue Ridge Mountains of Virginia. The sunlight was dazzling on the trail, throwing the leaf colors into brilliant contrast, and some even reflected white light back to the eye. These three mosaic panels show a semi-abstracted patterning of those leaves. I manipulated the color, shape, and orientation of the leaf forms to give each composition an internal rhythm and to suggest that nature reveals its own language of theme and variation in each collection of like objects. ***Encoded II and III*** were designed as two panels of a triptych, and the first panel of the three was sold to a collector.

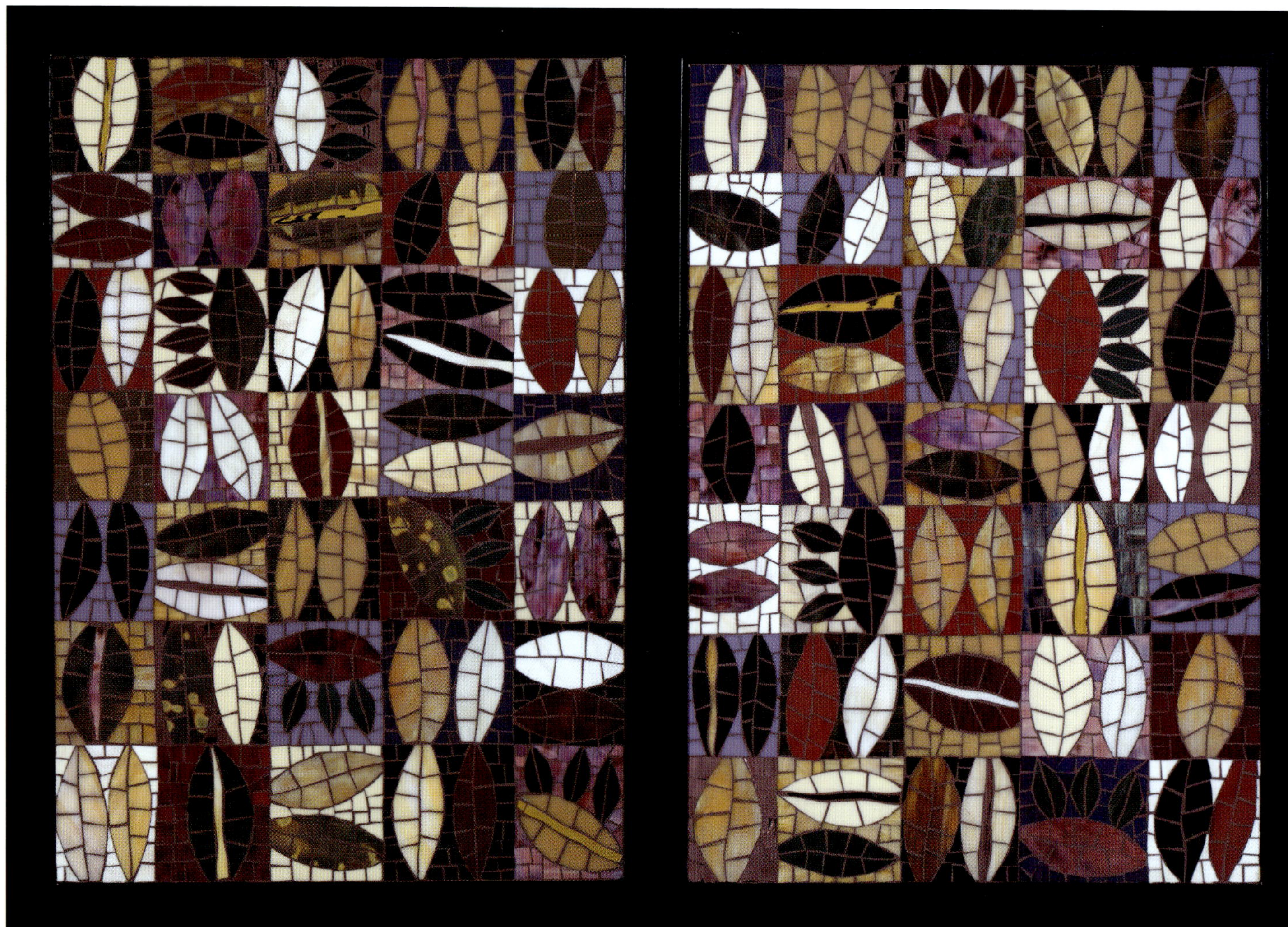

Rhonda Heisler. *Encoded II and III*. One-of-a-kind two-panel mosaic, semi-abstract. 2007. Stylized leaf pattern in hand cut opaque and metallic stained glass. Each panel 28" x 20". *Photo by Ross Stout*

Sukkothai was inspired by a trip to Thailand, where I walked the ruins of a 700-year-old temple complex. The colors and textures of decayed brick and stone at the site were a stark contrast to the grandeur and vitality that once existed there.

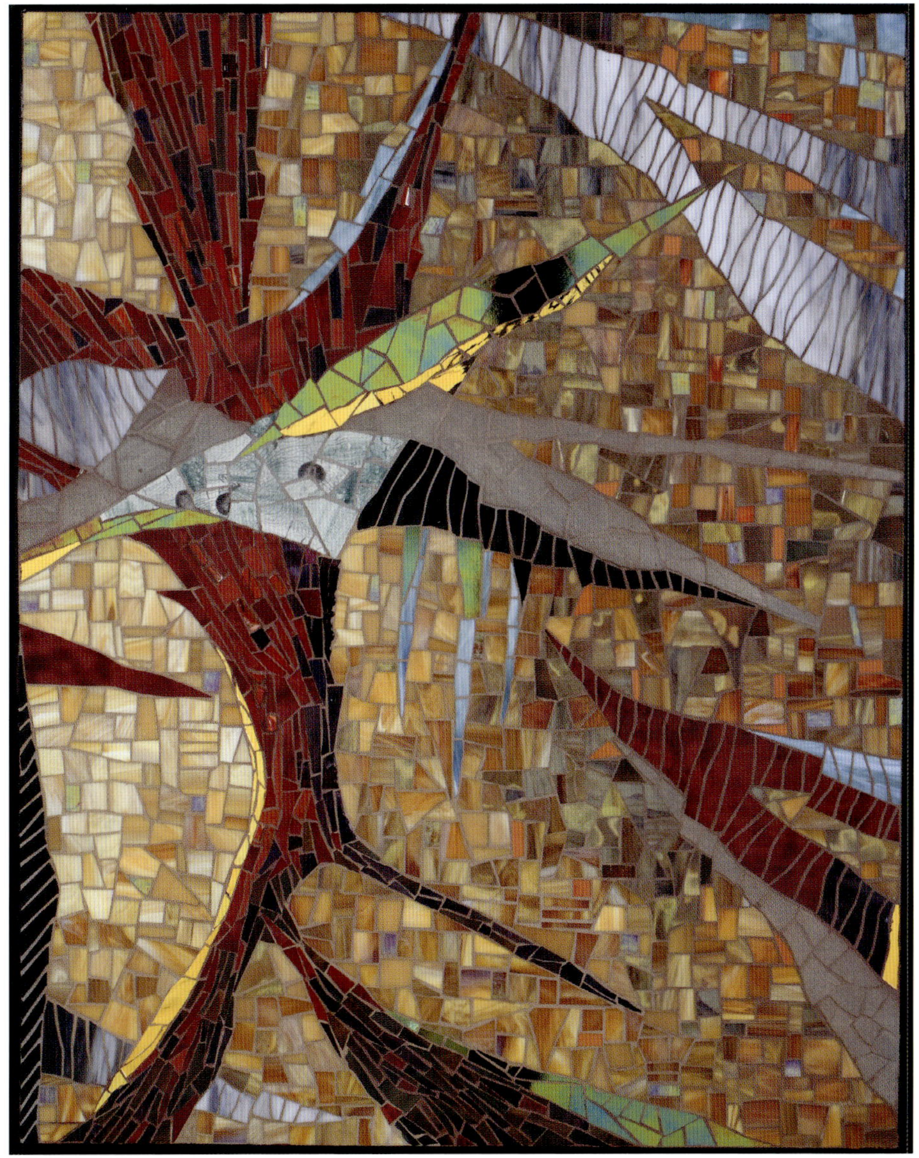

Rhonda Heisler. *Sukkothai.* One-of-a-kind single-panel mosaic abstract. 2008. Hand cut opaque and metallic stained glass, slate, raku-fired ceramic, red jasper. 36" x 29.5". *Photo by Ross Stout*

Gail Hercher

Honolulu, Hawaii, clayhawaii@aol.com

Artist's Statement

As a result of living on the tiny Island of Oahu in Hawaii, I am extremely conscious of environmental problems. Solid waste disposal, for example, is such a dire situation (no more landfill area) that the State of Hawaii recently contracted to send it to the Mainland (thereby adding to the problem by using fuel). Water pollution—from agricultural activities, an old, leaking sewer system, and street runoff—is causing coral reefs, marine habitats, and local fish populations to be destroyed.

My contribution (albeit small) to the solution of the solid waste problem is to use only recycled materials in my work. I have abandoned painting, printmaking, and papermaking, and no longer use paints, inks, poisonous solvents or other toxic materials. Instead, I now create mosaic pieces that are made with recycled materials. Car radiators, used bowls, hub caps, and fan covers serve as substrates; broken plates and found objects become the tesserae in the *pique assiette* technique. One intention of these mosaic pieces is to remind the viewer to consume and waste less!

The Artwork

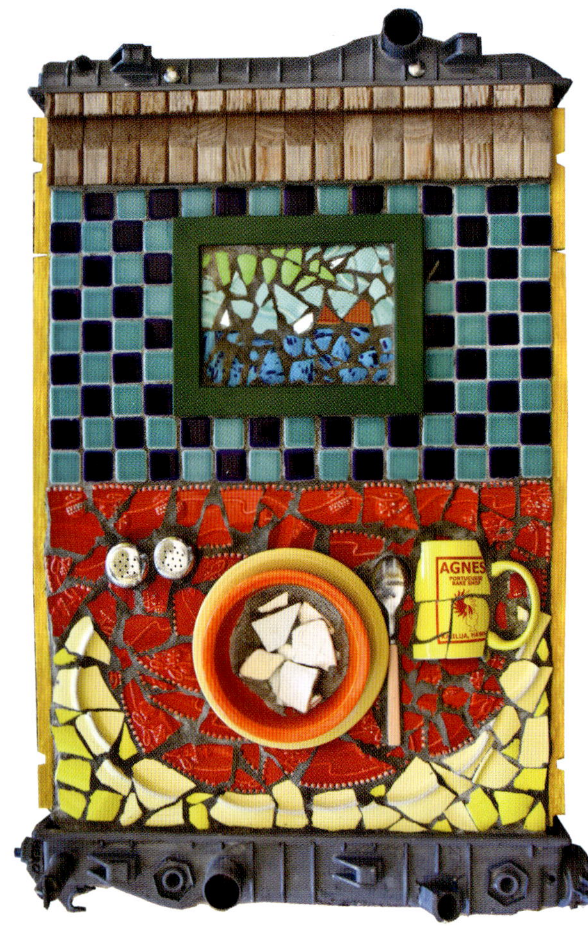

Gail Hercher. *Breakfast in Kailua*. 2010. Car radiator with *pique assiette*. 20" x 36".

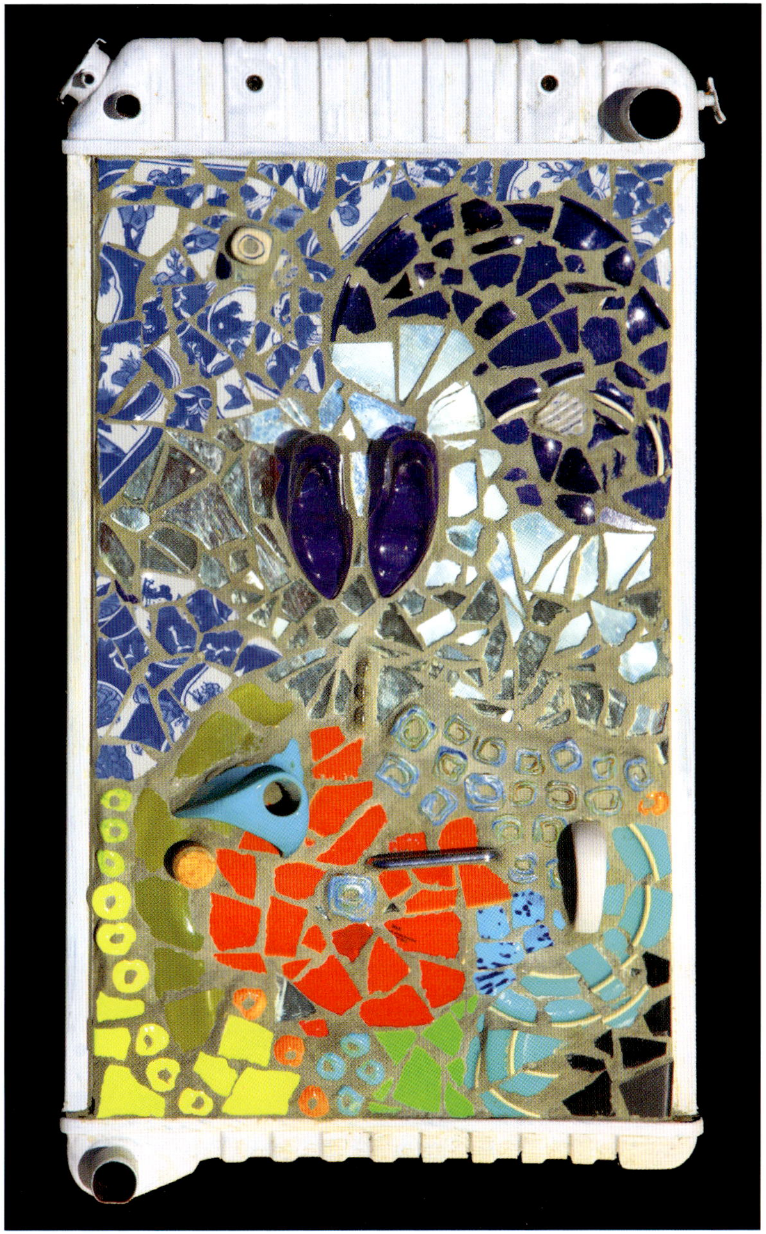

Gail Hercher. *Entering the City*. 2010. Car radiator with *pique assiette*. 20" x 36".

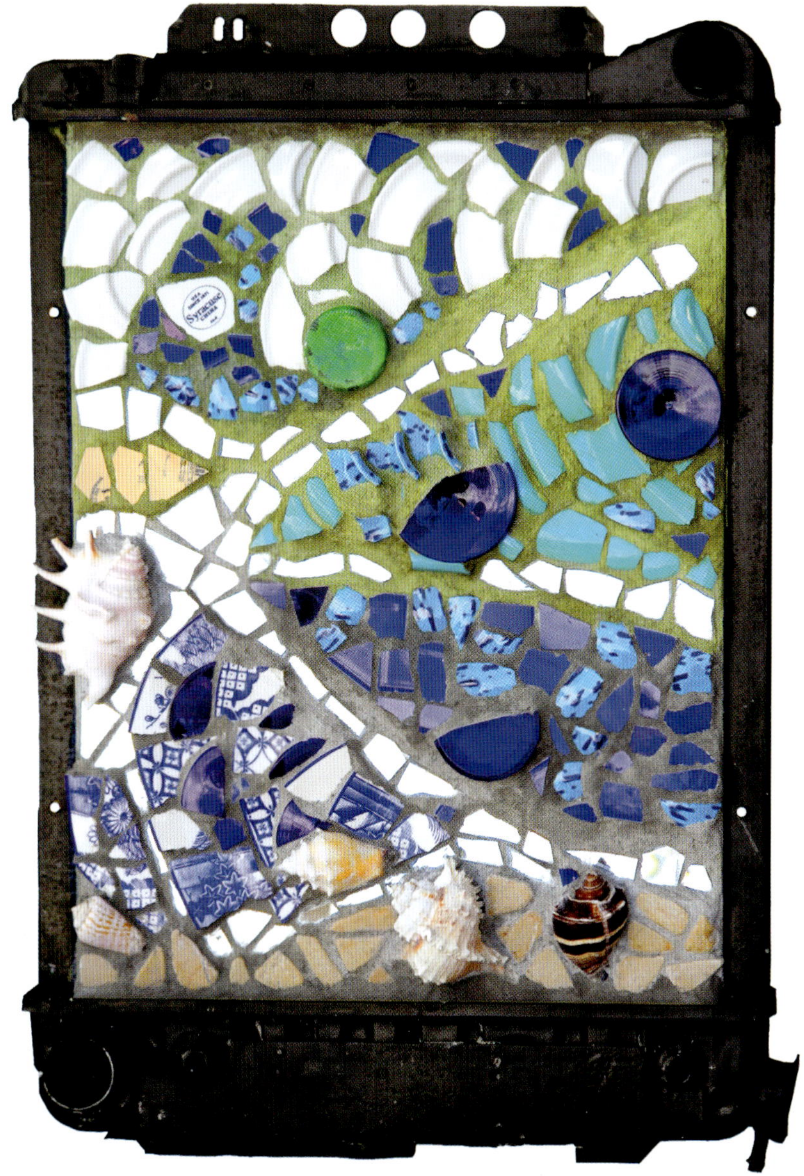

Gail Hercher. *Ocean & Sky*. 2010. Car radiator with *pique assiette*. 20" x 36".

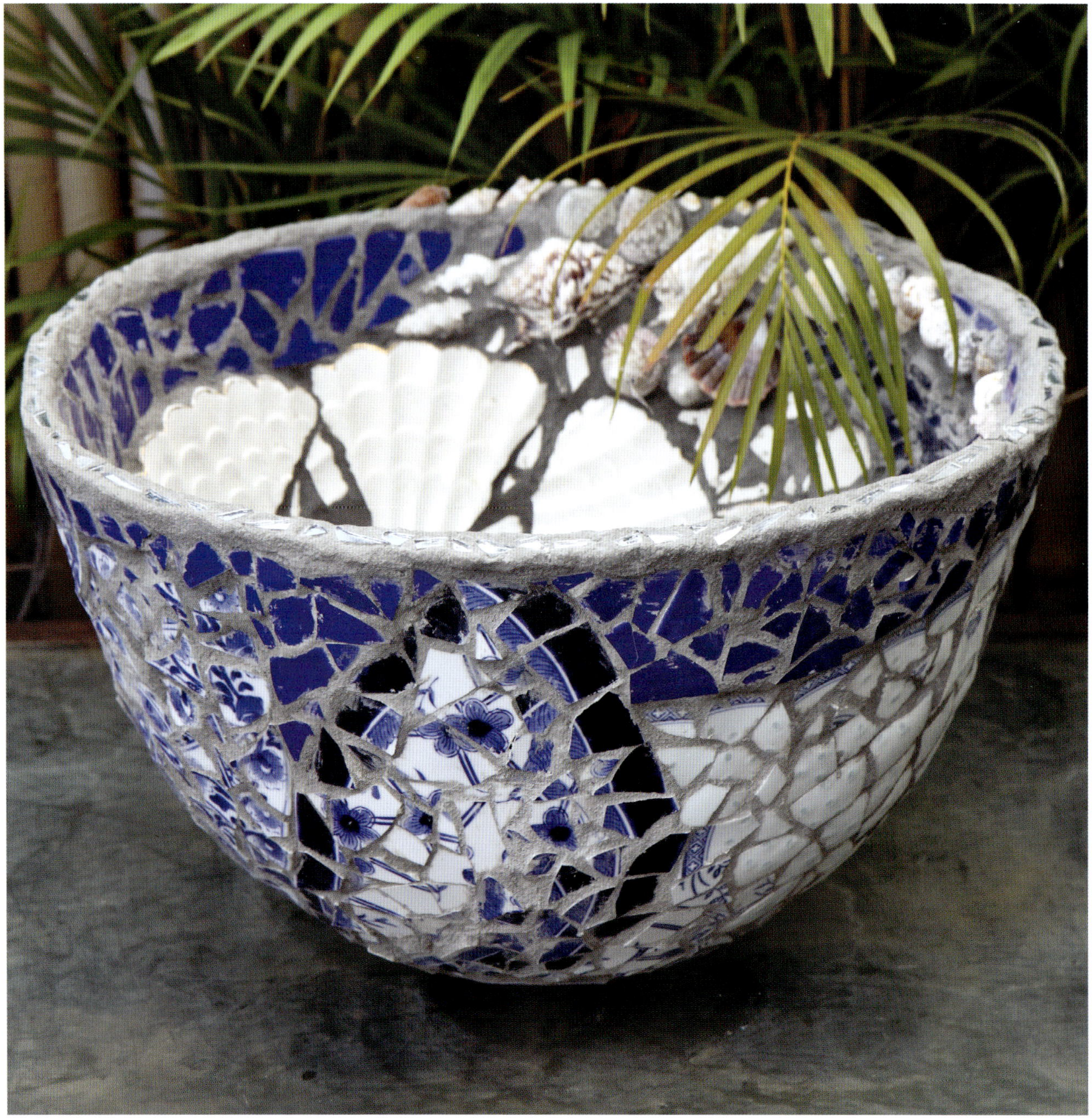

Gail Hercher. *Large Koi Bowl*. 2010. Bowl with *pique assiette.* 22" x 18".

Pamela Irving

Melbourne, Australia

About the Artwork

Dreaming With Open Eyes: Luna Park is an iconic theme park and tourist attraction in Melbourne. It was built in 1912 and has National Trust Classification due to its historic and cultural importance. This mosaic installation was completed in December 2010. It was commissioned by Melbourne's Luna Park Trust to celebrate Luna Park's 98th birthday. The work is located on the façade of the "Luna Palace" Building. The building is an original feature of the Park. The inside of the Luna Palace houses the Dodgem cars and Penny Arcade.

The work is made from recycled china, dinnerware and vitreous tiles. The substrate is a combination of cement sheeting, wire, concrete, and fiberglass. I work with a mapei adhesive system.

This mosaic installation is meant to induce a smile of delight in both the young and the aged. The work consists of large, giggly heads surrounded by many of my personal characters developed over years of working in clay, mosaic, and drawing. Many of the pieces utilize recycled ceramic objects. The character of a piece is often determined by the objects at hand.

My work is often described as quirky and playful. This work is a good example of this approach.

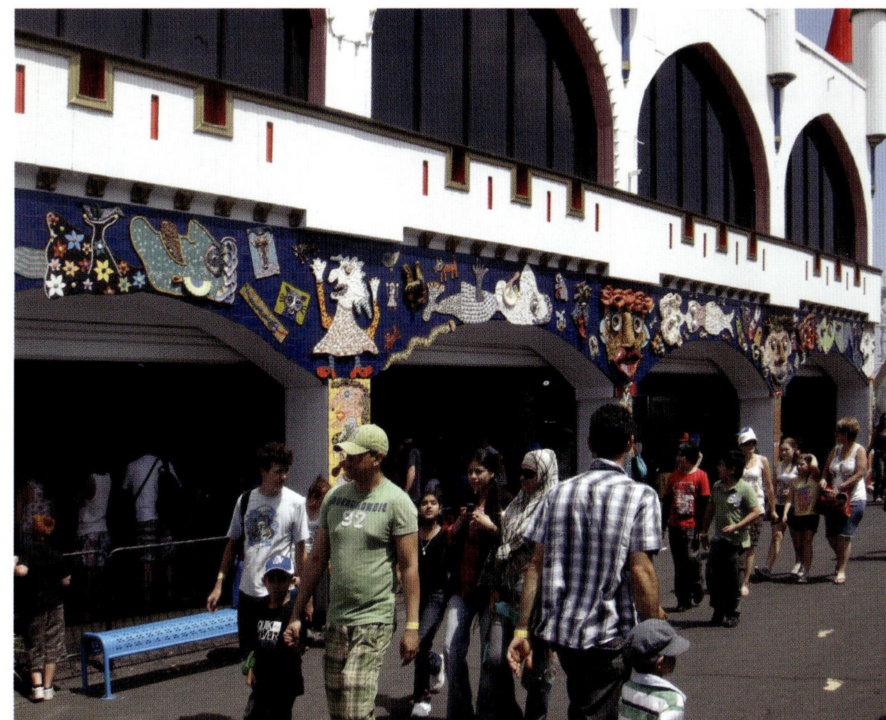

Pamela Irving. *Dreaming With Open Eyes*. Mosaic installation. (above and following two pages)

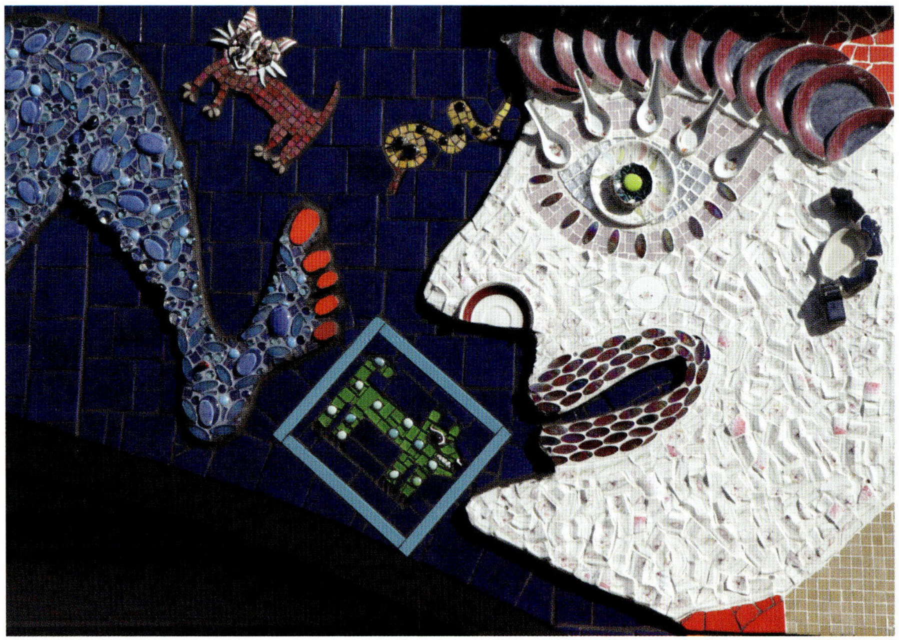

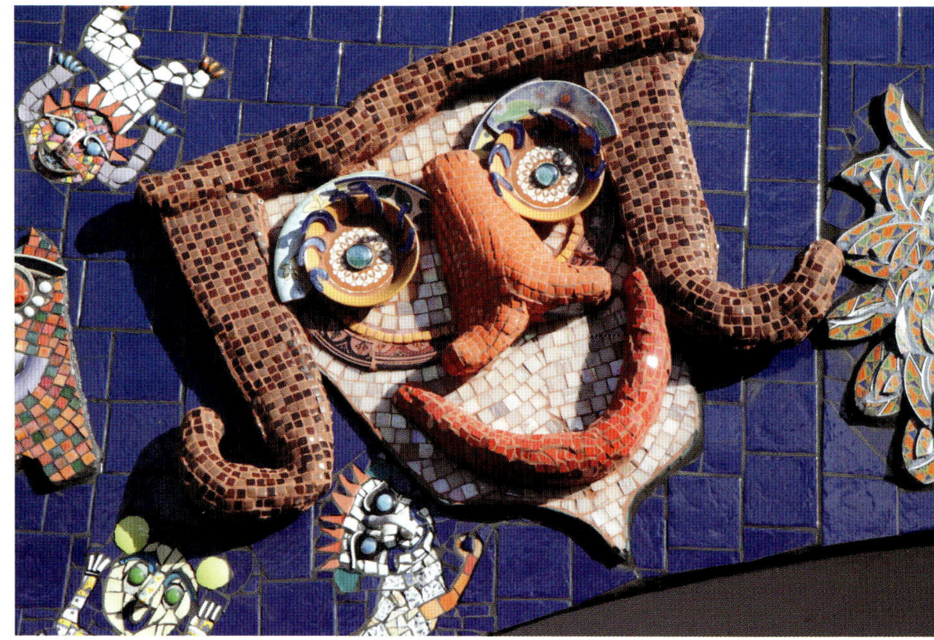

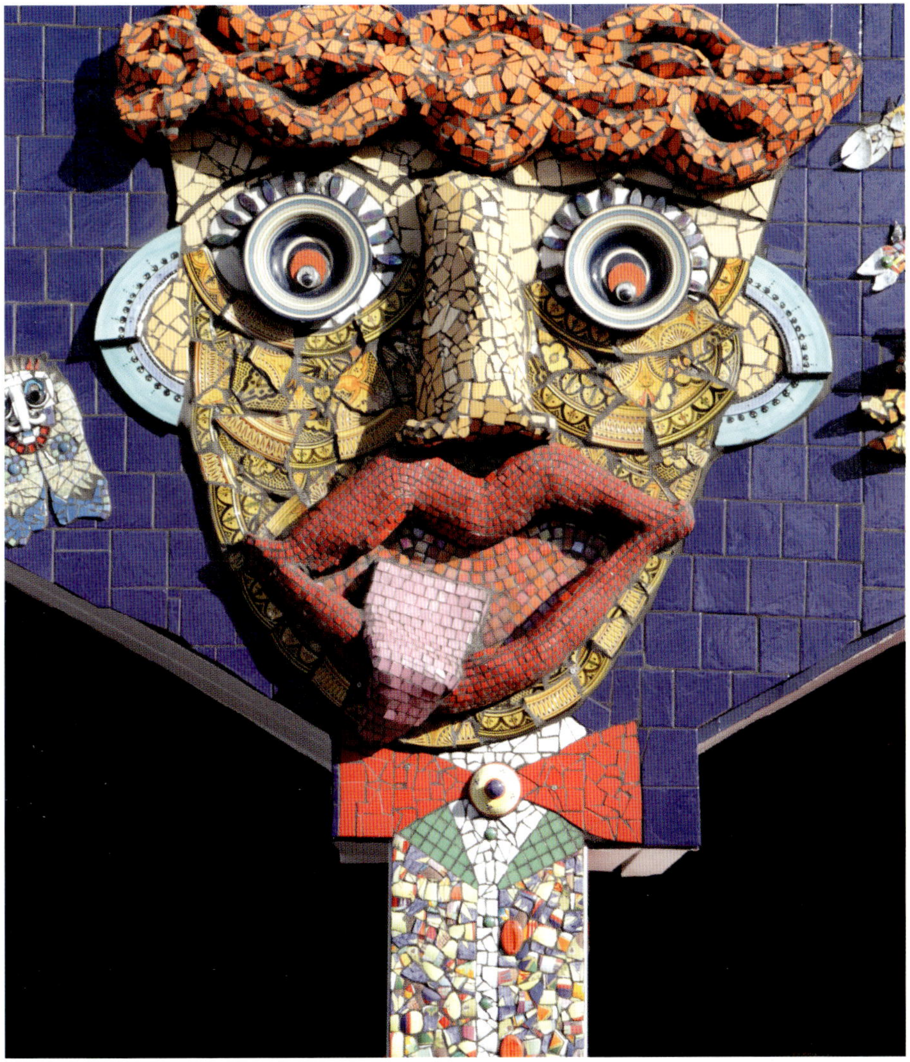

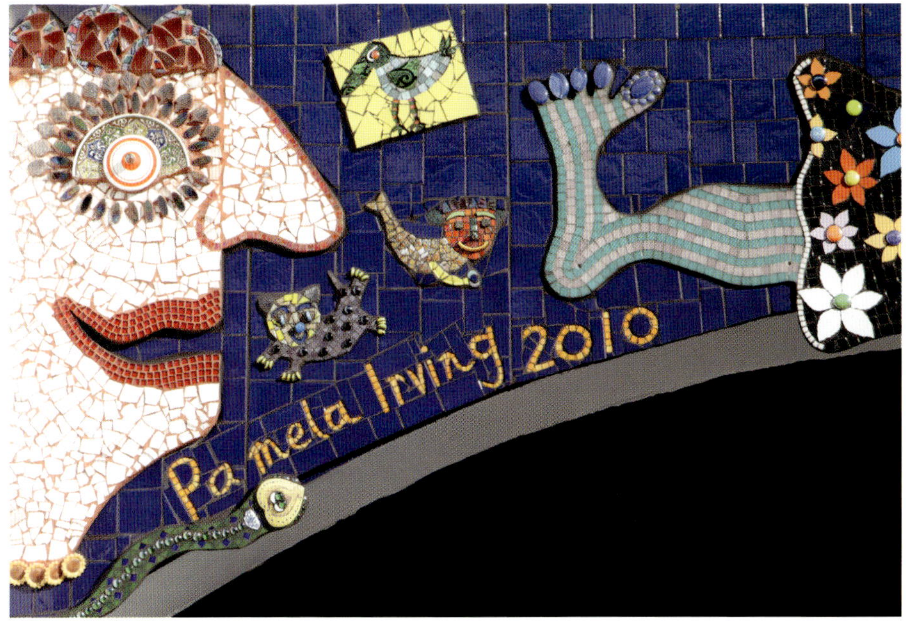
Pamela Irving 2010

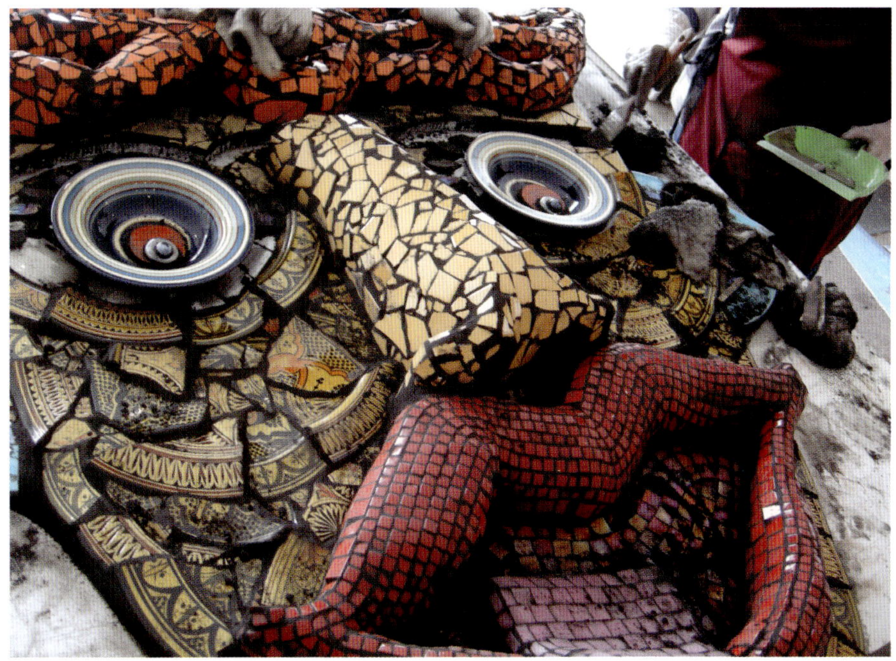

Minal Jeswani

Redwood City, California, Minalsj@gmail.com

About the Artwork

Desert Rose is one of a series of mosaics called *Introspection. Desert Rose* grew out of the concept of impermanence. The life of a rose is fragile and fleeting. I deliberately chose to juxtaposition fabric with granite. Fabric is relatively impermanent and fragile in comparison with granite. Line, color, and shape form an integral part of this composition. Working with different materials keeps me challenged and focused.

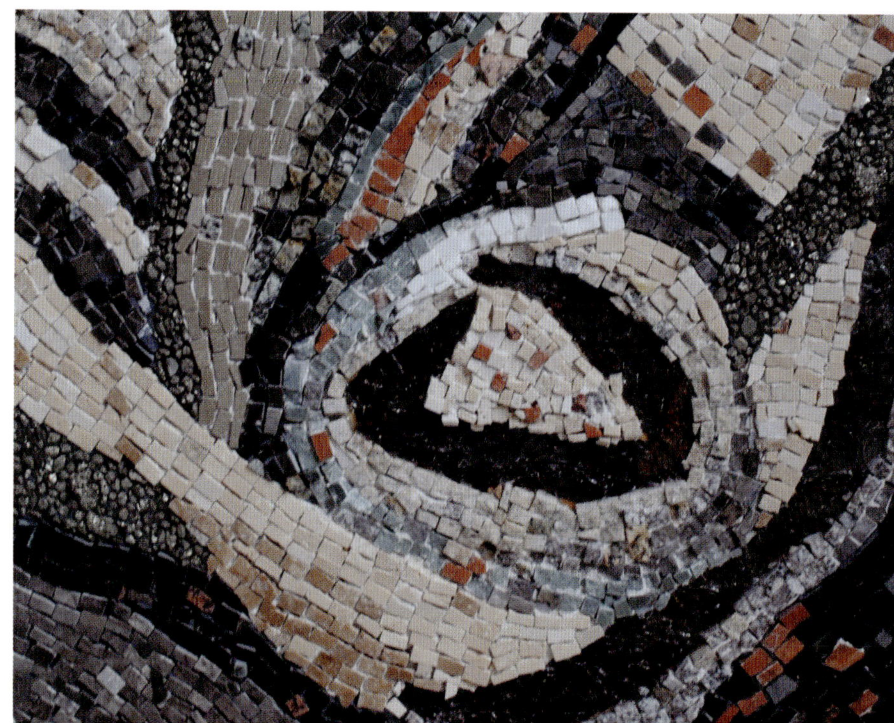

Minal Jeswani. *Desert Rose*. Mosaic. 16" x 20".

Rivers and Tides is one of a series of a body of work that I call "*introspection*." This mosaic was inspired by the idea of change. Just as the tides in the rivers are constantly changing and fluctuating, so is every moment of our lives. The waters of the rivers are constantly in motion, forever restless, ever searching; so is human nature, always in search of happiness.

Capturing movement was one of the goals of this mosaic. The colors are subtle and muted, with emphasis on line. Balance, rhythm, and repetition are some of the key design elements I focused upon when creating this mosaic.

Inner Landscape portrays various states of mind. The human mind has the capacity to remain calm or indulge in flights of fantasy, sometimes flights of terror. Thoughts are in constant flow. Occasionally there is a pause or gap between the thoughts, when the mind becomes quite and peaceful. I have tried to capture the essence of this calmness in *Inner Landscape*.

Some of the materials I have used are marble, granite, silk brocade, and safety glass.

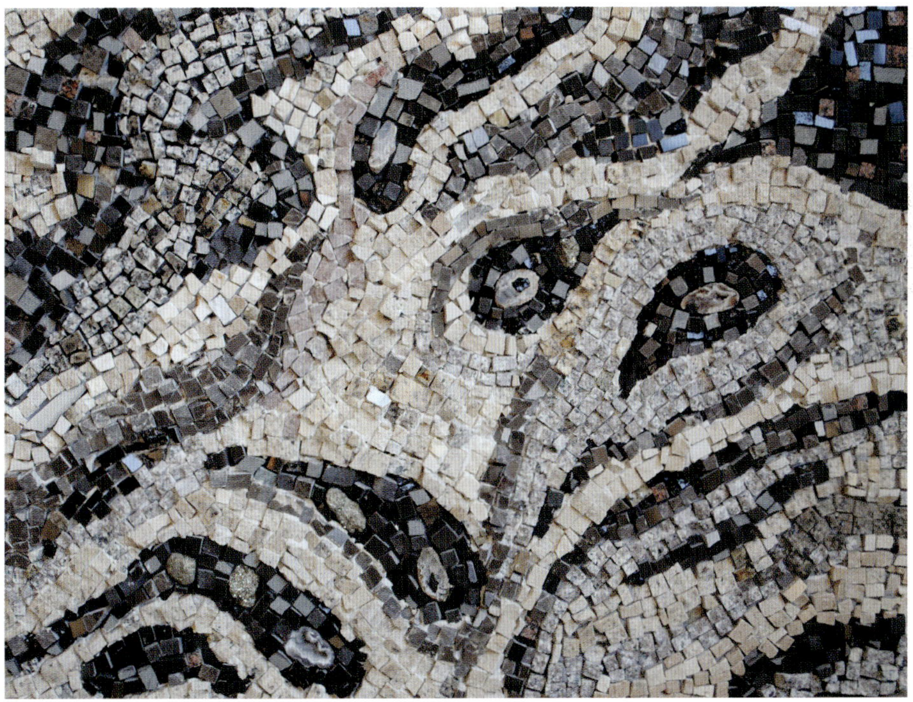

Minal Jeswani. *Rivers and Tides*. Mosaic. 18" x 24".

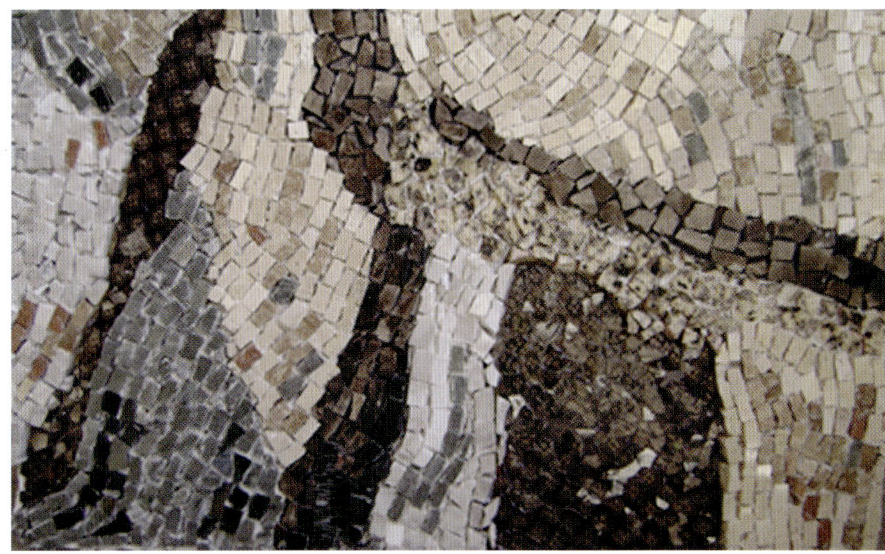

Minal Jeswani. *Inner Landscape*. Mosaic. 12" x 24".

Sands of the Desert was inspired by the deserts of our planet that sing. There are thirty five desert locations on earth that have recorded sands that sing, including Eureka and Kelso Dunes of the Mojave National preserve in California. The intent of this mosaic was to reflect the richness and the varied colors and textures of the desert sands and in some way to capture the haunting music of the desert sands.

Sands of the Desert is a celebration of earth's beauty and the many mysterious and unexplainable phenomena and wonder that we invariably experience when we come in close contact with nature.

Water portrays transparency. Water is fluid in its movements. Water can be muddy, blue, green or clear. Water has the capacity to absorb and reflect any color or surface it lays on. I used white pebbles, and blue sea glass, and gray marble to represent some of these traits. Water is a life sustainer, but it can also destroy lives. Water can be still or flowing. It can be liquid, solid or in the form of gas. Its properties never cease to amaze me.

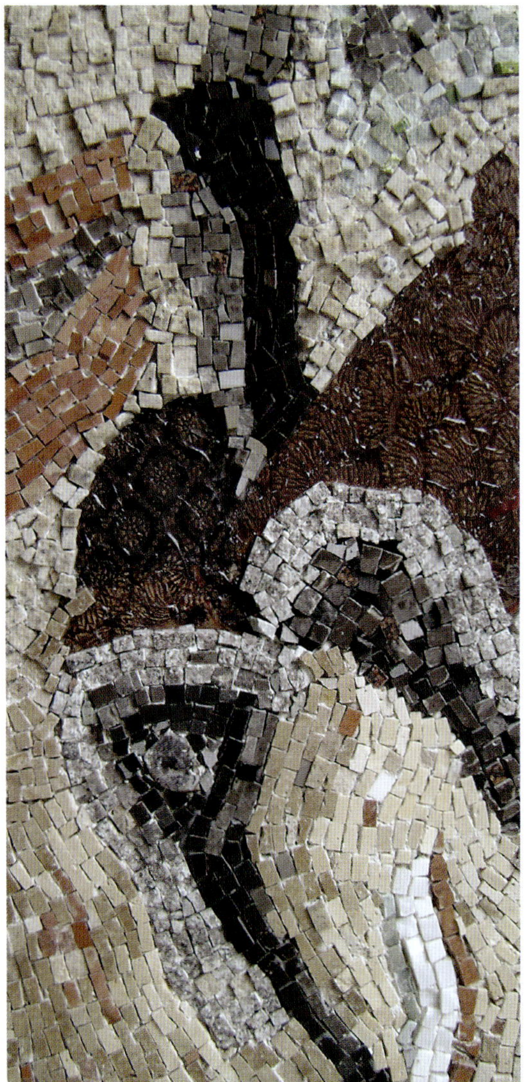

Minal Jeswani. *Sands of the Desert.* Mosaic. 24" x 12".

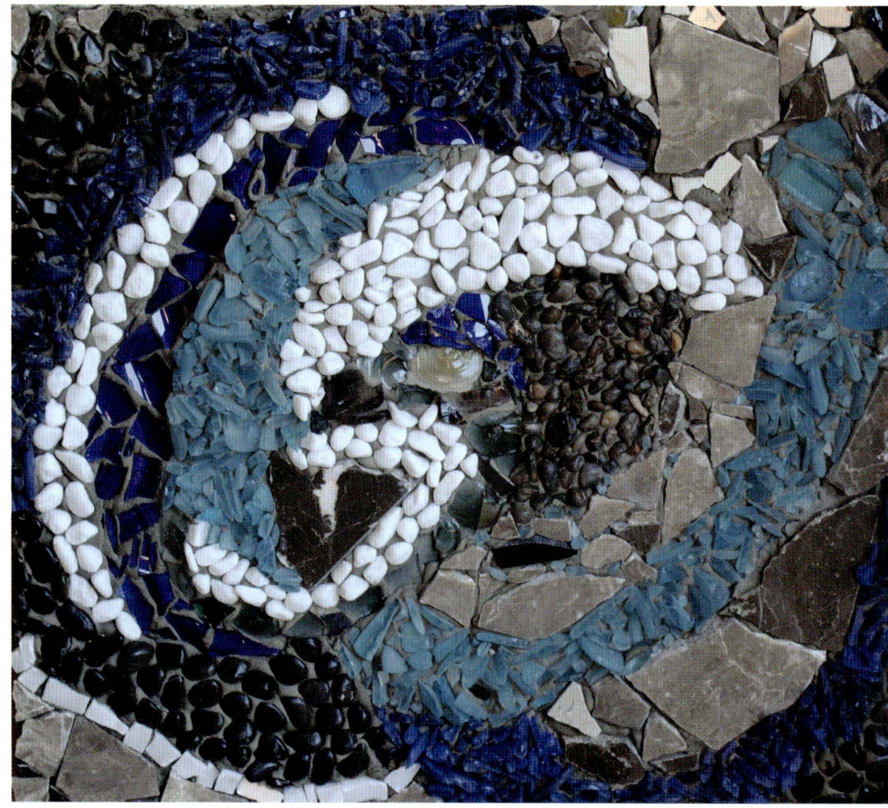

Minal Jeswani. *Water.* Mosaic. Pebbles, beach glass, marble, glass. 18" x 20".

Anju Jolly

DuBois, Pennsylvania, anjujolly@comcast.net

Artist's Statement

All of our lives are mosaics, fragments of experiences that come together to make us whole. As a mosaic artist I aim to bring my own fragments together—childhood in India, devotion to dance and music, adulthood in America, my faith, career as a professor, roles as wife and mother—into pieces that reflect how I live my life now. I make liberal use of vibrant colors and texture to capture the emotions of life being lived in dancers, in nature, in floral designs and in timeless themes. My hope is that as my audience experience images of my work, it may help them see life as a little more beautiful and enlightening.

In the beginning I plan my pieces with much precision but as the mosaic progresses, the objects, the colors, the shapes, and the motion in my pictures take on a life of their own, as if to help me discover the beauty in their symbiosis.

About the Artwork

I Love to Read: This mosaic is created on a piece of 1/2" birch wood sealed with three coats of wood sealer. It was then strengthened at the back with metal strips. The mosaic was done on "No Days" mesh and then glued with a thin set mortar. The mosaic has six different colors of grouts. It weighed about 38 pounds, and was hung with a metal cleat.

This picture is designed to look like a picture book illustration. The clients wanted a multi-cultural piece where children look excited about reading. So the central picture consists of five children each with a distinct appearance yet friendly. The toughest part was to show excitement on children's faces and also provide them a personality. I found that the eyes are at the heart of any facial expression.

Also, generally when making a tree, one makes the branches first and then the leaves. Here instead I spread the leaves out first, and then added tiles to give it branches. Being that the piece was three feet wide, I had to create the tree from the top side working backwards. (See following page.)

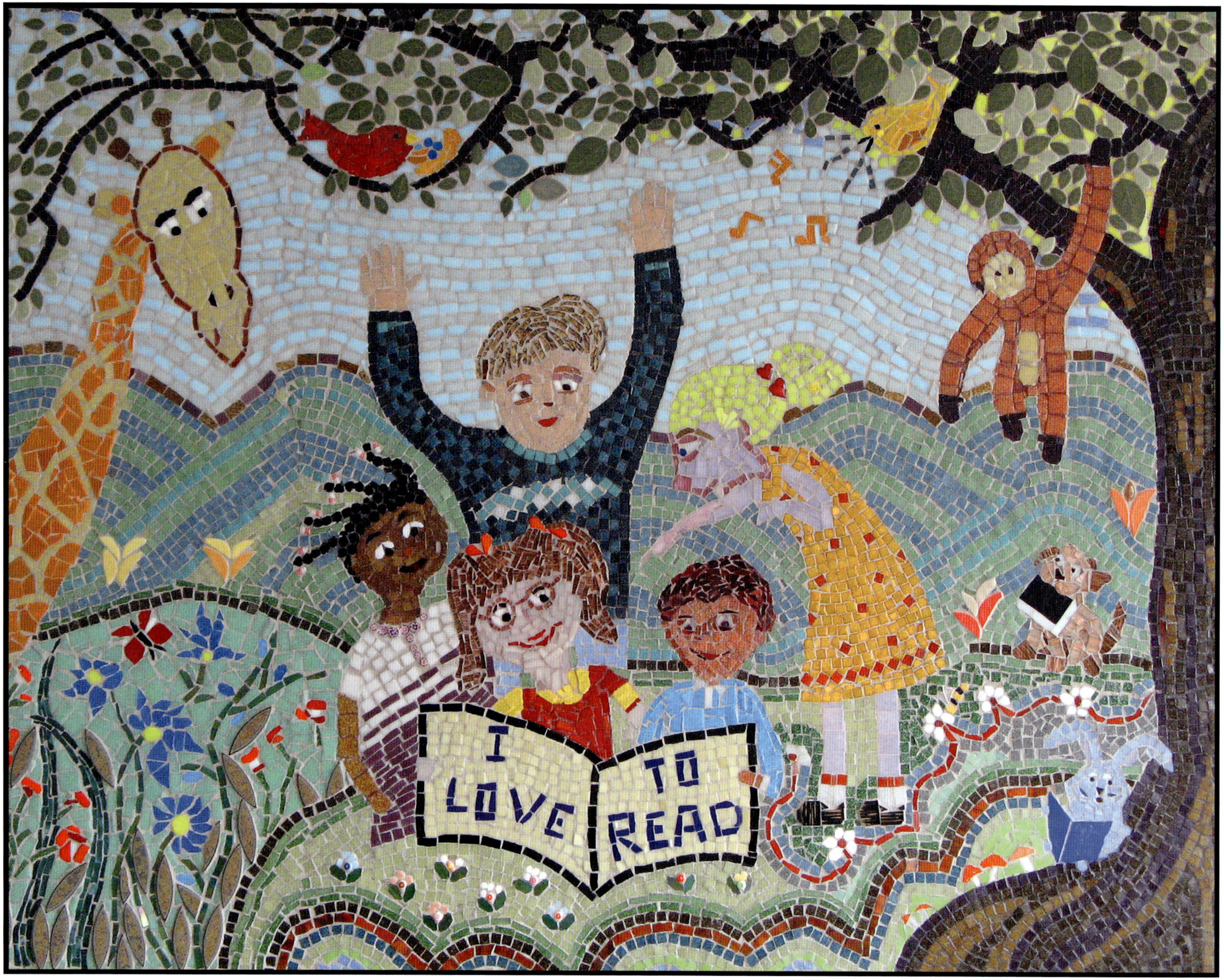

Anju Jolly. *I Love to Read*. Vitreous tiles, glass tiles, stained glass, ceramic tiles, and beads. 3' x 4'. A cluster of five children reading a book surrounded by animals. This is a commission made for a children's library. *Photo by Anju Jolly*

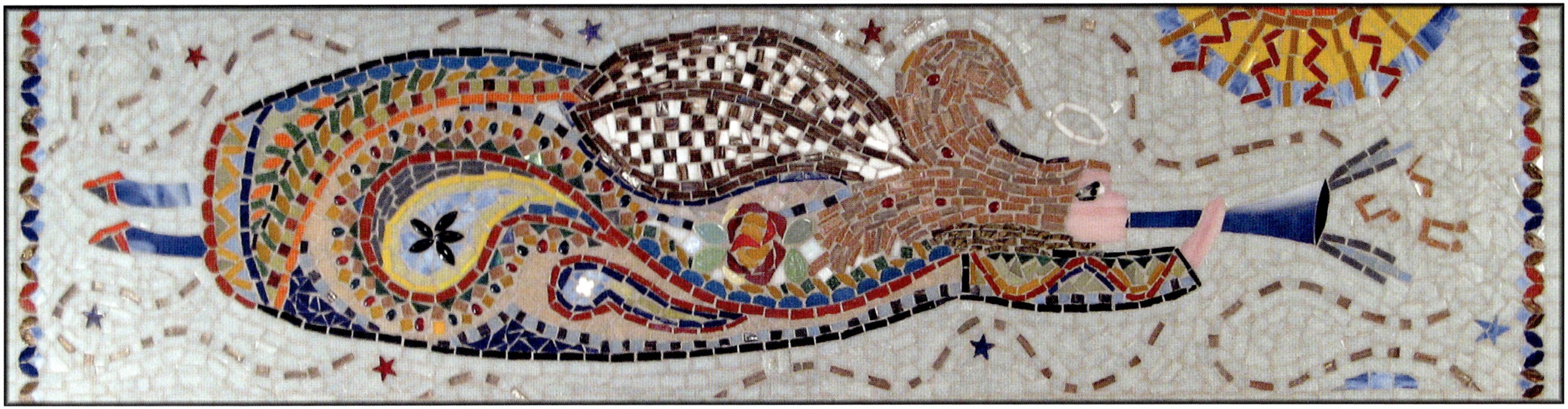

Sophie (Angel): This is a very special commission piece because making it was a journey in discovering my creative process. Prior to this piece, my mosaic drawings began with a cartoon and I simply filled in the spaces in the cartoon with tiles as attractively as I could. For this piece, however, I started with a very nebulous drawing of an angel and decided to allow the details of the picture to emerge as I added layers of colors working with the curves of the lines. The beauty of mosaics is in the details but I did not want to preplan the details, rather weave them as I went along. I discovered a rhythm in weaving those details in. Two steps forward and then a step backward, followed by three steps forward and then two steps backward and so on. I also learned that with careful use of solid and contrasting colors one can achieve movement and that lines and the boundaries between the lines have the power to express emotion, a joyous one in this case.

Half way through the mosaic, I felt compelled to call her Sophie. Later I was surprised and delighted to find out that the client's, for whom the commission was made, grandmother's name was Sophie.

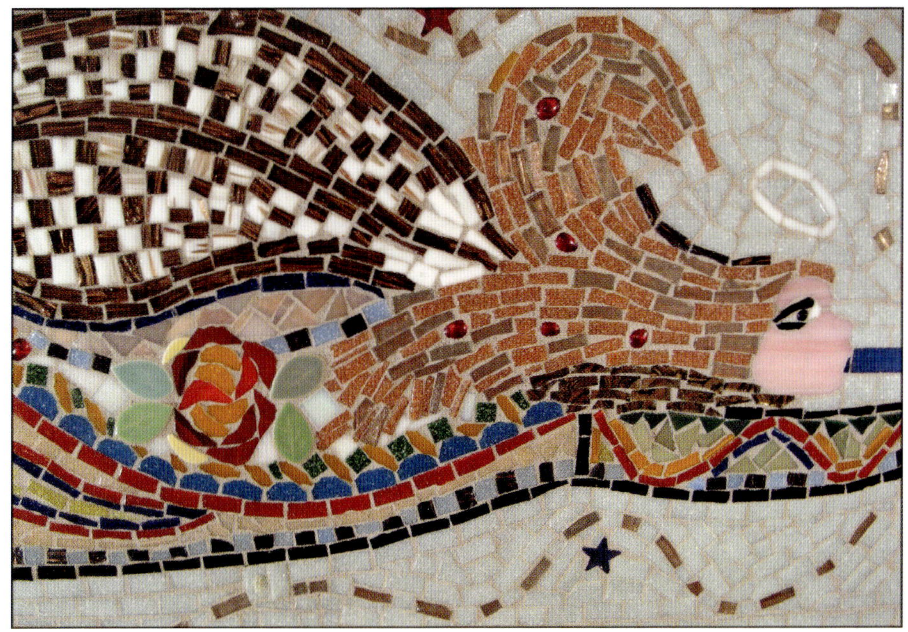

Anju Jolly. *Sophie (Angel).* Vitreous tiles, glass tiles, stained glass, ceramic tiles, and beads. 13" x 52" piece created to be installed above a fire place. *Photo by Anju Jolly*

Sonia King

Dallas, Texas, sonia@mosaicworks.com

Artist's Statement

Mosaic is hard. Art is harder. Mosaic's constant interplay between intellectual stimulation and the tactile pleasure of shaping and placing each piece keeps me in the studio. It's up to me and my ability to master the materials and create a work that captures something elusive. I'm fascinated with an altered view of the earth, landscapes both familiar and unreal. The illusion and contradiction fascinate me: Is this a slide under a microscope or an image from outer space? I work with a complex mix of materials using the tesserae, interstices, and andamento to create environments that are complex and serene, positive and negative. Much happens in the "spaces between," just as much of life is in the gaps. It's like trying to hear the silence between musical notes, straining to catch what I have no evidence exists.

Technically, I'm exploring two challenges with the goal of intensifying the viewers' experience. One is creating a sense of serenity from a complex blend of varying materials, shapes, spaces, scale, and reflectivity. The second involves reducing mosaic to its purest expression, freeing the elements to interact tessera-to-tessera.

I work to create art that demonstrates the power of my personal expression: heart and soul and emotion; art that can only be created at this particular point in my artistic journey; art that has the power and impact resulting from the intense and intimate struggle between the medium and my vision. The work is engrossing, consuming and challenging and I wouldn't do anything else.

About the Artwork

Nebula Chroma is the focal point of the new multi-story, main lobby at Children's Medical Center of Dallas, one of the largest pediatric healthcare providers in the United States. The dynamic mosaic mural has multiple viewing points across the light-filled, three-story circular atrium and from the stairs to the cafeteria.

My goal was to create a dramatic and engaging expression of contemporary mosaic art that would appeal to viewers of all ages, remain pleasing for caregivers and families after multiple viewings and, most importantly, offer a moment of pleasure during possibly stressful times. Plus the artwork had to integrate seamlessly into the dramatic architectural setting of the hospital's main lobby.

The visual impact of *Nebula Chroma* intensifies from the unexpected juxtapositions of one tessera next to another, interacting in multiple ways: color, scale, texture, reflectivity, and more. Over 200 different materials were used to create the complex "nebula." They float on a rhythmic background enhanced by my hand-colored "fresco grout" technique that I developed on a set of earlier walls for Children's Medical Center. The shifting colors add depth and visual stimulation while natural light from the three-story glass wall and the ceiling's fiber optic "stars" play off the varying levels of reflectivity.

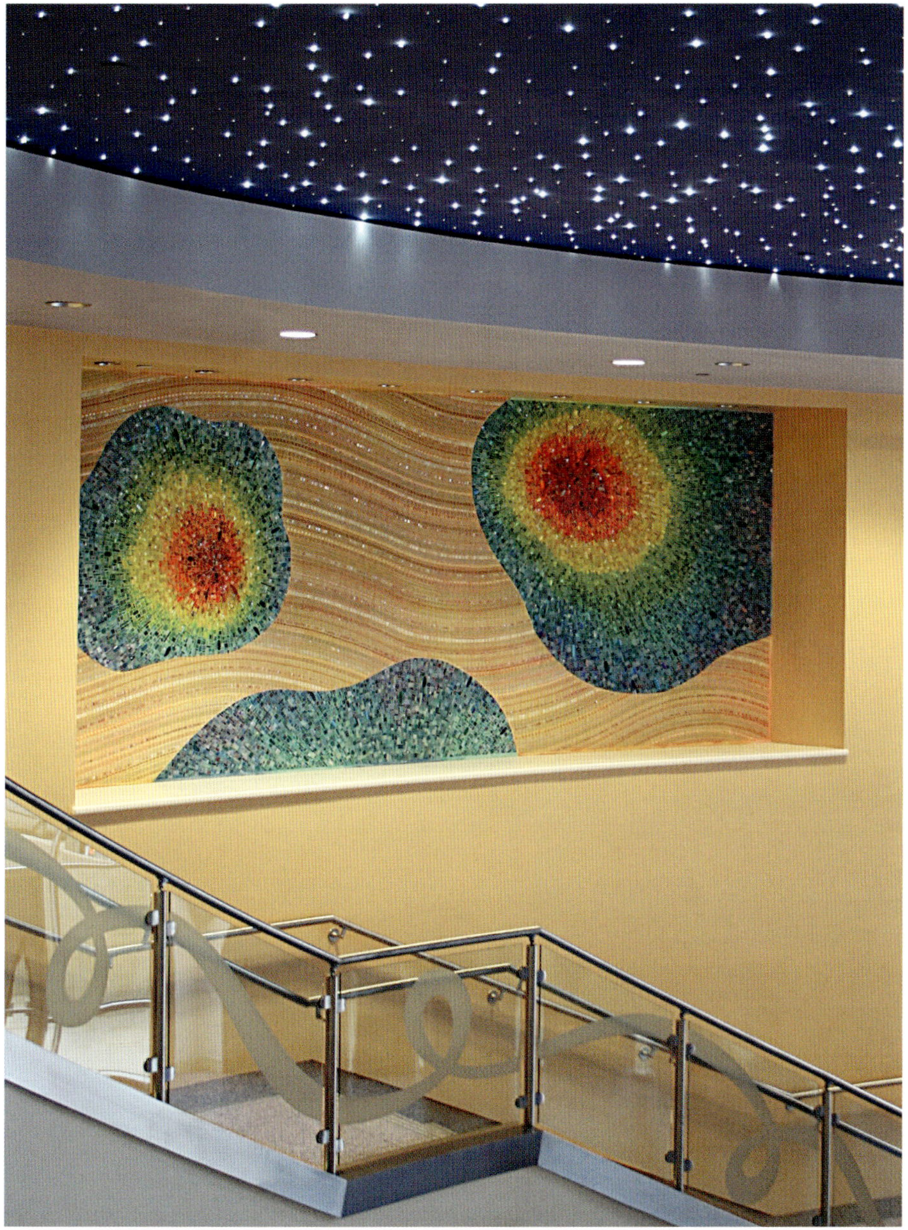

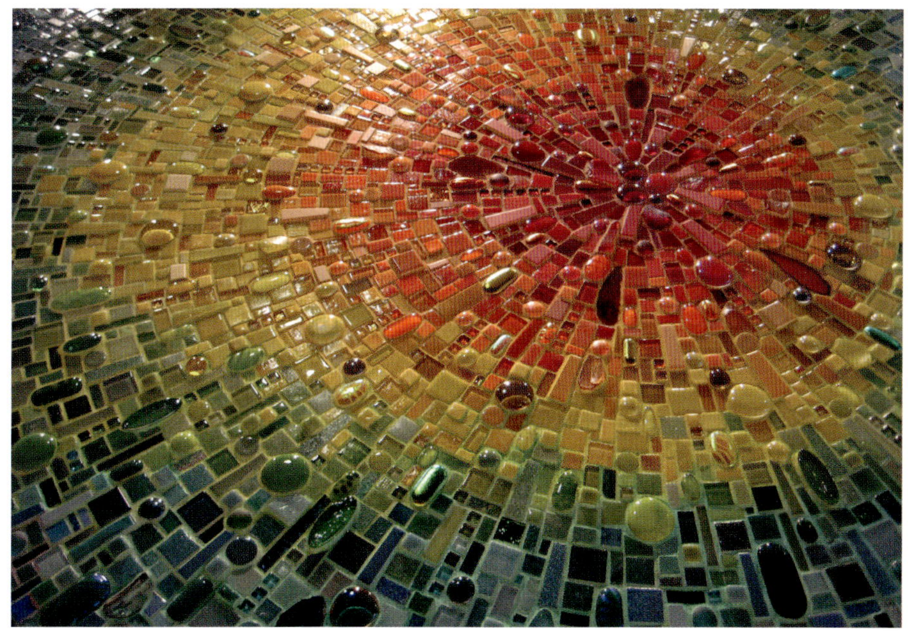

Sonia King. *Nebula Chroma*. Mosaic architectural installation for the main lobby of Children's Medical Center of Dallas. 2008. Glass, ceramic, agate slices, marble gems, dichroic glass fusions, shell. Double-direct onto mesh. 8' x 17'. *Images by Sonia King*

Nebula Aqua is a site-specific, mosaic installation in a private home. The project offered the opportunity to explore eliminating the constraints and arbitrary boundaries imposed by framed work. Using the stucco as "background" and playing with positive/negative space concentrates the impact of the mosaic elements and focuses the viewers' experience of the art. The mosaic elements were created in the studio on mesh and later installed directly onto the wall. Because the edges of the mosaic "nebulae" are critical to the illusion of the floating elements, the artist developed techniques for installation that maintained a perfect edge, even over the textured stucco. The mosaic integrates a huge range of materials in a limited color palette, emphasizing the relationships and interstices between the tesserae. During the day, natural light from the skylights shows off the texture and various reflective qualities of the materials. At night, *Nebula Aqua* glows, radiating an unworldly attraction. Developing a way to create, mount, and edge the independent mosaic elements allows me to transition my artistic expression into larger settings.

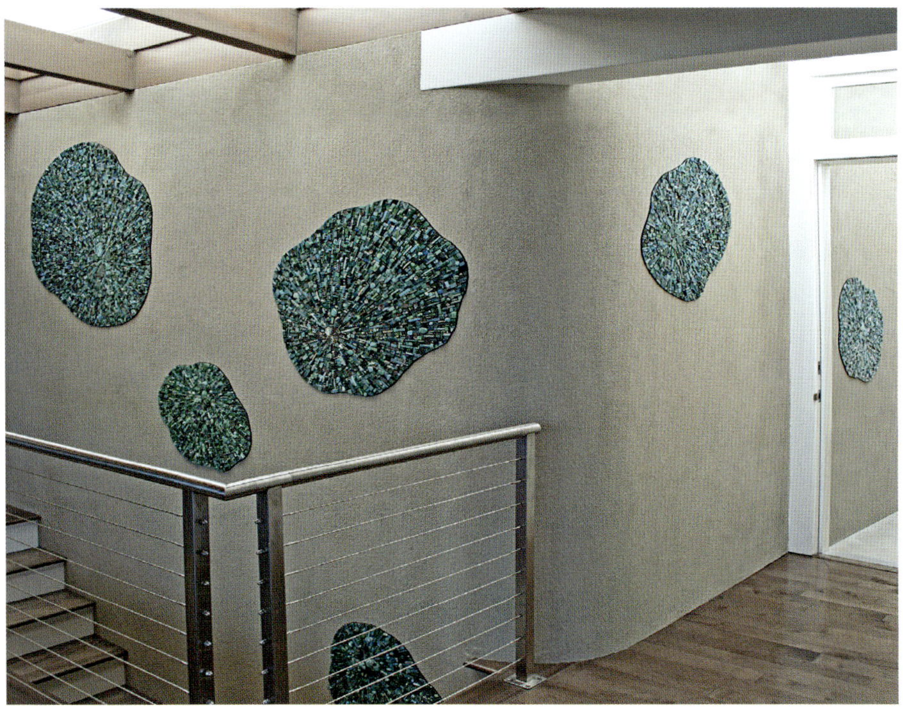

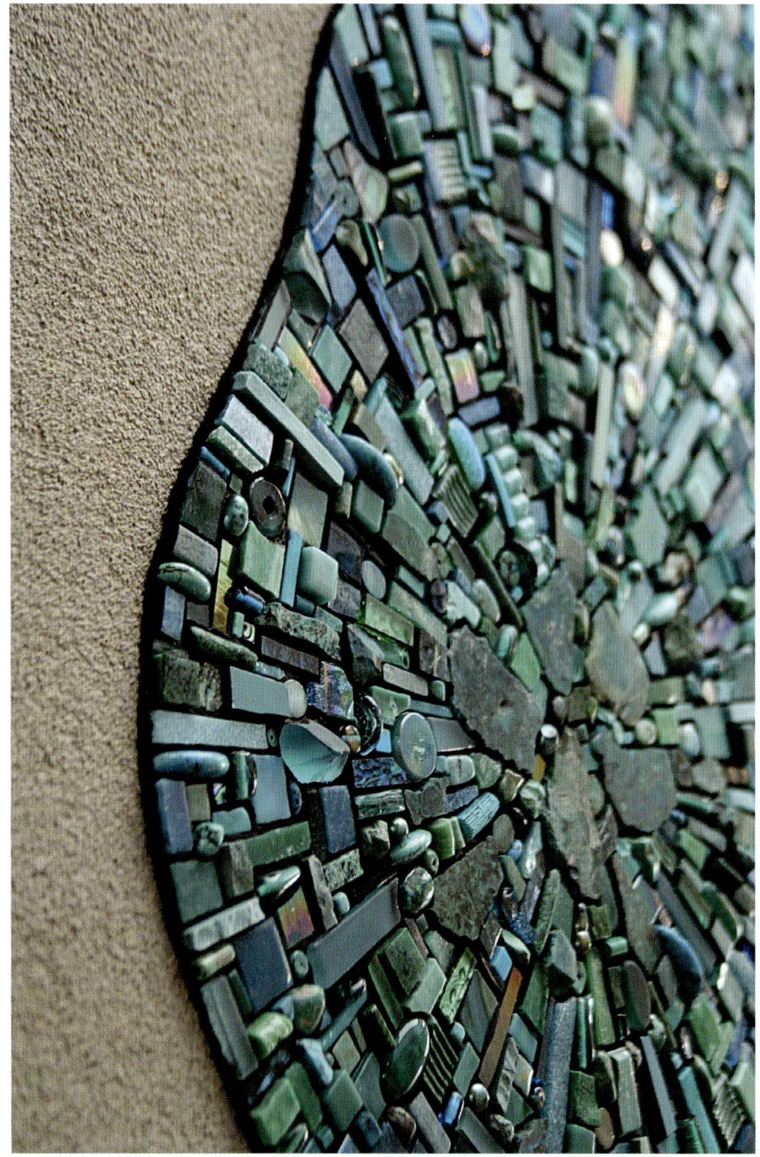

Sonia King. *Nebula Aqua*. Mosaic architectural installation for a private residence. 2009. Glass, ceramic, Paua shell, golds, smalti, turquoise, malachite, labradorite, pebbles, chrysocolla, crystals, pearls, beach glass, amazonite, stainless steel, abalone. Double-direct into cement-based adhesive. 15' x 25'. *Image by Sonia King*

Permafrost creates a world that doesn't exist, a cold world that evokes ice floes drifting in the Arctic, galaxies moving through space or perhaps microscopic life forms breaking free. The juxtaposition of precious stones, gold, and pearls interspersed between recycled scraps of ceramic, glass, abalone, and more continually offers differing views with multiple points of interest, creating endless interactions.

Permafrost takes a wide variety of materials into the third dimension, draping light and shadow, matte and shiny, smooth and irregular tesserae over an undulating, hand-formed substrate. It was a challenge to create a deceptively calm and tranquil work from a complex mix of materials, laid in a complex way. Each new tessera changed the rhythm, attracting and repelling other materials. Additionally, the difficulty of keeping the illusion of a background smoothly rolling across complex curves increased with the choice of opus palladianum, or crazy paving, as the laying style. As one side of a tessera shifted up, the other end tipped down and that happened in multiple directions at the same time. Working became a process of thinking backwards and forwards at the same time, remaining open to what the materials were communicating, judging the consequence of each added piece and balancing the tension between aesthetic and technical considerations.

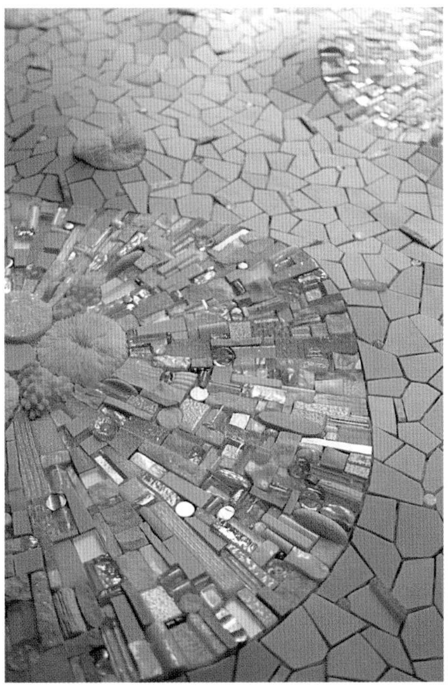

Sonia King. *Permafrost*. 3-D wall hanging. 2009. Glass, ceramic, coral, white gold, smalti, quartz, silver, marble, rock crystal, seashell, pearls, aluminum, selenite, abalone, pebbles. Direct over hand-formed, undulating surface. 24" x 18". *Image by Sonia King*

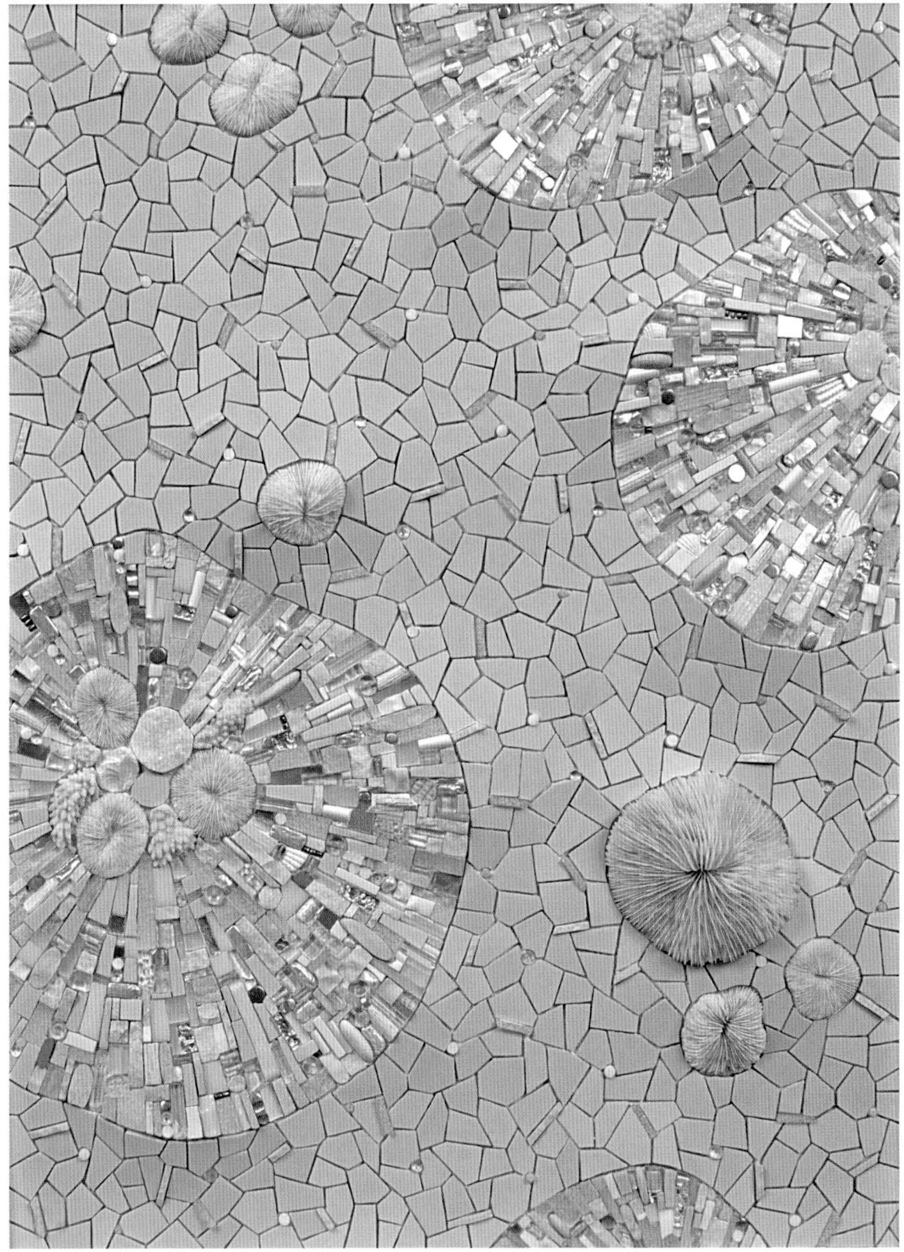

Outlier continues my quest to free the elements of mosaic to interact at the most basic level: tessera-to-tessera. I created a handmade, free form substrate to eliminate the arbitrary edge imposed by a frame. The substrate has a raison d'être of its own, establishing an environment for the mosaic elements. The rust-colored tesserae are presented without visible evidence of adhesion. The pieces rise and fall without apparent support, integrating shapes and textures freely in a dimensional way. I hope the viewers' experience of the artwork will be direct and focused.

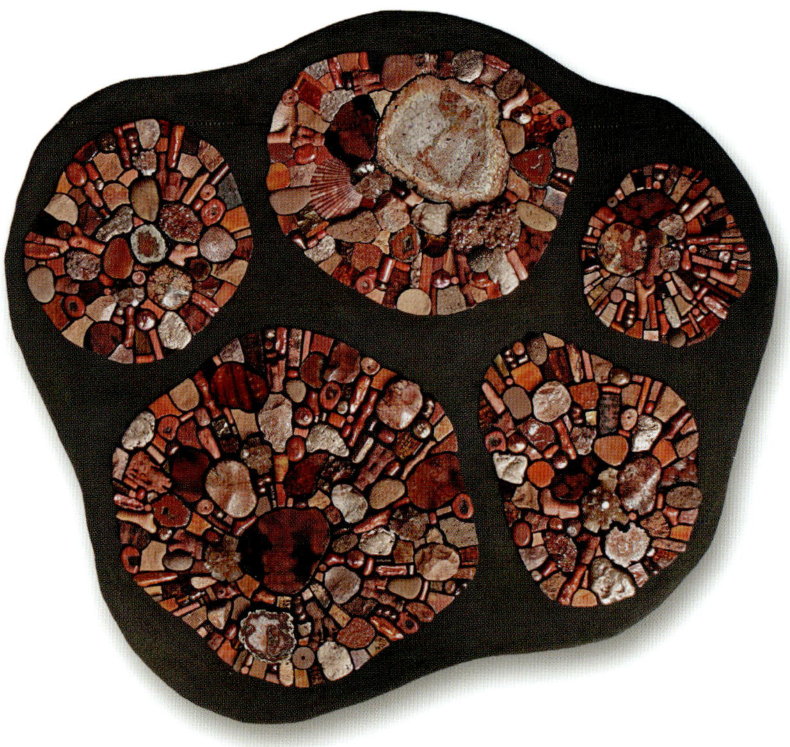

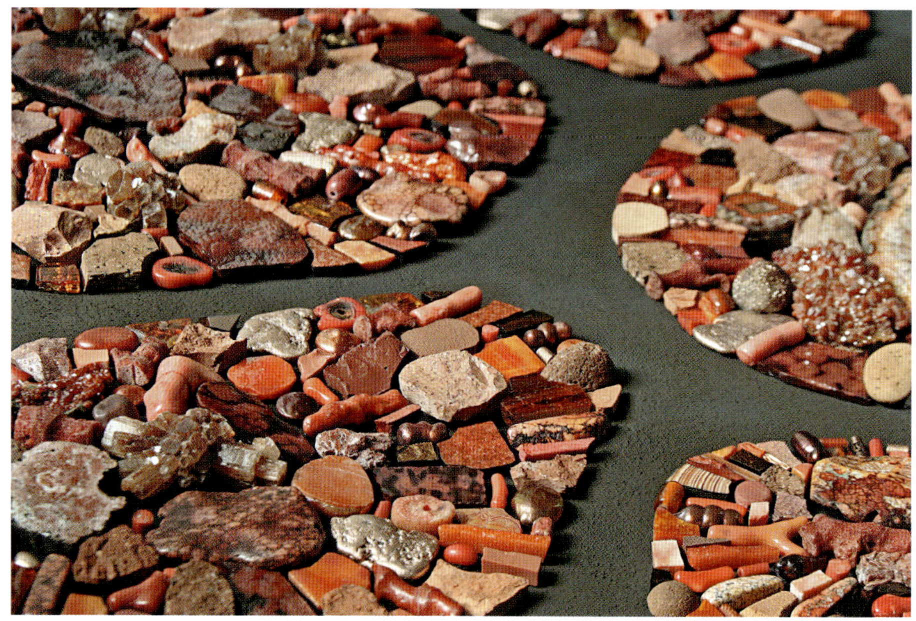

Sonia King. *Outlier.* 2-D wall hanging. 2009. Glass, ceramic, marble, copper, gold, aragonite, coral, citrine, petrified palm wood, magnesite, smalti, pearls, pebbles, terracotta, vanadanite, seashells, bone, pumice, rhyolite, raku pottery. Direct onto hand-formed substrate without visible evidence of adhesive. 18" x 22". *Image by Sonia King*

Coded Message 51423 is the first in a new series of work. I've been thinking about coded messages, secrets, cryptic communications, misunderstandings, unspoken thoughts, sounds of static, and undercurrents for a while. The neutral-colored tesserae are presented without visible evidence of adhesion. It seems possible that the pieces could reconfigure when one's back is turned and the message could change at any moment. The matte black tesserae form a subtext, perhaps expressing the real message. I hope each viewer will interpret the message in their own way, experiencing the work on their own terms and thinking about the tenuous hold and assumptions we make about communication.

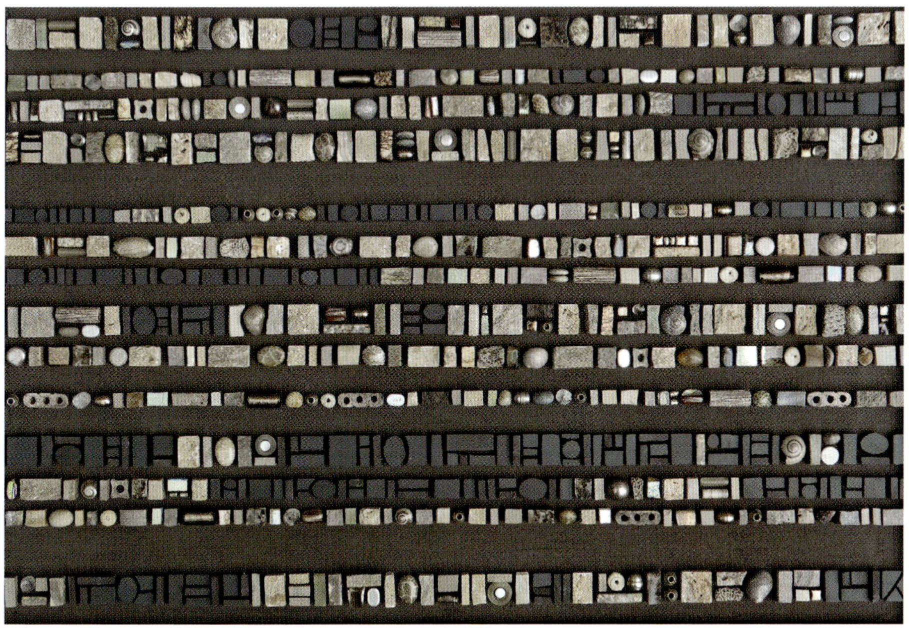

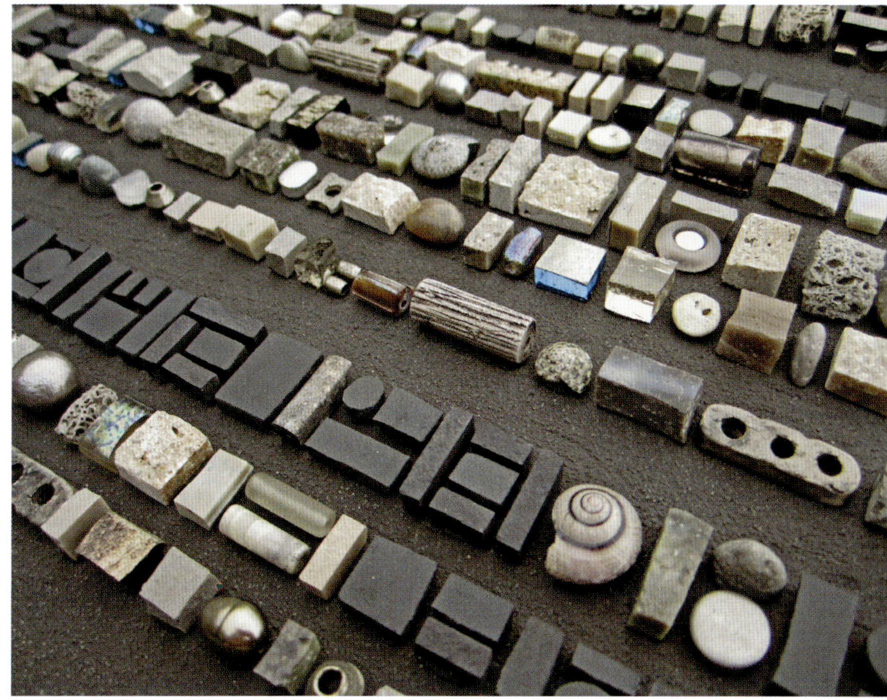

Sonia King. *Coded Message 51423.* 2-D wall hanging. 2010. Glass, ceramic, shells, golds, smalti, bone, jasper, fossils, pebbles, aluminum, laminate, pearls, metal, horn, coral, abalone. Direct without visible evidence of adhesive. 12" x 18". *Image by Sonia King*

Jonathan Mandell

Bala Cynwyd, Pennsylvania, fineartmosaics@aol.com

About the Artwork

Bar Scene: The majority of this mosaic (48" x 28") is created using ceramic tile. Various semiprecious stones and minerals were also used to embellish the imagery. Cosmopolitans are made using a combination of rose quartz and white quartz. Draft beers are pictured using either orange calcite or blue tiger-eye. The clothing of the patrons feature: turquoise, sodalite, chevron amethyst, unakite, turritella agate, blue lace agate, chrysocolla, and orange gneiss. The liquor bottles are made with Australian tiger-eye, leopardskin jasper, yellow jasper, red agate, pietersite, mookite jasper, ruby in zoisite, and picture jasper. The bar is made with a nickel tile and the serving trays and beer taps are made with a brass tile. The perspective used in the figures contrasts the flat lack of perspective in the floor. This flatness and the use of color allows the floor set a pulsating "bar scene" tone to the piece.

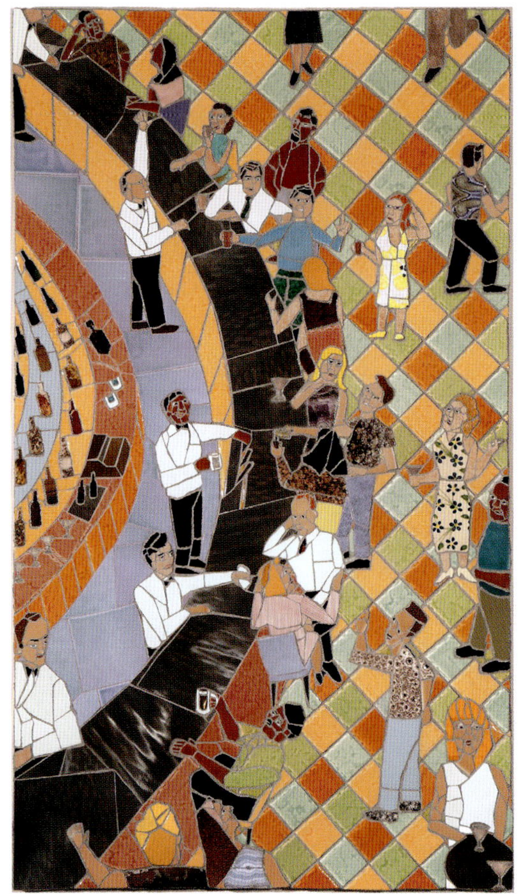

Jonathan Mandell. *Bar Scene*. Wall mounted mosaic. 2001. 48" x 24" x 2".

Citizens Bank Park: This 8' by 6' mosaic was commissioned by the Philadelphia Phillies organization as permanent artwork for the new Citizens Bank Park. The mosaic is located in the main concourse by section 125 (behind home plate). This mosaic is made with a range of semiprecious stones and minerals along with ceramic tile, glass, and metal. The sky is made from sodalite (blue) with a white calcite matrix. Additionally there is blue quartz mixed in the sodalite. The fan vision tower is made with sodalite as the sky. Snowflake obsidian (volcanic glass) is used to represent the scoreboards. The Coke sign to the left is made with leopardskin jasper and rose quartz. Beneath this is a piece of marble representing an advertising sign. To the right there are three stones used to depict a series of three signs. From bottom to top they are mookite jasper, leopardskin jasper and serpentine. Above this is a piece of white quartz which represents the light tower. To the right of the fan vision tower is a representation of the clock tower. This is made from spinel crystals in matrix (red crystals in black and white matrix). The advertising signs along the outfield wall are from left to right: howlite-white, red & gold jasper, aventurine-blue, hickoryite-red, white, and yellow. Next there is more snowflake obsidian to again depict the scoreboards. This is followed by crazy lace agate, and red brachiated jasper as the remaining advertising signs on the fence level. On the next tier up from right to left there is abalone as windowed boxes followed by rainbow fluorite, snowflake obsidian, and rainbow calcite silica as more advertising and score information. There is also abalone on the left side of the mosaic capturing more of the enclosed boxes. The hot dog vendor on the bottom right of the mosaic has a metal hot dog caddy made from nickel tile. His eyes are made from tiger eye and his hair is bronzite. Some of the fans in the bleachers above him have clothes made from blue lace agate, chevron amethyst (purple and white), thulite (pink), rhodonite (pink and black), and unakite (green and pink). The cotton candy vendor by the visitor's dugout has cotton candy made from rose quartz. The ball, which is approaching the outfield wall, is made from iridescent glass.

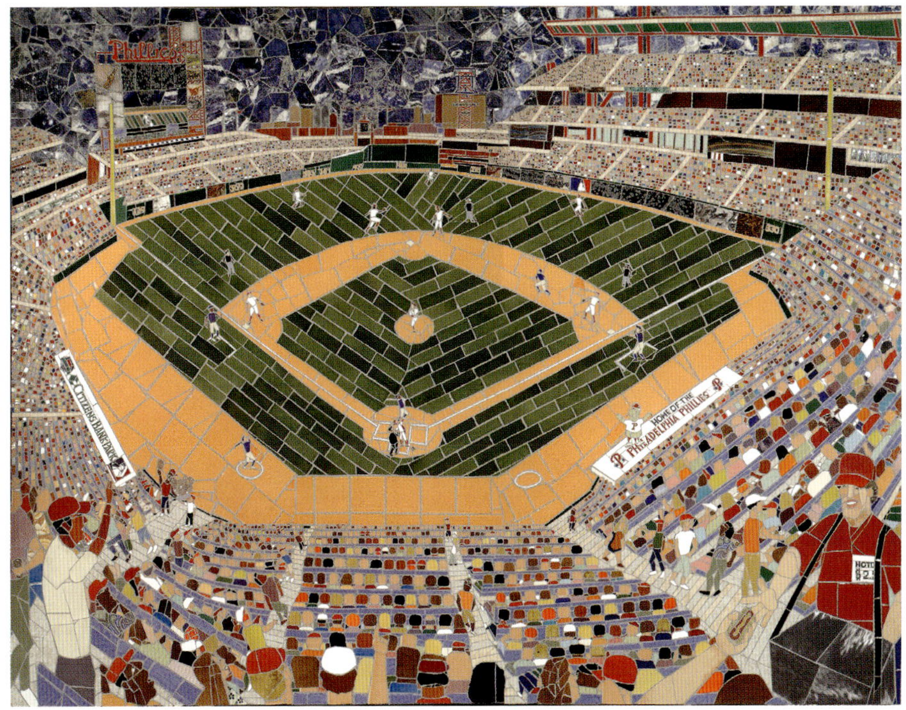

Jonathan Mandell. *Citizens Bank Park.* Wall mounted mosaic. 2004. 96" x 72" x 2".

Mountainscape with Flowers: This 38" x 30" x 3" mosaic is made using glass shards, which are gathered from broken vessels. The glass is convex and concave so it allows for topography to form over the surface of the mosaic. Additionally, various semiprecious stones and minerals are added to the mosaic to enliven the image. This mosaic features amethyst spheres, magnesite (burgundy) spheres, a rhodonite sphere (pink), howlite (white with gray veins), a banded red jasper sphere, and rose quartz. This mosaic features a nearscape of flowers with a vista mountain view in the distance.

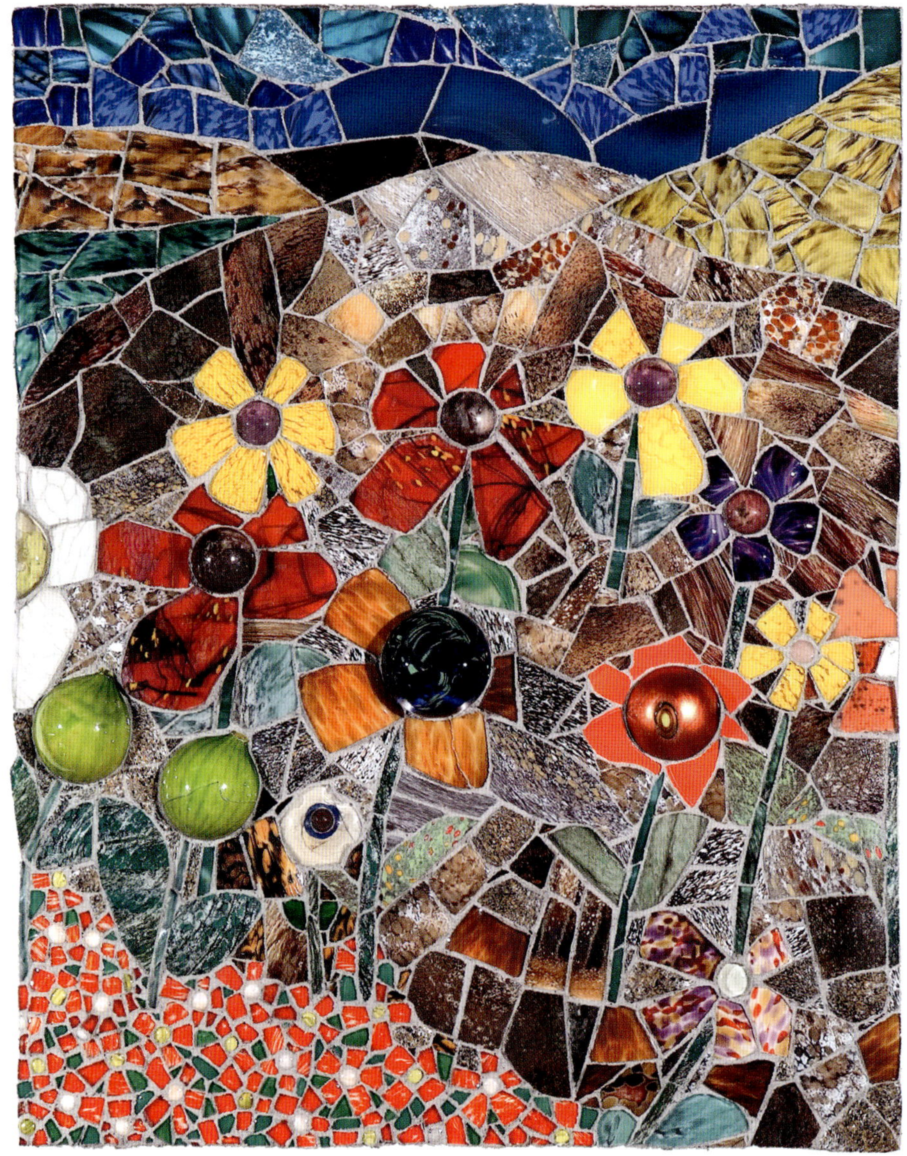

Jonathan Mandell. *Mountainscape with Flowers.* Wall mounted mosaic. 2006. 38" x 33" x 3".

Lost Highway: This 36" x 24" x 3" mosaic panel was made using ceramic tile, glass shards, and mirror. The grout joints act as drawing lines, creating a sense of depth. This mosaic was designed to be used as artwork for a wine label for Vine Street Importer's Lost Highway label.

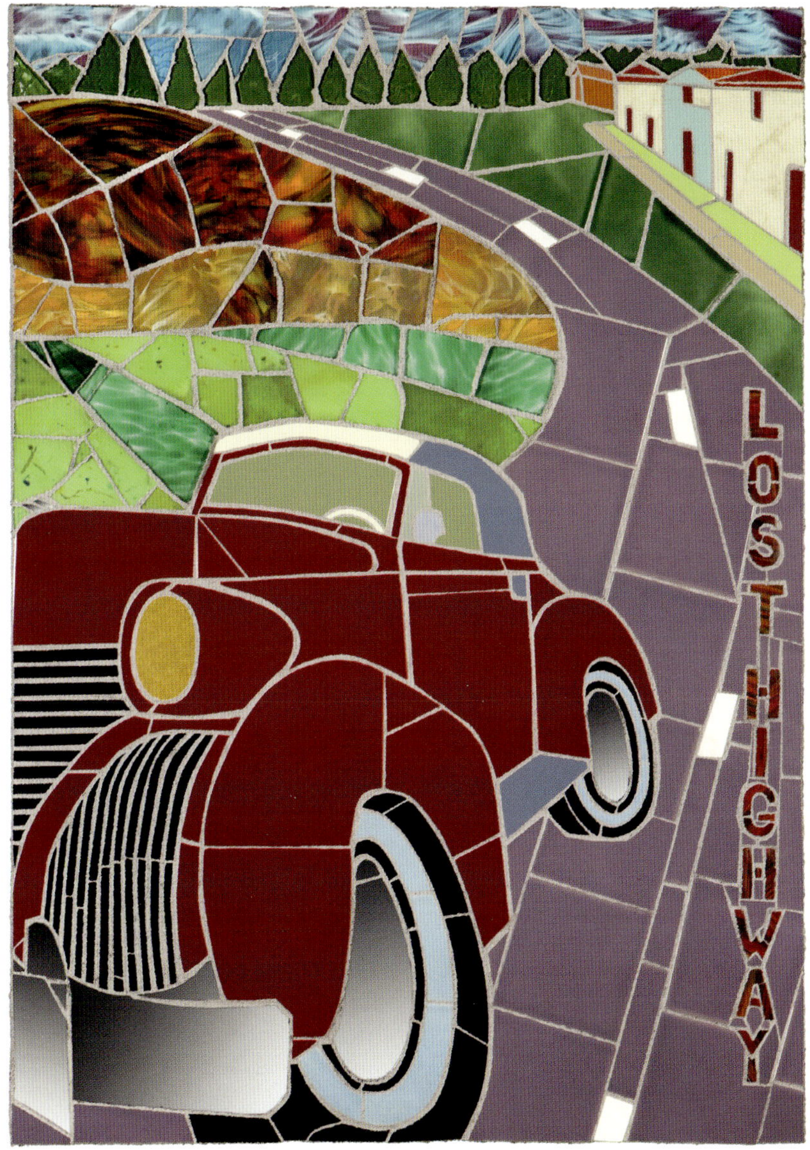

Jonathan Mandell. *Lost Highway*. Wall mounted mosaic. 2008. 36" x 24" x 3".

We the People: National Constitution Center Mosaic. The imagery of this 10' x 6' mosaic features the Preamble to the Constitution at the bottom. Above this are the three branches of government set behind mirror so people see themselves reflected in the government. The White House has white quartz as the windows. The flag flying is made using sodalite and a glass shard. The landscaping is amazonite. The fountain is blue lace agate. Above this is the NCC logo with its utilization of the US flag. The montage on top features images highlighting the rites of democracy: voting, jury service, military service, serving in political office, as well as individuals who forwarded the constitutional rights process. The first scene features immigrants looking at the Statue of Liberty from Ellis Island. The Statue of Liberty is made using iridescent glass. Next is the Seneca leader Osceola. Below this a scene of people engaging in protest. Their signs are made using yellow opalite, zebra marble, agate, and leopardskin jasper. The woman in the foreground has a dress made from rose quartz. Above this scene is a jury panel. The two people in the front row to the right have sweaters made from turetella agate (fossilized sea shell) and lavender pinite. The neckties are made from glass shards. Below this Clarence Gideon, who secured legal representation to those who could not afford it otherwise by personally petitioning the Supreme Court. Next is Dr. King. His eye is made from stromatalite (fossilized algae). Below this a Japanese-American soldier circa W.W.II. His buttons are made with brass. Next is a swearing in ceremony. The blue of the flag is made with blue quartz. Under this scene is an image of Brown vs. Board of Education. The newspaper is made using zebra marble. The sky is blue sodalite. The next image is a soldier. His glasses are made with glass gems. Below him is a first responder. The crest on his helmet is agate. The gauges on the fire truck are glass gems. Above is a woman voting. The voting booth is made using snowflake obsidian, leopardskin jasper, and aluminum. The remainder of the mosaic is ceramic tile.

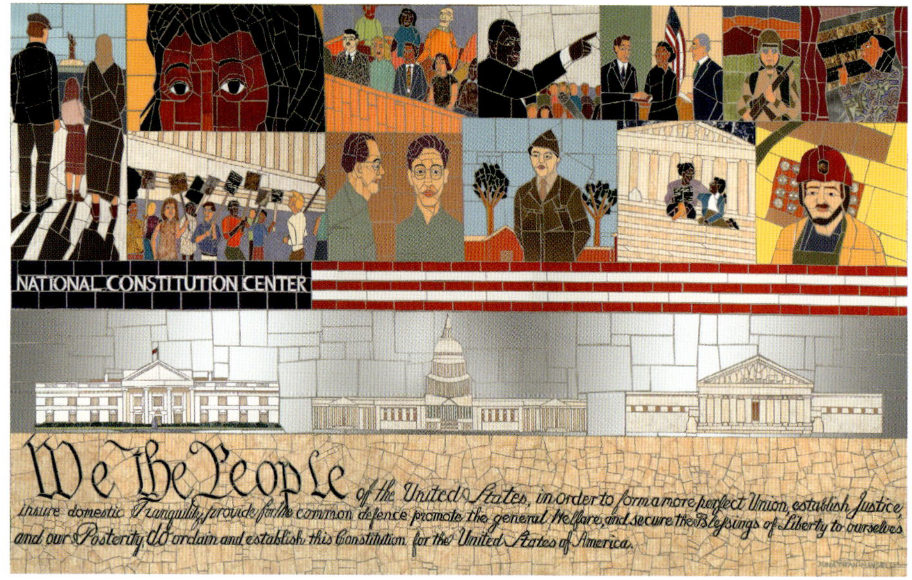

Jonathan Mandell. *We the People.* National Constitution Center.
Wall mounted mosaic. 2008. 120" x 72" x 3".

Rejoice: This 24" x 36" x 4" mosaic was made using glass shards and citrine. The glass shards are convex and concave. They were salvaged from broken glass art. The curved quality of the glass creates a bas-relief or topographic feature across the mosaic surface. This mosaic was created for the National Liberty Museum's 10th annual Glass Now Auction, held in October 2009.

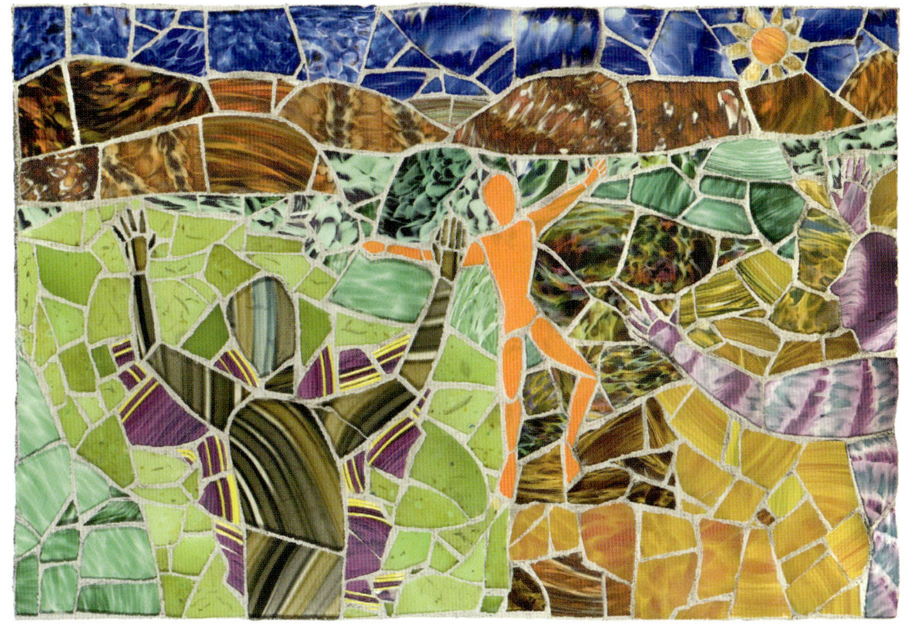

Jonathan Mandell. *Rejoice.* Wall mounted mosaic. 2009. 36" x 24" x 3".

Vickie Morrow

Scottsdale, Arizona, Vickie@tileartmosaic.com

Artist's Statement

Growing up in New Mexico I only knew of the blue, blue sky that transformed to a rich orange, magenta, and deep red at sunset. I watched the desert change from brown and ocher to the many colors of green and the bright desert flowers after a midafternoon summer rain. I love the colors, elements, and textures of the Native American arts and have never been able to get enough of the fiesta colors and handcraft from south of the border. Even as a child I assembled by color, textures, shapes, sizes, manmade, from nature, to an order of symmetry or an abstract balance. Then and now, I am constantly rearranging to make the assemblage more pleasing to the eye, creating an element of surprise or a restful place to feast the eyes.

Most of my work has been practical, evolving from recreating boxes, transforming fabric into wonderful quilts, making the useful artful. With my mosaics, I hand make each piece of ceramic tile. The composition of the finished art piece is created considering the recycled object as the base of my design and the handmade tile mosaic becoming one piece.

Each creation is influenced by the style or shape of the table base, tray, container or frame. My inspiration may come from a group of tile pieces lying in a tray in my studio, a photograph, and nature's design of pebbles, seeds, and sand after the stream has dried, or a memory of the texture of a basket or woven fabric. Textures are embossed into my handmade tile from hand carved stamps used in other lands or woven textiles and baskets from the world's continents and islands that I have collected from artisans all over the world. Lately architectural elements are showing up, reflective of ancient buildings in Europe.

Smoothing the edges of a newly cut tile, touching the shaped lines of a hand carved stamp, hand filling the grout between the tiles, running my hand over the texture of a completed mosaic piece is only part of the pleasure of the creative process. There is an element of surprise in every piece, whether it be the result of the fired glazes (color applied to the tiles) or an unanticipated design because of the way the tiles did or did not fit together as planned, and the final transformation as the grout is cleaned from the tile and the final mosaic appears.

I hand make most of the tile in my mosaic pieces. Occasionally I use elements I have picked up on morning walks, bits of broken glass, pebbles, small rusting castoffs, rescued tile and ceramic pieces, beads, stones, and fossils. Table bases, fine mirrors and frames, door knobs, and small boxes keep showing up for me to repurpose to be more artful. There are always two to six projects under way in my studio and another several dozen in my sketchbook.

About the Artwork

Kitchen Backsplash: Wonderful mosaic designs spiraling around the columns of the Duomo in Orvieto, Umbria, Italy, are the inspiration for this kitchen backsplash. What a wonder to feast your eyes on. Now Mediterranean colors in the same design, straightened and enlarged, make this kitchen bright and inviting. This project was sketched and a variety of color combinations and order combinations were tried before the final pallet decision was made. Each tile was hand cut and glazed specifically for this project. Tiles left from the backsplash were randomly set on the bistro table to complement the overall kitchen mosaic design.

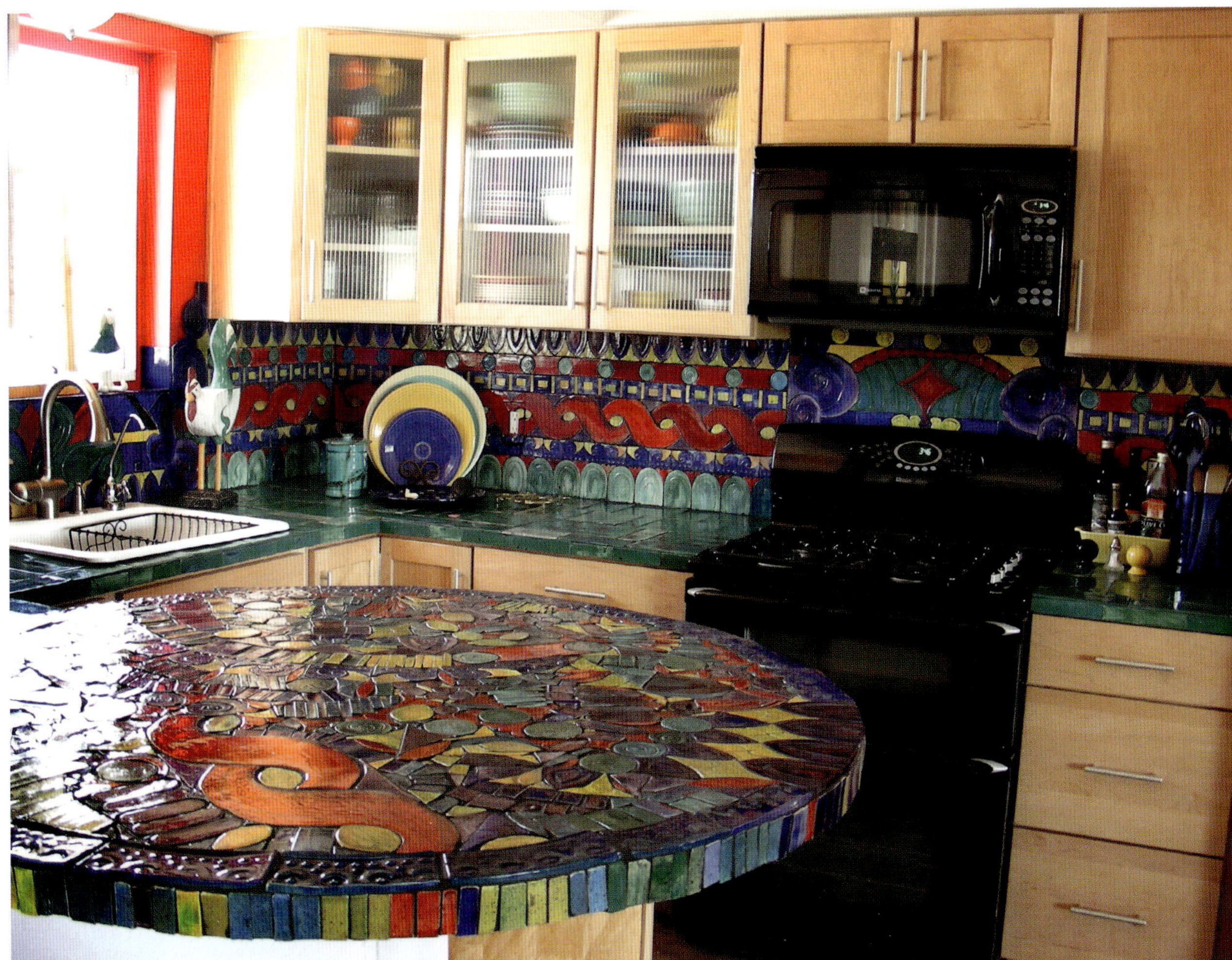

Vickie Morrow. Kitchen Backsplash. 2007. Handmade tile. 18" x 23'. Bistro table top 36" dia. x 1 1/2".

Intersection is a mosaic composition where one can feel the textures of a daily activity, whether approaching a stop light when in your car or the things that come up in your life demanding a decision. There are abrupt stops, curves in the road; sometimes we just go in circles or from a dark place to something much lighter and brighter. Intersection is the first mosaic in the Community Series. When working on the mosaics for this series I start with the title in mind. I select two to four tiles to anchor the composition and set them on the board (canvas). From there my senses go to work. My hands are grabbing tiles from the trays set on the table and arranging them on the canvas. There is no thought or decision involved. When the board is covered I walk away. Later I will come back to see what I created. There were no adjustments on *Intersection*.

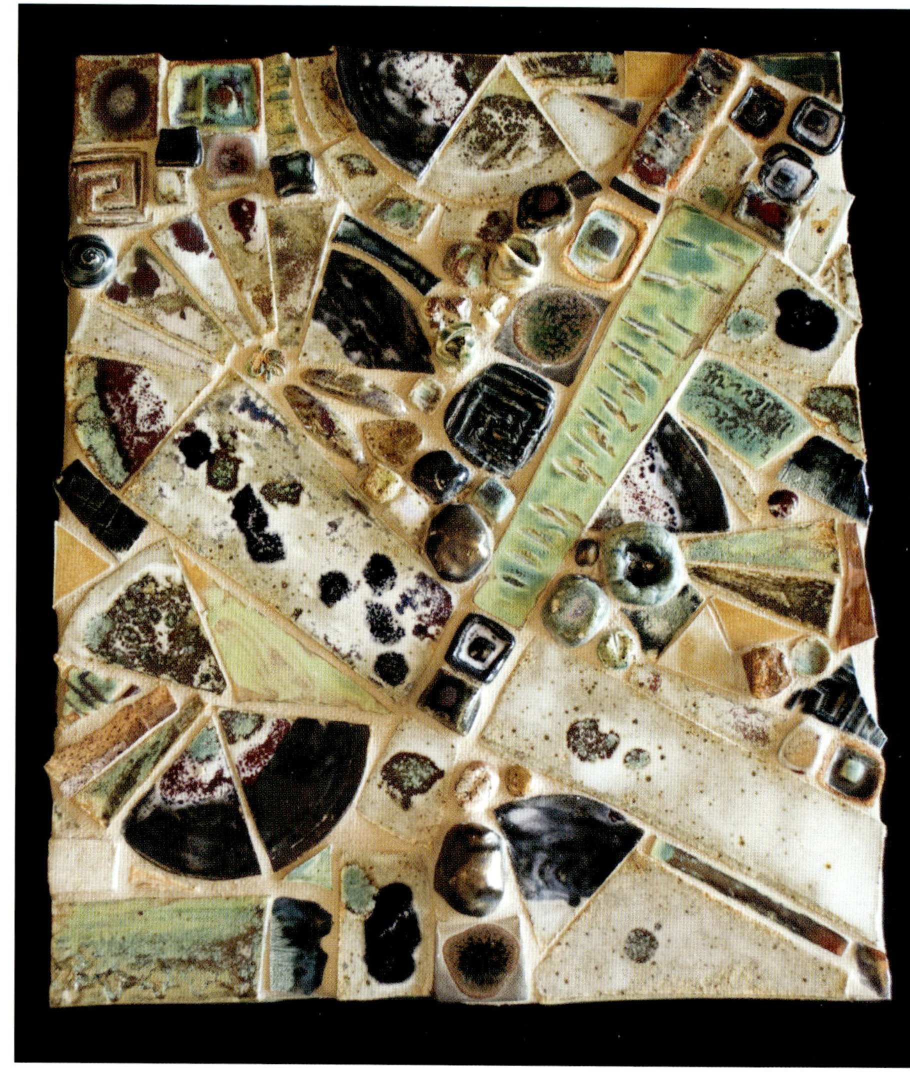

Vickie Morrow. *Intersection.* 2010. Handmade tile mosaic. Board with turndown edges. 11" x 7". *Photo by Judy Nichols*

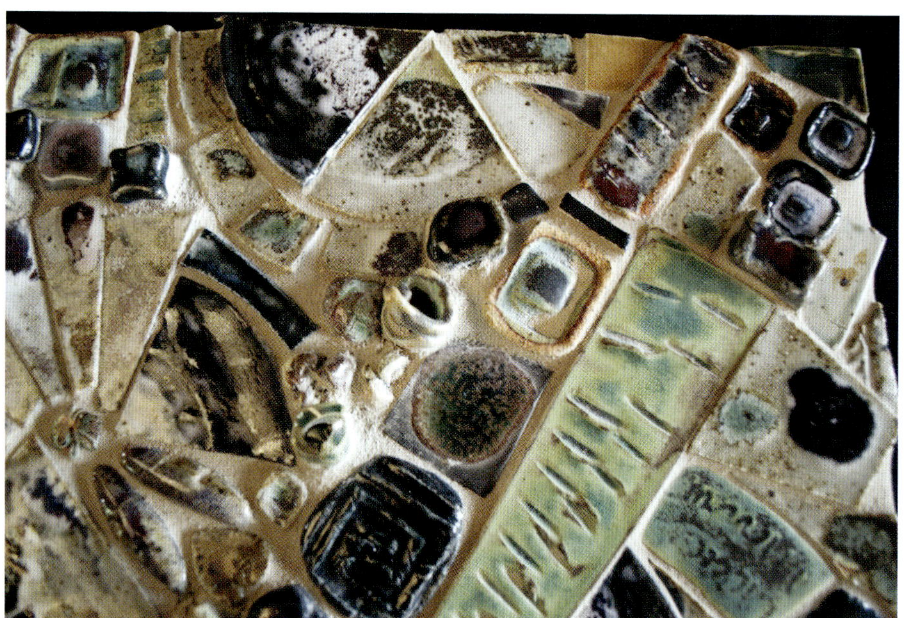

Two Left Standing: Curving continuous lines of heavily textured and stubby shapes of deep colored tiles create a feast for the eyes on these rescued, beautifully shaped candle holders. Glazes deep in the texture of the larger accent tiles give strength and an anchoring element to the mosaic composition. Large round tiles were created as one piece with a textured pattern from an eastern antique fabric stamp and glazed to top the two making them a pair. These beauties can stand as sculpture or be topped with pillar candles.

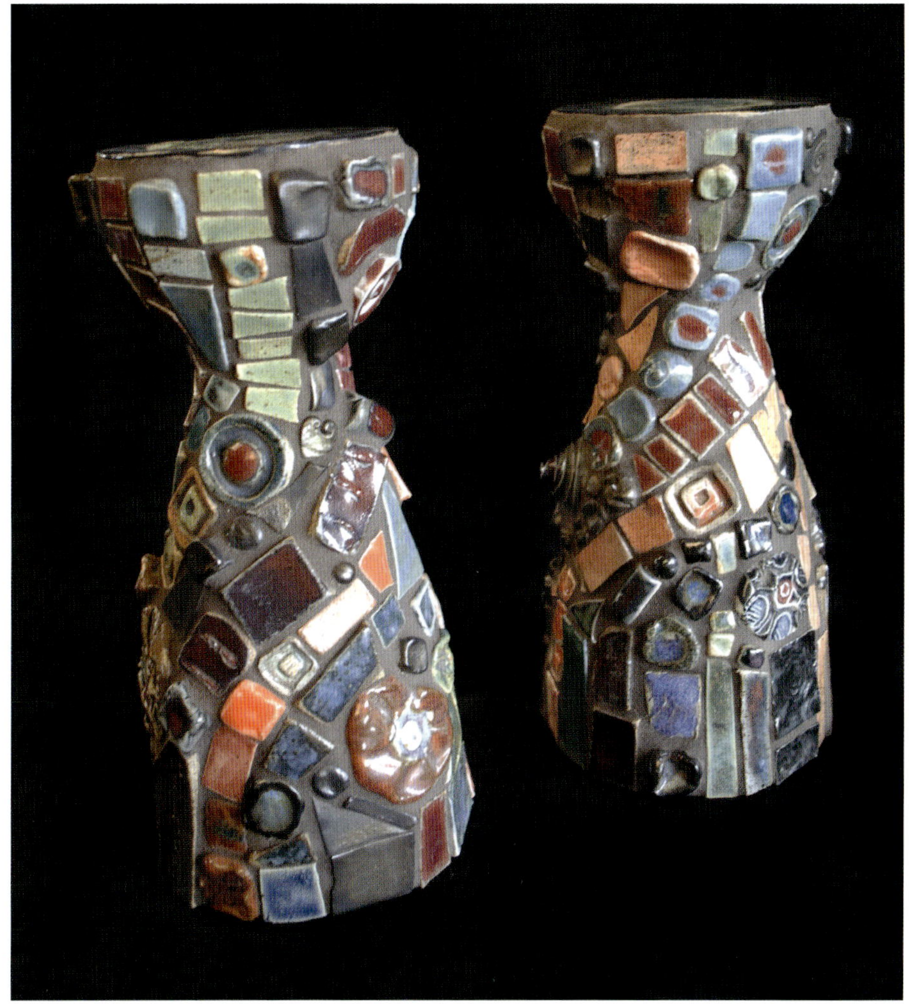

Vickie Morrow. *Two Left Standing.* 2010. Handmade tile on found, battered candle holders. 10" x 5" dia. *Photo by Judy Nichols*

Two Wine Glasses is one mosaic of the Vineyard Series. This handmade tile mosaic is made as a puzzle. The clay is rolled like cookie dough. The mosaic picture is cut free hand without a pattern, dried, fired to bisque, and then glazed. Using high fire glazes on this series, I am always in wonder and pleased with the result of the layered colors, never to be duplicated again. After the glaze firing, the handmade tiles are set in the puzzle design on a fiber/cement board with a tile turned down edge made at the same time as the picture, grouted, and hung. Great for a wine cellar, bar, dining room or kitchen.

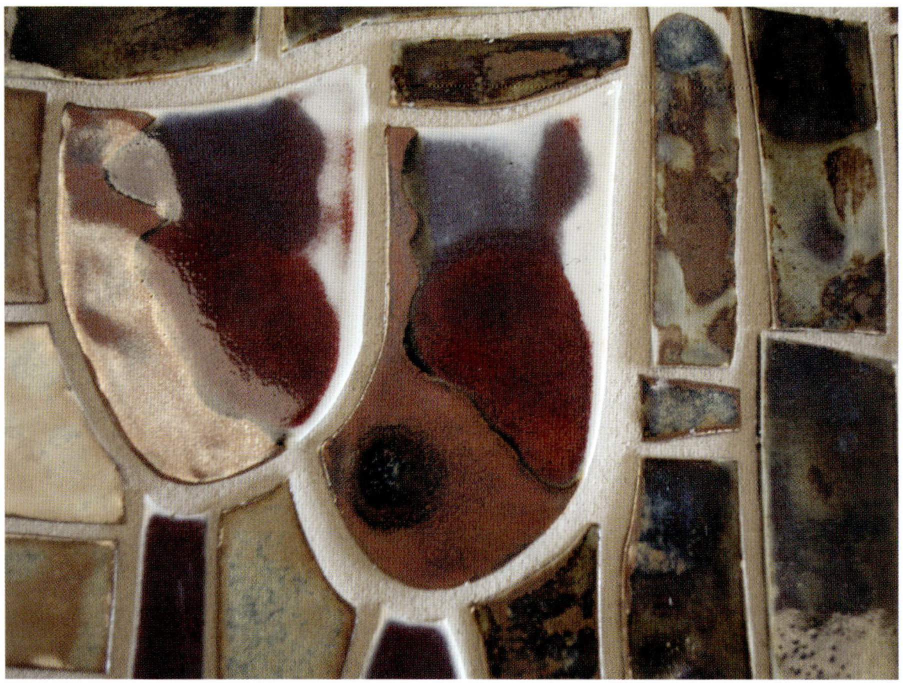

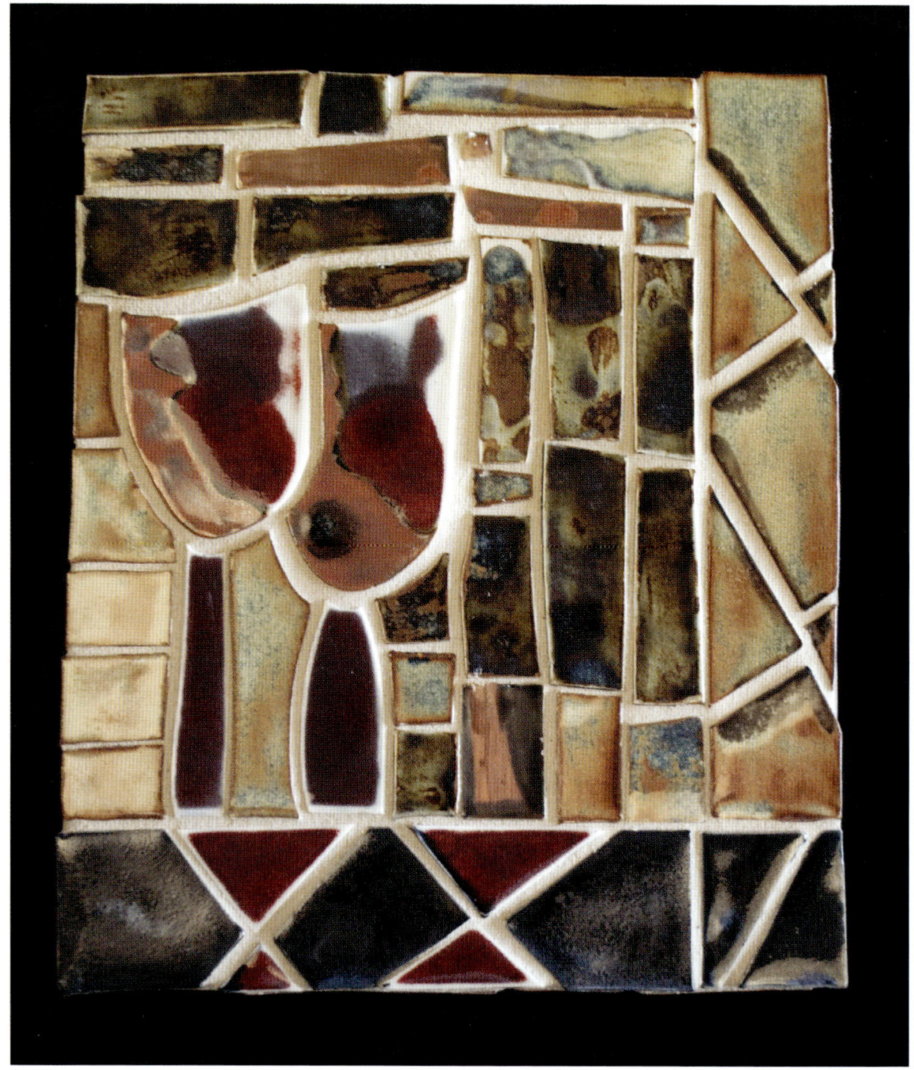

Vickie Morrow. *Two Wine Glasses*. 2010. Handmade tile on fiber/cement board. 9" x 12". *Photo by Judy Nichols*

Shawn Newton

Wallingford, Connecticut, snewtonart@aol.com

Artist's Statement

My interest in mosaics grew out of a renewed desire to utilize raw materials to create art after a long career in graphic design, though I admit I enjoy the assistance of computer technology in the initial creative process.

I employ small glass shards as paint strokes and often enhance them by building a sculptural bas relief foundation that serves as a stage to present a moment in time. I prefer to establish a relationship between my art and the viewer by using traditional subjects that soothe or amuse and, for a few moments, can transport one to another world.

As I continue my journey through thousands of pieces of glass, I intend to expand upon my sculptural technique in order to feature the beauty of glass on a dimensional surface. My greatest reward is the reaction of viewers who do not equate the word mosaics to my work. Their surprise assures me of a new appreciation of this art form as a legitimate contemporary medium of expression.

About the Artwork

Celebration: After completing and naming this work showing two red crested cranes, I happened to see a film clip of them and experienced the joy of seeing the pair come to life. In just a few seconds, the jubilant behavior of these beautiful birds reaffirmed my title choice.

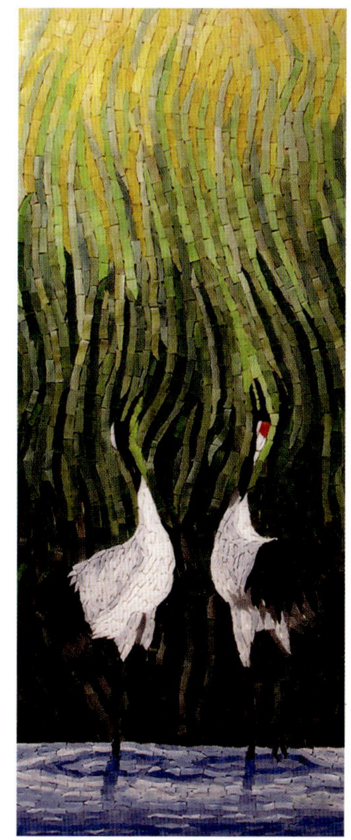

Shawn Newton. *Celebration.* 2007. Stained glass. 32" x 15".

Waiting: I am truly inspired by the Dutch masters and have been determined to utilize the quality of stained glass to attempt to replicate their magic. The mood of this image is enhanced through the strong use of light and dark and while most of the story takes place indoors, an old window frame directs attention to a lovely landscape and an imminent arrival.

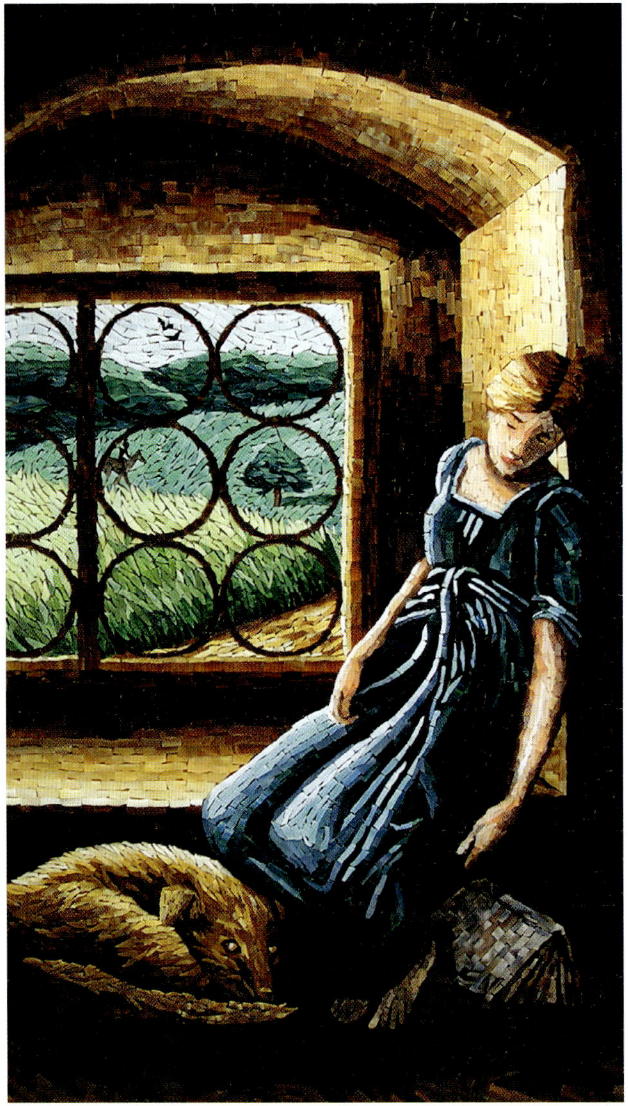

Shawn Newton. *Waiting*. 2009. Stained glass. 32" x 19".

Leftovers: While exploring the possibilities of glass on bas relief, it has been a challenge to transform subjects from a flat surface to dimensional shapes. Creating the relief requires one to pull objects out of the substrate, then stop when halfway out. After the usual recutting, regluing, and grumbling, the tessare is applied and the result is magical! This scene incorporates some of my favorite subjects: old buildings graced by flowering vines, the local dogs, and the everyday pleasures of life.

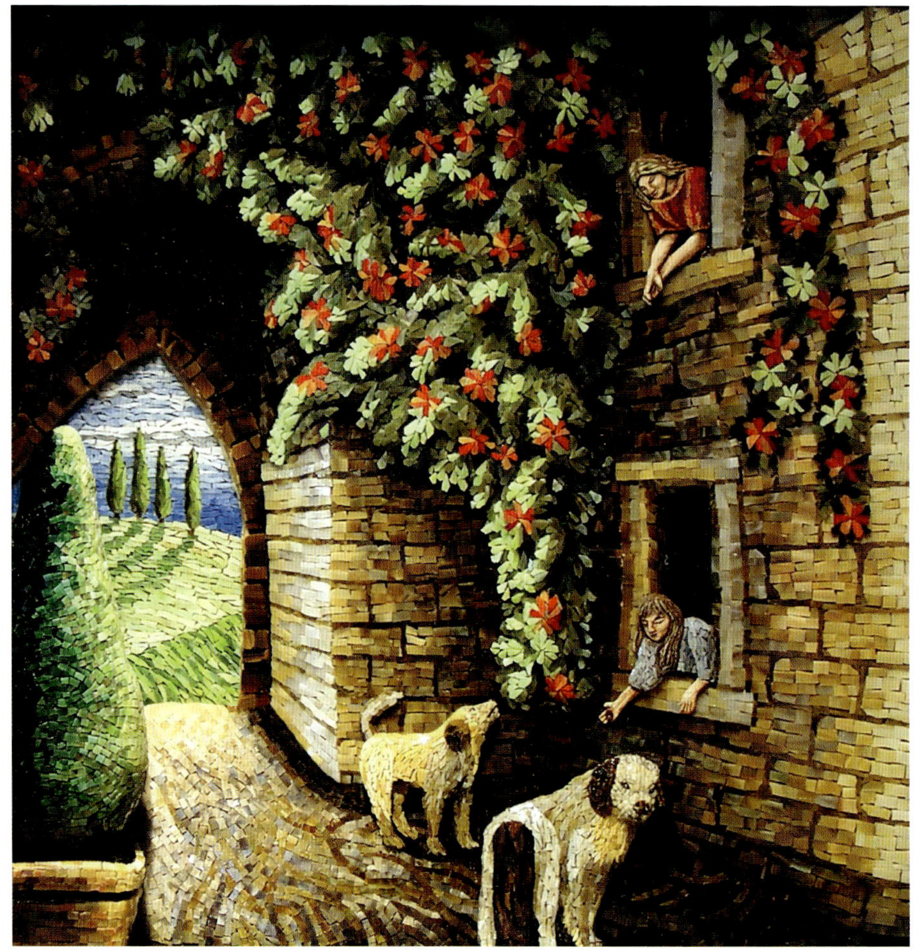

Shawn Newton. *Leftovers*. 2008. Stained glass on sculptural bas relief of styrofoam & clay. 25" x 25" x 5".

"I live while I skate; I feel every motion; all the muscles speak and answer me, as it were. I talk with my arms, my shoulders, with all my limbs, and think of music—of flying, if you will."
—George Meagher (1895)

Best Friends: The narrative is about the pure joy of skating. Being a skater myself I am drawn to the interest of our predecessors in this wintertime sport and the stories illustrated by prints of the era. Here, a young girl shares the spirit of Meagher's statement with her exuberant best friend. All that is needed is an old set of sheets and a clear patch of ice.

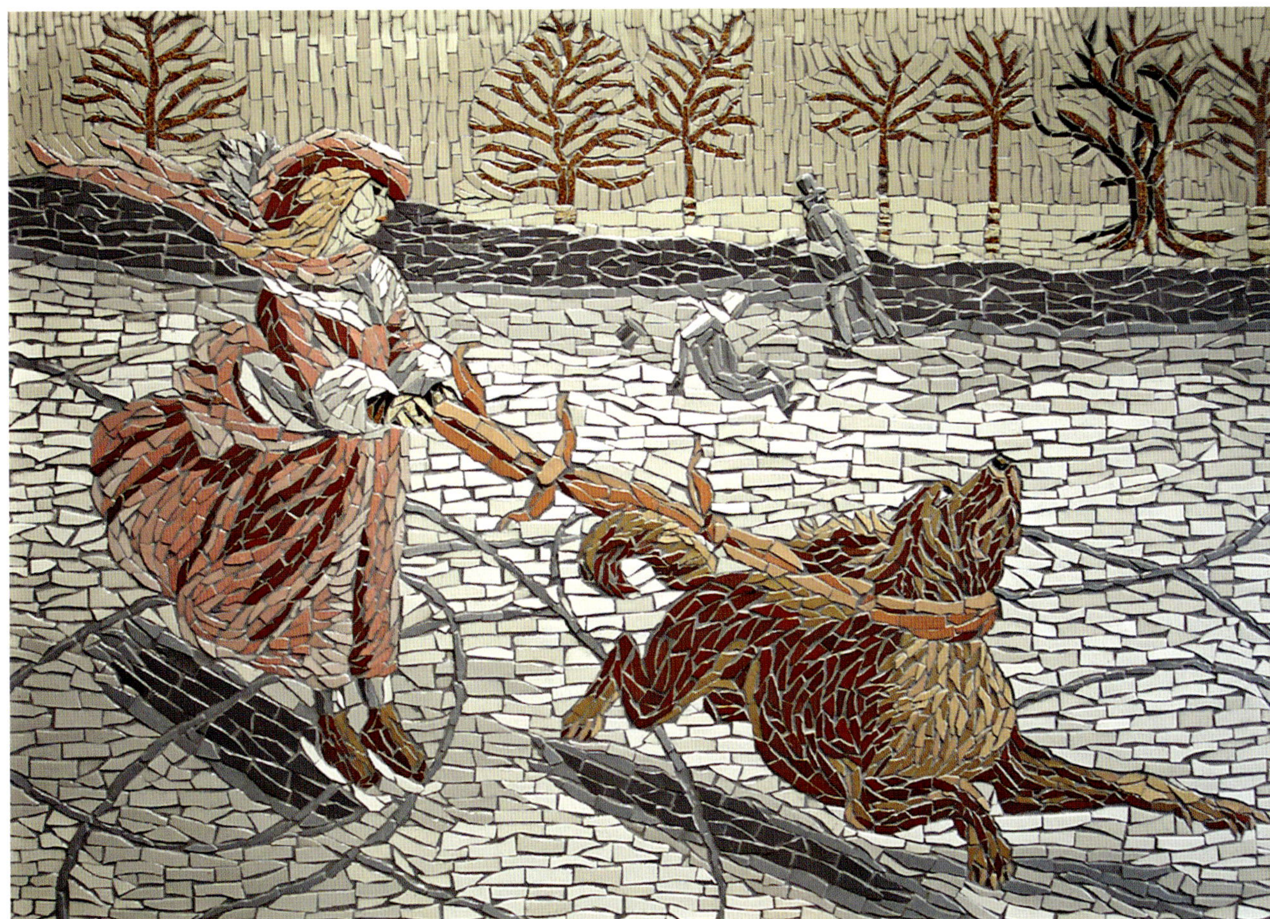

Shawn Newton. *Best Friends*. 2010. Unglazed porcelain tile. 12" x16".

Buddha: This portrait was a wedding gift.

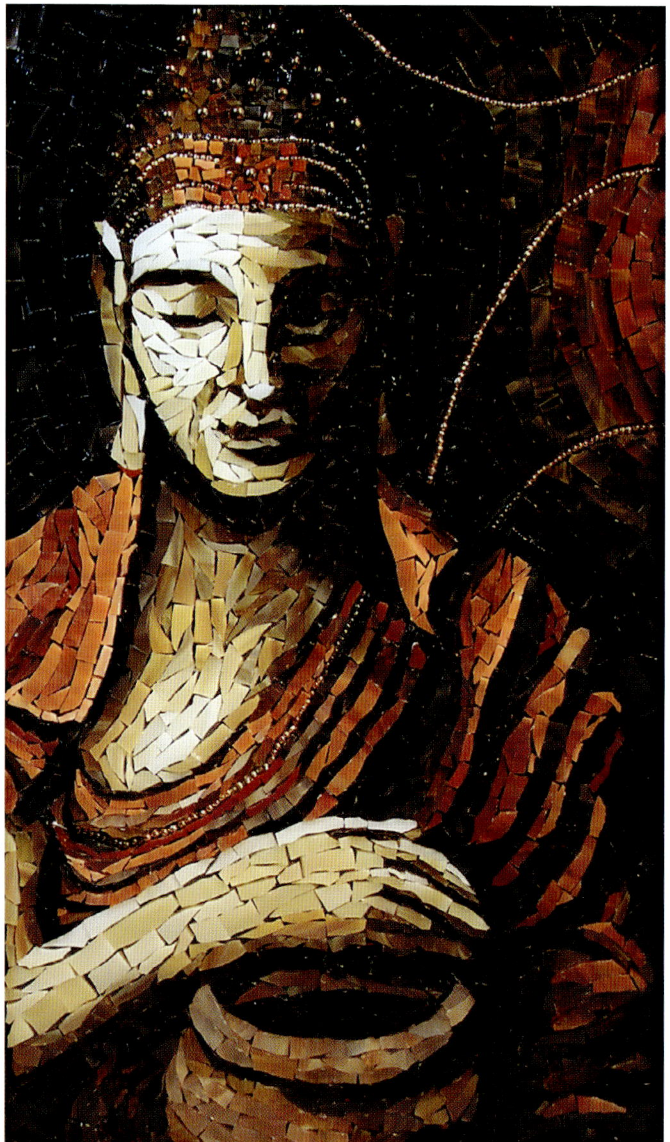

Shawn Newton. *Buddha.* 2010. Stained glass, glass beads. 10" x 7".

Sarla: My goal in this portrait was twofold: To use smalti exclusively for the first time and to make Sarla happy! I look forward to my future relationship with the material and am pleased to report a satisfied subject.

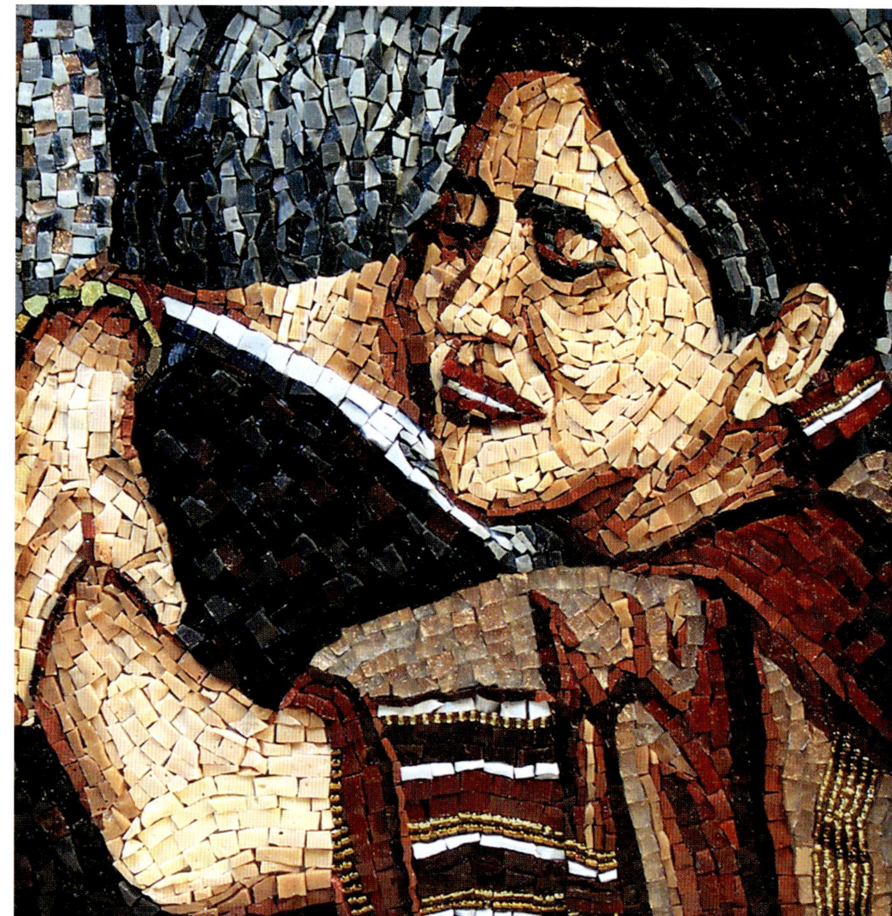

Shawn Newton. *Sarla*. 2010. Smalti, glass beads. 12" x 12".

Anne Oshman

Montclair, New Jersey, studio@anneoshman.com

Artist's Statement

The ancient art of mosaic is created by combining small pieces of "tesserae" to form a larger image. I use this ancient medium to capture twenty-first century reflections of ourselves. My work has often been derived from photographs, capturing moments and bits and pieces of individual narratives. Using 3/8" micro mosaic tile, marble and/or glass, these portraits express the relationship between people and their surroundings. Details that would otherwise go unnoticed are highlighted, yet the feeling of anonymity creates a sense of voyeurism for the viewer. A more recent evolution of my work has shifted toward the sculptural, both real and organic; an interesting extraction from materials that are solid and impervious by nature. The "ancient medium," it seems, is a wonderful avenue to reveal my views of contemporary life.

About the Artwork

Cupcakes: I thought this would be fun. The cupcake craze had begun, and shops were popping up all around.

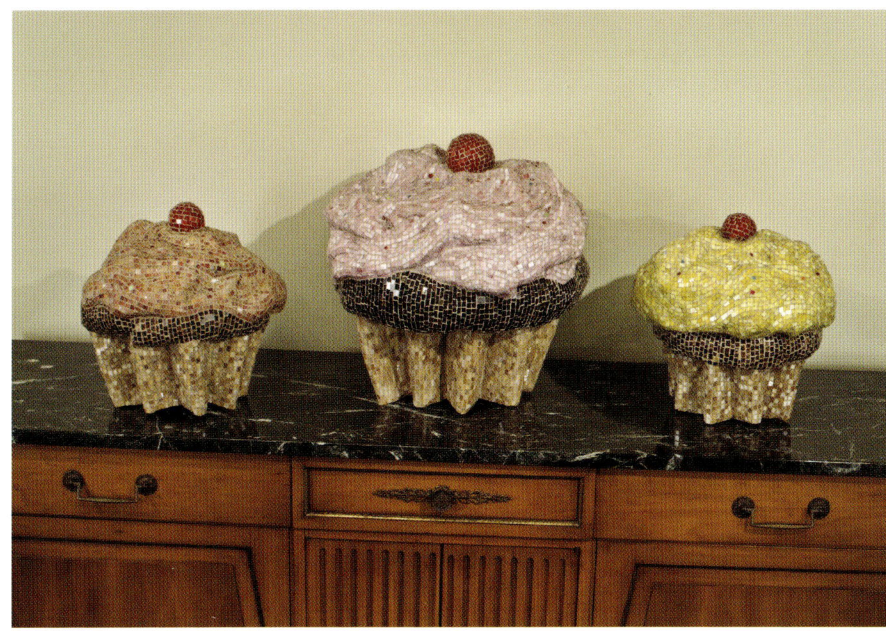

Anne Oshman. *Cupcakes.* 2007. Stained glass, wire mesh, towels, fiberglass and resin. Direct method. Small cupcakes, 13" x 13", large cupcake 20" x 20". *Greg Leshe, photographer.*

Nature's Berth, small scale, was my application in a public art competition for the Port of San Diego entitled *Urban Trees*. I wanted to make something sweet, colorful, family friendly, and safe, while giving a nod to its location. It is part of the Urban Trees 7 exhibition, and remained there until October 2011. This piece took five months to complete.

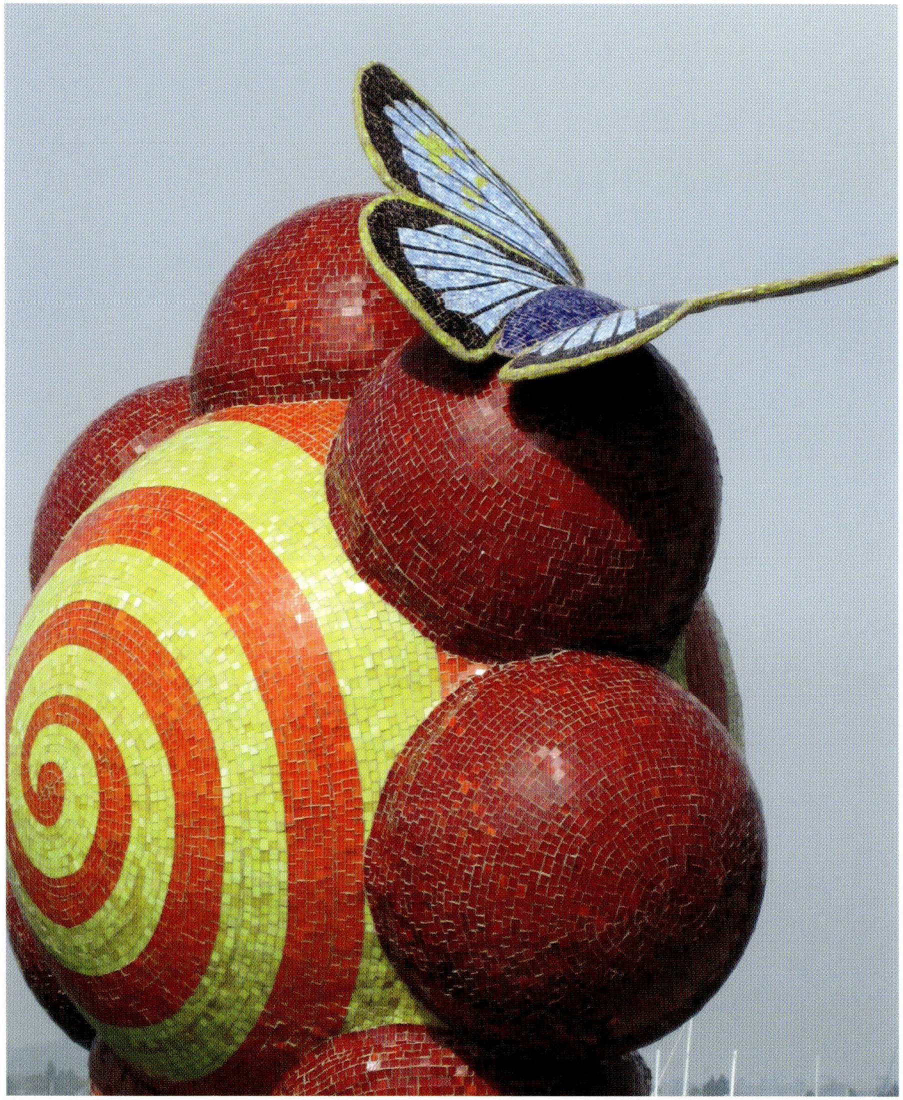

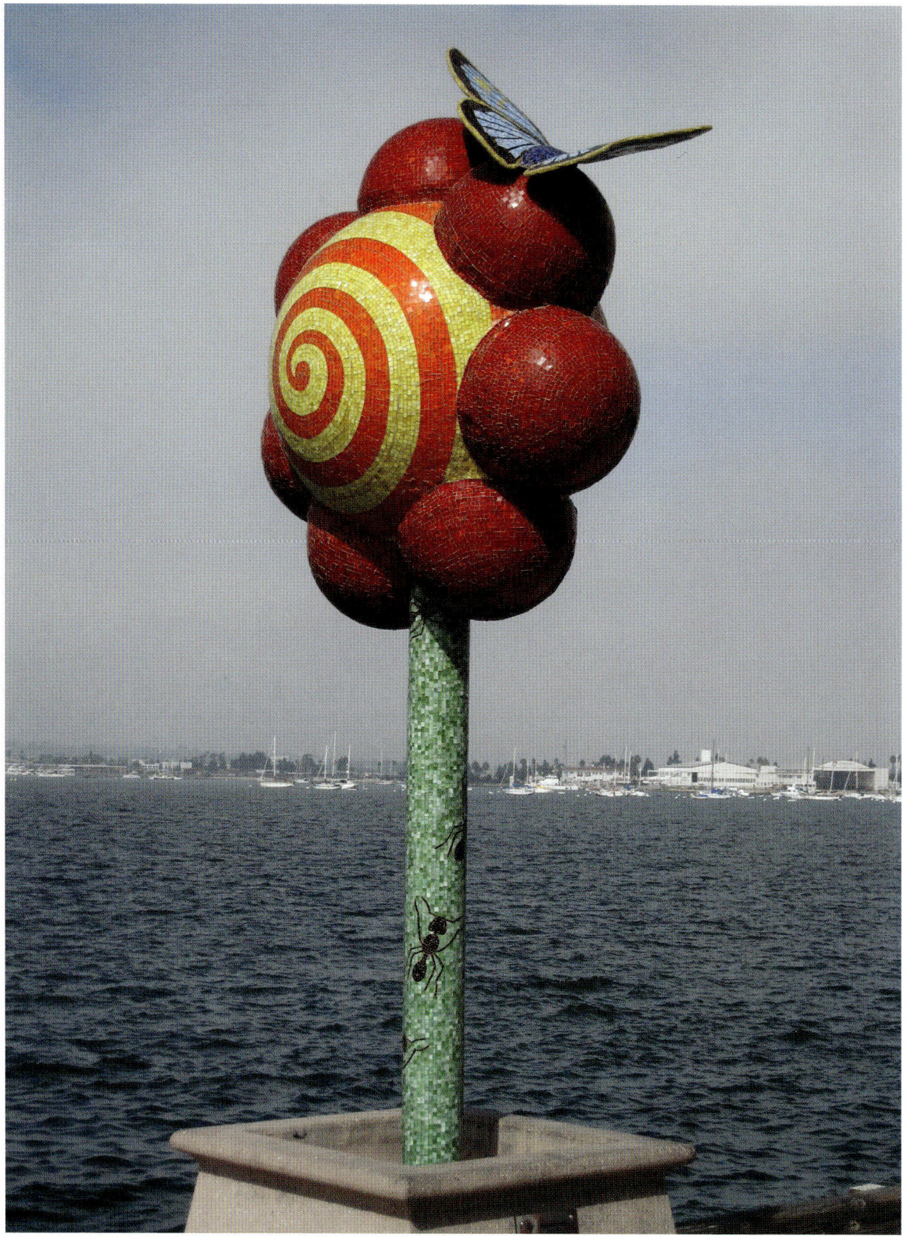

Anne Oshman. *Nature's Berth*. Grand scale flower with ants crawling up the stem and a butterfly sitting on a petal. 2010. Stained glass, Styrofoam, fiberglass, and resin. Direct method. 14.5' x 5'. *Anne Oshman, photographer*

Landscape: I created this large scale piece for visitors to rest and regroup.

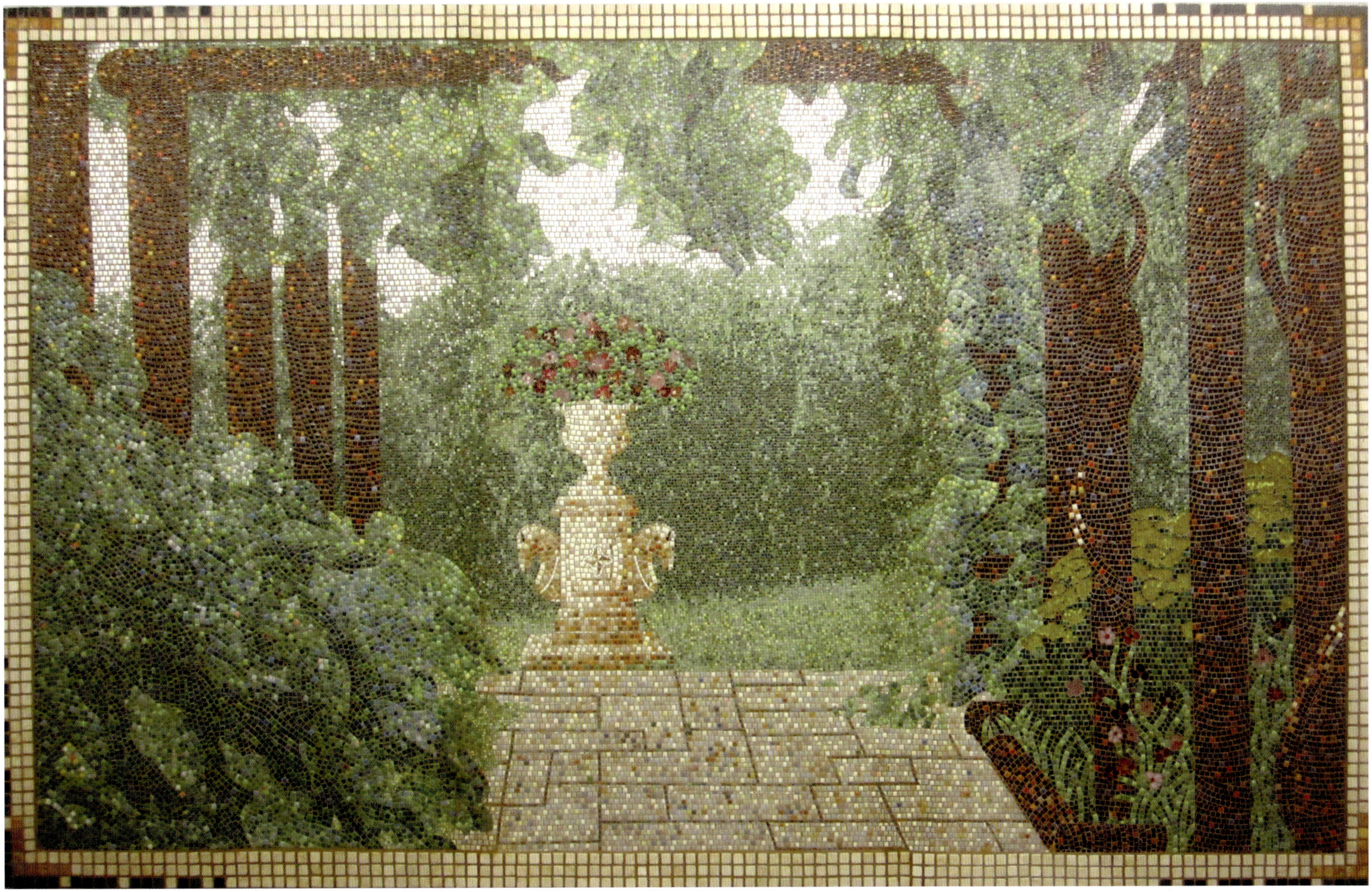

Anne Oshman. *Landscape.* A garden view. 2011. Micro mosaic ceramic tile (3/8"), and marble frame. Direct method. 6' x 10'. This piece was created for the Patio Café at St. Francis Heart Hospital in Roslyn, New York. *Anne Oshman, photographer*

Nancy Pollock

Beaufort, South Carolina

Artist's Statement

The art of mosaic is the creation of a puzzle, fitting small pieces together to form an imagc that can be cold to the touch but deep and warm in its color and texture. There are infinite possible combinations of materials, colors, and forms that almost change their physical properties as they become part of a unified piece of art. My first mosaic explorations were with utilitarian forms, floors and tables. The pieces emanated from my earlier career as a weaver, developing patterns based on blocks, color, and texture.

I became drawn to three-dimensional work that fed on the interplay of texture and shape in fantasy figures and forms. I need to smile when I look at a finished sculpture. I get great satisfaction from creating huge, imposing forms and then balancing that with something very small and precious. I love excessive accessorizing dating from my fashion years, or sometimes it is a whimsical combination of birds and fish in a totem form. Many of my pieces have been inspired by music, from Mambo Kings to Norah Jones. I love the refracted images created by small mosaic mirrors and the iridescence of glass tile. Today, I have an interest in recycled items—antique radios, musical instruments, and phones that have lost their original finish or their technology has become outdated. I love the new form and seeing these iconic forms return to a new, modern place in our homes. My attraction to human-sized figures relates to my sense of being a woman and a mother. All of my mosaics come together into a form that instinctively reflects the pieces of my earlier careers and my life.

About the Artwork

Bello Cello: Richard Roger's musical *NO STRINGS* was the first live Broadway musical I saw when it came to Kansas City when I was sixteen. Today the guitar, violin, mandolin, and cello immediately became a series I had to call "no strings." The recognizable shapes and the interplay of surfaces make them a great medium for mosaics. I am fascinated by the concept of colors in music, where both the composers and conductors refer to color tones to describe music tonality or the interpretation of a musical passage. (opposite page)

My Mother, Myself: The vanity mirror that is the "face" is clear on one side and fractured on the other. The skirt dazzles but the sharp pointed ends indicate danger. There is an apple from the Garden of Eden on the back and a serpent on the shoulder, which speaks to me of historical views about women and knowledge. It all somehow reflects my view of womanhood, just as it represents my mother's views in Kansas City over a period of ninety years. My fleeing to New York City at the age of twenty-three represented some sense of escape, but I realize now that we all truly are our mothers.

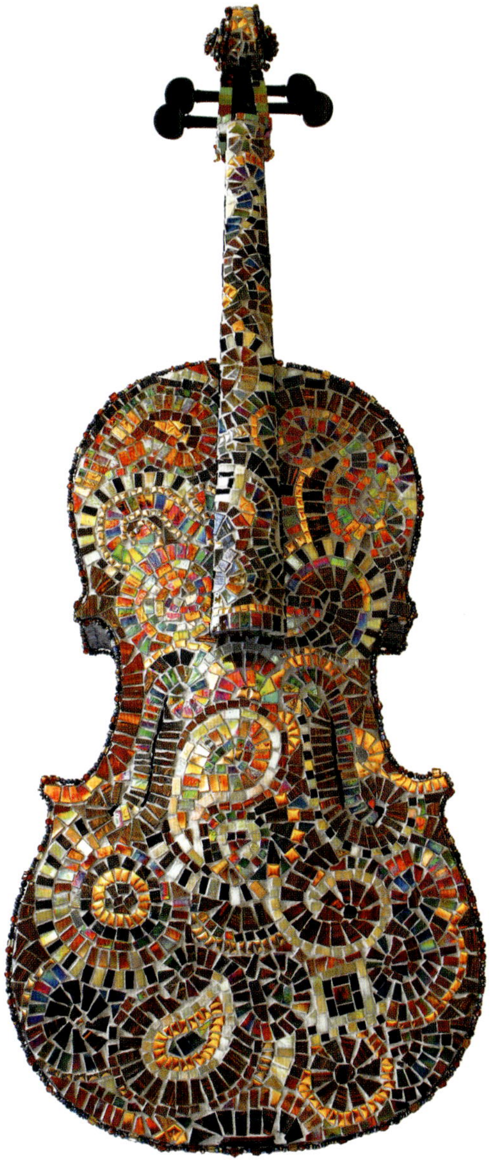

Nancy Pollock. *BELLO CELLO.* 2008. Glass and ceramic on cello. 8" x 17" x 44". *Photography by Cesar Garcia / Lifestyle Photography*

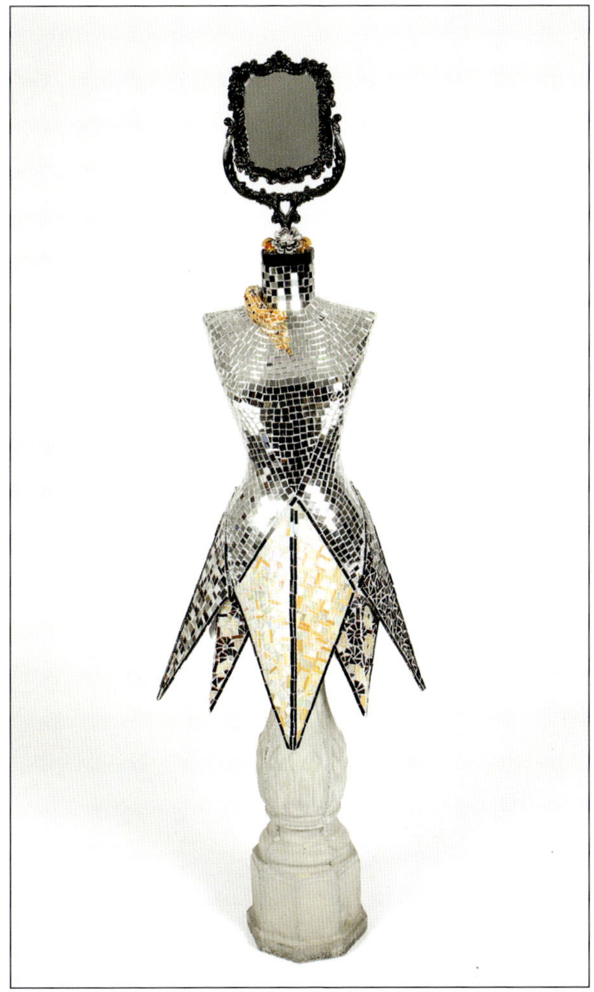

Nancy Pollock. *My Mother, Myself.* 2008. 5' x 2' x 22". *Photography by Cesar Garcia / Lifestyle Photography*

EASTER SUNDAY, 1957: Growing up in the 1950s, Easter was the only time you were permitted to buy a new outfit: a dress, shoes, hat, and maybe a new purse. Our family album had a series of photos with the children showing off their Easter outfits; each year it was the same picture with a new outfit. One of those pictures is in a frame behind the Easter bonnet among the Easter eggs.

Esperanza: This piece represents different aspects of a woman's ego. Her arms reach out in a joyous, beckoning embrace. She is both elegant and mysterious. All my female figures have mirrored faces, breaking the image into facets and reflecting back a fractured image of the viewer. *Esperanza* is the showgirl, the dance partner, the diva. From her conception, I always heard a female voice singing. She is a sort of t performance piece; I play recordings of the songs I heard from a small device hidden in the mix of old phonograph records at her base.

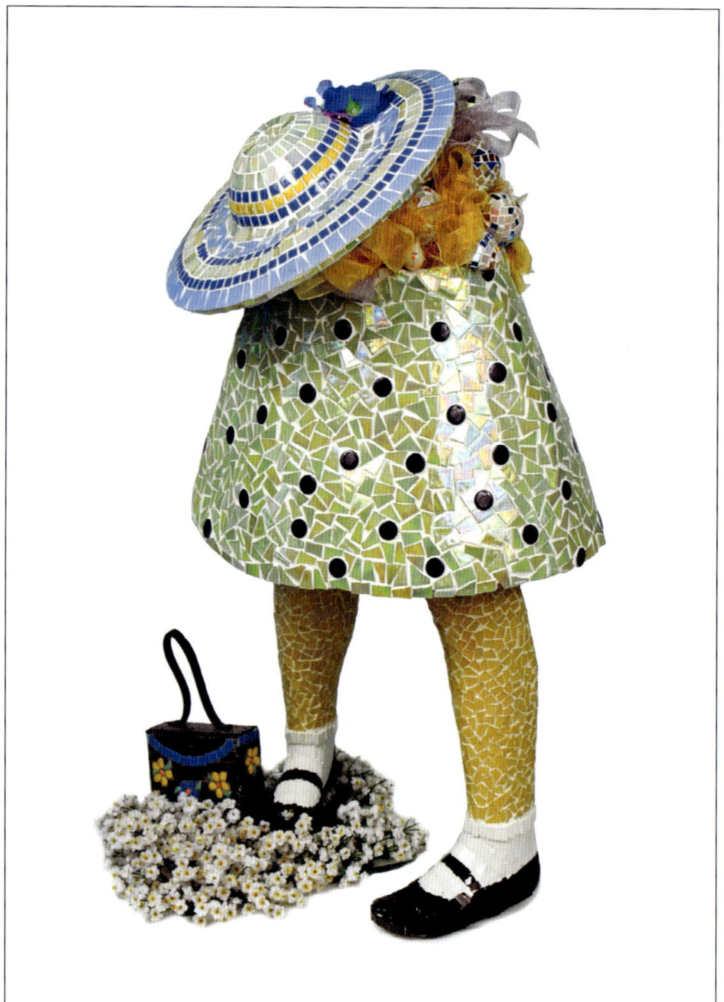

Nancy Pollock. *EASTER SUNDAY, 1957*. 2009. Glass and ceramic on fiberglass. 36" x 24" x 22". *Photography by Cesar Garcia / Lifestyle Photography*

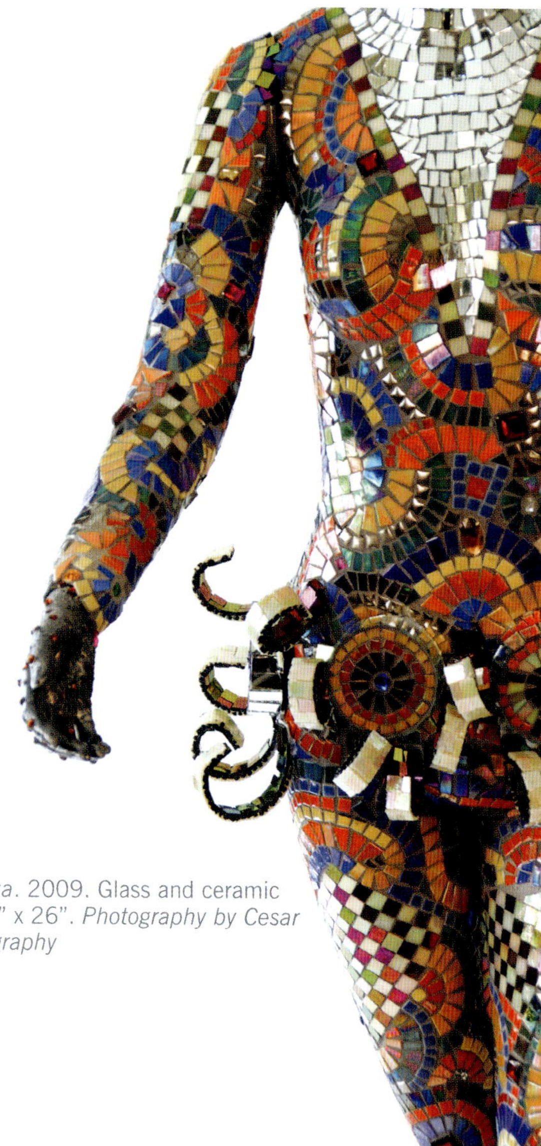

Nancy Pollock. *Esperanza*. 2009. Glass and ceramic on fiberglass. 6' 8" x 43" x 26". *Photography by Cesar Garcia / Lifestyle Photography*

Formal Dining: I remember a restaurant in Brooklyn where waiters wore military-type uniforms with ribbons for their years of service. This maitre d' proudly wears his awards of flatware and china. He hosts a great seafood restaurant where the signature fish is his culinary trademark. The toothpicks in the tail and fins could serve an entire party.

Martini Bar: Antique radios that have been battered and broken become mosaic pieces that maintain a sense of the past when people would gather around the radio for entertainment. We went to the Stork Club in New York before it closed in 1970. It was still so cosmopolitan and debonair. For me, the radio bars I have made evoke Fred Astaire doing Rogers and Hart, or Miles Davis, or sometimes the Mambo Kings. I like that this is recycled art.

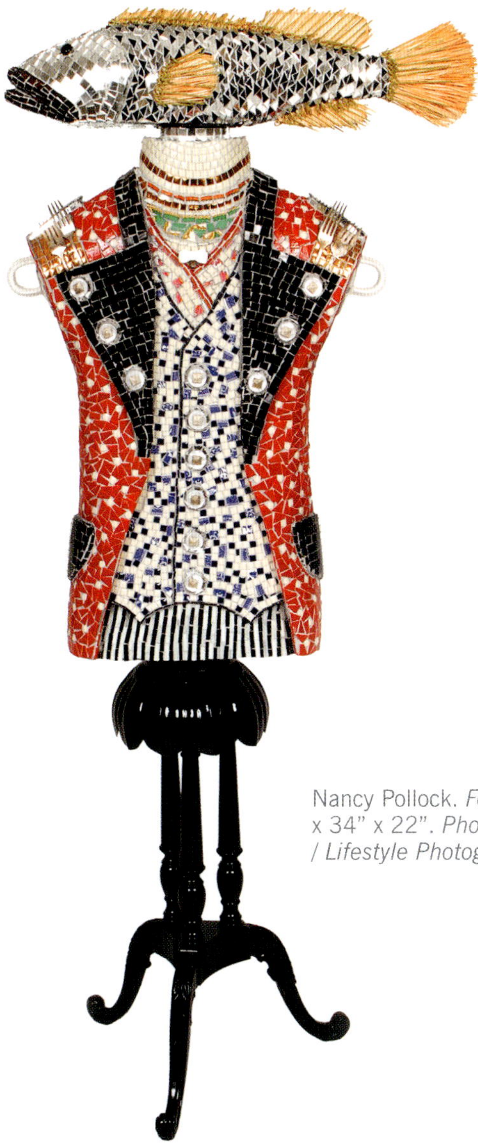

Nancy Pollock. *Formal Dining*. 2009. 5'7" x 34" x 22". *Photography by Cesar Garcia / Lifestyle Photography*

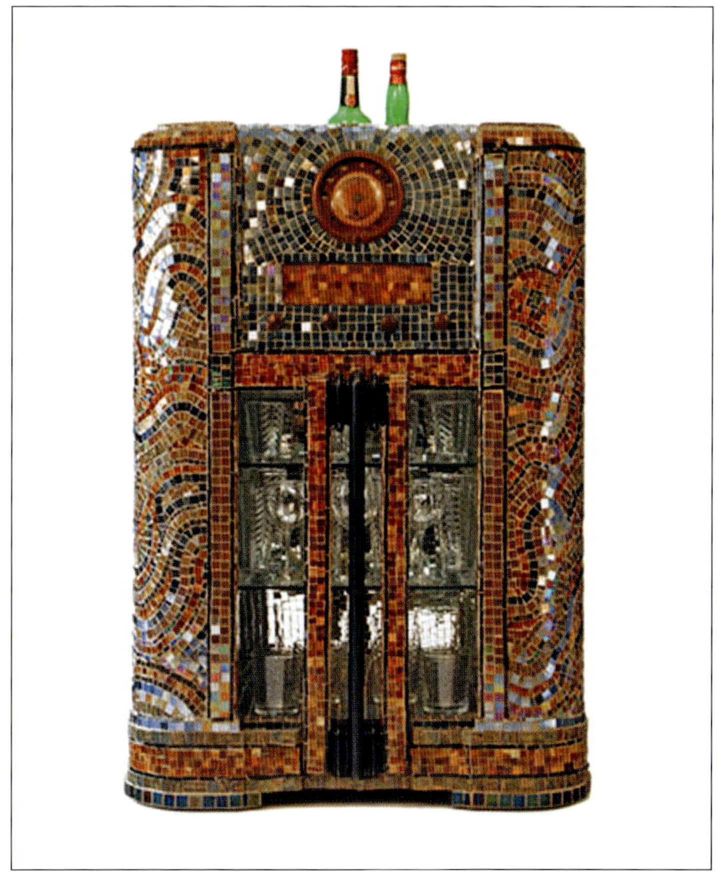

Nancy Pollock. *Martini Bar*. 2010. Ceramic and glass on antique radio; glass shelves, ice bucket, and bottle storage in top. 30" x 45" x 14". *Photography by Cesar Garcia / Lifestyle Photography*

Julie Groschen Richey

Irving, Texas, julierichey@mac.com

About the Artwork

Night Shirt is an evocative view based on a memory of San Francisco Bay as seen at 3 a.m. with friends at a mosaic conference. The skyline of the city asleep is depicted in stained and mirrored glass, dichroic glass, millefiori, and smalti. The shirt form was sculpted using several materials to attain the wrinkled, loose shirt effect. The entire relief sculpture was then coated in gray thinset and mesh, giving it a very rigid surface. The mosaic is Venetian glass smalti, cut so as to be only a very thin veneer of glass, undulating with the folds of the "cloth." I utilized primarily transparent smalti, so I had to tint the thinset in each section to keep the background color true.

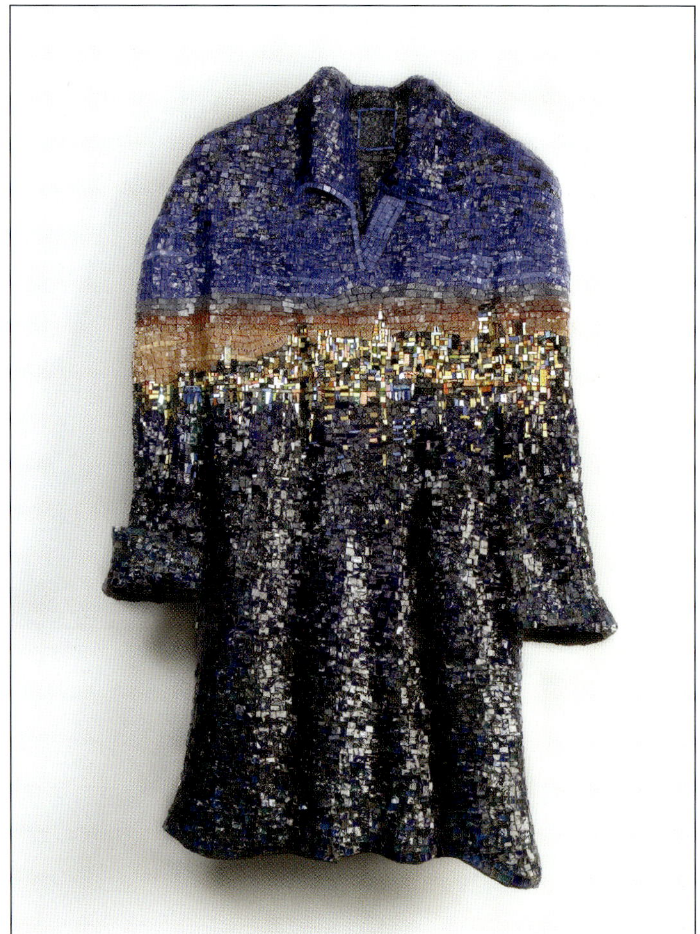

Julie Richey Mosaics, LLC. *Night Shirt*. 2008. Italian and Mexican smalti, stained and dichroic glass, 24k gold smalti, and millefiori on mixed media base. 32.5" x 21" x 2.5". *Photo by Stacy Bratton, www.stacybrattonphotography.com* (Right and opposite page.)

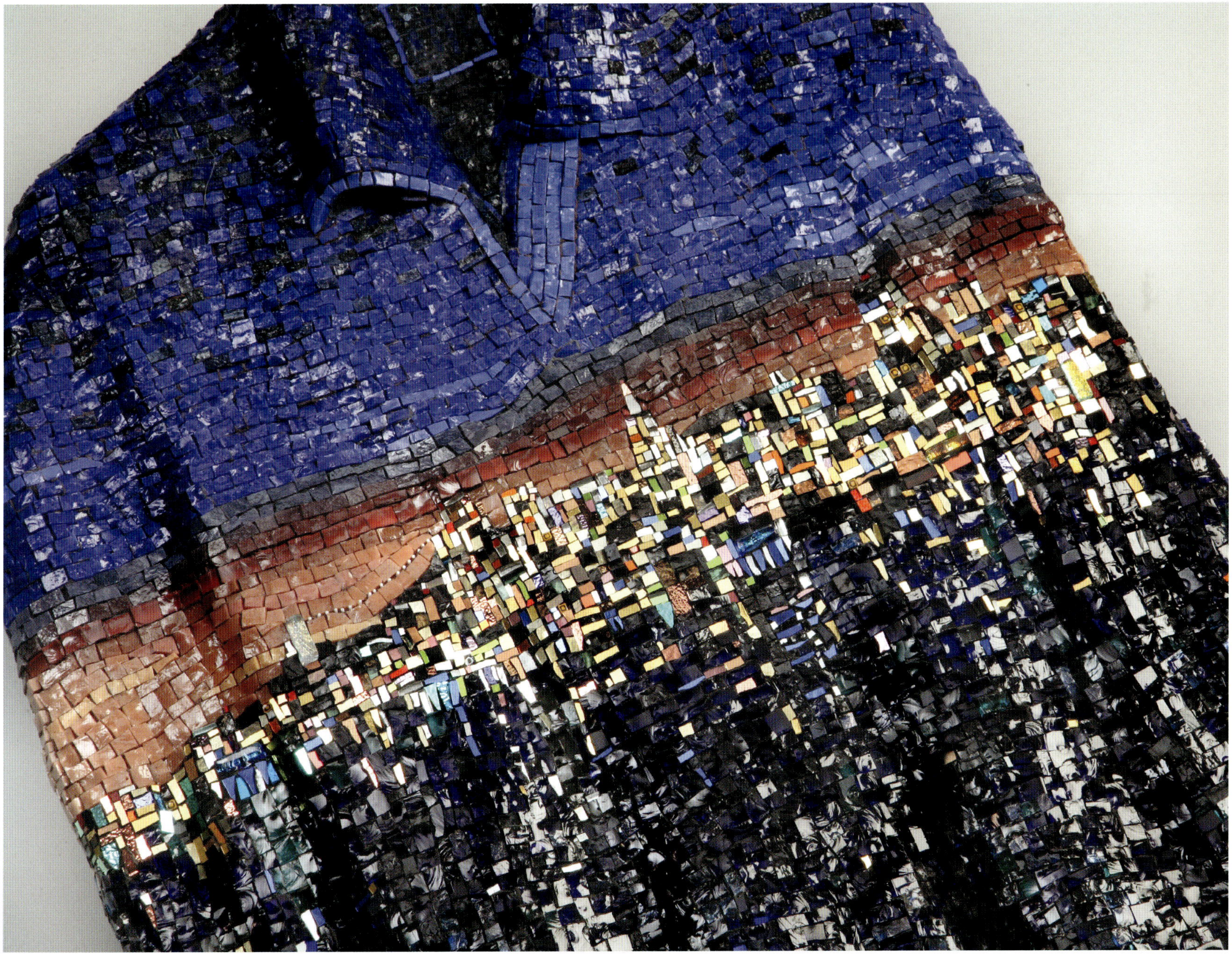

La Corrente: My work utilizes the innate opulence of mosaic materials—24k gold smalti, marble, semi-precious stones—to embellish sculptural forms in unexpected ways. The discovery of dentalia shells inspired the densely-packed under skirt. *La Corrente*, which means *The Current* in Italian, is about beauty amidst destruction. The giant Asian sea kelp adorning her gown swirls in the strong gulf currents. Although rich in nutrients, the kelp is an invasive species threatening the balance of plant and marine life in the region. While humanity overtly destroys the Gulf with oil, pollution, and fertilizer runoff, another destructive force creeps in with the current. *La Corrente* is a three-dimensional dress form I built up using Styrofoam, fiberglass mesh, and thinset. Once the form was the right shape, I adhered finely-cut tesserae made from marble, smalti, 24k white gold smalti, and seashells. From an art conservator friend, I learned a special technique to attach the dentalia shell underskirt. Each "sea tusk" was attached individually with tweezers.

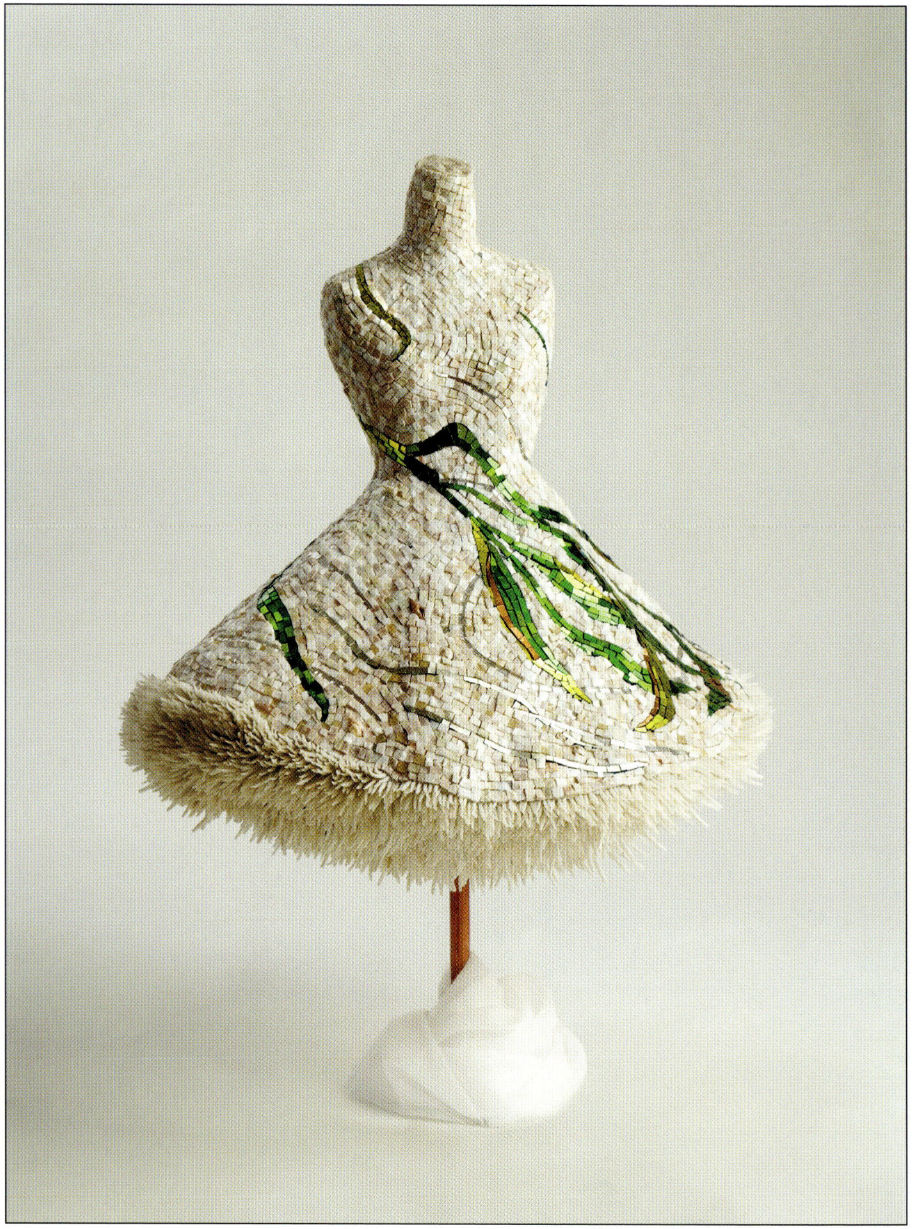

Julie Richey Mosaics, LLC. *La Corrente (The Current).* 2010. Marble, Italian, and Mexican smalti, 24k gold leaf smalti, chalcedony, and seashells on mixed media base. 29" x 22" x 22". *Photos by Stacy Bratton, www.stacybrattonphotography.com* (right and opposite page)

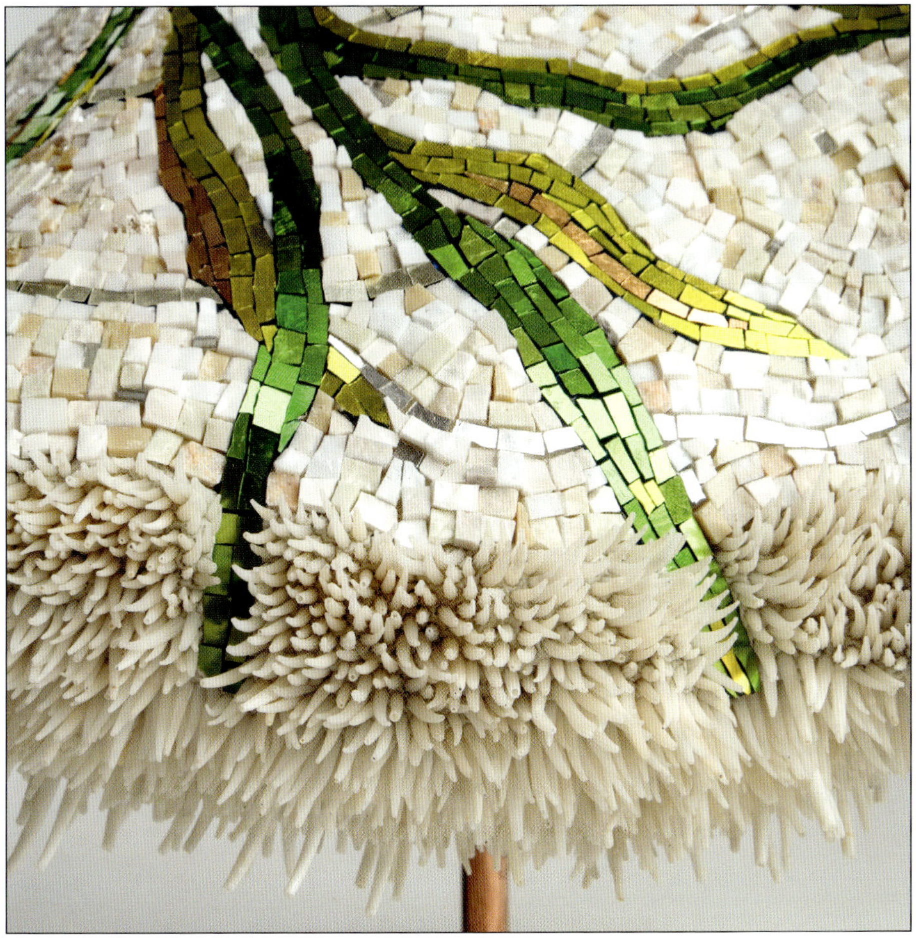

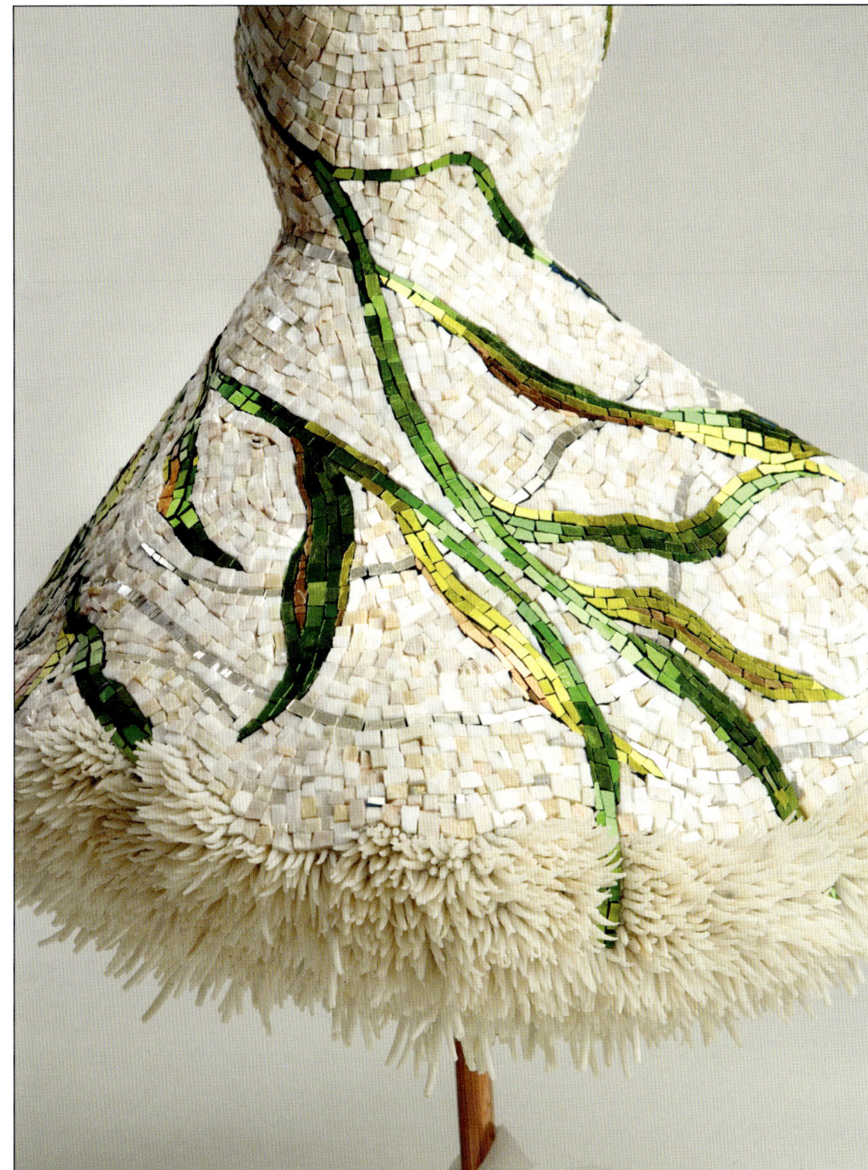

Four Seasons Floating Orbs: All four of these orbs, *Spring, Summer, Winter,* and *Fall*, were created for one client who wanted outdoor mosaics for his garden. Unlike traditional mosaic garden balls, these are made over a lightweight, hollow, cast foam core. They are waterproofed and covered with a thin veneer of iridized and vitreous glass mosaics, as well as millefiori. The result is surprisingly lightweight. As I was constructing the first orb, *Winter,* a friend suggested that they were probably light enough to float. We calculated their mass and sure enough, when we filled the bathroom tub, they surprised us by floating and spinning when the jets were turned on!

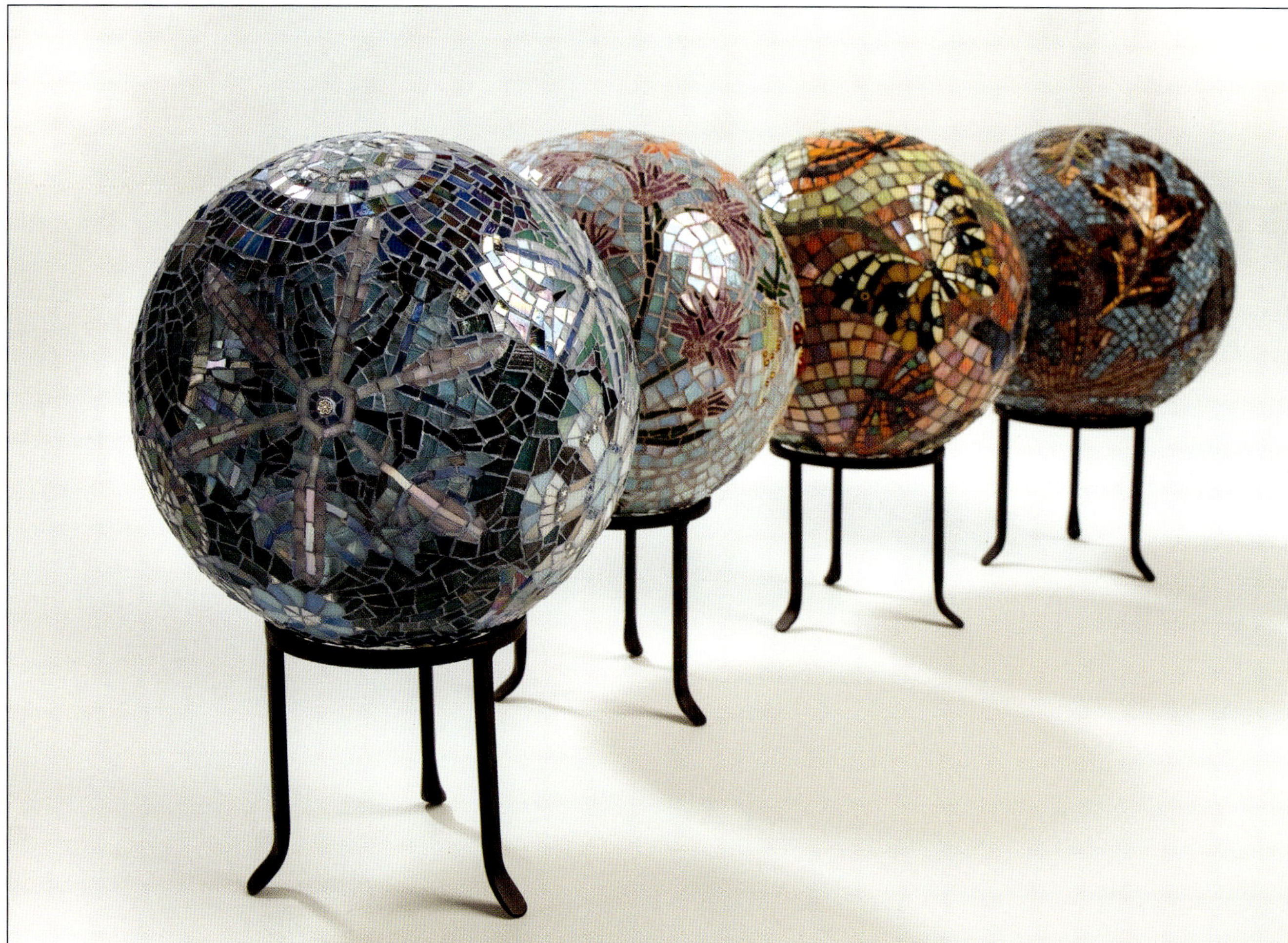

Julie Richey Mosaics, LLC. *Four Seasons Orbs: Winter, Summer, Spring, and Fall.* 2010. Glass and millefiori on foam base. 12". *Photos by Stacy Bratton, www.stacybrattonphotography.com* (right and opposite page)

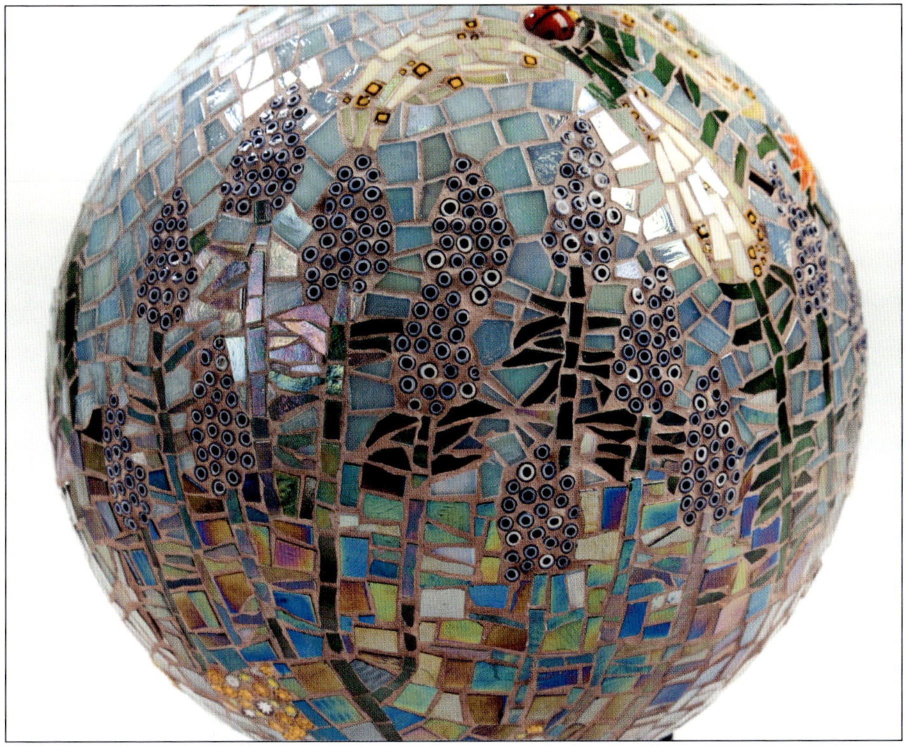

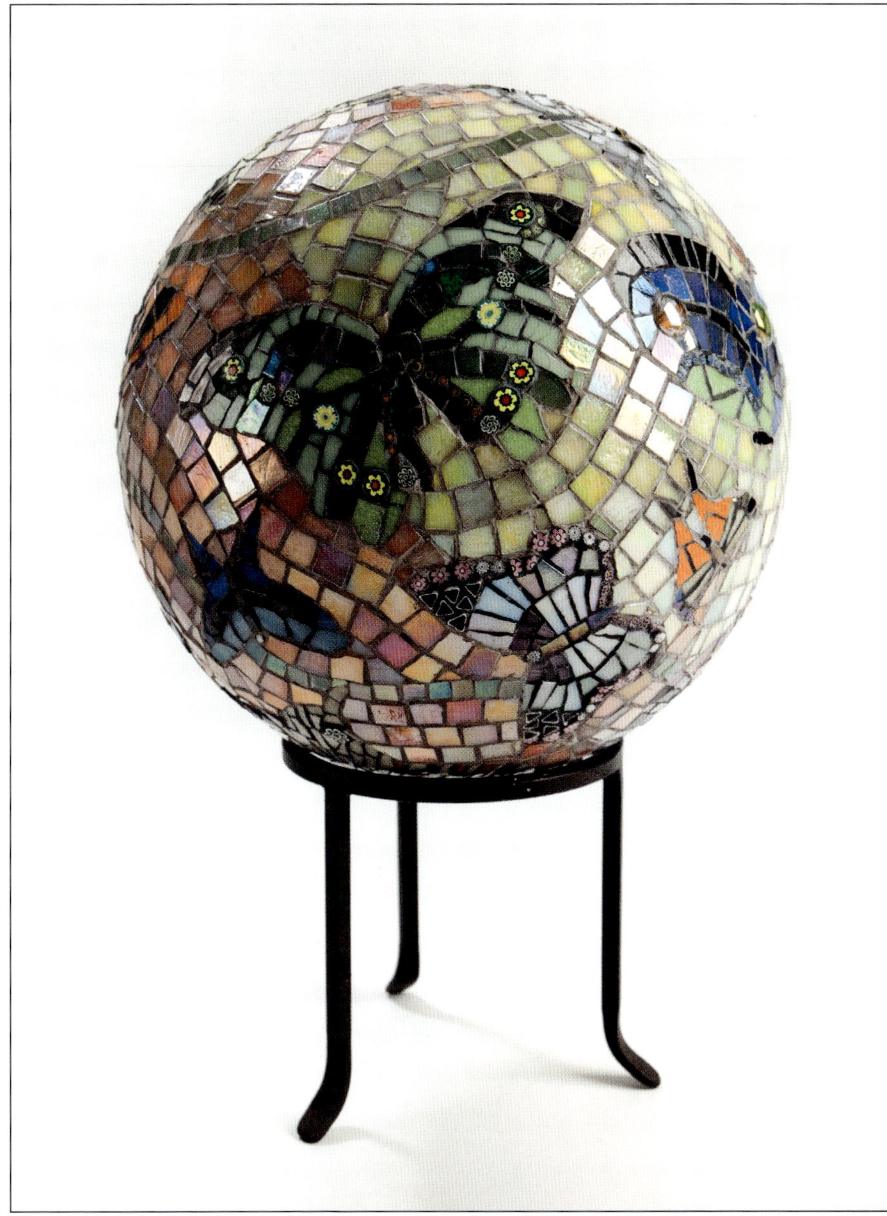

Laura Robbins

Placitas, New Mexico, laura@laurarobbinsmosaics.com

Artist's Statement

About My Mosaic Process: My mosaics are primarily made from ceramics and glass. I might incorporate stones, fossils, turtle shells or metal found objects as well. The clay forms are individually crafted, bisque fired, painted with glazes and fired again at a high temperature. They are then ready to be placed on the prepared surface. The mosaic wall pieces and some sculptures are created on foam covered with fiberglass mesh and polymer cement. Most work is weatherproof year round.

The glass pieces are created by precision cutting, random shaping or fusing. I tend to approach the placement of glass pieces as marks or brushstrokes. I have ideas before I begin, but except for certain commission work that requires specific imagery, I rarely plan or sketch beforehand, even though I love to draw! Each piece placed into the greater whole of the mosaic responds to the one before it, as well as to the negative spaces that will later be filled in by grout, the last step. Some of my series are entirely spontaneous designs. Other series are extremely personal, iconic fantasy where nature is home. Awareness of the miracle of being part of this planet in the greater universe is always present in my work. Also, because I am committed to helping identify and protect the wildlife passageways of New Mexico, much of my imagery includes animals, flora, and fauna. I co-spearhead an extensive, cooperative community mosaic to raise awareness to this end.

About the Artwork

Fireplace: This bright floral imagery decorates an outdoor kiva fireplace at a private home in Albuquerque. It includes cut glass and ceramic forms. The lower banco is also covered with pond imagery.

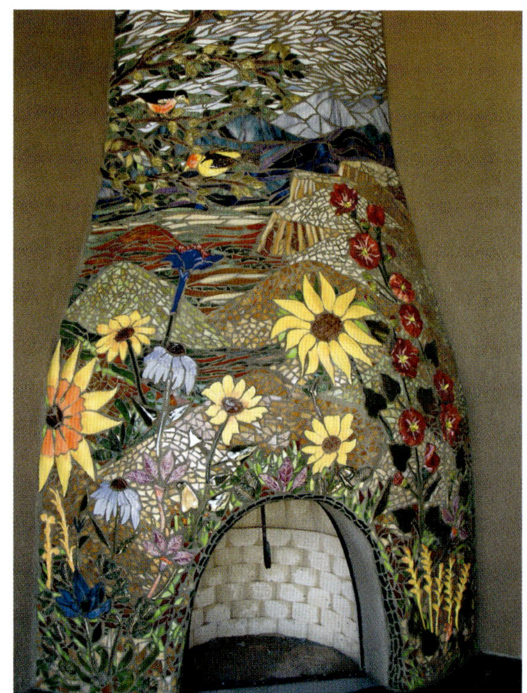

Laura Robbins. *Fireplace*.

House Beautiful One: I inherited some old tools and incorporated them into mosaics I call the *Tool Series*. My father was a great admirer of Frank Lloyd Wright and I think the combination of the old metal auger and wooden plane in combination with the glass design is a tribute to my dad and all the tools we humans use for our building processes.

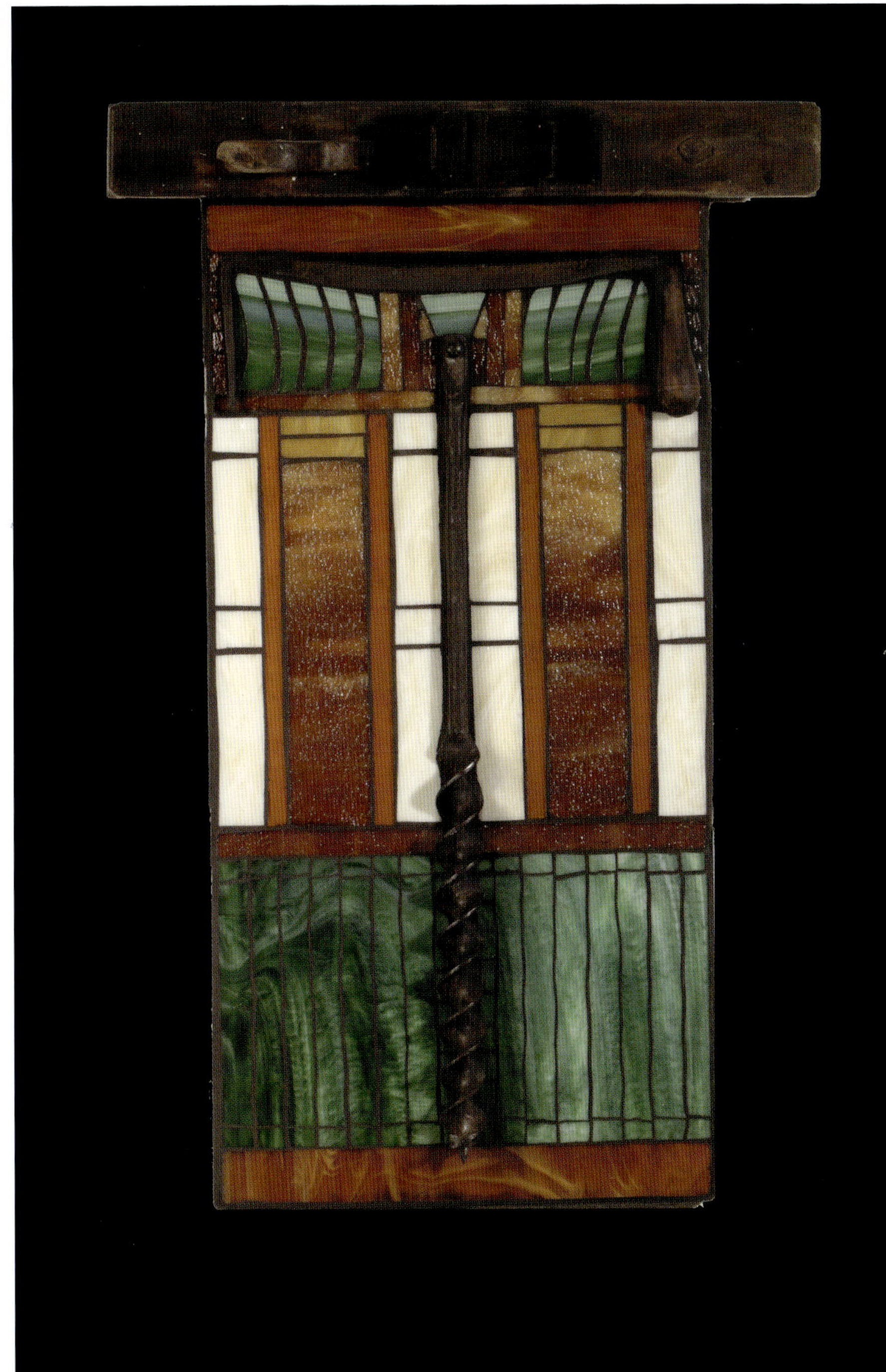

Laura Robbins. *House Beautiful One.* 2009. Approximately 32" x 21.5".

Gray Water Kitchen: This free-standing, 8.5' x 4.5' installation piece took me about two and a half years to complete. I wanted to extend it to include a bathtub and garden, but after it took four people to move it for a show—even in parts—I thought I'd wait until it found a permanent home to add anything else! The piece is structurally made from foam (insulation foam and even pool noodles) and strengthened by fiberglass mesh, polymer cement, and some joining metals and wires. Many of the forms are ceramic, such as the flowers and pot. Water from the faucet and pipe going to roots under the cabinet is fused glass, as are the leaves of the tree and some garden flowers. The curtains are slumped glass. It was a learning process of exploratory play to figure out how to construct and complete my visions. Home is an important theme in my work. The kitchen scene plays with not separating what is inside from what is outside as the earth is our home. Recycling my kitchen sink water to a part of our high desert garden inspired its creation!

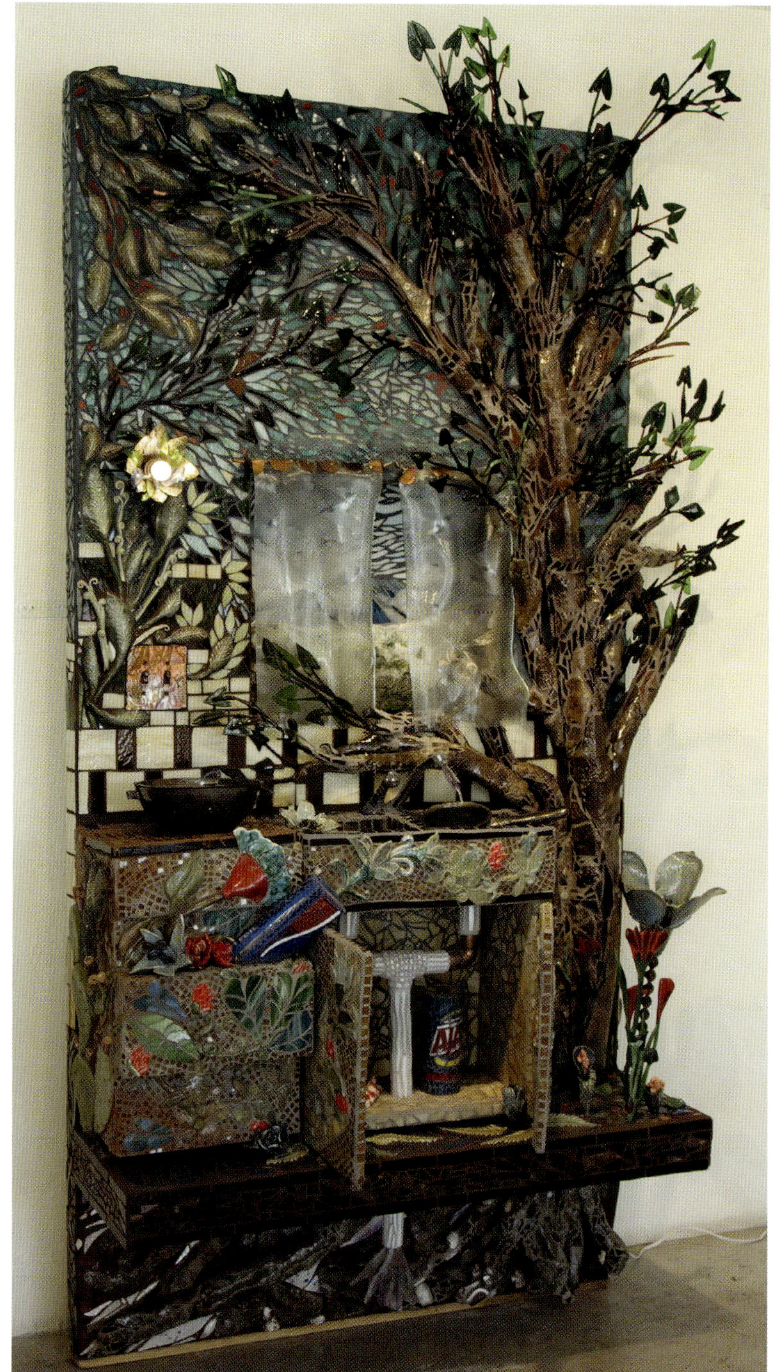

Laura Robbins. *Gray Water Kitchen.* 2010. 8.5' x 4.5' x 1.5'. (right and opposite page)

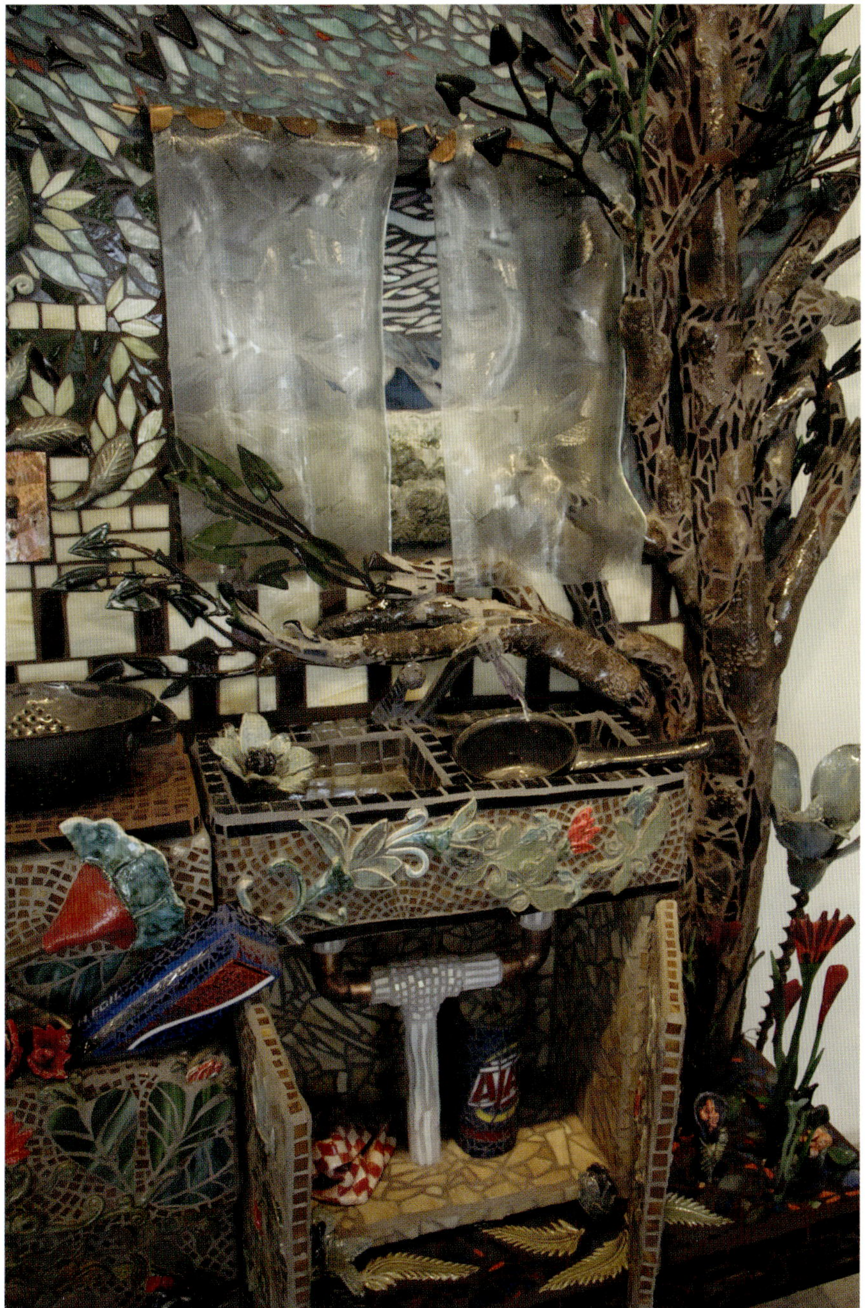

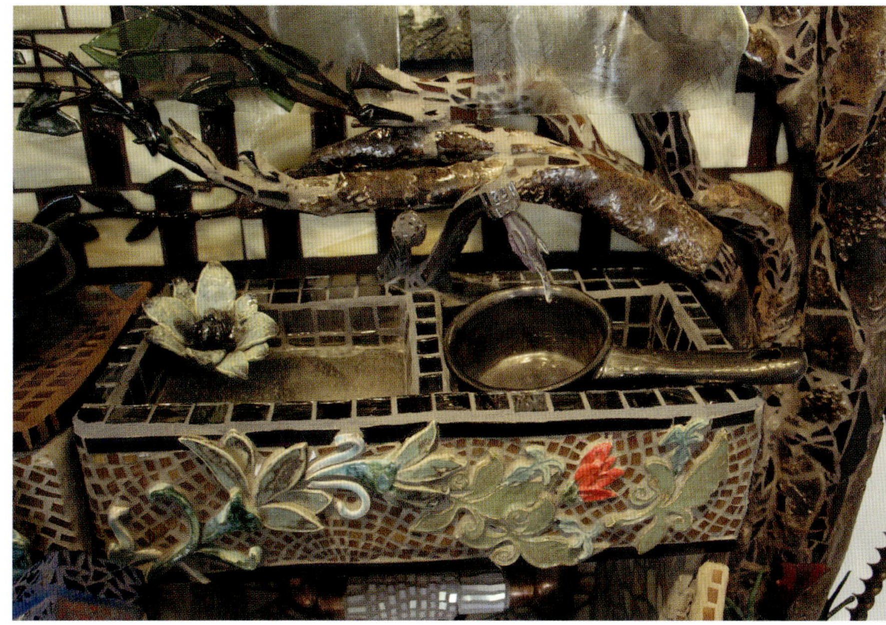

Night House also uses some of these old tools (compasses, etc.) and keys. It is a very textural piece. Ceramic leaves, textural glass, cement nails, and a fossil are components.

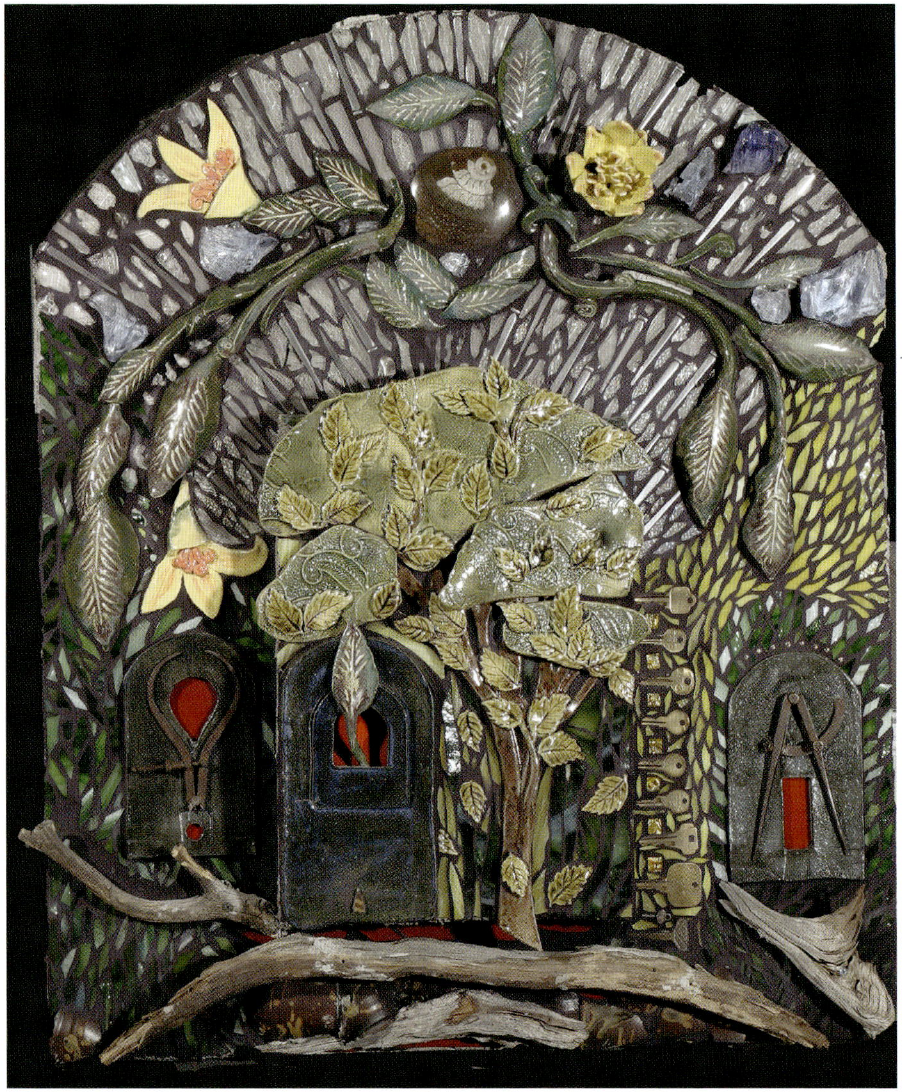

Laura Robbins. *Night House*. 2010. 37" x 31" x 4.5".

House of Song: I was asked to make a mosaic to be used for the 2011 Globalquerque Music Festival, where world music is highlighted. There was no real planning on this piece, except the ideas of the world as a home with roots of the songs of people, plants, and animals. All musical instruments (ancient and modern) also come from these roots.

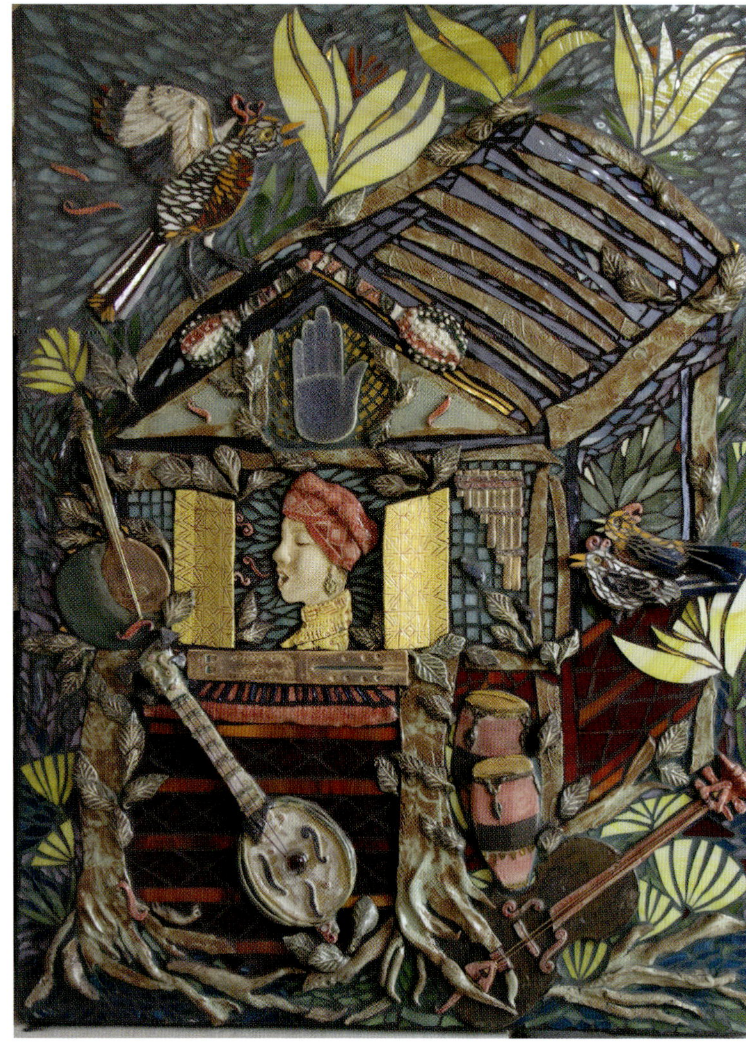

Laura Robbins. *House of Song*. 2011. 4' x 3' x 4".

After Ravenna: The initial creation of clay forms inspires the spontaneous glasswork as mark-making. These two compositions weren't planned but evolved until the pieces were completed. As always, the grout filled spaces are important to the movement and color.

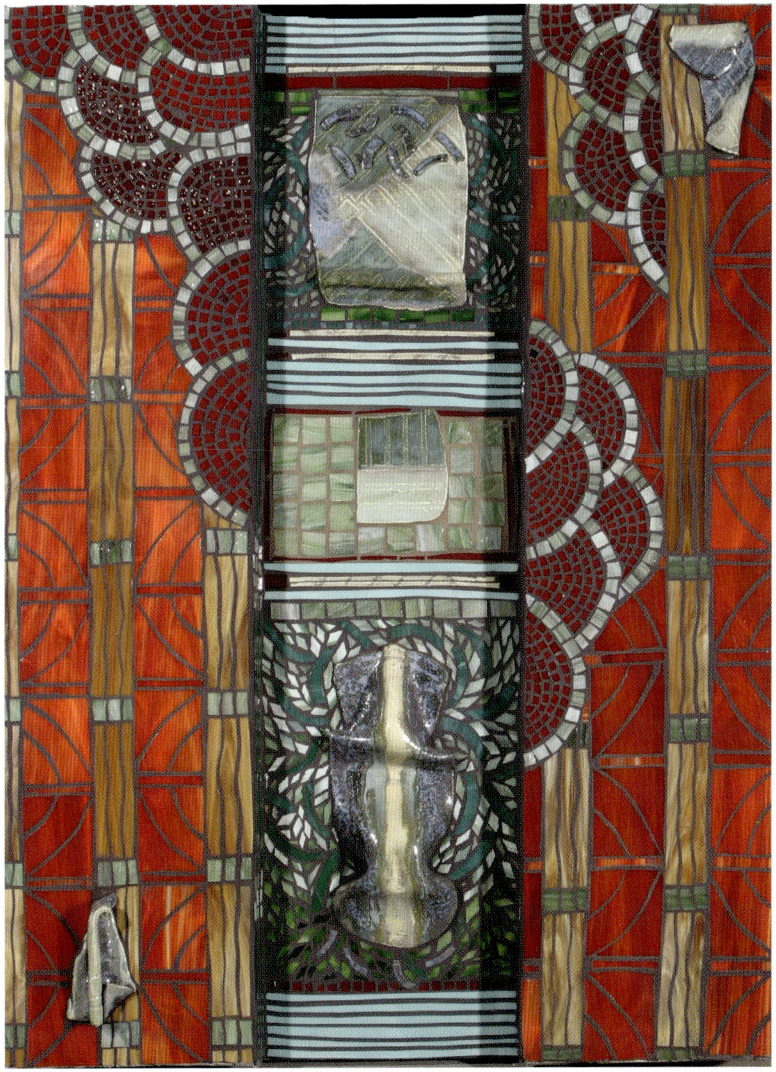

Laura Robbins. *After Ravenna*. 2010. 4' x 3' x 5".

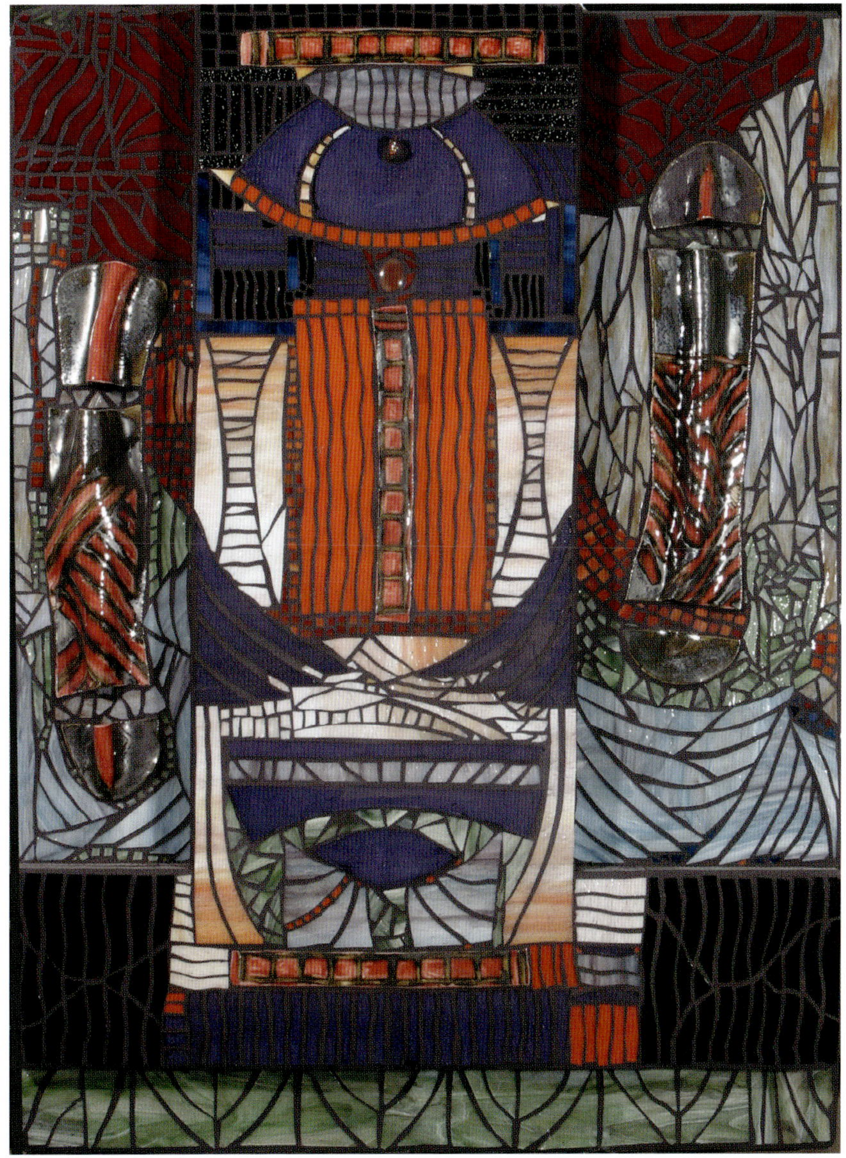

Laura Robbins. *Los Rincones*. 2010. 4' x 3' x 5".

Jackie Russo

Allegan, Michigan, jackie@jackierusso.com

About the Artwork

Fire In My Soul: One day I was cutting large sheets of art glass into smaller pieces for one of my "Harmony Poles" when I noticed a pleasing flowing pattern on the back side of a red sheet of glass. I couldn't bring myself to cut it into pieces so I propped it up in my studio to ponder it. It sat patiently waiting for several weeks while I waited for inspiration! One day I just knew what I had to do; I carefully cut out the red/orange flowing section of glass and used it as the starting point for this design. Although this design is not typical of my style, the design was spontaneous and just flowed.

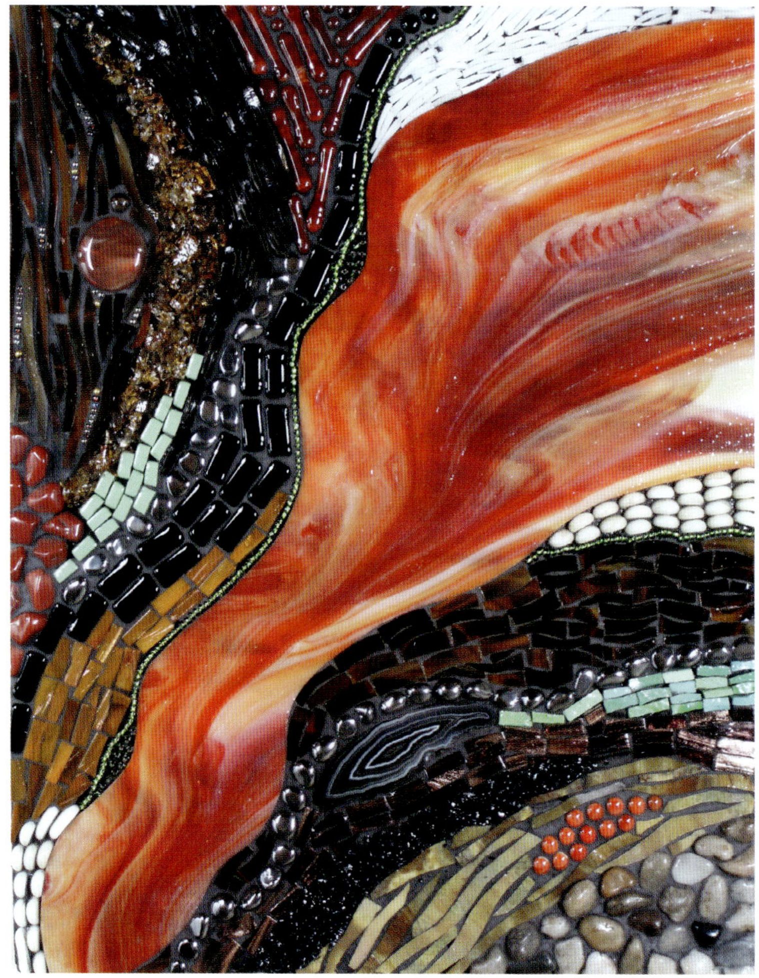

Jackie Russo. *Fire In My Soul*. Art glass, hematite, sea spines, tile, fused glass, beads, frit, smalti, agate slice on expanded polystyrene. 14" x 18".

Harmony Poles: Two years ago I broke my right arm and could only cut a straight line, no complex curves like my work usually incorporated. I needed to continue working as I had to prepare for the upcoming Art Fair season. Thus the *Harmony* collection was born. It was successful. I have continued to develop it and have not returned to my previous style of work.

The *Harmony* collection illustrates how elements not normally seen together can create a harmonious whole. They are a metaphor for how each of the cultures in the world contributes to a rich life experience; each adding its unique flavor and texture.

The pieces in this collection are created using mosaic techniques on a base of expanded polystyrene, making them very lightweight, about five pounds each. I create all of the fused glass elements used in the pieces and string all the beads.

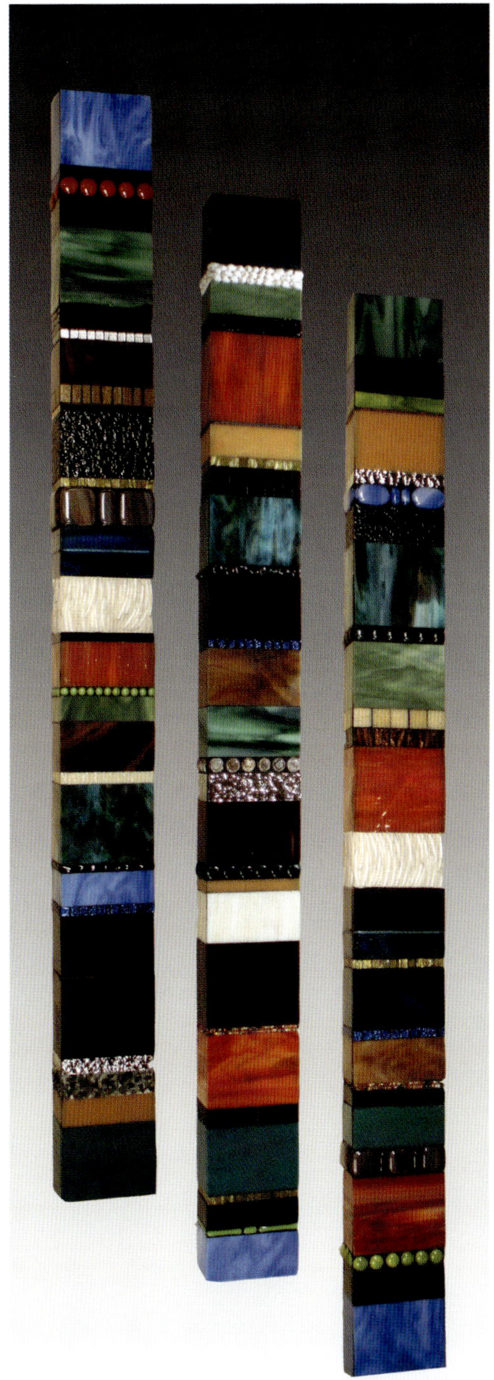

Jackie Russo. *Harmony Poles.* Art glass, fused glass, acrylic, tusk shells, hematite, gravel, tile, mirrored glass, beads, and shells on expanded polystyrene. 48" x 4" x 2".

Harmony Towers: The *Harmony Towers* are the newest addition to the *Harmony* collection. They are created with the same materials and techniques as the *Harmony Poles* but they are hollowed out and filled with cement to create a weighted piece.

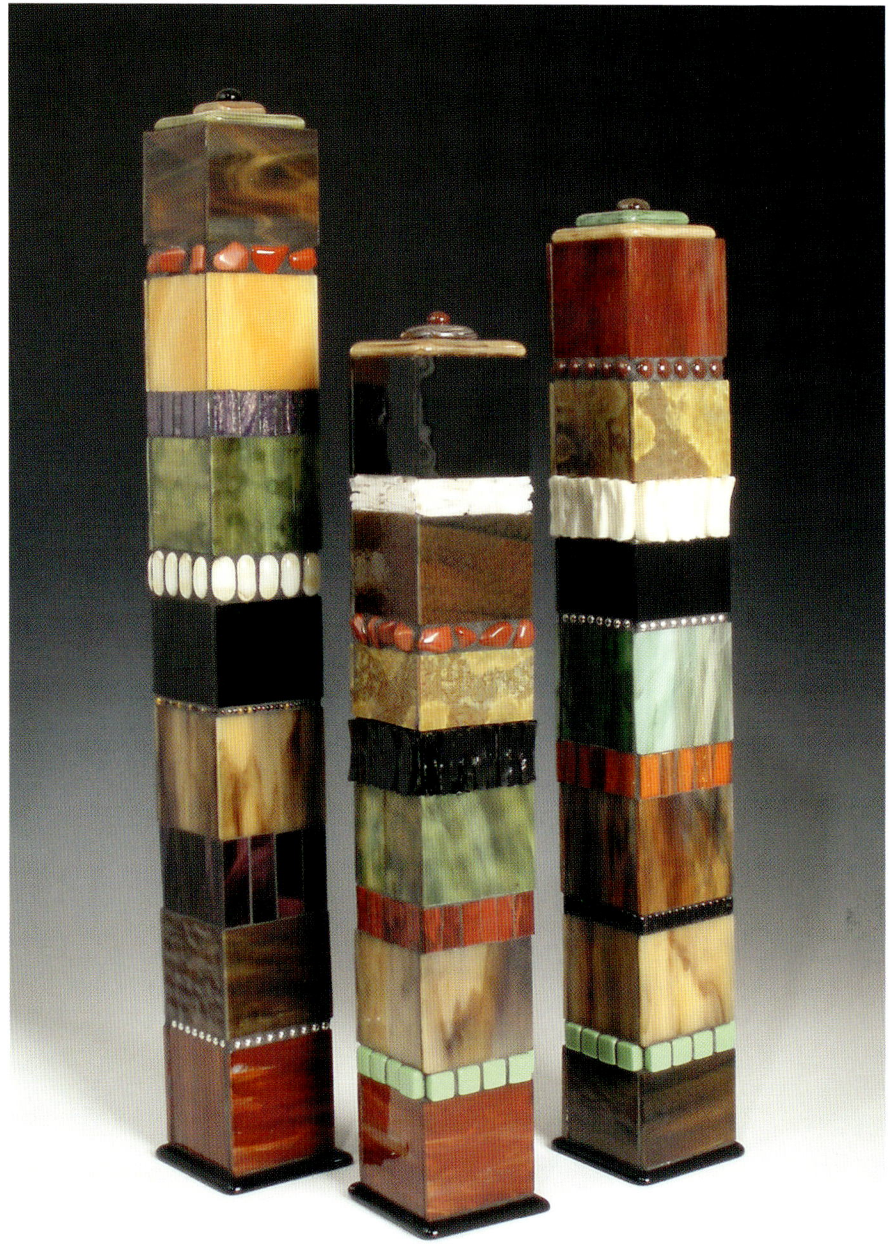

Jackie Russo. *Harmony Towers.* Stained glass, jasper, tile, fused glass, beads, ball chain, tusk shells on expanded poly styrene filled with cement. 19" x 2" x 2", 17" x 2" x 2", 15" x 2" x 2".

Listen To My Heart: This piece was created to raise funds for the Esther Benjamins Trust, which has a mosaic studio in Nepal that provides employment for young workers rescued as children by the Trust.

Mosaic artists from around the world each created an 8" x 8" (20cm x 20cm) mosaic with a circular feature. All the mosaics will be combined to create a larger mosaic, which will be donated to Central Middlesex Hospital in London. The final installation will be in the transport lounge where patients often wait for long hours.

My design was created from an abstraction of the inner ear, which I thought was appropriate for a hospital setting. Having been hospitalized as a child, I understand how scary it can be and how important it is to be heard as a patient. Children often don't know how to express or identify the overwhelming feelings of being ill and hospitalized; we need to listen to what is unsaid as much as to what is said. I chose the hues of blue and pink to use in this piece as they are calming and refreshing; blue is also my favorite color!

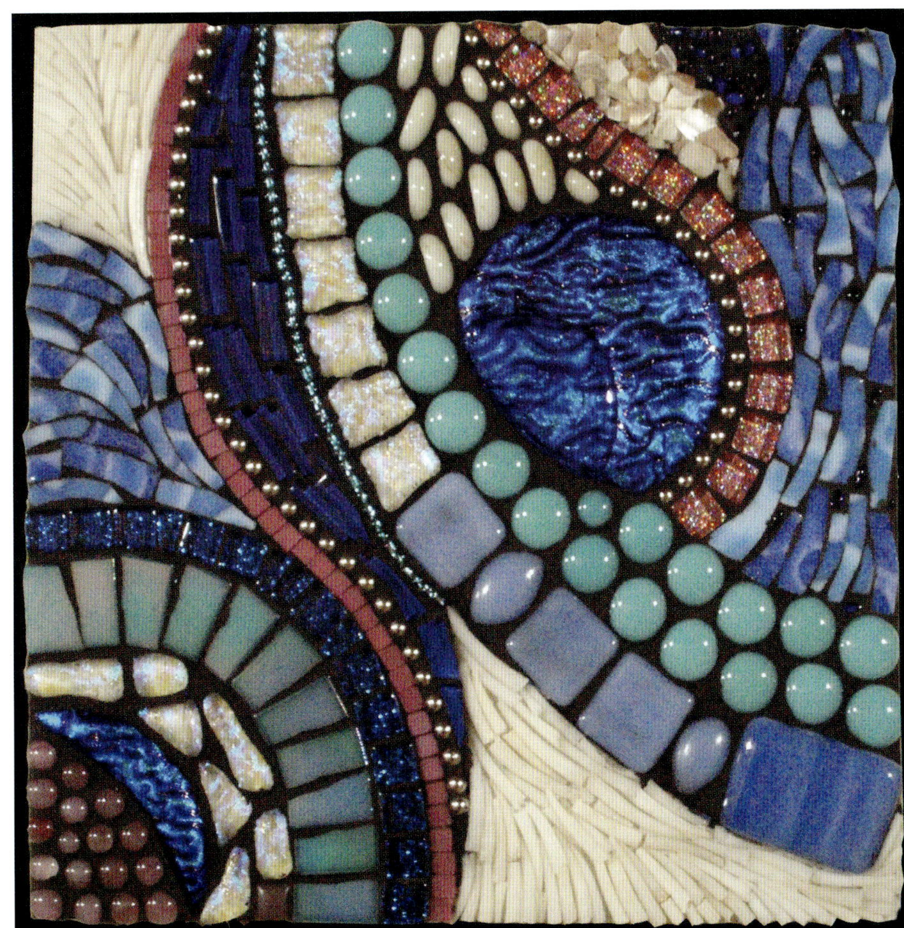

Jackie Russo. *Listen To My Heart*. Fused glass, tile, beads, tusk shells, crushed shells, ball chain, tile, dichroic glass, acrylic. 8" x 8".

Galina Rychagova & Vitaly Kulsh

Pushkin, St. Petersburg, rytotia@gmail.com

Artist's Statement

Our studio "TEVI" was named in honor of a beautiful cape on the eastern sea coast of Kamchatka (Russia) near an agate deposit. The two of us, Galina Rychagova and Vitaly Kulsh, work together. We make pictures and souvenirs from natural precious stones in a technique of Florentine Mosaic. This art blossomed out in the twelfth century in Florence. With the lapse of time, the concept of "Florentine mosaic" has come to signify not only the place of origin, but expressive and original ways of working with stones.

For over fourteen years we have been developing this exciting and difficult artwork. We use rare stones from Kamchatka to make our mosaics, including agate, chalcedony, kacholong, cornelian, jasper, obsidian, flint, and more. The process of stone mosaic development is long and complex. Sometimes it takes months or years to create a single work of art. The stone passes through several steps. We also obtain Kamchatka precious stones ourselves. This is important to the quality of the work. Several steps are required to create a work of art. We begin with draft development, move on to stone material selection and cutting, move on to adjustment and assembly, and end with the final treatment. In adjustment and assembly from sawed plates details for the future picture are cut out and adjusted thoroughly to each other. Then, details are glued together with epoxy resin. From the back side of the image, the base is attached. In the final treatment, the completed image is polished.

About the Artwork

Burning Bush: The icon was presented to the Russian Prime Minister V. Putin by the governor of the Kamchatka region in 2007.

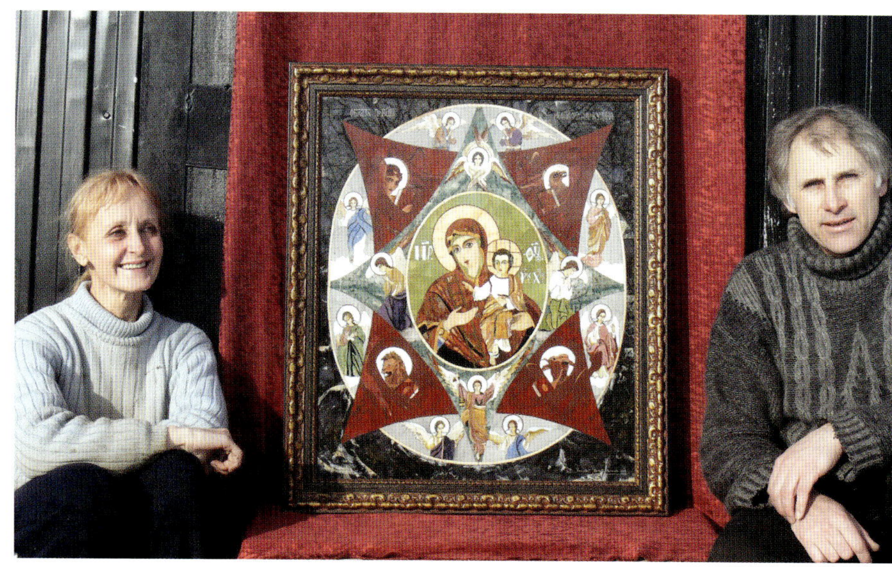

Galina Rychagova and Vitaly Kulsh. *Burning Bush.* Icon. Florentine mosaic. Agate, mossy agate, flint, lapis lazuli, rhodonite, kacholong, skarn, jasper. 20" x 24" (50cm x 62cm).

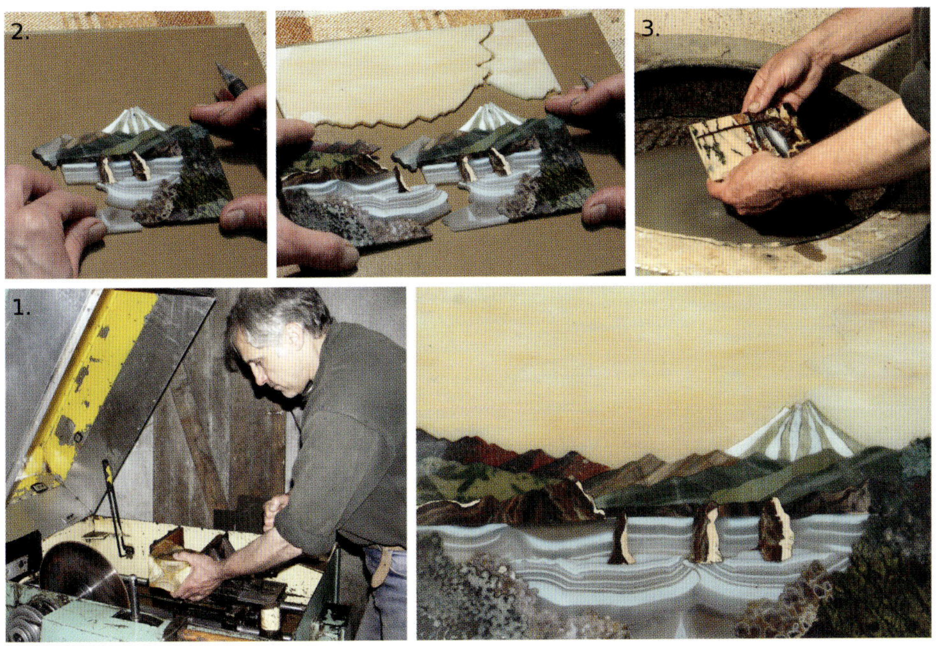

Galina Rychagova and Vitaly Kulsh. The process of creation. 1. Our master Vitaly Kulsh is cutting stone for plate samples. 2. Stone details are adjusted to each other. 3. A picture is polished.

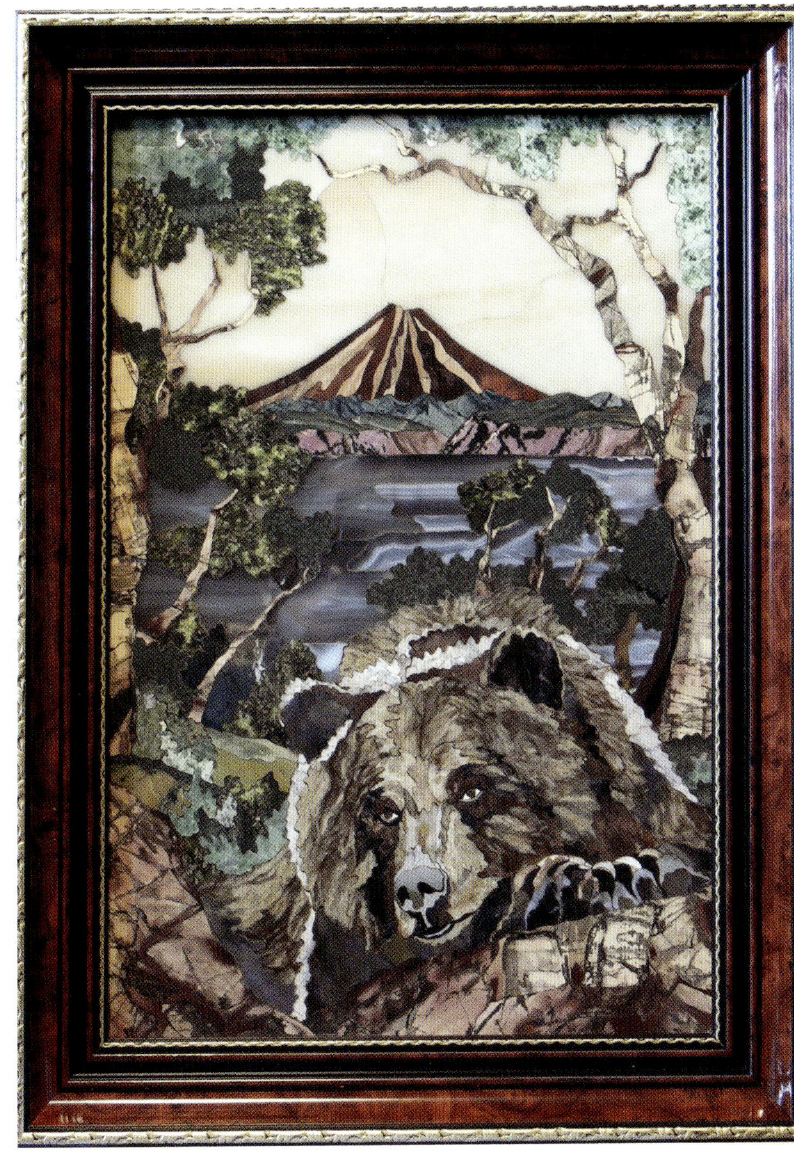

Galina Rychagova and Vitaly Kulsh. *Kamchatka Bear*. Florentine mosaic. Jasper, agate, obsidian, marble, serpentine, flint. 10" x 14 1/2" (25cm x 37cm).

Occasion: The picture was made over two months.

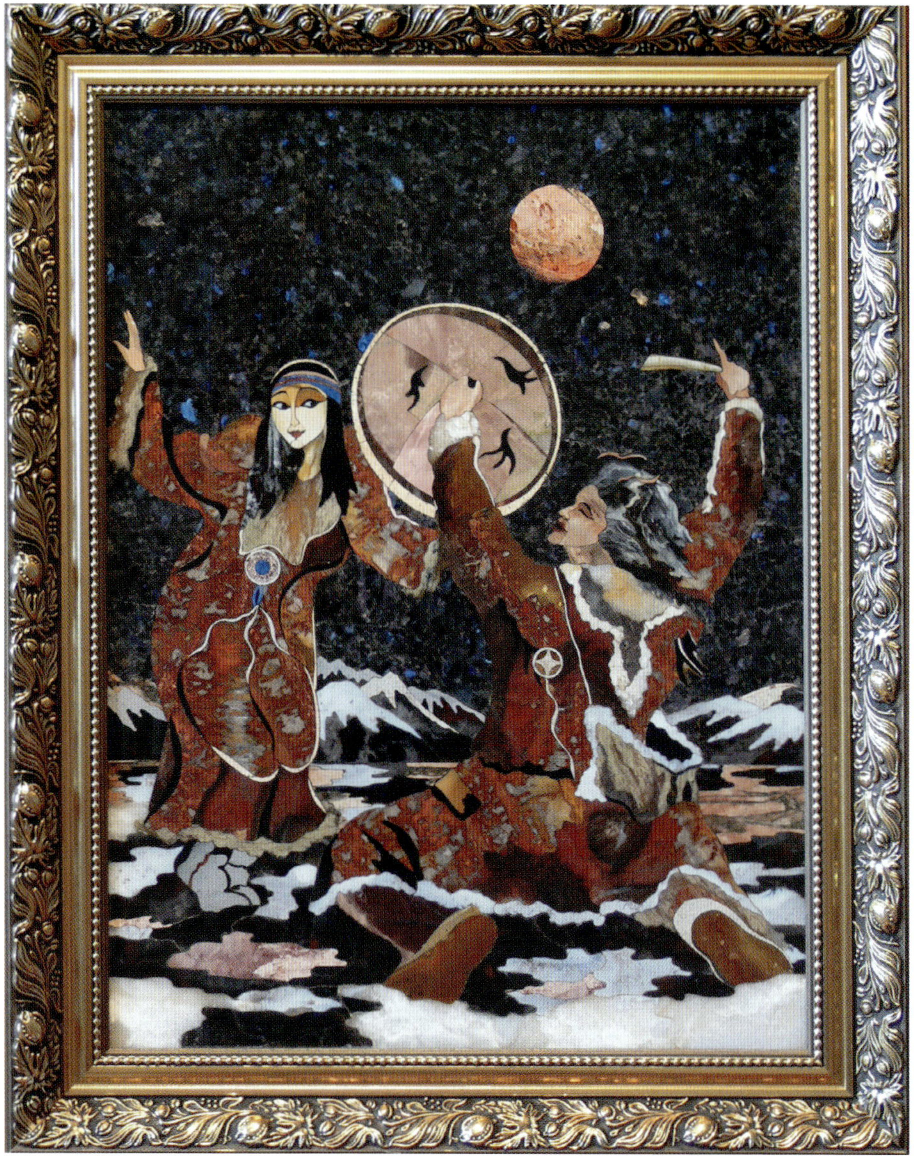

Galina Rychagova and Vitaly Kulsh. *Occasion*. Florentine mosaic. Jasper, mossy agate, lapis lazuli, fossil wood, flint, skarn, kacholong. 18 1/2" x 24" (47cm x 60cm).

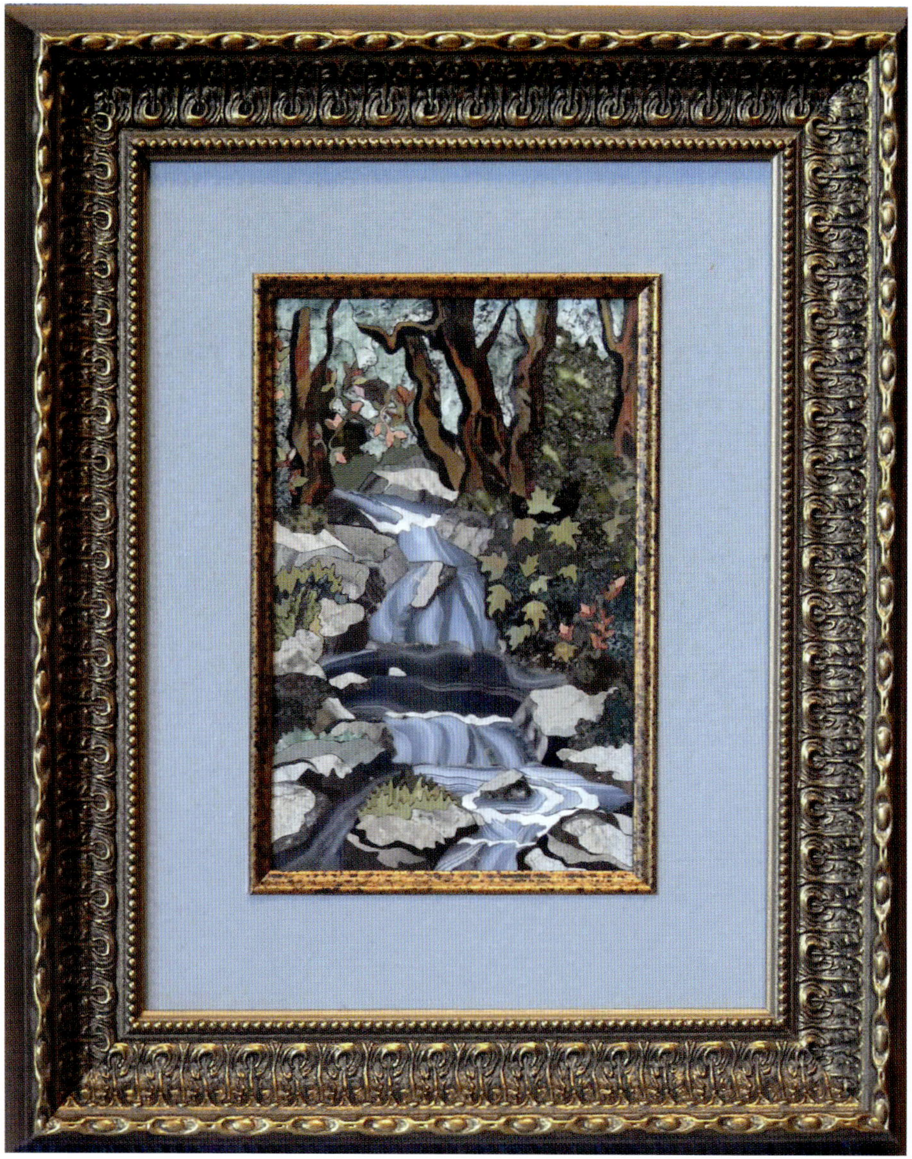

Galina Rychagova and Vitaly Kulsh. *Waterfall*. Florentine mosaic. Agate, jasper, marble, serpentine, ophiocalcite, chalcedony. 10" x 7" (25cm x 18cm).

Portrait of V. Samarsky: Was made in 2 1/2 months. The portrait was made in honor of a legendary pilot and is now presented in the portrait gallery "The Tablets of Kamchatka" (Petropavlovsk – Kamchatsky, Kamchatka).

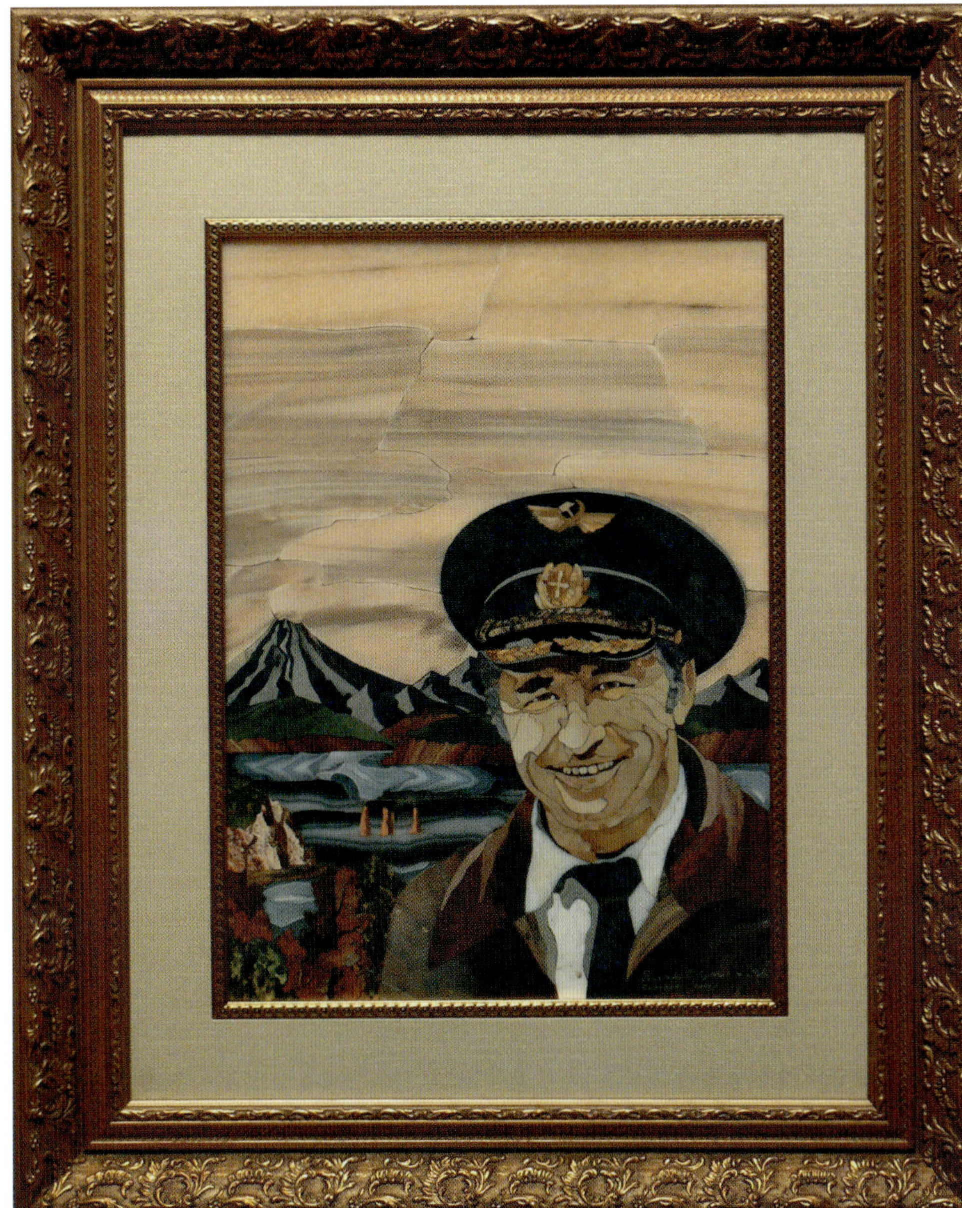

Galina Rychagova and Vitaly Kulsh. *Portrait of V. Samarsky, the Legendary Pilot of Kamchatka (Russia).* Florentine mosaic. Jasper, agate, kacholong, flint, chalcedony, marble. 22" x 17" (57cm x 44cm).

Patrizia Salles

Houston, Texas, ps@patriziaart.com

About the Artwork

Three Square: In contrast to night, these three pieces are representative of the sun filled days off the Mediterranean coastline of Spain. The modern geometric design, in variance with the flowing nightscape, balances the work with a vibrancy of color and exactness—the preciseness of the square. *Three Square* is also a composition on subtleties of color, paying homage to the more progressive attitudes and art of Spain.

Patrizia Salles. *Three Square.* Ceramic tile, glass tile, glass bubbles. 3" - 12" squares. *Photo by Hedda Wienpahl*

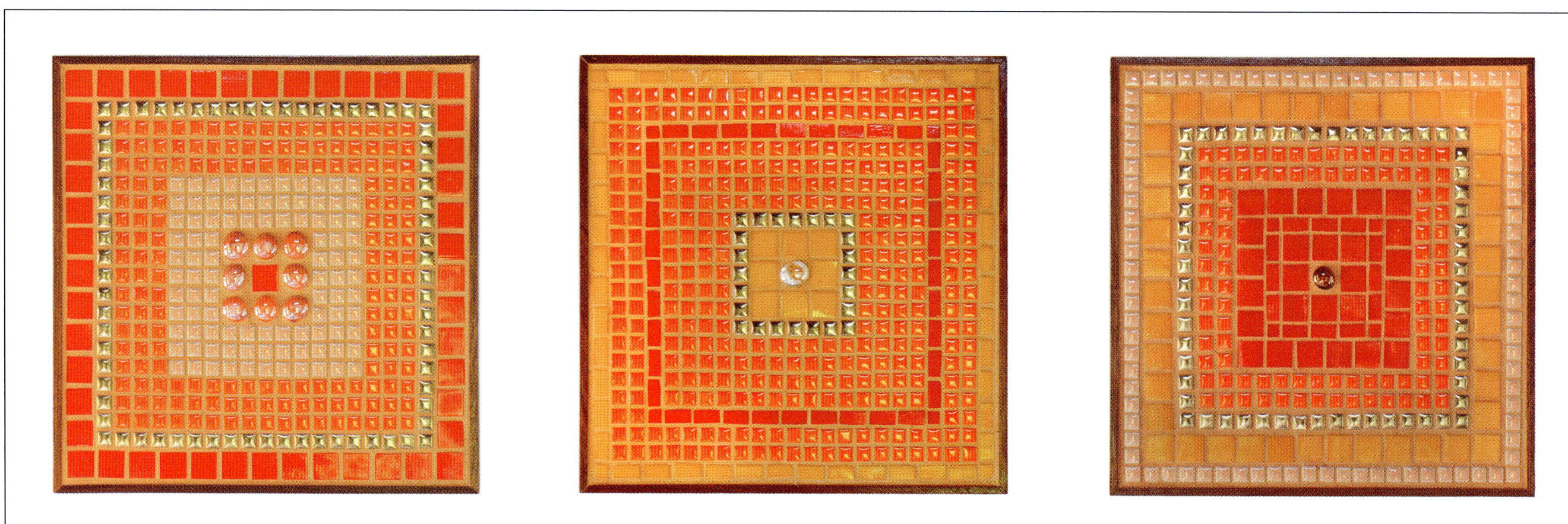

Four Elements. Earth, Wind, Fire, and Water: I had just started dabbling in multi media mosaics. I was interested in the assembly of several types of materials, from rock to ceramics to glass and glass bubbles, mixing the media to bring the piece alive not only with color, but texture. I couldn't wait to do the *Earth* panel, mixing the stones with the glass and other earthy colors. *Wind* was the most challenging. How to lay in the pieces and colors to illustrate the strength and motion found in the Da Vinci drawings while maintaining the transparency of air. Delicate hues that are imagined more than seen. Most of the panels were created in the Caribbean, so you can imagine the ease of working the *Water. Fire* came naturally in fierce-hot color.

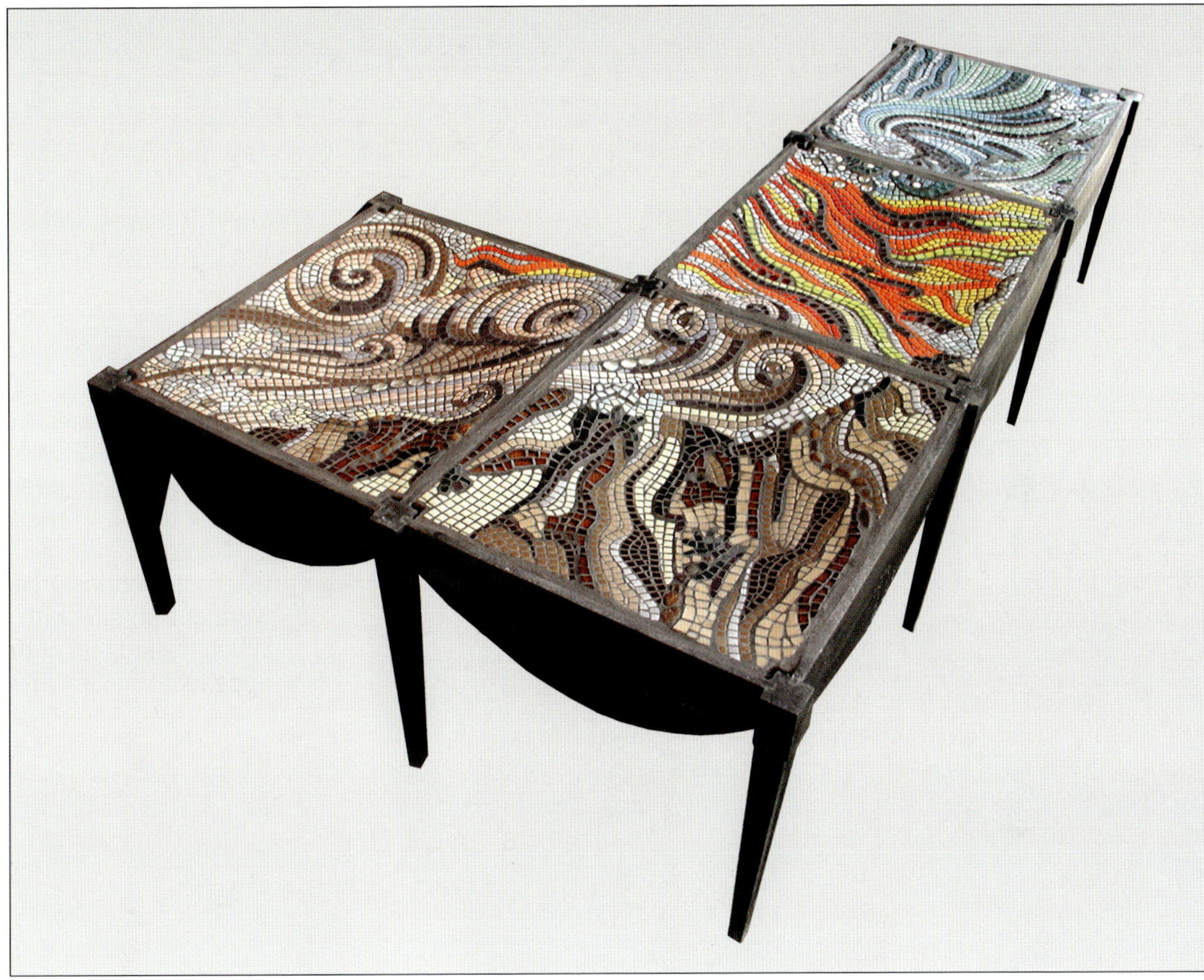

Patrizia Salles. *Four Elements. Earth, Wind, Fire, and Water*. Amen L-shaped Bench–Aluminum Base by Kelly Amen. 2005. 19" x 21" each. Finished Size: 60" x 48" x 19". *Photo by Hedda Wienpahl*

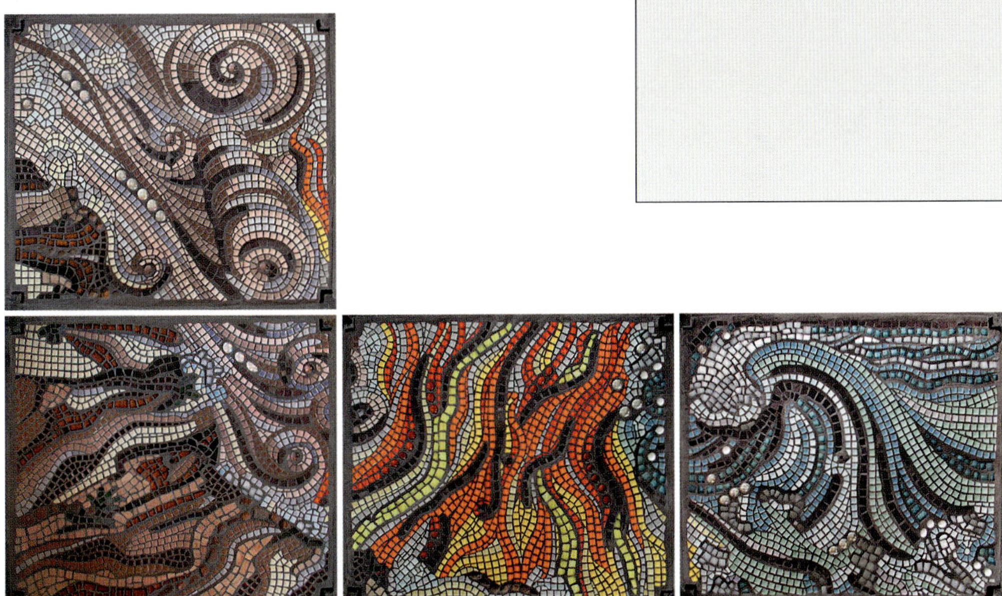

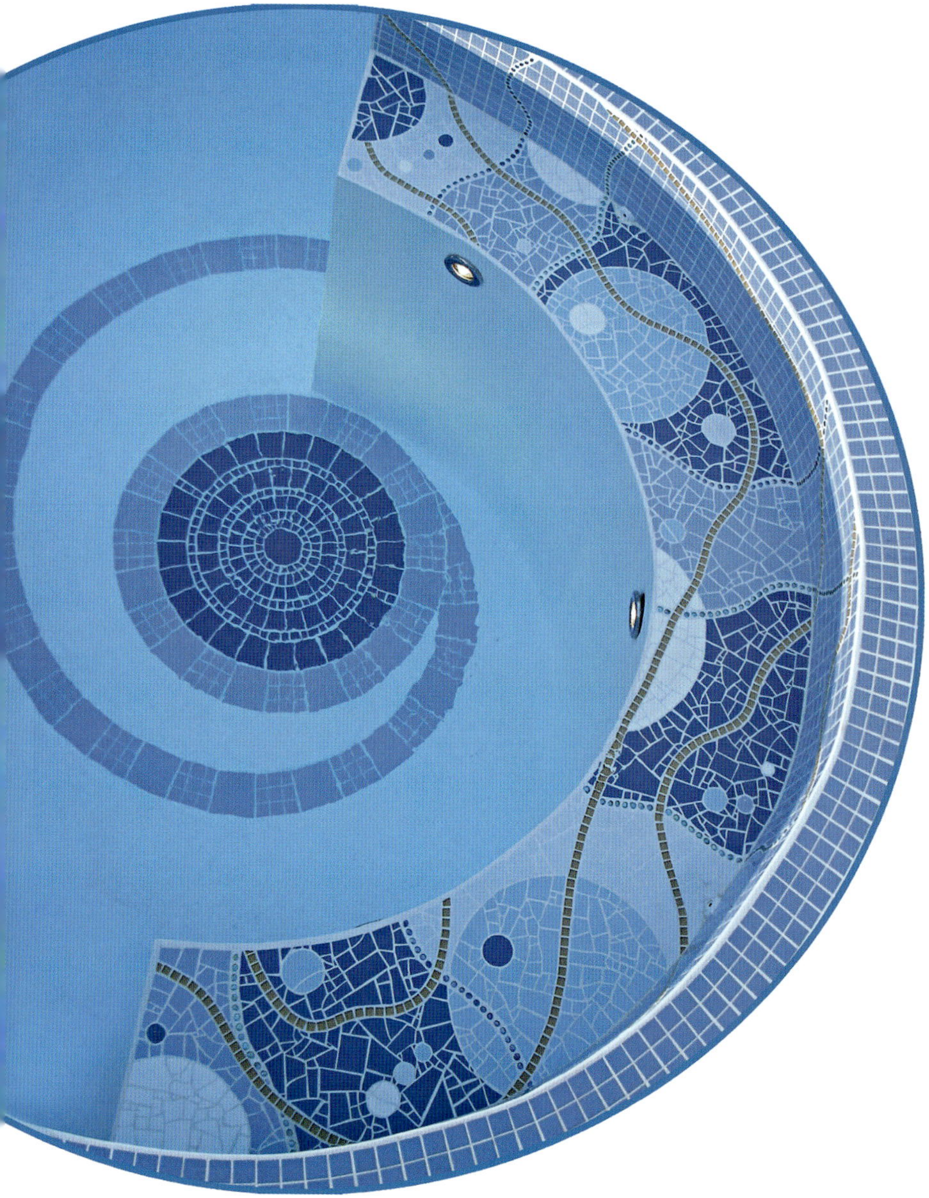

Patrizia Salles. Thompson Pool. 2007. Bench and back wall: 40" x 20'. Bottom swirl: 3' diameter.

Thompson Pool: At the edge of a cliff, Thompson Pool overlooks the Caribbean Sea, fish and turtles visible in the crystal clear aquamarine waters forty feet below. The architecture of the main house could be considered modern in a Caribbean vernacular kind of way. Based on the setting, I knew the best approach was to bring the transparency and movement of the ocean—with its stunning and varied shades of aqua-greens to cobalt blues—into the pool, creating a seamless transition from sea below to pool above, in a modern, flowing style. At the client's request, gold was added—to run through a design of circles, bubbles, and flowing water in ribbons and layers. White adds dimension and contrast to the design, and once the pool was filled yet another subtle shade of blue.

A three-dimensional model was created to help the client visualize the mosaic, as I was working from architectural drawings. The mosaic was produced in the studio, the hand cut ceramic tile, glass bubbles, and gold-colored glass glued to mesh. The finished mosaic was separated into two-foot sections, installed and grouted on site. The bottom circle and swirl were cut on-site with a tile saw and laid in before the pool crew finished. When walking up or down the steps on the side of the pool, the bottom swirl appears to move with you. The motion of the ocean was achieved.

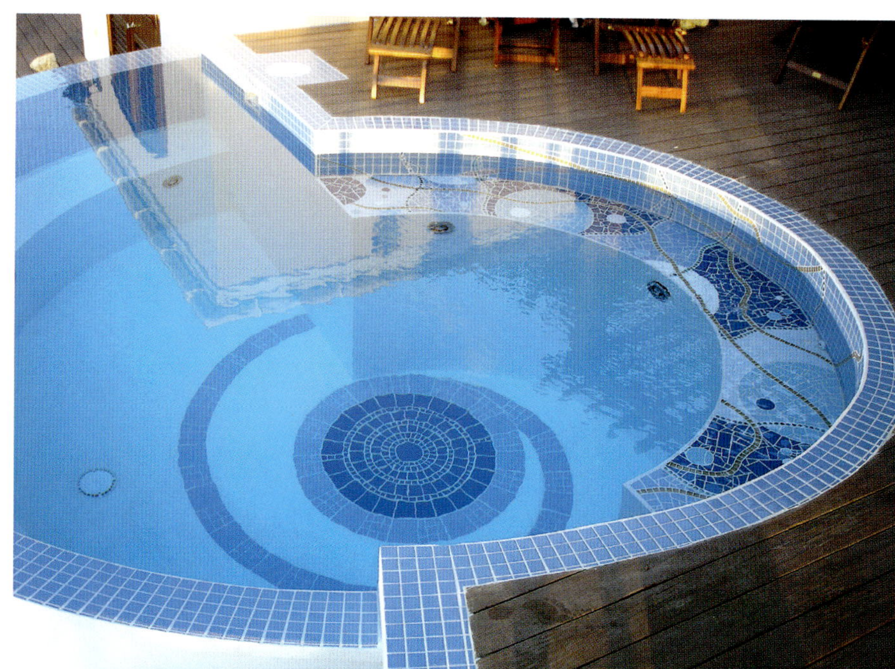

Barcelona Nights: Following the wonder of Antonio Gaudi in Barcelona, I hit Park Guell at dawn, on my last day. It was an exhilarating trek up the hill to see sculptured mosaics, park benches, towers, and slanting, maze-like outdoor rooms. On my way down to the Metro I happened upon a sign for a bar that planted the seed for *Barcelona Nights*.

The work is more than the sum of all parts (if that is possible) or the coalescence of famous Spanish artists such as El Greco, Goya, Miro, Picasso, and architect Gaudi. It is the ancient Catalunya Center and the progressive "La Ciudad de Las Damas." It adds up to a multi-faceted work on multiple planes with a night cast against the brilliance of color. It is the reflection of the vitality of a city, a richness of history, its food, and artisans that traverse life in Barcelona.

The choice between fine Bisazza glass tile and everyday ceramics, glass beads and iridescent gold, contrast the city fabric of narrow urban streets with fine opera houses, retail boutiques, opulent buildings, and century old ham makers and bakers.

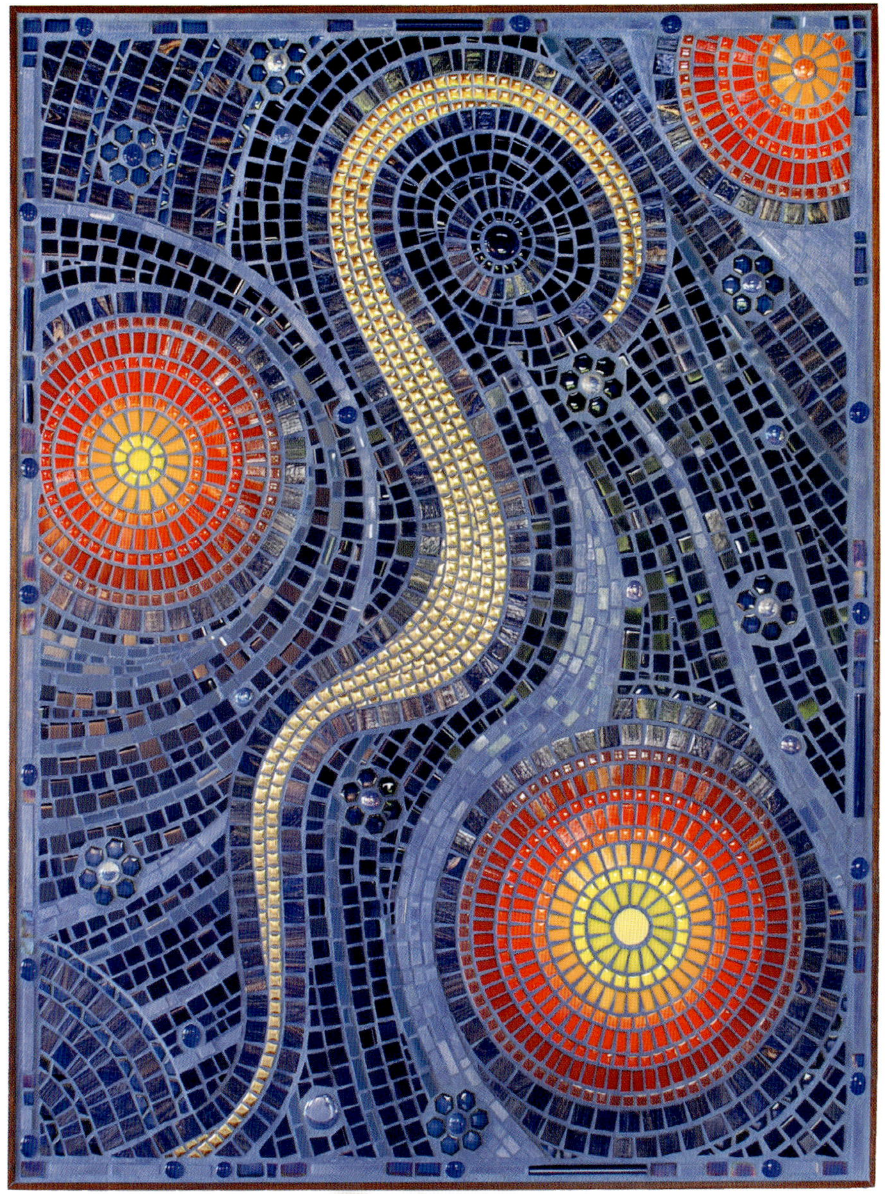

Patrizia Salles. *Barcelona Nights.* Barcelona Series: A work of four pieces. 2010. Ceramic tile, glass tile, glass bubbles. 32" x 42". *Photo by Hedda Wienpahl*

Marie A. Dresser: Living and working in the Caribbean, you collect a lot of shells. The Marie A. Dresser started as a way to use natural, found seashells and finding ways to mix them with everyday ceramic tile, vibrantly colored glass tiles, and gems. The piece was to be a kitchen glass cabinet, but once the mosaic evolved, I realized it was much too feminine and delicate for the kitchen and a high-traffic area and better suited for a ladies room.

The inclusion of the glass tile, especially the aquamarine, coupled with the glass gems, adds an opulence and luxuriousness to the dresser. The fine pieces—some of the iridescent shells and glass mosaics are not over a quarter of inch in diameter—are reminiscent of intricate details found in high renaissance boudoirs.

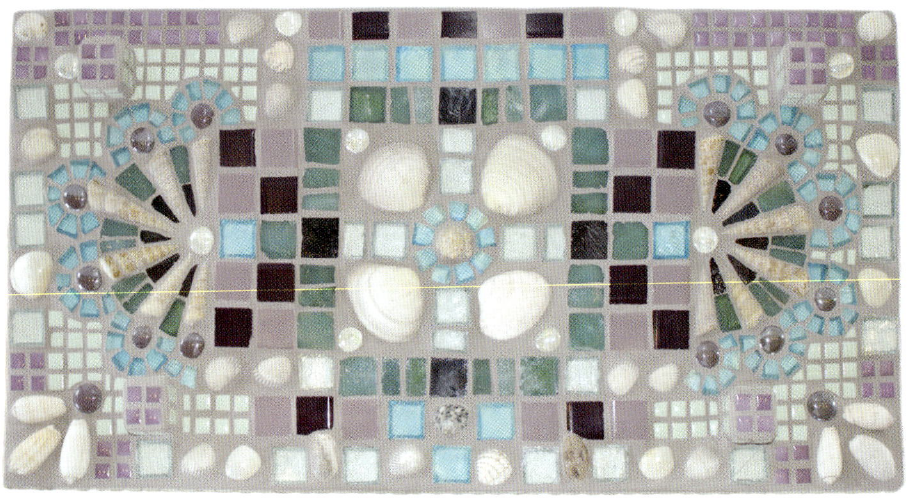

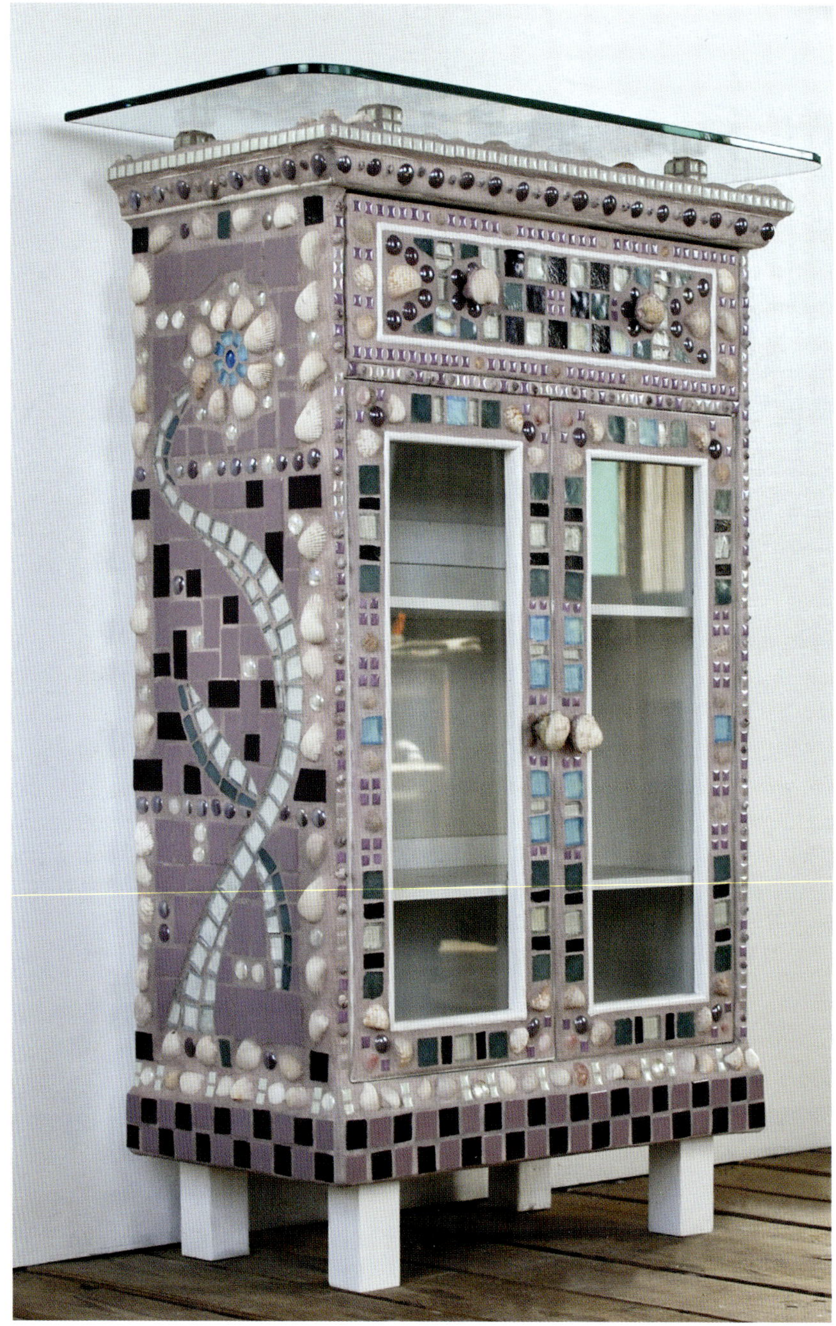

Patrizia Salles. *Marie A. Dresser.* 2010. Mixed media with seashells, ceramic tile, glass tile, and glass beads. 12" x 24" x 32". *Photo by Hedda Wienpahl*

Gretchen Schaefer

Portland, Maine, greatbluemosaic@gmail.com

Artist's Statement

An artist since childhood, exploring all manner of media from fiber to metalwork to painting, I turned to mosaic in the mid-2000s after making several visits to northern Italy. Seeing ancient pebble mosaic pavements in close proximity to vibrant glass and marble wall mosaics inspired me to combine these two styles in my own work.

Mosaic allows me to combine my love of texture, color, and fine craftsmanship to create images inspired by the natural world. My influences are diverse, from the patterns and stylized forms of Roman and Byzantine mosaic to the paintings of Gustav Klimt, with their juxtaposition of naturalistic portraiture against atomized, abstract fields.

I concentrate on natural images, notably wildlife found where land and water meet—fish, dragonflies, and, in particular, herons, to which I have dedicated a series of mosaics. The use of natural stone in combination with classic mosaic materials such as smalti, porcelain, marble, and glass allows me to contrast color, texture, and reflectivity in my work. The tension inherent in the juxtapositions of smooth and rough, dull and shiny, manufactured and natural, provides areas of both visual excitement and repose.

The Artwork

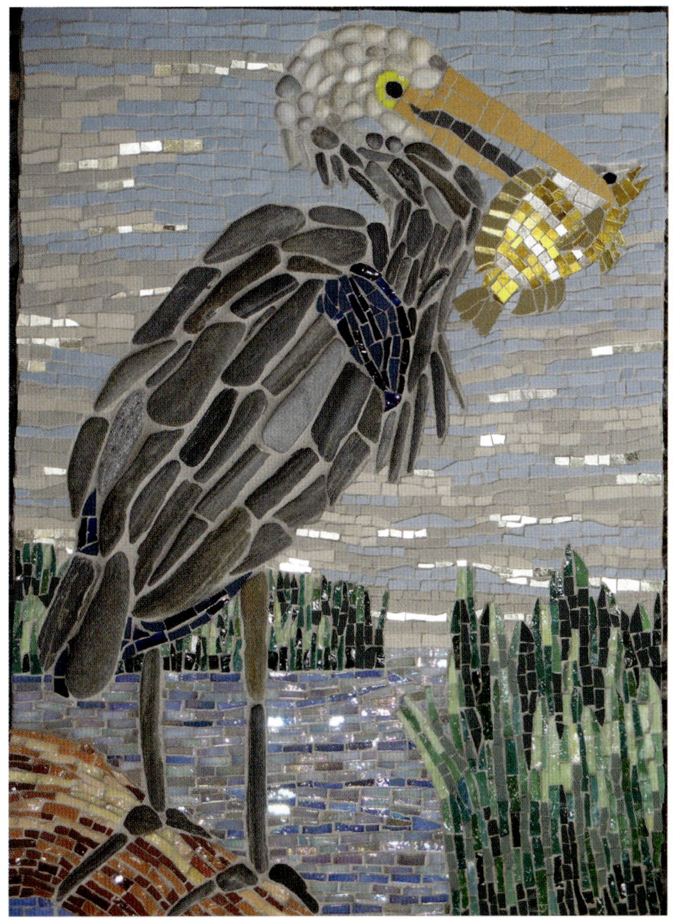

Gretchen Schaefer. *The Punkinseed*. Wall piece. 2008. Mixed media mosaic. 17" x 12.5".

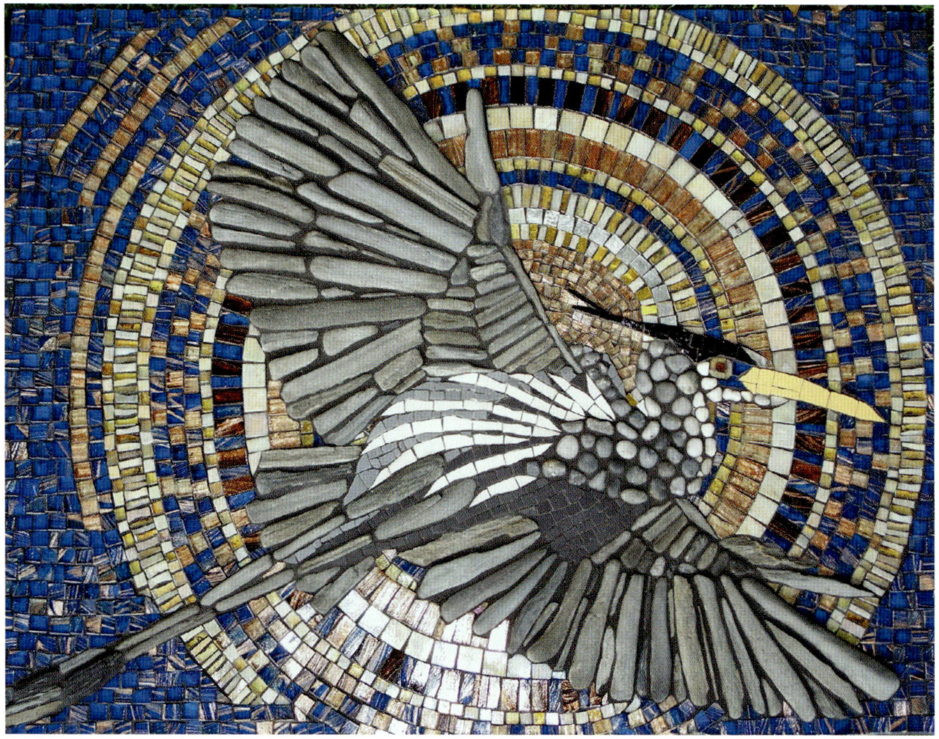

Gretchen Schaefer. *Blue Moon*. Wall piece. 2009. Mixed media mosaic. 18" x 20".

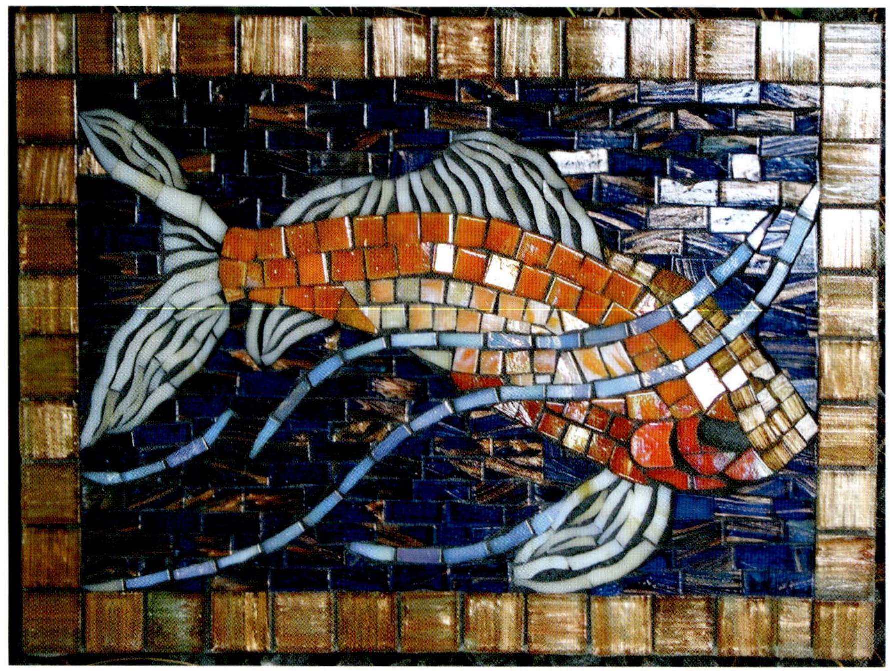

Gretchen Schaefer. *Goldfish*. Wall piece. 2010. Glass mosaic. 8" x 11".

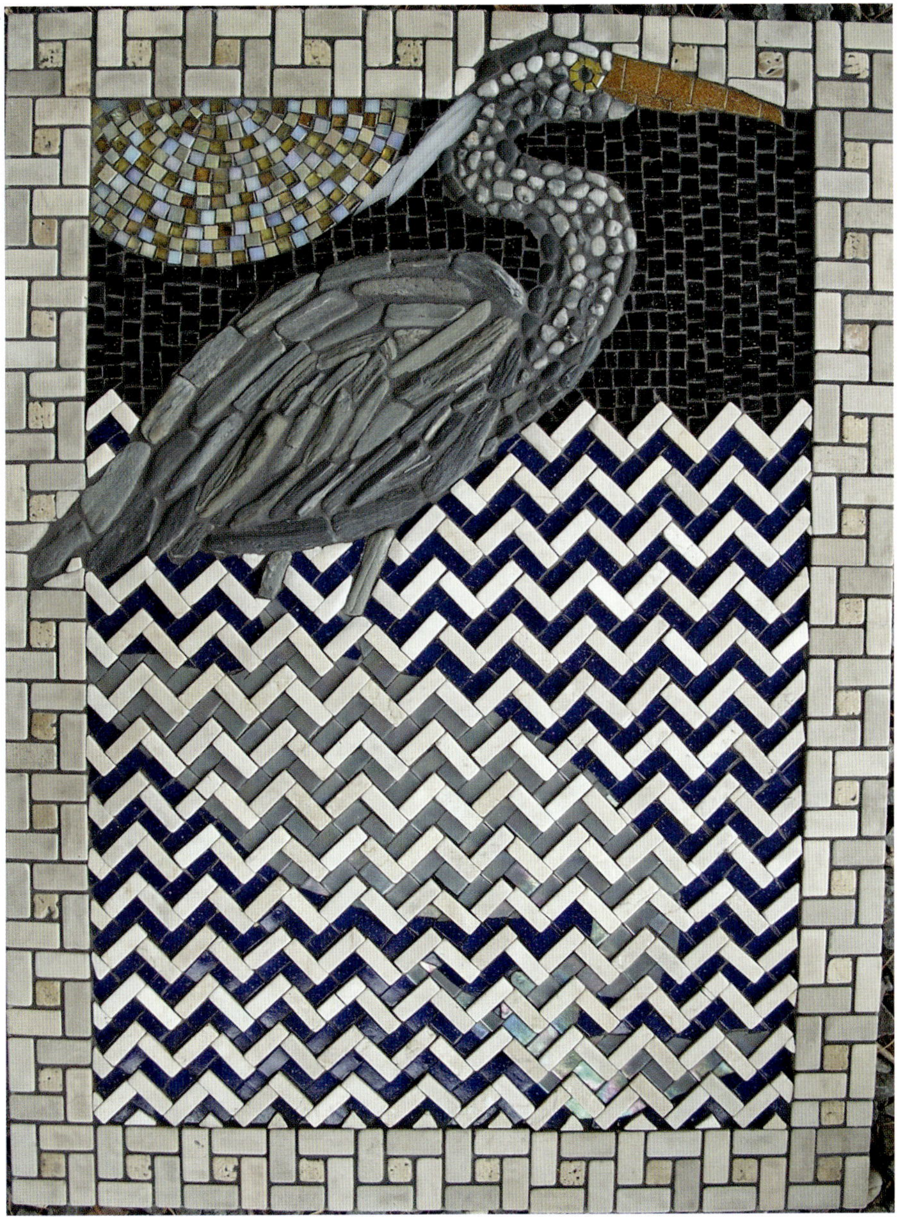

Gretchen Schaefer. *Reflection*. Wall piece. 2010. Mixed media mosaic. 26" x 20".

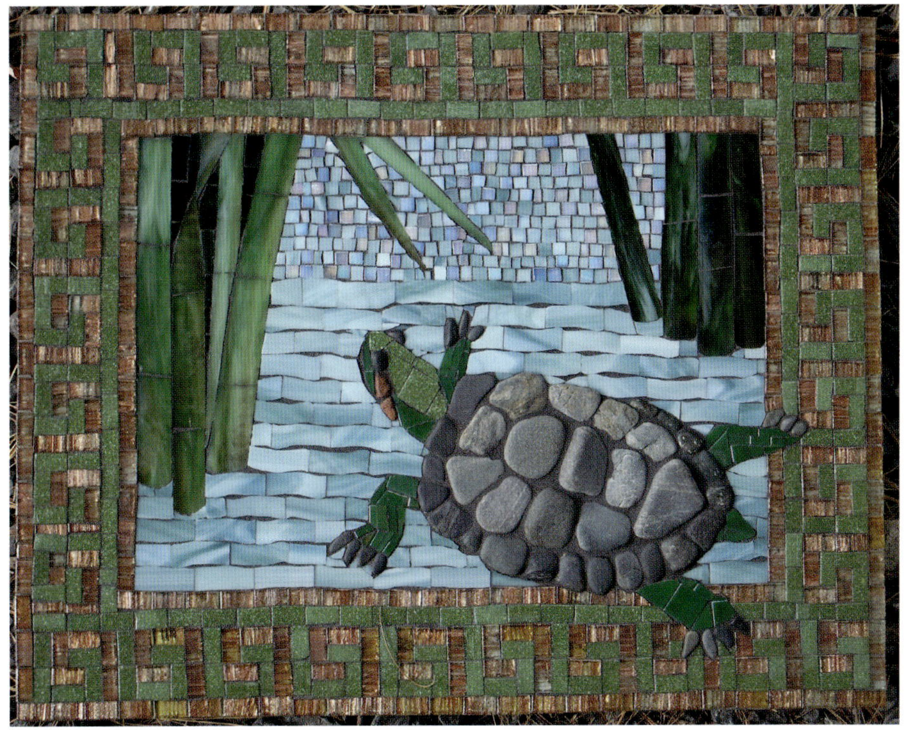

Gretchen Schaefer. *The River*. Wall piece. 2010. Mixed media mosaic. 16" x 20".

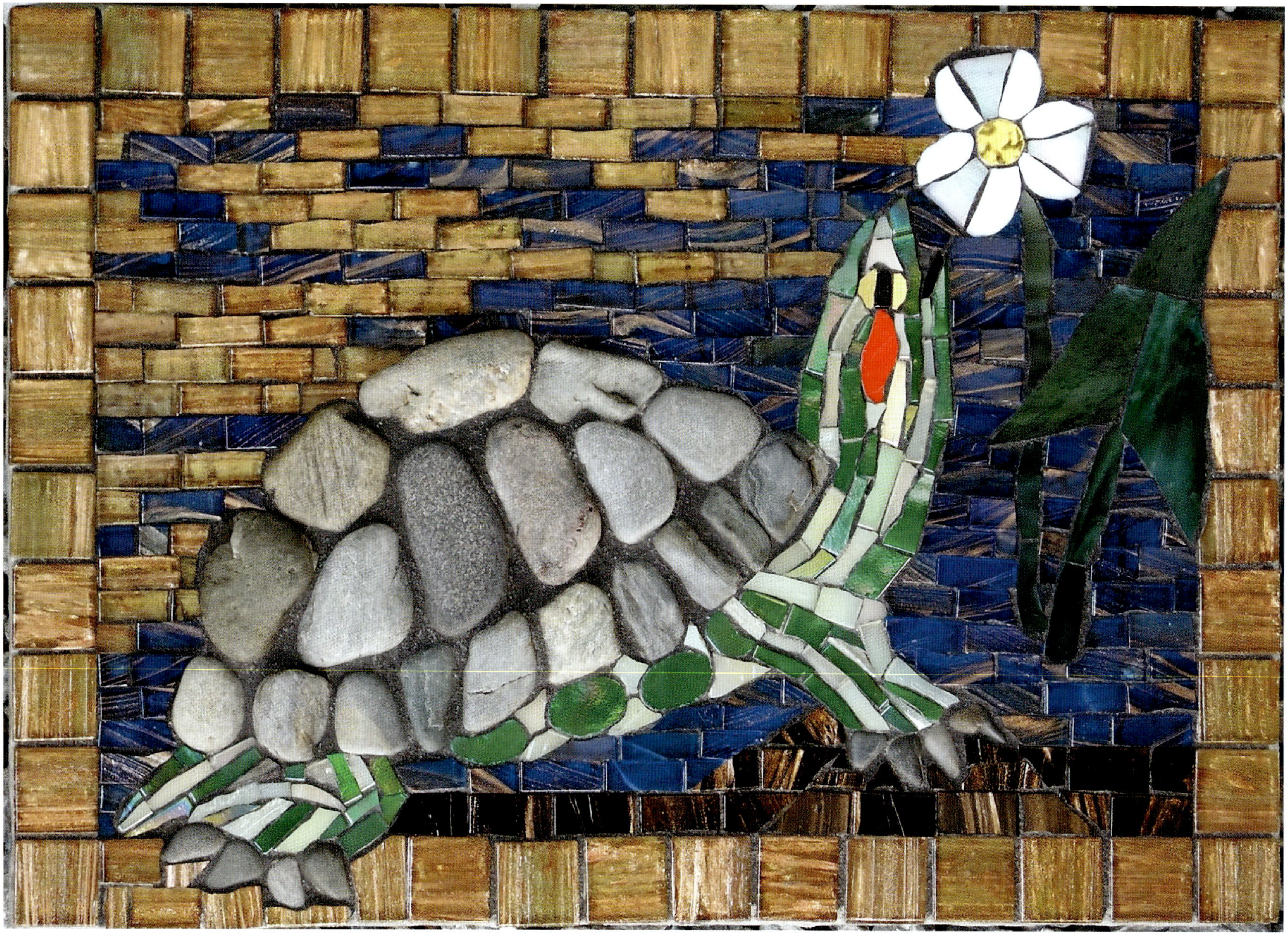

Gretchen Schaefer. *Turtle*. Wall piece. 2010. Mixed media mosaic. 8.5" x 12".

Linda C. Smith

Livermore, California, lcsartist@sbcglobal.net

Artist's Statement

Taken as an intellectual exercise, I like the idea of confining an artwork within a circle. Somehow the circle seems much more challenging than a rectangle. Most paintings are done in either a rectangular or square format, although there are some pretty impressive exceptions in Middle Ages art.

I have a series of drawings that have the tree as their subject. Some of them are just one tree, some have several. All are stylized or abstracted—I consider myself to be an *abstract colorist*—and the challenge is to confine these trees within the circle. Imagine thick trunks with rippling roots fighting their way around the circle looking for depth. Imagine the broad leaf heads vying with the sun or moon within the circle for space and prominence. Now imagine these images done not in paint, but in mosaic tiles. I have found a supplier of flat top, light weight, wooden plates to use as the support, along with a supplier of very *tiny tiles*. These tiles are made in Morocco of earthenware, glazed and fired at over 1000 degrees Celsius. I use these tiles and supports to produce my series of *tree mandalas*. I don't grout my mosaics as I don't think they need it as the tiles are placed pretty closely together; also I want light to reach every part of each tile. I don't want the color of the grout to dilute the colors in the tiles. Even the most neutral grout is a *color*.

About the Artwork

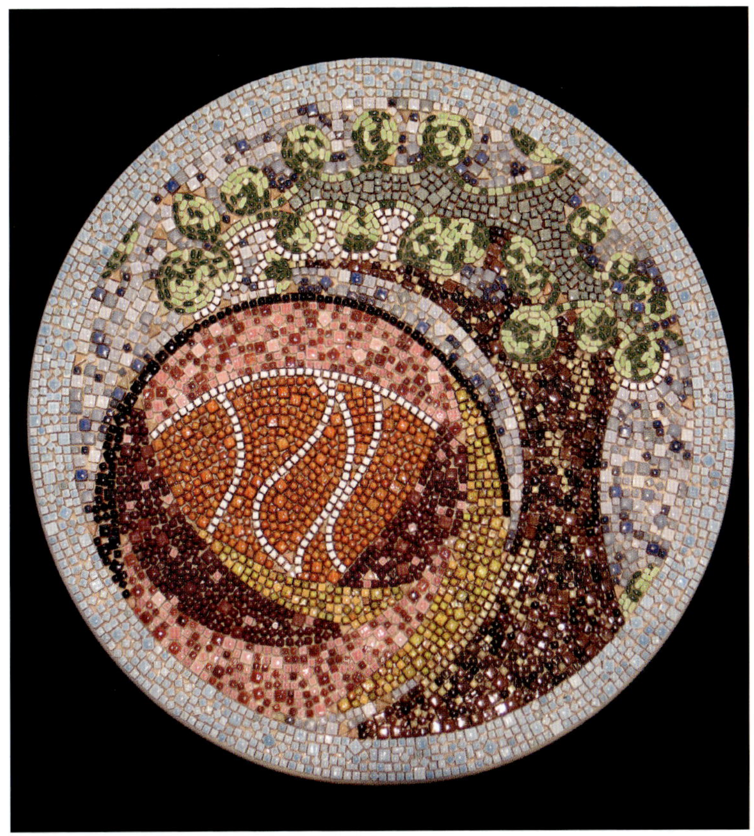

Linda C. Smith. *Sunset Mandala*. Mosaic. 2010. Earthenware ceramic tile on wooden support. 12" diameter. *Photography: Linda C. Smith*

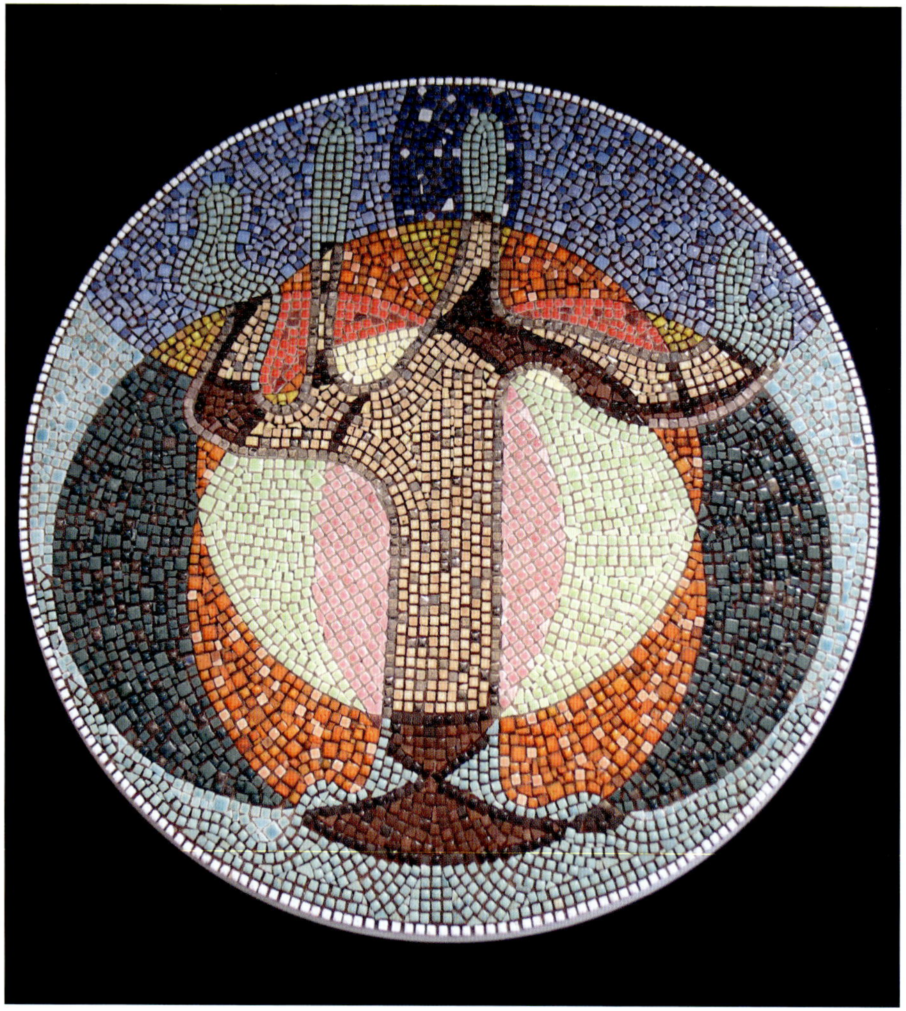

Linda C. Smith. *Night Cactus Mandala*. Mosaic. 2010. Earthenware ceramic tile on wooden support. 12" diameter. *Photography: Linda C. Smith*

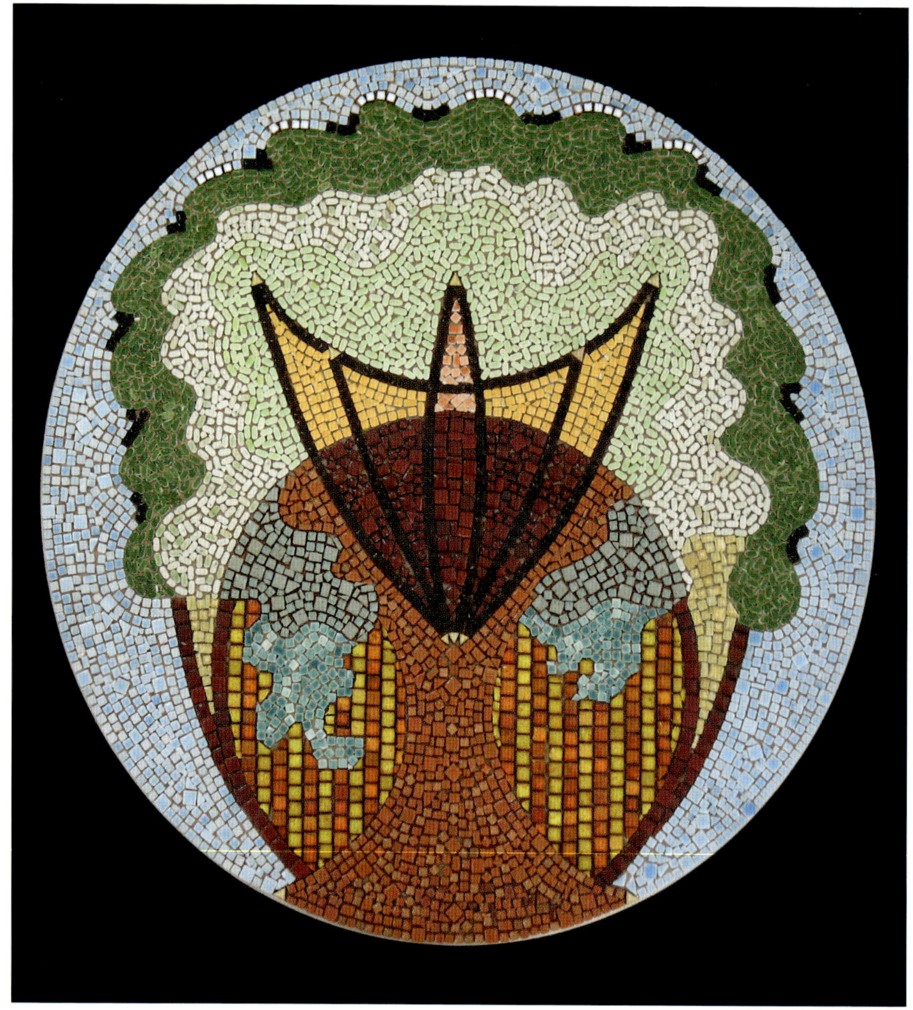

Linda C. Smith. *Tulip Tree Mandala*. Mosaic. 2010. Earthenware ceramic tile on wooden support. 12" diameter. *Photography: Linda C. Smith*

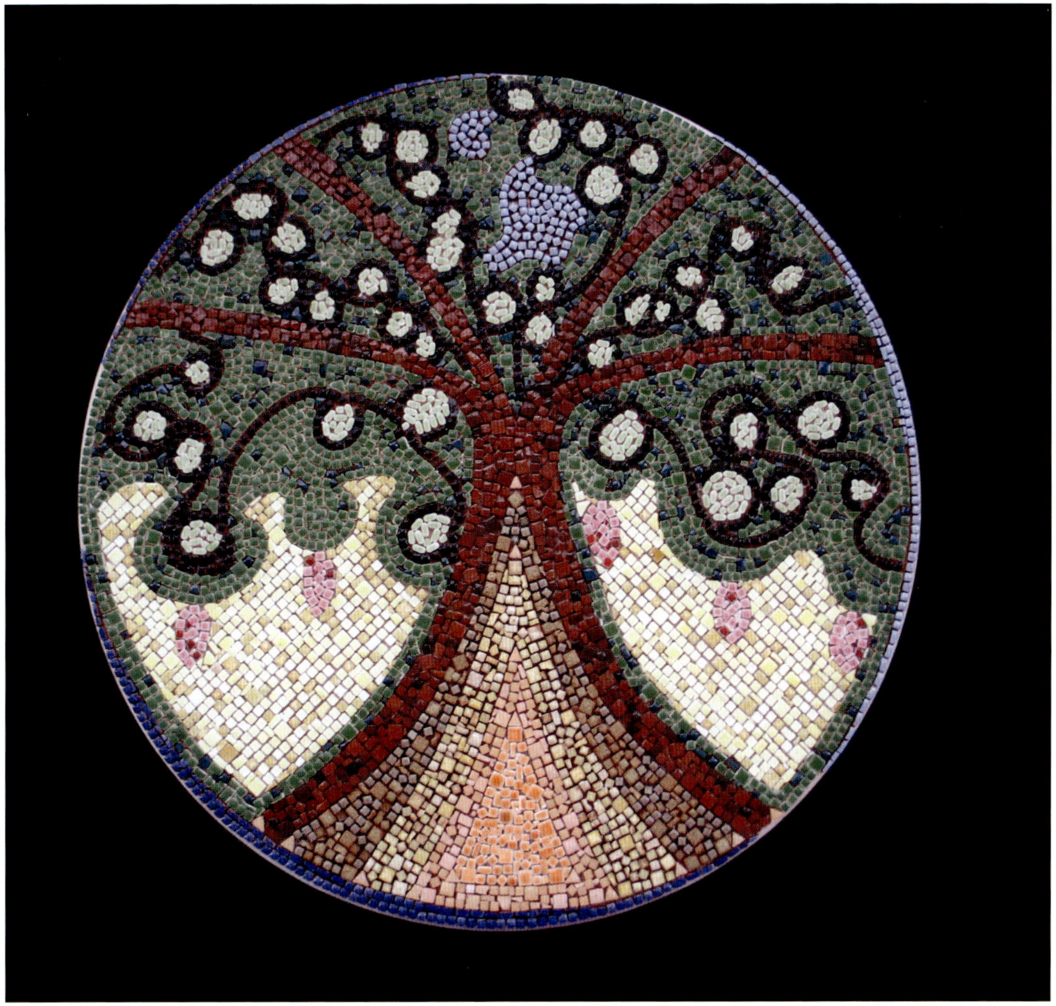

Linda C. Smith. *Fruit Tree Mandala*. Mosaic. 2010. Earthenware ceramic tile on wooden support. 12" diameter. *Photography: Linda C. Smith*

Mother Tree Mandala: One of the joys of working with these tiny tiles (1/8" and 1/4" squares and ovals) is that they flow in patterns so easily. This allowed me to design sections that are circular swirls. The uppermost section of the mosaic is darker blue squares that are regimented ... tightly lined up. Then come very light greens in their circular swirls; then a "grass" green with spiral patterns in among the random pieces—lots of movement.

Another section that I like is the lower foliage on the right side (as you look at it). This is a complex section that has lots of color and much movement. There are the light greens in the circular swirl section; a "grass" green area with a tracing of white tiles through it; then the reds, representing the fruit of the tree. All is held in the loving embrace of the blues of the sky.

And finally, look at the light blue of the sky that lights up the foliage and hugs the trunk ... these little tiles allow designs of movement in their placement. It's a joy to place each one.

Morning Sentinels Mandala is an abstract work done in a 14" round wood support. There are several thousand tiny ceramic tiles in this piece. I love abstract. Let me explain how it works here. For instance, if you were to look at a tree's foliage in nature, you would see not just a monochromatic green. You would see various shades of greens and you'd see contrasts of light and dark. To abstract the foliage of these two trees, I flattened all those elements. The whitish areas in the foliage are a light green; the stripes represent shadows.

The tree trunks are mottled brown and revealed are their roots ... this gives the idea that the trees are rooted deeply in the ground. The sun rises above the green hillside, which is dotted with white flowers. Around the circle is a border in reds done in an intricate pattern. The pattern in the reds is a fun contrast to the random and layering techniques used in the main body of the work.

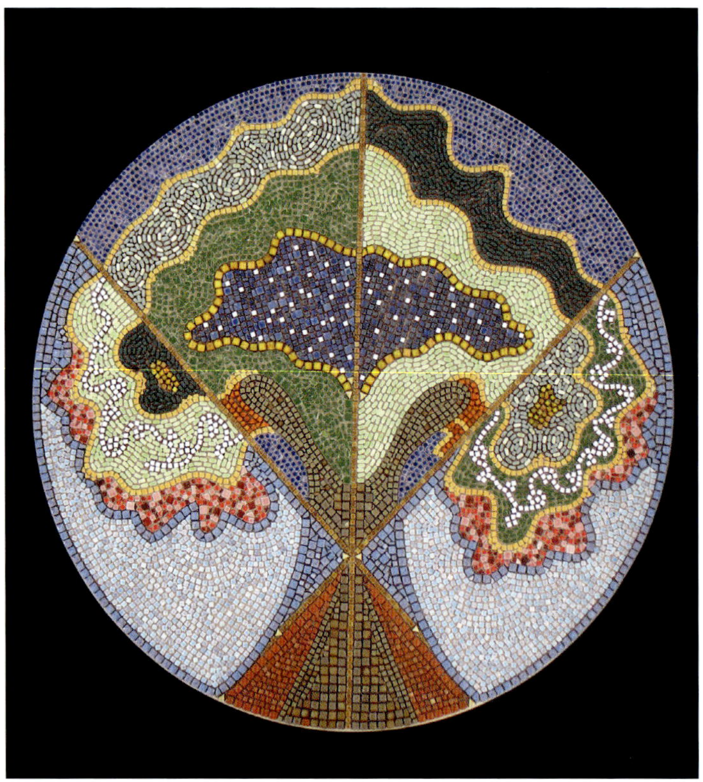

Linda C. Smith. *Mother Tree Mandala*. Mosaic. 2011.
Earthenware ceramic tile on wooden support. 16" diameter.
Photography: Linda C. Smith

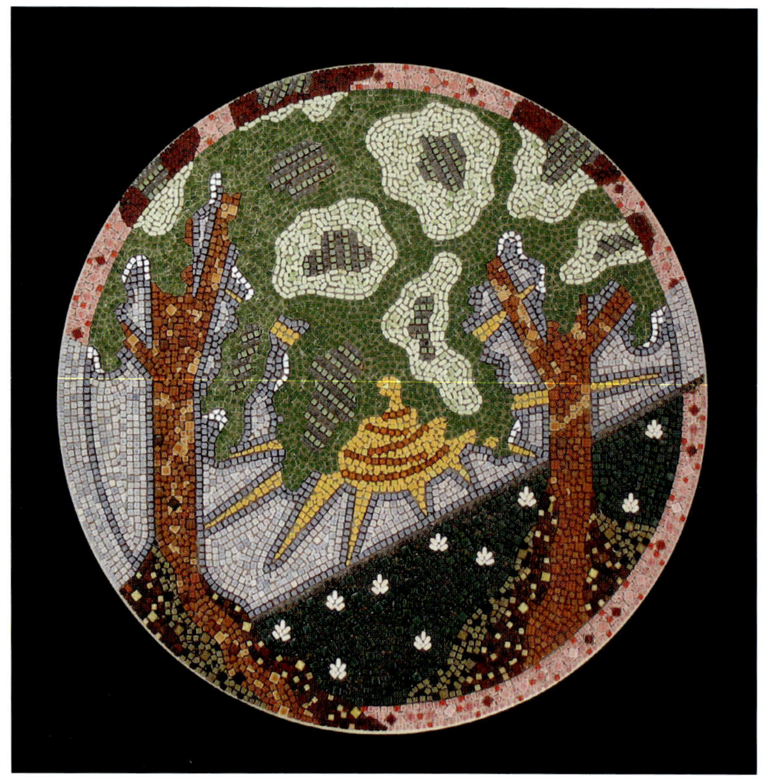

Linda C. Smith. *Morning Sentinels Mandala*. Mosaic. 2011.
Earthenware ceramic tile on wooden support. 14" diameter.
Photography: Linda C. Smith

John D. Sollinger

Ashland, Oregon, sollinger@jeffnet.org

Artist's Statement

From the hinterland betwixt and between art and science, I intuitively express the wonder I see in native landscapes. My studies in forestry and plant biology have enriched my visual vocabulary for describing the natural. I dabbled with acrylic painting and stained glass window-making before combining the two in the assembly of mosaics. Monet and Van Gogh have guided my aesthetic appreciation, but I draw my inspiration from da Vinci for seeing no divide between art and science. If my work furthers others' appreciation for the aesthetics' nature, then I will be content. But, if my work informs others about the wonders of nature, then I will rejoice.

About the Artwork

Mutation—a Study of Van Gogh's Irises of Arel: Van Gogh's emphatic brush mark, brilliant hues, grout lining, and highlighting inspired me to see if I could make glass appear as paint, which is the reverse of Vincent's desire to have his paint appear like stained glass. This work was named for the image inversion, errors in transcription, and Vincent's lone white iris.

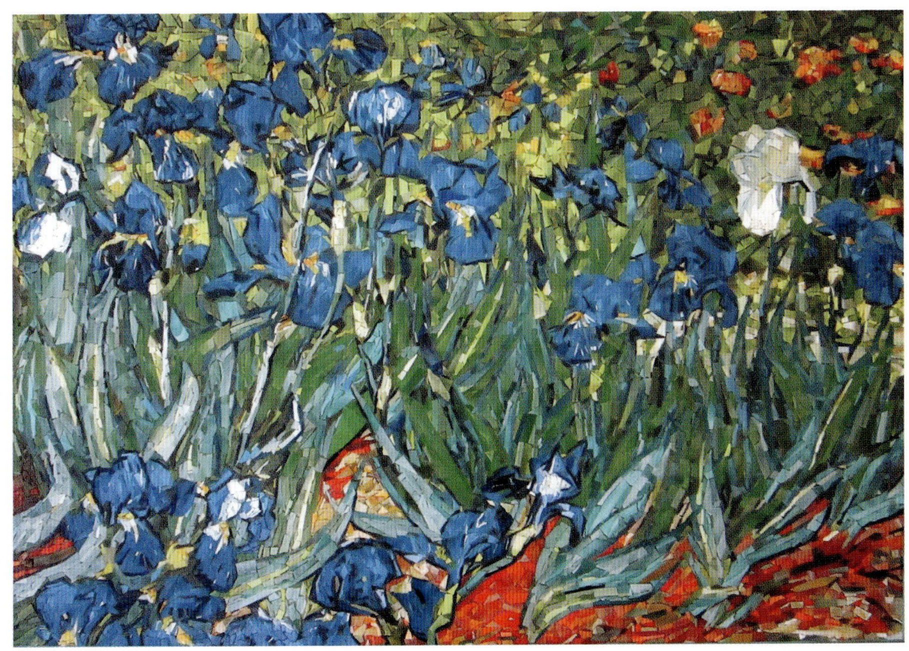

John D. Sollinger. *Mutation—A Study of Van Gogh's Irises of Arel*. 2009. Stained glass on tempered glass. Indirect method. 36" x 48" x 1".

Inspiration for ***Astir*** came from Drakesbad horse-camp and lodge in Lassen National Park. Before I tackled the sky, I carelessly kicked the mosaic (I glue after assembling most pieces, so it is "fluid" until then). After rearranging tessera in all but the center field, I saw Turmoil. Serendipity demanded that I fracture the sky and add clouds of oil (some pieces are iridescent, which resembles petroleum on water, as in the Gulf of Mexico).

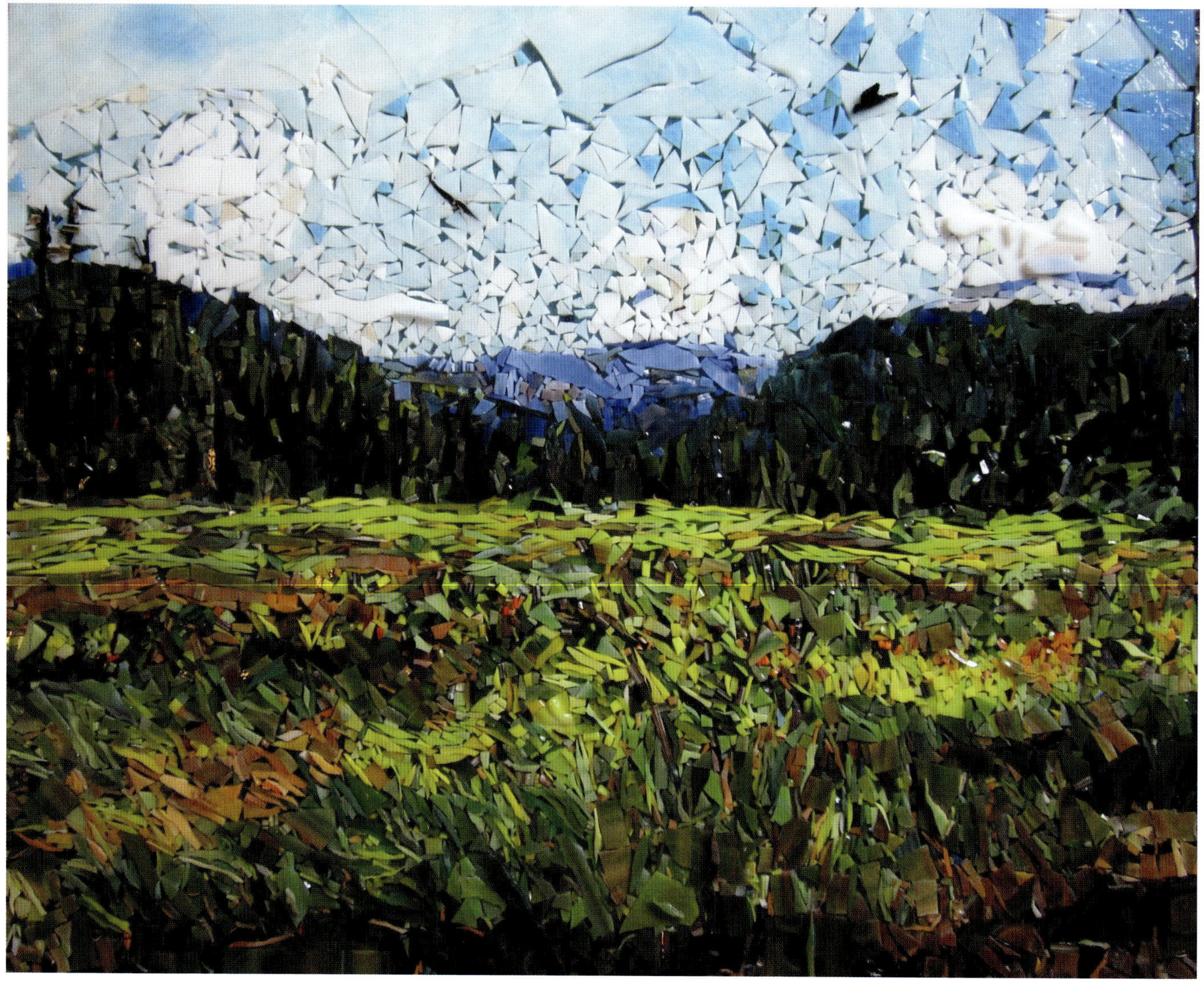

John D. Sollinger. *Astir.* 2010. Layered (1-3) glass on glass. Fluid double indirect method. 20" x 16" x 1".

Old Growth: In the finished mosaic, I layered several pieces of glass. Made to scale (inch = inch), this is a close up of the side of a large cedar tree trunk, adorned with lichens and moss, where it meets the forest floor. A lichen-covered fallen branch reflects the curve of the trunk. Otherwise, asymmetry reins.

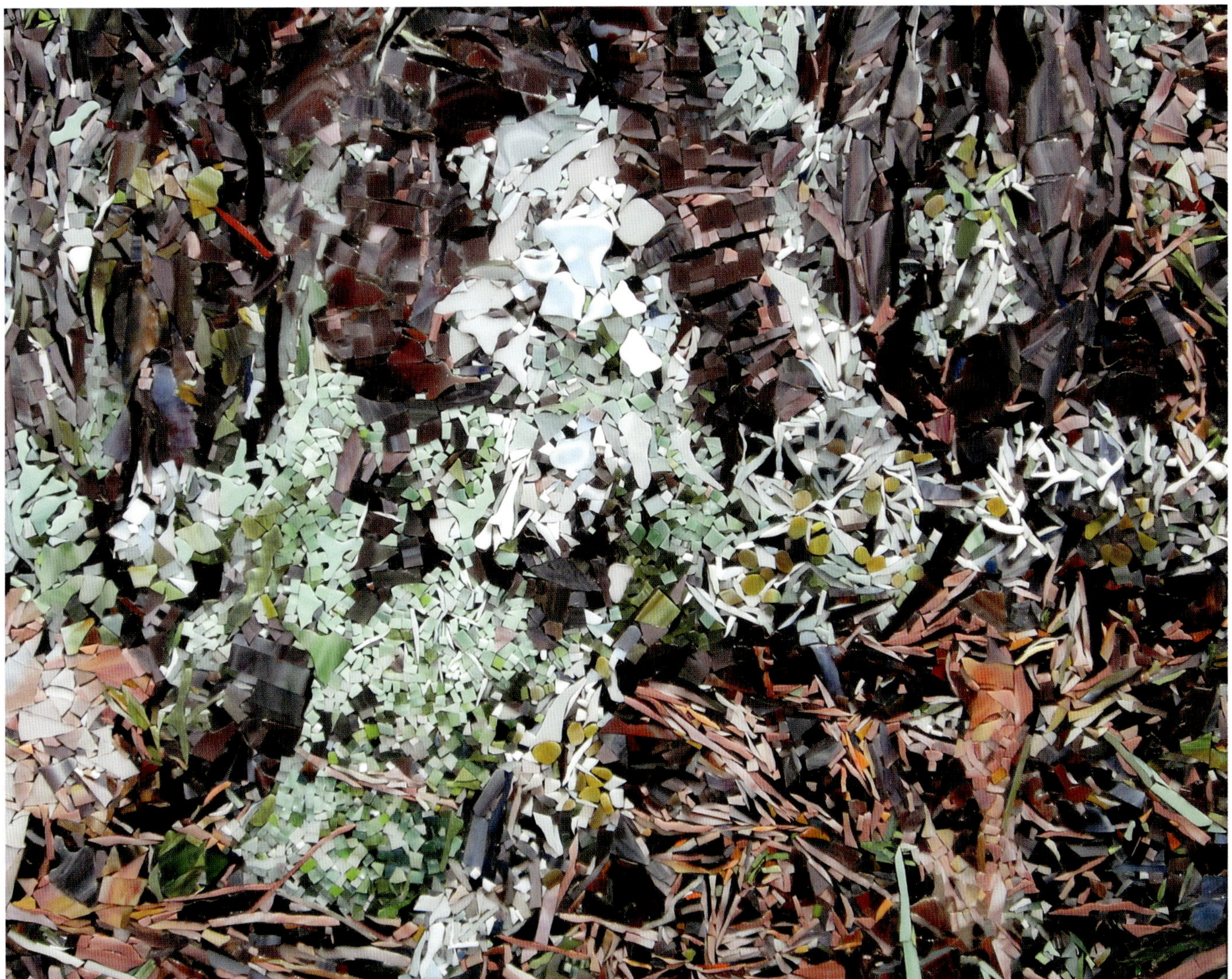

John D. Sollinger. *Old Growth.* 2010. Stained glass and native sand. Fluid double indirect method. 20" x 16" x 1".

Radiance is the first in a four part series of works based on natural, visible patterns in relatively pristine states. Inspiration came from a floral display in the Cascade-Siskiyou National Monument, which was established to protect the incredible diversity of life forms in this small intersection of three bioregions at the Oregon-California border. On center stage is a ridge-top cluster of *Arnica* on a midsummer noon.

Radiance was named for the radial pattern of the petals within each flower and the circular grouping of flowers in the clump, the play of light, and the sunflower, icon of the sun.

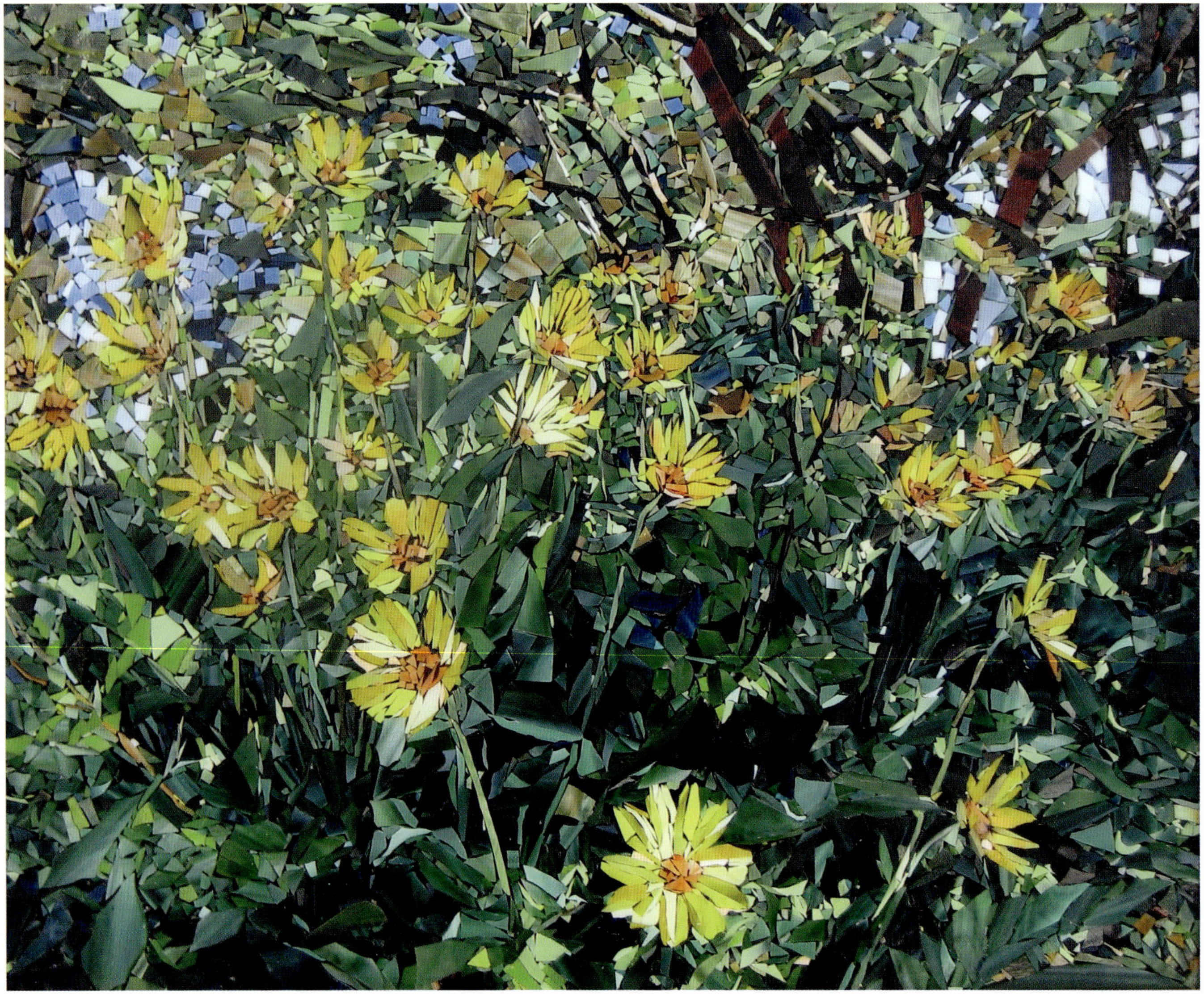

John D. Sollinger. *Radiance*. 2010. Stained glass. Indirect method. 20" x 16" x 1".

Carol Soritz-Shelkin

Drexel Hill, Pennsylvania

Artist's Statement

My work as an artist is mostly representational. I unite my background in painting and ceramics, using my favorite tool, wheeled nippers, hand cutting each piece of glass to resemble my familiar brush strokes. This is my way of capturing reflections of light with materials I use, which incorporate a mixture of stained glass, including iridescent glass, textured glass, wispy stained glass, shiny, matte, mirrored glass, translucent, opaque or transparent stained glass. I'm always being pulled to develop art that is alive with color, enhanced by reflective light, designed with texture revealing its uniqueness and longevity. I'm pulled to work on portraiture in stained glass and the human form.

The Artwork

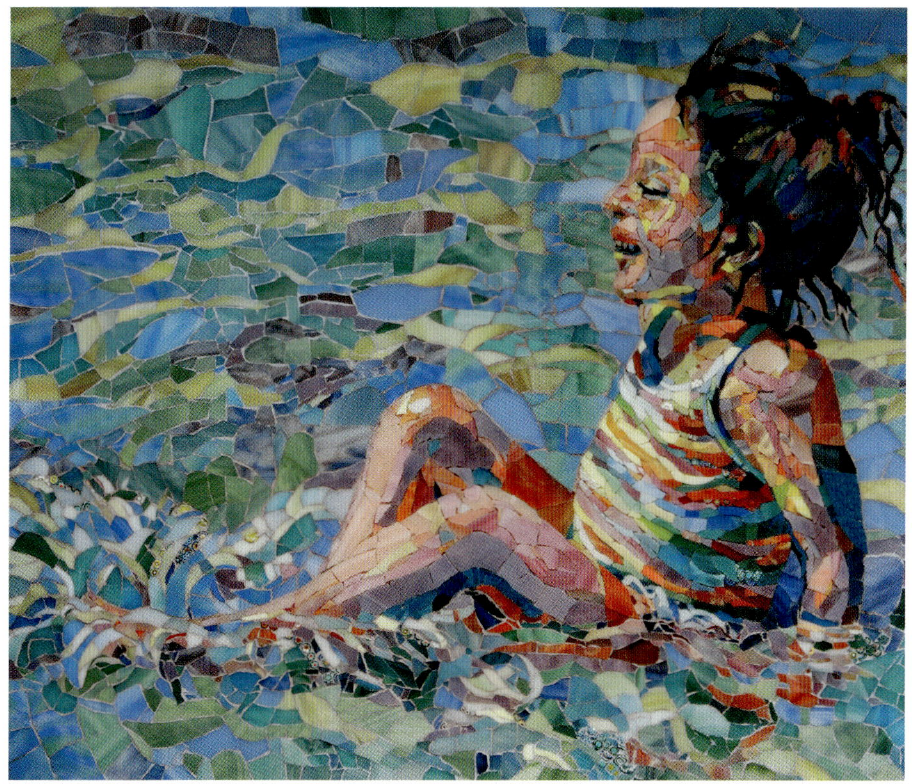

Carol Soritz-Shelkin. *Beautiful Day.* 2009. Stained glass, millefiori. 18" x 22".

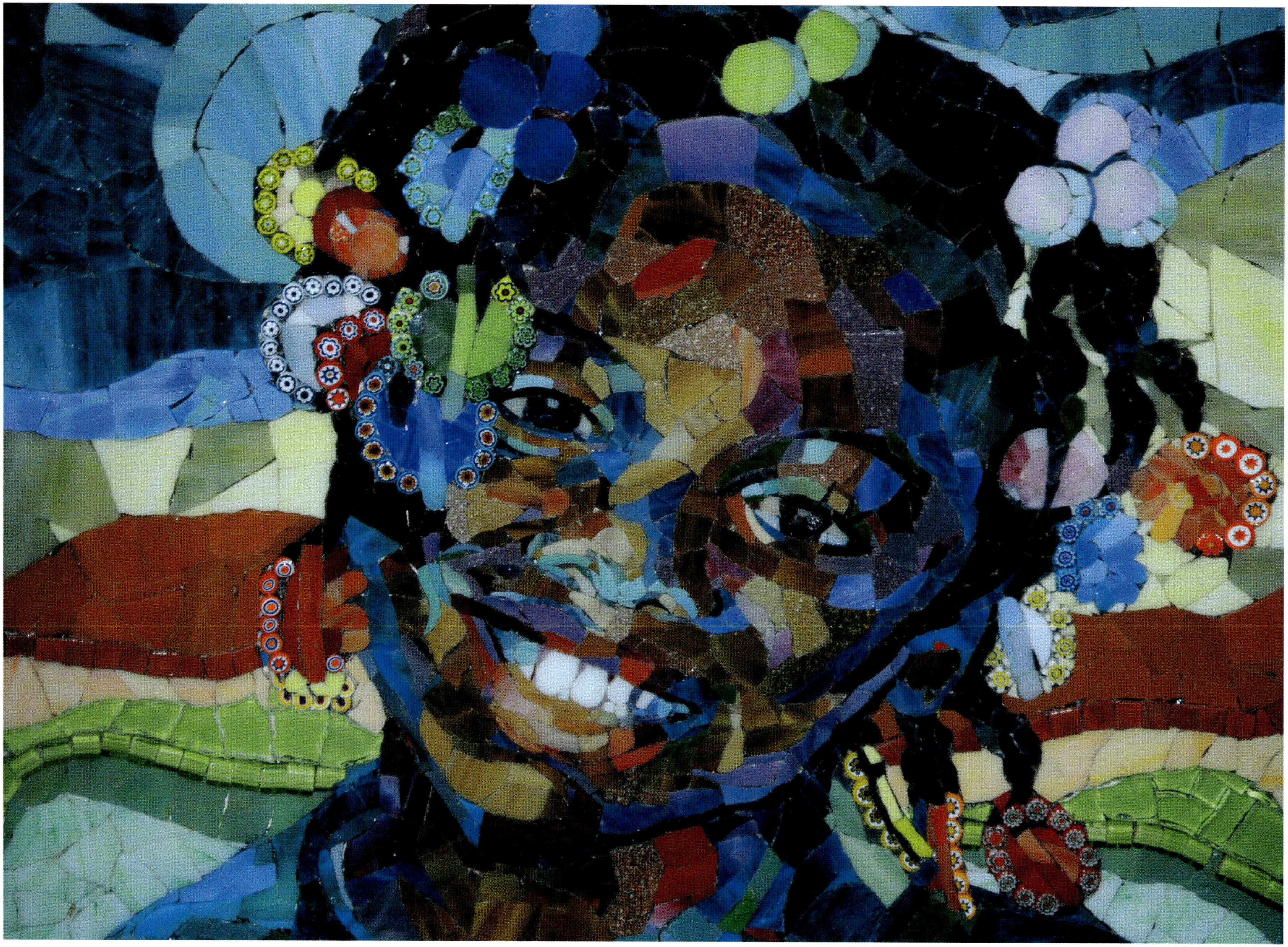

Carol Soritz-Shelkin. *Fabulous Hair*. 2009. Stained glass, glass beads, vitreous tiles, millefiori. 11" x 14".

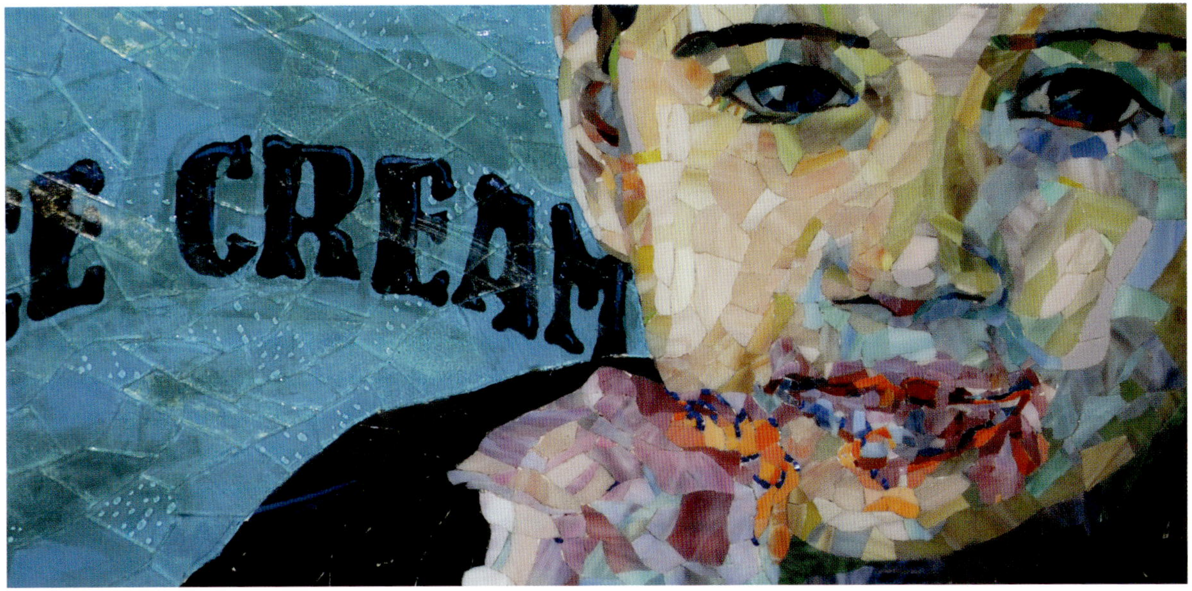

Carol Soritz-Shelkin. *Flavor of the Month.* 2011. Stained glass, glass beads, millefiori, paint. 12" x 18".

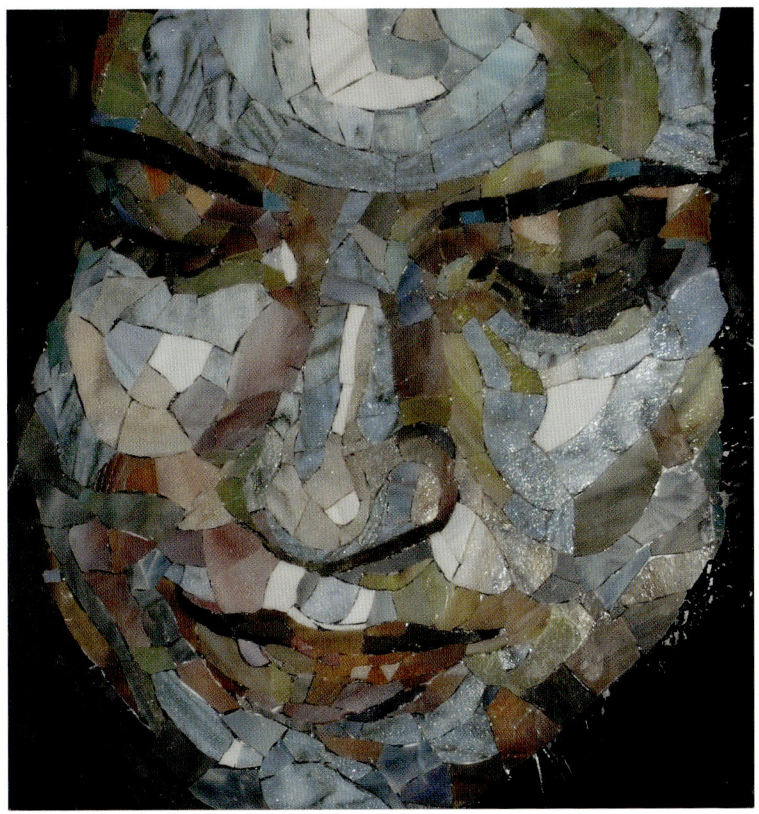

Carol Soritz-Shelkin. *Thinking.* 2010. Stained glass. 12" x 12".

Mary Trail

Hawthorne, California

About the Artwork

Adornment: This piece started with an idea of mixing various materials, different shapes, and using beads as grout to bring the whole piece together. Parts of this piece use grout with acrylic paint for color matching. It was really fun completing this piece. Amazing what you can do with beads, to create other projects besides jewelry.

Mary Trail. *Adornment*. Glass, glass tile, beads, semiprecious stones, ceramic tile, wood, mirror tile, shells, and tesserae. 16" diameter. (opposite page)

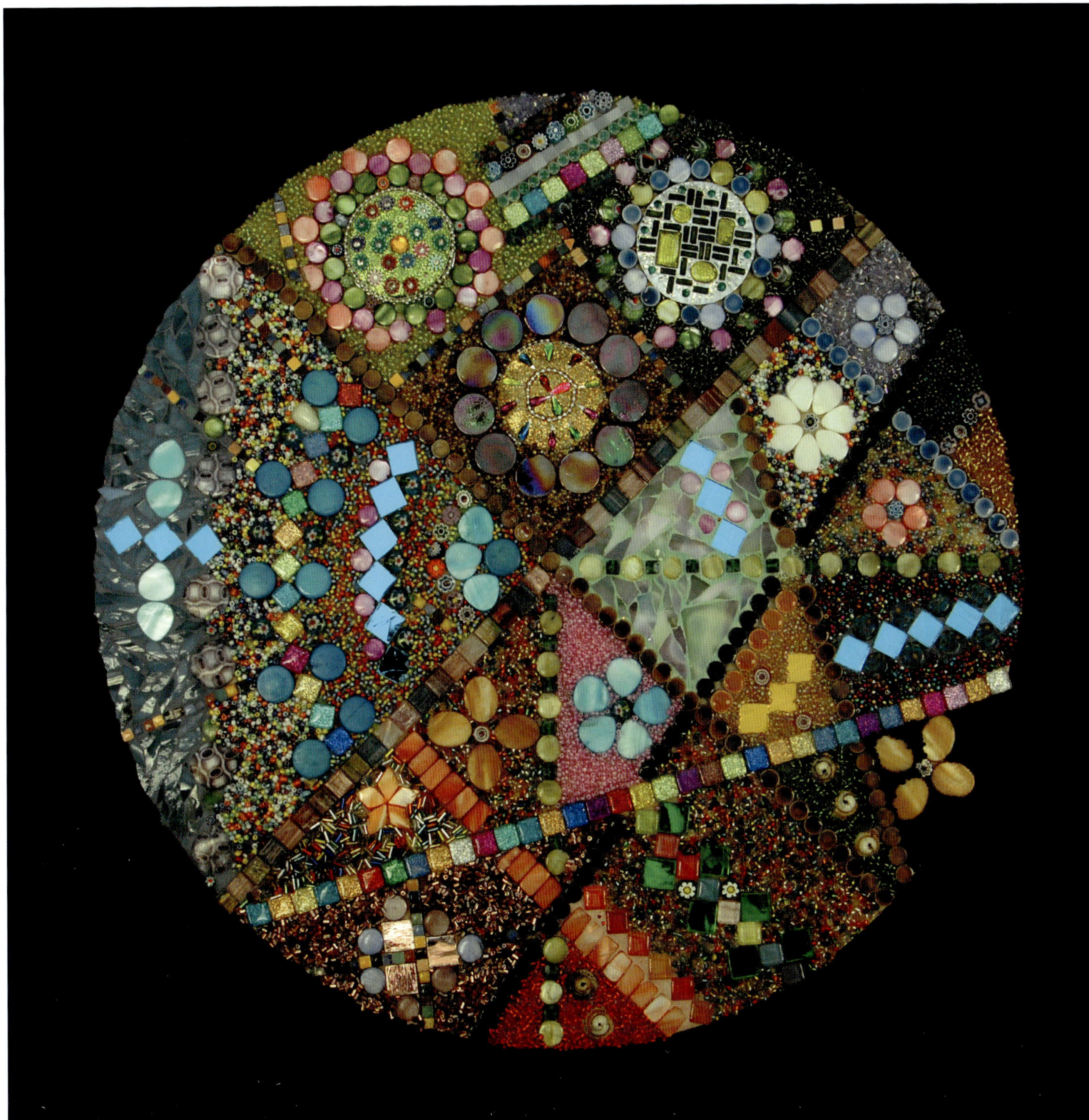

Ruth Helene Tyszka

Bloomfield Hills, Michigan, ruthtyszka@yahoo.com

Artist's Statement

Art has been a part of my life since I was a child and my mother forbade coloring books on the theory that coloring within the lines stifles creativity. Instead, I was given an endless supply of empty paper and all the tools to fill it. Decades later I was introduced to glass and mosaic art and I knew I was creatively home.

As I develop various series of works and techniques over the years, a common theme of my art is to allow one or more found or repurposed objects to inspire me, from which I use mosaic to create an environment, habitat or story around the object. The majority of my work is three-dimensional. I am challenged and delighted by exploring and developing the various views of three-dimensional art, and yet I may never obtain the satisfaction of seeing my entire creation at once, in a single view. In my most recent series, *Celebrate*, I explore cakes as a symbol of personal celebrations, events, and social gatherings.

About the Artwork

Cathedral Moment: One of my mosaic students used darkly colored cathedral glass in reds, blues, and purples with a dark grout in her first mosaic piece. When she grouted the piece, the dark grout with the glass gave an almost medieval stained glass effect to her design. This effect was part of the inspiration for creating the glass "windows" with grout mullions on *Cathedral Moment*. The effect of the clear yet colored glass in mosaics is enhanced by a white substrate with dark grout that replicates the effect of lead lines. The figure breaking out of the top of the piece is a "Neptune Man" from Neptune Glass. The base of the Neptune Man was chipped and I purchased him for a bargain. One of the benefits to working in mosaics is that I can exploit cracks and breaks and other leftover bits and pieces of objects in my art. (opposite page)

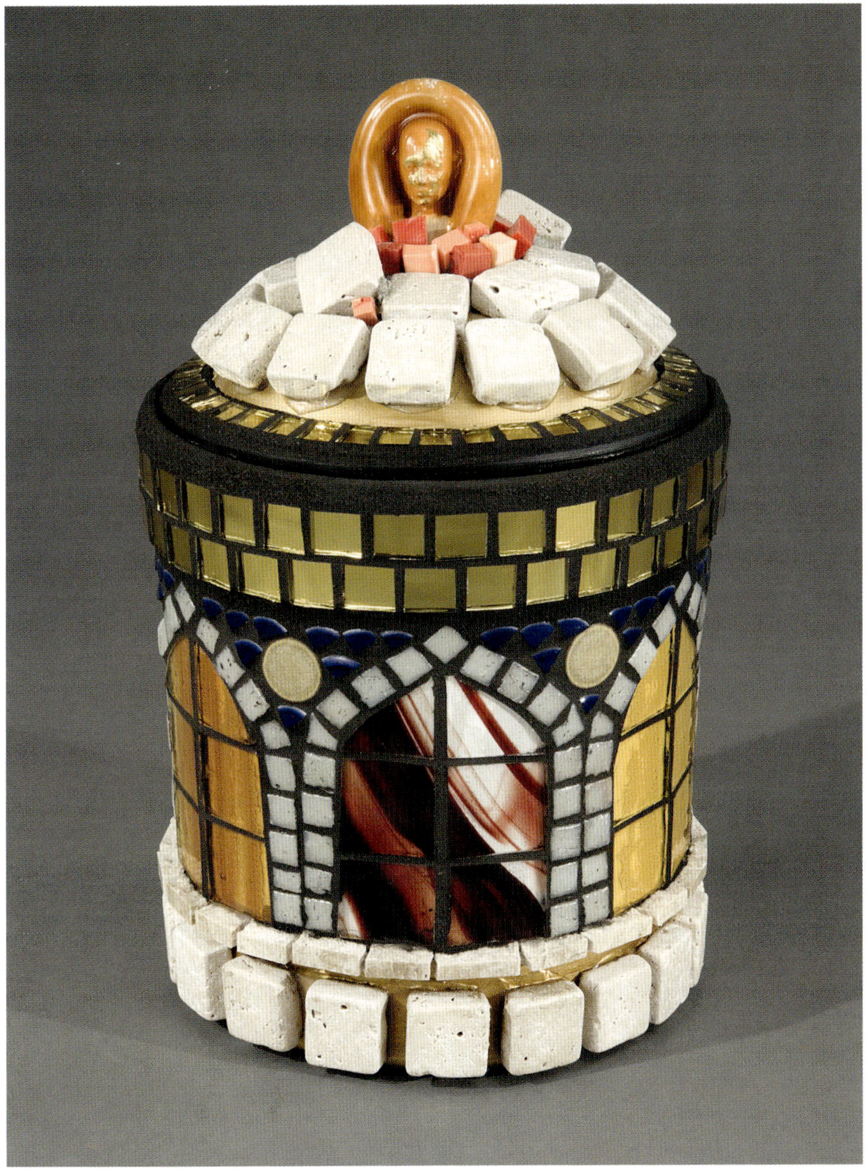

Ruth Helene Tyszka. *Cathedral Moment*. Canister with church window motif in red and amber. 2008. Functional canister with mosaic of ceramic tile, hand cut baroque and stained glass, marble, gold mirror, smalti and repurposed Neptune Man from Neptune Glass on glazed and fired bisqueware base. 11" x 7". *Photo by P.D. Rearick*

All Blues III: Mile Davis's *Kind of Blue* is one of my favorite albums and it is a staple in my art studio. "All Blues" is a piece on that album. The first of my *All Blues* series was a play on blue glass, metallic and iridescent embellishments, and blue grout, directly inspired by *Kind of Blue*. My artistic "default" color is blue, to which I return again and again, and I have continued with the "All Blues" theme. *All Blues III* was inspired by some wonderful shapes in broken china of an almost chartreuse color, which sings against the blue glass and tile. I used the broken china to create a focal point on each side of the four-sided pyramid. The piece was a sort of improvisational scat in materials: Millefiori, the play in the relief work of the smalti, some ceramic rounds, and the mirror along the bottom edge, which throws its own design onto the tabletop. Three-dimensional objects with such sharp edges always give me the challenge of how to treat the edge in the design. Here I built up the adhesive enough to use roughly cut bits of chartreuse stained glass up each edge, like large stitches.

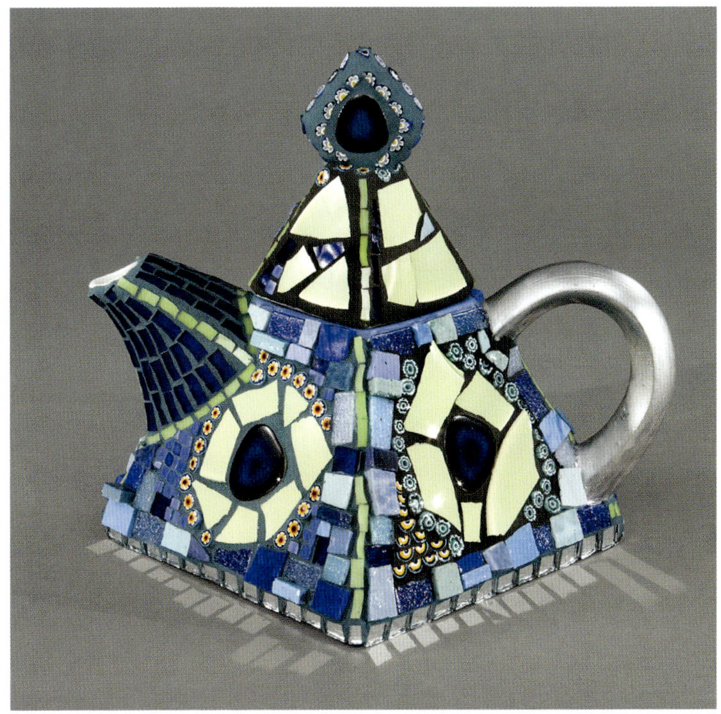

Ruth Helene Tyszka. *All Blues III*. Pyramid teapot with chartreuse tile and blue glass and tile. 2009. Functional mosaic teapot of repurposed broken china, millefiori, smalti, hand cut stained glass, ceramic tiles, and mirror tile on glazed and fired bisqueware base. 8.25" x 10" x 8". *Photo by P.D. Rearick*

Parisian Birthday: While the current trend in edible cakes is to challenge the boundaries of the medium to create cakes that look the least like a traditional cake, I continue to use very traditional cake decorating elements, tools, and scale to make my sculptures evoke the look of a cake. Graduated layers, mortar roping created with a cake-decorating gun and handmade clay flowers made with fondant cutters complete the illusion. The cakes are carefully planned out in detailed full color sketches first, and then I find the perfect tile and glass, create flowers and embellishments, and build the structure. I have reawakened my geometry skills in calculating the amount of a particular tile or glass needed to cover each cake layer; the cake layers are simply cubes and cylinders before they are art.

Tracy's Summer Patio Party: After creating my own mosaic wedding cake, I embarked on a series of cakes I call the *Celebrate* series, which explores the theme of cakes as a symbol of personal celebrations, milestones, and social gatherings. For each cake I have a particular image in mind of an occasion that the cake represents. The two-tier square cake is encrusted in millefiori, iridescent glass fan-shaped tiles, glitter tile, glass beads, mirror, metal bead chain, and sprinkled with crushed glass. The glass beads and crushed glass are added near the end of the process and they are blends of colors that I create for each specific cake.

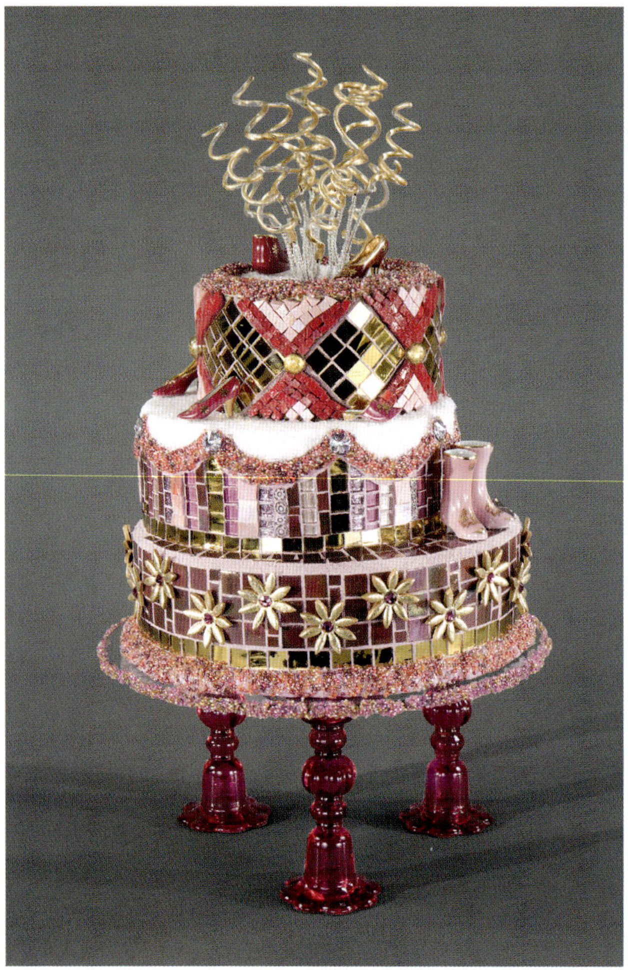

Ruth Helene Tyszka. *Parisian Birthday*. Three-tier cake sculpture. 2011. Glass tile, millefiori, smalti, crushed glass, glass beads, polymer clay flowers, vintage crystals, Austrian crystals, Italian cabochons and found and repurposed objects including Limoges shoe and boot figurines, candlesticks, and twisted glass rods on Styrofoam and mortar base. 21" x 12". *Photo by P.D. Rearick*

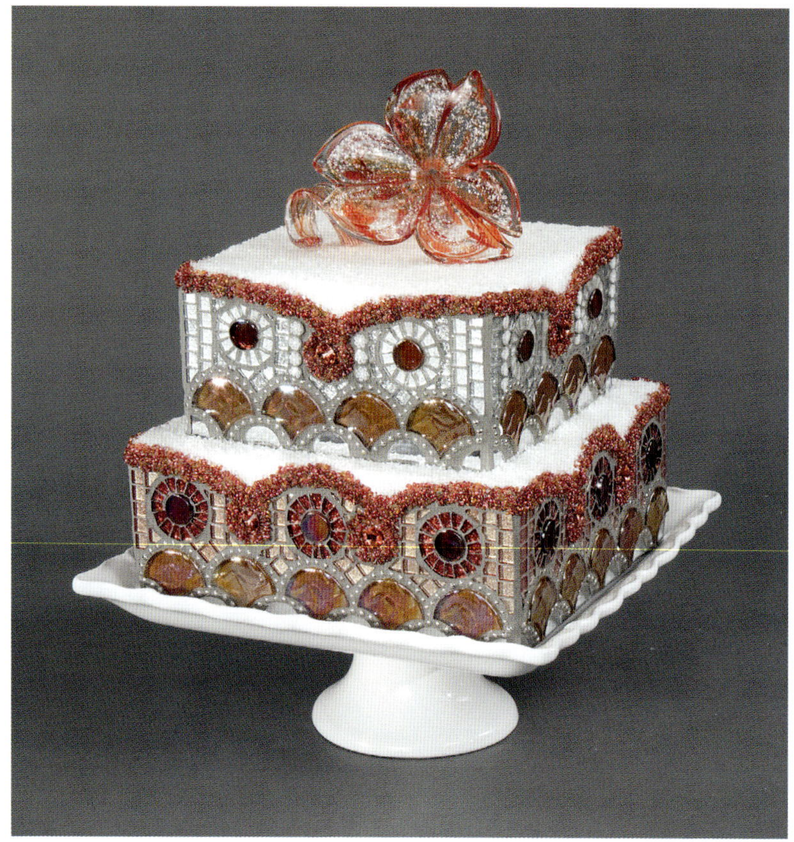

Ruth Helene Tyszka. *Tracy's Summer Patio Party*. Two-tier square cake sculpture. 2011. Glass tile, millefiori, Austrian crystals, crushed glass, glass beads, repurposed glass flower on Styrofoam and mortar base. 12" x 10" x 10". *Photo by P.D. Rearick*

Verdonna

Albuquerque, New Mexico, verdonna@gmail.com

Artist's Statement

I love to work with my hands. I like to piece things together. And, I like getting into the details. Mosaic is the perfect medium for me. Bold colors, tactile materials, lots of bits and pieces all melded together in original works, abstract, geometrical, some 3D and practical.

I can't resist the smooth feel of glass tile, textured metal beads, and the 3D effect of millefiori or fused glass. A touch of rhinestone sparkle, the twinkling brilliance of gemstones, or the luminescence of a piece of abalone shell, I am not shy about using them all.

While many of my mosaics are wall plaques, I love boxes, too. I like to recycle wooden boxes and turn them into one-of-a-kind decorative, yet functional, collectibles.

About the Artwork

Hi Brow: The design for this mosaic was conceived by taking an ordinary shape, in this case the shape of an eyebrow, then turning it into an art piece. The color scheme for *Hi Brow* came about by looking at value only, just shades of gray. Then specific colors that matched the selected shades of gray were assigned. *Hi Brow* is made of several different kinds of glass tile to add texture, depth, and interest.

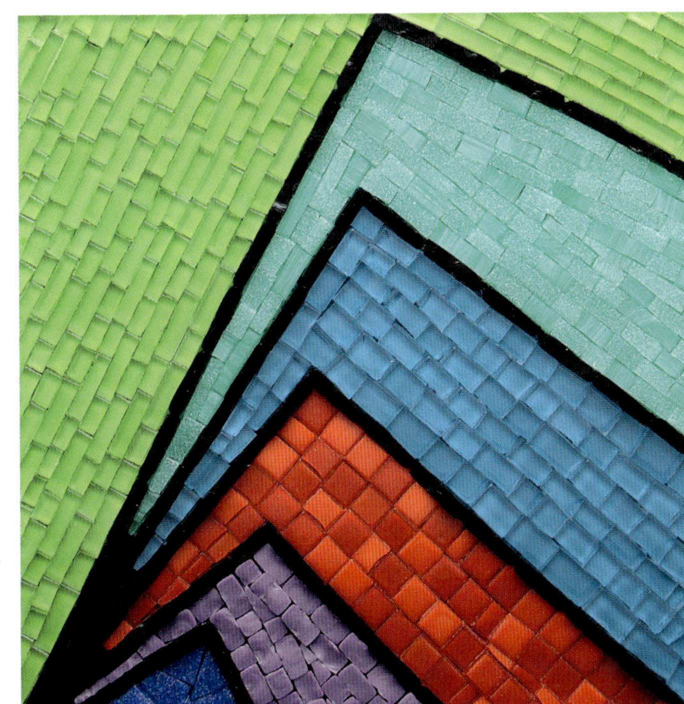

Verdonna. *Hi Brow*. Wall hanging. Opus Romano, venetian tile, Bisazza smalto, vitreous tile, glass tile, MDF base. 8" x 8". *Photograph by the author*

Marrakech: *Marrakech* was inspired after I saw a picture of colorful furnishings inside a Moroccan home. I couldn't help but fall in love with the luscious orange, blue, and silver hues. The base for *Marrakech* is a recycled handmade cedar wood cigar cask. I divided the cask into three horizontal rows and seven vertical columns. I gave each section its own geometrical design. Even the lid has seven different patterns. Glass tile, iridescent tile, pieces of mirror, flat back marbles, and silver beads give the cask its multi-textural Moroccan flair.

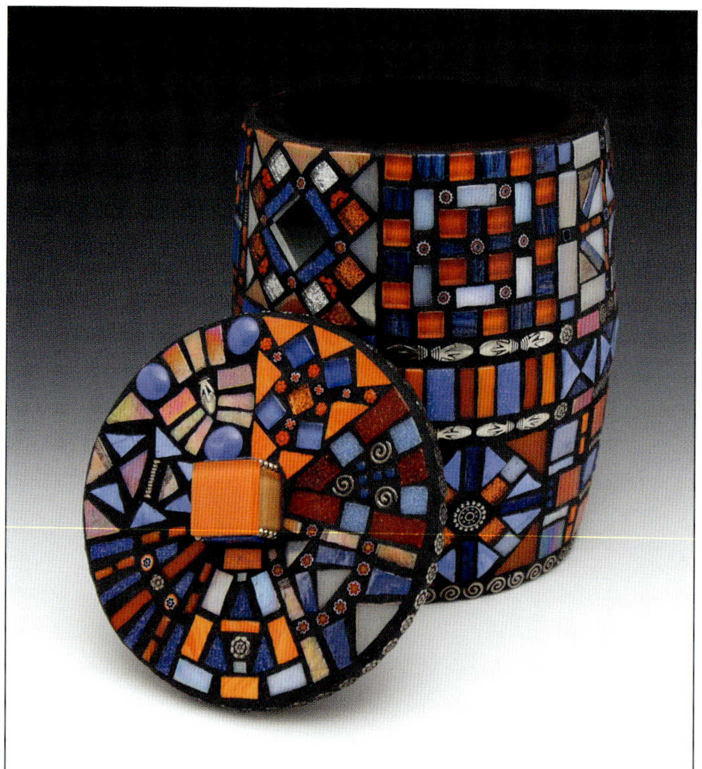

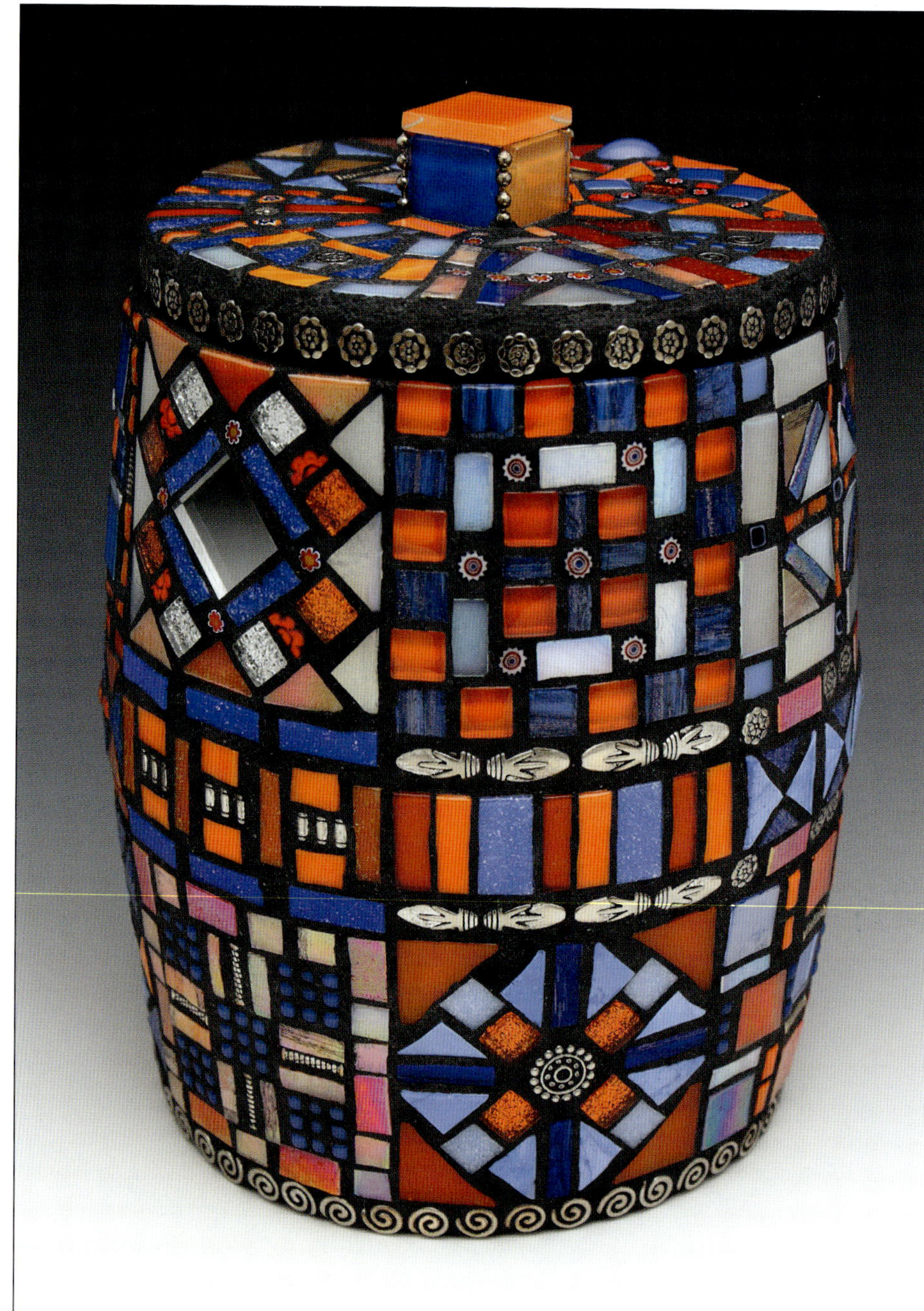

Verdonna. *Marrakech.* Cigar Cask. Millefiori, Sicis iridium tile, vitreous tile, glitter tile, venetian tile, glass tile, flat back marbles, Tibetan silver beads, mirror, ball chain, cedar wood cask. 8" x 6" x 6". *Photograph by the author*

Oeste del Sur: *Oeste del Sur* is Spanish for "south west." The American Southwest has its own distinct color palette, primarily influenced by the colors of the sky. As a resident of this region, I designed this piece to reflect the moments just after sunset, when the sky turns pale blue and peach. In the next moment, it mixes with bolder oranges, darker blues, and warm golds. Triangles, lines, and squares, which figure prominently in Native American art here, add to the Southwestern flavor and theme of *Oeste del Sur*.

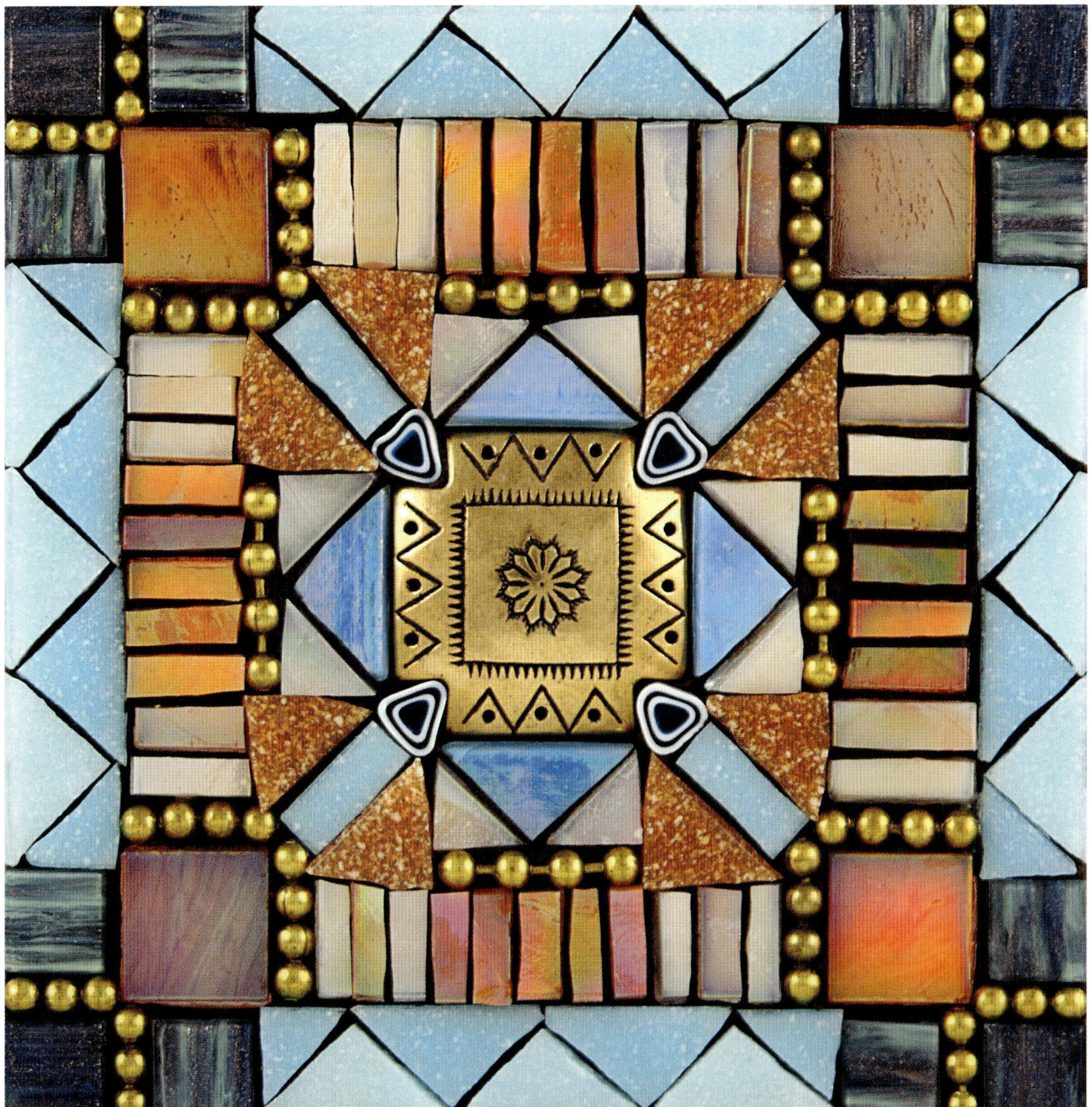

Verdonna. *Oeste del Sur.* Wall Plaque. Sicis iridium tile, vitreous tile, Bisazza metallic tile, vintage brass ball chain, millefiori, gold plated focal, ceramic tile base. 4" x 4". *Photograph by the author*

Wendy Viscarra

Los Angeles, California, mosaics@dslextreme.com

About the Artwork

Blue Pot: This flowerpot has a terra cotta base and ceramic tile and glass marbles added. I drew the design with a pencil on the actual terra cotta pot. I broke up the ceramic tile with a hammer. It is challenging to get the tile to stick to the pot due to the round surface, so I normally work in sections and do multiple pots at once. This allows me to make good use of my time and be productive. I find this system works for me and does not make me impatient waiting for pots to dry.

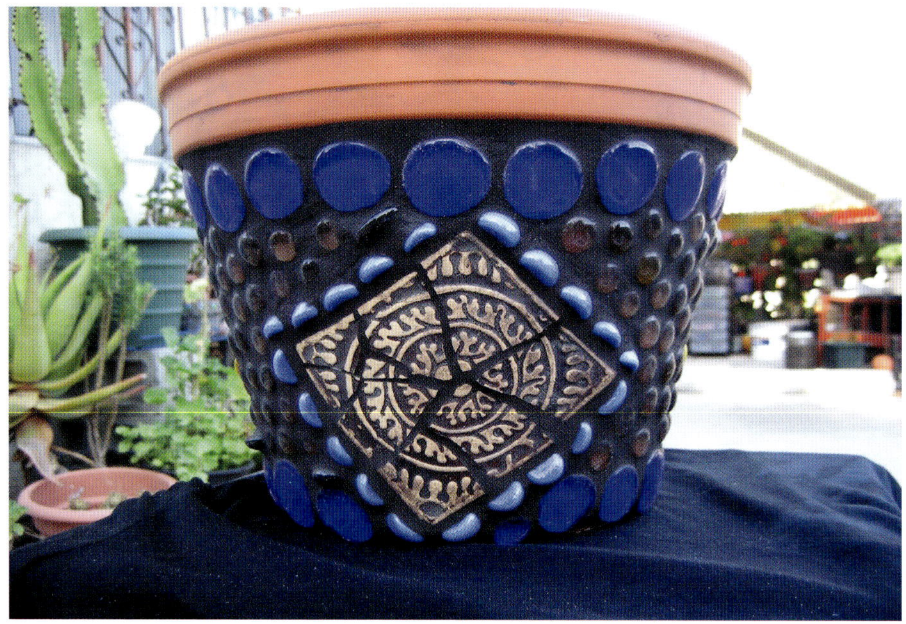

Wendy Viscarra. *Blue Pot*. Flowerpot. Terra cotta base, ceramic tile, glass marbles.

Nightmare Before Christmas: I created this design with the movie *Nightmare Before Christmas* in mind. I was attracted to Tim Burton's designs and it inspired me to put this idea on a table. I used very simple colors to portray the simplicity of it all.

This table has Spanish and Italian ceramic tile and it was put directly onto the wood base. It has a custom wrought iron base that is very heavy. This table was part of a series of tables that were custom made for an exhibit.

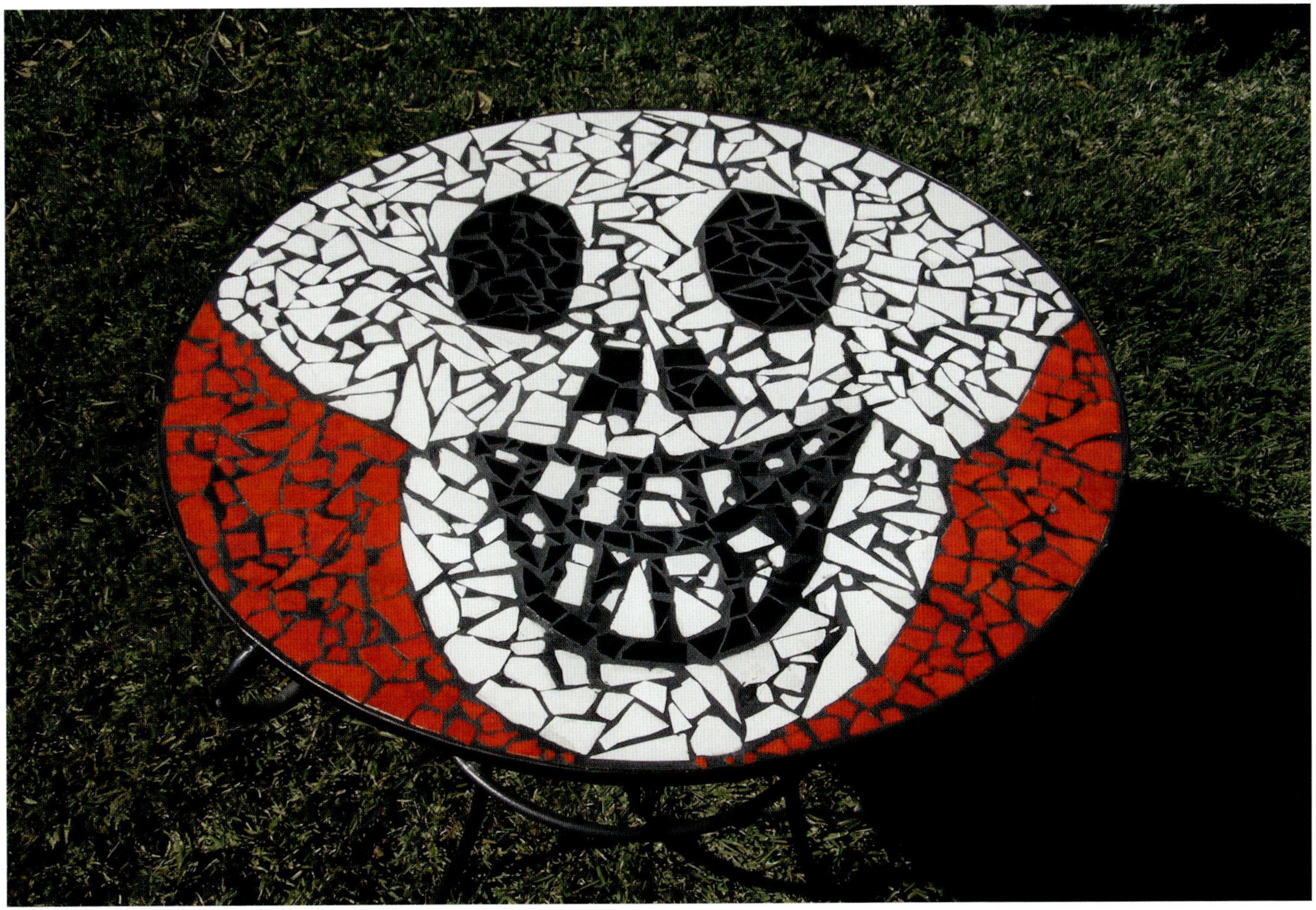

Wendy Viscarra. *Nightmare Before Christmas.* Table. Spanish and Italian ceramic tile, wood base. Custom iron base.

Rafael: I found this table on a sidewalk curb and I was just thrilled to have found it. It was in bad condition and had no top. I was immediately inspired to create a Day of the Dead image. I was also inspired by my friend, Rafael, in making this table. I designed the skeleton face and wanted to make him happy and colorful. The mosaic is created from stained glass put on a glass top base. The mosaic is visible from both sides of the table. I portrayed Rafael as having big teeth to emphasize them and the colorful stained glass colors around his head to indicate life.

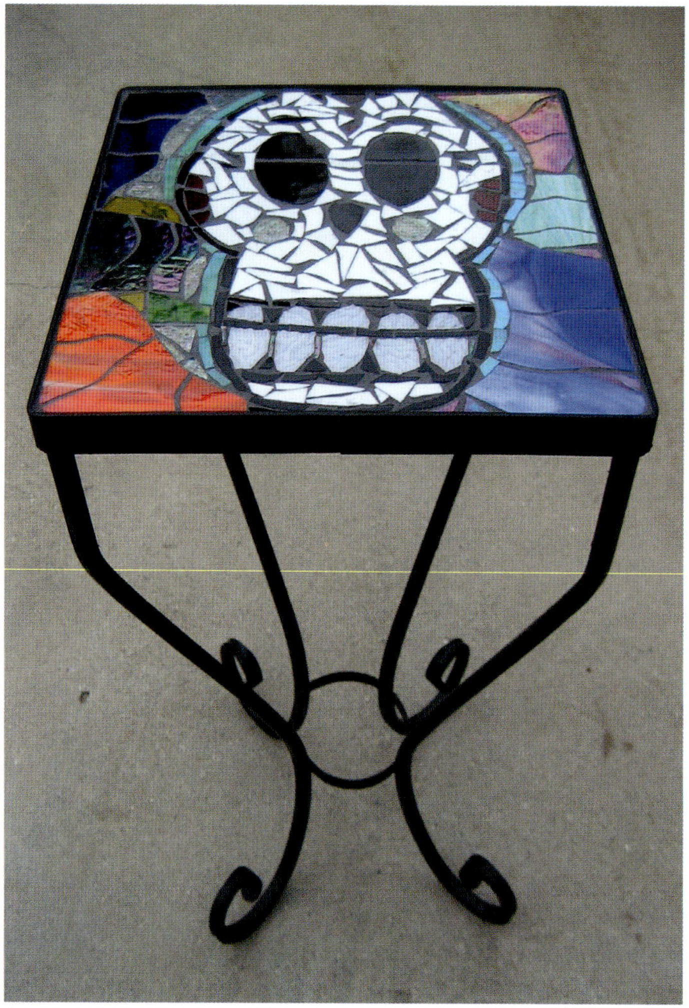

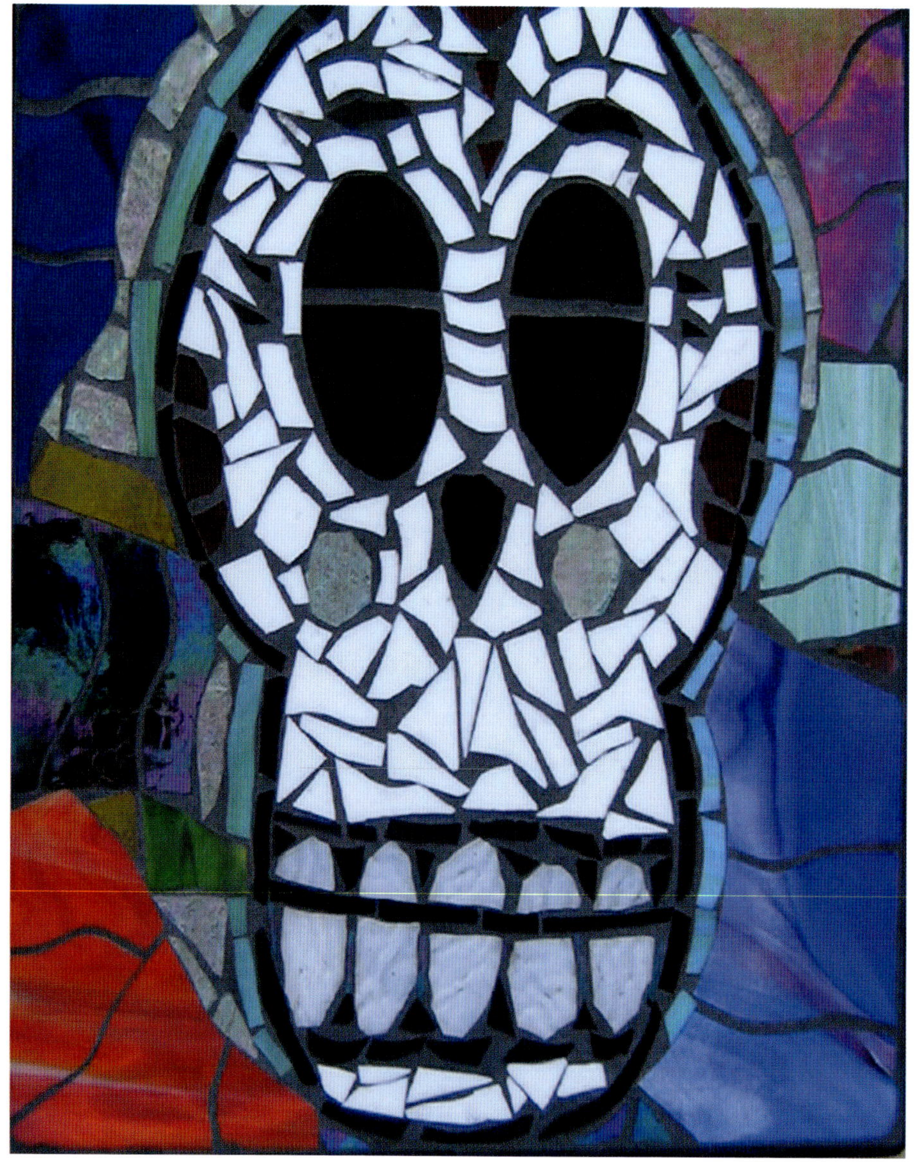

Wendy Viscarra. *Rafael.* Table. Stained glass mosaic, glass top base.

Liza Wheeler

Azuay, Ecuador, wheeler_lg@live.com

Artist's Statement

During graduate school (in Romania), my interest in producing fine figurative art increased each year. After attaining a degree in Design, I began the search for an art style and medium that would be most gratifying. In 1995 I joined a team of mosaic artists working principally in spiritual surroundings, largely producing icons and murals. I soon realized that this was the art form for which I had been searching, as it incorporates most major art forms, bringing a little of each into each mosaic. The years of inspiration and training received from some of Europe's most talented mosaic artists and masters taught me that by joining glass tiles, varying effects, and illusions could be created by their selection, cut, and placement, bringing life to a creation through the lines and reflection of light.

During the past several years, in an effort to make finer mosaics resembling Renaissance era micro mosaics, we have been cutting glass as small as 1 to 3 mm in width, which are joined very closely and include precious and semi-precious gemstones.

The Artwork

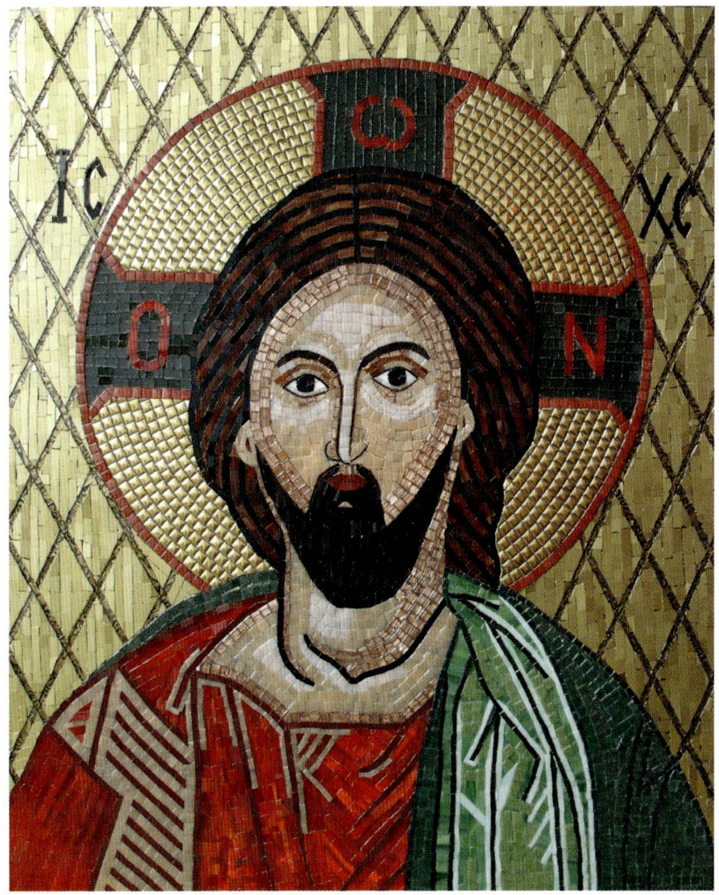

Liza Wheeler. *Christ.* 2D mosaic. 2006. Glazed glass, stain glass, Van Gogh glass, vitreous glass, metallic vitreous glass, and gold porcelain tiles on wood. Direct method. 39" x 33".

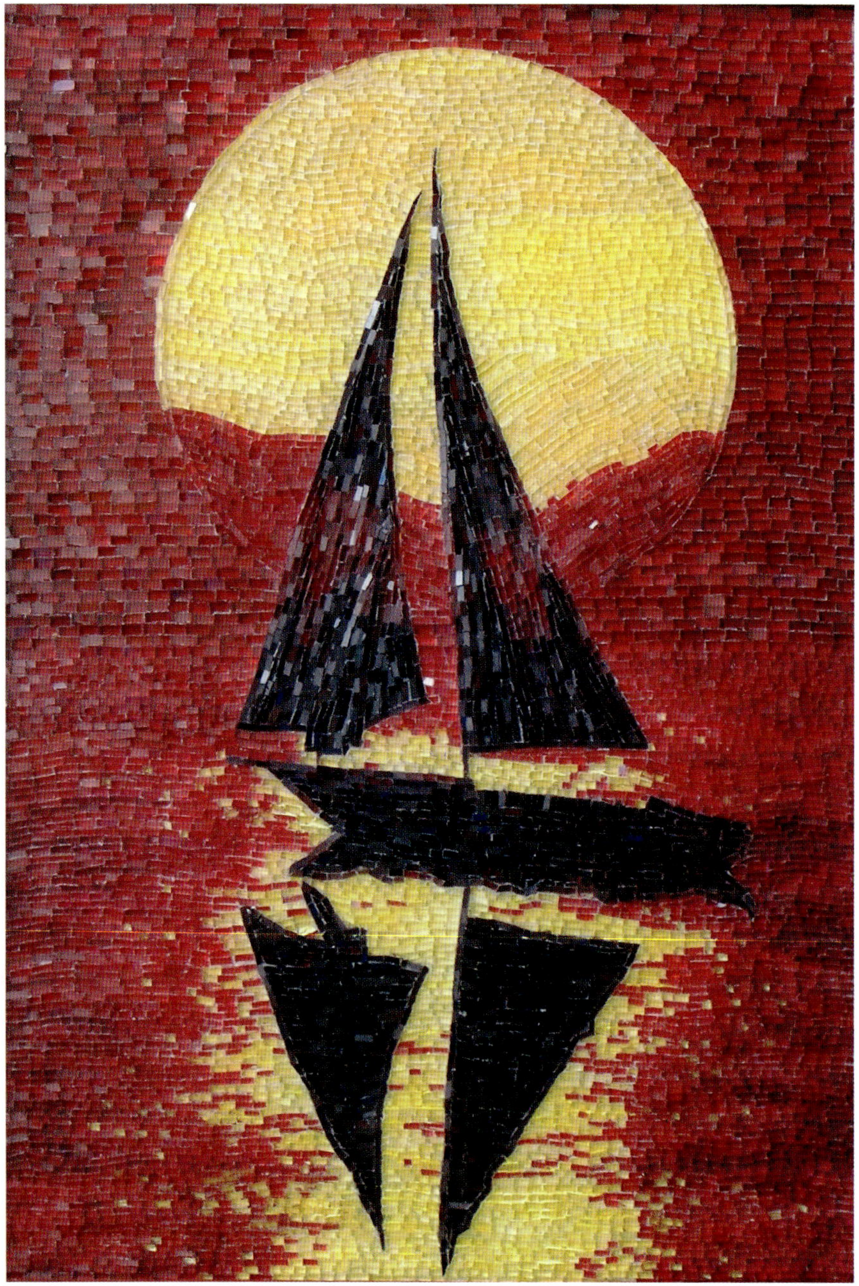

Liza Wheeler. *Enigma.* 2D, mosaic (micro mosaic pieces 1 to 3mm in width). 2009. Glazed glass on wood. Direct method. 22" x 15.5".

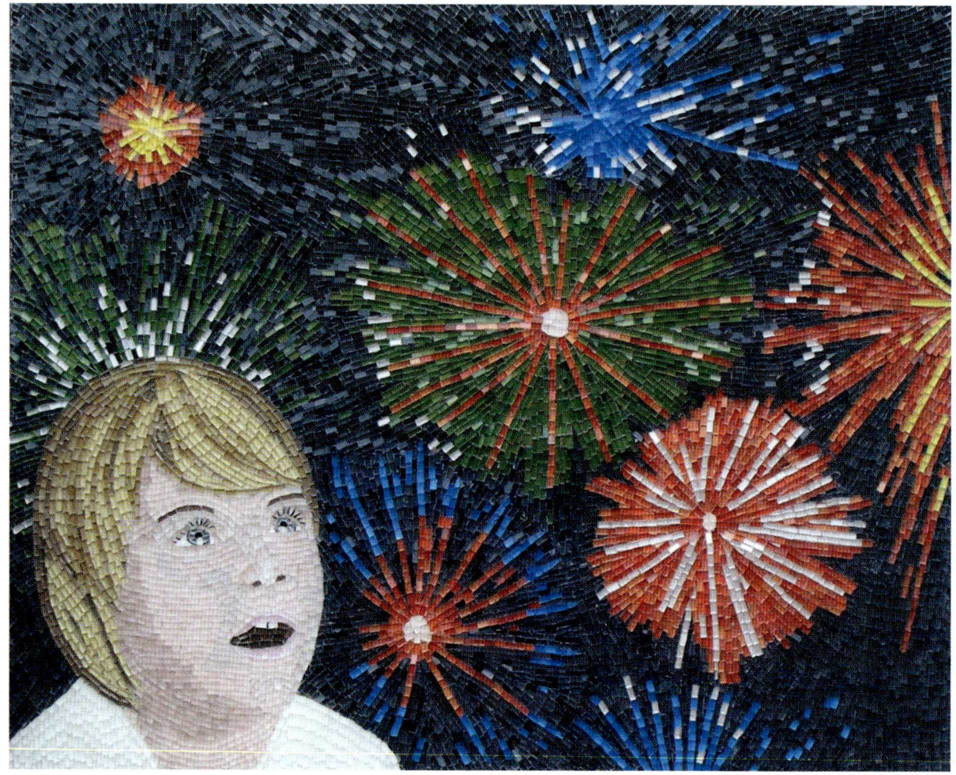

Liza Wheeler. *Carnival.* 2D, mosaic (micro mosaic, containing pieces from 1 to 3mm in width). 2010. Glazed glass on canvas. Direct method. 16" x 20".

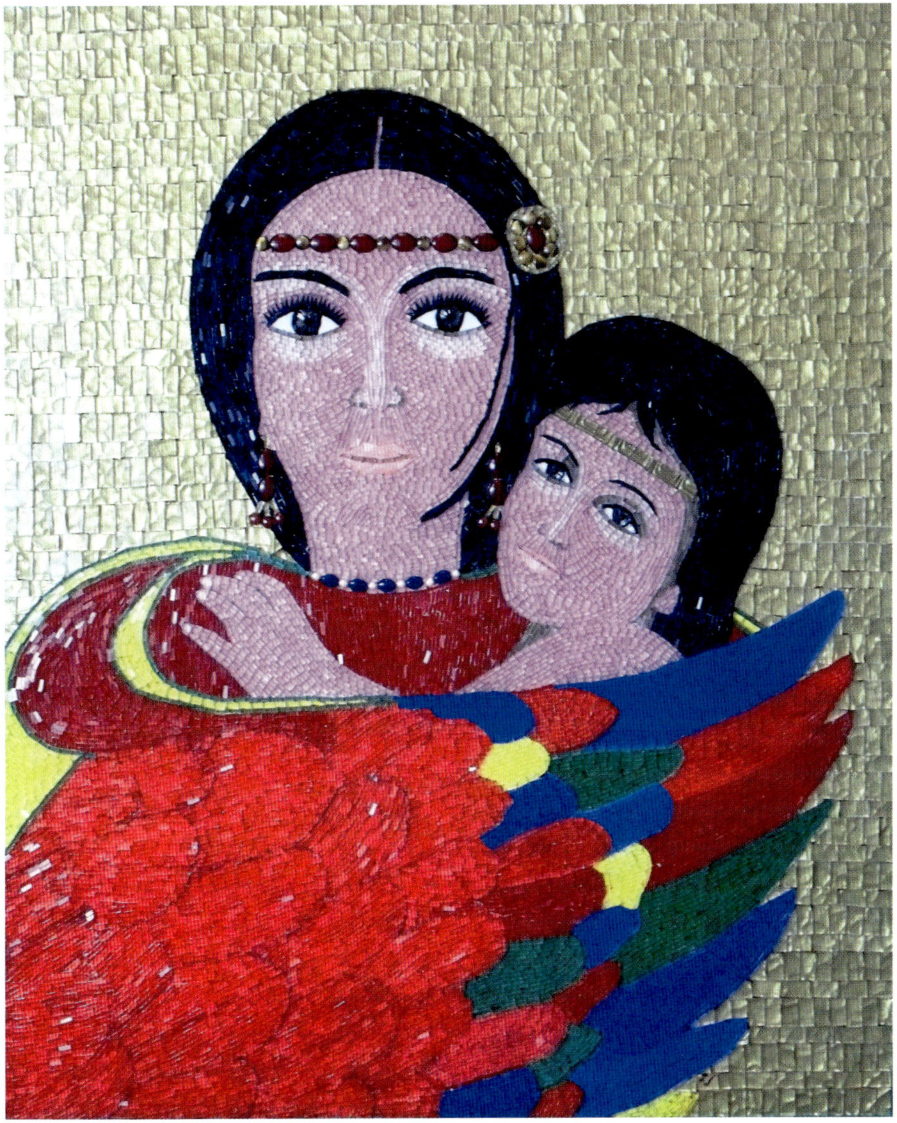

Liza Wheeler. *The First Canary*. 2D, mosaic (micro mosaic 1 to 3mm in width – excluding background). 2010. Glazed glass, Giorbello glass, stain glass, jade, and pearls on wood. Direct method. 31.5" x 26".

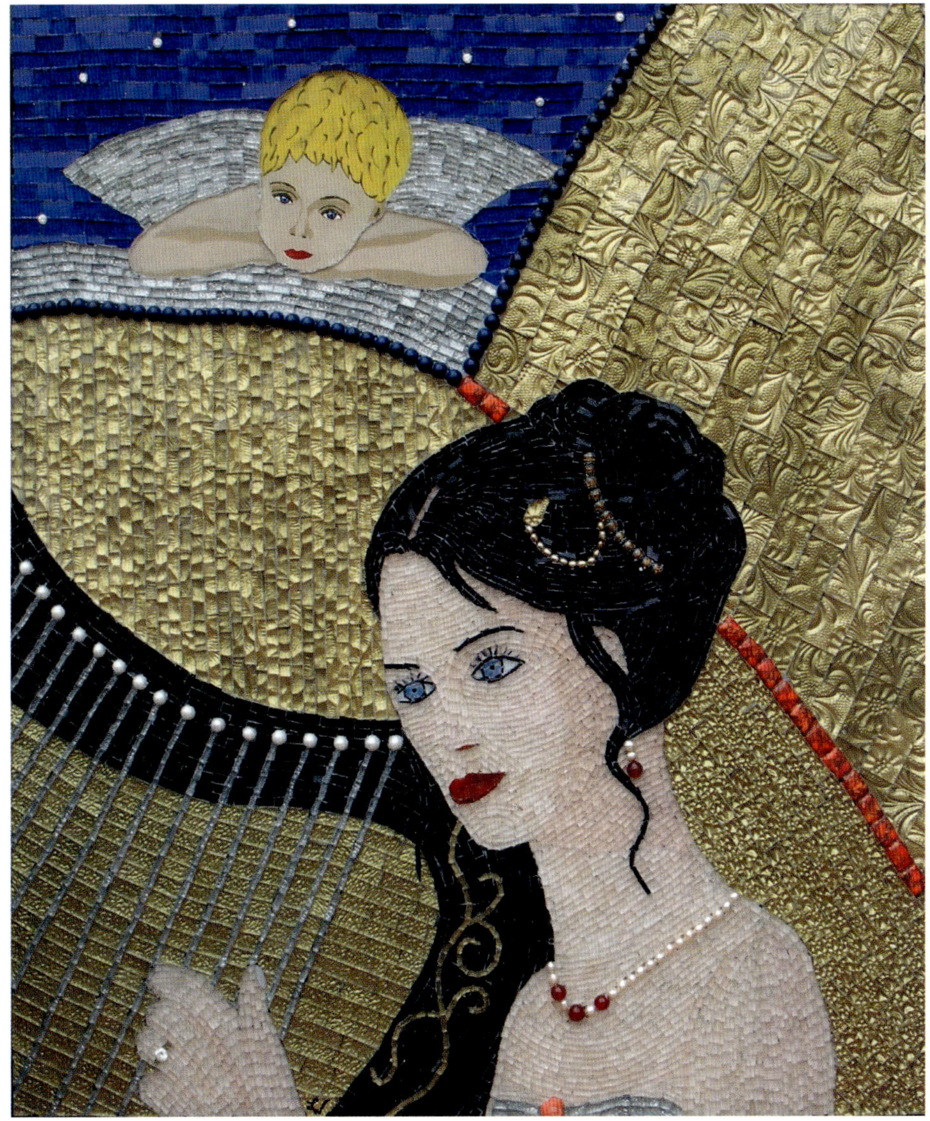

Liza Wheeler. *Music for an Angel*. 2D, mosaic (partial micro mosaic). 2010. Glazed glass, CZ, pearls, jade, carved coral, turquoise, and lapis lazuli on laminated Styrofoam. Direct method. 23" x 20".

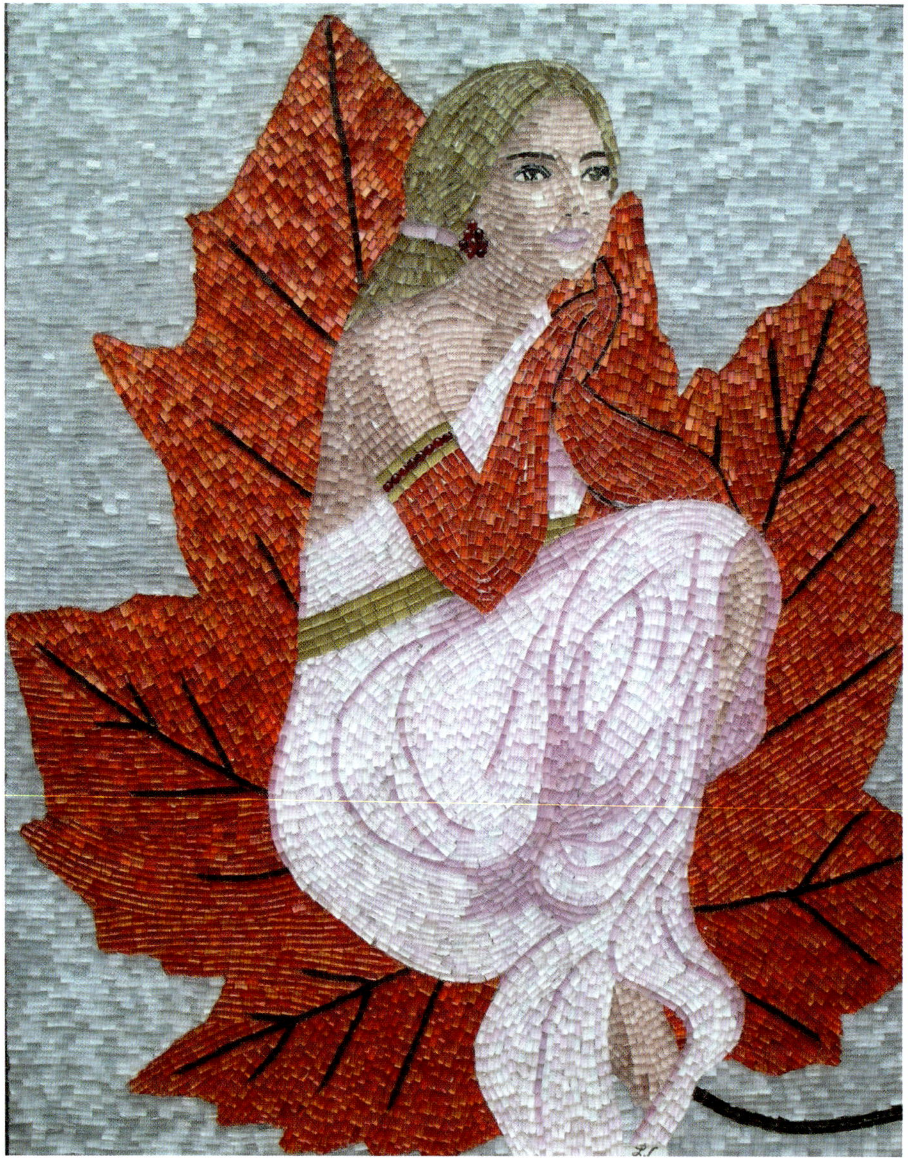

Liza Wheeler. *Tess Muse of Mosaic.* 2D, mosaic (micro mosaic pieces 1 to 3mm in width). 2010. Glazed glass and natural rubies on canvas. Direct method. 16" x 20".

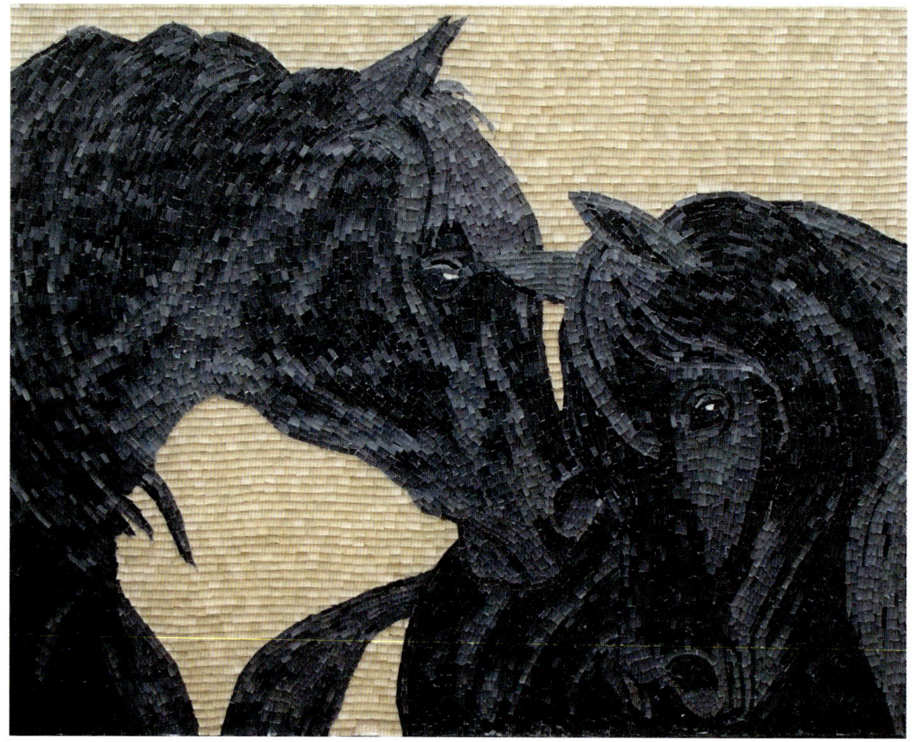

Liza Wheeler. *Tic & Toc.* 2D, mosaic (micro mosaic 1 to 4mm in width). 2010. Glazed glass on canvas. Direct method. 16" x 20".

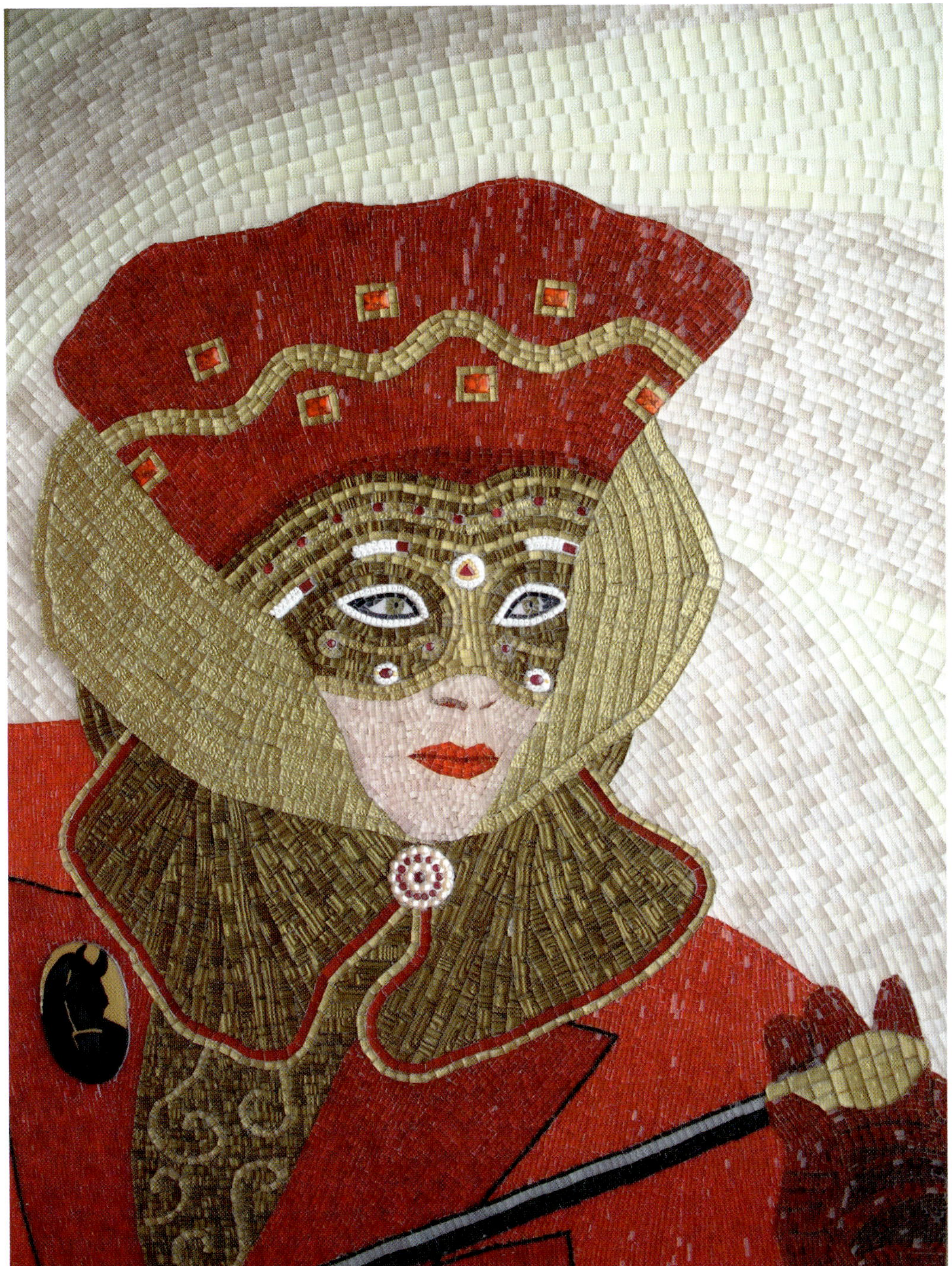

Liza Wheeler. *Venecia.* 2D, mosaic (partial micro mosaic). 2010. Glazed glass, Giorbello glass, jade, pearls, CZ, turquoise, and natural rubies on canvas. Direct method. 31" x 23".

Sylvia Witting

Fairfax, Virginia

Artist's Statement

An increasing appreciation for the marvelous natural world inspires much of my work. My art is a way of connecting with and absorbing the beauty of nature and honoring its creator. The endless variety of forms, colors, and textures are filtered through my sensibilities and become "abstract organic" designs. These forms grow in a spontaneous manner into the flowing lines and growing shapes that suggest the fantastic life found on the land and in the sea. They reflect my passion for gardening and the ocean. Shells and other natural materials as well as the handmade ceramic pieces contribute to the organic flow of the design with gold leaf, smalti, and colored glass providing accents.

About the Artwork

Burning Bush: I chose textured ceramic and rock to suggest the desert in this dramatic biblical story. The presence of God, which prevents the vivid ceramic and glass flames from consuming the green ceramic leaves, is symbolized by the radiating gold and crystal glass.

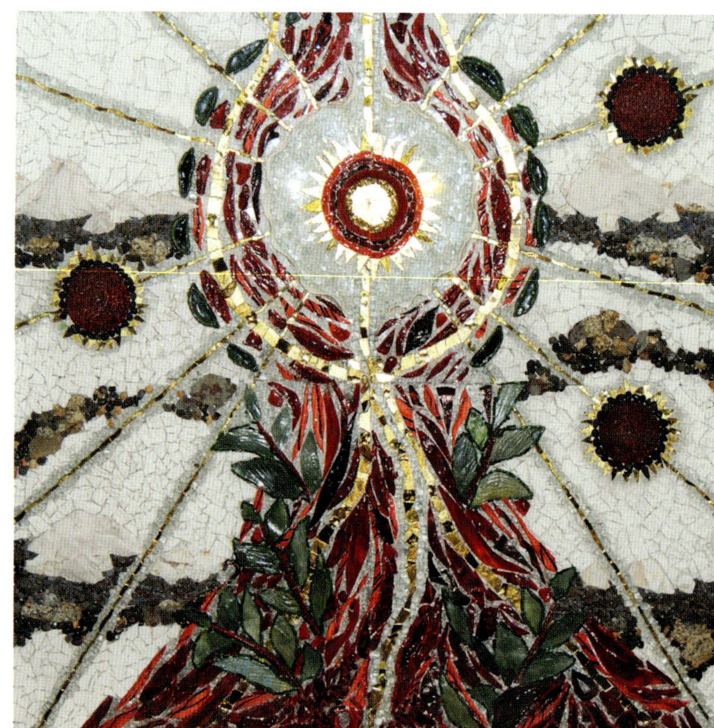

Sylvia Witting. *Burning Bush*. Pebbles, ceramic pieces, gold leaf, smalti, tempered and stained glass, and stone. 48" x 48". *Photographer: Megan Dwyer*

Living Ocean: I used the multiple oyster shells and barnacles to suggest living communities, with plant life and various fanciful sea creatures rendered in ceramic, shells, glass, and stone. The ceramic waves, glass, pebbles, and stone also create the underwater setting.

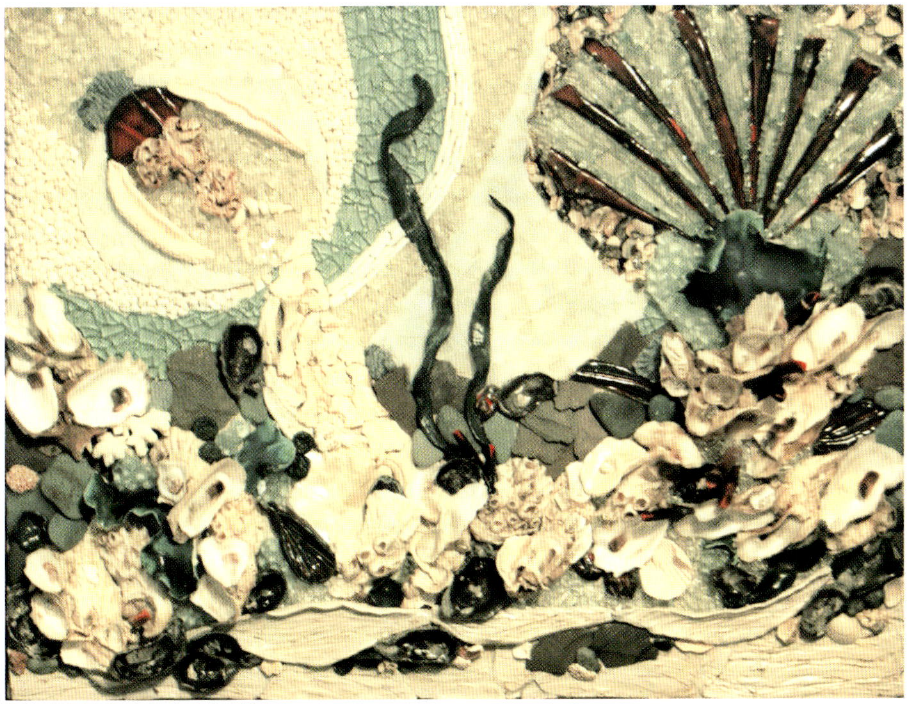

Sylvia Witting. *Living Ocean*. Ceramics, shells, coral, slate, pebbles, and glass. Two 18" x 24" panels. *Photographer: Megan Dwyer*

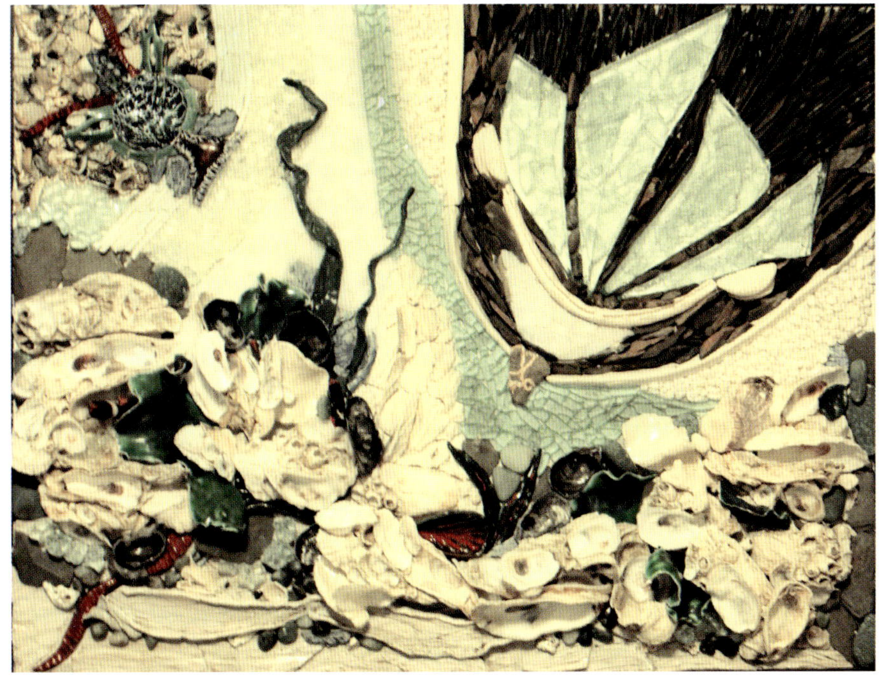

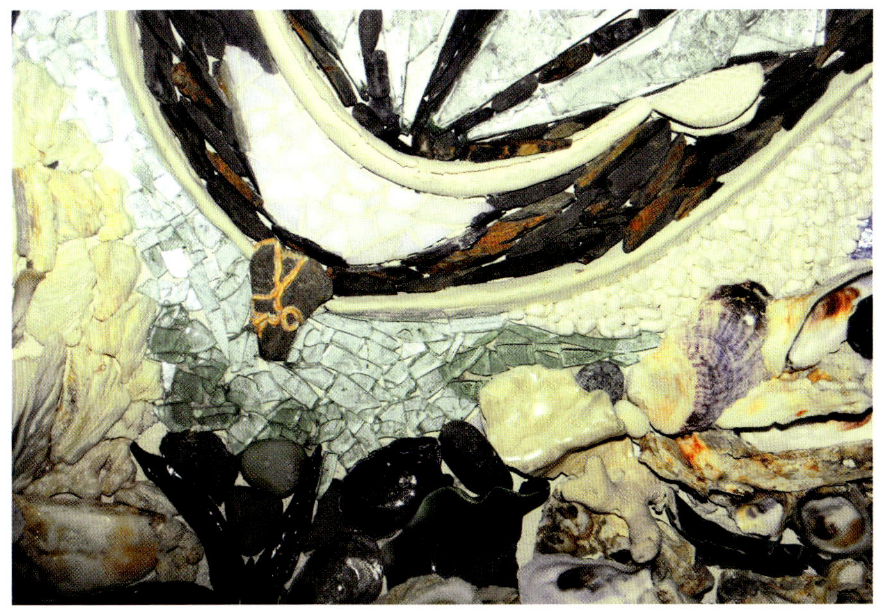

Ocean Commotion: This scene places fanciful underwater creatures in an environment that is not especially watery. The rather misplaced beings look crowded, captured, and confused.

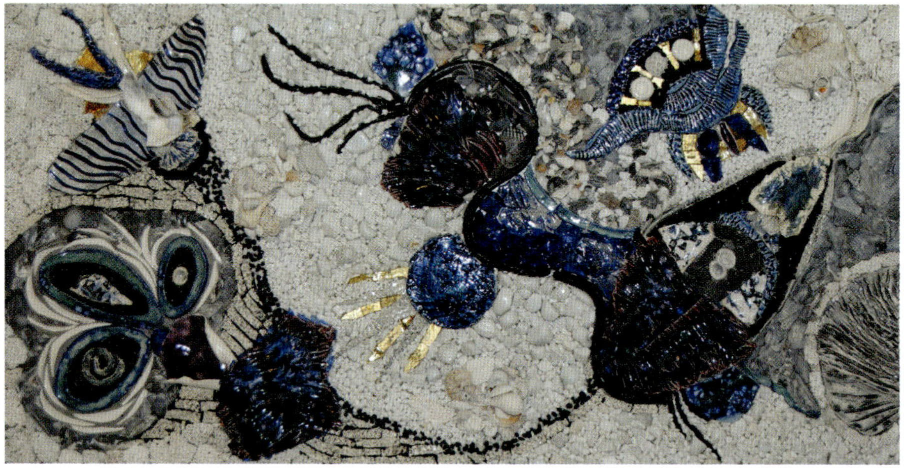

Sylvia Witting. *Ocean Commotion*. Ceramic, shells, coral, pebbles, gold foil, and mirror. 18" x 36". *Photographer: Megan Dwyer*

Ocean Odyssey II: Layers containing the remains of fascinating sea creatures, imaginative life forms, and light filtering down through the water currents are intruded upon by a bold ribbon of red representing a foreign influence that inhibits growth. This suggests a lingering indication of the careless invasion of man.

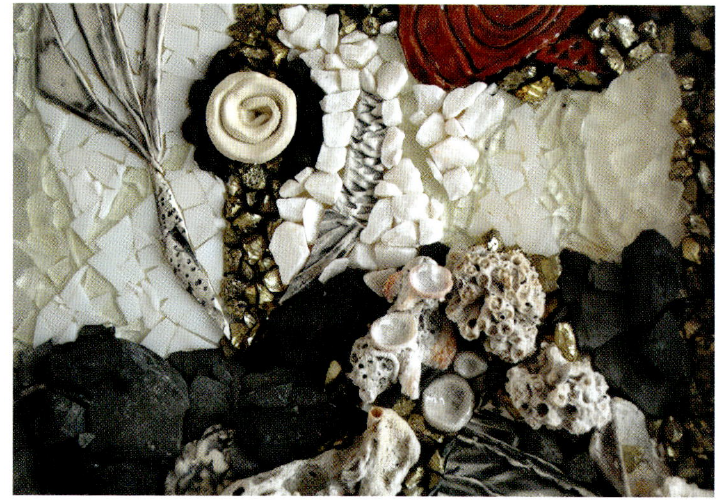

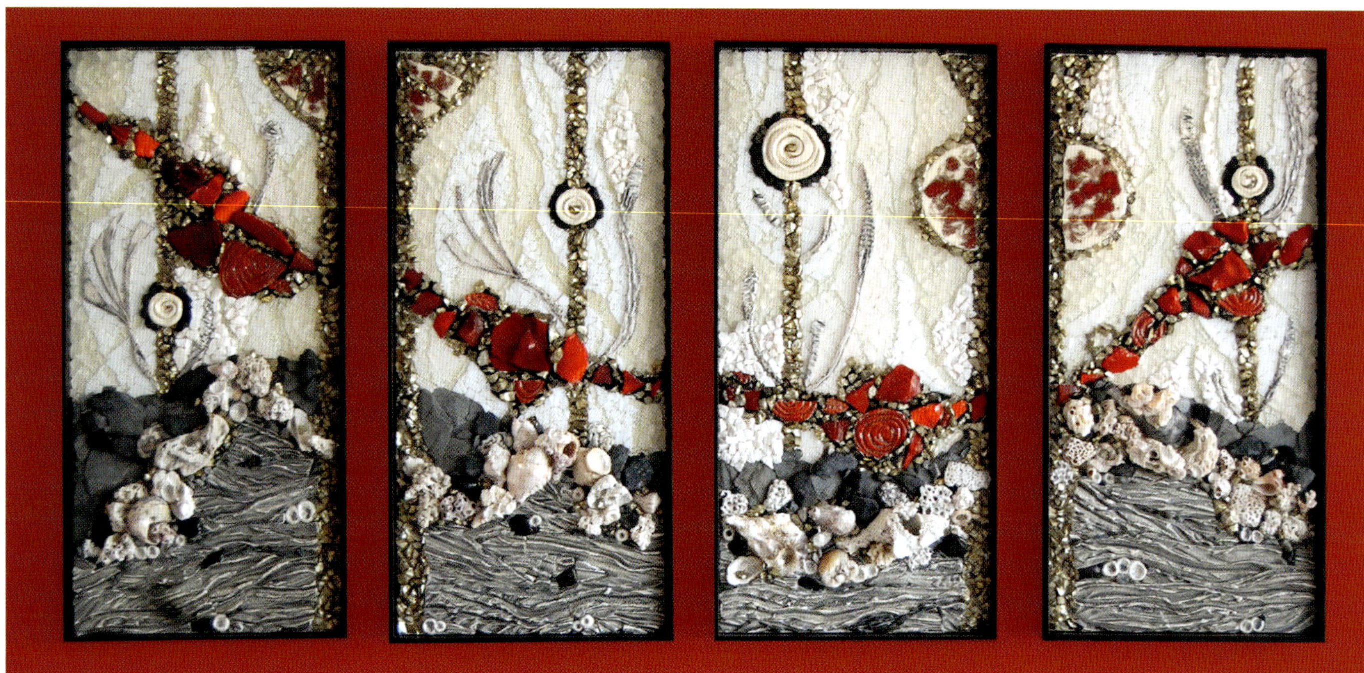

Sylvia Witting. *Ocean Odyssey II*. Pebbles, shells, barnacles, coral, ceramic pieces, recycled and stained glass. Four 12" x 24" panels. *Photographer: Megan Dwyer*

Kim Wozniak

Pulaski, Wisconsin

Artist's Statement

I am compelled to build. I am driven by the materials of construction and challenging these simple elements into unexpected forms. By juxtaposing them against each other they are given a voice. The permanence and tactile qualities of the materials allow me to entice my thoughts into a structure, and that structure to challenge the thoughts of others. To leave an impression that remains beyond me and my physical existence, like the hands of a child pressed into a freshly poured sidewalk.

Overall Description of Deconstruction and Reassembled Concrete Mosaics

Everything, and everyone, around us is broken or damaged in some way. When we see the flaws instinct tells us to cast it aside. Through my work I attempt to show the beauty in all that is broken, to encourage the viewer to look beyond the flaws and damage that surround us. To find the beauty that lies beneath, the story that the damage tells, the lesson that the fracture can teach us. Do the cracks make us weaker? Or are we stronger for having survived them?

The two most important materials in my work are concrete and glass. They both begin life as a mix of simple natural ingredients, and in the beginning they are both moldable and pliable.

Concrete is an amazing medium, a material of construction, and metaphor for life. You can move it, change it, teach it where you want it to go, but in a short amount of time it begins to set and you cannot stop it. It becomes hard and resistant to outside influence. We construct bridges, buildings, and whole cities with it. It gains strength as it ages; even as it cracks, it does not crumble. I hope this will be true of me as well.

Glass comes from almost the same simple elements as concrete and it too starts as a fluid form, but heat gives it the added brilliance of color and clarity. The price of the color is frailty. Even though glass is incredibly strong the slightest impact can cause it to shatter.

There is symbolism in the materials that give the art a voice and the viewer an opportunity to discover how that voice speaks to them.

About the Artwork

Emerging Aspirations was the beginning in many ways, the first cast concrete substrate, the first piece symbolizing the broken becoming whole again, the first piece accepted into a juried exhibition and the one in which I found my voice. It was created out of a major life change and speaks of my transformation from corporate prisoner to artist. The face of the new me emerges from within the pinstriped suit, wild, fearful, determined, and hopeful of the metamorphosis that is about to begin. (following page)

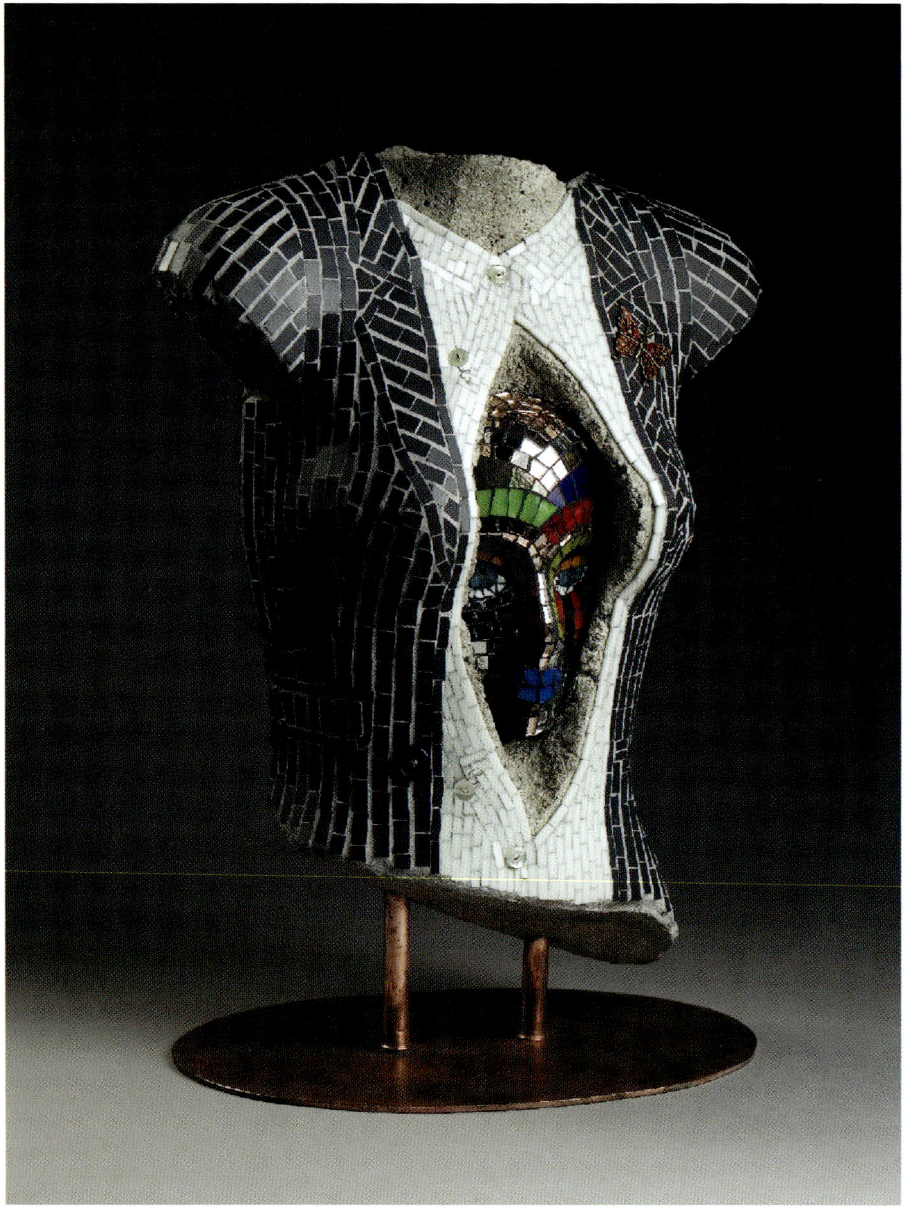

Kim Wozniak. *Emerging Aspirations.* Three-dimensional bust. 2005. Cast lightweight concrete, unglazed porcelain, stained glass, mirror, buttons, wire, and steel. 22" x 15" x 10". *Photo by Micheo Sangolies*

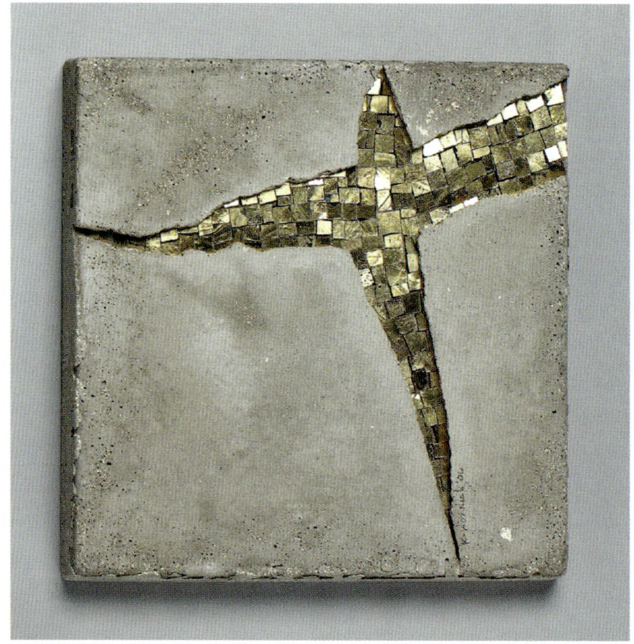

Kim Wozniak. *Phoenix.* 2006. Deconstructed and reassembled lightweight concrete, and gold smalti. 16" x 16" x 1.5". *Photo by Micheo Sangolies*

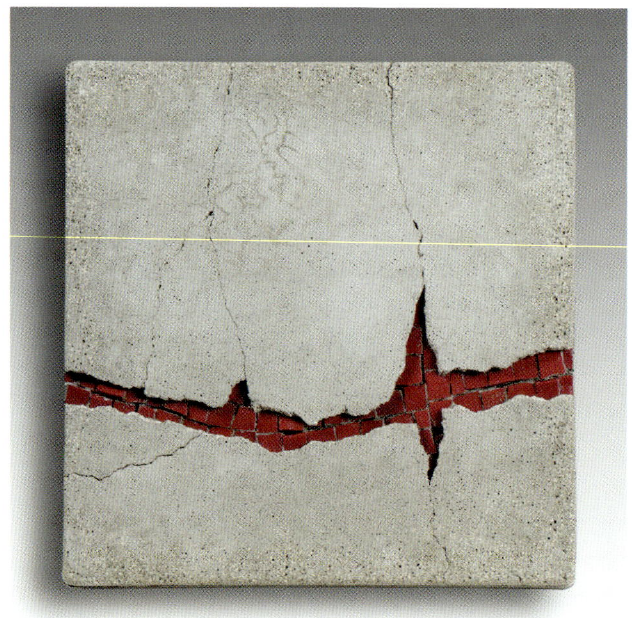

Kim Wozniak. *Cardiac Arrest*. Two-dimensional concrete with red inclusions. 2008. Deconstructed and reassembled lightweight concrete with Mexican smalti. 12" x 12" x 1.5". *Photo by Micheo Sangolies*

Love: Love, with all its facets. Who hasn't felt the bubbles of excitement as it begins, effervescent and beaming? In time the stress begins, cracks form, pieces break. The question is, "Are qualities that bound it together in the beginning enough to keep it from crumbling?"

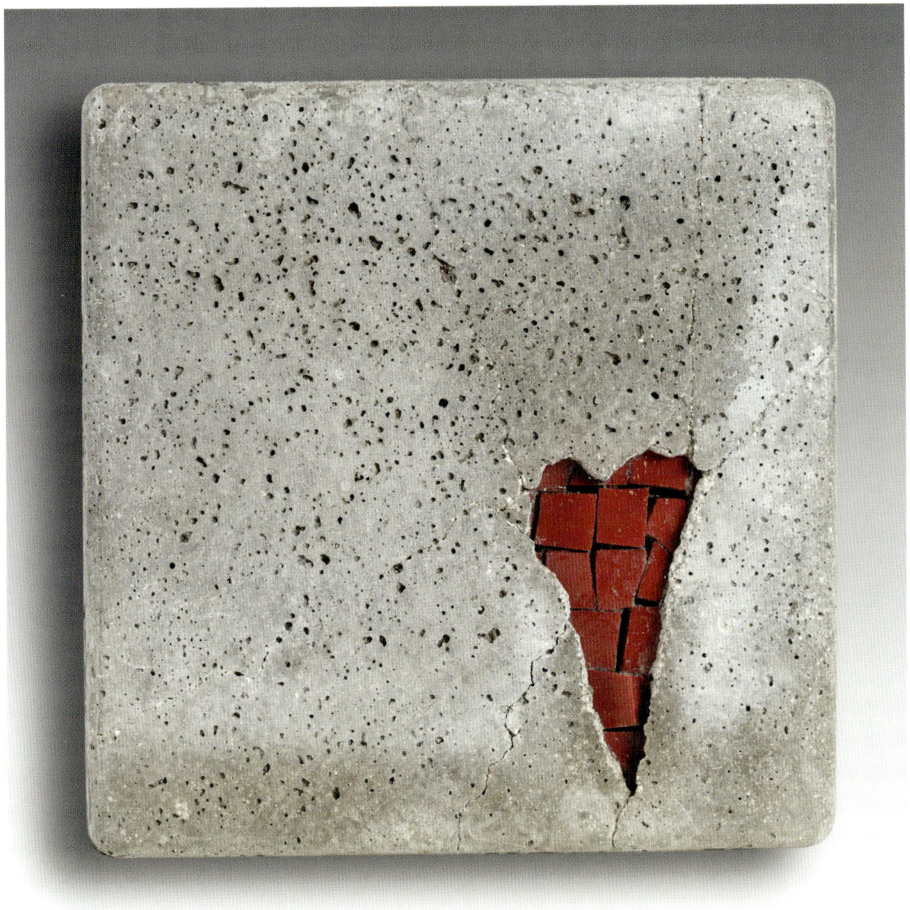

Kim Wozniak. *Love*. 2008. Deconstructed and reassembled lightweight concrete with Mexican smalti. 8" x 8" x 1.5". *Photo by Melanie Wishart*

The Guardian takes my broken and reassembled work into three-dimensional form. The protector, she is hard and soft, broken and whole, glowing from within. A sacred heart, tears, wings of steel, is she me or the one who protects me?

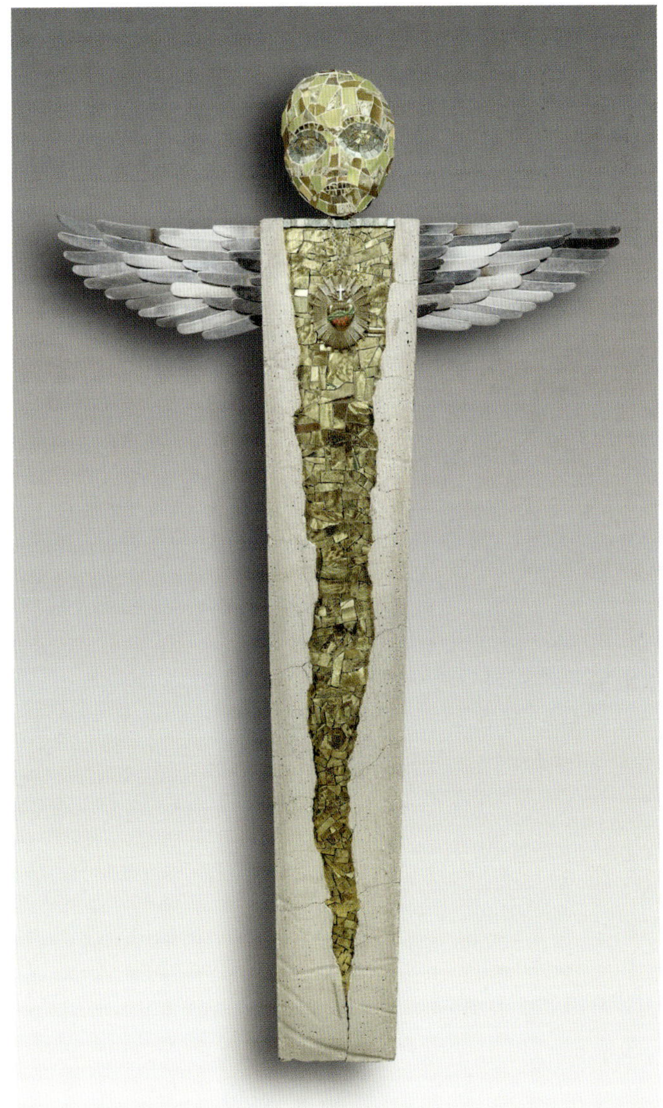

Kim Wozniak. *The Guardian*. 2009. Deconstructed and reassembled lightweight concrete, gold smalti, knives, and pottery shards. 53" x 34" x 10". *Photo by Melanie Wishart*

Intersections is the first in a series of new work that explores the roadway intersections we travel every day. At each intersection we must make a choice about which way to turn to get to our destination.

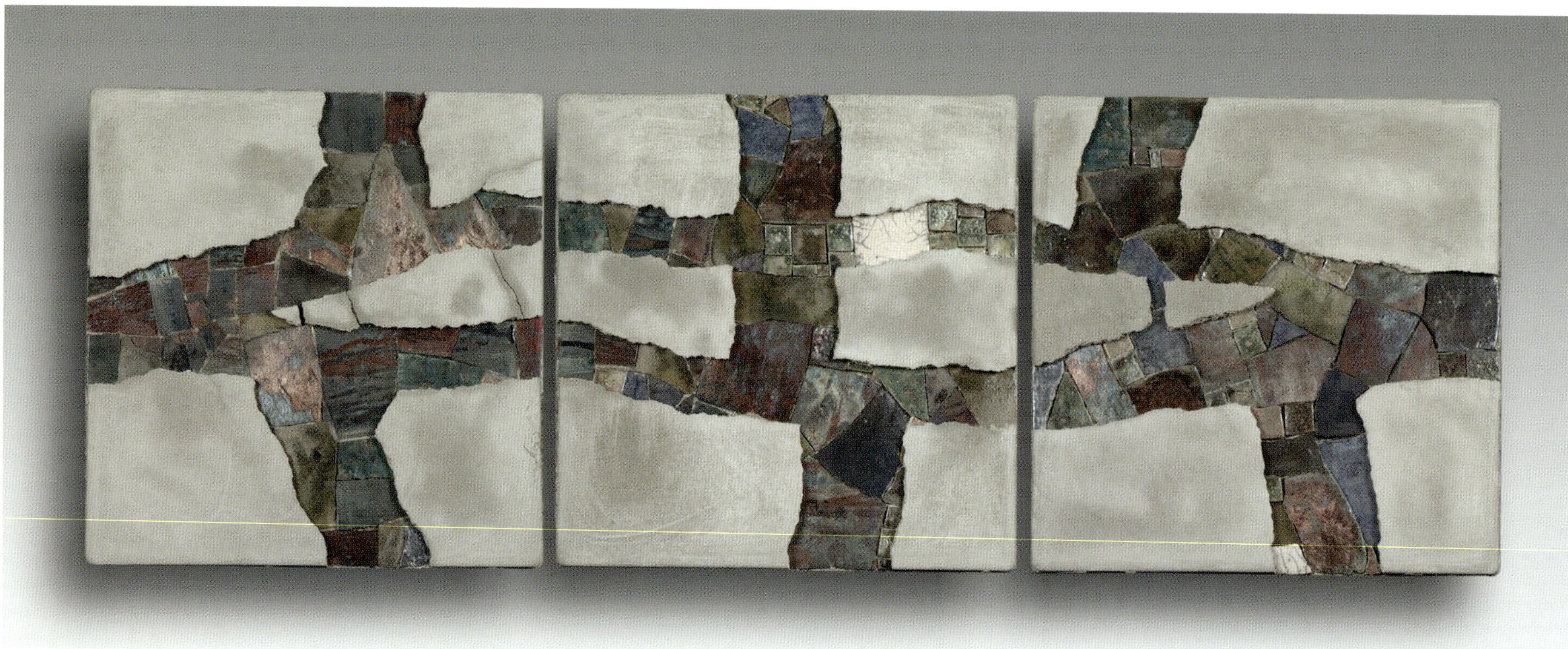

Kim Wozniak. *Intersections.* Two-dimensional concrete triptych with raku shards. 2009. Deconstructed and reassembled lightweight concrete with handmade raku shards. 12" x 37" x 1.5". *Photo by Melanie Wishart*

Wilma Wyss

Berkeley, California, wilma@wyssdesign.com

Artist's Statement

My freestanding concrete and mosaic sculptures merge fluidity and flimsiness with rigidity and weight. My work has been described as whimsical, joyous, and soothing. Mosaic in particular is carefully controlled and methodical, and working with concrete is unforgiving—challenges that I approach with my sense of order while using my creative energy to focus on color, texture, and shape.

The gathering of materials used to create the mosaic skin is an essential part of my process. Collecting found objects, contacting family and friends for contributions, relentlessly sorting and organizing lead me to see the objects purely in their shape and color. Evoking emotion through color and pattern has fascinated me since adolescence. I also find inspiration from colors I experience in nature, exploring the emotions and moods that different colors evoke.

My sculptural collages are influenced by the different settings and cultures I've experienced over the years. My childhood was a multicultural gyre: I was raised by Swiss parents in the U.S. and Africa, and often felt like an outsider, spiraling between continental divides. I'm inspired by the lively, colorful ornamentation in African culture that often draws from nature, even as it collides in my art with the Swiss tradition of orderliness and precision—a collision I hope infuses my work with intriguing contrasts and a dichotomy of order and the unexpected. As a resident of the Bay Area for twenty-five years, I also feel a strong connection to the western landscape, and often integrate natural materials in my work, including river rock, pebbles, beach glass, fossils, shells, and barnacles.

About the Artwork

Gramma Pat's Pillow, Hero Pillow and Penny Pillow, Parlor Pillow, Rust Easy Pillow, and ***Resilience Pillow:*** The sculptures in the *Pillow Series* are visual contrivances, three-dimensional *trompe d'œils*. The pillows are created out of concrete and then covered with mosaic using conventional tiling methods. Despite their rigid and hard surfaces, they bring to mind soft cloth and squishy pillows. The unusual and colorful mosaic patterns are whimsical and evocative of exotic tapestry, antique lace, and colorful fabric.

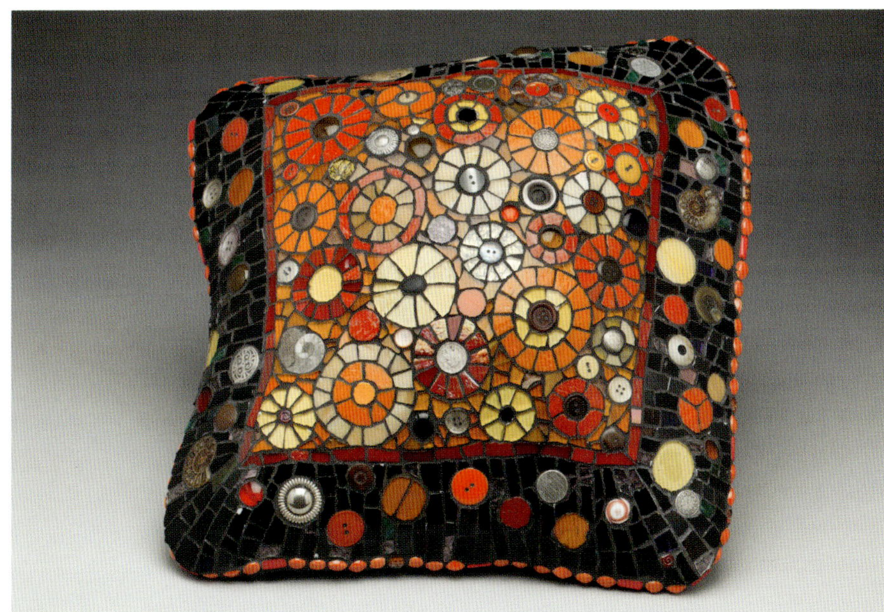

Wilma Wyss. *Parlor Pillow*. 2009. Concrete and mosaic of stained glass, glass tile, glass beads, buttons, broken jewelry, fossils, stone. 15" x 15" x 8". *Photographer: George P. Post*

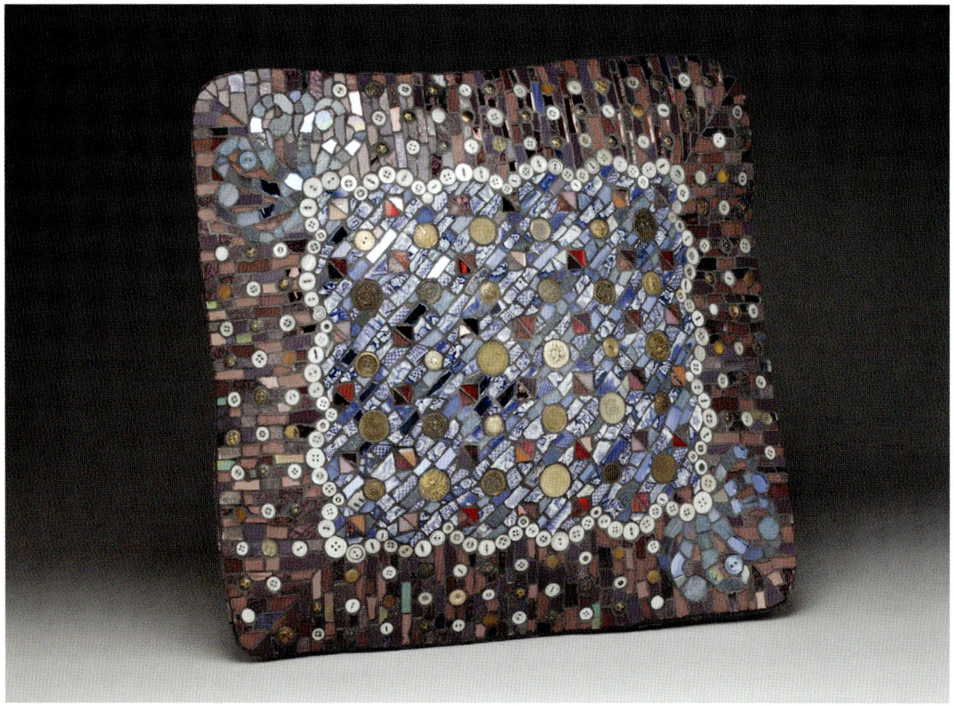

Wilma Wyss. *Gramma Pat's Pillow*. 2010. Concrete and mosaic of stained glass, glass tile, beach glass, ceramic dishes, mirror, buttons, coins, upholstery tacks. 16.5" x 18" x 5". *Photographer: George P. Post*

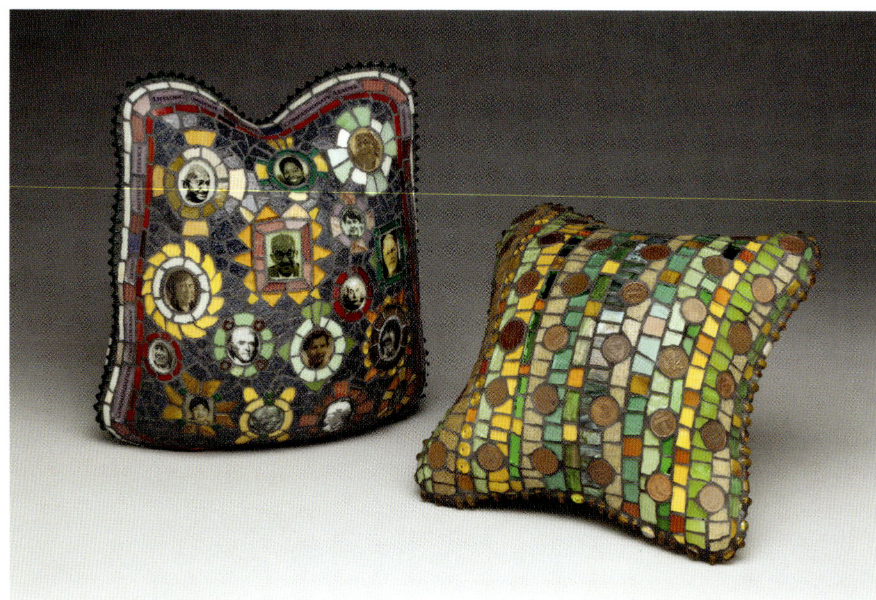

Wilma Wyss. *Hero Pillow* and *Penny Pillow*. 2010. Left: Concrete and mosaic of stained glass, glass tile, posterized black and white photos, glass beads. 11" x 10" x 6". Right: Concrete and mosaic of foreign coins, glass beads, stained glass, glass tile, mirror. 10" x 10" x 5". *Photographer: George P. Post*

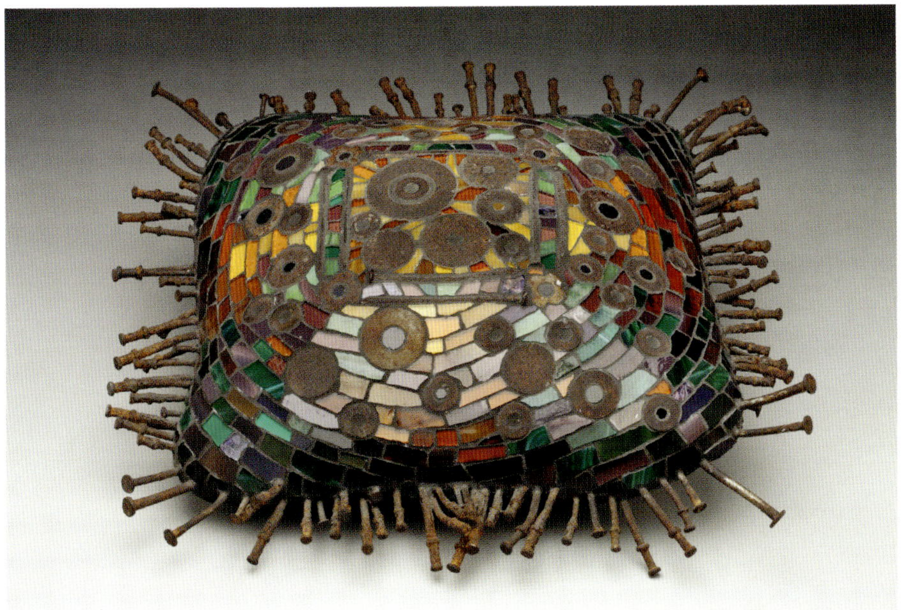

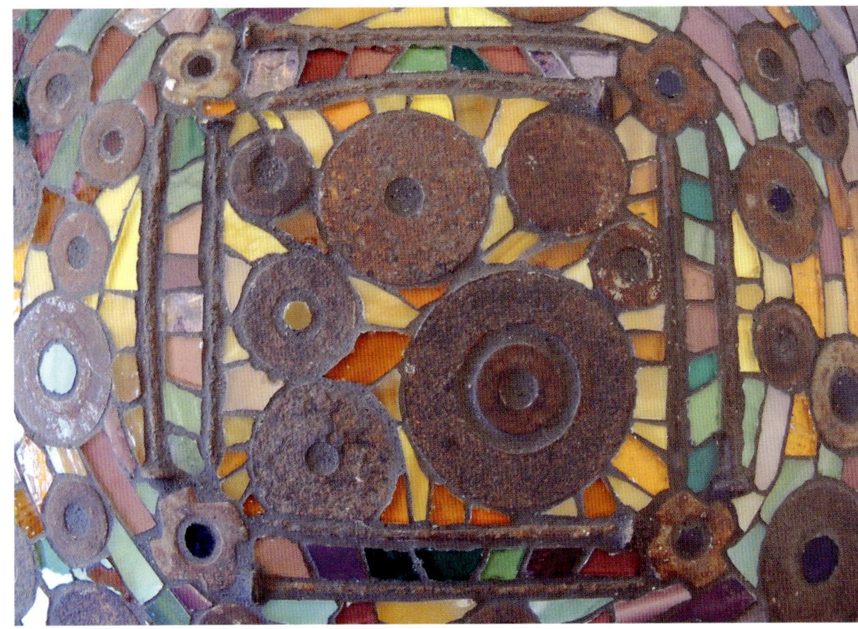

Wilma Wyss. *Rust Easy Pillow*. 2010. Concrete and mosaic of stained glass, glass tile, rusty nails, and washers. 15" x 15" x 6". *Photographer: George P. Post*

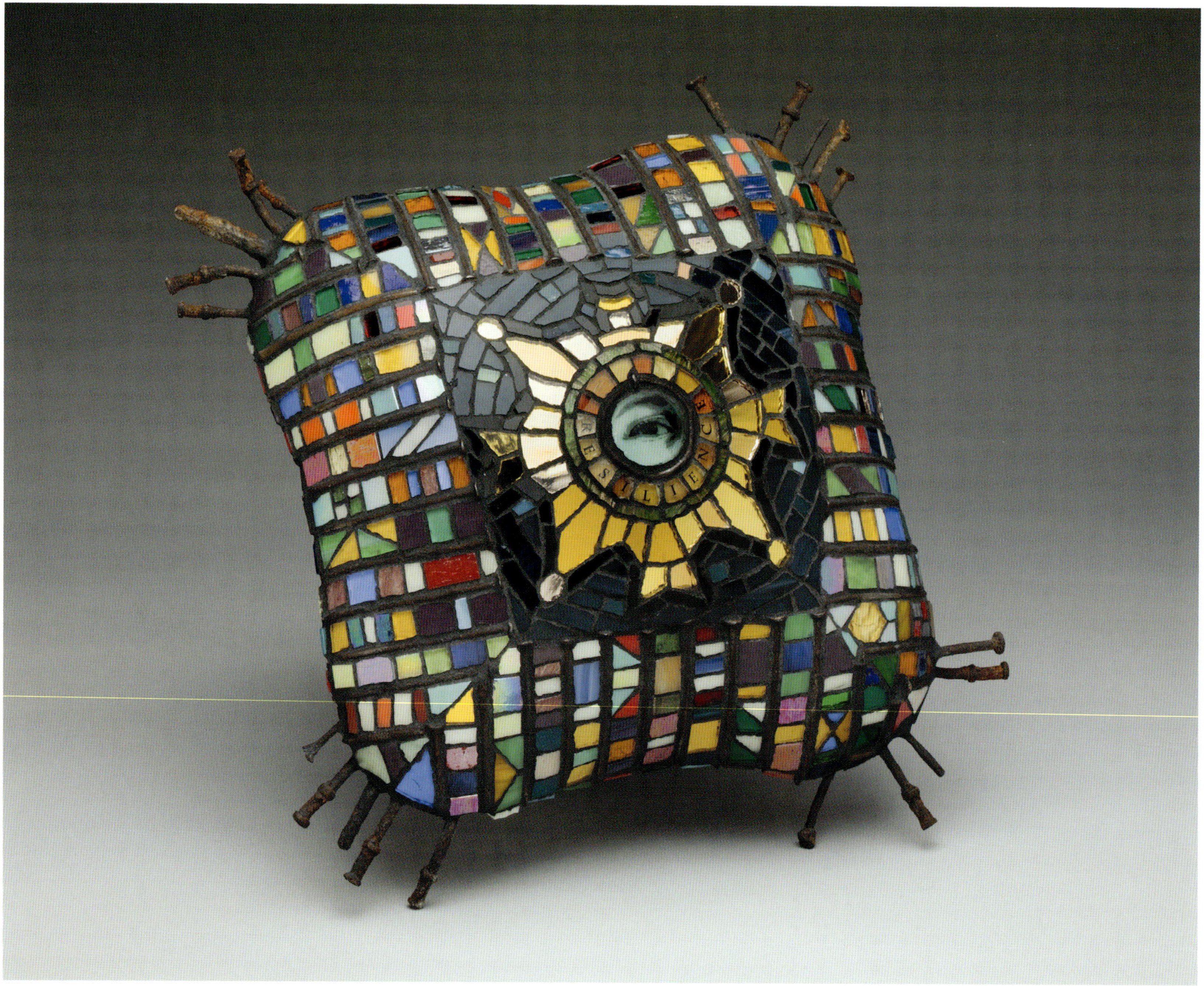

Wilma Wyss. *Resilience Pillow*. 2010. Concrete and mosaic of stained glass, glass tile, smalti, mirror, posterized black an white photo, and rusty nails. 11" x 11" x 5". *Photographer: George P. Post*

Gazing Cocoon: These small pieces are intended to be touched and picked up, to be examined more closely. These are seductive, cast-concrete forms that entice the viewer to explore them. Some viewers have called the texture against the palm of their hand soothing. Covered in a mosaic surface, they are a study of ornamentation, texture, and color using combinations of unusual, often recycled materials.

Awakening: Metamorphosis of Protective Thoughts: The pieces in this series of free-standing and wall mosaic sculptures are an illusion of flimsy and fluidity. The pieces deny the rigidity of mosaic and create a visual sense of graceful flowing movement. They are meant to be a visual contrivance, to give the illusion of a flexible organic form. One of my goals as an artist is to encourage the viewer to think about the emotions that are evoked by form and color, particularly since the pieces are abstract and don't intend to convey any specific message or agenda.

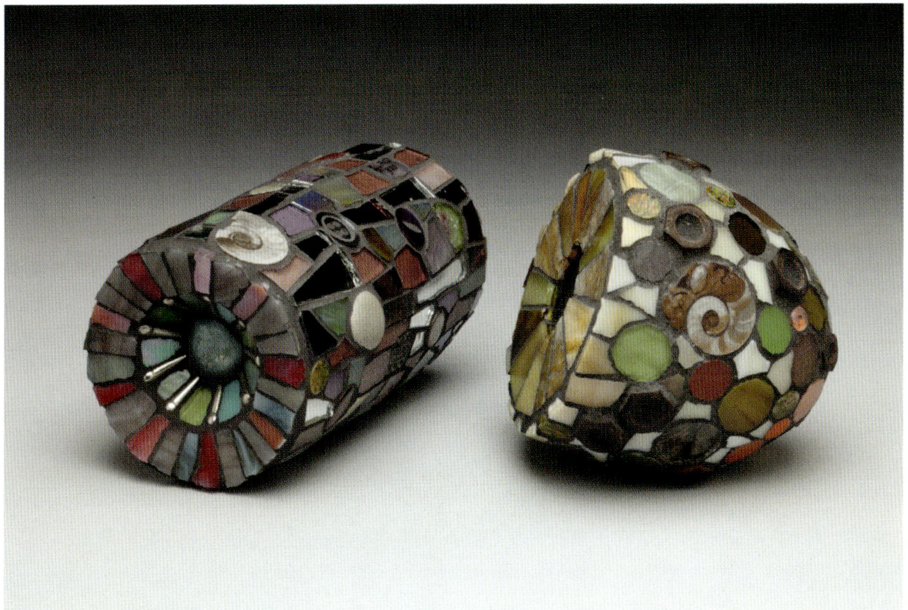

Wilma Wyss. *Gazing Cocoon*. 2010. Wire mesh and mosaic of stained glass and glass tile. 25.5" x 10" x 7.5". *Photographer: George P. Post*

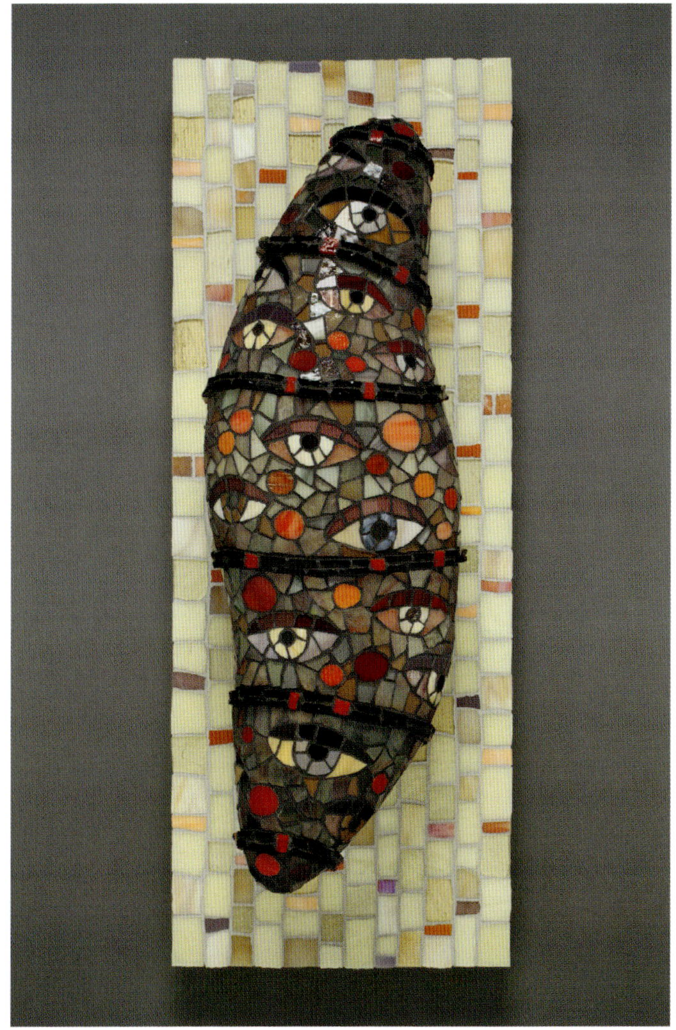

Wilma Wyss. *Awakening: Metamorphosis of Protective Thoughts*. 2010. Wire mesh and mosaic of stained glass and glass tile. 21" x 8" x 6". *Photographer: George P. Post*

Index